NORTE

Guimarães

Vila Re

GW00326553

0 kilometers   50

0 miles   25

DOURO AND TRÁS-OS-MONTES
Pages 232–261

• Viseu

• Guarda

CENTRAL PORTUGAL

imbra

Castelo Branco •

ESTREMADURA AND RIBATEJO
Pages 170–193

Portalegre •

THE BEIRAS
Pages 194–221

• Évora

• Beja

SOUTHERN PORTUGAL

ALENTEJO
Pages 290–313

ALGARVE
Pages 314–331

Faro

EYEWITNESS *TRAVEL GUIDES*

PORTUGAL

WITH MADEIRA & THE AZORES

DK EYEWITNESS *TRAVEL GUIDES*

PORTUGAL
WITH MADEIRA & THE AZORES

Main Consultant: MARTIN SYMINGTON

DORLING KINDERSLEY
LONDON • NEW YORK • MUNICH
MELBOURNE • DELHI
www.dk.com

A DORLING KINDERSLEY BOOK

www.dk.com

PROJECT EDITOR Ferdie McDonald
ART EDITOR Vanessa Hamilton
EDITORS Caroline Ball, Francesca Machiavelli
DESIGNERS Anthea Forlee, Carolyn Hewitson,
Nicola Rodway, Dutjapun Williams

MAIN CONTRIBUTORS
Susie Boulton, Christopher Catling, Clive Gilbert, Marion Kaplan,
Sarah McAlister, Alice Peebles, Carol Rankin, Norman Renouf,
Joe Staines, Robert Strauss, Nigel Tisdall, Edite Vieira

PHOTOGRAPHERS
Joe Cornish, Paul Harris, Robert Reichenfeld,
Linda Whitwam, Peter Wilson, Francesca Yorke

ILLUSTRATORS
Richard Draper, Paul Guest, Stephen Gyapay,
Claire Littlejohn, Maltings Partnership, Isidoro González-Adalid
Cabezas/Acanto Arquitectura y Urbanismo S.L.,
Paul Weston, John Woodcock, Martin Woodward

Reproduced by Colourscan, Singapore
Printed and bound by South China Printing Co. Ltd, China

First published in Great Britain in 1997
by Dorling Kindersley Limited
80 Strand, London WC2R 0RL
Reprinted with revisions in 1999, 2000, 2001, 2002

Copyright 1997, 2002 © Dorling Kindersley Limited, London
A Penguin Company

ALL RIGHTS RESERVED. NO PART OF THIS PUBLICATION MAY BE
REPRODUCED, STORED IN A RETRIEVAL SYSTEM, OR TRANSMITTED IN
ANY FORM OR BY ANY MEANS, ELECTRONIC, MECHANICAL,
PHOTOCOPYING, RECORDING OR OTHERWISE, WITHOUT THE
PRIOR WRITTEN PERMISSION OF THE COPYRIGHT OWNER.
A CIP CATALOGUE RECORD IS AVAILABLE FROM THE BRITISH LIBRARY.

ISBN 0 7513 4699 3

**The information in every
DK Eyewitness Travel Guide is checked regularly.**
Every effort has been made to ensure that this book is as up-to-
date as possible at the time of going to press. Some details,
however, such as telephone numbers, prices, gallery hanging
arrangements and travel information, are liable to change. The
publishers cannot accept responsibility for any consequences
arising from the use of this book, nor for any material on third-
party websites, and cannot guarantee that any website address in
this book will be a suitable source of travel information. We value
the views and suggestions of our readers highly. Please write to:
Senior Publishing Manager, DK Eyewitness Travel Guides,
Dorling Kindersley, 80 Strand, London WC2R 0RL.

◁ **Palácio da Pena rising above the wooded Parque da Pena, Sintra**

CONTENTS

HOW TO USE
THIS GUIDE 6

**Equestrian statue of José I
in Praça do Comércio, Lisbon**

INTRODUCING
PORTUGAL

PUTTING PORTUGAL
ON THE MAP *10*

A PORTRAIT OF
PORTUGAL *12*

PORTUGAL THROUGH
THE YEAR *30*

THE HISTORY OF
PORTUGAL *36*

LISBON

INTRODUCING
LISBON *60*

ALFAMA *68*

BAIXA *80*

BAIRRO ALTO
AND ESTRELA *88*

**Everyday scene in the Alfama,
the oldest quarter in Lisbon**

BELÉM *100*

FURTHER AFIELD *112*

LISBON STREET
FINDER *126*

CENTRAL PORTUGAL

INTRODUCING CENTRAL
PORTUGAL *142*

Typical blue-trim house near Beja in the Alentejo

THE LISBON COAST *148*

ESTREMADURA AND
RIBATEJO *170*

THE BEIRAS *194*

Entrance to the chapterhouse at
Alcobaça monastery, Estremadura

NORTHERN
PORTUGAL

INTRODUCING
NORTHERN PORTUGAL
224

DOURO AND TRÁS-
OS-MONTES *232*

MINHO *262*

SOUTHERN
PORTUGAL

INTRODUCING
SOUTHERN PORTUGAL
284

ALENTEJO *290*

ALGARVE *314*

PORTUGAL'S
ISLANDS

INTRODUCING
PORTUGAL'S ISLANDS *334*

MADEIRA *340*

THE AZORES *358*

TRAVELLERS'
NEEDS

WHERE TO STAY *374*

WHERE TO EAT *402*

SURVIVAL GUIDE

PRACTICAL
INFORMATION *426*

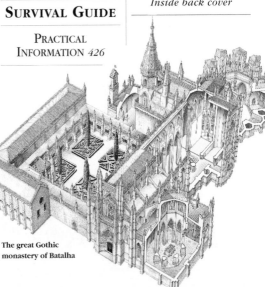

The great Gothic
monastery of Batalha

TRAVEL
INFORMATION *440*

GENERAL INDEX *450*

17th-century tile decoration
on Palácio Fronteira, Lisbon

PHRASE BOOK *479*

ROAD MAP
Inside back cover

HOW TO USE THIS GUIDE

THIS GUIDE helps you get the most from a visit to Portugal, providing expert recommendations as well as detailed practical information. The opening chapter *Introducing Portugal* maps the country and sets it in its historical and cultural context. Each of the nine regional chapters, plus *Lisbon*, describe important sights, using maps, pictures and illustrations. Features cover topics ranging from architecture and festivals to beaches and food. Hotel and restaurant recommendations can be found in *Travellers' Needs*. The *Survival Guide* contains practical information on everything from transport to personal safety.

LISBON

Lisbon has been divided into five main sightseeing areas. Each of these areas has its own chapter, which opens with a list of the major sights described. All sights are numbered and plotted on an *Area Map*. Information on the sights is easy to locate as the order in which they appear in the chapter follows the numerical order used on the map.

Sights at a Glance lists the chapter's sights by category: Churches, Museums and Galleries, Historic Buildings, Parks and Gardens.

1 Area Map
For easy reference, the sights covered in the chapter are numbered and located on a map. The sights are also marked on the Street Finder *maps on pages 126–39.*

A locator map shows clearly where the area is in relation to other parts of the city.

All the pages relating to Lisbon have red thumb tabs.

2 Street-by-Street Map
This gives a bird's-eye view of the heart of each of the sightseeing areas.

A suggested route for a walk is shown in red.

Stars indicate the sights that no visitor should miss.

3 Detailed Information
All the sights in Lisbon are described individually. Addresses and practical information are provided. The key to the symbols used in the information block is shown on the back flap.

THE LISBON COAST

1 Introduction
A general account of the landscape, history and character of each region is given here, explaining both how the area has developed over the centuries and what attractions it has to offer the visitor today.

PORTUGAL REGION BY REGION
Outside Lisbon, the rest of Portugal has been divided into nine regions, each of which has a separate chapter. The most interesting cities, towns and sights to visit are located and numbered on a *Pictorial Map*.

Exploring the Lisbon Coast

2 Pictorial Map
This shows the main road network and gives an illustrated overview of the region. All entries are numbered and there are also useful tips on getting around the region.

Each area of Portugal can be identified quickly by its colour coding, shown on the inside front cover.

3 Detailed Information
All the important towns and other places to visit are described individually. They are listed in order, following the numbering given on the Pictorial Map. Within each entry, there is further detailed information on important buildings and other sights.

Story boxes explore specific subjects further.

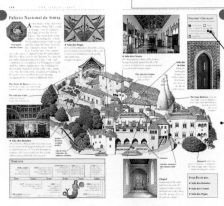

Palácio Nacional de Sintra

For all the top sights, a Visitors' Checklist provides the practical information you need to plan your visit.

4 The Top Sights
These are given two or more full pages. Historic buildings are dissected to reveal their interiors; museums and galleries have colour-coded floorplans to help you locate the most interesting exhibits.

INTRODUCING
PORTUGAL

PUTTING PORTUGAL ON THE MAP 10-11
A PORTRAIT OF PORTUGAL 12-29
PORTUGAL THROUGH THE YEAR 30-35
THE HISTORY OF PORTUGAL 36-57

Putting Portugal on the Map

SITUATED IN THE EXTREME southwest corner of Europe, Portugal occupies roughly one-sixth of the Iberian Peninsula with a population of just under 10 million. To the north and east, a border measuring approximately 1,300 km (800 miles) separates Portugal from its only neighbouring country, Spain, and to the south and west, 830 km (500 miles) of coastline meets the Atlantic Ocean. The Atlantic archipelagos of Madeira and the Azores are included in Portugal's territory.

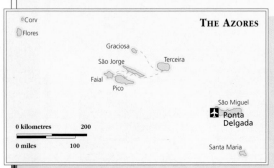

THE AZORES

Corv
Flores
Graciosa
São Jorge   Terceira
Faial
Pico
São Miguel
✈ Ponta Delgada
Santa Maria

0 kilometres   200
0 miles   100

The Azores

The Azores lie 1,300 km (800 miles) to the west of Lisbon in the Atlantic Ocean. Of volcanic origin, the islands are scattered over a distance of 650 km (400 miles).

MADEIRA

Porto Santo
Ilha do Porto Santo
Madeira
R101
R101
✈ Funchal

0 kilometres   20
0 miles   10

Madeira

Lying 965 km (600 miles) southwest of Lisbon in the Atlantic Ocean, the Madeiran archipelago has two inhabited islands, Madeira and Porto Santo.

KEY

✈ International airport
⚓ Ferry port
═ Motorway
═ Major road
═ Minor road
— Main railway line
–•– International boundary

ATLANTIC
OCEAN

0 kilometres   100
0 miles   50

Pontevedra
Vigo
Ourense
N525
Minho
A52
N13
Braga
Guimarães
Oporto (Porto) ✈
A4
Douro
IC1
A1
IP5
Viseu
N2
N109
Figueira da Foz
Coimbra
Zêzere
IP3
Mondego
P O R
IP6
N8
A15
Tejo
Santarém
A1
N10
LISBON (Lisboa) ✈
N4
Setúbal
A6
Évora
IP1
Sado
A2
IP8
IP2
Sines
Beja
N120
Portimão
N125
IP1

◁ **Landscape near Lagos in the Algarve by Sir Cedric Morris (1889–1982)**

EUROPE

NORWAY · SWEDEN · ESTONIA · LATVIA · LITHUANIA · DENMARK · UNITED KINGDOM · REPUBLIC OF IRELAND · NETHERLANDS · BELGIUM · LUXEMBOURG · GERMANY · POLAND · CZECH REPUBLIC · SLOVAKIA · AUSTRIA · HUNGARY · SLOVENIA · SWITZERLAND · FRANCE · ITALY · PORTUGAL · Lisbon · SPAIN · TUNISIA · MOROCCO · ALGERIA · LIBYA · Azores · Madeira

Bragança · Chaves · Real · Guarda · GAL · Castelo Branco · Portalegre · N246 · Badajoz · Mérida · Cáceres · Plasencia · SPAIN · MADRID · Sevilla · Huelva · Jerez de la Frontera · Málaga · Granada

GREATER LISBON

Odivelas · Sacavém · Queluz · Amadora · Belém · Cacilhas · Montijo · Trafaria · Almada · Barreiro · Moita · Costa de Caparica · Seixal · Coina · Tejo

0 kilometres 10
0 miles 5

Greater Lisbon
The capital of Portugal is a hilly city on the Tagus estuary. The country's main port and business centre, Greater Lisbon has a population of around two million.

A PORTRAIT OF PORTUGAL

OST VISITORS TO PORTUGAL *head for the sandy coves, pretty fishing villages and manicured golf links of the Algarve. But beyond the south coast resorts lies the least explored corner of Western Europe: a country of rugged landscapes, sophisticated cities, rural backwaters and sharply contrasting traditions.*

Portugal appears to have no obvious geographical claim to nationhood, yet this western extremity of the Iberian Peninsula has existed within borders virtually unchanged for nearly 800 years. Its ten million people speak their own language, follow their own unique cultural traditions, and have a centuries-old history of proud independence from, and deep distrust of neighbouring Spain.

Horseman at festival in Vila Franca de Xira, Ribatejo

For a small country, the regions of Portugal are immensely varied. The rural Minho and Trás-os-Montes in the north are the most traditional – some would say backward. Over the last few decades many inhabitants of these neglected regions have been forced to emigrate in search of work.

The south of the country could not be more different. The Algarve, blessed with beautiful sandy beaches and a wonderful, warm Mediterranean climate all year round, has been transformed into a holiday playground for North Europeans.

Two great rivers, the Tagus and the Douro, rise in Spain and then flow westwards across Portugal to the Atlantic Ocean. From the wild upper reaches of the Douro valley, comes Portugal's most famous product – port wine, from steeply terraced vineyards hewn out of the mountainsides. The Tagus, by contrast, is wide and languid, often spilling out over the flat, fertile, Ribatejo flood plain where fine horses and fighting bulls graze.

Crowded beach at high season at Albufeira in the Algarve

◁ Traditional agriculture on smallholdings near Ponte de Lima in the Minho

Rolling grassland of the Alentejo with village and medieval castle of Terena

At the mouths of the Tagus and Douro stand Portugal's two major cities, Lisbon and Oporto respectively. Lisbon, the capital, is a cosmopolitan metropolis with a rich cultural life and many national museums and art galleries. Oporto is a serious rival to Lisbon, especially in terms of commerce and industry. Most centres of population, however, are very much smaller: from the fishing communities on the Atlantic coast to the tiny medieval villages in the vast sunbaked plains of the Alentejo and the mountainous interior of the Beiras.

Woman stripping osiers for wickerwork in Madeira

Far out in the Atlantic Ocean lie two remote archipelagos that are self-governing regions of the Portuguese state: warm, luxuriant Madeira off the coast of Morocco, and the nine rainy, green, volcano tips that make up the Azores, about one third of the way across the Atlantic between Lisbon and New York.

POLITICS AND ECONOMICS

In the final quarter of the 20th century, a new era of Portuguese history began. From the late 1920s, under the long dictatorship of António Salazar, the country was a virtual recluse in the world community. The principal concern of foreign policy was the ultimately futile defence of Portugal's African and Asian colonies. Domestic industry and commerce were dominated by a few wealthy families, in an economic framework of extreme fiscal tightness.

The Carnation Revolution of 1974 brought this era to an end. At first the re-establishment of democracy was a painful process, but since the 1980s Portugal has assumed an increasingly confident Western European demeanour. Entry into the European Community in 1986 was welcomed at all levels of society, and led to an explosion of new construction,

Barredo quarter of Oporto, Portugal's second city

the like of which Portugal had never seen. Traditional exports, such as cork, resin, textiles, tinned sardines and wine, have been joined by new, heavier industries such as vehicle construction and cement manufacturing.

Grants and loans from the EU have funded the building of new roads, bridges and hospitals, and brought significant improvements in agriculture. National confidence in Europe is high, particularly since Oporto was the European Capital of Culture in 2001 and in July 2002 the euro became Portugal's currency.

Luxury yachts in the harbour at Vilamoura in the Algarve

THE PORTUGUESE WAY OF LIFE

Travellers in Portugal will find a mild-mannered, easy-going people. At the same time they have an innate sense of politeness, a quality they respect in others. The Portuguese also tend to dress well, if rather conservatively, and to use formal modes of address: for example, only the young will call new acquaintances by their Christian names.

Collecting seaweed for fertilizer in the Ria de Aveiro lagoon

In spite of this, they are gregarious, folk, often to be seen eating, drinking and making merry in large groups – at a *festa*, or in a restaurant celebrating a birthday or a first communion. There is a special weakness for children, who are cherished, indulged and welcomed everywhere. Visitors to the country who bring their youngsters with them will discover an immediate point of contact with their hosts. Nevertheless, behind the smiles and the good humour, there is a deep-rooted aspect of the national psyche which the Portuguese themselves call

View from the mountaintop village of Monsanto near the border with Spain

Farmworkers breaking for a picnic lunch in the fields of the Alentejo

The family is the bosom of Portuguese daily life. Although old customs are gradually changing, especially in the cities, it is quite common for three generations to live under one roof, and it is normal for both men and women to stay living in the family home until they marry. One thing that has changed dramatically is family size. A generation ago, families of ten or more children were commonplace – especially in remote, rural areas. Nowadays, one or two children constitute an average-sized family, often looked after by a grandmother while both parents go out to work.

saudade, a sort of ethereal, aching melancholy which seems to yearn for something lost or unattainable.

In so far as these generalizations hold true, so too do a couple of Portuguese characteristics which can prove irritating. The first is a relaxed attitude to time: no visitor should interpret lack of punctuality as a personal slight. The second is the fact that many Portuguese men tend to discard their native courtesy completely when they are behind the wheel of a car. Reckless driving, particularly high-speed tailgating, is a national pastime.

Town gate of Óbidos with shrine of Nossa Senhora da Piedade, lined with 18th-century tiles

Catholicism is at the heart of Portuguese life, especially in the north, where you will see a crucifix or the image of a saint watching over most homes, cafés and

Tiled housefront in Alcochete, a small town on the Tagus estuary

barbers' shops. Weddings and first communion services are deeply religious occasions. Although church attendance is in decline, particularly in the cities, national devotion to Our Lady of Fátima remains steadfast, as does delight in festivals *(romarias)* honouring local saints, another tradition that is strongest in the north.

LANGUAGE AND CULTURE

There are few faux pas more injurious to national esteem, than to suggest that Portuguese is a mere dialect of Spanish. Great pride is taken in the language and literature. *Os Lusíadas*, the national epic by 16th-century poet Camões, is studied reverentially, while many Portuguese also delight in the

Religious procession in the village of Vidigueira in the Alentejo

detached, ironic portrait of themselves in the 19th-century novels of Eça de Queirós. Pride too, is taken in *fado*, the native musical tradition which expresses the notion of *saudade*. In rural areas, especially the Minho, there is still an enthusiastic following for folk dancing.

There are several excellent newspapers, but the country's best-selling daily is *A Bola*, which is devoted exclusively to sport, football being a national obsession. Bullfighting too has its adherents, although with nothing like the passion found in Spain.

Transport in the remote Beira Alta

The Portuguese have long been avid watchers of television and are now producing many home-grown soap operas, films and documentaries. Up until just a few years ago, virtually all of these were imported from abroad.

The country has become more forward-looking in recent years, but most aspects of heritage hark back to the Discoveries. The best-loved monuments are those built in the one uniquely Portuguese style of architecture, the Manueline, which dates from this period. Many *azulejo* tile paintings, another cherished tradition, also glory in Portugal's great maritime past.

When the Portuguese joined the European Community in 1986, Commission President Jacques Delors solemnly warned them that they should think of themselves as "Portuguese first, and European second". Typically, the Portuguese were too polite to laugh out loud. How could anyone have imagined that this little country was in danger of suddenly throwing overboard centuries of culture nurtured in staunch independence.

Open-air café in Praça da Figueira in Lisbon's Baixa

Vernacular Architecture

Window in Marvão *(see p294)*

PORTUGAL'S RURAL ARCHITECTURE differs greatly according to climatic conditions and locally available building materials. In the north, thick-walled granite houses are built to give protection from cold winters and rain. The Beiras have a milder climate, but their houses, made of brick or limestone, usually face south to avoid the north wind. In the Alentejo and the Ribatejo, clay houses are long and low, hiding from the hot summer sun and chilly winters. Hills protect the Algarve from these extremes, and houses of clay or stone are built to enjoy the Mediterranean climate.

Yellow-trimmed houses below walls of Óbidos *(see pp174–5)*

Chimneys are small or non-existent. Instead, smoke escapes through openings in the roof.

Roofs are constructed of slate or schist tiles, or occasionally thatch.

Village houses in the Minho (see p263) *and Trás-os-Montes regions* (see p233) *are two-storeyed and usually built with the staircase on the outside. The veranda is used for extra living space.*

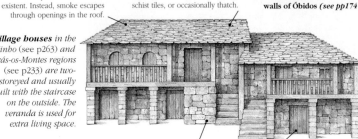

Local granite is used for rustic stonework.

The ground floor is used to keep animals and for storage.

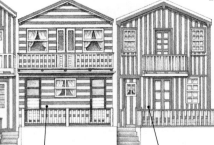

Fishermen's houses found in the Costa Nova region south of Aveiro (see p201) *are painted in brightly coloured stripes. Forests planted to prevent the sand dunes from encroaching on the land provide the raw material.*

Raised platforms guard against flooding.

Modern examples use tiles or painted façades to continue the tradition of striped houses.

Different coloured stripes painted onto the wood allowed the fishermen to identify their houses through the region's frequent mists.

Rooftops of Castelo de Vide in the Alentejo *(see p295)*

TILED ROOFS

Throughout Portugal, red clay roof tiles give towns and villages a memorable skyline. The most traditional and widely used type of roof tile is the *telha de canudo* or tubu-

Telhados de quatro águas, **the distinctive tiled roofs found in Tavira, the Algarve** *(see p330)*

lar tile. Originating from the Moors, these half-cylindrical tiles are plac in two layers: the first is placed with the concave side facing up and t second with the concave side facing down, covering the joints of the fir

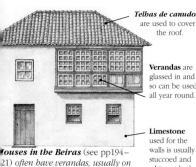

Telhas de canudo are used to cover the roof.

Verandas are glassed in and so can be used all year round.

Limestone used for the walls is usually stuccoed and whitewashed.

Houses in the Beiras (see pp194–221) often have verandas, usually on the first floor. These are built to face the sun, at the same time affording protection from the cold north winds.

Portugal's Windmills

Windmills are thought to have been used in Portugal since the 11th century. Many still dot the hillsides of the country, particularly in coastal regions.

Most windmills have a cylindrical brick or stone base. The upper section revolves to catch the wind in its canvas sails. Estremadura (see pp170–93) has good examples.

Wooden beams

Thatched houses in the Sado estuary (see p169) are now rare. Surviving examples have walls that consist of a wooden frame supporting woven sections made of straw and reed. The simple houses use only local materials.

Azorean windmills, such as this example on Faial (see p370), are fairly similar to the Portuguese model, but show the clear influence of early Dutch and Flemish settlers in their sail design.

Some roof tiles can be removed in summer for more light.

Wooden windows have a painted surround.

Huge chimneys provide spaces for smoking hams and sausages.

Colour-trimmed houses of the Alentejo and Ribatejo regions are mainly constructed of clay. Long and oblong in shape, they have few openings, to ensure that the heat is trapped in winter and kept out in summer.

Whitewashing protects the walls, deflects the hot summer sun and acts as a deterrent for pests and vermin. Many householders consider it a point of honour ro renew their whitewash each year.

Chimneys of the Algarve

These are an important decorative feature of houses in the Algarve (see pp314–31). The Moorish influence can be seen in their cylindrical or prismatic shapes and the geometric designs perforating the clay. The chimneys are whitewashed and many have details picked out in colour to accentuate their ornamentation.

Manueline Architecture

THE STYLE OF ARCHITECTURE that flourished in the reign
of Manuel I *(see pp46–9)* and continued after his
death is essentially a Portuguese variant of Late Gothic. It
is typified by maritime motifs inspired by Portugal's Age
of Discovery, and by elaborate "all-over" decoration.
The artists behind it include João de Castilho and
Diogo Boitac, renowned for the cloister of the Mosteiro
dos Jerónimos *(see pp106–7)*, and Francisco and Diogo
de Arruda, designers of the Torre de Belém *(see p110).*

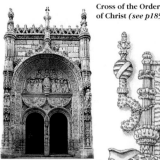

**Twisted Manueline pillory
in Chaves** *(see pp256–7)*

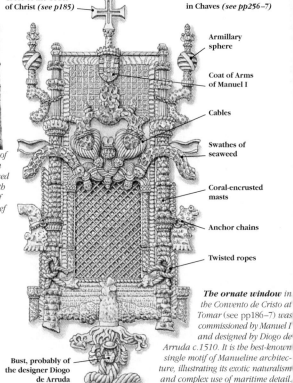

**Cross of the Order
of Christ** *(see p185)*

**Armillary
sphere**

**Coat of Arms
of Manuel I**

Cables

**Swathes of
seaweed**

**Coral-encrusted
masts**

Anchor chains

Twisted ropes

***The portal** of the church of
Conceição Velha in Lisbon*
(see p87) *was commissioned
by Manuel in the early 16th
century. The king himself
appears in the carved relief
in the tympanum.*

***The ornate window** in
the Convento de Cristo at
Tomar* (see pp186–7) *was
commissioned by Manuel I
and designed by Diogo de
Arruda c.1510. It is the best-known
single motif of Manueline architecture, illustrating its exotic naturalism
and complex use of maritime detail.*

**Bust, probably of
the designer Diogo
de Arruda**

***Gil Vicente** created the
Belém Monstrance (1506)
from the first gold brought
back from India. Made for
Santa Maria de Belém (see
p107), its superstructure
echoes the south portal.*

DECORATIVE DETAILS

The most important motifs
in Manueline architecture
are the armillary sphere, the
Cross of the Order of Christ
and twisted rope. Naturalistic
and fantastic forms are often
used, as well as flatter, finely
crafted designs similar to
those found on contempo-
rary Spanish silverware. Later
Manueline schemes some-
times incorporate Italian
Renaissance ornamentation.

The armillary sphere was
a navigational device that
became the emblem of
Manuel I himself.

**The Cross of the
Order of Christ**
was the emblem of
a military order that helped to
finance early voyages. It also
emblazoned sails and flags.

REBUILDING THE MANUELINE PORTAL OF MADRE DE DEUS

The Manueline portal of the church of Madre de Deus in Lisbon *(see p123)* was destroyed in the 1755 earthquake, but it was not until 1872 that João Maria Nepomuceno was commissioned to rebuild it. For accuracy, he referred to an early 16th-century painting by an unknown artist, *The Arrival of the Relics of Santa Auta at the Church of Madre de Deus*, now in the Museu Nacional de Arte Antiga *(see pp96–9)*. The splendid procession in the picture is shown heading towards the Manueline portal of the church, which is clearly depicted. Like others of that period, it stands proud of the building and dominates the façade. The Manueline style favoured rounded rather than pointed arches and this one has an interesting trefoil shape.

Portal of Madre de Deus church today

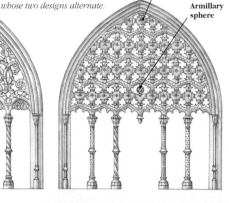

The painting of *The Arrival of the Relics* showing the original 16th-century portal

---

Curving branches and crinkled exotic foliage recall Indian sculptural motifs.

In the Royal Cloister of Batalha (see pp182–3), *early 15th-century pointed Gothic arches incorporate exquisite Manueline screens on colonnettes, probably by Diogo Boitac, whose two designs alternate.*

Soft limestone allowed complex patterns to be carved in the tracery.

Cross of the Order of Christ

Armillary sphere

The colonnettes have all-over ornamentation, with repeated patterns of pearls, shells and coil motifs.

Pillars of plaited colonnettes were used by architects such as Boitac in the Igreja de Jesus in Setúbal *(see p168)*.

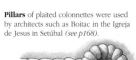

Twisted ropes decorate ceiling vaults, columns and arches, and girdle entire buildings inside and out.

The Buçaco Palace, *today a luxury hotel (see p210), was originally built as a royal hunting lodge about the end of the 19th century. An extraordinary building, the palace incorporates every conceivable element of Manueline architecture and decoration, illustrating the persistence of the style in Portuguese design, which continues to this day.*

Azulejos – Painted Ceramic Tiles

THE IDEA OF COVERING walls, floors and even ceilings with tiles was introduced to Spain and Portugal by the Moors. From the 16th century onwards, Portugal started producing its own decorative tiles. By the 18th century, no other European country was producing as many tiles, for such a variety of purposes and in so many different designs; the blue and white tiles of the Baroque era are considered by many to be the finest. *Azulejos* became and still remain a very important addition to the interior and exterior architecture of Portuguese buildings.

1716 *Detail from Panel of Christ Teaching in the Temple*
Around 1690 blue and white story-telling tiles began to be produced. These figures are from a typical scheme by António de Oliveira Bernardes (c.1660–1732), the greatest master of the genre. The central panels are surrounded by a complex architectural border (*Igreja Da Misericórdia , Évora, see p303*).

c.1520 *Frieze of Spanish-made Tiles*
These Moorish-style tiles were produced by compartmental techniques using raised and depressed areas to prevent the tin-glaze colours from running (*Palácio Nacional de Sintra, see pp158–9*).

c.1680 *Hunting Cat*
Naturalistic panels of this period were often naively drawn, but used a wide range of colours (*Museu Nacional do Azulejo, see pp122–3*).

1500	1600	1700
RENAISSANCE	**MANNERIST**	**BAROQUE**
1500	1600	1700

1565 *Susannah and the Elders*
The mid-16th century saw the introduction of the maiolica technique. This allowed artists to paint directly onto prepared flat tiles using several colours, as these did not run in the firing process. This panel of a biblical episode is one of the earliest produced in Portugal. The decorative details are typical of the Renaissance (*Quinta da Bacalhoa, see p167*).

c.1650 *Carpet Tiles*
So-called because they imitated the patterns of Moorish rugs, these were produced mainly in blue, yellow and white. They often covered whole walls (*Museu Nacional do Azulejo, see pp122–3*).

1736 *Capela de São Filipe*
The small chapel inside Setúbal's castle a fine example of a complete decorati scheme using blue and white tiles. Th panels, illustrating the life of St Philip are signed by Policarpo de Oliveira Bernardes, son of the great António (*Castelo de São Filipe, see p168*).

c.1670 *Tiled Altar Frontal*
The exuberant scheme incorporates Hindu motifs and other exotic themes inspired by the printed calicoes and chintzes brought back from India (*Museu Nacional do Azulejo, see pp122–3*).

1865 *Viúva Lamego Tile Factory, Lisbon*
For the first half of the 19th century, relatively few tiles were produced. The fashion then returned for covering whole surfaces with tiles, and simple stylized designs were used to decorate shop fronts and residential areas. This naive, chinoiserie figure is part of a scheme dating from 1865 that covers the entire façade of the factory.

c.1970 *Tile Pattern*
The original design for this strikingly modern scheme by architect Raúl Lino dates from about 1910. Many of Portugal's leading modern artists have worked with *azulejos* (*Museu Nacional do Azulejo, see pp122–3*).

c.1770–84 *Corredor das Mangas*
The Rococo period saw the reintroduction of polychromatic *azulejos*. This antechamber in the royal palace at Queluz has tiled panels showing hunting scenes, the seasons and the continents (*Palácio de Queluz, see pp164–5*).

1927 *Battle of Ourique*
The early years of the 20th century saw a revival of large-scale historical scenes in traditional blue and white. This panel is by Jorge Colaço (*Carlos Lopes Pavilion, Parque Eduardo VII, Lisbon, see p115*).

1800	1900

NEO-CLASSICAL ART NOUVEAU MODERN

1800	1900

c.1800 *The Story of António Joaquim Carneiro, Hatmaker*
Delicate Neo-Classical ornamentation surrounds the blue and white central subject matter in this charming tale of a shepherd boy who makes his fortune as a hatmaker in the big city. Sophisticated designs of this kind disappeared during the upheavals of the Peninsular War (*see p54*) at the beginning of the 19th century (*Museu Nacional do Azulejo, see pp122–3*).

TILES IN DOMESTIC ARCHITECTURE

Art Nouveau friezes and decorations in deep colours enliven the façade of this early 20th-century house in Aveiro. To this day, tiles are used to cover façades of houses. They are relatively cheap to produce, long-lasting and need little maintenance. Tiled houses brighten up many Portuguese towns and villages. The town of Ovar (*see pp198–9*) is particularly striking.

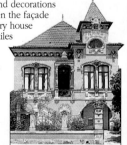

Vila Africana, Aveiro (*see p200*)

c.1770 *Gatekeeper*
"Cut out" figures like this musketeer are an amusing feature of tile schemes in many palaces and mansions from the 18th century onwards. They stand guard at the entrance, on landings or on staircases (*Museu Nacional do Azulejo, see pp122–3*).

Decorated Ceramics

S MALL, TRADITIONAL local potteries *(olarias)*, many of them family concerns, are found in most parts of Portugal. Different regions have their own distinct styles and attractive pottery can be bought from factories and local markets throughout the country. Choose from a variety of wares which include the excellent, practical brown earthenware, brightly coloured figurines *(bonecos)*, intricate hand-painted designs and fine porcelain.

Barcelos (see p273) *is the northern centre for pottery. Terracotta jars, vases, flowerpots and lanterns, and figurines in paintbox colours, are made in country workshops.*

The finest porcelain *in Portugal, famous for its delicacy, is made at Vista Alegre* (see p201). *The factory is well worth visiting for its museum that charts the evolution of the art.*

The faïence tradition *of Coimbra* (see pp202–5) *and its environs continues today in numerous factories, such as Estrela de Conimbriga, south of the city, where this candlestick was made. Detailed Moorish, 17th- and 18th-century designs are painted by hand onto all kinds of domestic objects and artefacts.*

Caldas da Rainha (see p175) *prides itself on its cabbage ware and other lookalike vegetable, fish and fruit ceramics, such as these "gourds". The factory also makes dinner sets with reliefs of flowers and foliage.*

Ceramic art *in Cascais* (see p162) *was revived by Luís Soares in the 1970s. He used the ancient technique of drawing a free design on the soft clay with a sharp stiletto, so no two designs are the same. High-quality glazes and a hot firing give an excellent finish.*

Porches Pottery *was founded in 1968 to revive a local craft and preserve ancient Iberian and Moorish patterns. Each piece is hand-glazed and painted in a free-flowing style, in blue, green and turquoise.*

MINH

ESTREMADURA
AND RIBATEJO

LISBON

THE LISBON
COAST

| 0 kilometres | 50 |
| 0 miles | 25 |

**DOURO AND
TRÁS-OS-MONTES**

BROWN EARTHENWARE

Matt and glazed earthenware, plain or painted with simple patterns, is widely used and sold at country fairs and markets throughout Portugal. The dishes make attractive and resilient cookware. They range from tall, lidded storage pots and sturdy, oven-proof casserole dishes to portable spirit-burners which are used for grilling *chouriço* sausages at the table.

THE BEIRAS

Bisalhães *and other villages near Vila Real (see p255) make an unusual black or dark grey pottery, coloured by wood smoke during slow firing. These tough pots are used for storing oil and olives, carrying water and cooking.*

White floral patterning *on plain terracotta is the hallmark of pottery from Nisa in the Alentejo. Shiny quartz or marble chips are painstakingly applied in lacy floral patterns reminiscent of embroidery.*

The red clay *of Estremoz (see pp300–1) is valued for its malleable qualities. Typical products are patterned in relief with bold decorative flourishes. Estremoz is also famous for its eccentric bonecos.*

The hand-painted pottery *of Redondo (see p300) has a distinctive homely style. Plates may be decorated with fresh floral designs or, as here, charming scenes of pastoral life.*

ENTEJO

GARVE

A potter *in São Pedro do Corval throws a jar "off the hump". This means she can produce, by eye, a number of equal sized jars from one large lump of clay. She is using a rib tool to shape and finish off the pot. Many small cooperative potteries can be found in the villages around Reguengos de Monsaraz (see p307).*

Harvesting the Ocean

A VITAL INDUSTRY IN PORTUGAL, fishing employs about 34,000 men, trawling treacherous coastal waters for a huge variety of fish, destined for local consumption or export. Among the best places to see fishermen at work are Viana do Castelo, Peniche, Nazaré, Sesimbra and Ericeira in the west; and Sagres, Lagos and Olhào in the south.

Terracotta octopus pots

Fishermen mend nets at Peniche (see p174), an important centre for sardines, which are at their best in the summer. About 250,000 tonnes are caught annually around the coast – for freezing, canning or eating fresh in seaside restaurants.

A quayside stall at Sesimbra (see p166) displays the local catch. In the foreground are several types of bream and bass. Traditionally, fishwives, or varinas, would sort the fish as it came in, ready for sale.

Ferragudo is a typical small Algarvian fishing community on the Arade estuary. Its tiny boats fish close to the coast mainly for local needs, leaving the heavy fishing to nearby Portimão, an important sardine centre on the Algarve.

Viana do Castelo

MINHO

Póvoa de Varzim
Oporto

DOURO AN
TRÁS-OS-MON

Aveiro

THE BEIRAS

Figueira da Foz

Nazaré

ESTREMADURA
AND RIBATEJO

Peniche

Ericeira

LISBON   THE LISBON
COAST

Cascais   Setúbal

Sesimbra

ALENTEJO

Sines

ALGARVE
Portimão
Lagos   Olhão   Ta
Sagres

FISHING BOATS

Of Portugal's 10,000 registered boats, many are ancient and weather-beaten. The largest, 24-m (80-ft) trawlers, have diesel engines and radios. Smaller trawlers are used for inshore fishing. At the other end of the scale is the oar-powered 5-m (16-ft) *meia-lua*, In some places this is hauled back up the beach by oxen.

A typical Algarve fishing boat, a small trawler (traineira), is less than 12 m (40 ft) long. This means that fishermen cannot go far out to sea or gather very large hauls.

The frail meia-lua (half-moon) with its fl bottom and high prou is still used on the we coast. It may be paint with a good luck sym such as the Cross of t Order of Christ (see p18

The festival of Nossa Senhora da Agonia at Viano do Castelo (see pp274–5) is one of several celebrations to honour the supreme guardian of fishermen. A statue of the Virgin is paraded through the streets, then carried out to sea in a flower-decked boat to bless the fleet.

At Cascais on the Lisbon coast, an auction is held each evening at the fish market to sell the day's catch. It is a noisy, bustling affair, and a major attraction for locals and visitors alike.

Clamdiggers return from the shellfish beds at Cabanas, east of Tavira in the Algarve. Clams, cockles, whelks and razor shells all flourish here in the warm, shallow waters of the lagoon, and are gathered at low tide.

The trawler (traineira), *fishes furthest offshore, mainly for sardines. In a tradition dating back to the Phoenicians, trawlers are usually painted in bright colours, making them easily recognizable out at sea.*

TYPES OF FISH

The choice of fish in Portugal seems almost endless, from the ubiquitous, delicious sardine through bream, bass, mullet and tuna, to members of the eel and octopus families. Strangely, the national favourite is neither Portuguese nor eaten fresh: dried, salted cod *(bacalhau)* is known as *o fiel amigo*, the faithful friend, and has inspired countless recipes.

Sardines *(sardinhas)* or young pilchards are the leading fresh fish catch. Trawlers catch them with purse-seine nets as they swim in shoals 25–40 m (80–130 ft) below the surface.

Horse mackerel *(carapau)*, favoured for its cheapness and abundance, is baked, grilled or fried. It can also be marinated after cooking to improve flavour.

Tuna *(atum)* can reach 4 m (13 ft) and are found in schools near the Azores and the Algarve – the smaller the fish, the larger the school. Tuna is sold fresh, or canned for export.

Squid *(lulas)* occur plentifully all round the coast and are traditionally served in a stew, fried or grilled. The related cuttlefish *(chocos)* and octopus *(polvos)* are equally popular.

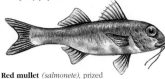

Red mullet *(salmonete)*, prized for its delicate flavour, frequents the coast around Setúbal, where the most famous recipes come from.

Scabbard fish *(peixe espada)* is a tasty, long, thin fish particular to Sesimbra and Madeira. It should not be confused with the similar-sounding but chunkier *espadarte* or swordfish, which tastes quite different.

The Wines of Portugal

SINCE JOINING THE EU in 1986, Portugal has been improving its range of wines. Long-established port *(see pp228–9)*, Madeira *(see p349)* and *vinhos verdes* or "green wines", so called because they are drunk when young, are unique to the country. The classic fruity reds of Bairrada and Dão regions are now gaining much wider recognition, while the last ten years have seen the high-quality reds of the Alentejo and Ribatejo regions win international popularity.

Rosés such as Mateus are Portugal's great export success. To obtain the pink colour, the skins of the red grapes remain in contact with the must (juice) for a short time after crushing.

WINE REGIONS

Each *região demarcada* (demarcated wine region) is designated by law and guarantees wine of high quality. The first region to be demarcated was the Douro, in the reign of King José (1750–77).

OPORTO

LISBON

KEY

- Vinhos Verdes
- Douro
- Dão
- Bairrada
- Bucelas
- Colares
- Moscatel de Setúbal
- Ribatejo
- Alentejo
- Lagoa

0 kilometres 50

0 miles 25

Vinho verde **vineyards in the village of Lapela, near Monção in the Minho**

Cellar of the Buçaco Palace Hotel *(see pp210–11)*, famous for its red wine

HOW TO READ A WINE LABEL

Apart from *branco*, *tinto* and *rosado* (white, red and rosé), terms to note on a wine label are *adamado* or *doce* (sweet), *seco* (dry), *bruto* (dry, sparkling), *licoroso* (fortified), and *maduro* (aged in a vat). *Generoso* indicates an apéritif or dessert wine, *clarete* a Bordeaux-style wine, and *novo* is used for a new or *nouveau* wine. *Reserva* is used for wines from an outstanding vintage year. The phrase *engarrafado na origem* indicates that the wine is estate-bottled, while the words *adega* (cellar) and *quinta* (estate) often appear on wine labels as part of the producer's name.

Vinhos Sogrape is the name of the producer responsible for bottling and distributing this wine.

This wine is a *vinho verde,* a light and slightly sparkling white. *Vinho verde* may also be red.

Denominação de origem controlada is the Portuguese equivalent of the French *appellation contrôlée*.

The alcohol content at 9.5 per cent is fairly high for *vinho verde*.

The style of wine shows it to be a "dry white".

Vinhos verdes *from the Minho are both red and white. The Portuguese drink more red than white, but it is the semi-sparkling white wines that are internationally famous. They are made from grapes grown high above the soil on fences or trees, and are best drunk young.*

White Bucelas *is produced just northwest of Lisbon, mainly from the Arinto grape, which grows especially well in the soil of this small district. Dry and exquisite, the wine has often been compared with Chablis, and goes well with fish dishes.*

Moscatel de Setúbal *is a world-famous dessert wine produced in the Arrábida hills around Palmela, mainly by the long-established firm of José Maria da Fonseca. Their cellars, where the wine is kept in oak casks for up to 50 years before bottling, are open to the public.*

The Douro *has about 80,000 vine-yards along its valley, and although the region is more widely known for its port, just as many grapes are grown for making table wines. Portugal's most expensive table wine, the long-matured Barca Velha, comes from this region.*

The Ribatejo *is becoming a successful region for wine pro-duction, with red and white grapes growing abundantly on the sandy flood plain of the Tagus. The region of Almeirim is becoming highly regarded for its soft and fruity reds.*

Full-bodied red Dão *is the most abundant of Portugal's vinhos maduros. Containing at least 20 per cent of the Touriga Nacional grape, it is aged in wood for several years to ensure quality. Crisp white Dão, which accounts for ten per cent of the region's production, should be drunk relatively young.*

Picking grapes for *vinho verde* near Amarante (see pp248–9)

The Alentejo region *is now making many of Portugal's best new wines. Single estates produce limited quantities of superlative reds, and labels such as Borba, Redondo, Moura and Reguengos are all worth looking out for. Both reds and whites are high in alcohol content.*

Bairrada *wines from the Beiras have been famous for over 1,000 years. The predominant red grape variety is the Baga, yielding the fruity and intense red which rivals Dão and also requires years of ageing. White wines are fewer and not so successful, with the exception of a sparkling version.*

Colares *is a small, historic wine region near Sintra known for its vintage reds. A variety of problems (see p153) means that present-day reds are not as good as their full-bodied forebears, with their softened tannin flavours. Good vintages can still be found in shops.*

Lagoa *produces the best wine from the recently de-marcated region of the Algarve. It is a straightforward wine that does not travel well, but, especially when bought by the garrafão (flagon), it is very cheap and makes a suitable accompa-niment for the local fish dishes.*

PORTUGAL THROUGH THE YEAR

WHILE JULY and August are the most popular months for visiting, spring and autumn can be more rewarding if you want to tour and experience local culture.

Monção's Festa da Coca (June)

Free of excessive heat and crowds, the country is more relaxed. There is deep-rooted respect throughout the country for ancient traditions, which are most often reflected in religious festivals. *Festas* are held throughout the year, most frequently celebrating saints' days, but also marking the end of the harvest, or gastronomic and even sporting events. *Festas* call for prayers, processions, fireworks, eating and drinking, traditional folk dances and general merrymaking.

SPRING

FROM THE ALGARVE to Trás-os-Montes, the country erupts in wild flowers as warmer days set in. This is the time to see the countryside at its most beautiful, although rain can be expected until the end of May.

Easter is a time of great religious celebration, with Holy Week processions taking place all over the country.

MARCH

Open de Portugal de Golfe *(mid-Mar)*. Venue changes from year to year.
Festival Intercéltico do Porto *(end Mar or early Apr)*, Oporto. A festival of music from Portugal and Spain.

Funchal Flower Festival (April)

APRIL

Holy Week *(week before Easter)*, Braga. Events in the country's religious capital are particularly traditional and solemn. Torchlit processions are led by church authorities.

Fátima on 13 May, when 100,000 pilgrims gather every year

Easter Sunday is also the beginning of the bullfighting season throughout Portugal.
Mãe Soberana *(second Sun after Easter)*, Loulé, Algarve. Pilgrimage to Nossa Senhora da Piedade *(see p324)*.
FIAPE *(end Apr)* Estremoz. An international agricultural, cattle and handicrafts fair.

MAY

Festas das Cruzes *(early May)*, Barcelos. The Festival of the Crosses celebrates the day the shape of a cross appeared in the earth in 1504.
Flower Festival *(late Apr)*, Funchal, Madeira. Shops and houses are decorated with flowers. Ends with a parade of flower-covered floats.
Pilgrimage to Fátima *(12–13 May)*. Huge crowds make the pilgrimage to the place where the Virgin appeared to three children in 1917 *(see p184)*.
Queima das Fitas *(mid-May)*, Coimbra. Lively celebrations mark end of the university's academic year *(see p207)*.

Festa do Senhor Santo Cristo dos Milagres *(fifth Sun after Easter)*, Ponta Delgada, São Miguel, Azores. The largest religious festival in the Azores.
Festa do Espírito Santo *(Pentecost)*, Azores. High point of the festival of the Holy Spirit *(see p367)*.
Pilgrimage to Bom Jesus *(Pentecost)*, Braga. Penitents climb the spectacular staircase on their knees *(see pp278–9)*.
Algarve Music Festival *(May Jun–Jul)*, throughout region. Concerts and performances by the Gulbenkian Ballet.

Children carrying a cross at the Festas das Cruzes, Barcelos (May)

SUMMER

M OST VISITORS choose the summer months to visit Portugal. Since many businesses shut down in August, it is holiday time for locals too. Many families spend the entire summer by the seaside.

Summer is a good time to visit the cooler Minho, when the north is busy with saints' day festivals (see pp226–7).

The famed horsemen of the Ribatejo, Vila Franca de Xira (July)

JUNE

Festa de São Gonçalo (first weekend), Amarante. Young, unmarried men and women in the town swap phallus-shaped cakes as tokens of love.
Feira Nacional da Agricultura (early Jun), Santarém. A combination of agricultural fairs, bullfighting and displays of folk dancing.
Santo António (12–13 Jun), Lisbon. Celebrated in the Alfama district with singing and dancing, food and drink. Locals put up lanterns and streamers and bring out chairs for the thousands who arrive.
Festa da Coca (Thu after Trinity Sun), Monção. Part of the Corpus Christi Day celebrations, the festival features scenes of St George in comic battle with the dragon.
São João (23–24 Jun), Oporto. Mid-summer festivities include making wishes while jumping over small fires, and the barcos rabelos boat race (see pp226–7).
São Pedro (29 Jun), Lisbon. More street celebrations with eating, dancing and singing.
Festival de Música de Sintra (Jun–Jul), Sintra. Classical music concerts and ballet.

JULY

Festa do Colete Encarnado (first weekend), Vila Franca de Xira. Named after the red waistcoats of the Ribatejo horsemen, the festival consists of bullfights and bull running.
Festa dos Tabuleiros (mid-Jul, every two or three years), Tomar. Music, dancing, fireworks and a bullfight (see pp184–5). Four hundred women carry trays of decorated loaves on their heads.
Festa da Ria (all month) Aveiro. Folk dances, boat races and a best-decorated boat competition (see p201).
Festival da Cerveja (late Jul), Fábrica do Inglês, Silves. This is a lively beer festival with folk dancing.

AUGUST

Festas Gualterianas (first weekend), Guimarães. Three-day festival dating back to 1452. Torchlight procession, dancing, and medieval parade.
Madeira Wine Rally (first weekend), Funchal, Madeira. Car enthusiasts flock to this challenging car rally, one of the stages of the European championships.
Festa da Nossa Senhora da Boa Viagem (early Aug), Peniche. A crowd gathers at the harbour with lighted candles to greet a statue of the Virgin that

Festa dos Tabuleiros, Tomar

arrives by boat. Fireworks and dancing in the evening.
Jazz em Agosto (early Aug) Lisbon. Popular jazz festival with music in the gardens of the Gulbenkian Centre.
Semana do Mar (1 week in Aug), Horta, Faial, Azores. Food, music, crafts, water sports and lively competitions in this sea festival.
Festival do Marisco (mid-Aug), Olhão. A seafood festival, hosted by the largest fishing port in the Algarve.
Romaria de Nossa Senhora da Agonia (weekend nearest to 20 Aug), Viana do Castelo. Religious procession, followed by display of floats, drinking, folk dancing, fireworks and bands. There is also a Saturday afternoon bullfight, and a ceremonial blessing of the town's fishing boats.

Girl in traditional dress, Viana do Castelo

The sun-drenched Algarve, a major attraction for summer visitors

Procession at the Romaria de Nossa Senhora da Nazaré

AUTUMN

IN MANY WAYS, this is the best season for touring and sightseeing. From mid-September temperatures cool sharply, and autumn is usually drier than spring. This is a mellow, fruitful time of year with the countryside a collage of brown, gold and red.

September is also the start of the *vindima* (the vintage) season. Grapes are harvested and crushed to wine in a spirit of festivity, especially in the port-growing Douro region.

SEPTEMBER

Romaria de Nossa Senhora dos Remédios *(6–9 Sep)*, Lamego. The annual pilgrimage to this famous Baroque shrine is the main feature of three days of celebration. Activities include a torchlit procession and live bands.
Romaria de Nossa Senhora da Nazaré *(8 Sep and following weekend)*, Nazaré. Includes processions, folk dancing, and bullfights.
Feiras Novas *(mid-Sep)*, Ponte de Lima. A huge market with fairground, fireworks, carnival costumes and a brass band competition.
Festa de Senhora da Consolação *(throughout Sep)*, Sintra. A celebration of Portugal's patron saint with a month of parties, music and food in the Assafora area.

Portuguese Grand Prix, Estoril. This Formula One race is cancelled for the forseeable future.
National Folklore Festival *(mid-Sep)*, the Algarve. Colourful music and dance groups converge on the region's towns.
Wine Festival *(all month)*, Funchal and Estreito de Câmara de Lobos, Madeira. The Funchal festival is a lively, popular event, but the one in Estreito de Câmara de Lobos is more authentic.
Feira de São Mateus *(last week)*, Elvas. Festival offering a mixture of religious, cultural and agricultural events.

Musicians in regional costume at the National Folklore Festival in September

Damon Hill winning the Grand Prix at Estoril in 1995

OCTOBER

Feira de Outubro *(first or second week)*, Vila Franca de Xira. Bulls are run through the streets and bullfights staged.

Pilgrimage to Fátima *(12–13 Oct)*. Final pilgrimage of the year, on the date of the Virgin's last appearance.
Festival de Gastronomia *(last two weeks)*, Santarém. Sample the best of regional cooking at this food festival.
International Algarve Car Rally *(Oct–Nov)*, Algarve.

NOVEMBER

All Saints' Day *(1 Nov)*. Throughout the country candles are lit in churches and homes and flowers placed on graves to honour the dead.
Feira Nacional do Cavalo *(first 2 weeks)*, Golegã. Horse enthusiasts and bullfighters come to see horse parades and races. Included are celebrations for St Martin's Day *(11 Nov)* with a grand parade and running of bulls.
Encontros de Fotografia *(throughout-Nov)*, Coimbra. This is Portugal's biggest photography show and features exhibitions of the work of both world-famous and new photographers.

Horsemen at the Feira Nacional do Cavalo, Golegã

Wintry snow scene in the Serra de Montemuro, south of Cinfães *(see p249)*

WINTER

SEEKERS OF MILD, sunny climes fly south to the Algarve where many of the resorts remain alive in winter. For golfers too, the coolest months of the year are the most appealing. January and February also see the spectacular blossoming of almond trees right across southern Portugal.

Bolo rei, a cake enjoyed over the Christmas period

Other visitors migrate even further south to sub-tropical Madeira where winter, in particular Christmas and the New Year, is high season.

PUBLIC HOLIDAYS

New Year's Day (1 Jan)
Carnaval (Feb)
Good Friday
(Mar or Apr)
Dia 25 de Abril,
*commemorating 1974
Revolution* (25 Apr)
Dia do Trabalhador,
Labour Day (1 May)
Corpus Christi (6 Jun)
Camões Day (10 Jun)
Assumption Day
(15 Aug)
Republic Day (5 Oct)
All Saints' Day (1 Nov)
Dia da Restauração,
*commemorating
independence from Spain,
1640* (1 Dec)
**Immaculate
Conception** (8 Dec)
Christmas Day (25 Dec)

DECEMBER

Christmas *(25 Dec).* Everywhere churches and shops display cribs. On Christmas Eve *bacalhau* (salted dried cod) is eaten. Presents are opened, and people go to midnight mass. In Madeira traditional *bolo de mel* (honey cake) is made, and children plant wheat, maize or barley in pots. The pots are placed around the crib to symbolize renewal and plenty.

JANUARY

New Year. Celebrations all over Portugal with spectacular firework displays welcoming in the New Year.
Festa dos Rapazes *(25 Dec – 6 Jan),* around Bragança. Boys dress up in masks and rampage through their villages in an ancient pagan rite of passage. *(see p227).*
Epiphany *(6 Jan).* The traditional crown-shaped cake for

Men in Carnaval costume, Ovar

Epiphany, *bolo rei* (king's cake), is made with a lucky charm and a bean inside. The person who gets the bean must buy the next cake. *Bolo rei* is also made at Christmas.
Festa de São Gonçalinho *(2nd week),* Aveiro. Festival in which loaves of bread are thrown to the crowds from the top of a chapel in thanks for the safe return of a fisherman, or for finding a husband.

Almond trees in blossom in February, the Algarve

FEBRUARY

Fantasporto *(2 weeks in Feb),* Oporto. An important international film festival, showing many films by new directors, including science fiction films.
Carnaval *(varies according to Easter).* Celebrated all over Portugal with spectacular costumes and floats; particularly colourful parades take place in Ovar, Sesimbra, Torres Vedras, Funchal and Loulé. Loulé's festivities are connected with the annual Almond Gatherers' Fair.

The Climate of Portugal

MAINLAND PORTUGAL has a pleasant climate with long, hot summers and mild winters. In the north winters are cool and wet; heading further south temperatures increase and rainfall decreases all the way down to the Algarve where it rarely falls below freezing. Further inland a more Continental climate prevails with summers hotter and winters colder than coastal regions. Madeira is rainy in the north, warmer and drier in the south, and the Azores are mild with year-round rainfall and strong winds.

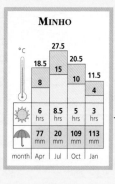

MINHO			
°C			
	27.5		
18.5	15	20.5	
		10	11.5
8			4
☀ 6 hrs	8.5 hrs	5 hrs	3 hrs
☂ 77 mm	20 mm	109 mm	113 mm
month Apr	Jul	Oct	Jan

THE AZORES

Flores

São Jorge
Faial · Pico
Terceira

São Miguel

0 kilometres 200
0 miles 100

ESTREMADURA AND RIBATEJO			
°C			
	20.5	19.5	
17	16	14.5	14
11.5			9
☀ 8 hrs	11 hrs	6.5 hrs	4.5 hrs
☂ 55 mm	2.5 mm	60 mm	92.5 mm
month Apr	Jul	Oct	Jan

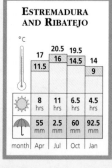

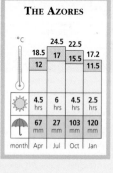

THE AZORES			
°C			
	24.5	22.5	
18.5	17	15.5	17.2
12			11.5
☀ 4.5 hrs	6 hrs	4.5 hrs	2.5 hrs
☂ 67 mm	27 mm	103 mm	120 mm
month Apr	Jul	Oct	Jan

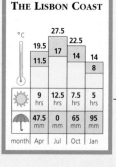

THE LISBON COAST			
°C			
	27.5		
19.5	17	22.5	
11.5		14	14
			8
☀ 9 hrs	12.5 hrs	7.5 hrs	5 hrs
☂ 47.5 mm	0 mm	65 mm	95 mm
month Apr	Jul	Oct	Jan

MADEIRA

Porto Santo

Madeira

Funchal

0 kilometres 20
0 miles 10

MADEIRA			
°C			
	24.5	24	
19.5	18	17.5	19
13.5			13
☀ 6 hrs	7.5 hrs	6 hrs	4.5 hrs
☂ 39 mm	2.5 mm	75 mm	103 mm
month Apr	Jul	Oct	Jan

Viana
do Castelo

Op

Av

BE
LITC

● Le

Santaré

LISBON

Setúbal

● S

Lag

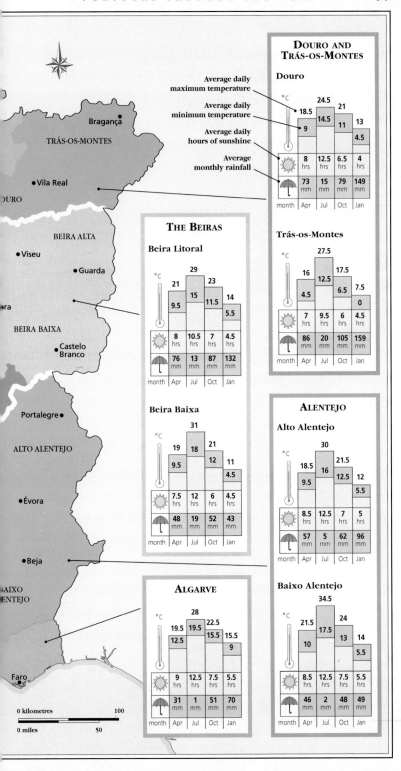

Bragança

TRÁS-OS-MONTES

Vila Real

DURO

BEIRA ALTA

Viseu

Guarda

ora

BEIRA BAIXA

Castelo Branco

Portalegre

ALTO ALENTEJO

Évora

Beja

AIXO
ENTEJO

Faro

0 kilometres 100

0 miles 50

DOURO AND TRÁS-OS-MONTES

Douro

Average daily maximum temperature

Average daily minimum temperature

Average daily hours of sunshine

Average monthly rainfall

°C	Apr	Jul	Oct	Jan
max	18.5	24.5	21	13
min	9	14.5	11	4.5
sunshine	8 hrs	12.5 hrs	6.5 hrs	4 hrs
rainfall	73 mm	15 mm	79 mm	149 mm

Trás-os-Montes

°C	Apr	Jul	Oct	Jan
max	16	27.5	17.5	7.5
min	4.5	12.5	6.5	0
sunshine	7 hrs	9.5 hrs	6 hrs	4.5 hrs
rainfall	86 mm	20 mm	105 mm	159 mm

THE BEIRAS

Beira Litoral

°C	Apr	Jul	Oct	Jan
max	21	29	23	14
min	9.5	15	11.5	5.5
sunshine	8 hrs	10.5 hrs	7 hrs	4.5 hrs
rainfall	76 mm	13 mm	87 mm	132 mm

Beira Baixa

°C	Apr	Jul	Oct	Jan
max	19	31	21	11
min	9.5	18	12	4.5
sunshine	7.5 hrs	12 hrs	6 hrs	4.5 hrs
rainfall	48 mm	19 mm	52 mm	43 mm

ALENTEJO

Alto Alentejo

°C	Apr	Jul	Oct	Jan
max	18.5	30	21.5	12
min	9.5	16	12.5	5.5
sunshine	8.5 hrs	12.5 hrs	7 hrs	5 hrs
rainfall	57 mm	5 mm	62 mm	96 mm

Baixo Alentejo

°C	Apr	Jul	Oct	Jan
max	21.5	34.5	24	14
min	10	17.5	13	5.5
sunshine	8.5 hrs	12.5 hrs	7.5 hrs	5.5 hrs
rainfall	46 mm	2 mm	48 mm	49 mm

ALGARVE

°C	Apr	Jul	Oct	Jan
max	19.5	28	22.5	15.5
min	12.5	19.5	15.5	9
sunshine	9 hrs	12.5 hrs	7.5 hrs	5.5 hrs
rainfall	31 mm	1 mm	51 mm	70 mm

OM MANVEL

per graça de dẽ Rey de portugall
dos. algaruee. daquem z dalẽ m
em africa. senor de guinee z da conquista nauegaçam z
merçio dethiopia arabia persia. z da jndia zc. ¶
quantoe. esto a perpetua memoria feito buem fazer
saber que assi como oproio z prinçipall cuydado dos
tem alguũ cargo deue ser trabalhar como ae cousae
lhee sam encarregadae sciam postae. no mare. prosp
z melhorado estado que ser possa. assy tanto maie. a
isto noe. Reie. z prinçepxe. fazello. quanto com maie. e
çellente preminençia sam per dẽ. postoe. na terra per
bem della z de seue. bassalloe. z para toda exceuçam z ex
plo de virtude. ☙ por que esta obrigaçam tam deuiꝺ

THE HISTORY OF PORTUGAL

PORTUGAL IS ONE of the oldest nation states in Europe: its foundation in 1139 predates that of its neighbour, Spain, by nearly 350 years. The Romans, who arrived in 218 BC, called the whole peninsula Hispania, but the region between the Douro and Tagus rivers was named Lusitania after the Celtiberian tribe that lived there. When the Roman Empire collapsed in the 5th century, Hispania was overrun first by Germanic tribes, then by Moors from North Africa in 711. Military reconquest by the Christian kingdoms of the north began in earnest in the 11th century and it was during this long process that Portucale, a small county of the kingdom of León and Castile, was declared independent by its first king, Afonso Henriques.

The new kingdom expanded southwards to the Algarve and Portuguese sailors began to explore the African coast and the Atlantic. Portugal's golden age reached its zenith in the reign of Manuel I with Vasco da Gama's voyage to India in 1498 and the discovery of Brazil in 1500. Eastern trade brought incredible wealth, but

Portuguese ship (c.1500)

military defeat in Morocco meant that the prosperity was short-lived. Spain invaded in 1580 and Spanish kings ruled Portugal for the next 60 years.

After Portugal regained independence, her fortunes were restored by the discovery of gold in Brazil. In the second half of the 18th century, the chief minister, the Marquês de Pombal, began to modernize the country and to limit the reactionary influence of the church. However, Napoleon's invasion in 1807 and the loss of Brazil in 1825 left Portugal impoverished and divided. Power struggles between Absolutists and Constitutionalists further weakened the country, and despite a period of stability from the 1850s, the debt crisis worsened. In 1910, a republican revolution overthrew the monarchy.

The economy deteriorated until a military coup in 1926 led to the long dictatorship of António Salazar, who held power from 1928 to 1968. The Carnation Revolution ended his rule in 1974 and democracy was restored in 1976. Portugal's depleted economy was gradually revived by an influx of funds through joining the EU in 1986.

Portuguese mariners' chart of the North Atlantic drawn on parchment (c.1550)

◁ **Illuminated frontispiece of the *Leitura Nova*, showing Portugal's coat of arms and portrait of Manuel I (c.1520)**

The Rulers of Portugal

AFONSO HENRIQUES declared himself Portugal's first king in 1139, but his descendants' ties of marriage to various Spanish kingdoms led to dynastic disputes. João I's defeat of the Castilians in 1385 established the House of Avis which presided over the golden age of Portuguese imperialism. Then in 1580, in the absence of a direct heir, Portugal was ruled by Spanish kings for 60 years before the Duke of Bragança became João IV. A Republican uprising ended the monarchy in 1910. However, in the first 16 years of the Republic there were 40 different governments, and in 1926 Portugal became a dictatorship under the eventual leadership of Salazar. Democracy was restored by the "Carnation" Revolution of 1974.

1481–95 João II

1211–23 Afonso II

1438–81 Afonso V

1185–1211 Sancho I

1248–79 Afonso III

1279–1325 Dinis

1100	1200	1300	1400	1500
HOUSE OF BURGUNDY			AVIS	
1100	1200	1300	1400	1500

1325–57 Afonso IV

1357–67 Pedro I

1367–83 Fernando I

1223–48 Sancho II

1139–85 Afonso Henriques (Afonso I)

1433–8 Duarte

1521 João

1385–1433 João I

1495–1521 Manuel I

1828–53 Maria II

1557–78 Sebastião

1750–77 José I

1932–68 António
Salazar (prime minister)

1621–40 Felipe III
(Philip IV of Spain)

1853–61
Pedro V

1640–56 João IV

1816–26
João VI (regent
from 1792)

**1976–8 &
1983–5**
Mário
Soares
(prime
minister)

1656–83 Afonso VI

1861–89
Luís I

1683–1706
Pedro II (regent
from 1668)

1600	1700	1800	1900	
HAPSBURG	BRAGANÇA			REPUBLIC
1600	1700	1800	1900	

1598–1621 Felipe II
(Philip III of Spain)

1985–95 Aníbal
Cavaco Silva
(prime minister)

1580–98 Felipe I
(Philip II of Spain)

1995–
António Guterres
(prime minister)

1578–80 Henrique

1777–1816
Maria I and Pedro III

1908–10
Manuel II

1826–28
Pedro IV

1706–50 João V

1889–1908 Carlos I

Prehistoric and Roman Portugal

FROM ABOUT 2000 BC Portugal's Stone Age communities were supplanted by foreign invaders, most notably the Iberians and the Celts. When Rome defeated the Carthaginians in 216 BC and took over all their territories in eastern Spain, she still had to subdue Celtiberian tribes living in the west. One of these, the Lusitani, put up fierce resistance. After their defeat in 139 BC, their name was preserved in Lusitania, a province of Roman Hispania, corresponding roughly to present-day Portugal. Romanization led to four centuries of stability and prosperity, but as the Roman Empire collapsed, Lusitania was overrun by Germanic tribes, first the Suevi and then the Visigoths.

Gold solidus (c.400 AD)

IBERIAN PENINSULA IN 27 BC

☐ *Roman provinces*

The amphitheatre probably dated from the building boom of the 1st century AD.

The forum and principal temple

Dolmen of Comenda
Dolmens such as this one near Évora were communal burial chambers. Many were built by the Neolithic peoples who lived in the Iberian Peninsula in the third millennium BC.

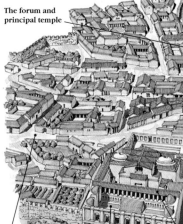

The main road led north to Aeminium (Coimbra).

Porca of Murça
Trás-os-Montes has preserved 16 statues of animals like this granite pig (see p257), probably used in Celtic fertility rituals.

Palestra (exercise area of the baths)

The Baths of Trajan had a spectacular view of the ravine below the city walls.

TIMELINE

c.2000 BC Iberian tribes arrive in the peninsula, probably from Africa

Iberian Gold gorget

139 BC Celtiberian resistance to Roman rule ends with the death of Viriatus, leader of the Lusitani tribe

3000 BC	2000 BC	1000 BC

2500 BC Portugal inhabited by late Stone Age people. Many megalithic tombs date from this time

Celtic stone warrior, 1st millennium BC

1000 BC Phoenicians set up trading stations and settlements along the southern coast

c.700 BC Celtic invaders settle in Portugal

218 BC The Romans invade the Iberian Peninsula

Floor Mosaic
Under Roman rule, the wealthy built lavishly decorated villas. This mosaic of a triton (1st century AD) comes from the House of the Fountains just outside the walls of Conimbriga.

WHERE TO SEE PREHISTORIC AND ROMAN PORTUGAL

The Alentejo is rich in Stone Age megaliths *(see p306)*, while the north has the two best examples of Celtiberian settlements at Sanfins *(p248)* and Briteiros. Many traces of the Roman period, including roads and bridges, are found throughout Portugal. Apart from Conimbriga, major sites, such as the villas at Pisões *(p311)* and Milreu *(p325)*, are mainly in the south. Faro's Museu Municipal *(p327)* has a good collection of local finds.

Roman Amphora
Garum, a popular, spiced sauce made of fermented fish, was manufactured at Tróia (see p169) and exported in 27-litre (6-gallon) amphorae like this one.

Aqueduct

Road east to Tomar

Citânia de Briteiros, a hilltop settlement founded around the 5th century AD, survived until well into the Roman period. It was discovered in 1874 (p281).

Visigothic Buckle
The Visigoths were warlike yet cultured people who strengthened the position of Christianity. However, their system of elective monarchy led to factional disputes.

A *domus*, private house with a garden

Évora's temple dates from the 2nd century AD (see p302). It is almost all that remains of an important Roman city.

RECONSTRUCTION OF CONIMBRIGA

The extensive remains of Conimbriga *(see p208)* give a vivid picture of how thoroughly Romanized Portugal became under the empire. The town expanded rapidly in the 1st century AD, when it achieved the self-governing status of a *municipium*. It fell to the Suevi in AD 468.

AD 73 Emperor Vespasian grants towns in the Iberian Peninsula same rights as Latin towns in Italy	**415** Visigoths invade the peninsula and drive out the Vandals and the Alani	**585** Visigoths take over the Suevian kingdom, fixing their capital at Toledo in Spain
	AD 200 Christianity becomes established in the peninsula	

D 1	**AD 200**	**AD 400**	**AD 600**

? BC During the rule of the mperor Augustus the Iberian ninsula is divided into three; sitania is the name given to central province south of e River Douro

409 Invasion by "barbarian" tribes from central Europe: the Vandals, the Alani and the Suevi

411 Suevian kingdom established in Galicia and northern Portugal

Visigothic chapel at São Frutuoso (see p277)

Moorish Domination and Christian Reconquest

IBERIAN PENINSULA IN 1100

- County of Portucale
- Kingdom of León and Castile
- Moorish kingdoms

Bronze Moorish oil lamp in the shape of a bird

WHEN MUSLIMS from North Africa defeated the Visigoths in 711, the Iberian Peninsula became a province of the Caliphate of Damascus. Then, in 756, Abd al Rahman established the independent kingdom of Al Andalus, his capital Córdoba becoming one of the world's great centres of culture. Moorish control of the peninsula remained virtually undisputed for the next 300 years until the small Christian kingdoms in the north began the Reconquest. In the 11th century, as Moorish power waned, "Portucale" was just a small county of the Kingdom of León and Castile, centred on the Douro. It became independent after Afonso Henriques defeated the Moors at Ourique in 1139.

Without the Virgin to watch over them, the Faro fishermen's nets are empty.

Moorish Plate
Vivid depictions of a hunting dog, a falcon and a gazelle decorate this 11th-century plate found at Mértola, a river port on the Guadiana used by eastern traders.

The fishermen set off with new hope.

Coexistence
Under Moorish rule, co-operation between the faiths was common. This miniature from the 13th century shows the friendly meeting of two knights, one a Christian, the other a Moor.

TIMELINE

711 Large Muslim army of Berbers and Arabs (the Moors) conquers Iberian Peninsula following dispute over Visigothic succession

10th-century Hispano-Moorish ivory casket

722 Christian victory at Covadonga in Asturias marks start of gradual reconquest

868 Vímara Peres takes Oporto from the Moors

878 Christian forces recapture Coimbra

AD 700	AD 800	AD 900	AD 100

756 Battle of Al Musara; Abd al Rahman defeats governor of Córdoba and founds kingdom of Al Andalus

Nora, a bucket wheel for raising water introduced by the Moors

955 Moorish leader Al Mansur retakes Coimbra, then forces Christian frontier back to the River Douro

1008–31 Civil war; Al Andalus divided into small kingdoms known as *taifas*

Stone Relief of São Tiago
In wars against the Moors, the apostle St James (São Tiago) assumed a special role. At Ourique in 1139, soldiers claimed to have seen him leading the Christian forces into battle.

12th-century Silver Dirham
This coin was minted at Beja by the Almohads, a Muslim sect even stricter than their forerunners, the Almoravids.

WHERE TO SEE MOORISH PORTUGAL

The influence of the Moors is strongest in the south, in towns like Lagos *(see p320)*, Faro *(p326)* and Silves, where they ruled for longer and the architecture *(p19)* retains many Arab features. In Mértola *(p313)*, the church preserves much of the old mosque. Further north, the Castelo dos Mouros, in Sintra *(p157)*, and many other fortresses were taken over and rebuilt by the Christians.

This cistern well was found on the site of the archaeological museum at Silves, a Moorish centre in the Algarve (p323).

The lost statue of the Virgin is recovered from the sea and restored to its rightful place on the walls.

Out at sea the fishermen's nets are full once more.

Capture of Lisbon
The Reconquest was given the status of a crusade by the pope. Lisbon was taken in 1147 with the aid of English troops bound for the Holy Land.

FARO UNDER MOORISH RULE

Christians who lived under Moorish rule were called Mozarabs. At Faro they placed a statue of the Virgin on the walls of the city, but resentful Muslims took the statue down. These four scenes from the *Cantigas de Santa Maria* tell the story of the miracle that followed.

1097 Alfonso VI of León and Castile entrusts ortucale to his son-in-law Henry of Burgundy

1086 Invasion of the Almoravids

1139 Battle of Ourique; Afonso Henriques declares himself King of Portugal

1143 Treaty of Zamora establishes Portugal's independence

1165–9 Geraldo sem Pavor captures a number of cities from the Almohads, including Évora and Badajoz

1050   **1100**   **1150**

1064 Christians regain Coimbra

1128 Battle of São Mamede; Afonso Henriques defeats his mother Teresa to win control of county of Portucale

1153 Founding of Cistercian Abbey at Alcobaça

1147 Fall of Lisbon to Crusader army; Almoravid empire falls to the Almohads

Henry of Burgundy

The New Kingdom

THE PORTUGUESE RECONQUEST was completed in 1249 when Afonso III captured Faro in the Algarve. His successor, King Dinis, encouraged agriculture and commerce, earning the nickname of the "farmer king". He also built castles to defend the border from Castilian attack and expanded the navy. Territorial disputes with Castile came to a head in 1383 when King Fernando died and his son-in-law, Juan I of Castile, claimed the Portuguese throne for his wife Beatriz. Juan's opponents favoured Pedro I's illegitimate son, João of Avis, elected king by the *cortes* (parliament) in Coimbra in 1385.

14th-century statue of armed knight

IBERIAN PENINSULA IN 1200

- ▨ *Kingdom of Portugal*
- ▢ *Spanish kingdoms*
- ▨ *Territory under Moorish rule*

Cancioneiro da Ajuda
King Dinis was a fine musician and poet. This illumination is from a collection of troubadour songs, many by the king himself.

Coat of arms of Portugal

The frieze shows scenes from the life of Pedro and Inês.

The aedicules contain finely carved scenes from the life of St Bartholomew, Dom Pedro's patron saint.

The faithful dog at the feet of the deceased a common feature of Gothic tombs.

Fortifications of Serpa
King Dinis had a chain of fortified towns and castles built along the borders with Castile and Moorish Spain. This 16th-century drawing shows the medieval walls and towers of Serpa (see p310).

TIMELINE

1185 Sancho I becomes king; his victories in the Algarve are reversed by Al-Mansur, the Almohad caliph

1211 First *cortes* (parliament) held at Coimbra

Leiria Castle

1254 The *cortes* held at Leiria includes representatives of the towns

1200

1250

1173 Remains of St Vincent brought from Cabo de São Vicente to Lisbon

1179 Portugal recognized as kingdom by the pope

Afonso III

1248 Anarchic reign of Sancho II ends in his deposition by his brother Afonso III

1249 Afonso III completes reconquest of the Algarve, but his claim to sovereignty is challenged by Castile

1256 Lisbon becomes capital of Portugal in place of Coimbra

St Isabel (1271–1336)
King Dinis did not approve of his wife's acts of charity. A legend tells how the bread Queen Isabel was about to distribute to the poor turned into roses when she was challenged by her husband.

Six angels support the recumbent king.

Cross of Sancho I
Sancho's reign (1185–1211) saw royal power and wealth increase despite disputes between the king and his bishops over papal authority.

Bartholomew is martyred by ing flayed alive.

TOMB OF PEDRO I
The Gothic carvings on the royal tomb at Alcobaça *(see pp178–9)* are the finest of their kind in Portugal. The forthright Pedro, who ruled from 1357–67, is remembered chiefly for the tragic tale of his murdered mistress, Inês de Castro, whose matching tomb stands facing Pedro's.

WHERE TO SEE MEDIEVAL PORTUGAL

Of the many castles built or rebuilt in this period, the most picturesque are at Almourol *(see p189)* and Óbidos. In the citadel of Bragança *(p 258–9)* stands the Domus Municipalis, a medieval meeting hall. Most surviving Romanesque buildings, however, are religious: the cathedrals in Oporto, Lisbon *(p74)* and Coimbra *(p204)* and many smaller churches in the north, such as those at Rates *(p272)*, Roriz *(p248)* and Bravães *(p267)*.

Óbidos Castle, *now a pousada, was rebuilt by King Dinis when he gave this fairy-tale town to his wife Isabel as a wedding present in 1282* (p172).

Oporto's Sé (p240) *has been much altered but the twin-towered west front retains its original 13th-century character.*

279–1325 King Dinis consolidates ortugal's independence

1288 Portugal's first university founded in Lisbon

1297 Castile recognizes Portugal's sovereignty over the Algarve

Knight of the Order of Christ

1300

1355 After murder of Inês de Castro, Pedro takes up arms against his father Afonso IV

1319 Foundation of the Order of Christ *(see p185)*

1336 Death of St Isabel of Portugal

1349 Following Black Death, a law is passed enforcing compulsory rural labour

1350

1357 Accession of Pedro I, who has murderers of Inês de Castro brutally executed

1383 João of Avis ends regency of Leonor Teles and proclaims himself defender of the realm

1384 Juan I of Castile invades Portugal

1372 Fernando I's unpopular marriage to Leonor Teles leads to riots

The House of Avis

AFTER JOÃO OF AVIS had defeated the Castilians in 1385 to become João I of Portugal, he strengthened his position through an important alliance with England. His long reign saw the start of Portuguese imperialism and the beginning of maritime expeditions promoted by his son, Henry the Navigator *(see pp48–9)*. Further voyages of discovery in the reign of Manuel I "the Fortunate", led to trade with India and the East and, following Afonso de Albuquerque's capture of Goa, initially brought great wealth. So, too, did the colonization of Brazil. However, the lure of overseas adventure weakened mainland Portugal, which suffered serious depopulation. The age of expansion ended when a foolhardy military expedition to Morocco, led by King Sebastião, was soundly defeated in 1578.

IBERIAN PENINSULA IN 1500

▨ *Portugal*

☐ *Spain (Castile and Aragon)*

16th-century Porcelain Plate
In 1557 the Portuguese were granted Macao as a trading post in China. This Chinese plate bears the arms of Matias de Albuquerque, a descendant of the great Afonso, conqueror of Goa.

Arms of English royal family

John of Gaunt used the alliance with Portugal to pursue his own claim to the throne of Castile.

Troops Landing at Arzila
The kings of the Avis dynasty constantly sought to extend their domains to Morocco, where they established a small colony around Tangier. This Flemish tapestry celebrates Afonso V's capture of Arzila in 1471.

Luís de Camões
After serving in India and Morocco, where he lost an eye, the poet wrote Os Lusíadas (see p188), an epic on the Discoveries.

TIMELINE

King Duarte

1385	c.1425	1441	1471	1482–3	1494	1495–1521	1496

1385 João I defeats Castilian army at Battle of Aljubarrota

1415 Capture of Ceuta in Morocco

c.1425 *Leal Conselheiro*, a treatise on courtly behaviour written by King Duarte

1441 Lagos is site of first slave market in modern Europe

1496 Jews expelled from the country or forcibly converted

1495–1521 Reign of Manuel I and great period of discoveries

1400	1425	1450	1475

1386 Alliance with England formalized by Treaty of Windsor

1418 Henry the Navigator made governor of the Algarve

1471 Conquest of Moroccan fortresses of Arzila and Tangier

1482–3 João II successfully resists the Conspiracy of the Nobles

1494 Spain and Portugal divide the Atlantic region by Treaty of Tordesillas

Wedding of Manuel I
Manuel's reign marked the highest point in Portugal's golden age of discovery and conquest. His marriages were made to reinforce ties with Spain. Shown here is his third: to Leonor, sister of Carlos I of Spain, in 1518.

João I drew support from the merchants of Lisbon and Oporto rather than the nobles, many of whom sided with Castile.

Archbishop of Braga

Portugal's bishops took João's side after the pope had refused to legitimize the children of Inês de Castro *(see pp44–5).*

WHERE TO SEE GOTHIC PORTUGAL

Many churches include Gothic elements, such as the cloister of the Sé in Oporto *(see p240)* and the richly sculpted portal of the Sé in Évora *(p304)*. Tomar's Convento de Cristo *(pp186–7)* is predominantly Gothic, as is the church at Alcobaça *(pp178–9)*. The finest church, however, is at Batalha, built in thanks for João I's victory at the Battle of Aljubarrota. It also contains major examples of Manueline architecture *(see pp20–21)*.

Batalha (pp182–3) incorporates a wide range of Gothic styles. The plain, lofty nave contrasts with the ornamented exterior.

JOÃO I AND THE ENGLISH

João's alliance with England against Castile led to his marriage in 1387 to Philippa of Lancaster, daughter of John of Gaunt, son of Edward III. This illustration from the chronicle of Jean de Wavrin shows the new king entertaining his father-in-law.

Battle of Alcácer-Quibir (1578)
King Sebastião saw his African expedition as a crusade against Islam. After Alcácer-Quibir, he and 8,000 of his troops lay dead, 15,000 captives were sold into slavery and the House of Avis dynasty was doomed.

Belém Monstrance (see p20)

1531 Inquisition introduced into Portugal

1510 Beginning of Portuguese empire in Asia; Goa conquered by Afonso de Albuquerque

1536 Death of Gil Vicente, Portugal's greatest dramatist

1572 Publication of *Os Lusíadas*, a verse epic celebrating Portugal's history by Luís de Camões

1500	**1525**	**1550**	**1575**

c.1502 Work starts on the Jerónimos monastery in Belém *(see pp106–7)*

1498 Vasco da Gama reaches India

1521–57 Reign of João III, known as "the Pious"

Gil Vicente

1559 Jesuit University established at Évora *(see p304)*

1578 King Sebastião's expedition to Morocco ends in his death and total defeat at the Battle of Alcácer-Quibir

The Age of Discovery

PORTUGAL'S ASTONISHING PERIOD of conquest and exploration began in 1415 with the capture of the North African city of Ceuta. Maritime expeditions into the Atlantic and along the West African coast followed, motivated by traditional Christian hostility towards Islam and desire for commercial gain. Great riches were made from the gold and slaves taken from the Guinea coast, but the real breakthrough for Portuguese imperialism occurred in 1498 when Vasco da Gama *(see p108)* reached India. Portugal soon controlled the Indian Ocean and the spice trade, and established an eastern capital at Goa. With Pedro Álvares Cabral's "discovery" of Brazil, Portugal became a mercantile super-power rivalled only by Spain.

Portuguese padrão

Armillary Sphere
This celestial globe with the ear[th] in its centre was used by navi[-] gators for measuring the positio[n] of the stars. It became the per- sonal emblem of Manuel I.

Magellan (c.1480–1521)
With Spanish funding, Portuguese sailor Fernão de Magalhães, known as Magellan, led the first circumnavigation of the globe (1519–22). He was killed in the Philippines before the voyage's end.

1500–1501 Gaspar Corte Real reaches Newfoundland.

1427 Diogo de Silves discovers the Azores.

1434 Gil Eanes rounds Cape Bojador (Western Sahara).

1460 Diogo Gomes discovers the Cape Verde archipelago.

1470s Discovery of island of São Tomé.

1482 Diogo Cão reaches the mouth of the Congo.

1500 Pedro Álvares Cabral reaches Brazil.

1485 On his third voyage Diogo Cão reaches Cape Cross (Namibia).

1488 Bartolom[eu] Dias rounds Ca[pe] of Good Hop[e].

African Ivory Salt Cellar
This 16th-century ivory carving shows Portuguese warriors supporting a globe and a ship. A sailor peers out from the crow's nest at the top.

The Adoration of the Magi
Painted for Viseu Cathedral shortly after Cabral returned from Brazil in 1500, this panel is attributed to Grão Vasco (see p213). The second king, Baltazar, is depicted as a Tupi Indian.

Japanese Screen (c.1600)
This screen shows traders unloading a nau, or great ship. Between 1575 and their expulsion in 1638, the Portuguese monopolized the carrying trade between China and Japan.

HENRY THE NAVIGATOR

Although he did not sail himself, Henry (1394–1460), the third son of João I, laid the foundations for Portugal's maritime expansion that were later built upon by João II and consolidated by Manuel I. As Master of the wealthy Order of Christ and Governor of the Algarve, Henry was able to finance expeditions along the African coast. By the time he died he had a monopoly on all trade south of Cape Bojador. Legend tells that he founded a great school of navigation either at Sagres *(see p320)* or Lagos.

KEY

– – – Discoverers' routes

1543 Portuguese arrive in Japan.

1513 Trading posts set up in China at Macau and Canton.

1510 Capture of Goa.

1498 Vasco da Gama reaches Calicut in India.

1518 Fortress built in Colombo (Sri Lanka).

1512 Portuguese reach Ternate in the Moluccas (Spice Islands).

Cloves

Pepper

Nutmeg

Cinnamon

The Spice Trade
Exotic spices were a great source of wealth for Portugal. The much-disputed Moluccas, or Spice Islands, were purchased from Spain in 1528.

PORTUGUESE DISCOVERIES

The systematic attempt to find a sea route to India, which led to a monopoly of the spice trade, began in 1482 with the first voyage of Diogo Cão, who planted a *padrão* (stone cross) on the shores where he landed.

Lateen-rigged Caravel
These ships with three triangular sails were favoured by the first Portuguese explorers who sailed close to the African coast. For later journeys across the open ocean, square sails were found more effective.

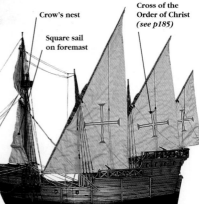

Crow's nest

Square sail on foremast

Cross of the Order of Christ *(see p185)*

Spanish Rule

Philip II of Spain

WHEN HENRIQUE, the Cardinal-King, died without an heir in 1580, Philip II of Spain successfully claimed the Portuguese throne through his mother, a daughter of Manuel I. Under Spanish rule, influential positions were held by Portuguese nobles, but a common foreign policy led to a steady loss of colonies to the Dutch. In 1640 a Portuguese revolt took place in Lisbon and the Duke of Bragança was chosen to become King João IV. Spain retaliated and the ensuing war continued until 1668. Meanwhile Portugal was forced to rely economically on her overseas territories.

Restoration of João IV
Two weeks after his supporters had ousted the Spanish in 1640, João was crowned on a platform outside the Royal Palace in Lisbon.

Spanish Armada
In 1588 Philip II of Spain hoped to invade England with his great fleet. It sailed from Lisbon where it had been equipped and provisioned.

The Graça fort was held by the Spanish.

António Vieira
Vieira (1606–97) was a Jesuit priest, writer and orator. He was sent on many diplomatic missions and clashed with the Inquisition over his support for Christianized Jews.

WAR OF INDEPENDENCE

Portugal's long war against Spain (1640–68) was fought mostly in the Alentejo. This *azulejo* panel from Palácio Fronteira in Lisbon *(see p125)* shows the Battle of Linhas de Elvas (1658). A Portuguese army besieged in Elvas *(see pp296–7)* was relieved by fresh troops from Estremoz, who soundly defeated the Spanish.

TIMELINE

1580 Battle of Alcântara; Spanish invade and Philip II of Spain becomes King of Portugal	**1614** Publication of the *Peregrinação* by Fernão Mendes Pinto, an account of his travels in Asia in the mid-16th century	**1624** Dutch capture Portuguese colony of Bahia in Brazil	**1631** Birth of painter Josefa de Óbidos
1588 Spanish Armada sets sail from Lisbon to invade England			
1580	**1600**		**1620**
1583 Philip returns to Spain leaving his nephew, Cardinal-Archduke Albert of Austria, as viceroy		*Church of São Vicente de Fora (see p72) by Filippo Terzi and Baltasar Álvares, completed in 1627*	**1626** Jesuit missionary António de Andrade crosses the Himalayas into Tibet
1581 The king invites Italian architect Filippo Terzi to Lisbon to remodel the Royal Palace and to build many churches			

Indo-Portuguese Contador

Luxury cabinets, known as contadores, *were made from teak and ebony in Portugal's overseas colonies. Many came from Goa. This fine 17th-century example is from the Museu Nacional de Arte Antiga (see pp96–9).*

The besieged Portuguese army at Elvas was retreating from a previous unsuccessful campaign in Spain.

Stout bastions deflected the attackers' cannon fire.

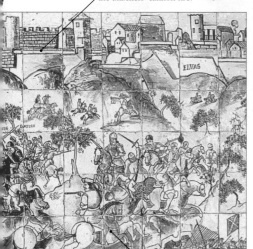

The relieving army from Estremoz surprised and routed the Spanish.

Josefa de Óbidos

Born in Spain, Josefa (1631–84) came to Óbidos (see pp174-5) when young. Trained by her father, she painted religious subjects and realistic still lifes.

WHERE TO SEE 17TH-CENTURY PORTUGAL

Under Spanish rule an austere style of architecture prevailed, typified by São Vicente de Fora *(see p72)* in Lisbon, the Sé Nova in Coimbra *(p204)* and Santarém's Jesuit church *(p191)*. At Vila Viçosa the style is evident in the long, plain façade of the palace of the Dukes of Bragança *(pp298–9)*. Colourful *azulejos* from the period can be seen at Palácio Fronteira *(p125)* and the Museu Nacional do Azulejo *(pp122–3)*.

Palácio dos Biscainhos in *Braga (p277) was built by rich emigrants returning from Brazil. Enlarged in later centuries, it retains its 17th-century core.*

The Inquisition

In the 16th and 17th centuries, the Inquisition, set up by the Catholic church, burned heretics in Lisbon's Terreiro do Paço to ensure religious conformity.

---

49 Portuguese vessels red from Japanese ports

1654 Fall of Pernambuco; Dutch driven from Brazil

1656 Death of João IV; his widow, Luisa de Guzmán, is regent for young King Afonso VI

1665 Spanish defeated at Battle of Montes Claros

1668 Spain recognizes Portuguese independence

1683 Pedro II becomes King

Pedro II

40 | **1660** | **1680**

Catherine of Bragança

40 The Restoration: Duke of Bragança owned King João IV er uprising against anish rule

1662 Catherine of Bragança marries Charles II of England

1667 Degenerate Afonso VI is deposed by his brother Pedro, who marries Afonso's French wife and becomes regent

1697 Gold discovered in Minas Gerais region of Brazil

1698 Last meeting of Portuguese *cortes*

The Age of Absolutism

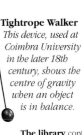

Tightrope Walker
This device, used at Coimbra University in the later 18th century, shows the centre of gravity when an object is in balance.

THE 18TH CENTURY was a period of mixed fortune for Portugal. Despite vast revenues from Brazilian gold and diamonds, João V almost bankrupted the country with his extravagance. In contrast, Pombal, chief minister of João's successor José I, applied the ideas of the Enlightenment, reforming government, commerce and education. When Maria I succeeded in 1777, she reversed many of Pombal's decrees. The French invasion of 1807 forced Maria, by then mad, and the royal family into exile in Brazil.

Gold coin of João V

The library contains richly carved Baroque bookcases and more than 40,000 volumes.

Marquês de Pombal (1699–1782)
After the 1755 earthquake (see pp62–3), Pombal insisted that Lisbon be rebuilt on strictly rational lines. Here he proudly presents the new city.

Queen's apartments

João V
This miniature (1720) by Castriotto shows João V drinking chocolate, a fashionable drink of the nobility, served to him by the Infante Miguel.

The basilica contains many marble statues made by Italian masters set amid a stunning scheme of yellow, pink, red and blue marble.

TIMELINE

Bom Jesus do Monte

1703 Methuen Treaty with Britain secures market for Portuguese wines in Britain, and for British woollen goods in Portugal

1706–50 Reign of João V "the Magnanimous", a period of great artistic extravagance

1723 Building of Baroque staircase of Bom Jesus near Braga (see pp278–9)

1730 Consecration of basilica at monastery-palace at Mafra

1733 First Portuguese opera, *The Patience of Socrates* by António de Almeida, performed at Royal Palace in Lisbon

1755 Earthquake devastates Lisbon and much of southern Portugal

1748 First water flows along Águas Livres aqueduct in Lisbon

1750 José I succeeds João V

| 1700 | 1720 | 1740 |

Águas Livres Aqueduct
Opened in 1748, the aqueduct was paid for by the citizens of Lisbon. João V had it built across the Alcântara valley against the advice of his engineers.

Monks' refectory

18th-Century Dressing Chair
This richly gilded walnut chair has sturdy cabriole legs, showing the influence of the English Queen Anne style.

The belltowers contain a carillon of 114 bells.

MONASTERY AT MAFRA
Begun in 1717, this vast monument to João V incorporates a royal palace, a church and a monastery (*see p152*). It took 38 years to complete and contains some 880 rooms and 300 monks' cells.

The King's apartments are separated from the Queen's by a long gallery.

WHERE TO SEE 18TH-CENTURY PORTUGAL

Baroque churches are found throughout Portugal, many with ornate interiors of gilded wood (*talha dourada*) such as São Francisco (*see p241*) and Santa Clara (*p239*) in Oporto. Tiled interiors are also very common (*pp22–3*). Coimbra University houses the glittering Capela de São Miguel and a fine Baroque library. As well as the palaces at Mafra and Queluz, many elegant country houses, notably the Casa de Mateus, date from this era (*pp254–5*).

Queluz Palace (pp164–5), *residence of Maria I, was begun in 1747. It is the finest example of Rococo architecture in Portugal.*

The Capela de São Miguel at *Coimbra University (pp206–7) was redecorated in Baroque style in the reign of João V.*

1756 Douro valley becomes world's first demarcated wine region

1759 Pombal expels Jesuits from Portugal

1760

1762 Spain declares war on Portugal

Statue of José I

1772 Pombal reorganizes Coimbra University, adding mathematics and natural sciences to the syllabus

1777 Accession of Maria I, who dismisses Pombal

1780

1775 Machado de Castro's statue of José I unveiled as centrepiece of reconstructed Lisbon

Maria I

1789 Portuguese suppress Brazilian independence movement in Minas Gerais

1808 French forced to retreat by Anglo-Portuguese force under Sir Arthur Wellesley; Treaty of Sintra

1800

1799 Maria I's son João named Regent

1807 The French, under Junot, invade Portugal; royal family flees to Brazil

Reform and Revolution

Portugal suffered many depredations during the upheavals of the Peninsular War, and after the loss of Brazil. A period of chaos culminated, in 1832, in civil war between the Liberal Pedro IV and the Absolutist Miguel: the War of the Two Brothers. Though the Liberals won, later governments were often reactionary. The second half of the century saw a period of stability and industrial growth, but attempts at expansion in Africa failed. By 1910, discontent with the constitutional monarchy was such that a Republican uprising forced King Manuel II into exile.

1820 Revolution
The revolution led to the royal family's return from Brazil and a new Liberal constitution. This proved unworkable and was revoked following an army coup in 1823.

Republican ships shell the king's palace in Lisbon.

Personification of Portuguese Republic

Zé Povinho
This long-suffering, Everyman figure first appeared in 1875, created by artist and potter Rafael Bordalo Pinheiro. He expressed the concerns of the average Portuguese working man.

Priests are led away by Republican soldiers.

Peninsular War (1808–14)
Napoleon tried twice to invade Portugal but was repulsed by an Anglo-Portuguese force led by Wellington. A key victory for the allies came at Buçaco (see pp210–11) in 1810.

THE BIRTH OF THE REPUBLIC

Republicanism spread among the middle classes and the army via a secret society called the Carbonária. The revolution took place in Lisbon in October 1910 and lasted less than five days. This contemporary poster celebrates the main events.

TIMELINE

1809–20 Regency dominated by Charles Stuart, British minister at Lisbon

1822 Radical new constitution. Brazil becomes independent under João VI's son Pedro

1826 Moderate charter introduced by Pedro IV, who then abdicates in favour of his young daughter Maria

1810 Battle of Buçaco

1828 Miguel, who is betrothed to his niece Maria, is crowned king

Teatro Nacional Dona Maria II

1842 Founding of National Theatre

1834 Monasteries dissolved

1832–4 War of the Two Brothers; defeat of Absolutist Miguel

1851–80 The Regeneration: period of industrial development

1853 First Portuguese postage stamps issued

1856 Opening of first railway from Lisbon to Carregado

5 Reis stamp

1810   1830   1850

The Drunkards by José Malhôa
Malhôa (1855–1933) created a virtual social history of the period in genre paintings like this one, showing a group of peasants sampling new wine.

King Manuel II flees to England from Ericeira aboard the royal yacht.

Portugal and Africa
Captain Serpa Pinto's crossing of southern Africa in 1879 led to a plan to form a Portuguese colony from coast to coast.

Republican troops set up barricades at key points in Lisbon. They meet with little opposition.

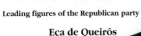

Leading figures of the Republican party

Eça de Queirós
The great novelist (1845–1900) painted a scathing picture of the Portuguese bourgeoisie. He spent many years abroad as a diplomat.

WHERE TO SEE 19TH-CENTURY PORTUGAL

Neo-Classicism, which dominated the early part of the century, can be seen in Lisbon's Palácio da Ajuda *(see p111)*. More Romantic historical styles emerged later in the century, ranging from the fantastical Neo-Gothic of the Palácio da Pena *(pp160–61)* in Sintra to the subtle Orientalism of Monserrate *(p155)*. Notable stations associated with the spread of Portugal's railways include Lisbon's Rossio and São Bento in Oporto *(p239)*.

Rossio station (p82) in Lisbon has a striking façade in Neo-Manueline style by José Luís Monteiro. Completed in 1887, the station contains one of the first iron vaults in Portugal.

Ponte de Dom Luís I (p242) in Oporto dates from 1886. Its two-tier design by Teófilo Seyrig was inspired by the nearby railway bridge built by Gustave Eiffel.

1865–8 Coalition of two main parties	**1888** Publication of *Os Maias* by Eça de Queirós, a satirical examination of Portuguese lethargy	*Manuel II*	**1910** Revolution: Manuel II abdicates and flees into exile
	1869 Slave trade abolished in all Portuguese territories		

1870	1890	1910

1861–89 Reign of moderate Luís I

1886 Building of Ponte de Dom Luís I in Oporto

1908 Carlos I and his heir, Luís, assassinated by Republicans

1877 Serpa Pinto sets out from Benguela in Angola to cross southern Africa

1890 Plan to link African colonies of Mozambique and Angola is thwarted by ultimatum from the British

Modern Portugal

Modern tiles decorating a Lisbon metro station

THE EARLY YEARS of the new Republic were marked by political and economic crisis, until a military coup in 1926 paved the way for the New State of 1933. Under the oppressive regime of prime minister António Salazar, the country was freed of its debts, but suffered poverty and unemployment. Portugal's reliance on its African colonies led to costly wars, unrest in the army and the overthrow of the government in 1974. The painful return to democracy was rewarded by admission to the European Community in 1986.

1935 Death of poet Fernando Pessoa who wrote under four different names, in four distinct styles. This portrait by José de Almada Negreiros is in Lisbon's Centro de Arte Moderna *(see p120)*

1922 First flight across the South Atlantic by Gago Coutinho and Sacadura Cabral

1933 Founding of the *Estado Novo* (New State), harsh dictatorship led by Salazar. Government bans all strikes and censors the press, crushing opposition through brutal secret police force, the PIDE

1949 Portugal signs the North Atlantic Treaty and becomes a founder member of NATO

1911 Women given the vote

1910	1920	1930	1940	1950
1910	1920	1930	1940	1950

1916 Portugal enters World War I on side of the British and French

1918 Assassination of President Sidónio Pais; postwar years are period of social unrest with frequent strikes and changes of government

1917 Three peasant children in Fátima claim to see Virgin Mary; site of vision becomes focus of major pilgrimage

1928 António Salazar made finance minister; he imposes austerity measures, balancing the budget by 1929. In 1932 he becomes prime minister

1949 Neurosurgeon António Egas Moniz wins Nobel Prize for Medicine for his work developing the prefrontal lobotomy

1942 Salazar meets Spanish dictator Franco to confirm mutual policy of non-aggression

1926 Coup puts military in charge of Republic; General Carmona is new president, holding office until his death in 1951

1939–45 In World War II Portugal is theoretically neutral but, after threats to her shipping, is forced to sell minerals to Germany. From 1943 Portugal permits British and American bases in the Azores. Here Salazar *(centre)* talks to troops stationed there

1966 Opening of Ponte Salazar (now Ponte 25 de Abril) across the Tagus (*see p114*)

1986 Portugal joins European Community. Soares becomes the first civilian president of Portugal in 60 years

1998 Lisbon hosts Expo '98; the mascot Gil embodies the theme of water and the oceans

1966 National football team with brilliant Eusébio (*centre, kneeling*) reach quarter-finals of World Cup

1985 Social Democrats, under Aníbal Cavaco Silva, come to power

1955 Armenian oil magnate Calouste Gulbenkian dies leaving £35 million escudos (£55 million) to set up a foundation for the arts and education

1974 Carnation Revolution: in a near bloodless coup, Marcelo Caetano's regime is overthrown by the MFA (Armed Forces Movement), a group of discontented left-wing army officers

1995 António Guterres of the Socialist Party elected prime minister

1960	1970	1980	1990	2000
1960	1970	1980	1990	2000

1961 India annexes Portuguese colonies of Goa, Damão and Diu

1968 Salazar retires after stroke and is succeeded by the more moderate Caetano

1976 In the first free elections for nearly 50 years, the Socialist Mário Soares becomes prime minister

1988 Rosa Mota (*centre*) wins women's marathon at the Olympic Games in Seoul

1958 In the presidential elections, the opposition candidate General Delgado wins so much support that the result is rigged against him. He is later assassinated

1975 All of Portugal's remaining colonies except Macau are granted independence, putting an end to long, unwinnable wars in Africa. Troops, such as these on patrol in the Angolan bush, are hastily brought home

THE CARNATION REVOLUTION

The revolution of 25 April 1974 gained its popular name when people began placing red carnations in the barrels of soldiers' guns. Led by army officers disaffected by the colonial wars in Africa, the revolution heralded a period of great celebration, as Portugal emerged from decades of insularity. The political situation, however, was chaotic: the new government pushed through a controversial programme of nationalization and land reform in favour of the peasants, but in November 1975 the left-wing radicals were ousted by a short-lived counter-coup.

GOLPE MILITAR
"MOVIMENTO DAS FORÇAS ARMADAS" DESENCADEIA ACÇÃO DE MADRUGADA

Newspaper headline announcing revolution

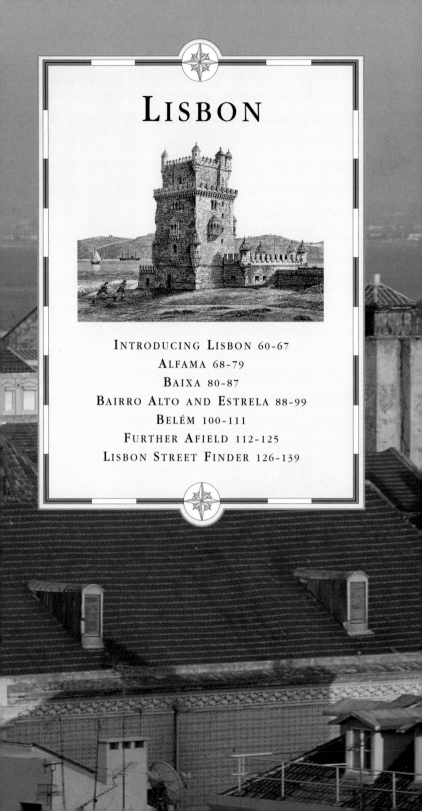

LISBON

INTRODUCING LISBON 60-67
ALFAMA 68-79
BAIXA 80-87
BAIRRO ALTO AND ESTRELA 88-99
BELÉM 100-111
FURTHER AFIELD 112-125
LISBON STREET FINDER 126-139

Lisbon at a Glance

PORTUGAL'S CAPITAL sits on the north bank of the Tagus estuary, 17 km (10 miles) from the Atlantic. The city has a population of about 550,000, but the conurbation of "Grande Lisboa", which has engulfed many surrounding villages, has nearly two million people. Razed to the ground by the earthquake of 1755 *(see pp62–3)*, the city centre is essentially 18th century, with carefully planned, elegant streets in the Baixa. On the hills on either side of the centre, the narrow streets of the Alfama and Bairro Alto make it a personal, approachable city. Since its days of glory during the Age of Discovery, when the city was at the forefront of world trade, Lisbon has been an important port. Today the docks have moved; however, the great monuments in Belém still bear witness to the city's maritime past.

The Museu Nacional de Arte Antiga *houses paintings, decorative art and sculpture. Of particular interest are the Flemish-influenced Portuguese paintings such as this* Apparition of Christ to the Virgin *by Jorge Afonso (see pp96–7).*

The Mosteiro dos Jerónimos *is a magnificent 16th-century monastery. Commissioned by Manuel I, much of it is built in the peculiarly Portuguese style of architecture, known as Manueline. The extravagantly sculpted south portal of the church, designed by João de Castilho in 1516, is one of the finest expressions of the style (see pp106–7).*

BELÉM
(See pp100–111)

The Torre de Belém *was a beacon for navigators returning from the Indies and the New World, and a symbol of Portuguese naval power (see p110).*

◁ Twin Romanesque towers of the Sé rising over the rooftops of the Baixa

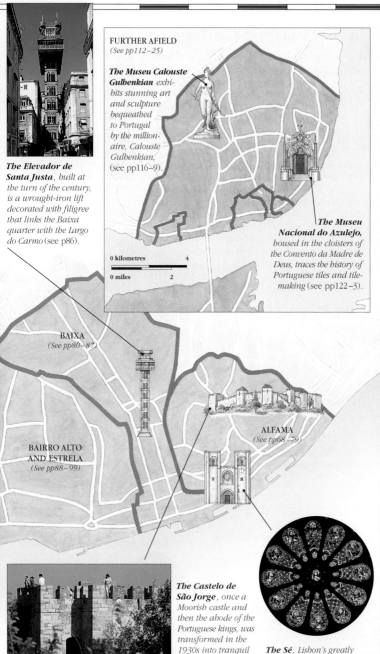

The Elevador de Santa Justa, built at the turn of the century, is a wrought-iron lift decorated with filigree that links the Baixa quarter with the Largo do Carmo (see p86).

FURTHER AFIELD
(See pp112–25)

The Museu Calouste Gulbenkian exhibits stunning art and sculpture bequeathed to Portugal by the millionaire, Calouste Gulbenkian, (see pp116–9).

The Museu Nacional do Azulejo, housed in the cloisters of the Convento da Madre de Deus, traces the history of Portuguese tiles and tile-making (see pp122–3).

0 kilometres   4

0 miles   2

BAIXA
(See pp80–87)

ALFAMA
(See pp68–79)

BAIRRO ALTO AND ESTRELA
(See pp88–99)

The Castelo de São Jorge, once a Moorish castle and then the abode of the Portuguese kings, was transformed in the 1930s into tranquil public gardens. The battlements afford spectacular views of the city (see pp78–9).

The Sé, Lisbon's greatly restored cathedral, is a sturdy Romanesque building noted for its beautiful rose window. Ecclesiastical robes and silver are among the many religious objects on display in the treasury (see p74).

0 metres   500

0 yards   500

The 1755 Lisbon Earthquake

Ex-voto tile panel offered by survivors

THE FIRST TREMOR of the devastating earthquake was felt at 9:30am on 1 November. A few minutes later there was a second, far more violent shock, reducing over half the city to rubble. Although the epicentre was close to the Algarve, Lisbon, as the most populated area, bore the worst. Over 20 churches collapsed, crushing the crowds who had assembled for All Saints' Day. A third shock was followed by fires which quickly spread. An hour later, huge waves came rolling in from the Tagus and flooded the lower part of the city. Most of Portugal suffered damage and the shock was felt as far away as Italy. Perhaps 15,000 people lost their lives in Lisbon alone.

This anonymous painting of the arrival of a papal ambassador at court in 1693 shows how Terreiro do Paço looked before the earthquake.

Some buildings that might have survived an earthquake alone were destroyed by the fire that followed.

The old royal palace, the 16th-century Paço da Ribeira, was utterly ruined by the earthquake and ensuing flood.

The royal family was staying at the palace in Belém, a place far less affected than Lisbon, and survived the disaster unscathed. Here the king surveys the city's devastation.

Ships crammed full of people fleeing the fire were wrecked and anchors thrown up to water level.

This detail is from an ex-voto painting dedicated to Nossa Senhora da Estrela, given by a grateful father in thanks for the sparing of his daughter's life in the earthquake. The girl was found miraculously alive after being buried under rubble for seven hours.

THE RECONSTRUCTION OF LISBON

Marquês de Pombal (1699–1782)

No sooner had the tremors abated than Sebastião José de Carvalho e Melo, chief minister to José I and later to become Marquês de Pombal, was outlining ideas for rebuilding the city. While philosophers moralized, Pombal reacted with practicality. "Bury the dead and feed the living" was his initial response. He restored order, then began a progressive town-planning scheme. His efficient handling of the crisis gained him almost total political control.

REACTIONS TO THE DISASTER

The earthquake had a profound effect on European thought. Eye-witness accounts appeared in the papers, many written by foreigners living in Lisbon. A heated debate arose as to whether the earthquake was a natural phenomenon or an act of divine wrath. Lisbon had been a flourishing city, famed for its wealth – also for its Inquisition and idolatry. Interpreting the quake as punishment, many preachers prophesied further catastrophes. Leading literary figures debated the significance of the event, among them Voltaire, who wrote a poem about the disaster, propounding his views that evil exists and man is weak and powerless, doomed to an unhappy fate on earth.

French author, Voltaire

The ancient castle walls succumbed to the reverberating shock waves.

Flames erupted as the candles lit for All Saints' Day ignited the city's churches. The fire raged for seven days.

Some of Lisbon's finest buildings were destroyed, along with gold, jewellery, priceless furniture, archives, books and paintings.

At 11am, tidal waves rolled into Terreiro do Paço. The Alcântara docks, to the west, bore the brunt of the impact.

Churches, homes and public buildings all suffered in the disaster. The Royal Opera House, here shown in ruins, was only completed in March the same year.

A CONTEMPORARY VIEW OF THE EARTHQUAKE

This anonymous German engraving of 1775 gives a vivid picture of the scale of the disaster. Many who fled the flames made for the Tagus, but were washed away in the huge waves which struck the Terreiro do Paço. The human and material losses were incalculable.

The reconstruction of the centre of Lisbon took place rapidly. By the end of November the Marquês de Pombal had devised a strikingly modern scheme for a grid of parallel streets running from the waterfront to Rossio. The new buildings are shown in yellow.

Modern-day Lisbon holds many reminders of the earthquake. Pombal's innovative grid system is clearly visible in this aerial view of the Baixa (see pp80–87). The scheme took many years to complete, and the triumphal arch spanning Rua Augusta was not finished until over a century later, in 1873.

ENTERTAINMENT IN LISBON

Though quite small compared to other European capitals, Lisbon boasts an outstanding cultural calendar. Chosen as Cultural Capital of Europe 1994, the city hosts both modern and traditional events from classical music, ballet and opera to street festivals, fairs and bullfights.

Pop and rock concerts are held all year round and traditional *fado (see pp66–7)* is widely performed. Football fans can spend an afternoon watching Benfica or Sporting. The city also offers excellent late-night entertainment, focused on lively, fashionable clubs and bars along the waterfront and in the Bairro Alto.

BOOKING TICKETS

Tickets can be reserved by phoning the Agência de Bilhetes para Espectáculos Públicos (**ABEP**). Pay in cash when you collect them from the kiosk. Cinemas and theatres will not take phone or credit card bookings – only the major cultural centres do.

ABEP kiosk selling tickets on Praça dos Restauradores

LISTINGS MAGAZINES

Previews of forthcoming events and listings of bars and clubs appear in several magazines in Lisbon. English-language publications on offer include the monthly *Follow Me Lisboa* and the quarterly *Lisboa Step By Step,* which are available free from tourist offices. The monthly *Agenda Cultural* is in Portuguese.

CINEMA AND THEATRE

Movie-goers are extremely well served in Lisbon. Films are shown in their original language with subtitles in Portuguese, and tickets are inexpensive. There are plenty of cinemas to choose from, and the futuristic **Amoreiras Shopping Centre** *(see p114)* has a multiplex centre with ten screens showing all the latest Hollywood releases. Cult movies and international art-house films can be seen at the

Cinemateca Portuguesa, which has a comprehensive monthly film calendar. Copies are available at the box office or tourist office. Most cinemas offer reductions on Mondays.

Theatre lovers can enjoy performances of Portuguese and foreign language plays at the **Teatro Nacional Dona Maria II** and the **Teatro da Trinidade**. For a less formal but entertaining event try Chapitô in the Alfama quarter, a circus school and theatre, which sometimes stages open-air shows.

CLASSICAL MUSIC, OPERA AND DANCE

Lisbon's top cultural centres are the modern **Centro Cultural de Belém** *(see p108)* and the **Fundação Calouste Gulbenkian** *(see pp116–19).* They host a variety of national and international events including concerts, ballet and opera. A calendar of events for each venue is available from the box office or the tourist office. Operas and classical concerts also take place at the **Teatro Nacional de São Carlos** *(see p93)* and the **Coliseu dos Recreios**.

Performance at the Chapitô, circus school, Alfama

WORLD MUSIC, JAZZ, FOLK AND ROCK

Though Lisbon's musical soul is *fado,* the city also swings to a variety of sounds from the rhythms of Africa and South America through contemporary jazz to heavy rock. For Brazilian music, try **Bar Pintaí** or **Pé Sujo** while **B. Leza** and **Lontra** are popular for African music.

Every summer the Fundação Calouste Gulbenkian puts on the International Jazz Festival. The **Hot Clube** is a favourite

The house orchestra playing at the Fundação Calouste Gulbenkian

Brazilian musician at Pé Sujo

jazz spot on a smaller scale, and it also plays host to a variety of popular folk singers and bands, such as Fausto and Sérgio Godinho.

Top pop and rock bands mostly play stadium concerts though some international bands appear at the Coliseu dos Recreios. Live rock is on offer at bars such as **Alcool Puro** and **Anos Sessenta**.

BARS AND CLUBS

FOR NIGHT-TIME DRINKING the most fashionable clubs and bars are largely concentrated in two areas of the city: the traditional nightspot of Bairro Alto and the riverside Avenida 24 de Julho. The Docas area, underneath Ponte 25 de Abril, has lively bars and cafés, which provide an ideal spot for an early evening drink. Bairro Alto has a range of clubs including **Portas Largas**, **Três Pastorinhos** and the hip club **Frágil**.

Avenida 24 de Julho is Lisbon's fastest-growing after-hours destination, with larger bars and nightclubs in converted warehouses and other attractive riverside buildings. The chic frequent fashionable **Kapital**, a club on three floors with a rooftop veranda.

Next door, Kremlin is a lively haunt playing techno music, while Plateau is geared towards fans of heavy rock. Lisbon's trendiest club by far is **Lux**.

SPORTS

MOST SPORTING action takes place outside the city, but one of Lisbon's two football teams (Benfica and Sporting) plays at home almost every Sunday, Benfica at **Estádio da Luz** and Sporting at **Estádio José Alvalade**. Portugal is hosting the 2004 European championships. Games in Lisbon will be held in these two stadia, which have been specially renovated for the event.

Bullfights are held from April to October in Lisbon's Campo Pequeno *(see p120)*.

DIRECTORY

BOOKING TICKETS

ABEP
Praça dos Restauradores.
Map 7 A2.
☏ 21-347 58 24.

CINEMA AND THEATRE

Amoreiras Shopping Centre
Avenida Engenheiro Duarte Pacheco.
Map 5 A5.
☏ 21-381 02 00.

Cinemateca Portuguesa
Rua Barata Salgueiro 39.
Map 5 C5.
☏ 21-354 62 79.

Teatro Nacional Dona Maria II
Praça Dom Pedro IV.
Map 7 B3.
☏ 21-347 22 46.

Teatro da Trinidade
Rua Nova da Trinidade 9.
Map 7 A3.
☏ 21-342 32 00.

CLASSICAL MUSIC, OPERA AND DANCE

Centro Cultural de Belém
Praça do Império.
Map 1 C5.
☏ 21-361 24 00.

Coliseu dos Recreios
Rua das Portas de Santo Antão 96.
Map 7 A2.
☏ 21-324 05 80.

Fundação Calouste Gulbenkian
Avenida de Berna 45.
Map 5 B2.
☏ 21-793 63 06 *(tickets)*.

Teatro Nacional de São Carlos
Rua Serpa Pinto 9.
Map 7 A4.
☏ 21-346 84 08.

WORLD MUSIC, JAZZ, FOLK AND ROCK

Anos Sessenta
Largo do Terreirinho 21.
Map 7 C2.
☏ 21-887 34 44.

Alcool Puro
Avenida Dom Carlos I 159.
Map 4 E3.
☏ 21-396 04 15.

B. Leza
Largo do Conde Barão 50.
Map 4 E3.
☏ 21-396 37 35.

Bar Pintaí
Largo da Trindade 22–3.
Map 7 A3.
☏ 21-342 48 02.

Hot Clube
Praça da Alegria 39.
Map 4 F1.
☏ 21-346 73 69.

Lontra
Rua de Sao Bento 157.
Map 4 E1.
☏ 21-369 10 83.

Pé Sujo
Largo de S Martinho 6–7.
Map 8 D4.
☏ 21-886 56 29.

BARS AND CLUBS

Frágil
Rua da Atalaia 128.
Map 4 F2.
☏ 21-346 95 78.

Kapital
Avenida 24 de Julho 68.
Map 4 E3.
☏ 21-395 71 01.

Lux
Avenida Infante Dom Henrique.
Map 8 D5.
☏ 21-882 08 90.

Pavilhão Chinês
Rua Dom Pedro V 89.
Map 4 F2.
☏ 21-342 47 29.

Portas Largas
Rua da Atalaia 105.
Map 4 F2.
☏ 21-346 63 79.

Três Pastorinhos
Rua da Barroca 111.
Map 4 F2.
☏ 21-346 43 01.

SPORTS

Estádio José Alvalade
Rua Francisco Stromp 2
☏ 21-756 79 30.

Estádio da Luz
Avenida General Norton Matos.
☏ 21-726 61 29.

Fado: the Music of Lisbon

A *guitarra* accompanist

LIKE THE BLUES, *fado* is an expression of longing and sorrow. Literally meaning "fate", the term may be applied to an individual song as well as the genre itself. The music owes much to the concept known as *saudade*, meaning a longing both for what has been lost, and for what has never been attained, which perhaps accounts for its emotional power. The people of Lisbon have nurtured this poignant music in back-street cafés and restaurants for over 150 years, and it has altered little in that time. It is sung as often by women as men, always accompanied by the *guitarra* and *viola* (acoustic Spanish guitar). *Fado* from Coimbra has developed its own light-hearted style.

A graphic depiction of the music's low-life associations from the 1920s

Argentina Santos is perhaps the leading traditional singer of today. All female *fadistas* wear a black shawl in memory of Maria Severa.

The *guitarrista* plays the melody and will occasionally perform a solo instrumental piece.

Maria Severa (1810–36) was the first great fadista *and the subject of the first Portuguese sound film in 1931. Her scandalous life and early death are pivotal to* fado *history, and her spiritual influence has been enormous, inspiring* fados, *poems, novels and plays.*

Most instruments have 12 paired strings, like this one. The double strings produce a resonant, silvery-sweet tone.

Delicate mother-of-pearl inlaid flower motifs

Mother-of-pearl finger plate

THE GUITARRA

Peculiar to Portuguese culture, the *guitarra* is a flat-backed instrument shaped like a mandolin, with eight, ten or twelve strings arranged in pairs. It has evolved from a simple 19th-century design into a finely decorated piece, sometimes inlaid with mother-of-pearl. The sound of the *guitarra* is an essential ingredient of a good *fado*, echoing and enhancing the singer's melody line.

Alfredo Duarte *(1891–1982) was a renowned writer of* fado *lyrics dealing with love, death, longing, tragedy and triumph. Affectionately known as* O Marceneiro *(the master carpenter) because of his skill as a joiner, he is still revered and his work widely performed.*

A cultural icon *for the Portuguese, Amália Rodrigues (1921–99) has been the leading exponent of* fado *for over 50 years. She crystallized the music's style in the postwar years, and made it known around the world.*

kinds of themes may occur in fado.
s song of 1910, for example, celebrates
dawning of the liberal republic. Such
gsheets remained a favoured means of
emination, even after the first records
e made in 1904.

The *viola* provides rhythm accompaniment, but the player will never take a solo.

The music has long inspired *great writers and painters.* O Fado *(1910) by José Malhôa (see p55) shows it in an intimate setting with the* fadista *captivating his listener. The air of abandonment underlines the earthiness of many of the songs.*

E FADO HOUSE

on's best *fado* houses, such as
famous Parreirinha de Alfama,
ch belongs to Argentina Santos
own above), are run by the
istas themselves for love of the
sic, not as a tourist attraction.
y continue the tradition that
an originally in the Alfama,
ereby cafés and restaurants
e the music of the people a
ne. Such authentic venues still
vide a good meal and a sense
istory as well as entertainment.
e oldest is Luso, which has been
xistence since the 1930s.

WHERE TO ENJOY FADO IN LISBON

Any of these fado houses will offer you good food, wine and music – or visit the Casa do Fado for a fascinating exhibition of the history of Fado.

Adega Machado
Rua do Norte 91. **Map** 7 A3.
(21-322 46 40.

Casa do Fado
Largo do Chafariz de Dentro 1.
(21-882 34 70. 8, 28, 50. 10am–6pm Wed–Mon.

Lisboa à Noite
Rua das Gáveas 69.
Map 7 A3. **(** 21-346 85 57.

Luso
Travessa da Queimada 10.
Map 7 A3. **(** 21-342 22 81.

Parreirinha de Alfama
Beco do Espírito Santo 1.
Map 7 E4. **(** 21-886 82 09.

Senhor Vinho
Rua do Meio à Lapa 18.
Map 4 D3. **(** 21-397 74 56.

ALFAMA

Portugal's coat of arms in the treasury of the Sé

I T IS DIFFICULT TO BELIEVE that this humble neighbourhood was once the most desirable quarter of Lisbon. For the Moors, the tightly packed alleyways around the fortified castle comprised the whole city. The seeds of decline were sown in the Middle Ages when wealthy residents moved west for fear of earthquakes, leaving the quarter to fishermen and paupers. The buildings survived the 1755 earthquake (see pp62–3) and, although there are no Moorish houses still standing, the quarter retains its kasbah-like layout. Compact houses line steep streets and stairways, their façades strung with washing.

Long-overdue restoration is under way in the most dilapidated areas, but daily life still revolves around local grocery stores and small, cellar-like tavernas.

Above the Alfama, the imposing Castelo de São Jorge crowns Lisbon's eastern hill. This natural vantage point, a defensive stronghold and royal palace until the 16th century, is today a popular promenade, with spectacular views from its greatly restored ramparts.

West of the Alfama stand the proud twin towers of the Sé. To the north-east, the domed church of Santa Engrácia and the white façade of São Vicente de Fora dominate the skyline.

SIGHTS AT A GLANCE

Museums and Galleries
Museu de Artes
    Decorativas **2**
Museu Militar **6**

Historic Buildings
Casa dos Bicos **7**
Castelo de São Jorge pp78–9 **10**

Churches
Santo António à Sé **9**

Santa Engrácia **5**
São Vicente de Fora **3**
Sé **8**

Belvederes
Miradouro da Graça **11**
Miradouro de Santa Luzia **1**

Markets
Feira da Ladra **4**

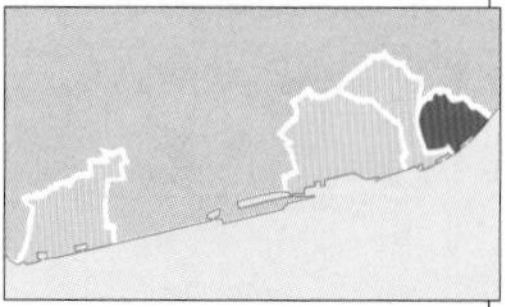

GETTING THERE

The 12 and 28 trams rattle up the narrow streets of the Alfama from the Baixa. Bus 37 does a circuit from the Castle to Rossio. Many buses run east along Avenida Dom Infante Henrique to Santa Apolónia station, and west to Belém.

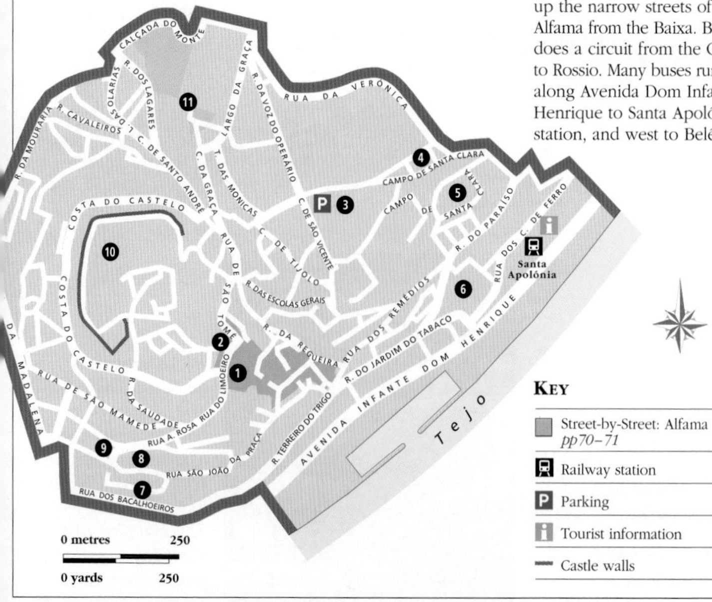

KEY

	Street-by-Street: Alfama pp70–71
🚊	Railway station
P	Parking
i	Tourist information
—	Castle walls

```
0 metres      250
0 yards       250
```

◁ **Ironwork balconies on a house in Rua dos Bacalhoeiros, beside the Casa dos Bicos**

Street-by-Street: Alfama

A FASCINATING QUARTER at any time of day, the Alfama comes to life in the late afternoon and early evening when the locals emerge at their doorways and the small tavernas start to fill. Many African immigrants live here and several venues play music from Mozambique and the Cape Verde Islands. Given the steep streets and steps of the quarter, the least strenuous approach is to start at the top and work your way down. A walk around the maze of winding alleyways will reveal picturesque corners and crumbling churches as well as panoramic views from the shady terraces, such as the Miradouro de Santa Luzia.

On Largo das Portas do Sol, café tables look out over the Alfama towards the Tagus estuary. Portas do Sol was one of the entrance gates to the old city.

The church of Santa Luzia has 18th-century blue and white *azulejo* panels on its south wall.

A modern statue of St Vincent holding the emblem of Lisbon, a boat with two ravens (*see p74*), stands in Largo das Portas do Sol.

Castelo de São Jorge

★ Museu de Artes Decorativas
Set up as a museum by the banker Ricardo do Espírito Santo Silva, the 17th-century Palácio Azurara houses fine 17th- and 18th-century Portuguese furniture and decorative arts ❷

KEY

– – – Suggested route

0 metres　　　25

0 yards　　　25

STAR SIGHTS

★ Miradouro de Santa Luzia

★ Museu de Artes Decorativas

★ Miradouro de Santa Luzia
The view from this bougainvillea-clad terrace spans the tiled roofs of the Alfama toward the Tagus. This is a pleasant place to rest after a walk around the area's steep streets ❶

Beco dos Cruzes, like most of the alleyways *(becos)* that snake their way through the Alfama, is a steep cobbled street. Locals often hang washing between the tightly packed houses.

LOCATOR MAP
See Lisbon Street Finder map 8

Rua de São Pedro is the scene of a lively early-morning fish market where the *varinas* sell the catch of the day. *Peixe espada* (scabbard fish) is one of the fish sold here.

Largo do Chafariz de Dentro is named after the 17th-century fountain *(chafariz)* that was originally placed within *(dentro)* rather than outside the 14th-century walls.

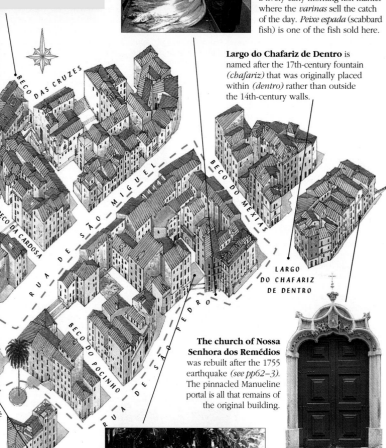

BECO DAS CRUZES

BECO DA CARDOSA

RUA DE SÃO MIGUEL

BECO DO MEXIAS

BECO DO POCINHO

RUA DE SÃO PEDRO

Sé

LARGO
DO CHAFARIZ
DE DENTRO

The church of Nossa Senhora dos Remédios was rebuilt after the 1755 earthquake *(see pp62–3)*. The pinnacled Manueline portal is all that remains of the original building.

São Miguel was rebuilt after it was damaged in the 1755 earthquake. It retains a few earlier features, including a fine ceiling of Brazilian jacaranda wood.

Popular restaurants hidden in the labyrinth of alleyways spill out onto open-air patios. The *Lautasco (see p404)*, in Beco do Azinhal, serves excellent Portuguese food.

Tile panel showing pre-earthquake Praça do Comércio, Santa Luzia

Miradouro de Santa Luzia ❶

Rua do Limoeiro. **Map** 8 D4. ⊞ 28.

THE TERRACE by the church of Santa Luzia provides a sweeping view over the Alfama and the River Tagus. Distinctive landmarks, from left to right, are the cupola of Santa Engrácia, the church of Santo Estêvão and the two startling white towers of São Miguel. While tourists admire the views, old men play cards under the bougainvillea-clad pergola. The south wall of Santa Luzia has two modern tiled panels, one of Praça do Comércio before it was flattened by the earthquake, the other showing the Christians attacking the Castelo de São Jorge *(see pp78–9)* in 1147.

Museu de Artes Decorativas ❷

Largo das Portas do Sol 2. **Map** 8 D3.
[21-888 19 91/881 46 00. ⊟ 37.
⊞ 12, 28. ◯ 10am–5pm Sun–Fri.
● 1 Jan, Easter, 1 May, 25 Dec. ▨ &

ALSO KNOWN AS the Ricardo do Espírito Santo Silva Foundation, the museum was set up in 1953 to preserve the traditions and increase public awareness of the Portuguese decorative arts. The foundation was named after a banker who bought the 17th-century Palácio Azurara in 1947 to house his fine collection of furniture, textiles, silver and ceramics. Among the 17th- and 18th-century antiques displayed in this handsome four-storey mansion are many fine pieces in exotic woods, including an 18th-century rosewood back-gammon and chess table. Also of note are the collections of 18th-century silver and Chinese porcelain, and the Arraiolos carpets *(see p301)*. The spacious rooms still retain some original ceilings and *azulejo* panels.

18th-century china cutlery case, Museu de Artes Decorativas

Workshops are housed in the adjoining building, where visitors can watch artisans preserving the techniques of cabinet-making, gilding, book-binding and other traditional crafts. Temporary exhibitions, lectures and concerts are also held in the palace.

Stone figure of a woman praying by the tomb of Carlos I in São Vicente de Fora

São Vicente de Fora ❸

Largo de São Vicente. **Map** 8 E3.
[21-882 44 00. ⊟ 12. ⊞ 28.
◯ 9am–12:30pm, 3–6pm daily.
[⊡ ▨ to cloisters.

ST VINCENT was proclaimed Lisbon's patron saint in 1173, when his relics were transferred from the Algarve *(see p319)* to a church on this site outside *(fora)* the city walls. Designed by Italian architect Filippo Terzi, and completed in 1627, the off-white Italianate façade is sober and symmetrical, with towers either side and statues of saints Vincent, Augustine and Sebastian over the entrance.

Inside, one is drawn immediately to Machado de Castro's Baroque canopy over the altar, flanked by life-size wooden statues.

The adjoining former Augustinian monastery, reached via the nave, retains its 16th-century cistern and vestiges of the former cloister but is visited for its 18th-century *azulejos*.

Among the panels in the entrance hall off the first cloister there are lively, though historically inaccurate, tile scenes of Afonso Henriques attacking Lisbon and Santarém. Around the cloisters the tiled rural scenes, surrounded by floral designs and cherubs, illustrating the fables of La Fontaine. A passageway leads behind the church to the old refectory, transformed into the Bragança Pantheon in 1885. The stone sarcophagi of almost every king and queen are here, from the first of that dynasty, João IV, who died in 1656, to Manuel II, last king of Portugal. Only Maria I and Pedro IV are not buried here. A stone mourner kneels at the tomb of Carlos I and his son Luís Felipe, assassinated in Praça do Comércio in 1908.

Feira da Ladra 4

Campo de Santa Clara. **Map** 8 F2. ○
7:30am–1pm Tue & Sat. ▦ 12. ▦ 28.

THE STALLS of the so-called
"Thieves' Market" have
occupied this site on the edge
of the Alfama for over a century, laid out under the shade
of trees or canopies. As the
fame of this flea market has
grown, bargains are increasingly hard to find amongst the
mass of bric-a-brac, but a few
of the vendors have interesting
wrought-iron work, prints and
tiles, as well as second-hand
clothes. The influence of the
African colonies can be seen
in some of the stalls selling
statuary, masks and jewellery.
Fish, vegetables and herbs are
sold in the nearby wrought-
iron marketplace.

Bric-a-brac for sale in the Feira da Ladra

Santa Engrácia 5

Campo de Santa Clara. **Map** 8 F2.
▌ 21-885 48 20. ▦ 12. ▦ 28. ○
10am–6pm Tue–Fri, 10am–7pm Sun.
● public hols. ▨ ▨

ONE OF LISBON'S most striking
landmarks, the soaring
dome of Santa Engrácia punc-
tuates the skyline in the east
of the city. The original church
collapsed in a storm in 1681.
The first stone of the new
Baroque monument, laid in
1682, marked the beginning
of a 284-year saga which led
to the invention of a saying
that a Santa Engrácia job was
never done. The church was
not completed until 1966.
    The interior, paved with
coloured marble and crowned
by a giant cupola, emanates
a feeling of space. As the
National Pantheon, it houses
cenotaphs of heroes of Portuguese history, such as Vasco da

Gama *(see p108)* and Afonso
de Albuquerque, Viceroy of
India (1502–15) on the left,
and on the right Henry the
Navigator *(see p49)* and Luís
Vaz de Camões *(see p188)*. On
request you can take the lift up
to the dome and enjoy a 360-
degree panorama of the city.

Museu Militar 6

Largo dos Caminhos de Ferro.
Map 8 F3. ▌ 21-884 25 69. ▦ 12,
46, 107. ▦ 28. ○ 10am–5pm
Tue–Sun. ● public hols. ▨

APTLY LOCATED on the site of
a 16th-century cannon
foundry and arms depot, the
military museum contains an
extensive display of arms,
uniforms and historical military
documents. Visits begin in the
Vasco da Gama Room
with a collection of old
cannons and modern
murals depicting the dis-
covery of the sea route
to India. The Salas da
Grande Guerra, on the
first floor, display World
War I related exhibits.
Other rooms are de-
voted to the evolution
of weapons in Portugal,
from primitive flints
through spears to rifles.
    The large courtyard,
flanked by cannons, tells the
story of Portugal in tiled
panels, from the Christian Reconquest to World War I. The
Portuguese artillery section in
the oldest part of the museum
displays the wagon used to
transport the triumphal arch to
Rua Augusta *(see p87)*.

**The multicoloured marble interior
beneath Santa Engrácia's dome**

Casa dos Bicos 7

Rua dos Bacalhoeiros. **Map** 8 D4.
▌ 21-881 09 00. ▦ 9, 28, 46, 59.
▦ 18, 25. ○ 9:30am–5:30pm Mon–
Fri (ground floor only). ● public hols.

THIS CONSPICUOUS house,
faced with diamond-shaped
stones *(bicos)*, was built in
1523 for Brás de Albuquerque,
illegitimate son of Afonso,
Viceroy of India and conqueror
of Goa and Malacca. The
façade is an adaptation of a
style popular in Europe during
the 16th century. The two top
storeys, ruined in the earthquake of 1755, were restored
in the 1980s, recreating the
original from old views of
Lisbon in tile panels and
engravings. In the interim the
building was used for salting
fish (Rua dos Bacalhoeiros
means street of the cod fishermen). The modern interior of
the lower floors is used for
temporary exhibitions.

The curiously faceted Casa dos Bicos, and surrounding buildings

The façade of the Sé, the city's cathedral

Sé ❽

Largo da Sé. **Map** 8 D4. 📞 21-886
67 52. 🚋 37. 🚌 12, 28. ⏰ 9am–
7pm Tue–Sat (cloister & treasury
10am–5pm), 9am–5pm Sun, Mon &
public hols. 🔼 📷 ♿ to cloister
& treasury.

IN 1150, THREE YEARS after
Afonso Henriques recap-
tured Lisbon from the Moors,
he built a cathedral for the first
bishop of Lisbon, the English
crusader Gilbert of Hastings,
on the site of the old mosque.
Sé is short for Sedes Episco-
palis, the seat (or see) of a
bishop. Devasted by three
earth tremors in the 14th century, as well as the earthquake

of 1755, and
renovated over the
centuries, the
cathedral you see
today blends a
variety of archi-
tectural styles.
The façade, with
twin castellated
belltowers and a
splendid rose win-
dow, retains its
solid Romanesque
aspect. The gloomy
interior, for the most
part, is simple and
austere, and hardly
anything remains
of the embellish-
ment lavished
upon it by King
João V in the first
half of the 18th
century. Beyond
the renovated Romanesque
nave the ambulatory has nine
Gothic chapels. The Capela de
Santo Ildefonso contains the
14th-century sarcophagi of
Lopo Fernandes Pacheco,
companion in arms to King
Afonso IV, and his wife, Maria
Vilalobos. The bearded figure
of the nobleman, sword in

**Detail of the Baroque nativity scene
by Joaquim Machado de Castro**

hand, and his wife, clutching
a prayer book, are carved
onto the tombs with their
dogs sitting faithfully at their
feet. In the adjacent chancel
are the tombs of Afonso IV
and his wife Dona Beatriz.
  The Gothic **cloister**, reached
via the third chapel in the ambulatory, has elegant double
arches with some finely carved
capitals. One of the chapels is
still fitted with its 13th-century
wrought-iron gate. Archaeological excavations in the
cloister have unearthed various
Roman and other remains.
  To the left of the cathedral
entrance the
Franciscan chapel
contains the font
where the saint
was baptized in
1195 and is decor-
ated with a charm-
ing tiled scene of St
Antony preaching
to the fishes. The
adjacent chapel
contains a Baroque
nativity scene made of cork,
wood and terracotta by
Machado de Castro (1766).
  The **treasury** is at the top
of the staircase on the right.
It houses silver, ecclesiastical
robes, statuary, illustrated
manuscripts and a selection
of relics associated with St
Vincent, which were transferred to Lisbon from Cabo de
São Vicente in 1173 (see p319).
Legend has it that two sacred
ravens kept a permanent vigil
over the boat that transported
the relics, and the raven became the symbol of Lisbon's
liberation from Muslim rule
used on the city's coat of
arms. The descendants of the
two ravens used to live in the
cloisters of the cathedral.

**Carved tomb of the 14th-century nobleman Lopo
Fernandes Pacheco in chapel in the ambulatory**

SANTO ANTÓNIO (c.1195–1231)

To the chagrin of the Lisboetas, their best-loved
saint is known as St Antony of Padua. Although
born and brought up in Lisbon, he spent
the last months of his life in Padua, Italy.
  St Antony joined the Franciscan Order
in 1220, impressed by some crusading friars he
had met at Coimbra where he was studying.
The Franciscan friar was a learned and passionate preacher, renowned for his devotion
to the poor and his ability to convert heretics.
Many statues and paintings of St Antony depict
him carrying the Infant Jesus on a book, while
others show him preaching to the fishes, as
St Francis preached to the birds. He is also
often called upon to help find lost objects.
  In 1934 Pope Pius XI declared St Antony
a patron saint of Portugal. The year 1995 saw
the 800th anniversary of his birth – a cause
for major celebrations throughout the city.

Santo António à Sé 9

Largo Santo António à Sé, 24. **Map**
7 C4. 🎫 *21-886 91 45.* 🚌 *37.*
🚊 *12, 28.* 🕐 *8am–7:30pm daily.*
⬤ *public hols.* 🏛 **Museu Antoniano**
🎫 *21-886 04 47.* 🕐 *10am–1pm,
2–6pm Tue–Sun.* 📷

Tʜᴇ ᴘᴏᴘᴜʟᴀʀ ʟɪᴛᴛʟᴇ church
of Santo António allegedly
stands on the site of the house
in which St Antony was born.
The crypt, reached via the
tiled sacristy on the left of the
church, is all that remains of
the original church destroyed
by the earthquake of 1755.
Work began on the new
church in 1757 headed by
Mateus Vicente, architect of
the Basílica da Estrela *(see
p95)* and was partially funded
by donations collected by
local children with the cry
"a small coin for St Antony".
Even today the floor of the tiny
chapel in the crypt is strewn
with escudos and the walls
are scrawled with devotional
messages from worshippers.

The church's façade blends
the undulating curves of the
Baroque style with Neo-
Classical Ionic columns on
either side of the main portal.
Inside, on the way down to the
crypt, a modern *azulejo* panel
commemorates the visit of
Pope John Paul II in 1982. In
1995 the church was given a
facelift for the saint's eighth
centenary. It is traditional for
young couples to visit the

church on their wedding day
and leave flowers for St Antony
who is believed to bring good
luck to new marriages.

Next door the small **Museu
Antoniano** houses artefacts,
relating to St Antony, as well
as gold and silverware which
used to decorate the church.
The most charming exhibit is a
17th-century tiled panel of St
Antony preaching to the fishes.

Castelo de São Jorge 10

See pp78–9.

The Miradouro and Igreja da Graça seen from the Castelo de São Jorge

Miradouro da Graça 11

Map 8 D2. 🚌 *37.* 🚊 *12, 28.*

Tʜᴇ ᴡᴏʀᴋɪɴɢ-ᴄʟᴀss quarter
of Graça developed at
the end of the 19th century.
Today, it is visited chiefly for
the views from its *miradouro*
(belvedere). The panorama
of rooftops and skyscrapers is
less spectacular than the view
from the castle, but it is a
popular spot, particularly
in the early evenings when
couples sit at café tables
under the pines. Behind the
miradouro stands an Augustinian monastery, founded in
1271 and rebuilt after the
earthquake. Once a flour-
ishing complex, the huge
building is now used as
barracks but the church, the
Igreja da Graça, can still be
visited. Inside, in the right
transept, is the *Senhor dos
Passo*s, a representation of
Christ carrying the cross on
the way to Calvary. This figure,
clad in brilliant purple clothes,
is carried on a procession
through Graça on the second
Sunday in Lent. The *azulejos*
on the altar front, dating from
the 17th century, imitate the
brocaded textiles usually
draped over the altar.

Tiled panel recording Pope John Paul II's visit to Santo António à Sé

Castelo de São Jorge ⑩

Stone head of Martim Moniz

FOLLOWING THE RECAPTURE of Lisbon from the Moors in 1147, King Afonso Henriques transformed their hilltop citadel into the residence of the Portuguese kings. In 1511 Manuel I built a more lavish palace in what is now the Praça do Comércio and the castle was used variously as a theatre, prison and arms depot. After the 1755 earthquake the ramparts remained in ruins until 1938 when Salazar *(see pp56–7)* began a complete renovation, rebuilding the "medieval" walls and adding gardens and wildfowl. The castle may not be authentic but the gardens and the narrow streets of the Santa Cruz district within the walls make a pleasant stroll and the views are the finest in Lisbon.

The Periscópio projects views of Lisbon onto the walls of this tower.

★ Battlements
Visitors can climb the towers and walk along the reconstructed ramparts of the castle walls.

Casa do Leão Restaurant
Part of the former royal residence can be booked for evening meals and parties (see p404).

A multimedia exhibit called Olispónia recreates 16th-century Lisbon here.

★ Observation Terrace
This large shaded square affords spectacular views over Lisbon and the Tagus. Local men play backgammon and cards under the trees.

KEY

— — — Suggested route

◁ **Delightful hidden courtyard among the run-down houses in Santa Cruz, within the castle walls**

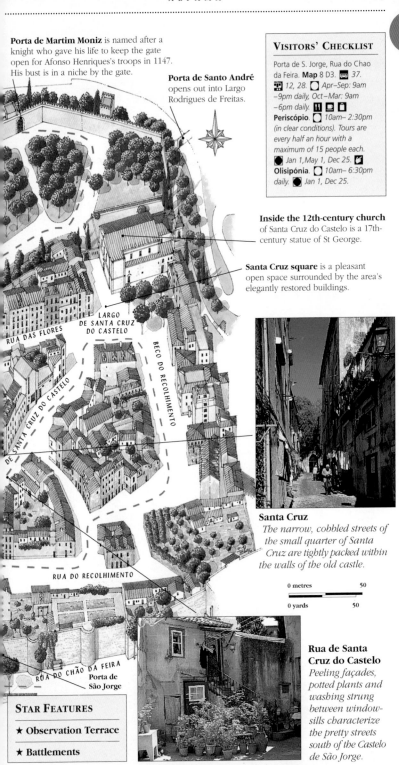

Porta de Martim Moniz is named after a knight who gave his life to keep the gate open for Afonso Henriques's troops in 1147. His bust is in a niche by the gate.

Porta de Santo André opens out into Largo Rodrigues de Freitas.

VISITORS' CHECKLIST

Porta de S. Jorge, Rua do Chao da Feira. **Map** 8 D3. 🚌 37. 🚋 12, 28. ◐ Apr–Sep: 9am –9pm daily, Oct–Mar: 9am –6pm daily. 🍴 🛒 🏛 **Periscópio.** ◐ 10am– 2:30pm (in clear conditions). Tours are every half an hour with a maximum of 15 people each. ● Jan 1, May 1, Dec 25. 🎫 **Olisipónia.** ◐ 10am– 6:30pm daily. ● Jan 1, Dec 25.

Inside the 12th-century church of Santa Cruz do Castelo is a 17th-century statue of St George.

Santa Cruz square is a pleasant open space surrounded by the area's elegantly restored buildings.

LARGO DE SANTA CRUZ DO CASTELO

RUA DAS FLORES

BECO DO RECOLHIMENTO

DE SANTA CRUZ DO CASTELO

RUA DO RECOLHIMENTO

Santa Cruz
The narrow, cobbled streets of the small quarter of Santa Cruz are tightly packed within the walls of the old castle.

| 0 metres | 50 |
| 0 yards | 50 |

RUA DO CHÃO DA FEIRA
Porta de São Jorge

STAR FEATURES

★ Observation Terrace

★ Battlements

Rua de Santa Cruz do Castelo
Peeling façades, potted plants and washing strung between window-sills characterize the pretty streets south of the Castelo de São Jorge.

BAIXA

ROM THE RUINS of Lisbon, devastated by the earthquake of 1755 *(see pp62–3)*, the Marquês de Pombal created an entirely new centre. Using a grid layout of streets, he linked the stately, arcaded Praça do Comércio beside the Tagus with the busy central square of Rossio. The streets were flanked by uniform, Neo-Classical buildings and named according to the shopkeepers and craftsmen who traded there.

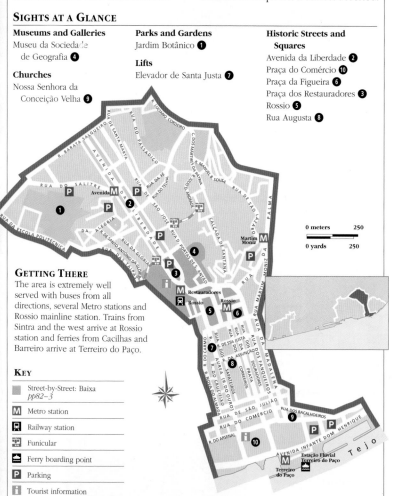

Detail on statue of José I in Praça do Comércio

The Baixa (lower town) is still the commercial hub of the capital, housing banks, offices and shops. At its centre, Rossio is a popular meeting point with cafés, theatres and restaurants. The geometric layout of the area has been retained, but most of the buildings constructed since the mid-18th century have not adhered to Pombaline formality. The streets are crowded by day, particularly the lively Rua Augusta, but after dark the quarter is almost deserted.

SIGHTS AT A GLANCE

Museums and Galleries
Museu da Sociedade de Geografia **4**

Churches
Nossa Senhora da Conceição Velha **9**

Parks and Gardens
Jardim Botânico **1**

Lifts
Elevador de Santa Justa **7**

Historic Streets and Squares
Avenida da Liberdade **2**
Praça do Comércio **10**
Praça da Figueira **6**
Praça dos Restauradores **3**
Rossio **5**
Rua Augusta **8**

GETTING THERE

The area is extremely well served with buses from all directions, several Metro stations and Rossio mainline station. Trains from Sintra and the west arrive at Rossio station and ferries from Cacilhas and Barreiro arrive at Terreiro do Paço.

KEY

▢	Street-by-Street: Baixa *pp82–3*
M	Metro station
▤	Railway station
▦	Funicular
⚓	Ferry boarding point
P	Parking
ℹ	Tourist information

0 meters 250
0 yards 250

Street-by-Street: Baixa

THIS IS THE BUSIEST PART of the city, especially the central squares of Rossio and Praça da Figueira. Totally rebuilt after the earthquake of 1755 *(see pp62–3)*, the area was one of Europe's first examples of town planning. Today, the large Neo-Classical buildings on the wide streets and squares house business offices. The atmosphere and surroundings are best absorbed from one of the busy pavement cafés. Rua das Portas de Santo Antão, a pedestrianized street where restaurants display tanks of live lobsters, is more relaxing for a stroll.

Tiled panel on façade of the Tabacaria Monaco

Palácio Foz, once a magnificent 18th-century palace built by the Italian architect Francesco Fabri, now houses a tourist office.

The Elevador da Glória is a bright yellow funicular that rattles up the hill to the Bairro Alto as far as the Miradouro de São Pedro de Alcântara *(see p94).*

Praça dos Restauradores
This large tree-lined square, named after the men who gave their lives during the War of Restoration, is a busy through road with café terraces on the pat-terned pavements ❸

Restauradores

RUA
T. DE SANTO A
RUA
PRAÇA DOS
RESTAURADORES

Rossio station, designed by José Luís Monteiro, is an eye-catching late 19th-century Neo-Manueline building with tw Moorish-style horseshoe arche

KEY

– – – Suggested route

STAR SIGHT

★ **Rossio**

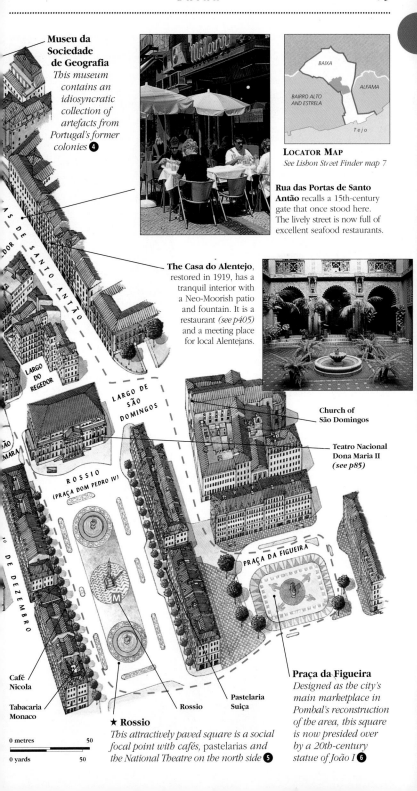

Museu da Sociedade de Geografia
This museum contains an idiosyncratic collection of artefacts from Portugal's former colonies ④

LOCATOR MAP
See Lisbon Street Finder map 7

Rua das Portas de Santo Antão recalls a 15th-century gate that once stood here. The lively street is now full of excellent seafood restaurants.

The Casa do Alentejo, restored in 1919, has a tranquil interior with a Neo-Moorish patio and fountain. It is a restaurant *(see p405)* and a meeting place for local Alentejans.

LARGO DO REGEDOR

LARGO DE SÃO DOMINGOS

Church of São Domingos

Teatro Nacional Dona Maria II *(see p85)*

ROSSIO (PRAÇA DOM PEDRO IV)

PRAÇA DA FIGUEIRA

Café Nicola

Tabacaria Monaco

Rossio

Pastelaria Suiça

0 metres   50
0 yards   50

★ **Rossio**
This attractively paved square is a social focal point with cafés, pastelarias and the National Theatre on the north side ⑤

Praça da Figueira
Designed as the city's main marketplace in Pombal's reconstruction of the area, this square is now presided over by a 20th-century statue of João I ⑥

Bridge and pond shaded by trees in the Jardim Botânico

Jardim Botânico ❶

Rua da Escola Politécnica 58. **Map** 4 F1.
☎ 21-392 1800. 🚌 15, 58, 100.
Ⓜ Avenida. **Gardens** ◷ 9am–6pm
(Apr–Sep: 8pm) Mon–Fri, 10am–6pm
(Apr–Sep: 8pm) Sat & Sun. ● 1 Jan,
25 Dec. 🅿 ♿ **Museu de História
Natural** ◷ for exhibitions only. 🎫
Museu da Ciência ◷ 10am–1pm,
2–5pm Mon–Fri, 3–6pm Sat.
● public hols. 🎫

THE COMPLEX, owned by the
university, comprises two
museums and four hectares
(10 acres) of gardens. The
botanical gardens, which slope
down from the upper level by
the main entrance towards Rua
da Alegria, have a distinct air
of neglect. However, it is worth
paying the entrance fee to
wander among the exotic trees
and dense shady paths of the
gardens as they descend to the
second entrance. A magnificent
avenue of lofty palms connects
the two different levels.

The **Museu de História
Natural** (Natural History
Museum) opens only for temporary exhibitions and these
are well advertised throughout
the city. The **Museu da
Ciência** (Science Museum),
whose exhibits demonstrate
basic scientific principles, is
popular with school children.

Avenida da Liberdade ❷

Map 7 A2. 🚌 2, 9, 36 & many other
routes. Ⓜ Restauradores, Avenida.

FOLLOWING THE earthquake
of 1755 (see pp62–3), the
Marquês de Pombal created
the Passeio Público (public
promenade) in the area now
occupied by the lower part
of Avenida da Liberdade and
Praça dos Restauradores.

Despite its name,
enjoyment of the
park was restricted to
Lisbon's high society
and walls and gates
ensured the exclu-
sion of the lower
classes. In 1821,
when the Liberals
came to power, the
barriers were pulled
down and the
Avenida and square
became open to all.

The boulevard
you see today was
built in 1879–82
in the style of the
Champs-Elysées
in Paris. The wide
tree-lined avenue
became a focus for
pageants, festivities
and demonstrations.
A war memorial
stands as a tribute to
those who died in
World War I. The
avenue still retains
a certain elegance
with fountains and
café tables shaded by trees,
however, it no longer makes
for a peaceful stroll. The once
majestic thoroughfare, 90 m
(295 ft) wide and decorated
with abstract pavement patterns, is now divided by seven
lanes of traffic linking Praça
dos Restauradores and Praça
Marquês de Pombal to the
north. Some of the original
mansions have been preserved,
including the Neo-Classical
Tivoli cinema at No. 188, with
an original 1920s kiosk outside,
and Casa Lambertini with its
colourful mosaic decoration at
No. 166. However, many of
the Art Nouveau façades have
unfortunately given way to
newer ones occupied by
offices, hotels or shopping
complexes.

**Detail from the memorial to the dead of
World War I in Avenida da Liberdade**

**19th-century monument in honour of the
Restoration in Praça dos Restauradores**

Praça dos Restauradores ❸

Map 7 A2. 🚌 2, 9, 36, 46 & many
other routes. Ⓜ Restauradores.

THE SQUARE, distinguished by
its soaring obelisk, erected
in 1886, commemorates the
country's liberation from the
Spanish yoke in 1640 (see
pp50–51). The bronze figures
on the pedestal depict Victory,
holding a palm and a crown,
and Freedom. The names and
dates inscribed on the obelisk
are those of the battles of the
War of Restoration.

On the west side the Palácio
Foz, now housing a tourist
office, was built by Francesco
Savario Fabri in 1755–
77 for the Marquês
de Castelo-Melhor.
It was renamed
after the Marquês
de Foz, who lived
here in the 19th century.
The smart Avenida Palace
Hotel (see p381) stands on
the southwest side of the
square. This building was
designed by José Lúis
Monteiro (1849–1942),
who also built Rossio
railway station (see p82).

Museu da Sociedade de Geografia ❹

Rua das Portas de Santo Antão 100.
Map 7 A2. 🄲 *21-342 54 01.* 🚌 *9, 80, 90.* Ⓜ *Restauradores.* 🄾 *11am & 3pm Tue–Thu.* 🄲 *compulsory.*

Located in the Geographical Society building, the museum houses an idiosyncratic ethnographical collection brought back from Portugal's former colonies. On display are circumcision masks from Guinea Bissau, musical instruments and snake spears. From Angola there are neckrests to sustain coiffures and the original *padrão* – the stone pillar erected by the Portuguese in 1482 to mark their sovereignty over the colony. Most of the exhibits are arranged along the splendid Sala Portugal, a large hall used also for conferences.

Rossio ❺

Map 6 B3. 🚌 *2, 36, 44, 45 & many other routes.* Ⓜ *Rossio.*

Formally called Praça de Dom Pedro IV, this large square has been the nerve centre of Lisbon for six centuries. During its history it has been the stage of bullfights, festivals, military parades and gruesome *autos da fé (see p51)*. However, today there is little more than an occasional political rally and the sober

Teatro Nacional Dona Maria II in Rossio illuminated by night

Pombaline buildings, disfigured on the upper level by rusting neon advertisements, are occupied at street level by small souvenir shops, jewellers and cafés. Centre stage stands a statue of Dom Pedro IV, the first emperor of independent Brazil *(see p54)*. At the foot of the statue, the four female figures are allegories of Justice, Wisdom, Strength and Moderation – qualities dubiously attributed to Dom Pedro.

In the mid-19th century the square was paved with wave-patterned mosaics which gave it the nickname of "Rolling Motion Square". The hand-cut grey and white stone cubes were the first such designs to decorate the city's pavements. Today, only a small central section of the design survives.

On the north side of the square is the Teatro Nacional Dona Maria II, named after Dom Pedro's daughter. The Neo-Classical structure was built in the 1840s by the Italian architect Fortunato Lodi. The interior was destroyed by fire in 1964 and reconstructed in the 1970s. On top of the pediment is Gil Vicente (1465–1536), the founder of Portuguese theatre.

Café Nicola on the west side of the square was a favourite meeting place among writers, including the poet Manuel du Bocage (1765–1805), who was notorious for his satires.

Praça da Figueira ❻

Map 6 B3. 🚌 *14, 43, 59, 60 & many other routes.* 🚋 *15.* Ⓜ *Rossio.*

Before the 1755 earthquake *(see pp62–3)* the square next to Rossio was the site of the Hospital de Todos-os-Santos (All Saints). In Pombal's new design for the Baixa, the square took on the role of the city's central marketplace. In 1885 a covered market was introduced, but this was pulled down in the 1950s. Today, the four-storey buildings are given over to hotels, shops and cafés and the square is no longer a marketplace. Perhaps its most eye-catching feature is the multitude of pigeons that perch on the pedestal supporting Leopoldo de Almeida's bronze equestrian statue of João I, erected in 1971.

Bronze statue of King João I in Praça da Figueira

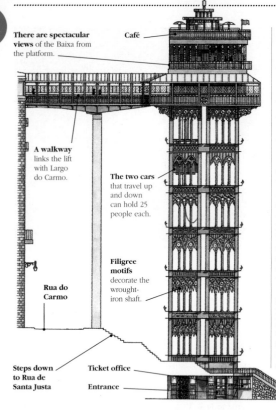

There are spectacular **views** of the Baixa from the platform.

Café

A walkway links the lift with Largo do Carmo.

The two cars that travel up and down can hold 25 people each.

Filigree motifs decorate the wrought-iron shaft.

Rua do Carmo

Steps down to Rua de Santa Justa

Ticket office

Entrance

Elevador de Santa Justa ❼

Rua de Santa Justa & Largo do Carmo.
Map 7 B3. 21-363 20 21.
8:30am–9:30pm. (call to check because of building works).

ALSO KNOWN as the Elevador do Carmo, this Neo-Gothic lift, built at the turn of the century by the French architect

Café on the top platform of the Elevador de Santa Justa

Raoul Mesnier du Ponsard, an apprentice of Alexandre Gustave Eiffel, is one of the more eccentric features of the Baixa. Made of iron, and embellished with filigree, the lift within a tower provides a regular service between the Baixa and the Bairro Alto, 32 m (105 ft) above, and is the most convenient way to reach the upper part of town. Two smart wood-panelled cabins with brass fittings travel up and down within the tower depositing passengers on a walkway leading to the nearby Largo do Carmo and the ruined Igreja do Carmo *(see p92)*.

The very top of the tower, reached via a tight spiral stairway, is given over to café tables. This high vantage point commands splendid views of Rossio, the grid pattern of the Baixa, the castle on the opposite hill, the river and the nearby ruins of the Carmo church. The fire that gutted the Chiado district in 1988 *(see p92)* was extinguished very close to the lift.

Rua Augusta ❽

Map 7 B4. Rossio. 2, 14, 36, 40 & many other routes.

ALIVELY PEDESTRIANIZED street decorated with mosaic pavements and lined with boutiques and open-air cafés, Rua Augusta is the main tourist thoroughfare and the smartest in the Baixa. Street performers provide entertainment, while vendors sell lottery tickets, books and souvenirs. The eye is drawn to the triumphal Arco da Rua Augusta framing the equestrian statue of José I in Praça do Comércio. Designed by the architect Santos de Carvalho to commemorate the city's recovery from the earthquake *(see pp62–3)*, the arch was completed only in 1873.

The other main thoroughfares of the Baixa are Rua da Prata (silversmiths' street) and Rua do Ouro or Rua Aurea (goldsmiths' street). Cutting across these main streets full of shops and banks are smaller streets that give glimpses up to the Bairro Alto to the west and the Castelo de São Jorge *(see pp78–9)* to the east. Many of the streets retain shops that gave them their name: there are jewellers in Rua da Prata and Rua do Ouro, shoemakers in Rua dos Sapateiros and banks in Rua do Comércio.

The most incongruous sight in the heart of the Baixa is a small section of the Roman baths, located within the Banco Comercial Português in Rua dos Correeiros. The ruins and mosaics can be seen from the street window at the rear side of the bank; alternatively you can book ahead to visit the "museum" on 21-321 10 00.

Shoppers and strollers in the pedestrianized Rua Augusta

Nossa Senhora da Conceição Velha ❾

Rua da Alfândega. **Map** 7 C4.
📞 21-887 02 02. 🚌 9, 46, 90.
🚊 18. ⏰ 8am–6pm Mon-Fri, Sun
(services only). ⬛ Aug. ✝ 📷 ♿

THE ELABORATE Manueline doorway of the church is the only feature that survived from the original 16th-century Nossa Senhora da Misericórdia, which stood here until the 1755 earthquake. The portal is decorated with a profusion of Manueline detail including angels, beasts, flowers, armillary spheres and the cross of the Order of Christ *(see pp18–19)*. In the tympanum, the Virgin Mary spreads her protective mantle over various contemporary figures. These include Pope Leo X, Manuel I *(see pp46–7)* and his sister, Queen Leonor, widow of João II. It was Leonor who founded the original Misericórdia (alms-house) on the site of a former synagogue.

Detail from portal of Conceição Velha

Unfortunately, en-joyment of the portal is hampered by the stream of traffic hurtling along Rua da Alfândega and the cars that park right in front of the church. The gloomy interior has an unusual stucco ceiling; in the second chapel on the right is a statue of Our Lady of Restelo. This came from the Belém chapel where naviga-tors prayed before embarking on their historic voyages east.

destroyed in the earthquake of 1755. In the rebuilding of the city, the square became the *pièce de résistance* of Pombal's Baixa design. The new palace occupied spacious arcaded buildings that extended around three sides of the square. After the revolution of 1910 *(see pp54–5)* these were converted into government administrative offices and painted Republican pink. However, they have since been repainted royal yellow.

The south side, graced by two square towers, looks across the wide expanse of the Tagus. This has always been the finest gateway to Lisbon, where royalty and ambassadors would alight and take the marble steps up from the river. You can still experience the dramatic ap-proach by taking a ferry across from Cacilhas on the southern bank. However, today the spectacle is spoilt by the busy Avenida Infante Dom Hen-rique, which runs along the waterfront. In the centre of Praça do Comércio is the equestrian statue of King José I erected in 1775 by Machado de Castro, the leading Portuguese sculptor of the 18th century. The bronze horse, depicted trampling on serpents, earned the square its third name of "Black Horse Square", used by English tra-vellers and merchants. Over the years, however, the horse has acquired a green patina.

Shaded arcades along the north side of Praça do Comércio

The impressive triumphal arch on the north side of the square leads into Rua Augusta and is the gateway to the Baixa. Opened in January 2001, in the northwest of the square, the Lisboa Welcome Center has a tourist information ser-vice, gallery, restaurants and shops. In the opposite corner, stands Lisbon's oldest café, the Martinho da Arcada, formerly a haunt of the city's literati.

On 1 February 1908, King Carlos and his son, Luís Felipe, were assassinated as they were passing through the square *(see p55)*. In 1974 the square saw the first uprising of the Armed Forces Movement which overthrew the Caetano regime in a bloodless revolu-tion *(see p57)*. For many years the area was requisitioned as a car park, but today it has been reclaimed for the use of open-air cafés and stalls.

Praça do Comércio ❿

Map 7 C5. 🚌 2, 14, 40, 46 & many other routes. 🚊 15, 18.

MORE COMMONLY known by the locals as *Terreiro do Paço* (Palace Square), this huge open space was the site of the royal palace for 400 years. Manuel I transferred the royal residence from Castelo de São Jorge to this more convenient location by the river in 1511. The first palace, along with its library and 70,000 books, was

Praça do Comércio, between the Tagus and the Baixa (lower town)

BAIRRO ALTO AND ESTRELA

Tile panel in Largo Rafael Bordalo Pinheiro, Bairro Alto

L AID OUT IN A GRID pattern in the late 16th century, the hilltop Bairro Alto is one of the most picturesque districts of the city. First settled by rich citizens who moved out of the disreputable Alfama, by the 19th century it had become a run-down area frequented by prostitutes. Today, it retains a traditional way of life, with small workshops and family-run *tascas* (cheap restaurants).

Very different in character to the heart of the Bairro Alto is the elegant commercial district known as the Chiado, where affluent Lisboetas do their shopping. To the north-west, the Estrela quarter is centred on the huge domed basilica and popular gardens. The mid-18th century district of Lapa, to the southwest, is home to foreign embassies and large, smart residences.

SIGHTS AT A GLANCE

Museums and Galleries
Museu do Chiado **5**
Museu Nacional de Arte Antiga pp96–9 **11**
Museu Nacional da Marioneta **6**

Churches
Basílica da Estrela **13**
Igreja do Carmo **2**
São Roque **1**

Historic Buildings and Districts
Chiado **3**
Palácio de São Bento **10**
Solar do Vinho do Porto **7**
Teatro Nacional de São Carlos **4**

Gardens and Belvederes
Jardim da Estrela **12**
Miradouro de São Pedro de Alcântara **8**
Praça do Príncipe Real **9**

GETTING THERE
This area is reached effortlessly with the Elevador da Glória from Praça dos Restauradores or the Elevador de Santa Justa from the Baixa. Otherwise it is a steep, but pleasant walk. There is also a metro station on Largo do Chiado. From Bairro Alto, tram 28 goes to Estrela and Lapa.

KEY
- Street-by-Street: Bairro Alto *pp90–91*
- **M** Metro station
- **R** Railway station
- **Funicular**
- Ferry boarding point
- **P** Parking
- Railway line

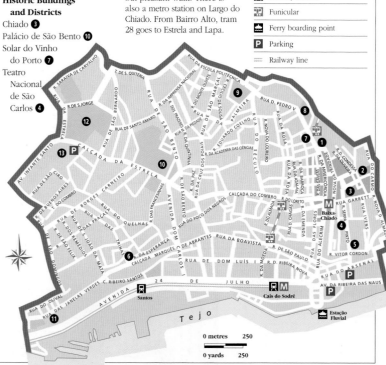

0 metres 250
0 yards 250

◁ **Art Nouveau decoration in the Chiado's Café Brasileira, once popular with writers and intellectuals**

Street-by-Street: Bairro Alto

T HE BAIRRO ALTO (high quarter) is a
fascinating area of cobbled streets,
adjacent to the Carmo and Chiado areas,
with peeling houses and tiny grocery
shops. Traditionally a bohemian quarter,
notorious for prostitution and gambling, today
the Bairro Alto is a residential area, with the
spirit of a close-knit community. In recent

Baroque cherub,
Igreja do Carmo

years it has become fashionable at night for its
bars and *casas de fado (see pp66–7).* In
contrast, the Chiado is an area of elegant
shops and old-style cafés that extends down from
Praça Luís de Camões towards Rua do Carmo
and the Baixa. Major renovation work has
taken place since a fire in 1988 *(see p92)*
destroyed many of the buildings.

Rua do Norte and Rua das
Gáveas marks the start of
the traditional Bairro Alto
where night-time rev-
ellers crowd the
bars after dark.

RUA DO NORTE

RUA DAS GÁVEAS

**Praça Luís
de Camões**

Chiado
*Once a haunt of writers
and intellectuals, this area
is now an elegant shop-
ping district. The 1920s
Brasileira café, on Largo
do Chiado, is adorned
with gilded
mirrors* ❸

RUA DO ALECRIM

LARGO DO CHIADO

**Largo do
Chiado** is flanked
by the churches
of Loreto and Nossa
Senhora da Encarnação.

Ⓜ
Baixa/Chiado

RUA GARRE[...]

**The statue of Eça de
Queirós** (1845–1900), by
Teixeira Lopes, was erected
in 1903. The great novelist
takes inspiration from a
scantily veiled muse.

Rua Garrett
is the main shopping
street of the Chiado.

```
0 metres          50
0 yards           50
```

KEY

– – – Suggested route

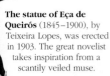

Tavares, at No. 37
Rua da Misericórdia
first opened as a
café in 1784. Today
it is an elegant res-
taurant *(see p405)*
decorated at the tur[n]
of the century with
mirrors and elabo-
rate stucco designs

Elevador da Glória

The Museu de Arte Sacra has an interesting exhibition of religious artefacts and explains the history of the treasures in the church of São Roque next door.

Cervejaria Trindade is a popular beer hall and restaurant decorated with *azulejo* panels.

Teatro da Trindade

★ São Roque
Opulent mosaics and semiprecious stones adorn the Baroque Capela de São João inside the 16th-century church of São Roque ❶

LOCATOR MAP
See Lisbon Street Finder map 7

BAIXA

BAIRRO ALTO AND ESTRELA

Tejo

The tile decoration on the façade of this house, erected in 1864 on Largo Rafael Bordalo Pinheiro, features allegorical figures of Science, Agriculture Industry and Commerce.

★ Igreja do Carmo
The graceful skeletal arches of this Carmelite church, once the largest in Lisbon, stand as a reminder of the earthquake of 1755. The chancel, the only part that remains intact, holds an archaeological museum ❷

Elevador de Santa Justa *(see p86)*

The shops in Rua do Carmo have been completely restored after the devastating fire in 1988 *(see p92)*.

STAR SIGHTS

★ São Roque

★ Igreja do Carmo

Ruins of the 14th-century Igreja do Carmo seen from the Baixa

São Roque ❶

Largo Trindade Coelho. **Map** 7 A3.
🄲 21-323 50 00. 🚌 58, 100 &
Glória lift. 🄾 9am–5pm (public hols:
1pm) daily. 🄵 **Museu de Arte
Sacra** 🄾 10am–5pm Tue–Sun.
⬤ public hols. ✎ 📷

São Roque's plain façade
belies a remarkably rich
interior. The church was
founded at the end of
the 16th century by
the Jesuit Order, then
at the peak of its
power. In 1742 the
Chapel of St John (last on
the left) was com-
missioned by the
prodigal João V from
the Italian architects
Luigi Vanvitelli and
Nicola Salvi. Con-
structed in Rome
and embellished with
lapis lazuli, agate, alabaster,
amethyst, precious marbles,
gold, silver and mosaics, the
chapel was given the Pope's
blessing in the church of
Sant'Antonio dei Portoghesi in
Rome, dismantled and sent to
Lisbon in three ships.

Among the many tiles in the
church, the oldest and most
interesting are those in the
third chapel on the right, dating
from the mid-16th century
and dedicated to São Roque
(St Roch), protector against
the plague. Other noteworthy
features of the church are the
painted *trompe l'oeil* ceiling,
showing a dome and scenes
of the Apocalypse, and the
sacristy, with its coffered
ceiling and painted panels of
the life of St Francis Xavier, the
16th-century Jesuit missionary.

**Tile detail in the
Chapel of St Roch**

Treasures from the Chapel of
St John, including the silver
and lapis lazuli altar front, can
be seen in the adjoining
Museu de Arte Sacra.

Igreja do Carmo ❷

Largo do Carmo. **Map** 7 B3. 🄲 21-
346 04 73. 🚋 28 & Santa Justa lift.
🄾 Apr–Sep: 10am–6pm Tue–Sun;
Oct–Mar: 10am–1pm, 2–5pm
Tue–Sun. ⬤ public hols. ✎

The gothic ruins
of this Carmelite
church, built on a
slope overlooking the
Baixa, are evocative
reminders of the dev-
astation left by the
earthquake of 1755.
Founded in the late
14th century by Nuno
Álvares Pereira, the
commander who
became a member of the
Carmelite Order, the church
was at one time the biggest in
Lisbon. Nowadays the roofless
nave, open to the sky, is all
that remains of the arches and
rubble that caved in on the
congregation as they were
attending mass. Roses grow
up its ancient pillars, pigeons
perch on the ruined arches
and cats wander among the
scattered statuary and capitals.

The chancel, whose roof
withstood the shock, is now
an **archaeological museum**
with a small, heterogeneous
collection of sarcophagi,
statuary, ceramics and mosaics.
Among the more ancient finds
from Europe are a remnant
from a Visigothic pillar and a
Roman tomb carved with
reliefs depicting the Muses.
There are also finds from
Mexico and South America,
including ancient mummies.

Outside the ruins, in the
Largo do Carmo, stands the
Chafariz do Carmo, an 18th-
century fountain designed by
Ângelo Belasco, elaborately
decorated with four dolphins.

Chiado ❸

Map 7 A4. 🚌 58. 🚋 28. Ⓜ Chiado.

Hypotheses abound for the
origin of the word Chiado,
in use since 1567. One of the
most interesting recalls the
creak *(chiar)* of the wheels of
the carts as they negotiated the
area's steep slopes. A second
theory refers to the nickname
given to the 16th-century poet
António Ribeiro, "O Chiado".
An area traditionally known

<hr>

The Chiado Fire

On 25 August 1988 a disastrous fire began in a store in
Rua do Carmo, the street that
links the Baixa with the Bairro
Alto. Fire engines were unable
to enter this pedestrianized
street and the fire spread into
Rua Garrett. Along with shops
and offices, many important
18th-century buildings were
destroyed, the worst damage
being in Rua do Carmo. The
renovation project, which is
now complete, has preserved
many original façades, and
was headed by Portuguese
architect, Álvaro Siza Vieira.

**Firemen attending the raging
fire in Rua do Carmo**

Stalls and circle of the 18th-century Teatro Nacional de São Carlos

for its intellectual associations, various statues of literary figures can be found here. Fernando Pessoa, Portugal's most famous 20th-century poet, is seated at a table outside the Café Brasileira. Established in the 1920s, this was a favourite rendezvous of intellectuals.

The name Chiado is often used to mean just Rua Garrett, the main shopping street of the area, named after the author and poet João Almeida Garrett (1799–1854). This elegant street, which descends from Largo do Chiado towards the Baixa, is known for its clothes shops, cafés and bookshops. Devastated by fire in 1988, the former elegance of this quarter has been recently restored.

On Largo do Chiado stand two Baroque churches: the Italian church, Igreja do Loreto, on the north side and opposite, Nossa Senhora da Encarnação, whose exterior walls are partly decorated with *azulejos*.

Teatro Nacional de São Carlos ❹

Rua Serpa Pinto 9. **Map** 7 A4. 21-346 84 08. 58. 28. Baixa-Chiado. ☐ for performances only.

REPLACING a former opera house which was ruined by the earthquake of 1755, the Teatro de São Carlos was built in 1792–5 by José da Costa e Silva. Designed on the lines of La Scala in Milan and the San Carlo in Naples, the building has a beautifully proportioned façade and an enchanting Rococo interior. Views of the exterior, however, are spoiled by the car park, invariably crammed, which occupies the square in front. The opera season lasts from September to June, but concerts and ballets are also staged here at other times of the year.

Museu do Chiado ❺

Rua Serpa Pinto 4–6. **Map** 7 A5. 21-343 21 48. 58. 24, 28. Baixa-Chiado. ☐ 10am–6pm Wed–Sun, 2–6pm Tue. 1 Jan, Easter, 1 May, 25 Dec.

THE NATIONAL MUSEUM of Contemporary Art, whose collection of 1850–1950 paintings could no longer be described as contemporary, changed its name in 1994 and moved to a stylishly restored warehouse. The paintings and sculpture are arranged over three floors in 12 rooms. Each room has a different theme illustrating the development from Romanticism to Modernism. The majority are works by Portuguese, often showing the marked influence from other European countries. This is particularly noticeable in the 19th-century landscape painters who had contact with artists from the French Barbizon School. The few international works of art on display include a collection of drawings by Rodin (1840–1917) and some French sculpture from the late 19th century. There are also temporary exhibitions which are held for "very new artists, preferably inspired by the permanent collection".

Grotesque puppet in Museu Nacional da Marioneta

Museu Nacional da Marioneta ❻

Convento das Bernardas, Rua da Esperança. **Map** 4 D3. 21-886 57 94. 27, 49. Cais do Sodré. ☐ 10am–1pm, 2–7pm Tue–Sun.

THIS SMALL, ECCENTRIC puppet museum moved to this elegantly refurbished convent building in 2001. The collection includes characters dating from 17th-and 18th-century theatre and opera, among them knights, jesters, princesses, devils and satirical figures. The puppets are finely crafted but a substantial proportion of them possess gruesome, contorted features, which are unlikely to appeal to small children. The museum explains the history of the art form and runs videos of puppet shows. It is worth calling ahead to see if a live performance is being held on the small stage set.

Art Nouveau façade of the popular Café Brasileira in the Chiado

The wide selection of port at the Solar do Vinho do Porto

Solar do Vinho do Porto ❼

Rua de São Pedro de Alcântara 45. **Map** 4 F2. 📞 21-347 57 07. 🚌 58. 🚋 28, Elevador da Glória. ⏰ 2pm–midnight Mon–Sat. ⬛ public hols.

THE PORTUGUESE WORD *solar* means mansion or manor house and the Solar do Vinho do Porto occupies the ground floor of an 18th-century mansion. The building was once owned by the German architect, Johann Friedrich Ludwig (Ludovice), who built the monastery at Mafra *(see p152)*. Similar to the Solar do Vinho do Porto in Oporto *(see p243)*, this bar has up to 6,000 varieties of port, including rare vintages dating back as far as 1937. You can try a selection of these rich fortified wines, from the younger red-coloured ruby port, through the lighter tawny, to the aristocratic vintages from the great shippers of Oporto *(see pp228–9)*. Although rather expensive, these can be tasted at the bar or in the comfort of armchairs in the club-like sitting room.

Miradouro de São Pedro de Alcântara ❽

Rua de São Pedro de Alcântara. **Map** 7 A2. 🚌 58. 🚋 28, Elevador da Glória.

THE BELVEDERE *(miradouro)* commands a sweeping view of eastern Lisbon, seen across the Baixa. A tiled map, conveniently placed against the balustrade, helps you locate the landmarks in the city below. The panorama extends from the battlements of the Castelo de São Jorge *(see pp78–9)*, clearly seen surrounded by trees on the hill to the southeast, to the 18th-century church of Penha da França in the northwest. The large monastery complex of the Igreja da Graça *(see p75)* is also visible on the hill, and in the distance São Vicente de Fora *(see p73)* is recognizable by the symmetrical towers that flank its white façade.

Benches and ample shade from the trees make this terrace a pleasant stop after the steep walk up Calçada da Glória from the Baixa. Alternatively, the yellow funicular, Elevador da Glória, will drop you off nearby.

The memorial in the garden, erected in 1904, depicts Eduardo Coelho (1835–89), founder of the newspaper *Diário de Notícias*, and below him a ragged paper boy running with copies of the famous

daily. This area was once the centre of the newspaper industry, however the modern printing presses have now moved to more spacious premises west of the city.

The view is most attractive at sunset and by night when the castle is floodlit and the terrace becomes a popular meeting point for young Lisboetas.

Praça do Príncipe Real ❾

Map 4 F1. 🚌 58, 100.

Playing cards in Praça do Príncipe Real

LAID OUT IN 1860 as a prime residential quarter, the square still retains an air of affluence. Smartly painted mansions surround a particularly pleasant park with an open-air café, statuary and some splendid robinia, magnolia and Judas trees. The branches of a huge cedar tree have been trained on a trellis, creating a wide shady spot for the locals who play cards beneath it. On the large square, at No. 26, the eye-catching pink and white Neo-Moorish building with domes and pinnacles is part of Lisbon university.

View across the city to Castelo de São Jorge from Miradouro de São Pedro de Alcântara

Attractive wrought-iron music pavilion in Jardim da Estrela

Palácio de São Bento ⑩

Rua de São Bento. **Map** 4 E2.
📞 21-396 01 41. 🚌 6, 49. 🚊 28
🕐 by appt only.

ALSO KNOWN as the Palácio da Assembleia Nacional, this enormous white Neo-Classical building is the seat of the Portuguese Parliament. It started life at the end of the 16th century as the Benedictine monastery of São Bento. After the dissolution of the religious orders in 1834, the building became the seat of Parliament, known as the Palácio das Cortes. The interior is suitably grandiose with marble pillars and Neo-Classical statues.

Museu Nacional de Arte Antiga ⑪

See pp96–9.

Jardim da Estrela ⑫

Praça da Estrela. **Map** 4 D2.
🚌 9, 20, 22, 38. 🚊 25, 28.
🕐 7am–midnight daily.

LAID OUT IN the middle of the 19th century, opposite the Basílica da Estrela, the popular gardens are a focal part of the Estrela quarter. Local families congregate here at weekends to feed the ducks and carp in the lake, sit at the waterside café or wander among the flower beds, plants and trees. The formal gardens are planted with herbaceous borders and shrubs surrounding plane trees and elms. The central feature of the park is a green wrought-iron bandstand, decorated with elegant filigree, where musicians strike up in the summer months. This was built in 1884 and originally stood on the Passeio Público, before the creation of Avenida da Liberdade *(see p44)*.
The English Cemetery to the north of the gardens is best known as the burial place of Henry Fielding (1707–54), the English novelist and playwright who died in Lisbon at the age of 47. The *Journal of a Voyage to Lisbon*, published posthumously in 1775, recounts his last voyage to Portugal made in a fruitless attempt to recover his failing health.

Basílica da Estrela ⑬

Praça da Estrela. **Map** 4 D2. 📞 21-396 09 15. 🚌 9, 20, 22, 38. 🚊 25, 28. 🕐 7:30am–12:30pm, 3–7:30pm daily. ✝ 📷

The tomb of the pious Maria I in the Basílica da Estrela

IN THE SECOND half of the 18th century Maria I *(see p165)*, daughter of José I, vowed she would build a church if she bore a son and heir to the throne. Her wish was granted and construction of the basilica began in 1779. Her son José, however, died of smallpox two years before the completion of the church in 1790. The huge domed basilica, set on a hill in the west of the city, is one of Lisbon's great landmarks. A simpler version of the basilica at Mafra *(see p152)*, the church was built by architects from the Mafra School in late Baroque and Neo-Classical style. The façade is flanked by twin belltowers and decorated with an array of statues of saints and allegorical figures.
The spacious, somewhat awe-inspiring interior, where light streams down from the pierced dome, is clad in grey, pink and yellow marble. The elaborate Empire-style tomb of Queen Maria I, who died in Brazil, lies in the right transept. Locked in a room nearby is Machado de Castro's extraordinary Nativity scene, composed of over 500 cork and terracotta figures. (To see it, ask the sacristan.)

Neo-Classical façade and stairway of Palácio de São Bento

Museu Nacional de Arte Antiga ⓫

Portugal's national art collection is housed in a 17th-century palace that was built for the counts of Alvor. In 1770 it was acquired by the Marquês de Pombal and remained in the possession of his family for over a century. Inaugurated in 1884, the museum is familiarly known to locals as the Casa das Janelas Verdes, referring to the former green windows of the palace. In 1940 a modern annexe (including the main façade) was added. This was built on the site of the St Albert Carmelite monastery, destroyed in the 1755 earthquake *(see pp62–3)*. The only surviving feature was the chapel, which has been integrated into the museum.

15th-century wood carving of St George

★ **St Jerome**
This masterly portrayal of old age by Albrecht Dürer expresses one of the central dilemmas of Renaissance humanism: the ephemeral nature of man (1521).

GALLERY GUIDE
The ground floor contains 14th–19th-century European paintings, as well as some decorative arts and furniture. Oriental and African art, Chinese and Portuguese ceramics and silver, gold and jewellery are on display on the first floor. The top floor is dedicated to Portuguese art and sculpture.

The Temptations of St Antony by Hieronymus Bosch

Stairs down to 🔲 🍴 👥

St Augustine by Piero della Francesca

60 61 62 59 63 58 64 57 65 56 66 55 54 68 53 67 69 52 51

The Virgin and Child and Saints
Hans Holbein the Elder's balanced composition of a Sacra Conversazione (1519) is set among majestic Renaissance architecture with saints in detailed contemporary costumes sewing or reading.

Ecce Homo
Painted in the late 15th century by an artist of the Portuguese school, the unusual depiction of the accused Jesus, with the shroud lowered over his eyes, retains an air of dignified calm, despite the crown of thorns, the rope and the specks of blood.

KEY TO FLOORPLAN
- ☐ European art
- ☐ Portuguese painting and sculpture
- ☐ Portuguese and Chinese ceramics
- ☐ Oriental and African art
- ☐ Silver, gold and jewellery
- ☐ Decorative arts
- ☐ Chapel of St Albert
- ☐ Temporary exhibitions
- ☐ Non-exhibition space

STAR EXHIBITS
- ★ **St Jerome by Dürer**
- ★ **Namban Screens**
- ★ **Adoration of St Vincent by Gonçalves**

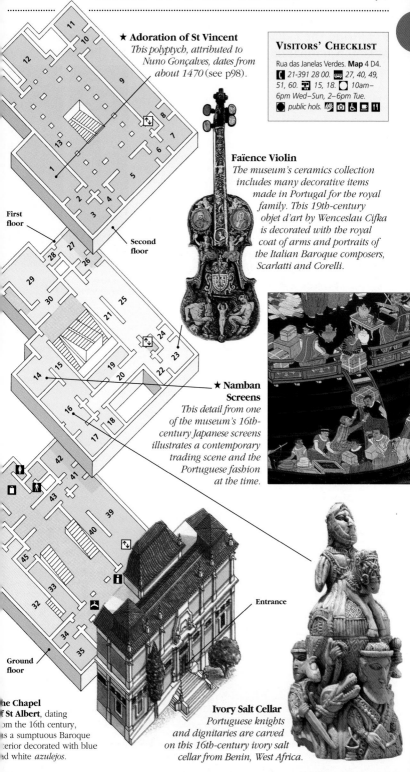

★ **Adoration of St Vincent**
This polyptych, attributed to
Nuno Gonçalves, dates from
about 1470 (see p98).

(see p98)

VISITORS' CHECKLIST

Rua das Janelas Verdes. **Map** 4 D4.
21-391 28 00. 27, 40, 49,
51, 60. 15, 18. 10am–
6pm Wed–Sun, 2–6pm Tue.
public hols.

Faïence Violin
The museum's ceramics collection
includes many decorative items
made in Portugal for the royal
family. This 19th-century
objet d'art by Wenceslau Cifka
is decorated with the royal
coat of arms and portraits of
the Italian Baroque composers,
Scarlatti and Corelli.

**First
floor**

**Second
floor**

★ **Namban
Screens**
This detail from one
of the museum's 16th-
century Japanese screens
illustrates a contemporary
trading scene and the
Portuguese fashion
at the time.

Entrance

**Ground
floor**

**he Chapel
f St Albert**, dating
om the 16th century,
as a sumptuous Baroque
terior decorated with blue
d white azulejos.

Ivory Salt Cellar
Portuguese knights
and dignitaries are carved
on this 16th-century ivory salt
cellar from Benin, West Africa.

Exploring the Collections of the Museu Nacional de Arte Antiga

THE MUSEUM has the largest collection of paintings in Portugal and is particularly strong on early religious works by Portuguese artists. The majority of exhibits came from convents and monasteries following the suppression of religious orders in 1834. There are also extensive displays of sculpture, silverware, porcelain and applied arts giving an overview of Portuguese art from the Middle Ages to the 19th century, complemented by many fine European and Oriental pieces. The theme of the discoveries is ever-present, illustrating Portugal's links with Brazil, Africa, India, China and Japan.

EUROPEAN ART

PAINTINGS by European artists, dating from the 14th to the 19th century, are arranged chronologically on the ground floor. Unlike the Portuguese art, most of the works were donated from private collections, contributing to the great diversity of works on display. The first rooms, dedicated to the 14th and 15th centuries, trace the transition from medieval Gothic taste to the aesthetic of the Renaissance.

The painters best represented in the European Art section are 16th-century German and Flemish artists. Notable works are *St Jerome* by Albrecht Dürer (1471–1528), *Salomé* by Lucas Cranach the Elder (1472–1553), *Virgin and Child* by Hans Memling (c.1430–94) and *The Temptations of St Antony* by the great Flemish master of fantasy, Hieronymus Bosch (1450–1516). Of the small number of Italian works, the finest are *St Augustine* by

the Renaissance painter, Piero della Francesca (c.1420–92) and a graceful early altar panel representing the Resurrection by Raphael (1483–1520).

Some Portuguese painters, including Josefa de Óbidos *(see p51)* and Gregório Lopes (1490–1550), are also displayed in the galleries of European art.

PORTUGUESE PAINTING AND SCULPTURE

MANY OF THE EARLIEST works of art are by the Portuguese primitive painters who were influenced by the realistic detail of Flemish artists. There had always been strong trading links between Portugal and Flanders and in the 15th and 16th centuries several painters of Flemish origin, for example Frey Carlos of Évora, set up workshops in Portugal.

Pride of place, however, goes to the São Vicente de Fora polyptych, the most important painting of 15th-century Portuguese art and one that has

Central panel of *The Temptations of St Antony* by Hieronymus Bosch

ADORATION OF ST VINCENT

Cistercian monks from Alcobaça *(see pp178–9)*

Friar

Fisherman

become a symbol of national pride in the Age of Discovery. Painted in about 1467–70, and generally believed to be by Nuno Gonçalves, the altarpiece portrays the *Adoration of St Vincent*, patron saint of Portugal, surrounded by dignitaries, knights and monks as well as fishermen and beggars. The accurate portrayal of contemporary figures makes the painting an invaluable historical and social document.

Later works include a 16th-century portrait of the young Dom Sebastião *(see pp46–7)* by Cristóvão de Morais and paintings by Neo-Classical artist Domingos António de Sequeira.

The museum's sculpture collection has many Gothic polychrome stone and wood statues of Christ, the Virgin and saints. There are also statues from the 17th century and an 18th-century nativity scene by Machado de Castro in the Chapel of St Albert.

PORTUGUESE AND CHINESE CERAMICS

THE EXTENSIVE collection of ceramics enables visitors to trace the evolution of Chinese porcelain and Portuguese faïence and to see the influence of oriental designs on

Nuno Gonçalves, self-portrait of the artist

Queen Eleonor of Aragon, the Queen mother

Henry the Navigator *(see p49)*

Archbishop of Lisbon, Jorge da Costa

Moorish knight

Jewish scholar

Beggar

Queen Isabel

Infante João (King João II)

King Afonso V

Infante Fernão, the king's brother

St Vincent

Knight

Duke of Bragança

Priest holding a fragment of St Vincent's skull

Portuguese pieces, and vice versa. From the 16th century Portuguese ceramics show a marked influence of Ming, and conversely the Chinese pieces bear Portuguese motifs such as coats of arms. By the mid-18th century individual potters had begun to develop an increasingly personalized, European style, with popular, rustic designs. The collection also includes ceramics from Italy, Spain and the Netherlands.

Chinese porcelain vase, 16th century

ORIENTAL AND AFRICAN ART

THE COLLECTION of ivories and furniture, with their European motifs, further illustrates the reciprocal influences of Portugal and her colonies. The 16th-century predilection for the exotic gave rise to a huge demand for items such as carved ivory hunting horns from Africa. The fascinating 16th-century Japanese Namban screens show the Portuguese trading in Japan. *Namban-jin* (barbarians from the south) is the name the Japanese gave to the Portuguese.

SILVER, GOLD AND JEWELLERY

AMONG THE MUSEUM's fine collection of ecclesiastical treasures are King Sancho I's gold cross (1214) and the Belém monstrance (1506) *(see p20)*. Also on display is the 16th-century Madre de Deus reliquary which allegedly holds a thorn from the crown of Christ. Highlight of the foreign collection is a sumptuous set of rare 18th-century silver tableware. Commissioned by José I from the Paris workshop of Thomas Germain, the 1,200 pieces include intricately decorated tureens, sauce boats and salt cellars. The rich collection of jewels came from the convents, originally donated by members of the nobility and wealthy bourgeoisie on entering the religious orders.

APPLIED ARTS

FURNITURE, tapestries and textiles, liturgical vestments and bishops' mitres are among the wide range of objects on display. The furniture collection has many examples from the reigns of King João V, King José and Queen Maria I, tracing the progress from Baroque to Neo-Classical styles. Of the foreign furniture, French pieces from the 18th century are the most prominent.

The textiles include 17th-century bedspreads, tapestries, many of Flemish origin, such as the *Baptism of Christ* (16th century), embroidered rugs and Arraiolos carpets *(see p301)*.

Gold Madre de Deus reliquary inlaid with precious stones (c.1502)

BELÉM

AT THE MOUTH of the River Tagus, where the caravels set sail on their voyages of discovery, Belém is inextricably linked with Portugal's Golden Age *(see pp46–9)*. When Manuel I came to power in 1495 he reaped the profits of those heady days of expansion, building grandiose monuments and churches that mirrored the spirit of the time. Two of the finest examples of the exuberant and exotic Manueline style of architecture *(see pp20–21)* are the Mosteiro dos Jerónimos and the Torre de Belém.

Generosity, **statue at entrance to Palácio da Ajuda**

Today Belém is a spacious, relatively green suburb with many museums, parks and gardens, as well as an attractive riverside setting with cafés and a promenade. On sunny days there is a distinct seaside feel to the embankment.

Before the Tagus receded, the monks in the monastery used to look out onto the river and watch the boats set forth. In contrast today several lanes of traffic along the busy Avenida da Índia cut central Belém off from the picturesque waterfront, and silver and yellow trains rattle regularly past.

SIGHTS AT A GLANCE

Museums and Galleries
Museu de Arte Popular ⑩
Museu da Marinha ⑦
Museu Nacional de Arqueologia ⑤
Museu Nacional dos Coches ②
Planetário Calouste Gulbenkian ⑥

Parks and Gardens
Jardim Agrícola Tropical ③
Jardim Botânico da Ajuda ⑭

Churches and Monasteries
Ermida de São Jerónimo ⑫
Igreja da Memória ⑬
Mosteiro dos Jerónimos pp106–7 ④

Historic Buildings
Palácio de Belém ①
Palácio Nacional da Ajuda ⑮
Torre de Belém p110 ⑪

Monuments
Monument to the Discoveries ⑨

Cultural Centres
Centro Cultural de Belém ⑧

KEY

▨	Street-by-Street: Belém *pp102–3*
🚉	Railway station
⛴	Ferry boarding point
P	Parking
═	Railway line

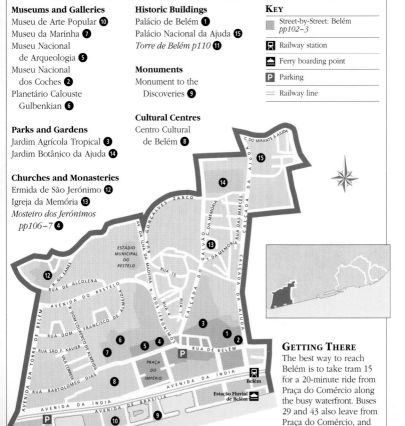

GETTING THERE

The best way to reach Belém is to take tram 15 for a 20-minute ride from Praça do Comércio along the busy waterfront. Buses 29 and 43 also leave from Praça do Comércio, and the 42 from Saldanha goes to Palácio da Ajuda. Slow trains from Cais do Sodré to Oeiras stop at Belém.

◁ **Nave of Santa Maria de Belém, the church of the Jerónimos monastery**

Street-by-Street: Belém

PORTUGAL'S FORMER maritime glory, expressed in the imposing, exuberant buildings such as the Jerónimos monastery, is evident all around Belém. In Salazar's

Stone caravel, Jerónimos monastery

(see p56) attempted revival of awareness of Portugal's Golden Age, the area along the water-front, which had silted up since the days of the caravels, was restructured to celebrate the former greatness of the nation. Praça do Império was laid out for the Exhibition of the Portuguese World in 1940 and Praça Afonso de Albuquerque was dedicated to Portugal's first viceroy of India. The royal Palácio de Belém, restored with gardens and a riding school by João V in the 18th century, briefly housed the royal family after the 1755 earthquake.

★ **Mosteiro dos Jerónimos**
Vaulted arcades and richly carved columns adorned with foliage, exotic animals and navigational instruments decorate the Manueline cloister of the Jerónimos monastery ❹

LARGO
DOS
JERÓNIMOS

PRAÇA DO IMPÉRIO

Museu Nacional de Arqueologia
Archaeological finds ranging from an Iron Age gold bracelet to Moorish artefacts are among the interesting exhibits on display ❺

Torre de Belém
(see p110)

STAR SIGHTS

★ **Mosteiro dos Jerónimos**

★ **Museu Nacional dos Coches**

KEY

– – – Suggested route

Praça do Império, an impressive square that opens out in front of the monastery, is lit up on special occasions with a colourful light display in the central fountain.

Vieira Portuense runs along a small park.
Colourful 16th- and 17th-century houses con-
with the typically imposing buildings in Belém.

**Jardim Agrícola
Tropical**
*Exotic plants and
trees gathered from
Portugal's former
colonies fill these
peaceful gardens
that were once part
of the Palácio de
Belém* ❸

LOCATOR MAP
*See Lisbon Street Finder
maps 1 & 2*

Antiga Confeitaria de Belém, a 19th-
century café, sells *pastéis de Belém*,
rich custard in a flaky pastry cup.

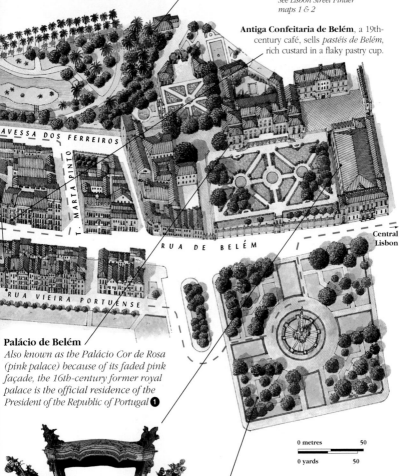

A VESSA DOS FERREIROS

T. MARTA PINTO

RUA DE BELÉM

RUA VIEIRA PORTUENSE

Central
Lisbon

Palácio de Belém
*Also known as the Palácio Cor de Rosa
(pink palace) because of its faded pink
façade, the 16th-century former royal
palace is the official residence of the
President of the Republic of Portugal* ❶

0 metres   50
0 yards   50

★ **Museu Nacional dos Coches**
*This 18th-century coach used by the ambassador
to Pope Clement XI is part of the collection in the
old riding school of the Palácio de Belém* ❷

**Praça Afonso de
Albuquerque** is
named after the
first Portuguese
viceroy of India.
A Neo-Manueline
column in the
centre bears his
statue, with scenes
from his life car-
ved on the base.

Palácio de Belém ❶

Praça Afonso de Albuquerque.
Map 1 C4. 🅒 21-361 46 00. 🚌 14, 28, 43, 49. 🚊 15. 🚇 Belém.
🔓 9am–1pm, 3rd Sun of month. 📷

BUILT BY the Conde de Aveiras in 1559 before the Tagus had receded, this summer palace once had gardens bordering the river. In the 18th century it was bought by João V, who had acquired vast wealth through gold from Brazil *(see pp52–3)*. He radically altered the palace, added a riding school and rendered the interior suitably lavish for his amorous liaisons.

When the great earthquake struck in 1755 *(see pp62–3)*, the king, José I, and his family were staying here and thus survived the devastation of central Lisbon. Fearing another earth tremor, the royal family temporarily set up camp in tents in the palace grounds and the palace interior was used as a hospital. Today the elegant pink building, which resembles a country estate, is the residence of the President of Portugal.

Pink façade of the Palácio de Belém, home of the President of Portugal

Museu Nacional dos Coches ❷

Praça Afonso de Albuquerque.
Map 2 D4. 🅒 21-361 08 50. 🚌 14, 28, 43, 49. 🚊 15. 🚇 Belém.
🔓 10am–5:30pm Tue–Sun. 🔴 1 Jan, Easter, 1 May, 25 Dec. 📷

THE MUSEUM'S collection of coaches is arguably the finest in Europe. Occupying the east wing of the Palácio de Belém, this was formerly the riding school built by the Italian architect Giacomo Azzolini in 1726. Seated in the upper gallery, the royal family used to watch their beautiful Lusitanian horses *(see p296)* performing in the arena. In 1905 the riding school was turned into a museum by King Carlos's wife, Dona Amélia, whose pink riding cloak is on display.

Made in Portugal, Italy, France, Austria and Spain, the coaches span three centuries and range from the plain to the preposterous. The main gallery, in Louis XVI style with splendid painted ceiling, is the setting for two straight, regimented rows of coaches created for Portuguese royalty.

The collection starts with the comparatively plain 17th-century red leather and wood coach of Philip II of Spain *(see pp50–51)*. The coaches become increasingly sumptuous, interiors lined with red velvet and gold, exteriors profusely carved and decorated with allegories and royal coats of arms. The rows end with three huge Baroque coaches made in Rome for the Portuguese ambassador to the Vatican, Dom Rodrigo Almeida e Menezes, the Marquês de Abrantes. The epitome of pomp and extravagance, but not necessarily of comfort, these 5-tonne carriages are embellished with a plush interior and life-size gilded statues.

The neighbouring gallery has further examples of royal carriages, including two-wheeled cabriolets, landaus and pony-drawn chaises used by young members of the royal family. There is also a 19th-century Lisbon cab, painted black and green, the colours of

Rear view of a coach built in 1716 for the Marquês de Abrantes, the Portuguese ambassador to Pope Clement XI

taxis right up to the 1990s. The 18th-century Eyeglass Chaise, whose black leather hood is pierced by sinister eye-like windows, was made during the era of Pombal *(see pp52–3)* when lavish decoration was discouraged. The upper gallery has a collection of harnesses, court costumes and portraits of members of the royal family.

Jardim Agrícola Tropical ❸

Largo dos Jerónimos. **Map** 1 C4.
🎫 21-362 02 10. 🚌 27, 28, 43, 51.
🚋 15. 🕐 10am–5pm Tue–Fri, 11am–6pm Sat & Sun. ⬤ public hols. 📷
🚻 **Museu Tropical** 🕐 by appt only.

ALSO KNOWN AS the Jardim do Ultramar, this peaceful park with ponds, waterfowl and peacocks, attracts surprisingly few visitors. Laid out at the beginning of the 20th century as the research centre of the Institute for Tropical Sciences, it is more of an arboretum than a flower garden. The emphasis is on rare tropical and subtropical trees and plants, many of them endangered species. Among the most striking are dragon trees, native to the Canary Islands and Madeira, monkey puzzle trees from South America and a handsome avenue of lofty Washington palms. The oriental garden with its streams, bridges and hibiscus is heralded by a large Chinese-style gateway which represented Macau in the Exhibition of the Portuguese World in 1940 *(see p102)*.

The research buildings and **Museu Tropical** are housed in the Palácio dos Condes da Calheta, an 18th-century mansion whose interior walls are covered with *azulejos* spanning three centuries. The museum has 50,000 dried plant specimens and 2,414 samples of wood.

Mosteiro dos Jerónimos ❹

See pp106–7.

Washington palms in the Jardim Agrícola Tropical

Museu Nacional de Arqueologia ❺

Praça do Império. **Map** 1 B4. 🎫 21-362 00 00. 🚌 28, 43, 49, 51. 🚋 15.
🕐 10am–6pm Wed–Sun, 2pm–6pm Tue. ⬤ 1 Jan, Easter, 1 May, 25 Dec.
📷 📷 🚻

THE LONG west wing of the Mosteiro dos Jerónimos *(see pp106–7)*, formerly the monks' dormitory, has been a museum since 1893. Reconstructed in the middle of the 19th century, the building is a poor imitation of the Manueline original. The museum houses Portugal's main archaeological research centre and the exhibits, from sites all over the country, include a gold Iron Age bracelet found in the Alentejo and Visigothic jewellery from Beja *(see p311)*.

Visigothic gold buckle, Museu de Arqueologia

Roman ornaments and early 8th-century Moorish artefacts. The main Egyptian and Greco-Roman section is strong on funerary art, featuring figurines, tombstones, masks, terracotta amulets and funeral cones inscribed with hieroglyphics alluding to the solar system. The dimly-lit Room of Treasures has an exquisite collection of coins, necklaces, bracelets and other jewellery dating from 1800–500 BC. Along with other parts of the museum, this room is being refurbished to allow more of the permanent collection to be shown. The new space is due to open at the end of 2001.

Planetário Calouste Gulbenkian ❻

Praça do Império. **Map** 1 B4. 🎫 21-362 00 02. 🚌 28, 27, 29, 43, 49, 51.
🚋 15. 🕐 for shows: 4pm & 6pm Sat & Sun (also school hols: 11am, 3pm & 4:15pm Wed & Thu). Special shows for children 11am Sun. ⬤
public hols. 📷 📷 🚻

FINANCED BY the Gulbenkian Foundation *(see p119)* and built in 1965, this modern building sits incongruously beside the Jerónimos monastery. Inside, the Planetarium reveals the mysteries of the cosmos. There are shows in Portuguese, English and French explaining the movement of the stars and our solar system, as well as presentations on more specialist themes, such as the constellations or the Star of Bethlehem (Belém).

The dome of the Planetário Calouste Gulbenkian

Mosteiro dos Jerónimos ❹

Armillary sphere in the cloister

A MONUMENT TO THE WEALTH of the Age of Discovery (see pp48–9), the monastery is the culmination of Manueline architecture (see pp20–21). Commissioned by Manuel I in around 1501, after Vasco da Gama's return from his historic voyage, it was financed largely by "pepper money", a tax levied on spices precious stones and gold.

Tomb of Vasco da Gama
The 19th-century tomb of the explorer (see p108) is carved with ropes, armillary spheres and other seafaring symbols.

Various masterbuilders worked on the building, the most notable of whom was Diogo Boitac, replaced by João de Castilho in 1517. The monastery was cared for by the Order of St Jerome (Hieronymites) until 1834, when all religious orders were disbanded.

The fountain is in the shape of a lion, the heraldic animal of St Jerome.

Refectory
The walls of the refectory are tiled with 18th-century azulejos. The panel at the northern end depicts the Feeding of the Five Thousand.

The modern wing, built in 1850 in Neo-Manueline style, houses the Museu Nacional de Arqueologia (see p105).

The west portal was designed by the 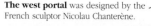 French sculptor Nicolau Chanterène.

Entrance to church and cloister

Gallery

View of the Monastery
This 17th-century scene by Felipe Lobo shows women at a fountain in front of the Mosteiro dos Jerónimos.

STAR FEATURES
★ **South Portal**
★ **Cloister**

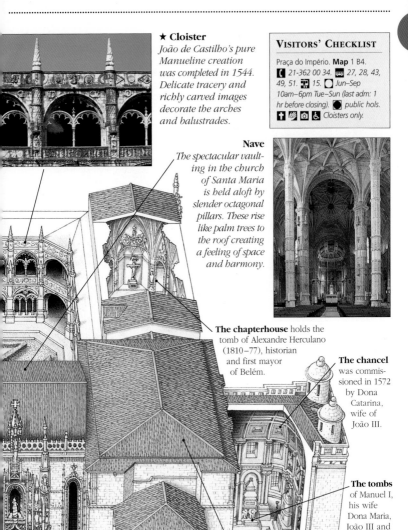

★ Cloister

João de Castilho's pure Manueline creation was completed in 1544. Delicate tracery and richly carved images decorate the arches and balustrades.

VISITORS' CHECKLIST

Praça do Império. **Map** 1 B4.
📞 21-362 00 34. 🚌 27, 28, 43, 49, 51. 🚊 15. 🕐 Jun–Sep 10am–6pm Tue–Sun (last adm: 1 hr before closing). ● public hols. ✝ 📷 🔲 ♿ Cloisters only.

Nave

The spectacular vaulting in the church of Santa Maria is held aloft by slender octagonal pillars. These rise like palm trees to the roof creating a feeling of space and harmony.

The chapterhouse holds the tomb of Alexandre Herculano (1810–77), historian and first mayor of Belém.

The chancel was commissioned in 1572 by Dona Catarina, wife of João III.

The tombs of Manuel I, his wife Dona Maria, João III and Catarina are supported by elephants.

★ South Portal

The strict geometrical architecture of the portal is almost obscured by the exuberant decoration. João de Castilho unites religious themes, such as this image of St Jerome, with the secular, exalting the kings of Portugal.

Tomb of King Sebastião
The tomb of the "longed for" Dom Sebastião stands empty. The young king never returned from battle in 1578 (see p47).

Façade of the Museu da Marinha

Museu da Marinha 🟢

Praça do Império. **Map** 1 B4. 🎧 21-362 00 19. 🚌 27, 28, 29, 43, 49, 51. 🚋 15. ⭘ 10am–6pm (Oct–Jun: 5pm) Tue–Sun. ⬤ public hols. ♿ 📷 ♿

THE MARITIME MUSEUM was inaugurated in 1962 in the west wing of the Jerónimos monastery *(see pp106–7)*. It was here, in the chapel built by Henry the Navigator *(see p49)*, that mariners took mass before embarking on their historic voyages. A hall about the Discoveries illustrates the rapid progress in shipbuilding from the mid-15th century, capitalizing on the experience of the long-distance explorers. Small replicas show the transition from the bark to the lateen-rigged caravel, through the faster square-rigged caravel, to the Portuguese *nau*. Also relating to the Discoveries are navigational instruments, astrolabes and replicas of 16th-century maps showing the world as it was known then. The stone pillars, carved with the Cross of the Knights of Christ, are replicas of the types of *padrão* set up as monuments to Portuguese sovereignty on the lands discovered. Beyond the Hall of Discoveries a series of rooms displaying models of modern Portuguese ships leads on to the Royal Quarters where you can see the exquisitely furnished wood-panelled cabin of King Carlos and Queen Amélia from the royal yacht *Amélia*, built in Scotland in 1900.

The modern, incongruous pavilion opposite houses original royal barges, the most extravagant of which is the royal brig built in 1780 for Maria I. The collection ends with a display of seaplanes, including the *Santa Clara* which made the first crossing of the South Atlantic in 1922.

Centro Cultural de Belém 🟢

Praça do Império. **Map** 1 B5. 🎧 21-361 24 00. 🚌 27, 28, 29, 43, 49, 51. 🚋 15. ⭘ 9am–10pm daily. ♿ **Exhibition Centre** ⭘ 11am–8pm. ♿ ♿

THE CONSTRUCTION of a stark modern building directly between the Jérónimos monastery and the Tagus was clearly controversial. Built in 1990 as the headquarters of the Portuguese presidency of the European Community, it opened as a cultural centre in 1993. It stresses music, performing arts and photography, with a large **Exhibition Centre** used for temporary displays and a permanent design museum. Both the café and restaurant overlook pleasant gardens and the river. At weekends, the centre's slightly austere atmosphere is enlivened by street performers, actors and rollerbladers.

The modern complex of the Centro Cultural de Belém

Monument to the Discoveries 🟢

Padrão dos Descobrimentos, Avenida de Brasília. **Map** 1 C5. 🎧 21-303 19 50. 🚌 28, 29, 43, 49, 51. 🚋 15. ⭘ 9am–5pm Tue–Sun. ⬤ public hols. ♿ for lift. 📷

STANDING PROMINENTLY on the Belém waterfront, this massive angular monument, the Padrão dos Descobrimentos, was built in 1960 to mark the 500th anniversary of the death of Henry the Navigator *(see p49)*. The 52-m (170-ft) high monument, commissioned by the Salazar regime, commemorates the mariners, royal patrons and all those who participated in the rapid development of the Portuguese Age

---

VASCO DA GAMA (c.1460–1524)

In 1498 Vasco da Gama sailed around the Cape of Good Hope and opened the sea route to India *(see pp48–9)*. Although the Hindu ruler of Calicut, who received him wearing diamond and ruby rings, was not impressed by his humble offerings of cloth and wash basins, da Gama returned to Portugal with a cargo of spices. In 1502 he sailed again to India, establishing Portuguese trade routes in the Indian Ocean. João III nominated him Viceroy of India in 1524, but he died of a fever soon after.

16th-century painting of Vasco da Gama in Goa

The huge pavement compass in front of the Monument to the Discoveries

of Discovery. The monument is designed in the shape of a caravel, with Portugal's coat of arms on the sides and the sword of the Royal House of Avis rising above the entrance. Henry the Navigator stands at the prow with a caravel in hand. In two sloping lines either side of the monument are stone statues of Portuguese heroes linked with the Age of Discovery. On the western face these include Dom Manuel I holding an armillary sphere, the poet Camões with a copy of *Os Lusíadas*, the painter Nuno Gonçalves with a paint pallet as well as famous navigators, cartographers and kings.

On the monument's north side, the huge mariner's compass cut into the paving stone was a present from the Republic of South Africa

in 1960. The central map, dotted with galleons and mermaids, shows the routes of the discoverers in the 15th and 16th centuries. Inside the monument a lift whisks you up to the sixth floor where steps then lead to the top for a splendid panorama of the river and Belém. The basement level is used for temporary exhibitions, but not necessarily related to the Discoveries.

The rather ostentatious Padrão is not to everyone's taste but the setting is undeniably splendid and the caravel design is imaginative. The monument looks particularly dramatic when viewed from the west in the light of the late afternoon sun.

Museu de Arte Popular ❿

Avenida de Brasília. **Map** 1 B5. 📞 *21-301 12 82.* 🚌 *27, 28, 29, 43, 49, 51.* 🚊 *15.* ⬜ *10am–12:30pm, 2–5pm Tue–Sun.* ⬤ *public hols.* 🖼

T HE DRAB BUILDING on the waterfront, between the Monument to the Discoveries and the Torre de Belém *(see p110)*, houses the museum of Portuguese folk art and traditional handicrafts, opened in 1948. The exhibits, which are arranged by province, include local pottery, agricultural tools, costumes, musical instruments, jewellery and brightly coloured saddles. The display gives a vivid indication of the diversity between the different regions.

Traditional costume from Trás-os-Montes

Each area has its speciality such as the colourful ox yokes and ceramic cocks from the Minho, basketware from Trás-os-Montes, cowbells and terracotta casseroles from the Alentejo and fishing equipment from the Algarve. If you are planning to travel around the country the museum offers an excellent preview to the traditional handicrafts of the provinces. The rooms housing the permanent collection are closed for alterations, but the displays will be the same when the museum reopens in 2002.

EASTERN FACE OF THE MONUMENT TO THE DISCOVERIES

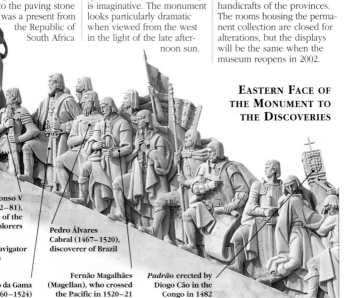

Afonso V (1432–81), patron of the first explorers

Henry the Navigator (1394–1460)

Pedro Álvares Cabral (1467–1520), discoverer of Brazil

Vasco da Gama (1460–1524)

Fernão Magalhães (Magellan), who crossed the Pacific in 1520–21

Padrão erected by Diogo Cão in the Congo in 1482

Torre de Belém ⓫

Arms of Manuel I

COMMISSIONED BY Manuel I, the tower was built as a fortress in the middle of the Tagus in 1515–21. Starting point for the navigators who set out to discover the trade routes, this Manueline gem became a symbol of Portugal's great era of expansion. The real beauty of the tower lies in the decoration of the exterior. Adorned with rope carved in stone, it has openwork balconies, Moorish-style watchtowers and distinctive battlements in the shape of shields. The Gothic interior below the terrace, which served as a storeroom for arms and a prison, is very austere but the private quarters in the tower are worth visiting for the loggia and the panorama.

VISITORS' CHECKLIST

Avenida da India. **Map** 1 A5.
📞 *21-362 00 34.* 🚌 *27, 28, 29, 43, 49, 51.* 🚊 *15.* 🚉
Belém. ⬜ *10am–5pm Tue–Sun (6pm Jun–Sep).* ⬤ *public hols.*
🚫 📷 ♿ *ground floor only.*

Renaissance Loggia
The elegant arcaded loggia, inspired by Italian architecture, gives a light touch to the defensive battlements of the tower.

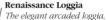

Armillary spheres and nautical rope are symbols of Portugal's seafaring prowess.

Royal coat of arms of Manuel I

Chapel

Battlements are decorated with the cross of the Order of Christ *(see pp20–21).*

Governor's room

Virgin and Child
A statue of Our Lady of Safe Homecoming faces the sea, a symbol of protection for sailors on their voyages of discovery.

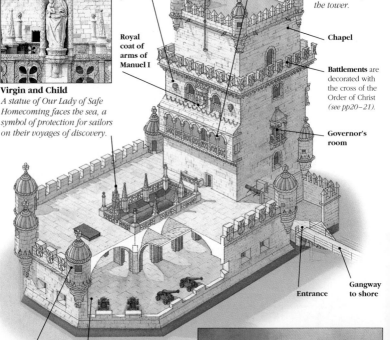

Entrance

Gangway to shore

Sentry posts

The vaulted dungeon was used as a prison until the 19th century.

The Torre de Belém in 1811
This painting of a British ship navigating the Tagus, by JT Serres, shows the tower much further from the shore than it is today. In the 19th century land on the north bank was reclaimed, making the river narrower.

The simple Manueline chapel, Ermida de São Jerónimo

Ermida de São Jerónimo 🔢

Rua Pedro de Covilhã. **Map** 1 A3.
📞 21-301 86 48. 🚌 27, 28, 41, 43, 49, 51. ⬜ by appt only.

ALSO KNOWN AS the Capela de São Jerónimo, this elegant little chapel was constructed in 1514 when Diogo Boitac was working on the Jerónimos monastery (see pp106–7). Although a far simpler building, it is also Manueline in style and may have been built to a design by Boitac. The only decorative elements on the monolithic chapel are the four pinnacles, corner gargoyles and Manueline portal. Perched on a quiet hill above Belém, the chapel has fine views down to the River Tagus and a path from the terrace winds down the hill towards the Torre de Belém.

Igreja da Memória 🔢

Calçada do Galvão, Ajuda. **Map** 1 C3.
📞 21-363 52 95. 🚌 14, 27, 29, 73.
⬜ 4–6pm Mon–Sat. ✝ ♿

BUILT IN 1760, the church was founded by King José I in gratitude for his escape from an assassination plot on this site in 1758. The king was returning from a secret liaison with a lady of the noble Távora family when his carriage was attacked and a bullet hit him in the arm. Pombal (see pp52–3), whose power had now become absolute, used this as an excuse to get rid of his enemies in the Távora family,

accusing them of conspiracy. In 1759 they were savagely tortured and executed. Their deaths are commemorated by a pillar in Beco do Chão Salgado, off Rua de Belém.

The Neo-Classical domed church has a marble-clad interior and a small chapel, on the right, containing the tomb of Pombal. He died at the age of 83, a year after he had been banished from Lisbon.

Jardim Botânico da Ajuda 🔢

Calçada da Ajuda. **Map** 1 C2. 📞 21-362 25 03. 🚌 14, 27, 29, 73. 🚋 18.
⬜ 9am–5pm Thu–Tue. ● Wed, public hols. 🎫 (free 9am–2pm Sun). ♿

LAID OUT on two levels by Pombal (see p15) in 1768, these Italian-style gardens provide a pleasant respite from the noisy suburbs of Belém. The entrance (wrought-iron gates in a pink wall) is easy to miss. The park comprises tropical trees and box-hedge gardens surrounding neat flower beds. Notable features are the 400-year-old dragon tree, native of Madeira, and the flamboyant 18th-century fountain decorated with serpents, winged fish, sea horses and mythical creatures. A majestic terrace looks out over the lower level of the gardens.

Palácio Nacional da Ajuda 🔢

Calçada da Ajuda. **Map** 2 D2. 📞 21-363 70 95. 🚌 14, 32,42, 60, 73. 🚋 18. ⬜ 10am–5pm Thu–Tue. ● 1 Jan, Easter, 1 May, 25 Dec. 🎫 ♿ 🖼

THE ROYAL PALACE, destroyed by fire in 1795, was replaced in the early 19th century by the Neo-Classical building you see today. This was left incomplete when the royal family was forced into exile in Brazil in 1807 (see pp52–3).

The palace only became a permanent residence of the royal family when Luís I became king in 1861 and married an Italian Princess, Maria Pia di Savoia. No expense was spared in furnishing the apartments. The ostentatious rooms are decorated with silk wallpaper, Sèvres porcelain and crystal chandeliers.

A prime example of regal excess is the extraordinary Saxe Room, a wedding present to Maria Pia from the King of Saxony, in which every piece of furniture is decorated with Meissen porcelain. On the first floor the huge Banqueting Hall, with crystal chandeliers, silk-covered chairs and an allegory of the birth of João VI on the frescoed ceiling, is truly impressive. At the other end of the palace, Luís I's Neo-Gothic painting studio is a more intimate display of intricately carved furniture.

19th-century throne from the Palácio Nacional da Ajuda

Manicured formal gardens of the Jardim Botânico da Ajuda

FURTHER AFIELD

THE MAJORITY of the outlying sights, which include some of Lisbon's finest museums, are easily accessible by bus or metro from the city centre. A ten-minute walk north from the gardens of the Parque Eduardo VII brings you to Portugal's great cultural complex, the Calouste Gulbenkian Foundation, set in a pleasant park. Few tourists go further north than the Gulbenkian, but the Museu da Cidade on Campo Grande is worth a detour for its fascinating overview of Lisbon's history.

***Azulejo** panel from
Palâcio Fronteira*

The charming Palácio Fronteira, decorated with splendid tiles, is one of the many villas built for the aristocracy that now overlook the city suburbs. Those interested in tiles will also enjoy the Museu Nacional do Azulejo in the cloisters of the Madre de Deus convent. Visitors with a spare half day can cross the Tagus to the Cristo Rei monument. Northeast of Lisbon is a vast oceanarium, Oceanário de Lisboa, built for Expo '98. The Expo site now includes residential, hotel and retail developments.

SIGHTS AT A GLANCE

Museums and Galleries
Centro de Arte Moderna **7**
Museu da Água **9**
*Museu Calouste Gulbenkian
pp116–19* **6**
Museu da Cidade **12**
*Museu Nacional do Azulejo
pp122–3* **10**

Modern Architecture
Amoreiras Shopping Centre **3**
Cristo Rei **1**
Ponte 25 de Abril **2**

Historic Architecture
Aqueduto das Águas Livres **14**
Campo Pequeno **8**
Palácio Fronteira **15**
Praça Marquês de Pombal **4**

Parks and Gardens
Parque Eduardo VII **5**
Parque do Monteiro-Mor **16**

Zoos
Jardim Zoológico **13**
Oceanário de Lisboa **11**

KEY

▨	Main sightseeing areas
✈	Airport
⛴	Ferry boarding point
▬	Motorway
▬	Major road
—	Minor road

0 kilometres   4

0 miles   2

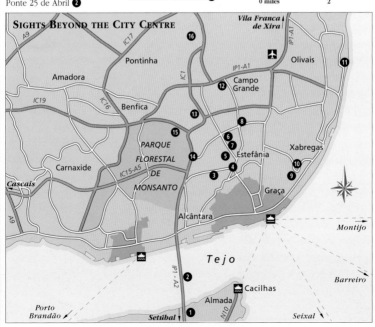

SIGHTS BEYOND THE CITY CENTRE

◁ **Nymph fountain among tropical vegetation inside the Estufa Fria, Parque Eduardo VII**

Cristo Rei ❶

Santuário Nacional do Cristo Rei, Alto do Pragal, Almada. 21-275 10 00. from Praça do Comércio & Cais do Sodré to Cacilhas then 101. **Lift** 9:30am–5:45pm daily.

M ODELLED ON the more famous Cristo Redentor in Rio de Janeiro, this giant-sized statue stands with arms outstretched on the south bank of the Tagus. The 28 m (92 ft) tall figure of Christ, mounted on a huge pedestal, was built by Francisco Franco in 1949–59 at the instigation of Prime Minister Salazar.

You can see the monument from various viewpoints in the city, but it is fun to take a ferry to the Outra Banda (the other bank), then a bus or taxi to the monument. (Rush hour is best avoided.) A lift, plus some steps, takes you up 82 m (269 ft) to the top of the pedestal, affording fine views of the city and river.

Ponte 25 de Abril ❷

Map 3 A5. 52, 53.

O RIGINALLY CALLED the Ponte Salazar after the dictator who had it built in 1966, Lisbon's suspension bridge was renamed (like many other

The towering monument of Cristo Rei overlooking the Tagus

monuments) to commemorate the revolution of 25 April 1974 which restored democracy to Portugal (see p57).

Inspired by San Francisco's Golden Gate in the United States, this steel construction stretches for 2 km (1 mile). The lower tier was recently

modified to accommodate a much-needed railway across the Tagus. The bridge's notorious traffic congestion has been partly resolved by the opening of the 12-km (7-mile) Vasco da Gama bridge. Spanning the river from Montijo to Sacavém, north of the Expo site, this bridge was completed in 1998. There is also a new traffic lane and rail link nearby.

Amoreiras Shopping Centre ❸

Avenida Engenheiro Duarte Pacheco. **Map** 5 A5. 21-381 02 00. 11, 18, 23, 48, 51, 53, 58, 74, 83. 10am–11pm daily. 25 Dec.

I N THE 18TH CENTURY, the Marquês de Pombal (see pp52–3) planted mulberry trees (amoreiras) on the western edge of the city to create food for silk worms. Hence the name of the futuristic shopping centre that was built here in 1985. This massive complex, with pink and blue towers, houses 370 shops, ten cinemas, and numerous cafés. Once an incongruous feature of Lisbon, it now draws the crowds, particularly the young, and has been joined by other new buildings and shopping centres in the area.

Ponte 25 de Abril linking central Lisbon with the Outra Banda, the south bank of the Tagus

Parque Eduardo VII **5**

Praça Marquês de Pombal. **Map** 5 B4.
[21-388 22 78. **M** Marquês de
Pombal. 2, 11, 12, 22, 36. **Estufa
Fria** ○ Apr–Sep: 9am–6pm daily; Oct–
Mar: 9am–5pm daily (last adm 30 mins
before closing). ● public hols.

Tropical plants in the Estufa Quente glasshouse, Parque Eduardo VII

Praça Marquês de Pombal **4**

Map 5 C5. **M** Marquês de Pombal.
1, 2, 12, 20, 38 & many other routes.

AT THE TOP of the Avenida da Liberdade (see p84), traffic thunders round the "Rotunda" (roundabout), as the praça is also known. At the centre rises the lofty monument to Pombal, unveiled in 1934. The despotic statesman, who virtually ruled Portugal from 1750–77, stands on the top of the column, his hand on a lion (symbol of power) and his eyes directed down to the Baixa, whose creation he masterminded (see pp62–3).

Allegorical images depicting Pombal's political, educational and agricultural reforms decorate the base of the monument. Standing figures represent Coimbra University where he introduced a new Faculty of Science. Although greatly feared, this dynamic politician propelled the country into the Age of Enlightenment. Broken blocks of stone at the foot of the monument and tidal waves flooding the city are an allegory of the destruction caused by the 1755 earthquake.

The sculptures on the pedestal and the inscriptions relating to Pombal's achievements can be seen by taking the underpass into the centre of the square (although this is often closed). Nearby, the well-tended Parque Eduardo VII extends northwards behind the square. The paving stones around the Rotunda are decorated with a mosaic of Lisbon's coat of arms. Similar patterns in small black and white cobbles decorate many of the city's streets and squares.

THE LARGEST PARK in central Lisbon was named in honour of King Edward VII of England who came to Lisbon in 1902 to reaffirm the Anglo-Portuguese alliance. The wide grassy slope, that extends for 25 hectares (62 acres) was laid out as Parque de Liberdade, a continuation of Avenida da Liberdade (see p84) in the late 19th century. Neatly clipped box hedging, flanked by mosaic patterned walkways, stretches uphill from the Praça Marquês de Pombal to a belvedere at the top. From here there are fine views of the city and the distant hills on the far side of the Tagus. On clear days it is possible to see as far as the Serra da Arrábida (see p167).

Located at the northwest corner, the most inspiring feature of this rather monotonous park is the jungle-like **Estufa Fria**, or greenhouse, where exotic plants, streams and waterfalls provide an oasis from the city streets. There are in fact two greenhouses: in the Estufa Fria (cold greenhouse), palms push through the slatted bamboo roof and paths wind through a forest of ferns, fuchsias, flowering shrubs and banana trees; the warmer Estufa Quente, or hot-house, is a glassed-over garden with lush plants, water-lily ponds and cacti, as well as tropical birds in cages.

Near the estufas a pond with large carp and a play area in the shape of a galleon are popular with children. On the east side the **Pavilhão Carlos Lopes**, named after the 1984 Olympic marathon winner, is now a venue for concerts and conferences. The façade is decorated with a series of modern tiled scenes, mainly of Portuguese battles. A pleasant waterside café lies to the north of the pavilion.

**Detail representing agricultural toil on the base
of the monument in Praça Marquês de Pombal**

Museu Calouste Gulbenkian ❻

Thanks to a wealthy Armenian oil magnate, Calouste Gulbenkian *(see p119)*, with wide-ranging tastes and an eye for a masterpiece, the museum has one of the finest collections of art in Europe. Inaugurated in 1969, the purpose-built museum was created as part of the charitable institution bequeathed to Portugal by the multimillionaire. The design of the building, set in a spacious park allowing natural light to fill some of the rooms, has recently undergone an extensive refurbishment and some displays may have changed.

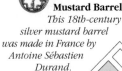

Mustard Barrel
This 18th-century silver mustard barrel was made in France by Antoine Sébastien Durand.

Lalique Corsage Ornament
The sinuous curves of the gold and enamel snakes are typical of René Lalique's Art Nouveau jewellery.

★ Diana
This fine marble statue (1780) by the French sculptor Jean-Antoine Houdon, was once owned by Catherine the Great of Russia but was considered too obscene to exhibit. The graceful Diana, goddess of the hunt, stands with a bow and arrow in hand.

Entrance

Stairs to

★ St Catherine
This serene bust of St Catherine was painted by the Flemish artist Rogier Van der Weyden (1400–64). The thin strip of landscape on the left of the wooden panel brings light and depth to the still portrait.

STAR EXHIBITS

★ Portrait of an Old Man by Rembrandt

★ Diana by Houdon

★ St Catherine by Van der Weyden

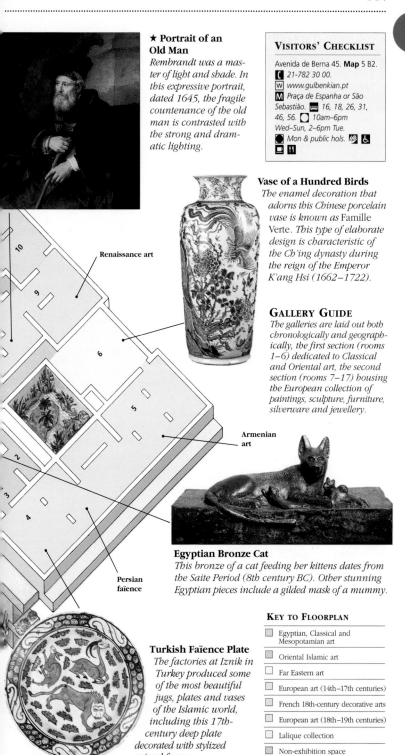

★ Portrait of an Old Man
Rembrandt was a master of light and shade. In this expressive portrait, dated 1645, the fragile countenance of the old man is contrasted with the strong and dramatic lighting.

VISITORS' CHECKLIST

Avenida de Berna 45. **Map** 5 B2.
21-782 30 00.
www.gulbenkian.pt
Praça de Espanha or São Sebastião. 16, 18, 26, 31, 46, 56. 10am–6pm Wed–Sun, 2–6pm Tue. Mon & public hols.

Vase of a Hundred Birds
The enamel decoration that adorns this Chinese porcelain vase is known as Famille Verte. *This type of elaborate design is characteristic of the Ch'ing dynasty during the reign of the Emperor K'ang Hsi (1662–1722).*

GALLERY GUIDE
The galleries are laid out both chronologically and geographically, the first section (rooms 1–6) dedicated to Classical and Oriental art, the second section (rooms 7–17) housing the European collection of paintings, sculpture, furniture, silverware and jewellery.

Renaissance art

Armenian art

Persian faïence

Egyptian Bronze Cat
This bronze of a cat feeding her kittens dates from the Saite Period (8th century BC). Other stunning Egyptian pieces include a gilded mask of a mummy.

Turkish Faïence Plate
The factories at Iznik in Turkey produced some of the most beautiful jugs, plates and vases of the Islamic world, including this 17th-century deep plate decorated with stylized animal forms.

KEY TO FLOORPLAN

- Egyptian, Classical and Mesopotamian art
- Oriental Islamic art
- Far Eastern art
- European art (14th–17th centuries)
- French 18th-century decorative arts
- European art (18th–19th centuries)
- Lalique collection
- Non-exhibition space

Exploring the Gulbenkian Collection

Housing CALOUSTE GULBENKIAN'S unique collection of art, the museum ranks with the Museu de Arte Antiga *(see pp96–9)* as the finest in Lisbon. The exhibits, which span over 4,000 years from ancient Egyptian statuettes, through translucent Islamic glassware, to Art Nouveau brooches, are displayed in spacious and well-lit galleries, many overlooking the gardens or courtyards. The museum is quite small, however each individual work of art, from the magnificent pieces that make up the rich display of Oriental and Islamic art, to the selection of European paintings and furniture, is worthy of attention.

Late 16th-century Persian faïence tile from the School of Isfahan

EGYPTIAN, CLASSICAL AND MESOPOTAMIAN ART

Priceless treasures chart the evolution of Egyptian art from the Old Kingdom (c.2700 BC) to the Roman Period (lst century BC). The exhibits range from an alabaster bowl of the 3rd Dynasty to a surprisingly modern-looking blue terracotta torso of a statuette of *Venus Anadyomene* from the Roman period.

Outstanding pieces in the Classical art section are a magnificent red-figure Greek vase and 11 Roman medallions, found in Egypt. These are believed to have been struck to commemorate the Olympic games held in Macedonia in AD 242 in honour of Alexander the Great. In the Mesopotamian art section the large Assyrian

5th-century BC Greek vase

alabaster bas-relief represents the winged genius of Spring, carrying a container of sacred water (9th century BC).

ORIENTAL ISLAMIC ART

Being armenian, Calouste Gulbenkian had a keen interest in art from the Near and Middle East. The Oriental Islamic gallery has a fine collection of Persian and Turkish carpets, textiles, costumes and ceramics. In the section overlooking the courtyard, the Syrian mosque lamps and bottles commissioned by princes and sultans, are beautifully decorated with coloured enamel on glass. The Armenian section has some exquisite illustrated manuscripts from the 16th to 18th centuries, produced by Armenian refugees in Istanbul, Persia and the Crimea.

FAR EASTERN ART

Calouste Gulbenkian acquired a large collection of Chinese porcelain between 1910 and 1930. One of the rarest pieces is the small blue-glazed bowl from the Yüan Dynasty (1279–1368), on the right as you go into the gallery. The majority of exhibits, however, are the later, more exuberantly decorated *famille verte* porcelain and the K'ang Hsi biscuitware of the 17th and 18th centuries. Further exhibits from the Far East are translucent Chinese jades and other semi-precious stones, Japanese prints, brocaded silk hangings and bound books, and lacquerwork.

EUROPEAN ART (14TH–17TH CENTURIES)

Illuminated manuscripts, rare printed books and medieval ivories introduce the section on Western art. The delicately sculpted 14th-century ivory diptychs and triptychs, made in France, show scenes from the lives of Christ and the Virgin.

The collection of early European paintings starts with panels of *St Joseph* and *St Catherine* by Rogier van der Weyden, leading painter of the mid-15th century in Flanders. Italian Renaissance painting is represented by Cima da Conegliano's *Sacra Conversazione* from the late 15th century and Domenico Ghirlandaio's *Portrait of a Young Woman* (1485).

The collection progresses to Flemish and Dutch works of the 17th century, including two works by Rembrandt: *Portrait of an Old Man* (1645),

French ivory triptych of
Scenes from the Life of the Virgin **(14th century)**

a masterpiece of psychological penetration, and *Alexander the Great* (1660), said to have been modelled on Rembrandt's son, Titus, and previously thought to have portrayed the Greek goddess Pallas Athena. Rubens is represented by three paintings, the most remarkable of which is the *Portrait of Hélène Fourment* (1630), the artist's second wife.

The gallery beyond the Dutch and Flemish paintings has tapestries and textiles from Italy and Flanders, Italian ceramics, rare 15th-century medallions and sculpture.

FRENCH 18TH-CENTURY DECORATIVE ARTS

SOME REMARKABLY elaborate Louis XV and Louis XVI pieces, many commissioned by royalty, feature in the collection of French 18th-century furniture. The exhibits, many of them embellished with laquer panels, ebony and bronze, are grouped together according to historical style with Beauvais and "chinoiserie" Aubusson tapestries decorating the walls.

The French silverware of the same period, much of which once adorned the dining tables of Russian palaces, includes lavishly decorated soup tureens, salt-cellars and platters.

Louis XV chest of drawers inlaid with ebony and bronze

EUROPEAN ART (18TH–19TH CENTURIES)

THE ART of the 18th century is dominated by French painters, including Watteau (1684–1721), Fragonard (1732–1806) and Boucher (1703–70). The most celebrated piece of sculpture is a statue of *Diana* by Jean-Antoine Houdon. Commissioned in 1780 by the Duke of Saxe-Gotha for his

***View of the Molo with the Ducal Palace* (1790) by Francesco Guardi**

gardens, it became one of the principal exhibits in the Hermitage in Russia during the 19th and early 20th centuries.

One whole room is devoted to views of Venice by the 18th-century Venetian painter Francesco Guardi, and a small collection of British art includes works by leading 18th-century portraitists, such as Gainsborough's *Portrait of Mrs Lowndes-Stone* (c.1775) and Romney's *Portrait of Mrs Constable* (1787). There are also two stormy seascapes by JMW Turner (1775–1851). French 19th-century landscape painting is well represented here, reflecting Gulbenkian's preference for naturalism, with works by the Barbizon school, the Realists and the Impressionists. The best-known paintings in the section, however, are probably Manet's *Boy with Cherries*, painted in about 1858 at the beginning of the artist's career, and *Boy Blowing*

Bubbles, painted about 1867. Renoir's *Portrait of Madame Claude Monet* was painted in about 1872 when the artist was staying with Monet at his country home in Argenteuil, in the outskirts of Paris.

LALIQUE COLLECTION

THE TOUR of the museum ends with an entire room filled with the flamboyant creations of French Art Nouveau jeweller, René Lalique (1860–1945). Gulbenkian was a close friend of Lalique's and he acquired many of the pieces of jewellery, glassware and ivory on display here directly from the artist. Inlaid with semi-precious stones and covered with gold leaf or enamel, the brooches, necklaces, vases and combs are decorated with the dragonfly, peacock or sensual female nude motifs characteristic of Art Nouveau.

CALOUSTE GULBENKIAN

Born in Scutari (Turkey) in 1869, Gulbenkian started his art collection at the age of 14 when he bought some ancient coins in a bazaar. In 1928 he was granted a 5 per cent stake in four major oil companies, including BP and Shell, in thanks for his part in the transfer of the assets of the Turkish Petroleum Company to those four companies. He thereby earned himself the nickname of "Mr Five Percent". With the wealth he accumulated, Gulbenkian was able to indulge his passion for fine works of art. During World War II, he went to live in neutral Portugal and, on his death in 1955, bequeathed his estate to the Portuguese in the form of a charitable trust. The Foundation supports many cultural activities and has its own orchestra, libraries, ballet company and concert halls.

Henry Moore sculpture in garden of the Centro de Arte Moderna

Centro de Arte Moderna ❼

Rua Dr Nicolau de Bettencourt.
Map 5 B3. 🄲 *21-782 30 00.*
Ⓦ *www.gulbenkian.pt* Ⓜ *São Sebastião.* 🚌 *16, 26, 31, 46, 56.*
◻ *10am–6pm Wed–Sun, 2–6pm Tue.* ● *Mon & public hols.* 🈲 🄵

T HE MODERN ART MUSEUM lies across the gardens from the Calouste Gulbenkian museum and is part of the same cultural foundation *(see p119)*. The permanent collection housed in the centre features paintings and sculpture by Portuguese artists from the turn of the 20th century to the present day. The most famous painting is the striking portrait of poet Fernando Pessoa in the Café Irmãos Unidos (1964) by José de Almada Negreiros (1893–1970), a main exponent of Portuguese Modernism. Also of interest are paintings by Eduardo Viana (1881–1967), Amadeo de Sousa Cardoso (1887–1910), as well as contemporary artists such as Paula Rego, Rui Sanches, Graça Morais and Teresa Magalhães.

The museum is light and spacious with pleasant gardens and a popular cafeteria.

Campo Pequeno ❽

Map 5 C1. Ⓜ *Campo Pequeno.* 🚌 *22, 45.* **Bullring** 🄲 *21-793 24 42.* ◻ *Easter–Oct: for bullfights.* 🈲 🄵

T HIS SQUARE is dominated by the red-brick Neo-Moorish bullring built in the late 19th century. Currently closed until 2003, the building is undergoing major works that are expected to create an underground car park and shops. Much of the bullring's distinctive architecture, such as its keyhole-shaped windows and double cupolas will be retained. For information on bullfights at other venues call the telephone number listed above.

Renovated 19th-century steam pump in the Museu da Água

Museu da Água ❾

Rua do Alviela 12. 🄲 *21-810 02 15.* 🚌 *35, 104, 105, 107.*
◻ *10am–6pm Mon–Sat.* ● *public hols.* 🈲 📷

D EDICATED TO the history of Lisbon's water supply, this small but informative museum was imaginatively created around the city's first steam pumping station. It commemorates Manuel da Maia, the 18th-century engineer who masterminded the Águas Livres aqueduct *(see p124)*. The excellent layout of the museum earned it the Council of Europe Museum Prize in 1990.

Pride of place goes to four lovingly preserved steam engines, one of which still functions (by electricity) and can be switched on for visitors. The development of technology relating to the city's water supply is documented with photographs. Particularly interesting are the sections on the Águas Livres aqueduct and the Alfama's 17th-century Chafariz d'El Rei, one of Lisbon's first fountains. Locals used to queue at one of six founts, depending on their social status.

Museu Nacional do Azulejo ❿

See pp122–3.

Neo-Moorish façade of the bullring in Campo Pequeno

Oceanário de Lisboa ⑪

Esplanada D Carlos I, Parque das Nações. 【 21-891 70 02. M *Oriente.* 18, 28, 50, 82. ☐ *Gare do Oriente.* ○ 10am–7pm daily. 🎫 &

O N THE BANKS of the Tagus, centrally located within the Parque das Nações, this innovative exhibit is the largest in Europe and the second biggest in the world. Built for Expo '98, to illustrate the theme of "The Oceans: A Heritage for the Future", the "oceanarium" was conceived by an American architect, Peter Chermayeff. His aim was to enhance public awareness of the diversity of the oceans' vast natural resources and to encourage mankind's responsibility to preserve the seas for future generations.

The central feature is the gigantic aquarium, the "Open Tank", with a volume of water equivalent to that of four Olympic swimming pools. Representing the open ocean, this features the fauna of the high seas, from shoals of sardines to sharks. Around the main tank four smaller aquariums reconstruct the ecosystems of the Atlantic, Antarctic Pacific and Indian oceans. Each one features life specific to the ocean, from seals in the Antarctic to the coral reefs of the Indian Ocean.

Museu da Cidade ⑫

Campo Grande 245. 【 21-759 16 17. M *Campo Grande.* 1, 3, 7, 33, 36, 47, 50, 101. ○ 10am–1pm, 2–6pm Tue –Sun. ● public hols. 🎫 &

P ALÁCIO PIMENTA was allegedly commissioned by João V (*see pp52–3*) for his mistress Madre Paula, a nun from the nearby convent at Odivelas. When the mansion was built, in the middle of the 18th century, it occupied a peaceful rural site outside the capital. Nowadays it has to contend

Original 18th-century tiled kitchen in the Museu da Cidade

18th-century Indian toy, Museu da Cidade

with the teeming traffic of Campo Grande and the city's main east-west flyover nearby. The house itself, however, still retains its period charm, and the city museum, established here in 1979, is one of the most interesting in Lisbon.

The displays follow the development of the city, from prehistoric times, through the Romans, Visigoths and Moors, traced by means of tiles, drawings, paintings, models and historical documents. Visits also take you through the former living quarters of the mansion, including the kitchen, decorated with blue and white tile panels of fish, flowers and hanging game. Other rooms contain period furniture, paintings and toys. A collection of 18th-century ceramics includes intricately modelled statuettes, tureens and plates made at the royal china factory in Rato.

Some of the most fascinating exhibits are those depicting the city before the earthquake of 1755, including a highly detailed model made in the 1950s and

an impressive 17th-century oil painting by Dirk Stoop (1610–86) of *Terreiro do Paço*, as Praça do Comércio was known then (*see p87*). One room is devoted to the Águas Livres aqueduct (*see p124*) with detailed architectural plans for its construction as well as prints and watercolours of the completed aqueduct by foreign and Portuguese artists.

The earthquake theme is resumed with pictures of the city amid the devastation and various plans for its reconstruction. The museum introduces the 20th century with a large colour poster celebrating the Revolution of 1910 and the proclamation of the new republic (*see pp54–5*). Several other exhibits depict life and customs in 20th-century Lisbon, including an evocative painting of *O Fado* (1910) by José Malhôa (*see p67*).

Detail of Dirk Stoop's 17th-century view of the Terreiro do Paço, Museu da Cidade

Museu Nacional do Azulejo ⑩

Pelican on the Manueline portal

DONA LEONOR, widow of King João II, founded the Convento da Madre de Deus in 1509. Originally built in Manueline style, the church was restored under João III using simple Renaissance designs. The striking Baroque decoration was added by João V. The convent cloisters provide a stunning setting for the National Tile Museum. Decorative panels, individual tiles and photographs trace the evolution of tile-making from its introduction by the Moors, through Spanish influence and the development of Portugal's own style *(see pp22–3)*, up to the present day.

Panorama of Lisbon
A striking 18th-century panel, along one wall of the cloister, depicts Lisbon before the 1755 earthquake (see pp62–3). This detail shows the royal palace on Terreiro do Paço.

First floor

Hunting Scene
Artisans rather than artists began to decorate tiles in the 17th century. This detail shows a naive representation of a hunt.

Ground floor

KEY TO FLOORPLAN

- ▢ Moorish tiles
- ▢ 16th-century tiles
- ▢ 17th-century tiles
- ▢ 18th-century tiles
- ▢ 19th-century tiles
- ▢ 20th-century tiles
- ▢ Temporary exhibition space
- ▢ Non-exhibition space

STAR FEATURES

★ **Madre de Deus**

★ **Manueline Cloister**

★ **Nossa Senhora da Vida**

★ **Nossa Senhora da Vida**
This detail showing St John is part of a fine 16th-century maiolica altarpiece. The central panel of the huge work depicts The Adoration of the Shepherds.

Tiles from the 17th century with oriental influences are displayed here.

Café Tiles
The walls of the restaurant are lined with 20th-century tiles showing hanging game, including wild boar, pheasant and sausages.

VISITORS' CHECKLIST

Rua da Madre de Deus 4. **C** 21-814 77 47. **=** 18, 42, 104, 105. **O** 2–6pm Tue, 10am–6pm Wed–Sun (last adm: 30 mins before closing). **●** 1 Jan, Easter, 1 May, 25 Dec. **⊠ ◉ ▣ ▯ ₶**

Moorish Tiles
Bold, geometric designs were characteristic of Moorish azulejo patterns. These 15th-century tiles, decorated with stylized animal motifs, were probably made by Moorish artisans in Seville.

Entrance

The Renaissance cloister
is the work of Diogo de Torralva (1500–66).

★ **Madre de Deus**
Completed in the mid-16th century, it was not until two centuries later, under João V, that the church of Madre de Deus acquired its ornate decoration. The sumptuous Rococo altarpiece was added after the earthquake of 1755.

GALLERY GUIDE
The rooms around the central cloister are arranged chronologically, from the Moorish tiles near the entrance to the 20th-century tiles upstairs. A room on the ground floor explains the history of the museum and tile-making techniques.

The carved Manueline portal *(see p21)* was recreated from a 16th-century painting.

Exhibition on museum's history

★ **Manueline Cloister**
An important surviving feature of the original convent is the graceful Manueline cloister. Fine geometrical patterned tiles were added to the cloister walls in the 17th century.

Jardim Zoológico  ⑬

Estrada de Benfica 158–60. 🎫 *21-723 29 00.* Ⓜ *Jardim Zoológico.* 🚌 *16, 34, 54, 68 & other routes.* 🕐 *9am–6pm (Apr–Sep: 8pm) daily.* 🌐 📷

THE GARDENS of the Jardim Zoológico are as much a feature as the actual zoo. Opened in 1905, the zoo has recently been revamped and the majority of its aviaries and cages now provide more comfortable conditions for the inmates. The most bizarre feature is the dogs' cemetery, complete with tombstones and flowers. Current attractions of the zoo include a cable car which tours the park, a reptile house and dolphin shows. The area is divided into four zones and the admission charge is based on how many you visit.

Dolphins performing in the aquarium of the Jardim Zoológico

Aqueduto das Águas Livres ⑭

Best seen from Calçada da Quintinha. 🕐 *for guided tours by appt (Apr–Oct only), phone Museu da Agua das Amoreiras.* 🎫 *21-813 55 22.* **Mãe d'Água das Amoreiras** 🎫 *21-325 16 46.* 🕐 *10am–6pm Mon–Sat.*

CONSIDERED THE most beautiful sight in Lisbon at the turn of the century, the impressive structure of the Aqueduto das Águas Livres looms over the Alcântara valley to the northwest of the city. The construction of an aqueduct to bring fresh water to the city gave João V *(see pp52–3)* an ideal opportunity to indulge his passion for grandiose building schemes, as the only area of Lisbon with fresh drinking water was the Alfama. A tax on meat, wine, olive oil and other comestibles funded the project, and although not complete until the 19th century, it was already supplying the city with water by 1748. The main pipeline measures 19 km (12 miles), but the total length, including all the secondary channels, is 58 km (36 miles). The most visible part of this imposing structure are the 35 arches that cross the Alcântara valley, the tallest of which rise to a spectacular 65 m (213 ft) above the city.

The public walkway along the aqueduct, once a pleasant promenade, has been closed since 1853. This is partly due to Diogo Alves, the infamous robber who threw his victims over the edge. Today, visitors may take a lively, informative guided tour over the Alcântara arches. There are also occasional tours of the Mãe d'Água reservoir and trips to the Mãe d'Água springs, the source of the water supply. These tours can be irregular, so it is best to contact the Museu da Água *(see p120)* for details of the trip on offer.

At the end of the aqueduct, the **Mãe d'Água das Amoreiras** is a castle-like building which once served as a reservoir for the water supplied from the aqueduct. The original design of 1745 was by the Hungarian architect, Carlos Mardel, who worked under Pombal *(see pp62–3)* in the rebuilding of the Baixa. Completed in 1834, it became a popular meeting place and acquired a reputation as the rendezvous for kings and their mistresses. Today the space is used for art exhibitions, fashion shows and other events.

Imposing arches of the Aqueduto das Águas Livres spanning the Alcântara valley

Palácio Fronteira ⓕ

Largo São Domingos de Benfica 1.
C 21-778 20 23. **M** Jardim
Zoológico. **☐** 72. **R** Benfica. **☐**
Mon–Sat. **✔** Jun–Sep: 10:30, 11, &
11:30am & noon; Oct–May: 11am &
noon. **●** public hols. **✔ ☐**

Tiled terrace leading to the chapel of the Palácio Fronteira

T
HIS DELIGHTFUL country
manor house was built as
a hunting pavilion for João de
Mascarenhas, the first Marquês
de Fronteira, in 1640. Although
skyscrapers are visible in the
distance, it still occupies a
quiet spot, by the Parque
Florestal de Monsanto. Both
house and garden have *azulejo*
decoration whose subjects
include battle scenes and
trumpet-blowing monkeys.

Although the palace is still
occupied by the 12th Marquis,
some of the living rooms and
the library, as well
as the formal gar-
dens, are included
in the tour. The
Battles Room has
lively tiled panels
depicting scenes
of the War of
Restoration *(see
pp50–51)*, with
a detail showing
João de Fronteira
fighting a Spanish
general. It was his
loyalty to Pedro II
during this war that earned him
the title of Marquis. Interesting
comparisons can be made between these naive 17th-century
Portuguese tiles and the Delft
ones from the same period in
the dining room, depicting
naturalistic scenes. The dining
room is also decorated with
frescoed panels and portraits
of Portuguese nobility by artists
such as Domingos António de
Sequeira (1768–1837).

The late 16th-century chapel
is the oldest part of the house.
The façade is adorned with
stones, shells, broken glass and
bits of china. These fragments
of crockery are believed to
have been used at the feast
inaugurating the palace and
then smashed to ensure no one
else could sup off the same set.
Visits to the **garden** start at the
chapel terrace, where tiled
niches are decorated with
figures personifying the arts
and mythological creatures.

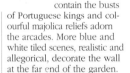
Bust of João I in gardens
of Palácio Fronteira

In the formal Italian garden the
immaculate box hedges are
cut into shapes to represent
the seasons of the year. To
one end, tiled
scenes of dashing
knights on horse-
back, representing
ancestors of the
Fronteira family,
are reflected in the
waters of a large
tank. On either
side of the water,
a grand staircase
leads to a terrace
above. Here,
decorative niches
contain the busts
of Portuguese kings and colourful majolica reliefs adorn
the arcades. More blue and
white tiled scenes, realistic and
allegorical, decorate the wall
at the far end of the garden.

Parque do Monteiro-Mor ⓖ

Largo Júlio Castilho. **C** 21-759 03 18.
☐ 1, 3, 4, 7, 36, 101, 108. **Park ☐**
10am–6pm Tue–Sun. **●** 1 Jan,
Easter, 1 May, 25 Dec. **Museu
Nacional do Traje ☐** 10am–6pm
Tue–Sun. **Museu Nacional do Teatro**
C 21-756 74 10. **☐** 10am–6pm
Wed–Sun, 2–6pm Tue. **✔** combined
ticket for park & museums. **☐ ☐**

M
ONTEIRO-MOR PARK was
sold to the state in 1975
and the 18th-century palace
buildings were converted to
museums. Relatively few
visitors come here because
of the distance from the city
centre, but the gardens are
attractive and rather more
romantic than the manicured
box-hedge gardens so typical
of Lisbon. Much of the land
is wooded, though the area
around the museums has
gardens with flowering shrubs,
duck ponds and tropical trees.

The rather old-fashioned
Museu Nacional do Traje
(costume museum) has a
varied collection of costumes
worn by musicians, politicians,
poets, aristocrats and soldiers.

The **Museu Nacional do
Teatro** has two buildings, one
devoted to temporary exhibitions, the other containing a
very small permanent collection. Photographs, posters
and cartoons feature famous
20th-century Portuguese actors
and one section is devoted to
Amália Rodrigues, the famous
fado singer *(see pp66–7)*.

Entrance to the theatre museum
in Parque do Monteiro-Mor

LISBON STREET FINDER

MAP REFERENCES given in this guide for sights and entertainment venues in Lisbon refer to the Street Finder maps on the following pages. Map references are also given for Lisbon's hotels *(see pp380–83)* and restaurants *(see pp404–7)*. The first figure in the map reference indicates which Street Finder map to turn to, and the letter and number which follow refer to the grid reference on that map. The map below shows the area of Lisbon covered by the eight Street Finder maps. Symbols used for sights and useful information are displayed in the key below. Lisbon's Metro network *(see pp448–9)* is being extended; and those stations marked on the map include those scheduled to open by 2001.

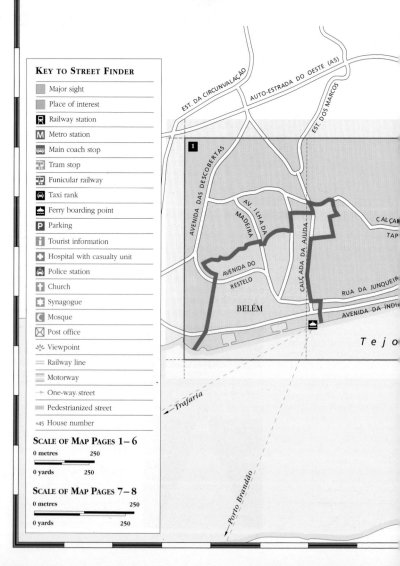

KEY TO STREET FINDER	
	Major sight
	Place of interest
🚉	Railway station
M	Metro station
🚌	Main coach stop
🚊	Tram stop
🚋	Funicular railway
🚕	Taxi rank
⛴	Ferry boarding point
P	Parking
i	Tourist information
✚	Hospital with casualty unit
🚓	Police station
✝	Church
✡	Synagogue
C	Mosque
✉	Post office
☼	Viewpoint
=	Railway line
▬	Motorway
→	One-way street
▬	Pedestrianized street
«45	House number

SCALE OF MAP PAGES 1–6

0 metres   250

0 yards   250

SCALE OF MAP PAGES 7–8

0 metres   250

0 yards   250

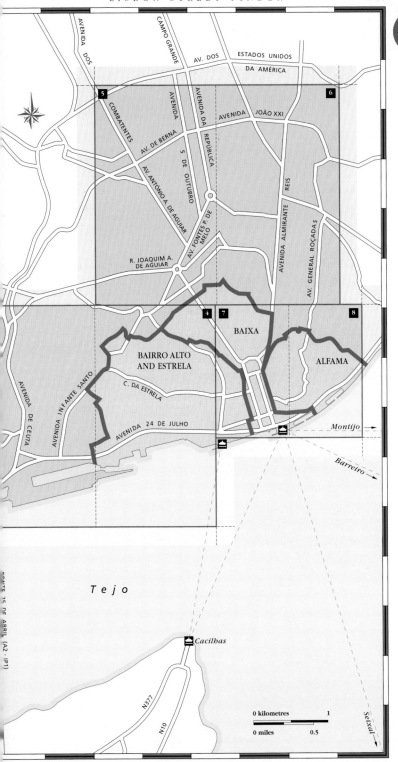

Street Finder Index

1º de Dezembro, Rua 7 B3
1º de Maio, Rua 3 A4
5 de Outubro, Avenida 5 C1
24 de Julho, Avenida 3 C4

A

Abade Faria, Rua 6 F2
Abílio Lopes do Rego, Rua 3 C3
Academia de Belas Artes, Largo da 7 B5
Academia das Ciências, Rua da 4 F2
Academia Recreativa de Santo Amaro, Rua 2 F3
Acesso à Ponte 3 A3
Açores, Rua dos 6 D3
Actor Isidoro, Rua 6 E2
Actor Taborda, Rua 6 D3
Actor Tasso, Rua 5 C4
Actor Vale, Rua 6 F3
Actriz Virgínia, Rua 6 E2
Açucenas, Rua das 1 C2
Adelas, Rua das 4 E2
Adro, Travessa do 7 B2
Afrânio Peixoto, Praça 6 E1
Afonso Costa, Avenida 6 F1
Afonso de Albuquerque, Praça 1 C4
Afonso Domingues, Rua 8 F1
Agostinho de Carvalho, Calçada de 7 C2
Águas Livres, Travessa 5 A5
Ajuda, Calçada de 2 D2
Ajuda, Calçada da 2 F2
Ajuda, Largo da 2 D2
Alcaide, Travessa do 4 F3
Alcântara, Rua de 3 A4
Alcolena, Rua de 1 A3
Alecrim, Rua do 7 A5
Alegria, Praça da 4 F1
Alegria, Rua da 4 F1
Alexandre Braga, Rua 6 D4
Alexandre Herculano, Rua 5 C5
Alexandre de Sá Pinto, Rua 2 D4
Alfândega, Rua da 7 C5
Alfredo Cortês, Rua 5 C1
Alfredo da Silva, Rua 2 D3
Alfredo Roque Gameiro, Rua 5 A1
Alfredo Soares, Rua 1 B2
Aliança Operária, Rua 2 E3
Almada, Rua da 4 F3
Almada, Travessa do 7 C4
Almas, Travessa das 3 C2
Almeida Brandão, Rua 4 D2
Almeida e Sousa, Rua 3 C1
Almirante Barroso, Rua 6 D3
Almirante Gago Coutinho, Avenida 6 E1
Almirante Reis, Avenida 6 E5
Alto do Duque, Rua do 1 A3
Álvaro Coutinho, Rua 6 E5
Álvaro Esteves, Rua 1 B3
Álvaro Pais, Avenida 5 B1
Alves Redol, Rua 6 D2
Alves Torgo, Rua (ao Areeiro) 6 E1
Alves Torgo, Rua (a Arroios) 6 E3
Alvito, Estrada do 2 F1
Alvito, Rua do 3 A3
Amendoeira, Rua da 8 D2
Américo Durão, Rua 6 F2
Amoreiras, Rua das (à Ajuda) 2 D3
Amoreiras, Rua das (ao Rato) 5 A5
Amoreiras, Travessa das (ao Rato) 5 B5

Amoreiras Shopping Center 5 A5
Anchieta, Rua 7 A4
Andaluz, Rua do 5 C4
Andrade, Rua 6 E5
Andrade Corvo, Rua 5 C4
André Brun, Rua 3 B2
Angelina Vidal, Rua 6 F5
Angola, Rua de 6 E4
Anjos, Rua dos 6 E5
Antão Gonçalves, Rua 1 A2
Antero de Quental, Rua 6 E5
António Abreu, Rua 1 A4
António Augusto de Aguiar, Avenida 5 B3
António Enes, Rua 5 C3
António Janeiro, Rua 1 A1
António José de Almeida, Avenida 6 D2
António Luís Inácio, Rua 6 F3
António Maria Cardoso, Rua 7 A5
António Pedro, Rua 6 E4
António Pereira Carrilho, Rua 6 E3
António de Saldanha, Rua 1 A2
António Serpa, Avenida 5 C1
Aqueduto das Águas Livres 5 A5
Arco, Rua do (a Alcântara) 3 B4
Arco, Rua do (a São Mamede) 4 E1
Arco do Cego, Rua do 6 D2
Arco do Chafariz das Terras, Rua do 3 C3
Arco do Carvalhão, Rua do 3 B1
Arco da Graça, Rua do 7 B2
Arco Grande de Cima 8 E2
Armador, Travessa do 2 D2
Arrábida, Rua da 4 D1
Arriaga, Rua da 3 C4
Arrochela, Travessa da 4 E2
Arroios, Calçada de 6 D3
Arroios, Rua de 6 E4
Arsenal, Rua do 7 B5
Artilharia Um, Rua 5 A4
Artur de Paiva, Rua 6 F4
Artur Lamas, Rua 2 E4
Assunção, Rua da 7 B4
Ataíde, Rua do 7 A5
Atalaia, Rua da 4 F2
Augusta, Rua 7 B3
Augusto Gil, Rua 6 D1
Augusto Gomes Ferreira, Rua 2 D2
Augusto Machado, Rua 6 E2
Augusto Rosa, Rua 8 D4
Áurea, Rua (Rua do Ouro) 7 B4
Azedo Gneco, Rua 3 C1

B

Bacalhoeiros, Rua dos 7 C4
Barão, Rua do 8 D4
Barão de Sabrosa, Rua 6 F2
Barata Salgueiro, Rua 5 C5
Barbadinhos, Calçada dos 8 F1
Barbosa du Bocage, Avenida 5 C2
Barracas, Rua das 6 E5
Barroca, Rua da 4 F2
Bartolomeu da Costa, Rua 8 F1
Bartolomeu Dias, Rua 1 A5
Basílica da Estrela 4 D2
Beatas, Rua das 8 E1

Bela Vista, Rua da (à Graça) 8 E1
Bela Vista, Rua da (à Lapa) 4 D2
Belém, Rua de 1 C4
Bempostinha, Rua da 6 D5
Beneficência, Rua da 5 A1
Benformoso, Rua do 7 C1
Berna, Avenida de 5 B2
Bernardim Ribeiro, Rua 5 C5
Bernardino Costa, Rua 7 A5
Bernardo Lima, Rua 5 C4
Betesga, Rua da 7 B3
Bica do Marquês, Rua da 2 D3
Boa Hora, Calçada da 2 E3
Boa Hora, Travessa da (ao Bairro Alto) 4 F2
Boa Hora, Travessa da (à Ajuda) 2 D3
Boavista, Rua da 4 F3
Bombarda, Rua da 7 C1
Bombeiros, Avenida dos 1 B1
Boqueirão do Duro, Rua 4 E3
Boqueirão de Ferreiros, Rua 4 E3
Borges Carneiro, Rua 4 D3
Borja, Rua de 3 B3
Braamcamp, Rua 5 B5
Brás Pacheco, Rua 6 D2
Brasília, Avenida de 1 A5
Brito Aranha, Rua 6 D2
Brotero, Rua 1 C3
Buenos Aires, Rua de 4 D3

C

Cabo, Rua do 4 D1
Cabo Verde, Rua de 6 E5
Caetano Alberto, Rua 6 D2
Caetanos, Rua dos 4 F2
Cais de Santarém, Rua do 8 D4
Calado, Travessa do 6 F4
Calouste Gulbenkian, Avenida 5 A2
Camilo Castelo Branco, Rua 5 C5
Caminhos de Ferro, Rua dos 8 D3
Campo dos Mártires da Pátria 6 D5
Campo de Ourique, Rua de 4 D1
Campo Pequeno 5 C1
Campo de Santa Clara 8 E2
Campolide, Rua de 5 A4
Capelão, Rua do 7 C2
Capelo, Rua do 7 A4
Capitão Afonso Pala, Rua 3 B3
Capitão Humberto de Ataíde, Rua 8 F1
Capitão Renato Baptista, Rua 7 B1
Cara, Travessa da 4 F2
Cardal à Graça, Rua do 8 E1
Cardal, Rua do 7 A1
Cardeal Cerejeira, Alameda 5 B4
Cardeal, Calçada do 8 F2
Cardeal Mercier, Rua 5 A1
Carlos Alberto da Mota Pinto, Rua 5 A5
Carlos Calisto, Rua 1 B2
Carlos José Barreiros, Rua 6 E3
Carlos da Maia, Rua 3 C1
Carlos Mardel, Rua 6 E3
Carlos Reis, Rua 5 B1
Carmo, Calçada do 7 A3
Carmo, Travessa do 7 A4
Carmo, Rua do 7 B4

Carrião, Rua do 7 A1
Carvalho, Travessa do 4 F3
Carvalho Araújo, Rua 6 F3
Casa dos Bicos 8 D4
Casal Ribeiro, Avenida 6 D3
Casal Ventoso de Baixo 3 B2
Casal Ventoso de Cima 3 B1
Casalinho da Ajuda, Rua do 2 E2
Cascais, Rua 3 B4
Cascão, Calçada do 8 F3
Caselas, Estrada de 1 B2
Castelo Branco Saraiva, Rua 6 F5
Castelo Picão, Calçada do 4 E3
Castelo Picão, Rua do 8 D4
Castilho, Rua 4 F1
5 A4
Cavaleiro de Oliveira, Rua 6 E3
Cavaleiros, Rua dos 7 C2
Cecílio de Sousa, Rua 4 F1
Cemitério da Ajuda 1 C2
Cemitério dos Prazeres 3 B4
Centro de Arte Moderna 5 B3
Centro Cultural de Belém 1 B5
Cesário Verde, Rua 6 F4
Cesteiros, Calçada dos 8 F2
Ceuta, Avenida de 3 A2
Chagas, Rua das 4 F3
Chaminés d'El Rei, Rua 1 C1
Chão da Feira, Rua do 8 D3
Chiado 7 A5
Chiado, Largo do 7 A4
Chile, Praça do 6 E3
Cidade Avintes, Travessa 8 F2
Cidade da Horta, Rua 6 E4
Cidade de Cardiff, Rua 6 E4
Cima dos Quartéis, Travessa de 3 C1
Clube Atlético e Recreativo do Caramão, Rua 1 C1
Clube de Ténis, Estrada do 3 A2
Coelho da Rocha, Rua 3 C1
Colégio de São José, Rua do 1 A2
Columbano Bordalo Pinheiro, Avenida 5 A2
Combatentes, Avenida dos 5 A1
Combro, Calçada do 4 F2
Combro, Travessa do 4 D3
Comércio, Praça do 7 C5
Comércio, Rua do 7 B5
Conceição, Rua da 7 B4
Conceição da Glória, Rua da 4 F1
Conde, Rua do 4 D3
Conde Barão, Largo do 4 E3
Conde de Monsaraz, Rua 6 F4
Conde de Pombeiro, Calçada do 6 E5
Conde da Ponte, Travessa do 3 A5
Conde de Redondo, Rua do 5 C5
Conde da Ribeira, Travessa do 2 F3
Conde de Valbom, Avenida 5 B2
Condes, Rua dos 7 A2
Condessa, Rua da 7 A3
Condessa do Rio, Travessa da 4 F3
Conselheiro Arantes Pedroso, Rua 7 B1
Conselheiro Fernando de Sousa, Avenida 5 A4
Conselheiro Martins de Carvalho, Rua 1 C2

Convento de Jesus,
Travessa do **4 F2**
Cordeiro de Sousa, Rua **5 C1**
Cordoeiros, Rua dos **4 F3**
Coronel Eduardo
Galhardo, Avenida **6 F4**
Castelo de São Jorge **8 D3**
Coronel Ferreira
do Amaral, Rua **6 E2**
Coronel Pereira da Silva,
Rua **2 D3**
Corpo Santo, Rua do **7 A5**
Correeiros, Rua dos **7 B4**
Correia Teles, Rua **3 C1**
Correio Velho,
Calçada do **7 C4**
Corvos, Rua dos **8 E3**
Costa, Rua da **3 B3**
Costa, Travessa da **3 B3**
Costa do Castelo **7 C3**
Costa Goodolfim, Rua **6 D2**
Costa Pimenta, Rua **3 B1**
Cova da Moura, Rua da **3 B3**
Cozinha Económica,
Rua da **3 A4**
Crucifixo, Rua do **7 B4**
Cruz, Estrada da
(ao Caramão) **1 B2**
Cruz , Rua da
(a Alcântara) **3 A3**
Cruz, Rua da (a Caselas) **1 A1**
Cruz, Travessa da
(do Torel) **7 B1**
Cruz da Carreira, Rua da **6 D5**
Cruz do Desterro,
Travessa **7 B1**
Cruz dos Poiais, Rua da **4 E2**
Cruz Vermelha, Rua da **5 B1**
Cruzeiro, Rua da **2 E2**
Cura, Rua do **4 D3**

D

Damão, Praça de **1 A4**
Damasceno Monteiro, **6 E5**
8 D1
David Melgueiro,
Rua **1 A4**
David de Sousa, Rua **6 D1**
Defensores de Chaves,
Avenida dos **5 C2**
Descobertas,
Avenida das **1 A2**
Desterro, Calçada do **7 C1**
Desterro, Rua do **7 B1**
Diário de Notícias, Rua **7 A4**
Dinis Dias, Rua **1 A4**
Dió, Praça de **1 A4**
Diogo Cão, Rua **2 E3**
Diogo Gomes, Rua **1 A4**
Diogo de Silves, Rua **1 B2**
Diogo de Teive, Rua **1 B2**
Dom Afonso Henriques,
Alameda **6 E2**
Dom Carlos I, Avenida **4 E3**
Dom Constantino de
Bragança, Rua **1 A3**
Dom Cristóvão da Gama,
Rua, **1 A4**
Dom Duarte, Rua **7 B3**
Dom Francisco
de Almeida, Rua **1 A4**
Dom Francisco Manuel
de Melo, Rua **5 A4**
Dom João V, Rua **4 D1**
Dom João de Castro,
Rua **2 E3**
Dom Lourenço
de Almeida, Rua **1 B4**
Dom Luís I, Rua **4 E3**
Dom Luís de Noronha,
Rua **5 A2**
Dom Pedro IV, Praça **7 B3**
Dom Pedro V, Rua **4 F2**
Dom Vasco, Rua de **2 D3**

Dom Vasco, Travessa de **2 D3**
Domingos Sequeira, Rua **4 D2**
Domingos Tendeiro, Rua **1 C3**
Dona Estefânia, Rua de **6 D3**
Dona Filipe de Vilhena,
Rua **6 D2**
Douradores, Rua dos **7 C4**
Doutor Almeida Amaral,
Rua **6 D5**
Doutor Álvaro de Castro,
Rua **5 A2**
Doutor Eduardo Neves,
Rua **5 C1**
Doutor Júlio Dantas, Rua **5 A3**
Doutor Mário Moutinho,
Avenida **1 B1**
Doutor Nicolau
de Bettencourt, Rua **5 B3**
Doutor Oliveira Ramos,
Rua **6 F3**
Doutor Silva Teles, Rua **5 B2**
Doutor Teófilo Braga,
Rua **4 D2**
Duarte Pacheco Pereira,
Rua **1 A4**
Duque, Rua do **7 A3**
Duque de Ávila, Avenida **5 C3**
Duque de Loulé, Avenida **5 C4**
Duque de Palmela, Rua **5 C5**
Duque de Saldanha,
Praça de **5 C3**
Duques de Bragança,
Rua dos **7 A5**

E

Eça de Queirós, Rua **5 C4**
Eduardo Bairrada, Rua **2 D2**
Eduardo Coelho, Rua **4 F2**
Eduardo da Costa, Rua **6 F4**
Egas Moniz, Rua **6 F2**
Elevador de Santa Justa **7 B3**
Elias Garcia, Avenida **5 C2**
Embaixador Teixeira de
Sampaio, Rua **3 C3**
Embaixador, Rua da **2 D4**
Emenda, Rua da **4 F3**
Engenheiro Duarte
Pacheco, Avenida **5 A5**
Engenheiro Miguel Pais,
Calçada **4 E1**
Engenheiro Santos
Simões, Rua **6 F2**
Engenheiro Vieira
da Silva, Rua **5 C3**
Entrecampos, Rua de **5 C1**
Entremuros do Mirante,
Rua de **8 F2**
Ermida de São Jerónimo **1 A3**
Escola Araújo,
Travessa da **6 D4**
Escola do Exército,
Rua da **6 D5**
Escola de Medicina
Veterinária, Rua da **6 D4**
Escola Politécnica,
Rua da **4 E1**
Escolas Gerais, Rua das **8 E3**
Espanha, Praça de **5 A2**
Espera, Travessa da **7 A4**
Esperança, Rua da **4 E3**
Esperança do Cardal,
Rua **7 A1**
Espírito Santo, Beco do **8 E4**
Estádio Municipal
do Restelo **1 B3**
Estrela, Calçada da **4 E2**
Estrela, Praça da **4 D2**
Estrela, Rua da **4 D2**

F

Fábrica dos Pentes,
Travessa da **5 B5**
Fala Só, Travessa do **7 A2**

Fanqueiros, Rua dos **7 C4**
Farinhas, Rua das **7 C3**
Fé, Rua da **7 A1**
Feira da Ladra **8 E2**
Feliciano de Sousa, Rua **3 A3**
Fernandes Tomás, Rua **4 F3**
Fernando Pedroso, Rua **6 D2**
Fernão Gomes, Rua **1 A3**
Fernão Lopes, Rua **5 C3**
Fernão Mendes Pinto,
Rua **1 A5**
Ferragial, Rua **7 A5**
Ferreira Borges, Rua **3 C1**
Ferreira Lapa, Rua **6 D4**
Ferreiro, Travessa do **3 C3**
Ferreiros, Rua dos **4 E2**
Ferreiros, Travessa dos **1 C4**
Fialho de Almeida, Rua **5 A3**
Fiéis de Deus,
Travessa dos **4 F2**
Figueira, Praça da **7 B3**
Filinto Elísio, Rua **2 F3**
Filipe da Mata, Rua **5 A1**
Filipe Folque, Rua **5 C3**
Flores, Rua das **7 A4**
Florindas, Travessa das **2 D3**
Fonseca Benevides, Rua **2 E2**
Fontainhas, Rua das **3 A4**
Fonte do Louro,
Azinhaga da **6 F1**
Fontes Pereira de Melo,
Avenida **5 C4**
Forno, Rua do **7 B2**
Forno do Tijolo, Rua do **6 E5**
Forte, Calçada do **8 F1**
Forte do Alto do Duque,
Estrada do **1 A2**
Fradesso da Silveira, Rua **3 A4**
Francesinhas, Rua das **4 E3**
Francisco de Holanda,
Rua **5 B1**
Francisco Metrass, Rua **3 C1**
Francisco Pedro Curado,
Rua **6 F4**
Francisco Ribeiro, Rua **6 E5**
Francisco Sá Carneiro
Praça, (ao Areeiro) **6 E1**
Francisco Sanches, Rua **6 E3**
Francisco Tomás
da Costa, Rua **5 B1**
Frei Amador Arrais, Rua **6 D1**
Frei Manuel do Cenáculo,
Rua **6 F5**
Frei Miguel Contreiras,
Avenida **6 E1**
Freiras, Travessa das
(a Arroios) **6 E3**
Freiras, Travessa das
(a Santa Clara) **8 F2**
Freitas Gazul, Rua **3 B1**
Fresca, Rua **4 E3**
Funil, Travessa do **8 D3**

G

Gaivotas, Rua das **4 E3**
Galé, Travessa da **3 A5**
Galvão, Calçada do **1 C3**
Garcia de Orta, Rua **4 D3**
Garrett, Rua **7 A4**
Garrido, Rua do **6 F2**
Gáveas, Rua das **7 A4**
General Farinha Beirão,
Rua **6 D4**
General Garcia Rosado,
Rua **6 D4**
General João de Almeida,
Rua **1 C3**
General Leman, Rua **5 A1**
General Massano
de Amorim, Rua **1 C3**
General Roçadas,
Avenida **6 F5**
Gervásio Lobato, Rua **3 B2**
Giestal, Rua do **2 E4**

Giestal, Travessa do **2 E3**
Gil Eanes, Rua **1 A3**
Gil Vicente, Rua **2 F3**
Gilberto Rola, Rua **3 B4**
Giovanni Antinori, Rua **2 E2**
Glória, Calçada da **7 A3**
Glória, Rua da **4 F1**
7 A2
Glória, Travessa da **7 A2**
Goa, Praça de **1 A3**
Gomes Freire, Rua **6 D4**
Gonçalo Nunes, Rua **1 B2**
Gonçalo Sintra, Rua **1 B2**
Gonçalo Velho Cabral,
Rua **1 B3**
Gonçalves Crespo, Rua **6 D4**
Gonçalves Zarco, Rua **1 C3**
Gorgel do Amaral, Rua **5 A5**
Graça, Calçada da **8 D2**
Graça, Largo da **8 D2**
Graça, Rua da **8 D1**
Gravato, Rua do **1 A1**
Gregório Lopes, Rua **1 B2**
Guarda, Travessa da **2 F4**
Guarda-Jóias, Rua do **2 D2**
Guarda-Jóias,
Travessa do **2 D3**
Guarda-Mor, Rua do **4 D3**
Guerra Junqueiro,
Avenida **6 E2**
Guilherme Braga, Rua **8 E3**
Guilherme Coussul,
Travessa de **7 A4**
Guilherme dos Anjos,
Rua **3 B1**
Guiné, Rua da **6 E4**
Gustavo de Matos
Sequeira, Rua **4 E1**

H

Heliodoro Salgado, Rua **6 F5**
Hellen Keller, Avenida **1 C2**
Henrique Alves, Rua **5 A3**
Henrique Cardoso,
Travessa **6 D1**
Heróis de Quionga, Rua **6 E3**
Horta, Travessa da **4 F2**
Horta e Silva, Rua **1 B1**
Horta Navia, Travessa da **3 B3**
Horta Seca, Rua da **7 A4**

I

Igreja do Carmo **7 B3**
Igreja da Memória **1 C3**
Igreja de Santo António
à Sé **7 C4**
Igreja de São Roque **7 A3**
Igreja de São Vicente
de Fora **8 E3**
Ilha do Faial, Praça da **6 D3**
Ilha da Madeira,
Avenida da **1 B2**
Ilha do Príncipe, Rua da **6 E4**
Ilha de São Tomé,
Rua da **6 E4**
Ilha Terceira, Rua **6 D3**
Império, Praça do **1 C4**
Imprensa, Rua da
(à Estrela) **4 E2**
Imprensa Nacional,
Rua da **4 E1**
Índia, Avenida da **1 A5**
Indústria, Rua da **2 F3**
3 A4
Infantaria Dezasseis,
Rua de **3 C1**
Infante Dom Henrique,
Avenida **8 D5**
Infante Dom Pedro,
Rua **5 C1**
Infante Santo, Avenida **3 C3**
Inglesinhos, Travessa
dos **4 F2**

Instituto Bacteriológico,
Rua do 7 B1
Instituto Industrial,
Rua do 4 E3
Intendente, Largo do 7 C1
Ivens, Rua 7 B4

J

Jacinta Marto, Rua 6 D4
Jacinto Nunes, Rua 6 F3
Janelas Verdes, Rua das 4 D4
Jardim, Travessa do 3 C2
Jardim Agrícola Tropical 1 C4
Jardim Botânico 4 F1
Jardim Botânico
da Ajuda 1 C2
Jardim Botânico,
Rua do 1 C3
Jardim Ducla Soares 1 A4
Jardim da Estrela 4 D2
Jardim do Tabaco, Rua 8 E4
Jasmim, Rua do 4 F2
Jau, Rua 2 F3
Jerónimos, Rua dos 1 C4
João XXI, Avenida 6 E1
João Afonso de Aveiro,
Rua 1 A4
João de Barros, Rua 2 F3
João Bastos, Rua 1 B4
João de Castilho, Rua 1 C3
João Coimbra, Rua 1 A3
João Crisóstomo,
Avenida 5 B3
João Dias, Rua 1 B2
João Fernandes Labrador,
Rua 1 B3
João de Menezes, Rua 6 F2
João do Outeiro, Rua 7 C2
João de Paiva, Rua 1 B3
João Penha, Rua 5 B5
João das Regras, Rua 7 B3
João do Rio, Praça 6 E2
João Villaret, Rua 6 D1
Joaquim António
de Aguiar, Rua 5 B5
Joaquim Bonifácio, Rua 6 D4
Joaquim Casimiro, Rua 3 C3
Jorge Afonso, Rua 5 A1
José Acúrcio das Neves,
Rua 6 F2
José Dias Coelho, Rua 3 A4
José Estêvão, Rua 6 E4
José Falcão, Rua 6 E3
José Fernandes,
Travessa 2 E2
José Malhôa, Avenida 5 A2
José Pinto Bastos, Rua 1 B1
José Ricardo, Rua 6 E3
Josefa Maria, Rua 8 D1
Josefa de Óbidos, Rua 5 B1
Julieta Ferrão, Rua 5 B1
Júlio de Andrade, Rua 7 A1
Júlio Dinis, Avenida 5 C1
Junqueira, Rua da 2 D4

L

Lagares, Rua dos 8 D2
Lagares, Travessa dos 8 D2
Lapa, Beco da 8 E3
Lapa, Rua da 4 D3
Latino Coelho, Rua 5 C3
Laura Alves, Rua 5 C1
Leão de Oliveira, Rua 3 A4
Leite de Vasconcelos,
Rua 8 F2
Liberdade, Avenida da 4 F1
5 C5
7 A2
Limoeiro, Rua do 8 D4
Livramento, Calçada do 3 B3
Lóios, Largo dos 8 D4
Londres, Praça de 6 E2
Loreto, Rua do 4 F3

Luciano Cordeiro, Rua 5 C4
Lucília Simões, Rua 6 E3
Lucinda do Carmo,
Rua 6 E2
Luís Bívar, Avenida 5 C3
Luís de Camões, Praça 7 A4
Luís de Camões, Rua 2 F3
Luís Derouet, Rua 3 C1
Luís Monteiro, Rua 6 F3
Luís Pedroso de Barros,
Rua 1 B3
Luísa Todí, Rua 2 F3
Lusíadas, Rua dos 2 F3
3 A4
Luz Soriano, Rua 4 F2

M

Macau, Rua de 6 E5
Machadinho, Rua do 4 E3
Machado, Rua do
(à Ajuda) 2 E3
Machado de Castro,
Rua 8 F1
Madalena, Rua da 7 C4
Madres, Rua das 4 E3
Madrid, Avenida de 6 E1
Mãe d'Água, Rua 4 F1
Maestro António Taborda,
Rua 3 C3
Malaca, Praça de 1 B4
Manuel Bento de Sousa,
Rua 7 B1
Manuel Bernardes, Rua 4 E2
Manuel da Maia,
Avenida 6 E2
Manuel Gouveia, Rua 6 F1
Manuel Soares Guedes,
Rua 7 C1
Manuelzinho d'Arcolena,
Rua 1 A1
Marconi, Avenida 6 D1
Marcos, Estrada dos 1 C1
Marcos, Largo dos 1 C2
Marcos, Rua dos 1 C2
Marechal Saldanha, Rua 4 F3
Margiochis, Rua dos 1 A1
Maria, Rua 6 E5
Maria Andrade, Rua 6 E5
Maria da Fonte, Rua 6 E5
Maria Luísa Holstein,
Rua 3 A4
Maria Pia, Rua 3 B1
Marquês de Abrantes,
Calçada 4 E3
Marquês de Fronteira,
Rua 5 A4
Marquês de Pombal,
Praça 5 C5
Marquês de Ponte de
Lima, Rua 7 C2
Marquês de Sá da
Bandeira, Rua 5 B3
Marques da Silva, Rua 6 E4
Marquês de Subserra,
Rua 5 A5
Marquês de Tancos,
Calçada do 7 C3
Marquês de Tomar,
Avenida 5 C2
Martim Moniz, Rua 7 C2
Martim Vaz, Rua de 7 B2
Martins Barata, Rua 1 B4
Martins Ferrão, Rua 5 C4
Martins Sarmento, Rua 6 F4
Mastros, Rua dos 4 E3
Mato Grosso, Rua 8 F1
Meio, Rua do (à Lapa) 4 D3
Mem Rodrigues, Rua 1 B4
Memória, Calçada da 1 C3
Memória, Travessa da 1 C3
Mercado 24 de Julho 4 F3
Merceeiras, Travessa
das 8 D4
Mercês, Rua das 2 D3

Mercês, Travessa das 4 F2
Mestre António Martins,
Rua 6 F4
Mexico, Avenida do 6 D2
Miguel Bombarda,
Avenida 5 C2
Miguel Lupi, Rua 4 E2
Milagre de Santo António,
Rua do 7 C4
Miradouro de São Pedro
de Alcântara 7 A2
Mirador, Rua do 2 E3
Miradouro da Graça 8 D2
Miradouro de
Santa Luzia 8 D4
Mirante, Beco do 8 F2
Mirante, Calçada do
(à Ajuda) 2 D2
Misericórdia, Rua da 7 A4
Moçambique, Rua de 6 E4
Moeda, Rua da 4 F3
Moinho de Vento,
Calçada 7 A1
Moinho de Vento,
Travessa do 3 C3
Moinho Velho,
Travessa do 2 E3
Moinhos, Travessa dos 2 E3
Monte, Beco do 7 C1
Monte, Calçada do 7 D1
Monte, Travessa do 8 D1
Monte Olivete, Rua do 4 E1
Morais Soares, Rua 6 F3
Mosteiro dos Jerónimos 1 C4
Mouraria, Rua da 7 C2
Mouros, Rua dos 4 F2
Mouzinho da Silveira,
Rua 5 B5
Mouzinho de Albuquerque,
Avenida 6 F4
Município, Praça do 7 B5
Museu de Arte Popular 1 B5
Museu de Artes
Decorativas 8 D3
Museu Calouste
Gulbenkian 5 B2
Museu do Chiado 7 A5
Museu da Marinha 1 B4
Museu da Marioneta 8 D3
Museu Militar 8 F3
Museu Nacional de
Arqueologia 1 B4
Museu Nacional de
Arte Antiga 4 D4
Museu Nacional
dos Coches 2 D4
Museu de Artilharia,
Rua do 8 F3

N

Navegantes, Rua dos 4 D2
Nazaré, Travessa de 7 C1
Necessidades,
Calçada das 3 C3
Necessidades, Rua das 3 B3
Newton, Rua 6 E4
Noronha, Rua do 4 E1
Norte, Rua do 7 A4
Nossa Senhora da
Conceição Velha 7 C4
Nova do Almada, Rua 7 B4
Nova do Calhariz, Rua 2 D3
Nova do Carvalho,
Rua 7 A5
Nova do Colégio,
Calçada 7 B2
Nova do Desterro, Rua 7 C1
Nova do Loureiro, Rua 4 F2
Nova da Piedade, Rua 4 E2
Nova de Santos,
Travessa 4 D3
Nova de São Domingos,
Travessa 7 B3

Nova de São Mamede,
Rua 4 E1
Nova da Trindade, Rua 7 A3
Nuno Tristão, Rua 1 A4

O

Ocidental, Largo 1 B1
Olaias, Rotunda das 6 F2
Olarias, Largo das 7 C2
Olarias, Rua das 7 C1
Olival, Rua do 3 C4
Olival, Travessa do
(à Graça) 8 F1
Oliveira, Rua da 7 A3
Oliveira Martins, Rua 6 D1
Oliveirinha, Rua 8 D3
Óscar Monteiro Torres,
Avenida 6 D1

P

Paço da Rainha, Largo 6 D5
Padre António Vieira,
Rua 5 A4
Padre Francisco Rua 3 C2
Padre Luís Aparício, Rua 6 D5
Padre Manuel Alves
Correia, Rua 2 E2
Padre Manuel da
Nóbrega, Avenida 6 E1
Padrão dos
Descobrimentos 1 C5
Paiva de Andrade, Rua 7 A4
Paiva Couceiro, Praça 6 F4
Palácio de Belém 1 C4
Palácio Nacional da
Ajuda 2 D2
Palácio de São Bento 4 E2
Palma, Rua da 7 B2
Palma, Travessa da 7 B2
Palmeira, Rua da 4 F2
Palmeira, Travessa da 4 E2
Palmira, Rua 6 E5
Pampulha, Calçada da 3 C4
Paraíso, Rua do 8 F2
Pardal, Travessa do 2 E2
Paris, Avenida de 6 E2
Parque Eduardo VII 5 B4
Parque Florestal de
Monsanto 1 B1
Particular, 2ª Rua 3 A4
Páscoa, Rua da 4 D1
Pascoal de Melo, Rua 6 D3
Passadiço, Rua 5 C5
7 A1
Passos Manuel, Rua 6 E4
Pasteur, Praça 6 E2
Patrocínio, Rua do 3 C2
Pau da Bandeira, Rua do 3 C3
Paulo da Gama, Rua 1 A3
Paulo Martins, Travessa 1 C3
Paz, Rua da 4 E2
Paz do Laranjal, Rua da 1 C3
Pedras Negras, Rua das 7 C4
Pedreiras, Rua das 1 C3
Pedro Alexandrino, Rua 8 F1
Pedro Álvares Cabral,
Avenida 4 D1
Pedro Augusto Franco,
Rua 1 B1
Pedro de Barcelos, Rua 1 B3
Pedro Calmon, Rua 2 F3
Pedro Escobar, Rua 1 A4
Pedro Fernandes
Queirós, Rua 1 A3
Pedro Nunes, Rua 5 C3
Pedro de Sintra, Rua 1 B2
Pedro Teixeira,
Estrada de 1 C1
Pedrouços, Rua de 1 A5
Pena, Travessa da 7 B2
Penha de França, Rua 8 E2
Pereira, Travessa da 8 E2

Pereira e Sousa, Rua 3 C1
Pero da Covilhã, Rua 1 B3
Pero de Alenquer, Rua 1 A3
Picoas, Rua das 5 C3
Pinheiro, Travessa do 4 D2
Pinheiro Chagas, Rua 5 C3
Pinto, Travessa do 2 F4
Pinto Ferreira, Rua 2 E4
Pinto Quartin, Rua 2 D2
Planetário Calouste
  Gulbenkian 1 B4
Poço da Cidade,
  Travessa do 7 A3
Poço dos Mouros,
  Calçada dos 6 F3
Poço dos Negros, Rua do 4 E3
Poiais de São Bento,
  Rua dos 4 E3
Ponte 25 de Abril 3 A5
Ponte, Avenida da 3 A4
Ponta Delgada, Rua 6 D3
Portas de Santo Antão,
  Rua das 7 A2
Portas do Sol, Largo 8 D3
Portugal Durão, Rua 5 A1
Possidónio da Silva, Rua 3 B2
Possolo, Rua do 3 C2
Possolo, Travessa do 3 C2
Praças, Rua das 4 D3
Praia, Escadinhas da 4 E3
Praia, Travessa da 2 F4
Praia de Pedrouços,
  Rua da 1 A5
Praia da Vitrouços,
  Rua da 1 A5
Prata, Rua da 7 B4
Prazeres, Estrada dos 3 B2
Prazeres, Rua dos 4 E2
Presidente Arriaga, Rua 3 C4
Pretas, Rua das 7 A1
Príncipe Real, Praça do 4 F1
Prior, Rua do 3 C3
Prior do Crato, Rua 3 B4
Professor Armando de
  Lucena, Rua 2 D2
Professor Cid dos Santos,
  Rua 2 D1
Professor Gomes
  Teixeira, Rua 3 C2
Professor Lima Basto,
  Rua 5 A2
Professor Sousa da
  Câmara, Rua 5 A5

Q

Quartéis, Rua dos 2 D3
Quatro de Infantaria, Rua 3 C1
Queimada, Travessa da 7 A3
Quelhas, Rua do 4 D3
Queluz, Estrada de 1 C1
Quinta do Almargem,
  Rua da 2 E2
Quinta do Jacinto,
  Rua da 3 A3
Quintinha, Rua da 4 E2
Quirino da Fonseca,
  Rua 6 E3

R

Rafael de Andrade, Rua 6 E5
Ramalho Ortigão, Rua 5 A3
Rato, Largo do 4 E1
Rebelo da Silva, Rua 6 D3
Regueira, Rua da 8 E4
Regueirão dos Anjos, Rua 6 E5
Remédios, Rua dos
  (a Alfama) 8 E3
Remédios, Rua dos
  (à Lapa) 4 D3

Remolares, Rua dos 7 A5
República, Avenida da 5 C1
Ressano Garcia, Avenida 5 A3
Restelo, Avenida do 1 A4
Restauradores, Praça dos 7 A2
Ribeira das Naus,
  Avenida da 7 B5
Ribeira Nova, Rua da 4 F3
Ribeiro Santos, Calçada 4 D3
Ribeiro Sanches, Rua 3 C3
Ricardo Espírito Santo,
  Rua 3 C3
Rio Seco, Rua do 2 E3
Rodrigo da Fonseca,
  Rua 5 A4
Rodrigo Rebelo, Rua 1 A2
Rodrigues Faria, Rua 3 A4
Rodrigues Sampaio, Rua 5 C5
Roma, Avenida de 6 D1
Rosa Araújo, Rua 5 C5
Rosa Damasceno, Rua 6 E3
Rosa, Rua da 4 F2
Rossio (Praça Dom
  Pedro IV) 7 B3
Rotunda das Olaias 6 F2
Rovisco Pais, Avenida 6 D3
Roy Campbell, Rua 2 E2
Rui Barbosa, Rua 8 F1
Rui Pereira, Rua 1 B3

S

Sá de Miranda, Rua 2 F3
Sabino de Sousa, Rua 8 F3
Sacadura Cabral, Avenida 6 D1
Saco, Rua do 7 B1
Sacramento, Calçada do 7 B4
Sacramento, Rua do
  (à Lapa) 3 C3
Sacramento, Rua do
  (a Alcântara) 3 B4
Sacramento, Travessa do
  (a Alcântara) 3 B4
Salitre, Rua do 4 F1
Salitre, Travessa do 4 F1
Salvador, Rua do 8 D3
Sampaio Bruno, Rua 3 B1
Sampaio e Pina, Rua 5 A4
Santa Bárbara, Rua de 6 E5
Santa Catarina, Rua de 4 F3
Santa Catarina,
  Travessa de 4 F3
Santa Cruz do Castelo,
  Rua 8 D3
Santa Engrácia 8 F2
Santa Justa, Rua de 7 B3
Santa Marinha, Rua de 8 D3
Santa Marta, Rua de 5 C5
Santa Marta,
  Travessa de 5 C5
Santa Quitéria,
  Travessa de 4 D1
Santana, Calçada 7 B2
Santana, Rua de
  (à Lapa) 3 C2
Santo Amaro, Calçada de 2 F3
Santo Amaro, Rua de 4 E2
Santo André, Calçada de 8 D2
Santo António, Rua de
  (à Estrela) 3 C2
Santo António,
  Travessa de (à Graça) 8 E1
Santo António da Glória,
  Rua 4 F1
Santo António da Sé,
  Rua de 7 C4
Santo Estêvão, Rua de 8 E3
Santos, Largo de 4 E3
Santos Dumont, Avenida 5 A2
Santos-o-Velho, Rua de 4 D3
São Bento, Rua de 4 E1

São Bernardino,
  Travessa 6 D5
São Bernardo, Rua de 4 D2
São Boaventura, Rua de 4 F2
São Caetano, Rua de 3 C3
São Ciro, Rua de 4 D2
São Domingos, Largo de 7 B3
São Domingos, Rua de 4 D3
São Félix, Rua de 4 D3
São Filipe Neri, Rua de 5 B5
São Francisco Xavier,
  Rua 1 A4
São Francisco,
  Calçada de 7 B5
São Gens, Rua de 8 D1
São João de Deus,
  Avenida 6 E1
São João da Mata,
  Rua de 4 D3
São João da Praça,
  Rua de 8 D4
São Jorge, Rua de 4 D2
São José, Rua de 7 A1
São Julião, Rua de 7 B4
São Lázaro, Rua de 7 B1
São Mamede, Rua de 7 C4
São Marçal, Rua de 4 E2
São Martinho, Largo de 8 D4
São Miguel, Rua de 8 E4
São Nicolau, Rua de 7 B4
São Paulo, Rua de 4 F3
  7 A5
São Pedro, Rua de 8 E4
São Pedro de Alcântara,
  Rua de 7 A3
São Pedro Mártir, Rua 7 C3
São Plácido, Travessa de 4 E2
São Sebastião da Pedreira,
  Rua de 5 C4
São Tiago, Rua de 8 D4
São Tomé, Rua de 8 D3
São Vicente, Calçada de 8 E3
São Vicente, Rua de 8 E3
São Vicente, Travessa de 8 D2
Sapadores, Rua dos 6 F5
Sapateiros, Rua dos 7 B4
Saraiva de Carvalho, Rua 3 C2
Sarmento de Beires, Rua 6 F1
Saudade, Rua da 8 D4
Sé 8 D4
Sebastião Saraiva Lima,
  Rua 6 F3
Sebeiro, Travessa do 3 A3
Século, Rua do 4 F2
Senhora da Glória, Rua 8 E1
Senhora da Graça,
  Travessa da 8 E1
Senhora da Saúde,
  Rua da 7 C2
Senhora do Monte,
  Rua da 8 D1
Serpa Pinto, Rua 7 B4
Sidónio Pais, Avenida 5 B4
Silva Carvalho, Rua 4 D1
  5 A5
Silva Porto, Rua 2 E3
Silva, Rua da 4 E3
Sítio ao Casalinho
  da Ajuda, Rua do 2 D2
Soares de Passos, Rua 2 F3
Sociedade Farmacêutica,
  Rua 5 C5
Soeiro Pereira Gomes,
  Rua 5 A1
Sol, Rua do (a Chelas) 8 F1
Sol, Rua do (à Graça) 8 E1
Sol, Rua do (ao Rato) 4 D1
Sol, Rua do (a Santana) 7 B1
Solar do Vinho do Porto 4 F2
Sousa Lopes, Rua 5 B1
Sousa Martins, Rua 5 C4

T

Taipas, Rua das 4 F1
Tapada da Ajuda 3 A1
Tapada das Necessidades 3 B3
Tapada, Calçada da 2 F3
  3 A3
Teatro de São Carlos 7 A4
Teixeira Júnior,
  Travessa de 3 A4
Teixeira Pinto, Rua 6 F4
Telhal, Rua do 7 A1
Tenente Espanca, Rua 5 B2
Tenente Ferreira Durão,
  Rua 3 C1
Tenente Valadim, Rua 3 B4
Terra, Calçada 6 F2
Terreirinho, Rua do 7 C2
Terreirinho, Travessa do 8 D2
Terreiro do Trigo,
  Rua do 8 E4
Tesouro, Travessa do 3 B3
Tijolo, Calçada de 4 F2
Tijolo, Calçadinha de 8 E3
Timor, Rua de 6 E5
Tomás da Anunciação,
  Rua 3 C1
Tomás Ribeiro, Rua 5 C3
Torel, Travessa do 7 B1
Torre de Belém 1 A5
Torre de Belém,
  Avenida da 1 A4
Torre, Largo da 2 D2
Torre, Rua da 2 D2
Torrinha, Azinhaga da 5 B1
Touros, Praça dos 5 C1
Trabuqueta, Travessa da 3 B4
Triângulo Vermelho, Rua 6 F5
Trinas, Rua das 4 D3
Trindade, Largo da 7 A3
Trindade, Rua da 7 A3
Tristão da Cunha, Rua 1 A4
Tristão Vaz, Rua 1 C2

V

Vaga-Lumes, Rua dos 1 B1
Vale de Santo António,
  Rua do 8 F1
Vale do Pereiro, Rua do 4 E1
Vale, Rua do 4 E2
Veloso Salgado, Rua 5 A1
Verónica, Rua da 8 E3
Vicente Borga, Rua 4 E3
Vicente Dias, Rua 1 A2
Vieira da Silva, Rua 3 B4
Vigário, Rua do 8 E3
Vila Berta 8 E2
Vila Correia 1 B4
Vila, Rua da 4 F2
Viriato, Rua 5 C4
Visconde de Santarém,
  Rua 6 D3
Visconde de Seabra, Rua 5 C1
Visconde de Valmor,
  Avenida 5 C2
Vítor Cordon, Rua 7 A5
Vítor Hugo, Rua 6 E1
Vitória, Rua da 7 B4
Voz do Operário, Rua da 8 E2

W

Washington, Rua 8 F1

X

Xavier Cordeiro, Rua 6 D2

Z

Zagalo, Travessa do 8 F3
Zaire, Rua do 6 E4

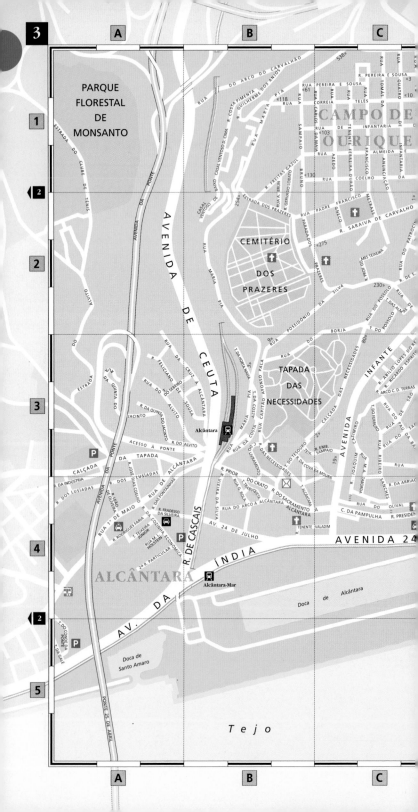

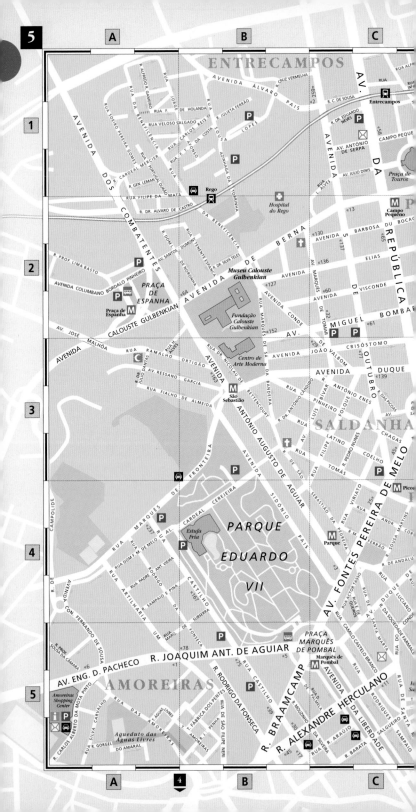

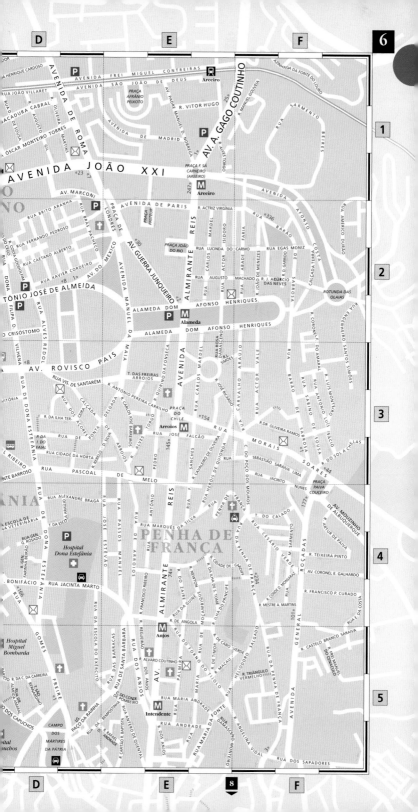

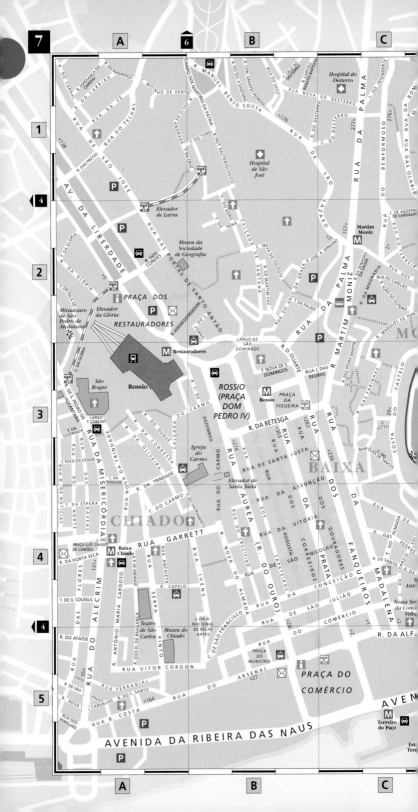

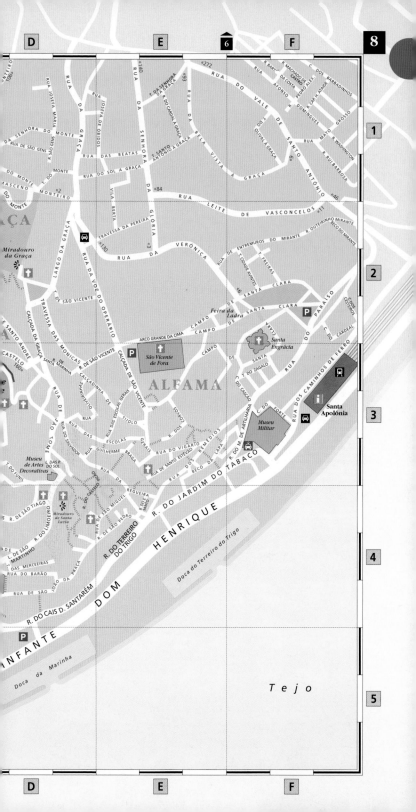

CENTRAL
PORTUGAL

INTRODUCING CENTRAL PORTUGAL 142-147
THE LISBON COAST 148-169
ESTREMADURA AND RIBATEJO 170-193
THE BEIRAS 194-221

Central Portugal at a Glance

BETWEEN PORTUGAL'S CAPITAL and its second city, Oporto, can be found some of the country's most impressive architecture and important historical sights. Near Lisbon are the fine palaces of Sintra and Queluz, and in Estremadura are several of Portugal's foremost religious sites. Estremadura and Beira Litoral mix empty beaches with quaint fishing villages and smart resorts, while the lush country stretching inland to the banks of the Tagus supports livestock and crops from grapes to fruit and rice. Further north, the Beiras are more varied, with the historic university town of Coimbra, the vine-clad valleys of the Dão wine region and the bleak highlands and fortress towns of Beira Alta and Beira Baixa. Dominating this remote region is the granite range of the Serra da Estrela.

Batalha *means "battle" and the monastery of Santa Maria da Vitória at Batalha was built to give thanks for victory over the Spanish at the Battle of Aljubarrota in 1385. Its delicate style makes it one of Portugal's finest Gothic buildings (see pp182–3).*

Alcobaça *is principally known for its abbey, founded in the 12th century by Portugal's first king, Afonso Henriques. The graceful, contemplative air of this great Cistercian house (see pp178–9) is exemplified by its huge vaulted dormitory.*

Sintra, *just west of Lisbon, is a cool wooded retreat from the heat of the capital. This is where the Portuguese monarchs chose to spend their summers. The Palácio Nacional is full of remarkable decorative effects, such as this painted "magpie" ceiling (see pp158–9).*

Estremadura

ESTREMADU
AND RIBAT
(See pp170–

LISBON
(See pp58–139)

THE LISBON CO
(See pp148–69

The Palácio de Queluz, *a masterpiece of Rococo architecture (see pp164–5), lies just outside Lisbon. The Lion Staircase leads up to the colonnaded pavilion named after its architect, Jean-Baptiste Robillion.*

0 kilometres

0 miles   25

◁ **Tomar's Templar fortress of Convento de Cristo overlooking the town**

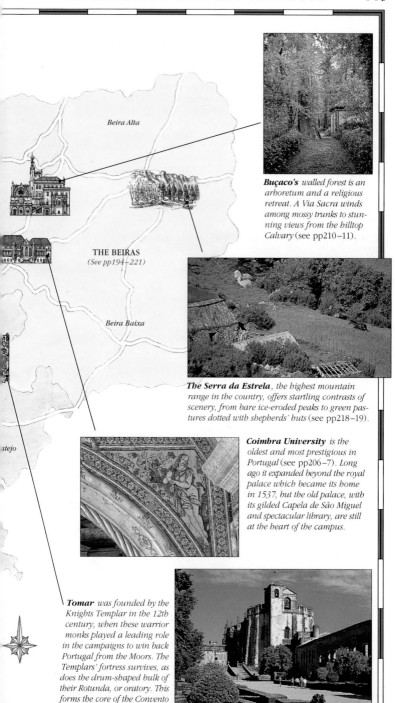

Buçaco's *walled forest is an arboretum and a religious retreat. A Via Sacra winds among mossy trunks to stunning views from the hilltop Calvary (see pp210–11).*

THE BEIRAS
(See pp194–221)

Beira Alta

Beira Baixa

atejo

The Serra da Estrela, *the highest mountain range in the country, offers startling contrasts of scenery, from bare ice-eroded peaks to green pastures dotted with shepherds' huts (see pp218–19).*

Coimbra University *is the oldest and most prestigious in Portugal (see pp206–7). Long ago it expanded beyond the royal palace which became its home in 1537, but the old palace, with its gilded Capela de São Miguel and spectacular library, are still at the heart of the campus.*

Tomar *was founded by the Knights Templar in the 12th century, when these warrior monks played a leading role in the campaigns to win back Portugal from the Moors. The Templars' fortress survives, as does the drum-shaped bulk of their Rotunda, or oratory. This forms the core of the Convento de Cristo which over the centuries was built up around the original church (see pp184–7).*

Horsemanship and Bullfighting

CLASSICAL DRESSAGE and bravura bullfighting in Portugal are linked to the Marquês de Marialva, the King's Master of the Horse from 1770 to 1799. He made famous the most advanced and difficult dressage techniques, including some in which the horse lifts itself off the ground like a ballet dancer. The Art of Marialva, as it is called, is of great use to horsemen in the bullring, and they will usually demonstrate some dressage movements for the entertainment of the crowd. The Ribatejo is the traditional centre of bullfighting, with events held from spring to autumn at annual fairs and towns such as Santarém, Vila Franca de Xira and Coruche. In Portugal, the bull is never killed in the arena.

Horseman at the national fair in Golegã

Advertising a summer bullfight in Santarém

Ribatejan herdsmen or *campinos, who round up the fighting bulls, here demonstrate their skills.*

Leading bullfighter João Moura salutes the crowd at a *tourada* with his tricorne hat.

The mane is plaited with ribbons for a beautifully groomed effect.

THE CAVALEIRO

The bullfighter or *cavaleiro* wears traditional 18th-century costume, including the satin coat of a grandee, and rides an elaborately adorned horse. He has to plant a number of darts (*farpas*) in the bull's shoulders, and his performance is judged on style and courage.

The costly saddle cloth is embroidered with João Moura's initials.

Tail tidying and decoration go back to the ornate French style of Louis XV.

Box stirrups are traditional, stylish and secure.

TRADITIONAL EQUESTRIAN SKILLS

Lisbon's Escola Portuguesa de Arte Equestre, and equestrian centres in the Ribatejo, today maintain the standards set by Marialva. The Lisbon school performs several times a year around the country. On Lusitanian horses of Alter Real stock (*see p296*), riders in 18th-century costume give superb dressage displays. Their movements resemble these illustrations of 1790 from a book on equestrianism, dedicated to Dom João (later João VI), himself a keen horseman.

Plaque of Lezíria Grande Equestrian Centre (see p192)

The Marquês de Marialva his horse in the *croupade* hind legs tucked up bene
as it sp
into t

THE BULLFIGHT

The *corrida* or *tourada* combines drama and daring. First, a team of bullfighters on foot *(peões de brega)* distracts the bull with capes, preparing it for the *cavaleiro*. He is followed by eight volunteer *forcados*, who aim to overcome the bull with their bare hands in what is known as the *pega*. Finally the bull is herded from the ring among a group of farm oxen.

At this opening ceremony in Montijo, the two cavaleiros line up with the forcados *on either side.*

The cavaleiro lodges long darts in the bull's shoulders.

The bull charges, provoked by the *cavaleiro* and the prancing horse. The bull's horns are blunted and sheathed in leather.

Partnership between man and horse is paramount. Most cavaleiros ride a Lusitanian, the world's oldest saddle horse and a classic warrior steed, famed for its courage, grace and strength. Its agility and speed are essential in the ring, and defenders of bull-fighting believe the spectacle has helped preserve the breed.

The horse's lower legs are strapped for support.

The leader of the *forcados* tackles the bull head on, throwing himself between its horns and gripping it around the neck.

The next in line assists the front man, while the others prepare to lend support.

The bullfight ends with the pega. The leader of the forcados *challenges the bull to charge, then launches himself over its head. The others try to hold him in place and use their combined weight to bring the bull to a standstill, with one of the men holding onto its tail. Eight times out of ten the* forcados *get tossed in all directions, then re-form to repeat the challenge. The crowd laughs, but applauds the men's skill and courage.*

Dom João himself demonstrates the *galope*, a difficult exercise with a change of direction at each step.

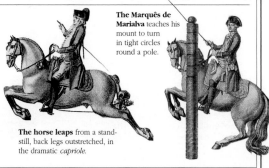

The Marquês de Marialva teaches his mount to turn in tight circles round a pole.

The horse leaps from a standstill, back legs outstretched, in the dramatic *capriole*.

Regional Food: Central Portugal

Ceramic honey pot

GASTRONOMICALLY, the central region of Portugal is immensely varied. Aveiro specializes in eel stews and the sweet delicacy of *ovos moles (see p200)*, while sucking pig is a feature on menus around Coimbra. Along the coast, shellfish is varied and abundant; inland, kid and lamb are succulent, spiked with *colorau* (paprika) and cooked in the region's rich red wines. Milk from sheep and goats is turned into a variety of local cheeses, the most famous being Serra, from the Serra da Estrela. The Ribatejo's melons are renowned for their sweetness and Setúbal grows muscat grapes for the table and for wines.

Pataniscas *are tasty salt-cod fritters.* Rissois, *half-moons filled with a seafood sauce, are favourites as party snacks.*

Pãezinhos
Papo seco
Queijo de ovelha
(ewe's milk cheese)
Requeijão

Sopa de pedra, *"stone soup", derives from a legend about a beggar monk. Full of vegetables and meats, it is tasty and filling.*

Fresh cheeses *made from ewe's or goat's milk are enjoyed with a variety of fresh rolls. Especially prized is Requeijão.*

Leitão à Bairrada, *roasted sucking pig with crisp crackling, is relished hot or cold, and can be bought in good delicatessens.*

Bife à café, *café-style steak, is tender steak with a creamy sauce, served with chips and topped with a fried egg.*

Frango à piri-piri, *a great favourite from Portugal's former colonies in Africa, is barbecued chicken with chilli.*

Bacalhau à Brás *binds shreds of salt cod* (bacalhau)*, potato and onion with scrambled egg to make a highly esteemed dish.*

CHEESES

Most cheeses are made with ewe's or goat's milk or both. The best (and most expensive) is undoubtedly the buttery Serra, which becomes harder and more piquant as it ages *(see p215)*. Rabaçal is a mild cheese from Coimbra, while Azeitão, from near Setúbal, is quite pungent and Saloio, dried fresh cheese, is favoured for its milky taste. Individual small cheeses may be kept in oil.

Rabaçal

Serra

Azeitão

Saloio

Shellfish *is plentiful and much enjoyed in Portugal. Lisbon is full of specialist seafood restaurants with artistic displays of lobsters, prawns of all sizes, crayfish, oysters and crabs, including the spiny-shelled spider crab. Lesser-known delicacies such as goose-necked barnacles will also appear on menus. Cockles and clams find their way into a variety of dishes, such as the rich seafood rice,* arroz de marisco.

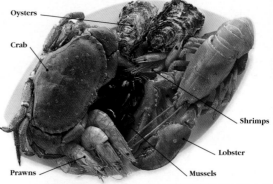

Oysters

Crab

Shrimps

Lobster

Prawns

Mussels

Açorda de marisco *is a special and unusual dish: shellfish are added to a thick soup of mashed bread, oil, garlic and coriander.*

Salmonete grelhado, *grilled red mullet, is a speciality in Setúbal, where it is served with a lemony butter sauce.*

LOCAL DRINKS

Central Portugal produces a number of wines *(see pp28–9)*, from which *aguardente* (brandy) is distilled. There are also local liqueurs, such as the herb-based Licor Beirão. From the region's many spas come a variety of mineral waters, of which Luso *(see p209)* is one of the most popular. Less known is the Lisbon area's beer-making tradition, and Lisbon itself has several *cervejarias* (beer houses).

Mousse de chocolate *needs to be made with really good dark chocolate, but can be excellent.*

Arroz doce, *creamy rice pudding rich with egg, is flavoured with lemon rind and vanilla.*

Aguardente Velha Reserva

Mineral water from Luso

Queijadas de Sintra (cheese tarts spiced with cinnamon)

Pastéis de nata (custard-cream tartlets)

Pastel de feijão (almonds, eggs and beans)

Broas (maize and almond)

Tartlets such as pastéis de nata *epitomize the region's infinite variety of cakes, many based on egg yolks, almonds and spices.*

Licor Beirão

Sagres beer

THE LISBON COAST

WITHIN AN HOUR'S DRIVE *northwest of Lisbon you can reach the rocky Atlantic coast, the wooded slopes of Sintra or countryside dotted with villas and royal palaces. South of Lisbon you can enjoy the sandy beaches and fishing towns along the coast or explore the lagoons of the Tagus and Sado river estuaries.*

Traders and invaders, from the Phoenicians to the Spanish, have left their mark in this region, in particular the Moors whose forts and castles, rebuilt many times over the centuries, can be found all along this coast. After Lisbon became the capital in 1256, Portuguese kings and nobles built summer palaces and villas in the countryside west of the city, particularly on the cool, green heights of the Serra de Sintra.

Across the Tagus, the less fashionable southern shore (Outra Banda) could be reached only by ferry, until the suspension bridge was built in 1966. Now, the long sandy beaches of the Costa da Caparica, the coast around the fishing town of Sesimbra and even the remote Tróia peninsula have become popular resorts during the summer months. Fortunately, large stretches of coast and unspoilt countryside are being protected as conservation areas and nature reserves.

Despite the region's rapid urbanization, small fishing and farming communities still flourish. Lively fish markets offer a huge variety of fresh fish and seafood; Palmela and the Sado region are noted for their wine; sheep still roam the unspoilt Serra da Arrábida, providing milk for Azeitão cheese; and rice is the main crop in the Sado estuary. Traditional industries also survive, such as salt panning near Alcochete and marble quarries at Pero Pinheiro.

Though the sea is cold and often rough, especially on west-facing coasts, the beaches are among the cleanest in Europe. As well as surfing, fishing and scuba diving, the region provides splendid golf courses, horse riding facilities and a motor-racing track. Arts and entertainment range from music and cinema festivals to bullfights and country fairs where regional crafts, such as hand-painted pottery, lace and baskets, are on display.

Tiled façades of houses in Alcochete, an attractive town on the Tagus estuary

◁ Brightly painted fishing boats moored in the harbour at Sesimbra

Exploring the Lisbon Coast

NORTH OF THE TAGUS, the beautiful hilltown of Sintra is dotted with historic palaces and surrounded by wooded hills, at times enveloped in an eerie sea mist. On the coast, cosmopolitan Cascais and the traditional fishing town of Ericeira are both excellent bases from which to explore the rocky coastline and surrounding countryside. South of the Tagus, the Serra da Arrábida and the rugged coast around Cabo Espichel can be visited from the small port of Sesimbra. Inland, the nature reserves of the Tagus and Sado estuaries offer a quiet retreat.

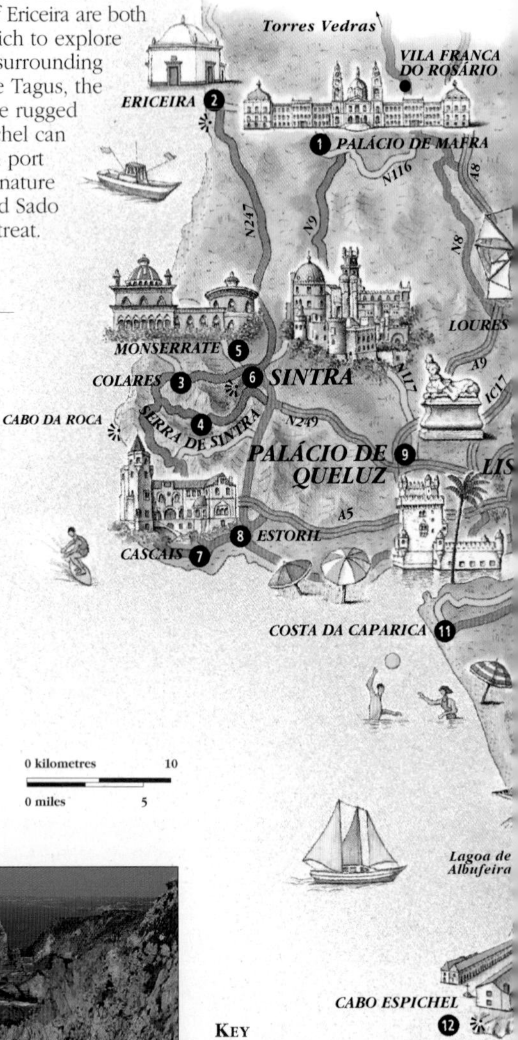

SIGHTS AT A GLANCE

Alcácer do Sal **18**
Alcochete **10**
Cabo Espichel **12**
Cascais **7**
Colares **3**
Costa da Caparica **11**
Ericeira **2**
Estoril **8**
LISBON pp58–139
Monserrate **5**
Palácio de Mafra **1**
Palácio de Queluz pp164–5 **9**
Palmela **14**
Península de Tróia **17**
Serra da Arrábida **15**
Sesimbra **13**
Setúbal **16**
Sintra pp156–61 **6**

Tours

Serra de Sintra **4**

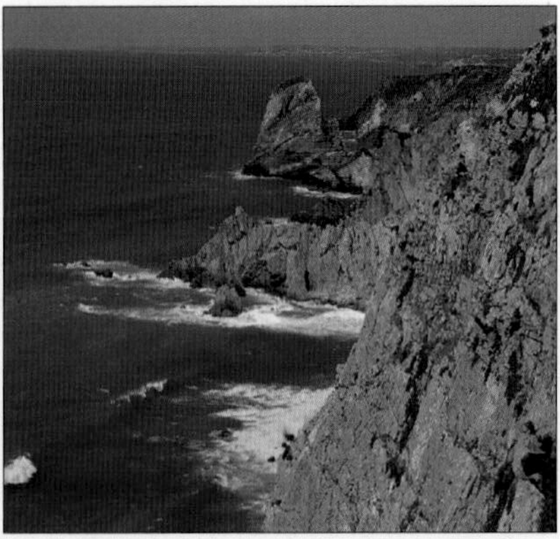

Torres Vedras

VILA FRANCA DO ROSÁRIO

ERICEIRA **2**

1 PALÁCIO DE MAFRA

MONSERRATE **5**

COLARES **3**

CABO DA ROCA

SERRA DE SINTRA **4**

6 SINTRA

LOURES

PALÁCIO DE QUELUZ **9**

LIS

CASCAIS **7**

8 ESTORIL

COSTA DA CAPARICA **11**

0 kilometres   10

0 miles   5

Lagoa de Albufeira

CABO ESPICHEL **12**

KEY

▬	Motorway
▬	Major road
▬	Minor road
▬	Scenic route
▬	River
- -	Ferry route
✳	Viewpoint

Cabo da Roca on the western edge of Serra de Sintra

**Convento da Arrábida in the hills
of the Serra da Arrábida**

GETTING AROUND

Motorways give quick access from
Lisbon to Sintra, Estoril, Palmela and
Setúbal. Main roads are generally
well signposted and surfaced, though
traffic congestion can be a problem,
particularly at weekends and holidays.
Watch out for potholes on smaller
roads. Fast, frequent trains run west
from Lisbon's Cais do Sodré station to
Estoril and Cascais, and from Rossio
station to Queluz and Sintra. For trains
south to Setúbal, Alcácer do Sal and
beyond, take a ferry to Barreiro on the
southern bank of the Tagus. There
are good bus services to all parts of
the region, most of which leave from
Lisbon's Praça de Espanha.

Santarém

Vila Franca de Xira

AVÉM

🔟 *ALCOCHETE*

TAIPADAS

MONTIJO

*SANTO ISIDRO
DE PEGÕES*

N4

*RREIRO
XAL*

MOITA

PINHAL NOVO

*Montemor-o-Novo
Évora*

ÃO FERRO

PALMELA 🔺14

MARATECA

N379

🔺15 🔺16 *SETÚBAL*

PALMA

BRA

SERRA DE ARRÁBIDA

TRÓIA

*PORTINHO
DA ARRÁBIDA*

🔺17 *PENÍNSULA
DE TRÓIA*

Sado

N253

ALCÁCER DO SAL 18

Grândola

**Fishing boats
in the harbour
at Sesimbra**

SEE ALSO

• *Where to Stay* pp384–6

• *Where to Eat* pp408–9

The stunning library in the Palácio de Mafra, paved with chequered marble

Palácio de Mafra ❶

Road map B5. Terreiro de Dom João V,
Mafra. 261-817 550. from
Lisbon. 10am–4:30pm Wed–Mon.
1 Jan, Easter, 1 May, 25 Dec.
free Sun am. compulsory.

THE MASSIVE BAROQUE palace
and monastery *(see also
pp52–3)*, which dwarfs the
small town of Mafra, was built
during the reign of Portugal's
most extravagant monarch,
João V. It began with a vow
by the young king to build a
new monastery and basilica,
supposedly in return for an
heir (but more likely, to atone
for his well-known sexual ex-
cesses). Work began in 1717
on a modest project to house
13 Franciscan friars but, as
wealth began to pour into the
royal coffers from Brazil, the
king and his Italian-trained
architect, Johann Friedrich
Ludwig (1670–1752), made
ever more extravagant plans.

No expense was spared: 52,000
men were employed and the
finished project housed not 13,
but 330 friars, a royal palace
and one of the finest libraries
in Europe, decorated with
precious marble, exotic
wood and countless
works of art. The
magnificent basilica
was consecrated on
the king's 41st birth-
day, 22 October 1730,
with festivities lasting
for eight days.

The palace was never
a favourite with the
members of the royal
family, except for those
who enjoyed hunting
deer and wild boar in
the adjoining *tapada*
(hunting reserve). Most
of the finest furniture
and art works were
taken to Brazil when
the royal family escaped the
French invasion in 1807. The
monastery was abandoned in
1834 following the
dissolution of all
religious orders,
and the palace itself
was abandoned in
1910, when the last
Portuguese king,
Manuel II, escaped
from here to the
Royal Yacht an-
chored off Ericeira.

Allow at least an
hour for the lengthy
tour which starts in
the rooms of the
monastery, through
the pharmacy, with

fine old medicine jars and
some alarming medical in-
struments, to the hospital,
where 16 patients in private
cubicles could see and hear
mass in the adjoining chapel
without leaving their beds.

Upstairs, the sumptuous
palace state rooms extend
across the whole of the monumental west façade, with the
King's apartments at one end
and the Queen's apartments
at the other, a staggering
232 m (760 ft) apart. Halfway
between the two, the long,
imposing façade is relieved
by the twin towers of the
domed basilica. The interior
of the church is decorated in
contrasting colours of marble
and furnished with six early
19th-century organs. Fine Baroque sculptures, executed by
members of the Mafra School
of Sculpture, adorn the atrium
of the basilica. Begun by José I
in 1754, many renowned
Portuguese and
foreign artists
trained in the
school under the
directorship of the
Italian sculptor
Alessandro Giusti
(1715–99). Further on,
the Sala da Caça has
a grotesque collection
of hunting trophies
and boars' heads.

Mafra's greatest
treasure, however,
is its magnificent
library, with a
patterned marble
floor, Rococo-style
wooden bookcases,
and a collection of
over 40,000 books in gold
embossed leather bindings,
including a prized first edition
of *Os Lusíadas* (1572) by the
Portuguese poet, Luís de
Camões *(see p46)*.

**Statue of St Bruno
in the atrium of
Mafra's basilica**

ENVIRONS: Once a week, on
Thursday mornings, the small
country town of **Malveira**,
10 km (6 miles) east of Mafra,
has the region's biggest market,
selling clothes and household
goods as well as food.

At the village of **Sobreiro**,
6 km (4 miles) west of Mafra,
Zé Franco's model village is
complete with houses, farms,
a waterfall and working windmill, all in minute detail.

The king's bedroom in the Royal Palace

Tractor pulling a fishing boat out of the sea at Ericeira

Ericeira ❷

Road map B5. 🚶 4,500. 🚌
🛈 Rua Mendes Leal (261-863 122).
🗓 Apr–Oct daily.

ERICEIRA IS AN OLD fishing village which keeps its traditions despite an ever-increasing influx of summer visitors, from Lisbon and abroad, who enjoy the bracing climate, clean, sandy beaches and fresh seafood. In July and August, when the population leaps to 30,000, pavement cafés, restaurants and bars around the tree-lined Praça da República are buzzing late into the night. Red flags warn when swimming is dangerous: alternative attractions include crazy golf in Santa Marta park and an interesting museum of local history, the **Museu da Ericeira**, exhibiting models of traditional regional boats and fishing equipment.

The unspoilt old town, a maze of whitewashed houses and narrow, cobbled streets, is perched high above the ocean. From Largo das Ribas, at the top of a 30-m (100-ft) stone-faced cliff, there is a bird's-eye view over the busy fishing harbour below, where tractors have replaced the oxen that once hauled the boats out of reach of the tide. On 16 August, the annual fishermen's festival is celebrated with a candlelit procession to the harbour at the foot of the cliffs for the blessing of the boats.

On 5 October 1910, Manuel II, the last king of Portugal (see pp54–5), sailed into exile from Ericeira as the Republic was declared in Lisbon; a tiled panel in the fishermen's chapel of Santo António above the harbour records the event. The banished king settled in Twickenham, southwest London, where he died in 1932.

🏛 Museu da Ericeira

Largo da Misericórdia. 📞 261-864 079. 🕐 Jun–Sep: Tue–Sun; Oct–May: Mon–Sat (pm only). ● public hols. 🖼

Colares ❸

Road map B5. 🚶 6,500. 🚌
🛈 Praça da República 23, Sintra (219-231 157).

ON THE LOWER SLOPES of the Serra de Sintra, this lovely village faces the sea over a green valley, the Várzea de Colares. A leafy avenue, lined with pine and chestnut trees, winds its way up to the village. A few vineyards here still make the famous Colares wine, once a robust, velvety red, but now a thin wine. The old vines grow in a sandy soil, with their roots set deep below in clay; these were the only vines in Europe to survive the disastrous phylloxera epidemic brought into Europe from America in the late 19th century with the first viticultural exchanges. The insect, which destroyed vineyards all over Europe by eating the tender roots, could not penetrate the dense sandy soil of the Atlantic coast and thus spared the vines around Colares. Wine can be sampled at the Adega Regional de Colares on Alameda de Coronel Linhares de Lima.

ENVIRONS: There are several popular beach resorts west of Colares. From the village of Banzão you can ride 3 km (2 miles) to **Praia das Maçãs** on the old tramway, which opened in 1910 and still runs in the summer months from 1 July to 30 September. Just north of Praia das Maçãs is the picturesque village of **Azenhas do Mar**, clinging to the cliffs; just to the south is the larger resort of **Praia Grande**. Both have natural pools in the rocks, which are filled by seawater at high tide. The unspoilt **Praia da Adraga**, 1 km (half a mile) further south, has a delightful beach café and restaurant. In the evenings and off-season, fishermen set up their lines to catch bass, bream and flat fish that swim in on the high tide.

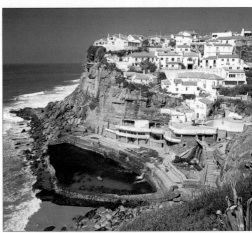

Natural rock pool at Azenhas do Mar, near Colares

Serra de Sintra Tour ④

THIS ROUND TRIP from Sintra follows a dramatic route over the top of the wooded Serra. The first part is a challenging drive with hazardous hairpin bends on steep, narrow roads that are at times poorly surfaced. It passes through dense forest and a surreal landscape of giant moss-covered boulders, with breathtaking views over the Atlantic coast, the Tagus estuary and beyond.

Tiled angels, Peninha chapel

After dropping down to the rugged, windswept coast, the route returns along small country roads passing through hill villages and large estates on the cool, green northern slopes of the Serra de Sintra.

Atlantic coastline seen from Peninha

Colares ⑥
The village of Colares rests on the lower slopes of the wooded Serra, surrounded by gardens and vineyards *(see p153)*.

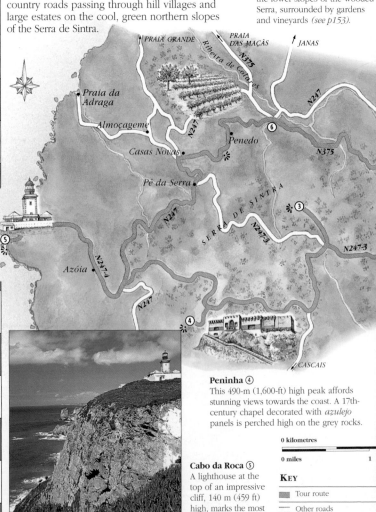

Peninha ④
This 490-m (1,600-ft) high peak affords stunning views towards the coast. A 17th-century chapel decorated with *azulejo* panels is perched high on the grey rocks.

Cabo da Roca ⑤
A lighthouse at the top of an impressive cliff, 140 m (459 ft) high, marks the most westerly point of the European mainland.

0 kilometres

0 miles   1

KEY

▬ Tour route

― Other roads

☼ Viewpoint

Tips for Drivers

Length: 36 km (22 miles).
Stopping-off points: There are wonderful picnic spots in the forests and in the Parque da Pena, with cool springs of drinking water and fountains along the mountain roads. At Cabo da Roca you will find a café, restaurant and souvenir shops; at Colares there are several delightful restaurants and bars. (See also pp444–5.)

Palace of Monserrate

Monserrate ❺

Road Map B5. Estrada de Monserrate.
📞 21-923 12 01. 🚌 to Sintra then taxi. ◻ 25 Mar–27 Oct:: 9am–7pm; 28 Oct–24 Mar: 9am–6pm (last adm one hour before closing). 🅰

eais ⑧
e elegant, pink palace, now
xury hotel and restaurant
e p386 & p409), was built in
18th century for the Dutch
sul, Daniel Gildemeester.

Monserrate ⑦
The cool, overgrown forest
park and elaborate 19th-century
palace epitomize the
romanticism
of Sintra.

Sintra ①
From the centre of the
old town the road winds
steeply upwards past
magnificent *quintas*
(country estates)
hidden among
the trees.

ERICEIRA
MAFRA
N247

Palácio
da Pena

N249   LISBOA

CRUZ ALTA

N9

ESTORIL
CASCAIS

Parque da Pena ②
This huge, exotic park can be
explored on foot (see p157).
It is also possible to drive as
far as Cruz Alta, the highest
point of the Serra de Sintra.

**Convento
dos Capuchos** ③
Two huge boulders guard
the entrance to this remote
Franciscan monastery,
founded in 1560, where
the monks lived in tiny
rock-hewn cells lined with
cork. There are stunning
views of the coast from
the hill above this austere,
rocky hideaway.

THE WILD, ROMANTIC garden
of this once magnificent
estate is a jungle of exotic trees
and flowering shrubs. Among
the sub-tropical foliage and
valley of tree ferns, the visitor
will come across a waterfall, a
small lake and a chapel, built
as a ruin, tangled in the roots
of a giant *Ficus* tree. Its history
dates back to the Moors, but it
takes its name from a small
16th-century chapel dedicated
to Our Lady of Montserrat in
Catalonia, Spain. The gardens
were landscaped in the late
18th century by a wealthy
young Englishman, the ec-
centric aesthete William
Beckford. They were later
immortalized by Lord
Byron in *Childe Harold's
Pilgrimage* (1812).

In 1856, the abandoned
estate was bought by
another Englishman, Sir
Francis Cook, who built
a fantastic Moorish-style
palace (which now stands
eerily empty) and trans-
formed the gardens with
a large sweeping lawn,
camellias and sub-tropical
trees from all over the
world. These include the giant
Metrosideros (Australian Christmas tree, covered in a blaze of
red flowers in July), the native
Arbutus (known as the strawberry tree because of its juicy
red berries), from which the
medronheira firewater drink
is distilled, and cork oak, with
small ferns growing on its bark.

The Friends of Monserrate is
an organization that has been
set up to help restore the sadly
neglected house and gardens
to their former glory.

Sintra ⑥

Visiting the sights of Sintra by horse-drawn carriage

SINTRA'S STUNNING setting on the north slopes of the granite Serra, among wooded ravines and fresh water springs, made it a favourite summer retreat for the kings of Portugal. The tall conical chimneys of the Palácio Nacional de Sintra *(see pp158–9)* and the fabulous Palácio da Pena *(see pp160–61)*, eerily impressive on its peak when the Serra is blanketed in mist, are unmistakable landmarks.

Today, the town (recognized as a UNESCO World Heritage site in 1995) draws thousands of visitors all through the year. Even so, there are many quiet walks in the wooded hills around the town, especially beautiful in the long, cool evenings of the summer months.

Exploring Sintra

Present-day Sintra is in three parts, Sintra Vila, Estefânia and São Pedro, joined by a confusing maze of winding roads scattered over the surrounding hills. In the pretty cobbled streets of the old town, Sintra Vila, which is centred on the **Palácio Nacional de Sintra**, are the museums and beautifully tiled **post office**. The curving **Volta do Duche** leads from the old town, past the lush **Parque da Liberdade**, north to the Estefânia district and the striking Neo-Gothic **Câmara Municipal** (Town Hall). To the south and east, the hilly village of São Pedro

spreads over the slopes of the Serra. The fortnightly Sunday **market** here extends across the broad market square and along Rua 1º de Dezembro.

Exploring Sintra on foot involves a lot of walking and climbing up and down its steep hills. For a more leisurely tour, take one of the horse and carriage rides around the town. The **Miradouro da Vigia** in São Pedro offers impressive views, as does the cosy **Casa de Sapa** café, where you can sample *queijadas*, the local sweet speciality *(see p147)*.

Fonte Mourisca on Volta do Duche

East of here, near the railway station, the **Museu de Arte Moderna** focuses on 20th-century works, including paintings by Andy Warhol.

The many fountains dotted around the town are used by locals for their fresh spring drinking water. Among the most striking is the tiled **Fonte Mourisca** (Arab Fountain), so-called for its Neo-Moorish decoration.

Toy Alfa Romeo, Museu do Brinquedo

🏛 Museu do Brinquedo

Rua Visconde De Monserrate. 📞 21-924 21 71. ⏱ 10am–6pm Tue–Sun. 🈲 🉐

This small museum, situated in a converted railway station, is bursting with a fine international collection of toys. Hundreds of toys are arranged over three floors and range from model planes, cars and trains, including 1930s Hornby sets, to battalions of toy soldiers, dolls and dolls' houses, tin toys and curious clockwork models of cars and soldiers. The museum is fun for a rainy day, particularly for nostalgic adults.

🏛 Museu Regional

Praça da República 23. 📞 21-924 47 72. ⏱ Mon–Fri (also: Sat & Sun pm). 🈲 Carnaval, 1 May, 22 Dec–2 Jan.

Sintra's regional museum is on two floors. The Art Gallery, used for temporary exhibitions, houses a small permanent collection of paintings and old prints showing views of Sintra, including two early views of Palácio da Pena in the 1860s.

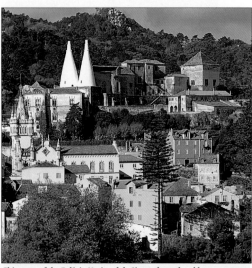

Chimneys of the Palácio Nacional de Sintra above the old town

♣ Castelo dos Mouros

Estrada da Pena. ○ *10am–6pm daily.* ● *1 Jan, 25 Dec.*

Standing above the old town, like a sentinel, the ramparts of the 8th-century Moorish castle, conquered by Afonso Henriques in 1147, snake over the top of the Serra. On a fine day, there are breathtaking views from the castle walls over the old town to Palácio da Pena, on a neighbouring peak, and far along the coast. Hidden inside the walls are a ruined chapel and an ancient Moorish cistern. For walkers, a steep footpath threads up through wooded slopes from the 12th-century church of **Santa Maria**. Follow the signs to a dark green swing gate where the footpath begins. The monogram "DFII" carved on the gateway is a reminder that the castle walls were restored by Fernando II *(see p161)* in the 19th century.

Battlements of the Castelo dos Mouros perched on the slopes of the Serra

VISITORS' CHECKLIST

Road map B5. ⌂ 23,000. 🚉 🚌 *Avenida Dr Miguel Bombarda.* 🛈 *Praça da República 23 (219-233 919).* 🛒 *2nd & 4th Sun of month in São Pedro.* 🎭 *Festival de Música (Jun–Jul).*

♣ Parque da Pena

Estrada da Pena. 📞 *21-923 07 46.* ○ *daily.* ● *1 Jan, 25 Dec.* ♿

A huge park surrounds the Palácio da Pena where footpaths wind among a lush vegetation of exotic trees and shrubs. Hidden among the foliage are gazebos, follies and fountains, and a Romantic chalet built by Fernando II for his mistress in 1869. Cruz Alta, the highest point of the Serra at 530 m (1,740 ft), commands spectacular views of the Serra and surrounding plain. On a nearby crag stands the statue of Baron Von Eschwege, architect of the palace and park.

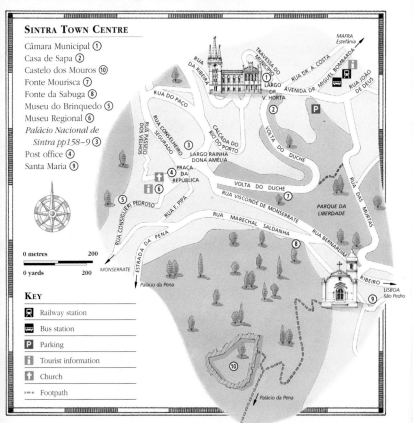

SINTRA TOWN CENTRE

Câmara Municipal ①
Casa de Sapa ②
Castelo dos Mouros ⑩
Fonte Mourisca ⑦
Fonte da Sabuga ⑧
Museu do Brinquedo ⑤
Museu Regional ⑥
Palácio Nacional de Sintra pp158–9 ③
Post office ④
Santa Maria ⑨

0 metres   200
0 yards   200

KEY

🚉 Railway station
🚌 Bus station
🅿 Parking
🛈 Tourist information
✝ Church
⚬⚬⚬ Footpath

Palácio Nacional de Sintra

Swan panel, Sala dos Cisnes

AT THE HEART of the old town of Sintra (Sintra Vila), a pair of strange conical chimneys rises high above the Royal Palace. The main part of the palace, including the central block with its plain Gothic façade and the large kitchens beneath the chimneys, was built by João I in the late 14th century, on a site once occupied by the Moorish rulers. The Paço Real, as it is also known, became the favourite summer retreat for the court, and continued as a residence for Portuguese royalty until the 1880s. Additions to the building by the wealthy Manuel I, in the early 16th century, echo the Moorish style. Gradual rebuilding of the palace has resulted in a fascinating amalgamation of various different styles.

★ Sala das Pegas
It is said that King João I had the ceiling panels painted as a rebuke to the court women for indulging in idle gossip like chattering magpies (pegas).

The Torre da Meca has dovecotes below the cornice decorated with armillary spheres and nautical rope.

The Sala das Galés (galleons) houses temporary exhibitions.

★ Sala dos Brasões
The domed ceiling of this majestic room is decorated with stags holding the coats of arms (brasões) of 74 noble Portuguese families. The lower walls are lined with 18th-century Delft-like tiled panels.

Jardim da Preta, a walled garden

Sala de Dom Sebastião, the audience chamber

TIMELINE

			1495–1521 Reign of Manuel I; major restoration and Manueline additions	**1683** Afonso VI dies after being imprisoned here for nine years by brother Pedro II	**1755** Parts of palace damaged in great earthquake *(see pp62–3)*
10th century Palace becomes residence of Moorish governor	**1281** King Dinis orders restoration of the Palácio de Oliva (as it was then known)				

800	1000	1200	1400	1600	1800

1147 Christian reconquest; Afonso Henriques takes over palace		**1385** João I orders complete rebuilding of central buildings and kitchens			**1880s** Maria Pia (grandmother of Manuel II) is last royal resident
8th century First palace established by Moors		*Siren, Sala das Sereias (c.1660)*			**1910** Palace becomes a national monument

★ Sala dos Cisnes
The magnificent ceiling of the former banqueting hall, painted in the 17th century, is divided into octagonal panels decorated with swans (cisnes).

The Sala dos Árabes is decorated with fine *azulejos*.

Sala das Sereias
Intricate Arabesque designs on 16th-century tiles frame this door in the Room of the Sirens.

VISITORS' CHECKLIST

Largo Rainha Dona Amélia. 21-910 68 40. 10am–5:30pm Thu–Tue (last adm: 30 mins before closing). 1 Jan, Easter, 1 May, 29 Jun, 25 Dec. (free 10am–1pm Sun).

The kitchens, beneath the huge conical chimneys, have spits and utensils once used for preparing royal banquets.

Entrance

Sala dos Archeiros, the entrance hall

Manuel I added the *ajimece* windows, a distinctive Moorish design with a slender column dividing two arches.

Chapel
Symmetrical Moorish patterns decorate the original 14th-century chestnut and oak ceiling and the mosaic floor of the private chapel.

STAR FEATURES

★ Sala dos Brasões

★ Sala dos Cisnes

★ Sala das Pegas

Sintra: Palácio da Pena

Triton Arch

O N THE HIGHEST PEAKS of the Serra de Sintra stands the spectacular palace of Pena, an eclectic medley of architectural styles built in the 19th century for the husband of the young Queen Maria II, Ferdinand Saxe-Coburg-Gotha. It stands over the ruins of a Hieronymite monastery founded here in the 15th century on the site of the chapel of Nossa Senhora da Pena. Ferdinand appointed a German architect, Baron Von Eschwege, to build his summer palace filled with oddities from all over the world and surrounded by a park. With the declaration of the Republic in 1910, the palace became a museum, preserved as it was when the royal family lived here. Allow at least an hour and a half to visit this enchanting place.

Entrance Arch
A studded archway with crenellated turrets greets the visitor at the entrance to the palace. The palace buildings are painted the original daffodil yellow and strawberry pink.

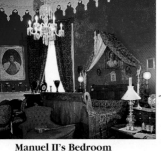

Manuel II's Bedroom
The oval-shaped room is decorated with bright red walls and stuccoed ceiling. A portrait of Manuel II, the last king of Portugal, hangs above the fireplace.

In the kitchen the copper pots and utensils still hang around the iron stove. The dinner service bears the coat of arms of Ferdinand II.

★ Ballroom
The spacious ball-room is sumptuously furnished with German stained-glass windows, precious Oriental porcelain and four lifesize turbaned torch-bearers holding giant candelabra.

★ Arab Room
Marvellous trompe-l'oeil frescoes cover the walls and ceiling of the Arab Room, one of the loveliest in the palace. The Orient was a great inspiration to Romanticism.

VISITORS' CHECKLIST

Estrada da Pena, 5 km (3 mile)
S of Sintra. 📞 21-910 53 40.
🚌 from Avenida Dr Miguel
Bombarda, Sintra.
🕙 10am–5pm Tue–Sun.
🔴 1 Jan, Easter, 1 May,
29 Jun, 25 Dec. 🎫 (free
10am–1pm Sun).

★ Chapel Altarpiece
The impressive 16th-century alabaster and marble retable was sculpted by Nicolau Chanterène. Each niche portrays a scene of the life of Christ, from the manger to the Ascension.

The Triton Arch is encrusted with Neo-Manueline decoration and is guarded by a fierce sea monster.

The cloister, decorated with colourful patterned tiles, is part of the original monastery buildings.

Entrance

FERDINAND: KING CONSORT
Ferdinand was known in Portugal as Dom Fernando II, the "artist" king. Like his cousin Prince Albert, who married the English Queen Victoria, he loved art, nature and the new inventions of the time. He was himself a watercolour painter. Ferdinand enthusiastically adopted his new country and devoted his life to patronizing the arts. In 1869, 16 years after the death of Maria II, Ferdinand married his mistress, the opera singer Countess Edla. His lifelong dream of building the extravagant palace at Pena was completed in 1885, the year he died.

STAR FEATURES

★ Arab Room

★ Ballroom

★ Chapel Altarpiece

Outdoor café in the popular holiday resort of Cascais

Cascais ❼

Road map B5. 👥 30,000. 🚌 🚐
🛈 Rua Visconde da Luz 14 (21-486 82 04). 🛒 1st & 3rd Sun of month.

A FAVOURED HARBOUR since prehistoric times, Cascais stands in a sheltered, sandy bay at the mouth of the River Tagus, once heavily defended against invaders. It became a fashionable resort in the 1870s, when Luís I converted the 17th-century citadel on the southwest corner of the bay into a summer palace.

Sea bathing became popular at the turn of the century and wealthy families built splendid holiday villas here. Nowadays it is a busy resort, with fashionable shops in the pleasant pedestrian streets of the old town, and plenty of cafés and restaurants in the new marina. Fishing is still an important activity, and the day's catch is auctioned near the harbour in the afternoon.

The **Museu do Conde de Castro Guimarães** in Gandarinha Park was once the palatial residence of the Conde de Castro Guimarães. Superbly sited on a small creek where the sea sweeps in at high tide, the house was built in 1892, when Cascais was at the height of fashion. The count and his wife died without children in the 1920s, and the house with its eclectic collection of Indo-Portuguese furniture, paintings, *azulejos*, porcelain and valuable books, was left to the State. The library has been moved to Casa da Horta de Santa Clara near the central market. Its prize exhibit is a rare 16th-century illustrated book by Duarte Galvão (1455–1517), *Chronicles of Dom Afonso Henriques*.

On a smaller scale, the **Museu do Mar** focuses on the life and history of Cascais with some fascinating old photographs, painted panoramas and finds from local shipwrecks.

Nearby, the church of **Nossa Senhora da Assunção** is decorated with paintings by Josefa de Óbidos (1631–84) *(see p51)*.

🏛 **Museu-Biblioteca**
Avenida Rei Humberto de Itália.
📞 21-482 54 07. **Museum** ◯
10am–5pm Tue–Sun. 📖 **Library**
Casa da Horta de Santa Clara (near
Cascais central market. ◯ 10am–7pm
Mon–Sat. ● public hols.

ENVIRONS: At **Boca do Inferno** (Mouth of Hell), about 3 km (2 miles) west on the coast road, the sea rushes into clefts and caves in the rocks making an ominous booming sound and sending up spectacular spray in rough weather. The place is almost obscured by a roadside market and cafés but a small platform gives a good view of the rocky arch with the sea roaring in below.

The magnificent sandy beach of **Guincho**, 10 km (6 miles) further west, is backed by sand dunes with clumps of umbrella pines, and a new cycle path. A small fort (now a luxury hotel) stands perched on the rocks above the sea. Atlantic breakers rolling in make this a paradise for experienced windsurfers and surfers, though beware of the strong currents.

Spectacular view of the weatherbeaten coastline at Boca do Inferno, near Cascais

Estoril ❽

Road map B5. 👥 40,000. 🚌 🚐
🛈 Arcadas do Parque (214-664 414).

E STORIL HAS THE AIR of a once prosperous resort, as indeed it was. Exiled royalty, including Italy's last king, Umberto II, Juan de Borbón of Spain, Karl Hapsburg, the last Austro-Hungarian emperor, and King Carol of Romania, settled here, and it grew from a small spa village into an elegant town, popular as a smart conference venue.

The proximity to Lisbon, the mild climate and its fame as a haunt of aristocrats have long attracted both summer and winter visitors to this "Portuguese Riviera". Today, grand villas, modern apartments and five-star hotels line the coast, following the long, breezy promenade behind the sandy beach that links Estoril with the town of Cascais, 3 km (2 miles) to the west.

Sandy beach and promenade along the bay of Estoril

Impressively sited at the top of the central park, the casino is flanked with tall, majestic date palms. Other entertainments include several superb golf courses, sailing and horse riding. In September, the drone of motor racing cars at the nearby Autodromo echoes round the hills.

Palácio de Queluz ❾

See pp164–5.

Alcochete ❿

Road map C5. 🏘 *13,000.* 🚌
ℹ *Largo da Misericórdia (212-340 080).*

T HIS DELIGHTFUL old town overlooks the wide Tagus estuary from the southern shore. Salt has long been one of the main industries here, and saltpans can still be seen to the north and south of the town, while in the town centre a large statue of a muscular salt worker has the inscription: "Do Sal a Revolta e a Esperança" (From Salt to Rebellion and Hope). On the outskirts of town, is a statue of Manuel I *(see pp46–7),* who was born here on 1 June 1469 and granted the town a Royal Charter in 1515.

Statue of a salt worker in Alcochete (1985)

ENVIRONS: The **Reserva Natural do Estuário do Tejo** covers a vast area of estuary water, salt marshes and small islands around Alcochete and is a very important breeding ground for water birds. Particularly interesting are the flocks of flamingos that gather here during the autumn and spring migration, en route from colonies such as the Camargue in France and Fuente de Piedra in Spain. Ask at the tourist office about boat trips to see the wildlife of the estuary, which includes wild bulls and horses.

🔱 **Reserva Natural do Estuário do Tejo**
Avenida dos Combatentes da Grande Guerra 1. 📞 *21-234 17 42.*

Pilgrims' lodgings, Cabo Espichel

Costa da Caparica ⓫

Road map B5. 🏘 *40,000.* 🚉 *to Pragal then bus.* ℹ *Av. da República 18 (21-290 00 71).*

L ONG SANDY beaches, backed by sand dunes, have made this a popular holiday resort for Lisboetas who come here to swim, sunbathe and enjoy the seafood restaurants and beach cafés. A railway, with open carriages, runs for 10 km (6 miles) along the coast during the summer months. The first beaches reached from the town are popular with families with children, while the furthest beaches suit those seeking quiet isolation. Further south, sheltered by pine forests, **Lagoa do Albufeira**, is a peaceful windsurfing centre and camp site.

Cabo Espichel ⓬

Road map B5. 🚌 *from Sesimbra.*

S HEER CLIFFS DROP straight into the sea at this windswept promontory where the land ends dramatically. The Romans named it Promontorium Barbaricum, alluding to its dangerous location, and a lighthouse warns sailors of the treacherous rocks below. Stunning views of the ocean and the coast can be enjoyed from this bleak outcrop of land but beware of the strong gusts of wind on the cliff edge.

In this desolate setting stands the impressive **Santuário de Nossa Senhora do Cabo**, a late 17th-century church with its back to the sea. On either side of the church a long line of pilgrims' lodgings facing inwards form an open courtyard. Baroque paintings, ex votos and a frescoed ceiling decorate the interior of the church. Although partly restored, the building still has a derelict air. A domed chapel, tiled with blue and white *azulejo* panels, is located nearby.

The site became a popular place of pilgrimage in the 13th century when a local man had a vision of the Madonna rising from the sea on a mule. Legend has it that the tracks of the mule can be seen embedded in the rock. The large footprints, on Praia dos Lagosteiros below the church, are actually believed to be fossilized dinosaur tracks.

Spring flowers by the saltpans of the Tagus estuary near Alcochete

Palácio de Queluz **⓿**

IN 1747, PEDRO, younger son of João V, commissioned Mateus Vicente to transform his 17th-century hunting lodge into a Rococo summer palace. The central section, including a music room and chapel, was built, but after Pedro's marriage in 1760 to the future Maria I, the palace was again extended. The French architect, Jean-Baptiste Robillion, added the sumptuous Robillion Pavilion and gardens, cleared space for the Throne Room and redesigned the Music Room. During Maria's reign, the royal family kept a menagerie and went boating on the *azulejo*-lined canal.

A sphinx in the gardens

Corridor of the Sleeves
Painted azulejo *panels (1784) representing the continents and the seasons, as well as hunting scenes, line the walls of the brigh Corredor das Mangas (sleeves)*

★ Sala dos Embaixadores
Built by Robillion, this stately room was used for diplomatic audiences as well as concerts. The trompe l'oeil *ceiling shows the royal family attending a concert.*

Neptune's Fountain

The Lion Staircase is an impressive and graceful link from the lower gardens to the palace.

STAR FEATURES

★ Throne Room

★ Sala dos Embaixadores

★ Palace Gardens

To canal

Lion Fountain

The Robillion Pavilion displays the flamboyance of the French architect's Rococo style.

Don Quixote Chamber
The royal bedroom, where Pedro IV (see p54) was born and died, has a domed ceiling and magnificent floor decoration in exotic woods, giving the square room a circular appearance. Painted scenes by Manuel de Costa (1784) tell the story of Don Quixote.

Music Room
Operas and concerts were performed here by Maria I's orchestra, "the best in Europe" according to English traveller, William Beckford. A portrait of the queen hangs above the grand piano.

VISITORS' CHECKLIST

Road map B5. Largo do Palácio.
21-435 00 39. Queluz-Belas or Queluz-Massama. from Lisbon, (Colégio Militar). 10am–5pm Wed–Mon. 29 Nov, Easter, 1 May, 25 Dec, 1 Jan. (free 10am–noon Sun). Cozinha Velha (see p409).

Chapel

The royal family's living rooms and bedrooms opened out onto the Malta Gardens.

★ Throne Room
The elegant state room (1770) was the scene of splendid balls and banquets. The gilded statues of Atlas are by Silvestre Faria Lobo.

Entrance

Malta Gardens

The Hanging Gardens, designed by Robillion, were built over arches, raising the ground in front of the palace above the surrounding gardens.

ARIA I (1734–1816)

...ria, the eldest daughter of José I, ...d at the palace in Queluz after ... marriage to her uncle, Pedro, in ...0. Serious and devout, she con-...entiously filled her role as queen, ... suffered increasingly from bouts ...melancholia. When her son José ...d from smallpox in 1788, she went ...pelessly mad. Visitors to Queluz ...re dismayed by her agonizing shrieks ... she suffered visions and hallucinations. ...er the French invasion of 1807, her younger son João ...clared regent in 1792) took his mad mother to Brazil.

★ Palace Gardens
The formal gardens, adorned with statues, fountains and topiary, were often used for entertaining. Concerts performed in the Music Room would spill out into the Malta Gardens.

Sesimbra ⑬

Road map C5. 🏘 *27,000.* 🚌
ℹ *Largo da Marinha 26–7 (21-223
57 43).* 🛒 *1st & 3rd Fri of month.*

A STEEP NARROW ROAD leads
down to this busy fishing
village in a sheltered south-
facing bay. Protected from
north winds by the slopes
of the Serra da Arrábida, the
town has become a popular
holiday resort with Lisboetas.
It was occupied by the Romans
and later the Moors until King
Sancho II *(see pp42–3)* conquered its heavily defended
forts in 1236. The old town is
a maze of steep narrow streets,
with the **Santiago Fort** (now
a customs post) in the centre
overlooking the sea. From the
terrace, which is open to the
public during the day, there
are views over the town, the
Atlantic and the wide sandy
beach that stretches out on
either side. Sesimbra is fast
developing as a resort, with
holiday flats mushrooming on
the surrounding hillsides and
plentiful pavement cafés and
bars that are always busy on
sunny days, even in winter.

The fishing fleet of brightly
painted boats is moored in the
Porto do Abrigo to the west
of the main town. The harbour
is reached by taking Avenida
dos Náufragos, a sweeping

Colourful fishing boats in the harbour at Sesimbra

promenade that follows the
beach out of town. On the
large trawlers *(traineiras)*, the
catch is mainly sardines, sea
bream, whiting and swordfish;
on the smaller boats, octopus
and squid. In the late afternoon, when the fishing boats
return from a day at sea, a
colourful, noisy fish auction
takes place on the quayside.
The day's catch can be tasted
in the town's excellent fish
restaurants along the shore.

High above the town is the
Moorish castle, greatly
restored in the 18th century
when a church and small
flower-filled cemetery were
added inside the walls. There
are wonderful views from the
ramparts, especially at sunset.

Palmela ⑭

Road map C5. 🏘 *14,000.* 🚌 🚃
ℹ *Castelo de Palmela (21-233 21 22).*
🛒 *every other Tue.*

T HE FORMIDABLE castle at
Palmela stands over the
small hilltown, high on a north-
eastern spur of the wooded
Serra da Arrábida. Its strategic
position dominates the plain
for miles around, especially
when floodlit at night. Heavily
defended by the Moors, it
was eventually conquered in
the 12th century and given by
Sancho I to the Knights of the
Order of Santiago *(see p43)*.
In 1423, João I transformed
the castle into a monastery for
the Order, which has now
been restored and converted
into a splendid *pousada (see
p385)*, with a restaurant in
the monks' refectory and a
swimming pool for residents,
hidden inside the castle walls.

From the castle terraces, and
especially from the top of the
14th-century keep, there are
fantastic views all around,
over the Serra da Arrábida to
the south and on a clear day
across the Tagus to Lisbon. In
the town square below, the
church of **São Pedro** contains
18th-century tiles of scenes
from the life of St Peter.

The annual wine festival, the
Festa das Vindimas, is held on
the first weekend of September
in front of the 17th-century
Paços do Concelho (town hall).
Traditionally dressed villagers,
press the wine barefoot and on
the final day of celebrations
there is a spectacular firework
display from the castle walls.

The castle at Palmela with views over the wooded Serra da Arrábida

Serra da Arrábida ⓯

Road map C5. 🚃 Setúbal.
🛈 Parque Natural da Arrábida, Praça da República, Setúbal (265-54 11 40).

THE PARQUE NATURAL da Arrábida covers the small range of limestone mountains which stretches east-west along the coast between Sesimbra and Setúbal. It was established to protect the wild, beautiful landscape and rich variety of birds and wildlife, including eagles, wildcats and badgers.

The name Arrábida is from Arabic meaning a place of prayer, and the wooded hillsides are indeed a peaceful, secluded retreat. The sheltered, south-facing slopes are thickly covered with aromatic and evergreen shrubs and trees such as pine and cypress, more typical of the Mediterranean. Vineyards also thrive on the sheltered slopes and the town of **Vila Nogueira de Azeitão** is known for its wine, especially the Moscatel de Setúbal.

The **Estrada de Escarpa** (the N379-1) snakes across the top of the ridge and affords astounding views. A narrow road winds down to **Portinho da Arrábida**, a sheltered cove with a beach of fine white sand and crystal clear sea, popular with underwater fishermen. The sandy beaches of **Galapos** and **Figueirinha** are a little further east along the coast road towards Setúbal. Just east of Sesimbra, the Serra da Arrábida drops to the sea in the sheer 380-m (1,250-ft) cliffs of Risco, the highest in mainland Portugal.

Portinho da Arrábida on the dramatic coastline of the Serra da Arrábida

🔒 Convento da Arrábida

Serra da Arrábida. 🕻 21-218 05 20. ◯ by appt only, via Fundação Oriente (phone 21-352 70 02). 📷
Half-hidden among the trees on the southern slopes of the Serra, this large 16th-century building was once a Franciscan monastery. The five round towers perched on the hillside were probably used for solitary meditation.

[map showing: LISBOA, Palmela, N379, N252, Vila Fresca de Azeitão, Vila Nogueira de Azeitão, N10, Setúbal, N379-1, N10-4, Convento ta Arrábida, Galapos, Figueirinha, Portinho da Arrábida, BAÍA DE SETÚBAL]

KEY

▬ Major road
▬ Minor road
▭ Other road

0 kilometres — 5
0 miles — 3

🏛 Museu Oceanográfico

Fortaleza de Santa Maria, Portinho da Arrábida. 🕻 265-54 11 40. ◯ 9am–noon, 2–5pm Tue–Fri. 📷
This small fort, just above Portinho da Arrábida, was built by Pedro, the Prince Regent, in 1676 to protect local communities from attacks by Moorish pirates. It now houses a Sea Museum and Marine Biology Centre where visitors can see aquaria containing many local sea creatures, including sea urchins, octopus and starfish.

🍷 José Maria de Fonseca

Rua José Augusto Coelho 11, Vila Nogueira de Azeitão. 🕻 21-219 89 40. ◯ 9am–noon, 2:30–5pm daily. ⬤ Dec 25–Jan 1. 📷 🚭 🔒
The long-established José Maria de Fonseca winery produces popular red table wines and is famous for its fragrant dessert wine, Moscatel de Setúbal (see p29). Tours of the winery explain the process of making moscatel and include being taken around a series of old cellars containing huge oak and chestnut vats. Tours last about 45 minutes and include a wine tasting.

Manueline interior of Igreja de Jesus, Setúbal

Setúbal ⑯

Road map C5. 🏘 *120,000.* 🚉 🚌
⛴ 🛈 *Casa do Corpo Santo, Praça
do Quebedo (265-53 42 22).*

ALTHOUGH THIS is an important
industrial town, and the
third largest port in Portugal
(after Lisbon and Oporto),
Setúbal can be used to
explore the area. To the south
of the central gardens and
fountains are the fishing harbour, marina and ferry port,
and a lively covered market.
North of the gardens is the
old town, with attractive
pedestrian streets and squares
full of shops and cafés.

The 16th-century **cathedral**,
dedicated to Santa Maria da
Graça, has glorious tiled panels
dating from the 18th century,
and gilded altar decoration.
Street names commemorate
two famous Setúbal residents:
Manuel Barbosa du Bocage
(1765–1805), whose satirical
poetry landed him in prison,
and Luísa Todi (1753–1833),
a celebrated opera singer.

In Roman times, fish-salting
was the most important industry here. Rectangular tanks,
carved from stone, can be
seen under the glass floor of
the Regional Tourist Office at
No. 10 Travessa Frei Gaspar.

🛐 Igreja de Jesus
Praça Miguel Bombarda. 📞 *265-52
41 50.* ◯ *9am–noon, 2–5pm Tue–
Sun.* ♿ **Museum** 📞 *265-52 47 72.*
◯ *Tue–Sat.* ● *public hols.*
To the north of the old town,
this striking Gothic church is
one of Setúbal's architectural
treasures. Designed by the

**Fisherman's boat on the shallow mud flats of
the Reserva Natural do Estuário do Sado**

architect Diogo Boitac in 1494,
the lofty interior is adorned
with twisted columns, carved
in three strands from pinkish
Arrábida limestone, and rope-
like stone ribs decorating the
roof, recognized as the earliest
examples of the distinctive
Manueline style *(see pp20–21).*

On Rua do Balneário, in
the old monastic quarters, a
museum houses 14 remarkable paintings of the life of
Christ. Painted in glowing
colours, the works are attributed to the followers of Jorge
Afonso (1520–30), influenced
by the Flemish school.

🏛 Museu de Arqueologia
e Etnografia
Avenida Luísa Todi 162. 📞 *265-239
365.* ◯ *Tue–Sat.* ● *public hols.*
The archaeological museum
displays a wealth of finds from
digs around Setúbal, including
Bronze Age pots, Roman coins
and amphorae made to carry
wine and *garum*, a sauce
made from fish marinated in
salt and herbs considered a
great delicacy in Rome. The
ethnography display shows
local arts, crafts and industries,
including the processing of salt
and cork over the centuries.

♟ Castelo de São Filipe
Estrada de São Filipe. 📞 *265-52 38
44.* ◯ *daily.*
The star-shaped fort was built
in 1595 by Philip II of Spain
during the period of Spanish
rule *(see pp50–51)* to keep a
wary eye on pirates, English
invaders and the local population. A massive gateway
and stone tunnel lead to the
sheltered interior, which now
houses a *pousada (see p385)*
and an exquisite small chapel,
tiled with scenes from the life
of São Filipe by Policarpo de
Oliveira Bernardes
(see p22). A broad
terrace offers mar-
vellous views over
the city and the
Sado estuary.

ENVIRONS: Setúbal is
an excellent starting
point for a tour by
car of the unspoilt
**Reserva Natural
do Estuário do
Sado**, a vast stretch
of mud flats, shallow

lagoons and salt marshes with patches of pine forest, which has been explored and inhabited since 3500 BC. Otters, water birds (including storks and herons), oysters and a great variety of fish are found in the reserve. The old tidal water mill at Mouriscas, 5 km (3 miles) to the east of Setúbal, uses the different levels of the tide to turn the grinding stones. Rice-growing and fishing are the main occupations today, and pine trees around the lagoon are tapped for resin.

Reserva Natural do Estuário do Sado
Praça da República, Setúbal (265-54 11 40).

Península de Tróia ⑰

Road map C5. 🚢 Tróia. ℹ Complexo Turístico de Tróia (265-49 43 12).

Thatched fisherman's cottage in the village of Carrasqueira

HIGH-RISE HOLIDAY apartments dominate the tip of the Tróia peninsula, easily accessible from Setúbal by ferry. The Atlantic coast, stretching south for 18 km (11 miles) of untouched sandy beach, lined with dunes and pine woods, is now the haunt of sunseekers in the summer.

Near Tróia, in the sheltered lagoon, the Roman town of **Cetóbriga** was the site of a thriving fish-salting business; the stone tanks and ruined buildings are open to visit. To the south, smart new holiday villas and golf clubs are springing up along the lagoon.

Further on, **Carrasqueira** is an old fishing community where you can still see traditional reed houses, with walls and roofs made from thatch. The narrow fishing boats

View over Alcácer do Sal and the River Sado from the castle

moored along the mud flats are reached by walkways raised on stilts. From here to Alcácer do Sal, great stretches of pine forest line the road, and there are the first glimpses of the cork oak countryside typical of the Alentejo.

Cetóbriga
N253-1. (265-49 43 18. ☐ daily.

Alcácer do Sal ⑱

Road map C5. 🏠 15,000. 🚉 🚌
ℹ Rua da República (265-610 070).
🗓 1st Sat of month.

BYPASSED by the main road, the ancient town of Alcácer do Sal (al-kasr from the Arabic for castle, and do sal from its trade in salt) sits peacefully on the north bank of the River Sado. The imposing castle was a hillfort as early as the 6th century BC.

The Phoenicians established an inland trading port here, and the castle later became a stronghold for the Romans. Rebuilt by the Moors, it was finally conquered by Afonso II in 1217. The restored buildings have now taken on a new life as a *pousada (see p384)*, with sweeping views over the rooftops and untidy storks' nests on the town's church roofs.

There are pleasant cafés along the riverside promenade and several historic churches. The small church of Espírito Santo now houses a **Museu Arqueológico** exhibiting local finds and the 18th-century **Santo António** holds a marble Chapel of the 11,000 Virgins. The bullring is a focus for summer events and hosts the agricultural fair in October.

Museu Arqueológico
Igreja do Espírito Santo, Praça Pedro Nunes. (265-61 00 70. ☐ daily.

BIRDS OF THE TAGUS AND SADO ESTUARIES

Many waterbirds, including black-winged stilts, avocets, Kentish plovers and pratincoles are found close to areas of open water and mud flats as well as the dried out lagoons of the Tagus and Sado estuaries. Reed-beds also provide shelter for nesting and support good numbers of little bitterns, purple herons and marsh harriers. From September to March, the area around the Tagus estuary is extremely important for wildfowl and wintering waders.

Black-winged stilt, a wader that feeds in the estuaries

ESTREMADURA AND RIBATEJO

ETWEEN THE TAGUS *and the coast lies Estremadura, an area of rolling hills that tumble down to rugged cliffs and sandy beaches. In contrast, the Ribatejo is a vast alluvial plain stretching along the banks of the Tagus. Portugal's finest medieval monasteries bear witness to the illustrious, if turbulent past of these regions.*

The name Estremadura comes from the Latin *Extrema Durii*, "beyond the Douro", once the border of the Christian kingdoms in the north. As Portugal expanded southwards in the 12th century, land taken from the Moors *(see pp42–3)* was given to the religious orders. The Cistercian abbey at Alcobaça celebrates Afonso Henriques's capture of the town of Santarém in 1147, and the Knights Templar began their citadel at Tomar *(see p185)* soon after.

Spanish claims to the Portuguese throne brought more fighting: Batalha's magnificent abbey was built near the site of João I's victory over the Castilians at Aljubarrota in 1385. More recently, in 1808–10, Napoleonic forces sacked many towns in the region, but were stopped by Wellington's formidable defences, the Lines of Torres Vedras.

Nowadays, Estremadura is an area of expanding commerce, where vineyards, wheatfields and market gardens flourish. In the Ribatejo (the name means "Banks of the Tagus") the river's vast flood plain provides fertile soil for agriculture and grazing land for Portugal's prized black fighting bulls and fine horses.

The area around Tomar and the river towns along the Tagus have thriving industries, while on the River Zêzere, the dam built at Castelo de Bode in the 1940s heralded a new era of hydro-electric power. The Atlantic coast is a popular holiday destination, especially the fishing village of Nazaré and the sandy beaches along the Pinhal de Leiria forest. Visitors also flock to Portugal's most important religious shrine at Fátima, scene of celebrated visions of the Virgin Mary in 1917.

Posters advertising the local bullfighting events in Coruche

◁ Austere Gothic columns in the nave of the Cistercian abbey church at Alcobaça

Exploring Estremadura and the Ribatejo

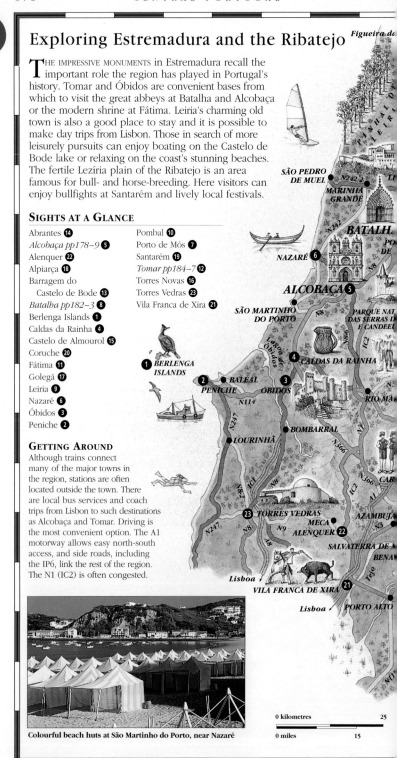

T HE IMPRESSIVE MONUMENTS in Estremadura recall the important role the region has played in Portugal's history. Tomar and Óbidos are convenient bases from which to visit the great abbeys at Batalha and Alcobaça or the modern shrine at Fátima. Leiria's charming old town is also a good place to stay and it is possible to make day trips from Lisbon. Those in search of more leisurely pursuits can enjoy boating on the Castelo de Bode lake or relaxing on the coast's stunning beaches. The fertile Lezíria plain of the Ribatejo is an area famous for bull- and horse-breeding. Here visitors can enjoy bullfights at Santarém and lively local festivals.

SIGHTS AT A GLANCE

Abrantes **14**

Alcobaça *pp178–9* **5**

Alenquer **22**

Alpiarça **18**

Barragem do
  Castelo de Bode **13**

Batalha *pp182–3* **8**

Berlenga Islands **1**

Caldas da Rainha **4**

Castelo de Almourol **15**

Coruche **20**

Fátima **11**

Golegã **17**

Leiria **9**

Nazaré **6**

Óbidos **3**

Peniche **2**

Pombal **10**

Porto de Mós **7**

Santarém **19**

Tomar *pp184–7* **12**

Torres Novas **16**

Torres Vedras **23**

Vila Franca de Xira **21**

GETTING AROUND

Although trains connect many of the major towns in the region, stations are often located outside the town. There are local bus services and coach trips from Lisbon to such destinations as Alcobaça and Tomar. Driving is the most convenient option. The A1 motorway allows easy north-south access, and side roads, including the IP6, link the rest of the region. The N1 (IC2) is often congested.

Colourful beach huts at São Martinho do Porto, near Nazaré

| 0 kilometres | 25 |
| 0 miles | 15 |

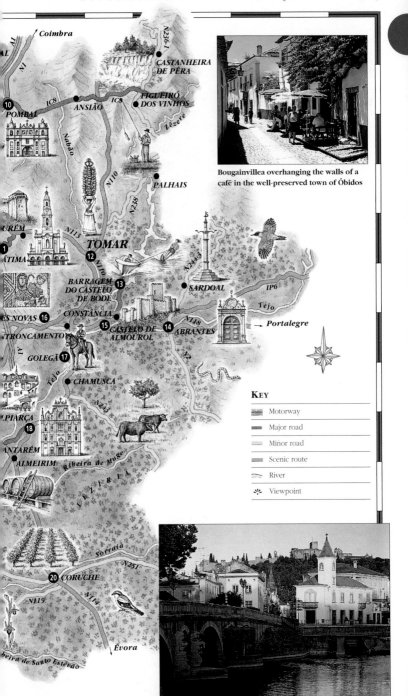

Bougainvillea overhanging the walls of a café in the well-preserved town of Óbidos

Key

Motorway
Major road
Minor road
Scenic route
River
✲ Viewpoint

The Renaissance bridge, Ponte Velha, over the River Nabão in Tomar, with the Convento de Cristo in the distance

See Also

• *Where to Stay* pp386–8

• *Where to Eat* pp410–11

Berlenga Islands ●

Road map B4. *from Peniche.*
ℹ *Peniche.*

Monks, a lighthouse keeper, fishermen and, recently, biologists have inhabited this rocky archipelago that juts out from the Atlantic Ocean 12 km (7 miles) from the mainland. Berlenga Grande, the biggest island, can be reached by ferry in about an hour. This island is a nature reserve with nesting sites for seabirds including guillemots and herring gulls.

On the southeast side of the island is the 17th-century pentagonal **Forte de São João Baptista**. This stark, stone fort suffered repeated assaults from pirates and foreign armies over the years. Today it is a basic hostel. Small boats can be hired from the jetty to explore the reefs and marine grottoes around the island. **Furado Grande** is the most spectacular of these; a 70-m (230-ft) tunnel, opening into the Covo do Sonho (Dream Cove) framed by imposing red granite cliffs.

Stone fortress of São João Baptista on Berlenga Grande

Peniche ●

Road map B4. 👥 *20,000.* 🚌
ℹ *Rua Alexandre Herculano (262-78 95 71).* 🛒 *Last Thu of the month (except Jul & Dec).*

Set on a peninsula, this small, pleasant town is partly enclosed by 16th-century walls. Totally dependent on its port, Peniche has good fish restaurants and deep-sea fishing facilities. At the water's edge on the south side of town stands the 16th-century **Fortaleza**, used as a prison during the Salazar regime *(see pp56–7)*. The fortress was made famous by the escape in 1960 of the communist leader, Álvaro Cunhal. Inside, the **Museu de Peniche** caters to popular interest with a tour that includes a look into the prison cells. In Largo 5 de Outubro, the **Igreja da Misericórdia** has 17th-century painted ceiling panels depicting the *Life of Christ*, and patterned *azulejo* panels from the same period.

🏛 Museu de Peniche
Campo da República. **☎** *262-78 01 16.* **◯** *Tue–Sun.* **●** *25 Dec.* 🔷

Environs: On the peninsula's western headland, 2 km (1 mile) from Peniche, **Cabo Carvoeiro** affords grand views of the ocean and the strange-shaped rocks along the eroded coastline. Here, the interior of the chapel of **Nossa Senhora dos Remédios** is faced with 18th-century tiles on the *Life of the Virgin* attributed to the workshop of António de Oliveira Bernardes *(see p22)*.

Along the coast, 2 km (1 mile) east of Peniche, **Baleal** is a small community with gorgeous beaches and an idyllic fishing cove across a causeway.

Óbidos ●

Road map B4. 👥 *600.* 🚊 🚌
ℹ *Rua Direita (262-95 92 31).*

This enchanting hilltown with pretty whitewashed houses is enclosed within 14th-century castellated walls. When King Dinis *(see pp44–5)* married Isabel of Aragon in 1282, Óbidos was among his wedding presents to her. At the time Óbidos was an important port, but by the 16th century the river had silted up and its strategic importance declined. It has since been restored and preserved as a picture-postcard town, popular with tourists.

Boats anchored in the old harbour at Peniche

The entrance into the town is through the southern gate, **Porta da Vila**, whose interior is embellished with 18th-century tiles. Rua Direita, the main shopping street, leads to Praça de Santa Maria. Here, a Manueline **pelourinho** (pillory) is decorated with a fishing net, the emblem of Dona Leonor, wife of João II. She chose this emblem in honour of the fishermen who tried in vain to save her son from drowning.

Opposite the pillory is the church of **Santa Maria**, with a simple Renaissance portal. The future Afonso V was married to his cousin Isabel here in 1441. He was ten years old, she eight. The interior of the church retains a simple clarity with a painted wooden ceiling and 17th-century tiles. In the chancel, a retable depicting the *Mystic Marriage of St Catherine* (1661) is by Josefa de Óbidos *(see p51)*. The artist lived most of her life in Óbidos and is buried in the church of **São Pedro** on Largo de São Pedro. Her work is also on display in the **Museu Municipal**.

Dominating the town is the **castle**, rebuilt by Afonso Henriques after he took the town from the Moors in 1148.

View of the castle over the whitewashed houses of Óbidos

Today it is a charming *pousada (see p387)*. The sentry path along the battlements affords fine views of the rooftops.

Southeast of town is the Baroque **Santuário do Senhor da Pedra**, begun in 1740 to a hexagonal plan. An early Christian stone crucifix on the altar remains a venerated item.

m Museu Municipal
Praça de Santa Maria. [262-95 50 10. [] daily. [] 1 Jan, 25 Dec. []

Caldas da Rainha ❹

Road map B4. [] 22,000. [] []
[] Praça da República (262-83 45 11). [] May–Nov. [] Mon.

THE "QUEEN'S HOT SPRINGS" is a sprawling spa town. It owes its prosperity to successes in three quite different fields: thermal cures, fruit farming and ceramics. The queen who gave her name to the town was Dona Leonor, founder of the **Misericórdia** hospital on Largo Rainha Dona Leonor. The original hospital chapel later became the impressive Manueline **Igreja do Populo**, built by Diogo Boitac *(see pp106–7)*. Inside is the chapel of São Sebastião, built in the 15th century and faced with 18th-century *azulejos*.

The market in Praça da República and shops in Rua da Liberdade sell local ceramics, including the green cabbage-leaf majolica ware *(see pp24–5)* typical of the town. Examples of the religious and humorous work of the caricaturist and potter, Rafael Bordalo Pinheiro (1846–1905), can be seen in the **Museu de Cerâmica**, housed in the ceramics factory.

m Museu de Cerâmica
Rua Dr Ilídio Amado. [262-840 280. [] Tue–Sun. [] public hols. []

ENVIRONS: The saltwater **Lagoa de Óbidos**, 15 km (9 miles) west of Caldas, is a popular lagoon for sailing and fishing.

Pillory in front of the Igreja de Santa Maria in Óbidos

The fairytale town of Óbidos encircled by medieval crenellated walls ▷

Alcobaça ❺

PORTUGAL'S LARGEST CHURCH, the Mosteiro de Santa Maria de Alcobaça, is renowned for its simple medieval architecture. Founded in 1153, the abbey is closely linked to the arrival of the Cistercian order in Portugal in 1138 as well as the birth of the nation. In March 1147, Afonso Henriques *(see pp42–3)* conquered the Moorish stronghold of Santarém. To commemorate the victory, the king fulfilled his vow to build a mighty church for the Cistercians. This massive task was completed in 1223. The monarchy continued to endow the monastery, notably King Dinis who built the main cloister. Among those buried here are the tragic lovers King Pedro and his murdered mistress Inês.

Sacristy Doorway
Exotic foliage and elaborate pinnacles adorn the Manueline doorway, attributed to João de Castilho (see p106).

Tomb of Inês de Castro

Dormitory

The chapterhouse was where the monks met to elect the abbot and discuss issues regarding the monastery.

The kitchen's huge chimney

The octagonal lavabo was where the monks washed their hands.

Refectory and Kitchen
Stairs lead up to the pulpit where one of the monks read from the Bible as the others ate in silence. In the vast kitchen next door, oxen could be roasted on the spit inside the chimney and a specially diverted stream provided a constant water supply.

★ Cloister of Dom Dinis
Also known as the Cloister of Silence, the exquisite cloister was ordered by King Dinis in 1308. The austere galleries and double arches are in keeping with the Cistercian regard for simplicity.

STAR FEATURES

★ Cloister of Dom Dinis

★ Tombs of Pedro I and Inês de Castro

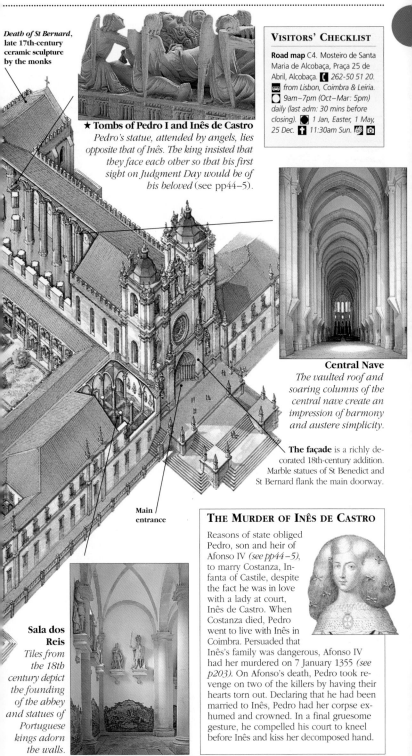

Death of St Bernard, late 17th-century ceramic sculpture by the monks

★ **Tombs of Pedro I and Inês de Castro**
Pedro's statue, attended by angels, lies opposite that of Inês. The king insisted that they face each other so that his first sight on Judgment Day would be of his beloved (see pp44–5).

VISITORS' CHECKLIST

Road map C4. Mosteiro de Santa Maria de Alcobaça, Praça 25 de Abril, Alcobaça. ☎ 262-50 51 20. 🚌 from Lisbon, Coimbra & Leiria. 🕓 9am–7pm (Oct–Mar: 5pm) daily (last adm: 30 mins before closing). ● 1 Jan, Easter, 1 May, 25 Dec. ✝ 11:30am Sun. 🎦 📷

Central Nave
The vaulted roof and soaring columns of the central nave create an impression of harmony and austere simplicity.

The façade is a richly decorated 18th-century addition. Marble statues of St Benedict and St Bernard flank the main doorway.

Main entrance

Sala dos Reis
Tiles from the 18th century depict the founding of the abbey and statues of Portuguese kings adorn the walls.

THE MURDER OF INÊS DE CASTRO

Reasons of state obliged Pedro, son and heir of Afonso IV *(see pp44–5)*, to marry Costanza, Infanta of Castile, despite the fact he was in love with a lady at court, Inês de Castro. When Costanza died, Pedro went to live with Inês in Coimbra. Persuaded that Inês's family was dangerous, Afonso IV had her murdered on 7 January 1355 *(see p203)*. On Afonso's death, Pedro took revenge on two of the killers by having their hearts torn out. Declaring that he had been married to Inês, Pedro had her corpse exhumed and crowned. In a final gruesome gesture, he compelled his court to kneel before Inês and kiss her decomposed hand.

The beach at Nazaré viewed from Sítio

Nazaré ❻

Road map C4. 🏚 10,000. 🚏
🛈 Avenida da República 17 (262-56 11 94). 🚢 Fri.

BESIDE A GLORIOUS BEACH in a sweeping bay backed by steep cliffs, this fishing village is a popular summer resort that has maintained some of its traditional character. Fishermen dressed in checked shirts and black stocking caps and fish-wives wearing several layers of petticoats can still be seen mending nets and drying fish on wire racks on the beach. The bright boats with tall prows that once were hauled from the sea by oxen are still used, although now they have a proper anchorage south of the beach. According to legend the name Nazaré comes from

Baroque church of Nossa Senhora da Nazaré in Sítio

a statue of the Virgin Mary brought to the town by a monk from Nazareth in the 4th century.

High on the cliff above the town is **Sítio**, reached by a funicular that climbs 110 m (360 ft). At the cliff edge stands the tiny **Ermida da Memória**. According to legend, this is where the Virgin Mary saved Dom Fuas Roupinho, a local dignitary, and his horse from following a deer that leapt off the cliff in a sea mist in 1182. Across the square, the 17th-century church of **Nossa Senhora da Nazaré**, with two Baroque belfries and 18th-century tiles inside, contains an anonymous painting of the miraculous rescue. The church also contains the revered image of Our Lady of Nazaré. In September this statue is borne down to the sea in a traditional procession, a colourful re-minder of the town's origins.

ENVIRONS: São Martinho do Porto, 13 km (8 miles) south of Nazaré, is a sandy beach on a curving, almost land-locked bay. The safe location makes it popular with families and chil-dren. The Visigothic church of **São Gião**, 5 km (3 miles) fur-ther south, has fine sculpting and well-proportioned arches.

Porto de Mós ❼

Road map C4. 🏚 6,000. 🚏
🛈 Jardim Principal (244-49 13 23). 🚢 Fri.

ORIGINALLY A MOORISH fort, and rebuilt over the cen-turies by successive Christian kings, the rather fanciful **castle** perches on a hill above the small town of Porto de Mós. Its present appearance, with green cone-shaped turrets and an exquisite loggia, was the inspired work of King Afonso IV's master builders in 1420. In the town below, the 13th-century church of **São João Baptista** retains its original

Romanesque portal. In the public gardens is the richly decorated Baroque church of **São Pedro**. Just off the Praça da República, the **Museu Municipal** displays a varied collection of local finds dating back to Roman remains and dinosaur bones. More modern exhibits include the local *mós* (millstones), as well as present-day ceramics and woven rugs.

🏛 **Museu Municipal**
Travessa de São Pedro. 🕻 244-49 96 15. 🕙 Tue–Sun. 🌑 public hols.

Donkey in the Serra de Aire nature reserve, south of Porto de Mós

ENVIRONS: South of the town, the 38,900-ha (96,000-acre) **Parque Natural das Serras de Aire e Candeeiros** covers a limestone landscape of pas-tures, olive groves and stone walls and is a nesting place for the red-beaked chough.

The area is also dotted with vast and spectacular under-ground caverns with odd rock formations and festoons of stalactites and stalagmites. The **Grutas de Mira de Aire**, 17 km (10 miles) southeast of Porto de Mós, are the biggest, descending 110 m (360 ft) into tunnels and walkways around subterranean lakes. A tour through caverns with names such as the "Jewel Room", past bizarre rocks dubbed "Chinese Hat" or "Jellyfish", ends in a theatrical light and water show.

🦇 **Grutas de Mira de Aire**
Mira de Aire, E.N. 243. 🕻 244-44 03 22. 🕙 daily. 🎫

Batalha ❽

See pp182–3.

Leiria 🟨

Road map C4. 🏠 *13,000.* 🚇 🚌
ℹ️ *Jardim Luís de Camões
(244-82 37 73).* 🚐 *every second Tue
& Sat.* 🆆 *www.rt-leiriafatima.pt*

EPISCOPAL CITY since 1545,
Leiria is set in attractive
countryside on the banks of
the River Lis. Originally the
Roman town of Collipo, it was
recaptured from the Moors by
Afonso Henriques *(see pp42–3)*
in the 12th century. In 1254
Afonso III held a *cortes* here,
the first parliament attended
by common laymen.

The resplendent hilltop
castle that crowns the city
houses a library and meeting
rooms. In the early 14th century, King Dinis restored the
castle and turned it into a
royal residence for himself
and his queen, Isabel of
Aragon. Within the castle
battlements stands the Gothic
church of **Nossa Senhora da
Pena**, today little more than a
roofless shell of dark granite
walls. A magnificent view from
the castle loggia overlooks the
wide expanse of pine forest,
the Pinhal de Leiria, and the
rooftops of the town below.

The old town below the
castle is full of charm, with
tiny dwellings over archways,
graceful arcades and the small
12th-century church of **São
Pedro** on Largo de São Pedro.
The Romanesque portal is all

that remains of the
original church. The
muted 16th-century
Sé above Praça
Rodrigues Lobo has
an elegant vaulted
nave and an altar-
piece in the chancel
painted in 1605 by
Simão Rodrigues.
From Avenida
Marquês
de Pombal, climbing
the hill opposite the
castle, an 18th-century stairway
takes you up to the elaborate
16th-century **Santuário de
Nossa Senhora da
Encarnação**. The small
Baroque interior is tightly
packed with colourful geometric *azulejo* panels and
17th-century paintings of the
Life of the Virgin.

Exposed and rugged coastline west of Leiria

♜ Castle
Largo de São Pedro. ☎ *244-81 39 82.*
🕐 *daily.* 🔴 *1 Jan, 25 Dec.* 🔲

ENVIRONS: West of Leiria is
the long coastal pine forest, the
Pinhal de Leiria, planted by
King Dinis, "the farmer king",
to supply wood for ship building. "A green and whispering
cathedral", in the words of
the poet Afonso Lopes Vieira
(1878–1946), the forest extends
northwards to the beach of
Pedrógão. **São Pedro de Muel**,
22 km (13 miles) to the west
of Leiria, is a small resort on a
marvellous beach.

Pombal 🟨

Road map C4. 🏠 *12,500.* 🚇 🚌
ℹ️ *Viaduto Guilherme Santos (236-
213 230).* 🚐 *Mon & Thu.*

CLOSELY ASSOCIATED with the
Marquês de Pombal *(see
pp52–3)* who retired here in
disgrace in 1777, this small
town of whitewashed houses
is overlooked by the stately
castle founded in 1171 by the
Knights Templar *(see p185)*.

The Marquis lived in what is
now Praça Marquês de Pombal.
Here the old prison and the
celeiro (granary) are adorned
with the Pombal family crest.
The former monastery of Santo
António contains the **Museu
Marquês de Pombal**. Its collection of documents and art
focuses on the Marquis.

🏛 Museu Marquês
de Pombal
Largo do Cardal. ☎ *236-212 018.*
🕐 *Mon–Fri.* 🔴 *public hols.* ♿

Arcaded loggia and castle towers guarding the town of Leiria

Batalha ●

João I's coat of arms on portal

Tᴴᴇ ᴅᴏᴍɪɴɪᴄᴀɴ ᴀʙʙᴇʏ of Santa Maria da Vitória at Batalha is a masterpiece of Portuguese Gothic architecture, famous for its Manueline elements. The pale limestone monastery celebrates the victory at Aljubarrota in 1385. João I had vowed that he would dedicate a magnificent church to the Virgin if he won the battle. Today, two unknown soldiers from World War I lie in the chapterhouse. The abbey was begun in 1388 under master builder Afonso Domingues, succeeded in 1402 by David Huguet. Over the next two centuries successive kings left their mark on the monastery: João's son, King Duarte, ordered a royal pantheon behind the apse, and Manueline additions include the Unfinished Chapels and much of the decoration of the abbey buildings.

Chapterhouse
Guards keep watch by the To... of the Unknown Soldiers bene... David Huguet's striking star-vaulted ceiling.

★ Royal Cloister
Gothic arches by Afonso Domingues and David Huguet around the cloister are embellished by Manueline tracery (see pp20–21) to achieve a harmony of form and decoration.

The lavabo, where monks washed their hands before and after meals, contains a fountain built around 1450.

Refectory

Main entrance

Portal
The portal was decorated by Huguet with religious motifs and statues of the apostles in intricate late Gothic style.

Sᴛᴀʀ Fᴇᴀᴛᴜʀᴇs

★ **Founder's Chapel**

★ **Royal Cloister**

★ **Unfinished Chapels**

★ Unfinished Chapels

Begun under King Duarte, the octagonal mausoleum was abandoned by Manuel I in favour of the Jerónimos monastery in Belém (see pp106–7).

VISITORS' CHECKLIST

Road map C4. Mosteiro de Santa Maria da Vitória, Batalha. **C** 244-76 54 97. from Lisbon, Leiria, Porto de Mós & Fátima. 9am–6pm (Oct–Mar: 5pm) daily. 1 Jan, Easter, 1 May, 24 & 25 Dec.

The stained-glass window behind the choir dates from 1514.

Manueline Portal

Most of the decoration of the Unfinished Chapels dates from the reign of Manuel I. This delicate portal was carved in 1509 by Mateus Fernandes.

Lofty nave by Afonso Domingues

The chapel is topped by an octagonal lantern.

★ Founder's Chapel

The tomb of João I and his English wife Philippa of Lancaster, lying hand in hand, was begun in 1426 by Huguet. Their son, Henry the Navigator, is also buried here.

THE BATTLE OF ALJUBARROTA

In 1383 Portugal's direct male line of descent ended with the death of Fernando I *(see pp44–5)*. Dom João, the illegitimate son of Fernando's father, was proclaimed king, but his claim was opposed by Juan of Castile. On 14 August 1385 João I's greatly outnumbered forces, commanded by Nuno Álvares Pereira, faced the Castilians on a small plateau near Aljubarrota, 15 km (9 miles) south of Batalha. João's spectacular victory ensured 200 years of independence from Spain. The monastery now stands as a symbol of Portuguese sovereignty and the power of the house of Avis.

Commander Nuno Álvares Pereira

João I's motto, *Por bem* (for good), is inscribed on his tomb.

Curved limestone gallery around the vast esplanade in front of the basilica at Fátima

Fátima ⑪

Road map C4. 🏘 *4,000.* 🚌
ℹ *Avenida Dom José Alves Correia da Silva (249-53 11 39).* 🚃 *Sat.*

THE SANCTUARY of Fátima is a devotional shrine on a prodigious scale, a pilgrim destination on a par with Santiago de Compostela in Spain or Lourdes in France. The Neo-Baroque limestone **basilica**, flanked by statues of saints, has a 65-m (213-ft) tower and an esplanade twice the size of St Peter's Square in Rome.

On 12 and 13 of May and October vast crowds of pilgrims arrive to commemorate appearances of the Virgin to three shepherd children (the three *pastorinhos*). On 13 May 1917, 10-year-old Lucia Santos and her young cousins, Jacinta and Francisco Marta, saw a shining figure in a holm oak tree. She ordered them to return to the tree on the same day for six months and by 13 October 70,000 pilgrims were with the children by the tree.

Only Lucia heard the three "Secrets of Fátima", spoken on her last appearance. The first talked of peace (this was during World War I); the second was about Russia; the third was divulged by Pope John Paul II at the Millenium, and interpreted as a message of hope. The Pope also beatified the two dead *Pastorinhos* in May 2000. Inside the basilica, begun in 1928, are the tombs of Jacinta and Francisco. Lucia, who became a Carmelite nun, is still alive today. The stained-glass windows show scenes of the sightings. In the esplanade, the **Capela das Aparições** marks the site of the apparition. Inside, the crown of the Virgin holds the bullet used in the assassination attempt on Pope John Paul II in 1981. East of the sanctuary, the childrens' homes have been preserved in the **Casa dos Pastorinhos**.

For most people, however, the most impressive sight is the intense emotion and faith of the penitents who approach the shrine on their knees. Wax limbs are burned as offerings for miracles performed by the Virgin and thousands of candles light the esplanade in the night-time masses.

🏠 **Casa dos Pastorinhos**
Aljustrel. 📞 *249-53 28 28.*
🕐 *daily.* ♿

ENVIRONS: The medieval town of **Ourém**, 10 km (6 miles) northeast of Fátima, is a walled citadel, dominated by the 15th-century castle of Ourém built by Afonso, grandson of Nuno Álvares Pereira *(see p183)*. His magnificent tomb is in the 15th-century Igreja Matriz. The town's name is said to derive from Oureana, a Moorish girl who, before she fell in love with a Christian knight and converted, was called Fátima.

Ruined secret passage connecting the towers of the castle in Ourém

Tomar ⑫

Road map C4. 🏘 *20,000.* 🚉 🚌
ℹ *Avenida Dr Cândido Madureira (249-32 24 27).* 🚃 *Fri.*

FOUNDED IN 1157 by Gualdim Pais, the first grand master of the Order of the Templars in Portugal, the town is dominated by the 12th-century castle containing the Convento de Cristo *(see pp186–7)*. The heart of this charming town is a neat grid of narrow streets. The lively shopping street, Rua Serpa Pinto, leads to the Gothic church of **São João Baptista** on Praça da República, the town's main square. The late 15th-century church has an elegant Manueline portal and is capped by an octagonal spire. Inside, there is a carved stone pulpit and 16th-century paintings including a *Last Supper* by Gregório Lopes (1490–1550). A particularly gory beheading of John the Baptist is also attributed to Lopes.

The area outside the church is the focus of the spectacular Festa dos Tabuleiros, a festival with pagan origins held

Church and clocktower of São João Baptista in Tomar's main square

in July, every two or three years, in which girls in white carry towering platters of bread and flowers on their heads. The festival has similar roots to the Festa do Espírito Santo *(see p366)*, popular in the Azores.

Nearby, in Rua Dr Joaquim Jacinto, stands one of the oldest **synagogues** in Portugal, built in 1430–60 with four tall columns and a vaulted ceiling. The building was last used as a place of worship in 1497 after which Manuel I *(see pp46–7)* banished all Jews who refused to convert to Christianity. It has since been a prison, a hay loft and a warehouse. Today, it holds a small Jewish museum, the **Museu Luso-Hebraico de Abraham Zacuto**, named after a renowned 15th-century astronomer and mathematician.

Further south stands the 17th-century church of São Francisco. Its former cloisters now house the **Museu dos Fósforos**, a match museum proudly boasting the largest collection in Europe – over 43,000 matchboxes from 104 countries of the world.

On the east side of the River Nabão, just off Rua Aquiles da Mota Lima, is the 13th-century church of **Santa Maria do Olival**, with a distinctive three-storey belltower. Restored various times over the centuries, the church preserves its Gothic façade and rose window. Inside are the graves of Gualdim Pais (died 1195) and other Templar Masters, and an elegant Renaissance pulpit. The church once had significance far beyond Tomar as the mother church for mariners in the Age of Discovery.

Heading north, Rua Santa Iria takes you to the **Capela de Santa Iria**, beside the 15th-century bridge, **Ponte Velha**. This Renaissance chapel is said to have been built where the saint was martyred in the 7th century *(see p191)*. A powerful stone retable depicting *Christ on the Cross* (1536) stands

Tomar's main shopping street, Rua Serpa Pinto, overlooked by the castle

above the altar in the Capela dos Vales. On an island in the river the shaded **Parque do Mouchão** is a pleasant walk; an allegedly Roman water-wheel turns with the passing water. Continuing northwards, past the octagonal 16th-century **Ermida de São Gregório** with its wild Manueline doorway, a huge flight of steps leads to a 17th-century chapel, **Nossa Senhora da Piedade**.

On the slopes of the hill leading up to the Convento do Cristo is the Renaissance basilica, **Nossa Senhora da Conceição**, built between 1530 and 1550. Its exterior simplicity contrasts with the elegantly proportioned and delicately carved Corinthian columns of the interior. The architect is believed to be Francisco de Holanda (1517–84), who worked for King João III.

🏛 **Museu Luso-Hebraico de Abraham Zacuto**
Rua Joaquim Jacinto. 📞 *249-32 26 01*. ⬜ *daily.* ⬤ *public hols.*
🏛 **Museu dos Fósforos**
Largo 5 de Outubro. 📞 *249-32 26 01*. ⬜ *daily.* ⬤ *public hols.* ♿

Pulpit in Santa Maria do Olival

THE ORDER OF CHRIST

During the 12th and 13th centuries, the crusading Order of the Knights Templar helped the Portuguese in battle against the Moorish "infidels". In return they were rewarded with extensive lands and political power. Castles, churches and towns sprang up under their protective mantle. In 1314, Pope Clement V was forced to suppress this rich and powerful Order, but in Portugal King Dinis turned it into the Order of Christ, which inherited the property and privileges of the Templars.

Cross of the Order of Christ

Ideals of Christian expansion were revived in the 15th century when their Grand Master, Prince Henry the Navigator, invested the order's revenue in exploration. The emblem of the order, the squared cross, adorned the sails of the caravels that crossed the uncharted waters *(see pp46–7)*.

Tomar: Convento de Cristo

Founded in 1162 by the Grand Master of the Templars, the Convent of Christ still retains some reminders of these monk-knights and the inheritors of their mantle, the Order of Christ *(see p185)*. Under Henry the Navigator, the Governor of the Order from 1418, cloisters were built between the Charola and the Templars' fortress, but it was the reign of João III (1521–57) that saw the

St Jerome, south portal

greatest changes. Architects such as João de Castilho and Diogo de Arruda, engaged to express the Order's power and royal patronage in stone, built the church and cloisters with dazzling Manueline flourishes, which reached a crescendo with the window in the west front of the church.

★ **Manueline Window**
Marine motifs entwine round this elaborate window. The carving at the base is thought to be either the architect (see p20) or the Old Man of the Sea.

Cloister of the Crows, flanked by an aqueduct

★ **Great Cloister**
Begun in the 1550s, probably by Diogo de Torralva, this cloister reflects João III's passion for Italian art. Concealed spiral stairways in the corners lead to the Terrace of Wax.

The "Bread" Cloister
was where loaves were handed out to the poor who came to beg at the monastery.

The Terrace of Wax, where honeycombs were left to dry

THE CHAROLA

The nucleus of the monastery is the 12th-century Charola, the Templars' oratory. Like many of their temples, its layout is based on the Rotunda of Jerusalem's Holy Sepulchre, with a central octagon of altars. In 1356, Tomar became the headquarters of the Order of Christ in Portugal, and the Charola's decoration reflects the Order's wealth. The paintings and frescoes (mostly 16th-century biblical scenes) and the gilded statuary below the Byzantine cupola have undergone much careful restoration.

The gilded octagon

When the Manueline church was built, an archway was created in the side of the Charola to link the two, making the Charola the church's main chapel.

STAR FEATURES

★ **Charola**

★ **Manueline Window**

★ **Great Cloister**

Manueline Church
Diogo de Arruda's church, begun in the early 16th century, is on two levels: this is the upper choir. The ornate ribbed vaulting incorporates the insignia and initials of Manuel I.

VISITORS' CHECKLIST

15 minute walk from Tomar centre. 249-31 50 89. from Lisbon, Coimbra & Leiria. Jun–Sep: 9:30am–6:30pm, daily; Oct–Apr: 9am–5:30pm, daily (last adm: 30 mins before closing). 1 Jan, Easter, 1 May, 25 Dec. (no flash/tripod).

★ Charola
The original Templar church, sometimes called the Rotunda, was built in the shape of a 16-sided drum.

Internal octagon of the Charola

Cemetery Cloister
Monks' tombstones pave the perimeter of this early 15th-century cloister, the first to be built here. In one corner stands a well.

The Laundry Cloister was built around a pair of large reservoirs, today planted with flowers.

Ruins of the former royal quarters

The south portal is initialled by João de Castilho.

Entrance

Castle keep

Templar Castle
In 1160 the Templars' Grand Master built this castle on land given to the Order for services in battle.

The defensive walls of the early 13th-century fortress at Abrantes

Barragem do Castelo de Bode ⑬

Road map C4. ▦ *to dam.* ▦ *from Castanheira.* 🚌 *Tomar (249-32 24 27).*

PERHAPS THERE ONCE was a "Castle of the Billygoat", but today the name refers to a large dam *(barragem)* that blocks the flow of the River Zêzere 10 km (6 miles) upstream from its confluence with the Tagus. Construction of the dam began in 1946 to serve the first of Portugal's hydroelectric power stations. Above the dam, a long, sprawling lake nestles between hills covered in pine and eucalyptus forests in which lie small, isolated villages. The valley is a secluded area popular for boating, fishing and water sports and it is possible to hire equipment from centres along the lake shore. Canoes, windsurf boards and water skis can be found at the Centro Naútico do Zêzere,

in Castanheira on the western side of the lake, and yachting facilities are usually available from the lakeside hotels such as the peaceful Estalagem Lago Azul *(see p386).* A cruise can also be taken from the hotel, stopping at the sandy beaches and the small islands.

Abrantes ⑭

Road map C4. 🏠 *15,000.* 🚉 🚌
🛈 *Esplanada 1° de Maio (241-362 555).* 🕯 *Mon.*

GRANDLY SITUATED above the Tagus, the town was once of strategic importance. It had a vital role in the Reconquest *(see pp42–3),* and during the Peninsular War *(see p54)* both the French General Junot and the Duke of Wellington made it a base. The ruined **fortress** that overlooks the town and the surrounding flatlands is a reminder of its status.

The 15th-century church of Santa Maria do Castelo, within the castle walls, is now the small **Museu Dom Lopo de Almeida**. Besides local archaeological finds, it houses the tombs of the Almeida family, counts of Abrantes. On Rua da República, the **Misericórdia** church, constructed in 1584, has six magnificent religious panels attributed to Gregório Lopes (1490–1550).

🏛 **Museu Dom Lopo de Almeida**
Rua Capitão Correia de Lacerda.
🅲 *241-37 17 24.* 🕙 *daily.*

Whitewashed houses in Constância above the banks of the Tagus

ENVIRONS: The 16th-century church of São Tiago e São Mateus, in the unspoiled town of **Sardoal**, 8 km (5 miles) north of Abrantes, holds a compelling thorn-crowned Christ by the 16th-century painter, the Master of Sardoal. An 18th-century tile panel on the façade of the Capela do Espírito Santo, in Praça da República, honours Gil Vicente, the 16th-century playwright born here.

The pretty whitewashed town of **Constância**, 12 km (7 miles) west of Sardoal, nurtures the memory of the poet Luís Vaz de Camões. Sent away from court for misbehaving with a court lady, he lived here briefly after 1546. The **Casa Memória de Camões**, the poet's home on the river bank, can be visited.

🏠 **Casa Memória de Camões**
Rua do Tejo. 🅲 *249-739 536.*
🕙 *call for opening times.*

LUÍS VAZ DE CAMÕES (1524–80)

The author of Portugal's celebrated epic poem, *Os Lusíadas*, had a passionate nature and was often in trouble. Banished from court, he enlisted in 1547 and set sail for North Africa, where he lost an eye. Imprisoned after another brawl, he agreed to serve his country in India, but his was the only ship from the fleet to survive the stormy seas. This experience gave his subsequent poem its vibrant power. A unique record of the Discoveries, this Classical-style epic charts the voyage of Vasco da Gama to India and recounts events and legends from Portuguese history. There was to be no success for Camões, however, and he passed bleak years in India yearning for Lisbon. His poem was published in 1572 but he died almost unnoticed.

Statue of Camões on the river bank at Constância

Castelo de Almourol ⑮

Road map C4. ⬜ *to Barquinha then taxi then ferry.* ⬜ *daily during daylight hours.* ℹ️ *Praça da República, Barquinha (249-72 03 50).*

The evocative ruins of the island fortress of Almourol

DRAMATICALLY SET on a tiny island in the Tagus, this enchanting castle was built over a Roman fortress in 1171 by Gualdim Pais (*see p185*). Legends of this magical place abound. A 16th-century verse romance called *Palmeirim de Inglaterra* weaves a tale of giants and knights and the fight of the crusader Palmeirim for the lovely Polinarda. Some say the castle is haunted by the ghost of a princess sighing for the love of her Moorish slave.

Over the centuries, the castle, surrounded by ramparts and nine towers, has never been taken by invading forces.

Torres Novas ⑯

Road map C4. 🏠 *16,000.* ⬜ ℹ️ *Largo dos Combatentes 4–5 (249-81 30 19).* 🚌 *Tue.*

ANIMATED STREETS and many fine churches cluster beneath the castle walls of this handsome town. The ruins of the 12th-century **fortress**, scene of bitter fighting between Moors and Christians during the Reconquest, now enclose a garden. Just below the castle is the 16th-century **Misericórdia** church with a Renaissance portal and an interior lined with colourful "carpet" *azulejos* from 1674. The **Igreja de Santiago**, on Largo do Paço, was probably built in 1203, although tiles and a gilded retable with a wood carving of the young Jesus assisting Joseph in his carpentry are 17th-century additions.

In the centre of town is the **Museu Municipal de Carlos Reis**, named after the painter Carlos Reis (1863–1940) who was born here. The museum contains paintings by 19th- and early 20th-century artists, a 15th-century Gothic figure of Nossa Senhora do Ó, as well as coins and bronze and ceramic artefacts from the Roman ruins at Vila Cardílio.

🏛 Museu Municipal de Carlos Reis
Rua do Salvador. 📞 *249-81 25 35.* ⬜ *Tue–Sun.*

ENVIRONS: Roman ruins dating from the 4th century AD at **Vila Cardílio**, 3 km (2 miles) southwest of Torres Novas, retain some superb mosaics and baths. On the northeast outskirts of town the **Grutas das Lapas**, large Neolithic caves, can be seen carved out of the rock. The small wetland **Reserva Natural do Paúl de Boquilobo**, 8 km (5 miles) south, between the Tagus and Almondo rivers, was declared a nature reserve in 1981. The willow trees and aquatic plants along the river shelter wildfowl in winter, and in spring it is an important nesting site for colonies of egrets and herons.

∩ Vila Cardílio
Off E.N.3. ⬜ *daily.* ♿
∩ Grutas das Lapas
Rua José Mota e Silva, Lapas. ⬜ *daily (ask for key in house opposite).*

Remains of the hypocaust, the Roman underfloor heating system, at Vila Cardílio outside Torres Novas

Portal of the Igreja Matriz in Golegã

Golegã ⑰

Road map C4. 🏠 *9,000.* 🚌
ℹ️ *Largo do Parque de Campismo
(249-976 742).* 🛒 *Wed.*

USUALLY A QUIET town, Golegã
is overrun during the first
two weeks of November by
thousands of horse enthusiasts
who throng to the colourful
annual horse fair, the Feira
Nacional do Cavalo. This coincides with the tasting of the
year's new wine on St Martin's
day (11 November). The fair
attracts Portugal's finest horses,
breeders and equestrians, while
the atmosphere is enlivened by
the joyful consumption of the
young wine and *agua-pé*
(literally, foot water).

In the centre of town, the
16th-century **Igreja Matriz**,
attributed to Diogo Boitac *(see
pp106–7)*, has an exquisite
Manueline portal and a calm
interior. The small **Museu de
Fotografia Carlos Relvas**
is housed in the elegant Art
Nouveau house and studio of
the photographer (1838–94).
A vivid modern art collection
can be seen in the **Museu de
Pintura e Escultura Martins
Correia** in the old post office.

🏛 **Museu de Fotografia
Carlos Relvas**
Largo Dom Manuel I. 📞 *249-979
050.* 🔴 *until further notice.* ♿
🏛 **Museu de Pintura e
Escultura Martins Correia**
Largo da Imaculada Conceição.
📞 *249-979 050.* 🔴 *Tue–Sun.*
🔴 *1 Jan, 25 Dec.* ♿ *to ground floor.*

Alpiarça ⑱

Road map C4. 🏠 *8,000.* 🚌
ℹ️ *Parque de Campismo de Alpiarça
(243-557 040).* 🛒 *Wed.*

SET IN THE VAST, fertile plain
known as the Lezíria, which
stretches east of the Tagus and
is famous for horse breeding,
Alpiarça is a small, neat town.
The fine twin-towered parish
church, on Rua José Relvas, is
dedicated to **Santo Eustáquio**,
patron saint of the town. Built
in the late 19th century, it
houses paintings from the 17th
century, including a charming *Divine Shepherdess* in
the sacristy in which the
young Jesus is shown
conversing with a sheep.
The stone cross in the
courtyard is dated 1515.

On the southern outskirts
of town is the striking **Casa
Museu dos Patudos** sur-
rounded by vineyards. This
was the residence of the
wealthy and cultivated José
Relvas (1858–1929), an art
collector and diplomat as well
as a politician and – briefly –
premier of the Republic. The
exterior of this eye-catching
country house, built for him
by Raúl Lino in 1905–9, has
simple whitewashed walls
and a green and white striped
spire. The colonnaded loggia,
reached via an outside staircase, is lined with colourful
azulejo panels. The museum
contains Relvas's personal collection of fine and decorative
art. Renaissance paintings include *Virgin with Child and
St John* by Leonardo da Vinci

and *Christ in the Tomb* by
Albrecht Dürer. There are also
paintings by Delacroix and
Zurbarán as well as many
works by 19th-century Portuguese artists, including 30 by
Relvas's friend, José Malhôa
(see p55). Relvas also collected
exquisite porcelain, bronzes,
furniture and Oriental rugs,
as well as early Portuguese
Arraiolos carpets, including a
particularly fine one in silk.

🏛 **Casa Museu dos Patudos**
2 km (1 mile) S, E.N.118. 📞 *243-556
444.* 🔴 *Tue–Sun.* 🔴 *public hols.* ♿

**Elegant façade of the country manor,
Quinta da Alorna, outside Almeirim**

ENVIRONS: **Almeirim**, 7 km
(4 miles) to the south, was a
favourite abode of the House
of Avis *(see pp46–7)*. Today
little of its royal past remains
and most visitors come here
to sample the famous *sopa de
pedra* (stone soup) *(see p146)*.

Many large estates and fine
stables extend across the vast
flat plains of this fertile horse
and cattle breeding area. The
Quinta da Alorna, a handsome 19th-century manor
house within walled gardens
and well known for its wines,
lies just outside Almeirim.

Tiled loggia of the Casa Museu dos Patudos, Alpiarça

he Tagus seen from the Jardim das Portas do Sol in Santarém

Santarém ⓳

Road map C4. 30,000.
Rua Capelo e Ivens 63 (243-304 479). *2nd & 4th Sun of month.*

THE LIVELY DISTRICT capital of the Ribatejo, overlooking the Tagus, has an illustrious past. To Julius Caesar it was an important bureaucratic centre, Praesidium Julium. To the Moors it was the stronghold of Xantarim – from Santa Iria, the 7th-century martyred nun from Tomar *(see pp184–5)* whose body was thrown into the River Nabão and allegedly reappeared here on the Tagus shore. To the Portuguese kings, who ousted the Moors in 1147, Santarém was a pleasing abode and the site of many gatherings of the *cortes* (parliaments).

At the centre of the old town, in Praça Sá da Bandeira, is the vast **Igreja do Seminário**, a multi-windowed Baroque edifice built by João IV for the Jesuits in 1640 on the site of a royal palace. The huge interior has a painted wooden ceiling and marble and gilt ornamentation. From here, Rua Serpa Pinto runs southeast past a cluster of older buildings. The lofty **Igreja do Marvila**, built in the 12th century and later altered, has a Manueline portal and is lined with dazzling early 17th-century diamond-patterned *azulejo* panels. The medieval, although much restored 22-m (72-ft) high **Torre das Cabaças**, stands opposite the **Museu Arqueológico**. Formerly the Romanesque church of São João de Alporão, the museum has many fine pieces covering the Roman and Moorish periods of the city's history. The star display is the elaborate tomb of Duarte de Meneses, heroic governor of Ceuta, a Christian stronghold in Morocco. He was hacked to death in 1464 in a disastrous campaign in Alcácer-Ceguer. The tomb is said to contain all that could be recovered – a single tooth.

Rua Serpa Pinto leads into Rua 5 de Outubro and up to the **Jardim das Portas do Sol**, built on the site of a Moorish castle. The gardens are enclosed by the city's medieval walls, and a terrace affords a panorama of the river and its vast meadowlands.

Returning into town, on Largo Pedro Álvares Cabral, the 14th-century **Igreja da Graça** has a spectacular rose window carved from a single stone. The church contains the tombstone of Pedro Álvares Cabral, who discovered Brazil *(see p48).* Further south, the 14th-century **Igreja do Santíssimo Milagre**, on Rua Braamcamp Freire, has a Renaissance interior and 16th-century *azulejos.* A small crystal flask in the sacristy is said to contain the blood of Christ. The belief stems from a 13th-century legend in which a holy wafer intended to help persuade a husband to stop beating his wife was miraculously transformed into blood.

Santarém is an important bullfighting centre with a modern bullring at the southwest corner of town. During the first ten days of June, the town hosts the Ribatejo Fair, Portugal's largest agricultural fair, in which there are bullfights and contests between the colourfully dressed herdsmen, *campinos.*

Museu Arqueológico
Rua Conselheiro Figueiredo Leal. *Tue–Sun.* *public hols.*

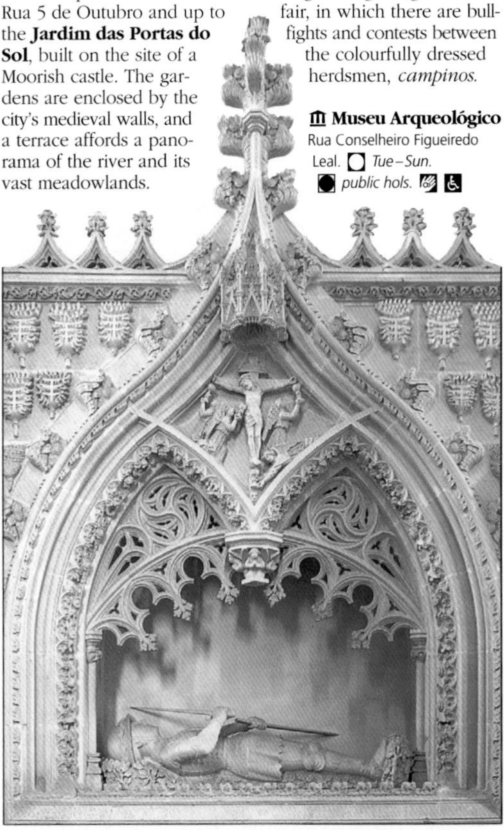

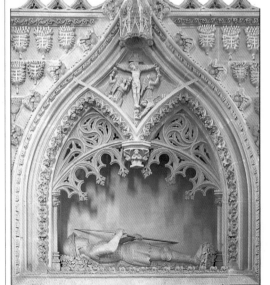

Tomb of Duarte de Meneses in the Museu Arqueológico, Santarém

Fields and vineyards in the low-lying Lezíria extending beyond Coruche

Coruche ⑳

Road map C5. 🏛 *3,500.* 🚉 🚌
🛈 *Porto João Felício (243-61 74 88).*
🛒 *last Sat of month.*

CORUCHE IS an attractive little town in the heart of the bullfighting country with a riverside location overlooking the Lezíria, the wide open plain that stretches east of the Tagus. The town, inhabited since Palaeolithic times, was razed to the ground in 1180 by the Moors as reprisal against the reconquering Christians.

In the central pedestrian street, Rua de Santarém, the **O Coruja** café is lined with vivid modern *azulejo* panels showing bulls in the Lezíria, the town's bullring and scenes of local life. A short walk up the street stands the tiny church of **São Pedro**. Its interior is completely covered with 17th-century blue and yellow carpet tiles. An *azulejo* panel on the altar front shows St Peter surrounded by birds and animals. Above the town

Chancel in the church of São Pedro covered in *azulejos*, Coruche

stands the simple 12th-century blue and white church of **Nossa Senhora do Castelo**. From here there are excellent views over the fertile agricultural land and cork oaks of the Sorraia valley and the Lezíria.

Bull-running *(largada)* in Vila Franca de Xira

Vila Franca de Xira ㉑

Road map C5. 🏛 *20,000.* 🚉 🚌
🛈 *Avenida Almirante Cândido dos Reis 147 (263-27 60 53).* 🛒 *Tue & Fri.*

SITTING BESIDE the Tagus, surrounded by the riverside industries that dominate this area, the town has a reputation larger than its modest appearance suggests. Traditionally the area has been the centre for bull and horse rearing communities. Twice a year crowds flock here to participate in the bull-running through the streets and watch the *tourada* and traditional horsemanship. The animated and gaudy Festa do Colete Encarnado (named after the red waistcoat worn by *campinos*, the Ribatejo

herdsmen) takes place over several days in early July. The festival is a lively occasion with folk dancing, boat races on the Tagus and sardines grilled in the street. A similar festival, the Feira de Outubro, takes place in October. The brightly coloured traditional costumes of the *campinos* and other exhibits related to bullfighting in Portugal are on display in the small **Museu Etnográfico**.

The town centre retains an exuberantly tiled covered **market** dating from the 1920s. Further east, on Largo da Misericórdia, striking 18th-century *azulejos* adorn the chancel of the **Misericórdia** church. South of town, the **Ponte Marechal Carmona**, built in 1951, is the only bridge across the River Tagus between Santarém to the north and Lisbon to the south.

🏛 **Museu Etnográfico**
Praça de Touros. ▌ *263-273 057.*
🔲 *Tue–Sun.* ⬤ *public hols.*

ENVIRONS: At the **Centro Equestre da Lezíria Grande** in Povos, 3 km (2 miles) south you can watch stylish displays of dressage on thoroughbred Lusitanian horses *(see p296).*

⬤ **Centro Equestre da Lezíria Grande**
E.N.1. ▌ *263-275 279.* 🔲
Tue–Sun. ⬤ *1 Jan, Easter, 25 Dec.*

Alenquer 22

Road map C5. 🚶 4,000. ☷
🛈 Avenida 25 de Abril (263-711 122). ☷ 2nd Mon of month.

V ILA ALTA, the old part of town, climbs steeply up the slopes of the hillside, high above the newer town by the river. In the central Praça Luís de Camões, the 15th-century church of **São Pedro** contains the tomb of the humanist chronicler and native son, Damião de Góis (1501–74). Pêro de Alenquer, a navigator for the explorers Bartolomeu Dias in 1488 and Vasco da Gama in 1497 (see pp48–9), was also born here. Uphill, near the ruins of a 13th-century castle, the monastery church of **São Francisco** retains a Manueline cloister and a 13th-century portal. Founded in 1222, during the saint's lifetime, this was the first Franciscan monastery in Portugal.

ENVIRONS: At **Meca**, 5 km (3 miles) northwest, is the huge pilgrimage church of Santa Quitéria, where a blessing of animals takes place each May.

Defensive walls and the castle overlooking Torres Vedras

Torres Vedras 23

Road map B5. 🚶 30,000. ☷ ☷
🛈 Rua 9 de Abril (261-31 40 94). ☷ 3rd Mon of month.

T HE TOWN IS CLOSELY linked with the Lines of Torres Vedras, fortified defenses built by the Duke of Wellington to repel Napoleon's troops during the Peninsular War (see p54). North of the town, near the restored fort of **São Vicente**, traces of trenches and bastions are still visible, but along most of the lines the forts and earthworks have gone, buried by time and rapid change.

Above the town, the restored walls of the 13th-century **castle** embrace a shady garden and the church of Santa Maria do Castelo. Down in the town, on Praça 25 de Abril, a memorial to those who died in the Peninsular War stands in front of the 16th-century Convento da Graça. Today the monastery houses the well-lit **Museu Municipal**. A room devoted to the Peninsular War displays a model of the lines; other interesting exhibits include a 15th-century Flemish School Retábulo da Vida da Virgem. Open for mass at weekends, the monastery church, **Igreja da Graça**, has a 17th-century gilded altarpiece. In a niche in the chancel is the tomb of São Gonçalo de Lagos (see p320).

Beyond the pedestrian Rua 9 de Abril, the Manueline church of **São Pedro** greets the visitor with an exotic winged dragon on the portal. The interior has a painted wooden ceiling, and colourful 18th-century azulejo panels depicting scenes of daily life adorn the walls. Behind the church, on Rua Cândido dos Reis, is a 16th-century water fountain, the **Chafariz dos Canos**.

🏛 **Museu Municipal**
Praça 25 de Abril. 📞 261-31 04 84.
🕐 Tue–Sun. 🔴 public hols. 📷

THE LINES OF TORRES VEDRAS

In October 1809, to save Lisbon from Napoleonic invasion, Arthur Wellesley (later the Duke of Wellington) ordered an arc of defensive lines (Linhas de Torres) to be built. When complete, over 600 guns and 152 redoubts (masonry forts) lay along two lines stretching from the sea to the River Tagus. One was 46 km (29 miles) long, from the Sizandra river mouth, west of Torres Vedras, to Alhandra, south of Vila Franca de Xira. The second line, running behind the first as far as the sea, was 39 km (24 miles) long. A short third line covered the possibility of retreat and embarkation. Construction of the lines took place in extraordinary secrecy: rivers had to be dammed, earthworks raised, hills shifted and homes and farms demolished, but within a year the chain of hilltop fortresses was complete. On 14 October 1810, General Masséna, at the head of 65,000 French troops, saw with astonishment the vastly altered and fortified landscape and realized it was impregnable. In November, the invaders fell back to Santarém (see p191) and in 1811, suffering hunger and defeat, withdrew beyond the Spanish border.

Flintlock pistol from Peninsular War

Portrait of the Duke of Wellington, 1814

THE BEIRAS

STRETCHING FROM THE SPANISH FRONTIER *to the sea, the Beiras are a bulwark between the cool green north and the parched south. This diverse region encompasses the heights of the Serra da Estrela and the salt marshes of the Ria de Aveiro, and its towns vary from lively Figueira da Foz to the stately old university town of Coimbra.*

The three provinces of the Beiras may not be a hub of tourism, but their past commercial and defensive significance has left its mark. In Beira Litoral, the elaborate prows of Aveiro's seaweed boats are a legacy of trade with the Phoenicians. All over Beira Baixa, from its capital, Castelo Branco, to little granite villages, there are relics of early foreign occupations, and Viseu, Beira Alta's capital, grew up at a crossroads of trading routes used by the Romans.

The Romans were never as firmly entrenched here as further south, but the ruins of Conímbriga speak eloquently of the elegant city that once stood here, and which gave its name to Coimbra, the principal city of Beira Litoral. Afonso Henriques, as king of the new nation of Portugal *(see p42)*, moved his court to Coimbra, the young country's capital for over a century.

The upheavals of the nation's founding and a hard-won independence have left a rich heritage of castles and fortified towns. Conscious of Spain's proximity and claim on their land, successive Portuguese kings constructed a great defensive chain of forts along the vulnerable eastern border. The seemingly impregnable walls of Almeida still stand as a reminder of the region's unsettled history. These border fortresses continued to prove vital in the fight for independence from Spain in the 17th century, and again against Napoleon's forces *(see p54)*. Even Buçaco, revered for the peace and sanctity of its forest, is known also as the site of Wellington's successful stand against Masséna.

Despite the unforgiving terrain and 20th-century depopulation, the Beiras are the source of some gastronomic treats: Portugal's favourite cheese is made in the Serra da Estrela, and the lush Bairrada district around Mealhada is renowned for its *leitão*, sucking pig. The region's red wines are among Portugal's best known: rich Bairradas and the oaky Dãos *(see pp28–9)*.

Distinctive candy-striped beach houses in Costa Nova, between the Ria de Aveiro and the sea

◁ **A stone *pelourinho* (pillory) in a quiet corner of Castelo Mendo, one of the border towns in Beira Alta**

Exploring the Beiras

THE BEIRAS, ENCOMPASSING some of Portugal's finest scenery, comprise three regions. Along the Beira Litoral are the sleepy backwaters of the Ria de Aveiro and, in contrast, the busy seaside resort of Figueira da Foz. The stately old university city of Coimbra repays exploration, and is a convenient base for visiting the historic forest of Buçaco and several of Portugal's spas.

Inland lies Viseu, the charming capital of Beira Alta, on the route to the medieval strongholds of Guarda, Trancoso and the border castles. The country's highest mountains, the Serra da Estrela, separate the Beira Alta from the little-visited Beira Baixa, where Monsanto, voted "most Portuguese village", and the handsome little city of Castelo Branco are contrasting attractions.

Coimbra's Museu Nacional Machado de Castro, with a fine sculpture collection

SIGHTS AT A GLANCE

Almeida ㉒
Arganil ⑭
Arouca ①
Aveiro pp200–1 ④
Belmonte ㉖
Buçaco pp210–11 ⑫
Caramulo ⑰
Castelo Branco ㉛
Celorico da Beira ㉑
Coimbra pp202–7 ⑧
Coneímbriga ⑨
Figueira da Foz ⑥
Guarda ㉔
Idanha-a-Velha ㉚
Lousã ⑪
Luso ⑬
Monsanto ㉙
Montemor-o-Velho ⑦
Oliveira do Hospital ⑯
Ovar ③
Penamacor ㉘
Penela ⑩
Piodão ⑮
Praia de Mira ⑤
Sabugal ㉗
Santa Maria da Feira ②
Sernancelhe ⑲
Serra da Estrela pp218–19 ㉕
Trancoso ⑳
Viseu ⑱

Tours
Border Castles Tour ㉓

0 kilometres   25

0 miles   15

Summer at the seaside in popular Figueira da Foz

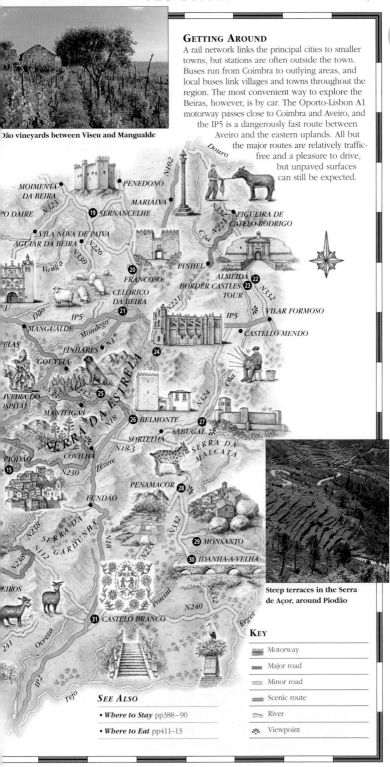

Dão vineyards between Viseu and Mangualde

GETTING AROUND

A rail network links the principal cities to smaller towns, but stations are often outside the town. Buses run from Coimbra to outlying areas, and local buses link villages and towns throughout the region. The most convenient way to explore the Beiras, however, is by car. The Oporto-Lisbon A1 motorway passes close to Coimbra and Aveiro, and the IP5 is a dangerously fast route between Aveiro and the eastern uplands. All but the major routes are relatively traffic-free and a pleasure to drive, but unpaved surfaces can still be expected.

MOIMENTA DA BEIRA
PENEDONO
MARIALVA
O DAIRE
SERNANCELHE 19
FIGUEIRA DE CASTELO RODRIGO
VILA NOVA DE PAIVA
AGUIAR DA BEIRA
PINHEL
FRANCOSO 20
ALMEIDA 22
BORDER CASTLES TOUR 23
CELORICO DA BEIRA
MANGUALDE 21
VILAR FORMOSO
LINHARES
CASTELLO MENDO
GOUVEIA
24
IVEIRA DO OSPITAL
25
MANTEIGAS
26 BELMONTE 27
SORTELHA
SABUGAL
SERRA DA ESTRELA
SERRA DA MALCATA
PIODÃO
15
COVILHÃ
PENAMACOR 28
FUNDÃO
SERRA DA GARDUNHA
MONSANTO 29
IDANHA-A-VELHA 30
EIROS
CASTELO BRANCO 31

Steep terraces in the Serra de Açor, around Piodão

KEY

▨▨▨	Motorway
▬▬	Major road
▬	Minor road
▨▨	Scenic route
⌐⌐	River
☼	Viewpoint

SEE ALSO

• **Where to Stay** pp388–90

• **Where to Eat** pp411–13

Arouca ❶

Road map C2. 🏛 2,400. 🚌
🛈 Praça Brandão de Vasconcelos
(256-94 35 75). 🛋 5 & 20 of month.

THIS SMALL TOWN in a green
valley owes its principal
attraction, the great **Convento
de Arouca**, to its saintly royal
benefactor, Mafalda. Princess
Mafalda was born in 1195, the
daughter of Sancho I. She was
betrothed to the teenage Prince
Enrique of Castile, but when
he died in an accident, Mafalda
took the veil in Arouca. Under
her, the convent became
Cistercian and Mafalda's
wealth and dedication
made the house highly
influential. She died in
1256, and her incorrupt
corpse was discovered
in 1616, leading to her
beatification in 1793.

For over a thousand
years the convent has
stood beside Arouca's
church on the cobbled
main square. In the early 18th
century the church underwent
costly redecoration: 104 carved
choir stalls are surmounted by
paintings in sumptuous gilded
panels, and the organ and
chancel retable are also heavily
gilded. Honoured with its own
altar is a recumbent effigy of
Santa Mafalda in a silver and
ebony casket; her mummified
remains lie below the casket.

Guided tours take visitors
round the convent's museum,
in which are displayed some
exquisite silver monstrances,
furniture and religious works
of art, including two paintings
by 18th-century artist André
Gonçalves, showing Mafalda
saving the monastery from
fire. The Neo-Classical double
cloister, begun in 1781, the
large refectory and kitchen and
a chapterhouse covered with
cheerful Coimbra tiles of rural
scenes can also be visited.

🔒 Convento de Arouca
Largo de Santa Mafalda. 📞 256-94
33 21. ◯ Tue–Sun. ⬤ 1 Jan, 2 May,
25 Dec. 🖼 ✔

**Silver and ebony casket in the convent church
at Arouca, containing the effigy of Santa Mafalda**

Santa Maria
da Feira ❷

Road map C2. 🏛 10,000. 🚉 🚌
🛈 Praça da República (256-37 08
00). 🛋 20 of month.

PROSPEROUS FROM CORK and
its thriving markets, Santa
Maria derives its name from
long tradition – a document
from 1117 refers to "Terra de
Santa Maria, a place people
call Feira", after the fairs held
here. A large market each
month in the broad Rossio
upholds the town's reputation.

A double stairway leads from
the Rossio to the **Igreja dos
Lóios**, with blue 17th-century
tiles decorating the façades of
its two symmetrical belltowers.
On the opposite side of the
Rossio, winding streets of solid
merchants' houses from the
18th and 19th centuries lead
to a decorative stairway with
an ornamental fountain. This
rises up to the 18th-century
Misericórdia church.

Crowning a wooded hill on
the southern edge of the town
is the fairytale **castle**. Although
much is a 20th-century reconstruction, it follows the
15th-century design of a
local, Fernão Pereira, and
his son. They added
crenellations and towers
to an 11th-century fort
which in turn had been
built over a temple to
a local god. The title of
Conde da Feira was bes-
towed on Pereira, and
the castle remained in his
family until 1700. There
is not much inside the castle
now, but it retains its
romantic air.

♦ Castle
Largo do Castelo. 📞 256-37 22 48.
◯ Tue–Sun. 🖼

Ovar ❸

Road map C2. 🏛 14,000. 🚉 🚌
🛈 Rua Elias Garcia (256-57 22 15).
🛋 Tue, Thu & Sat (general), 3rd Sun
of month (antiques).

VARINAS, the hardworking
Portuguese fishwives, take
their name from Var, or O Var,
this small town which earned
its living from the sea and the
Ria de Aveiro that spreads out
to the south (see p201). Industry has arrived in the shape of
foundries and steel mills, but
oxen still plod along the roads.

Gleaming tiles cover many
of the small houses, as well as
the twin-towered 17th-century
Igreja Matriz in Avenida do
Bom Reitor. In the town centre
the Calvary chapel of the 18th-
century **Capela dos Passos**
is adorned with woodcarvings
carrying a shell motif.

Ovar's Carnaval parade is
one of the most colourful in
Portugal, and its sponge cake,

The pinnacled and crenellated castle crowning Santa Maria da Feira

House façades in Ovar with their traditional eye-catching blue tiles

pão-de-ló, is highly esteemed. Tableaux in the **Museu de Ovar** recreate the lifestyle of a bygone era, alongside displays of regional costume and dolls. There are also mementoes of Júlio Dinis, a popular Portuguese novelist who lived in Ovar in the 19th century.

🏛 **Museu de Ovar**
Rua Heliodoro Salgado 11. 📞 256-57 28 22. ☐ Mon–Sat. ● public hols. 📷

Aveiro ❹

See pp200–1.

Praia de Mira ❺

Road map C3. 🏠 5,000. 🚌
ℹ Praça da República (231-47 11 00). 🎡 11 & 30 of month.

Fishing boat on the beach at Praia de Mira

TOURISM IS ONLY NOW making an impact on this stretch of coast backed by a wooded reserve, the Mata Nacional das Dunas de Mira. Praia de Mira, with the dunes and Atlantic on one side and the peaceful lagoon of Barrinha de Mira on the other, is a pretty fishing village developing as a resort. High-prowed fishing boats are still drawn up the spectacular beach by oxen, but leisure craft now cruise the shore and the

inland waterways, and the fishermen's striped *palheiros* (*see p18*), popular as seaside cottages, are fast vanishing amid shops, bars and cafés.

Figueira da Foz ❻

Road map C3. 🏠 35,000. 🚉 🚌 ℹ Avenida 25 de Abril (233-40 28 27). 🎡 daily.

LIVELY AND COSMOPOLITAN, if somewhat timeworn, this popular resort has a bustling marina, a casino and a wide, curving beach with breakers that attract intrepid surfers.

Although general jollity is the keynote, the town's **Museu Municipal Dr Santos Rocha** has a notable archaeological collection, and an eclectic display extending to Arraiolos carpets (*see p301*), a musical archive, fans and photographs.

The **Casa do Paço** has an amazing interior lined with 8,000 Delft tiles taken from a shipwreck in the late 17th century. Where the Mondego meets the sea stands the 16th-century fortress of **Santa Catarina**. The Duke of Wellington briefly made this little fort his base when he landed to retake Portugal from Napoleon in 1808 (*see p54*).

🏛 **Museu Municipal Dr Santos Rocha**
Rua Calouste Gulbenkian.
📞 231-40 28 40. ☐ 9:30am–5:15pm Tue–Sun. ● public hols.
🏛 **Casa do Paço** Largo Professor Vitor Guerra. 📞 233-42 21 59.
☐ 9am–5pm Mon–Fri.
● public hols.

Montemor-o-Velho ❼

Road map C3. 🏠 2,600. 🚌
ℹ Castelo de Montemor-o-Velho (239-68 03 80). 🎡 every other Wed.

THIS ATTRACTIVE and historic hillside town rises out of fields of rice and maize beside the River Mondego. Its **castle**, which served as a primary defence of the city of Coimbra (*see pp202–7*) is mostly 14th century, but it had previously been a Moorish stronghold, and the keep has fragments of Roman stonework. The church of **Santa Maria de Alcaçova** within its walls was founded in 1090. Restored in the 15th century, its naves and arches reflect the Manueline style.

Montemor was the birthplace of Fernão Mendes Pinto (1510–83), famous for the colourful accounts of his travels in the east. Another explorer, Diogo de Azambuja (died 1518), is buried here. Columbus is said to have sailed with Azambuja, who intrepidly navigated along the West African coast. His tomb, by the Manueline master Diogo Pires, is in the **Convento de Nossa Senhora dos Anjos** in the square of the same name (ask at the tourist office for key). Its 17th-century façade hides an earlier, more lavish interior, with Manueline and Renaissance influences.

♣ **Castle**
Rua do Castelo. ☐ Tue–Sun.

Enjoying café life in the spring sunshine of Figueira da Foz

Aveiro ❹

Tᴴɪꜱ ʟɪᴛᴛʟᴇ ᴄɪᴛʏ, once a great sea port, has a long history – Aveiro's salt pans were featured in the will of Countess Mumadona in AD 959. By the 16th century it was a considerable town, rich from salt and the *bacalhoeiros* fishing for cod off Newfoundland. When storms silted up the harbour in 1575 this wealth vanished rapidly, and the town languished beside an unhealthy lagoon, the *ria*. Only in the 19th century did Aveiro regain some of its prosperity; it is now ringed with industry and is home to an important university. The *ria* and canals give Aveiro its individual character.

Wooden barrel of *ovos moles*

Old Quarter

Tucked in between the Canal das Pirâmides and the Canal de São Roque are the neat, whitewashed houses of Aveiro's fishermen. In the early morning the focus of activity is the **Mercado do Peixe**, where the fish from the night's catch is auctioned.

Skirting the Canal Central, along Rua João de Mendonça, are Art Nouveau mansions and some of the many *pastelarias* selling Aveiro's speciality: *ovos moles*. Literally "soft eggs", these are a rich confection of sweetened egg yolk in candied casings shaped like fish or barrels. As so often in Portugal, the original recipe is credited to nuns. *Ovos moles* are sold by weight or in little barrels.

Bridge across the Canal de São Roque

Across the Canal Central

South of the Canal Central and the bustling Praça Humberto Delgado are the principal historic buildings of Aveiro. The **Misericórdia** church in the Praça da República dates from the 16th century, its façade of *azulejos* framing a splendid Mannerist portal. In the same square stands the stately 18th-century **Paços do Concelho**, or town hall, with its distinctive Tuscan-style pilasters.

Nearby, opposite the museum is Aveiro's modest 15th-century cathedral of **São Domingos**. The figures of the Three Graces over the door on the Baroque façade were added in 1719.

A short walk south lies the **Igreja das Carmelitas**, its nave and chancel decorated with paintings of the life of the Carmelite reformer, St Teresa.

🏛 Museu de Aveiro

Rua de Santa Joana Princesa.
📞 234-423 297. ⏱ 10am–5:15pm Tue–Sun. 🖼

The former Mosteiro de Jesus is full of mementoes of Santa Joana, who died here in 1490. The daughter of Afonso V, Joana retreated to the convent in 1472 and spent the rest of her life here. She was beatified in 1693 and her ornamental Baroque marble tomb, completed 20 years later, is in the lower choir. Simpler in style are the 18th-century paintings in the chapel, showing scenes of her life. This was once the needlework room where Santa Joana died. Among Portuguese primitive paintings is a superb 15th-century full-face portrait of the princess in court dress.

Also part of the museum are the superb gilded chancel (1725–9), 15th-century cloisters and refectory faced in Coimbra tiles. Between the refectory and chapterhouse lies the Gothic tomb of an armoured knight, Dom João de Albuquerque.

Colourful seaweed-collecting *moliceiros* moored along the Canal Central

Raking the salt as it dries in the pans fringing the Ria de Aveiro

ENVIRONS: Lying about 8 km (5 miles) south of Aveiro, at Ílhavo, is the modern block of the **Museu Marítimo e Regional de Ílhavo**, where the region's long seafaring history is told through displays of fishing craft and equipment, with maritime memorabilia from shells to model boats.

About 4 km (2 miles) further south a small sign points to the **Museu Histórico da Vista Alegre**. A name renowned in the world of porcelain *(see p24)*, the Vista Alegre factory was established in 1824 and samples of its fine porcelain can be bought from the factory shop. The museum traces the history of the factory, and has displays of porcelain (together with some crystal glass) from the 1850s to the present day.

VISITORS' CHECKLIST

Map C3. 70,000. Avenida Dr Lourenço Peixinho. Avenida Dr Lourenço Peixinho. Rua João Mendonça 8 (234-423 680). 14 & 28 of month. Jul–Aug: Festa da Ria. Aveiro–Torreira: once daily (Jun–Sep).

Museu Marítimo e Regional de Ílhavo
Avenida Rocha Madahil.
234-32 96 08. 9am–12:30pm, 2–5:30pm Wed– Sat, Tue & Sun pm. public hols.
Museu Histórico da Vista Alegre Signposted off N109.
234-32 07 60. for works.

RIA DE AVEIRO

Old maritime charts show no lagoon here, but in 1575 a terrible storm raised a sand bar that blocked the harbour. Denied access to the sea, Aveiro declined, its population cut down by the fever bred in the stagnant waters. It was not until 1808 that the *barra nova* was created, linking Aveiro once more to the sea.

The lagoon which remains covers some 65 sq km (25 sq miles), and is nearly 50 km (30 miles) long, from Furadouro south past Aveiro's salt pans and the nature reserve of São Jacinto to Costa Nova. Of the boats seen here the most elegant is the *moliceiro*. Despite the bright, often humorous, decoration on its high, curving prow, this is a working boat, harvesting *moliço* (seaweed) for fertilizer. Chemical fertilizers have drastically cut demand for *moliço*, but a few of the stately craft survive; the Festa da Ria is a chance to see them in full sail.

In summer a daily boat trip between Aveiro and Torreira explores this unique backwater, known as the Rota da Luz, the "route of light" running between gleaming salt flats, pale beaches and sparkling ocean.

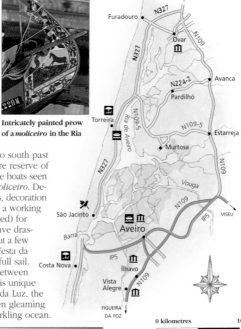

Intricately painted prow of a *moliceiro* in the Ria

The seaward waterfront at the fishing village of Torreira

KEY

Motorway
Major road
Minor road
Other road
Boat trips
Salt marsh

Coimbra ●

Tᴴᴇ ʙɪʀᴛʜᴘʟᴀᴄᴇ ᴏꜰ ꜱɪx ᴋɪɴɢꜱ and the seat of Portugal's oldest university, Coimbra arouses an affection in the Portuguese shared by no other city. To the Romans the town founded on Alcaçova hill was Aeminium, but as its importance grew it took on the mantle and name of nearby Coní2mbriga (see p208). Coimbra was wrested from the Moors in AD 878, only to come under their control again a century later, until finally freed by Ferdinand the Great of Castile in 1064. When Afonso Henriques, the first king of Portugal, decided to move his capital south from Guimarães in 1139 (see pp42–3), his choice was Coimbra, an honour it retained until 1256. For the Portuguese, Coimbra carries the roots of nationhood and, for visitors, a wealth of fascinating historic associations.

Student in May celebrations

Orientation
In the historic heart of the city, high above the Mondego, lie the cathedrals, university and a fine museum, but a first impression of Coimbra is likely to be of commerce, not culture. Shops, traffic and the railway rule the riverside and around the Praça do Comércio. The Largo da Portagem is a useful starting point, and river trips depart from nearby, alongside the Parque Dr Manuel Braga.

Tomb of Portugal's first king, Afonso Henriques, in Santa Cruz

The Lower Town
From Largo da Portagem, Rua Ferreira Borges leads past shops, lively bars, restaurants and *pastelarias* to the Praça do Comércio. In one corner of this bustling square stands the church of **São Tiago**. Its plain façade is a restoration of the 12th-century original, but inside is an exuberant Rococo altarpiece in gilded wood.

Running north of the Praça do Comércio, Rua Visconde da Luz leads to the Praça 8 de Maio and the historic church of **Santa Cruz** (see p205). Portugal's first two kings are buried here, and monks from the adjacent monastery of Santa Cruz tutored the first students at Coimbra university.

Beyond Praça 8 de Maio is Rua da Sofia, the "street of wisdom", named after the theological colleges that once stood here. The convent churches to which they were attached remain: the **Igreja do Carmo** (1597), with a 16th-century retable, and the **Igreja da Graça**, founded by João III in 1543. The nearby Pátio da Inquisição is a reminder that Coimbra, like Lisbon and Évora, was a seat in the 16th century of the fiercely intolerant Inquisition (see p51).

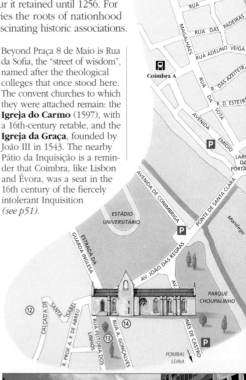

Café tables in the Praça do Comércio, overlooked by São Tiago

Pátio das Escolas, at the heart of Portugal's oldest university

VISITORS' CHECKLIST

Road map C3. ▒ *150,000*.
▒ *Coimbra A, Avenida Emídio
Navarro; Coimbra B, N of city,
on E.N.11.* ▒ *Avenida Fernão de
Magalhães.* ▒ *Praca da República
(239-83 32 02).* ▒ *Mon–Sat.*
▒ *early May: Queima das Fitas;
early Nov: Festa das Latas (a feast
to celebrate new students).*

are from the workshop of the
16th-century sculptor, Jean de
Rouen. The tower now houses
an arts and crafts gallery.

Among the houses lining the
maze of steep alleys that wind
up to the top of the hill are a
number of *repúblicas*, student
lodgings since medieval times.

Coimbra's two cathedrals, **Sé
Velha** and **Sé Nova** *(see p204)*,
lie in the shadow of the hilltop
university *(see pp206–7)*. Beyond is the upper town's main
square, Praça da República.

Across the Mondego

It is worth crossing the river
just to admire the view of
old Coimbra. The two con-
vents of **Santa Clara** *(see
p205)* on the southern
bank have close ties with
Santa Isabel, and with Inês
de Castro, Pedro I's luckless
lover, who was stabbed to
death here in 1355 *(see p179)*.
A romantic legend tells how a
spring, the **Fonte dos Amores**,
rose on the spot. This can be
seen in the garden of the 18th-
century Quinta das Lágrimas,
now a hotel *(see p389)*, just
south of Santa Clara-a-Velha.

The Upper Town

The altered and restored 12th-
century **Arco de Almedina**,
off the Rua Ferreira Borges, is
the gateway to the old city (in
Arabic *medina* means town).
Steps lead up past the **Torre
de Anto**, whose Renaissance
windows and medallions

KEY

▒	Railway station
▒	Bus station
▒	River boat service
▒ P	Parking
▒	Tourist information
▒	Church
▒	Aqueduct
▒	Steps

0 metres 200
0 yards 200

COIMBRA CITY CENTRE

Arco de Almedina ⑥
Igreja do Carmo ②
Igreja da Graça ①
Jardim Botânico ⑪
Museu Nacional Machado
    de Castro ⑧
Portugal dos Pequenitos ⑬
Santa Clara-a-Nova ⑫
Santa Clara-a-Velha ⑭
Santa Cruz ③
São Tiago ④
Sé Nova ⑨
Sé Velha ⑦
Torre de Anto ⑤
University ⑩

The Arco de Almedina arching
over the steps to the upper town

Exploring Coimbra

THAT THE CITIZENS of Coimbra fondly call their river, the Mondego, "O Rio dos Poetas" gives a clue to the affection they have for their vibrant and beautiful city. From the university *(see pp206–7)* at the top of Alcáçova hill, down the narrow streets and stairways to the lower town, the city is crammed with historic buildings and treasures (and, all too often, slow-moving traffic). Most sights are within walking distance of each other, and despite its steep hill, Coimbra is a city best appreciated on foot. Across the Mondego there are further historic sights and an unusual theme park for children.

Elaborate façade of the Sé Nova

The Sé Velha's gilded altarpiece

⛪ Sé Velha

Largo da Sé Velha. 239-82 52 73.
10am–noon, 2–6pm Sat–Thu,
10am–noon Fri. to cloister.

The fortress-style Old Cathedral is widely regarded as the finest Romanesque building in Portugal, a celebration in stone of the triumph over the Moors in 1064. The nation's first king, Afonso Henriques, made the city of Coimbra his capital and his son, Sancho I, was crowned here in 1185, soon after the cathedral was completed.

Inside, square piers lead the eye up the nave to the flamboyant retable over the altar. This was the work of Flemish woodcarvers in about 1502 depicting the birth of Christ, the Assumption and many saints. A 16th-century altarpiece in the south transept is also highly decorated, as is the Manueline font, thought to be by Diogo Pires the Younger. In contrast is the quiet restraint of the cloister, built in 1218 but restored in the 18th century.

The tomb of the city's first Christian governor, Sisinando (a Moslem convert who died in 1091), lies in the chapterhouse, and in the north aisle is the tomb of the Byzantine Dona Vetaça (died 1246), who was companion and tutor to the wife of King Dinis, the saintly Queen Isabel *(see p45)*.

⛪ Sé Nova

Largo da Feira. 239-82 31 38.
9am–noon, 2–5:30pm Tue–Fri.
public hols except for mass.

New is a relative term, as this church, a short walk from the university, was founded by the Jesuits in 1598. (Their adjacent Colégio das Onze Mil Virgens is today part of the sciences faculty.) The Jesuit Order was banned by the Marquês de Pombal in 1759 *(see p52)* but their church became the episcopal seat in 1772. Jesuit saints still look out from the façade.

The interior, more spacious than the Sé Velha, is barrel-vaulted, with a dome over the crossing. To the left of the entrance is a Manueline-style octagonal font brought, like the choir stalls, from the Sé Velha. The paintings above the stalls are copies of Italian masters. The altarpiece in the 17th-century chancel, featuring more Jesuit saints, is flanked by a pair of 18th-century organs.

Coimbra seen from the Mondego, with the university's landmark belltower crowning Alcáçova hill

🏛 Museu Nacional Machado de Castro

Largo Dr José Rodrigues. 📞 *239-82 37 27.* ⏱ *9:30am–12:30pm, 2–4:45pm Tue–Sun.* 📷

The elegant 16th-century loggias and lovely courtyards of the former bishops' palace are the setting for the display of some of Portugal's finest sculpture – Joaquim Machado de Castro (1731–1822) was himself a master sculptor. Among the medieval pieces is an endearing knight holding a mace. Also in the collection, together with furnishings and vestments, are paintings from the 12th to 20th centuries, including an early 16th-century work, *The Assumption of Mary Magdalen*, by the Master of Sardoal. An intriguing feature of the museum is the Cripto-portico de Aeminium, a maze of underground Roman passages containing a collection of Roman sculpture and stelae and Visigothic artefacts.

Claustro do Silêncio (Cloister of Silence) in the monastery of Santa Cruz

⛪ Santa Cruz

Praça 8 de Maio. 📞 *239-82 29 41.* ⏱ *9am–noon, 2–5:30pm Mon–Sat, 4–6pm Sun.* 📷 *to cloister.*

Founded in 1131, the church and monastery of Santa Cruz are rich in examples of the city's own early 16th-century school of sculpture. Carvings by Nicolau Chanterène and Jean de Rouen adorn the church's Portal da Majestade, designed by Diogo de Castilho in 1523. The chapterhouse by Diogo Boitac is Manueline in style, as are the Claustro do Silêncio and the choir stalls, carved in 1518 with a frieze on the theme of exploration. The first two kings of Portugal, Afonso Henriques and Sancho I, were reinterred here in 1520. Their elaborate tombs are thought to be by Chanterène, also buried here.

🌿 Jardim Botânico

Alameda Dr Júlio Henriques. ⏱ *daily.*

These, Portugal's largest botanical gardens, were created in 1772 when the Marquês de Pombal introduced the study of natural history at the University of Coimbra.

The entrance, near the 16th-century aqueduct of São Sebastião, leads into 20 ha (50 acres) devoted to a remarkable collection of some 1,200 plants, including many rare and exotic species. The gardens are used for research, but are laid out as pleasure gardens, with greenhouses and a wild area overlooking the Mondego.

Open-air study in the Jardim Botânico

⛪ Santa Clara-a-Velha

Santa Clara. ⏱ *for restoration.*

Santa Isabel, the widow of King Dinis, chose to rebuild the convent of Santa Clara for her retreat. She died in 1336 in Estremoz (*see p300*), but was buried here in the convent church. The murdered Inês de Castro was also laid to rest here 20 years later, but was re-entombed at Alcobaça (*see pp178–9*).

Almost from the day it was built, Santa Clara suffered from flooding the river and was finally abandoned in 1677. In 1696 Santa Isabel's remains were moved to safety in the Convent of Santa Clara-a-Nova. The original Gothic church has been in silted ruins since the end of the 17th century, but is now at last being restored.

⛪ Santa Clara-a-Nova

Calçada de Santa Isabel. 📞 *239-44 16 74.* ⏱ *9am–noon, 2–5pm Tue–Sun.* 📷 *to cloister.*

The vast "new" convent of the Poor Clares was built between 1649 and 1677 to house the nuns from Santa Clara-a-Velha on drier land uphill. The building was designed by a mathematics professor, João Turriano, and although intended as a convent, now serves in part as a barracks for the army. In the richly Baroque church, pride of place is given to the silver tomb of Santa Isabel, installed in 1696 and paid for by the people of Coimbra. The saint's original tomb, a single stone, lies in the lower choir and polychrome wooden panels in the aisles tell the story of her life. The convent's large cloister, built by the Hungarian Carlos Mardel, was contributed in 1733 by João V, a generous benefactor who was well-known for his charity to nuns.

🏛 Portugal dos Pequenitos

Santa Clara. 📞 *239-44 12 25.* ⏱ *daily.* ⬤ *25 Dec.* 📷 ♿

Markedly different in mood from the rest of Coimbra, Portugal dos Pequenitos is a children's wonderland. Here, set in a pretty park, is a world in miniature and children and adults alike can explore scaled-down versions of Portugal's finest national buildings, whole villages of typical regional architecture, and pagodas and temples representing the far-flung reaches of the former Portuguese empire.

Child-sized model of an Algarve manor house in Portugal dos Pequenitos

Coimbra University

An Atlas on the Via Latina

IN RESPONSE to an ecclesiastical petition, King Dinis founded a university, one of the world's oldest and most illustrious, in 1290. Vacillating between Lisbon and Coimbra, it was finally installed in 1537 in Coimbra's royal palace. Study was mostly of theology, medicine and law until the much-needed reforms by the Marquês de Pombal in the 1770s broadened the curriculum. A number of 19th-century literary figures, including Eça de Queirós *(see p55)*, were alumni of Coimbra. Many buildings were replaced after the 1940s, but the halls around the Pátio das Escolas echo with 700 years of learning.

Museu de Arte Sacra
As well as works of art on religious themes, the four rooms of the museum display vestments, chalices and books of early sacred music.

★ **Capela de São Miguel**
Although begun in 1517 the chapel's interior is mostly 17th and 18th century. The azulejos, ornate ceiling, even the fine Mannerist altar, are eclipsed by the dazzling organ, angels trumpeting its Baroque glory.

The portal of Capela de São Miguel is Manueline in style, the work of Marcos Pires before his death in 1521.

Portrait of João V (c.1730)

STAR FEATURES

★ **Biblioteca Joanina**

★ **Capela de São Miguel**

★ **Biblioteca Joanina**
Named after its benefactor, João V (whose coat of arms is over the door), the library was built in the early 18th century. Its rooms, rich in gilt and exotic wood, are lined with 300,000 books.

The belltower, symbol of the university, can be seen from all over the city. The best-known of its three bells, called *a cabra*, the goat, has summoned generations of students to lectures since the tower was completed in 1733.

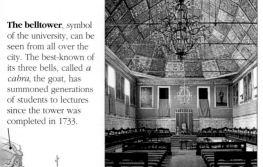

VISITORS' CHECKLIST

Universidade de Coimbra, Paço das Escolas. ☎ *239-85 98 00.* 🚌 *1 from Largo da Portagem.* ○ *9:30am–noon, 2–5pm daily.* ● *25 Dec.* ⓦ ◻

Sala Grande dos Actos
Also known as the Sala dos Capelos, this is where major events such as investitures are celebrated. Dons' benches line the walls below portraits of Portuguese monarchs.

The Via Latina is a colonnaded walkway added to the original palace in the 18th century. The Portuguese coat of arms above the double staircase is crowned by a statue of Wisdom, while below, figures of Justice and Fortitude flank José I, in whose reign (1750–77) the Marquês de Pombal modernized the university.

To ticket office

Sala do Exame Privado
José Ferreira Araújo's exuberant ceiling, painted in 1701, arcs above a frieze of portraits of past rectors in the private examination hall.

STUDENT TRADITIONS

When the university was first founded, the only subjects studied were canon and civil law, medicine and letters – grammar and philosophy. To indicate which faculty they belonged to, students began to pin coloured ribbons to their gowns: red for law, yellow for medicine, dark blue for letters. Much has changed in 700 years, but students are still initiated in rites whose origins are long forgotten, and in May, as the academic year ends, there is a ceremonial burning of ribbons, the Queima das Fitas.

Burning faculty ribbons in best scholastic tradition

Porta Férrea
Built in 1634, this heavy iron gate to the university pátio is flanked by figures representing the original faculties.

Conímbriga ❾

Road map C3. 2 km (1 mile) S of
Condeixa-a-Nova. 🚌 from Coimbra.
Site ◯ 9am–1pm, 2–8pm (Sep–Mar:
6pm) daily. ⬤ 25 Dec. **Museum**
📞 239-94 11 77. ◯ 10am–1pm,
2–7pm (Sep–Mar: 6pm) Tue–Sun.
⬤ 25 Dec. 📷 ♿ museum only.

Tᴴɪs, ᴛʜᴇ ʟᴀʀɢᴇsᴛ and most
extensively excavated
Roman site in Portugal *(see
pp40–41)*, was on the Roman
road between Lisbon (Olisipo)
and Braga (Bracara Augusta).
There is evidence of Roman
habitation as early as the 2nd
century BC, but it was under
Augustus, from
about 25 BC,
that Conímbriga
became a sub-
stantial town:
baths, a forum
and the aque-
duct have been
uncovered from
this era. The
finest buildings,
however, date
from the 2nd and 3rd centuries
AD, and they provide a vivid
image of a prosperous city.

The site is approached along
a section of Roman road that
led into the city from the east.
Just to the left cluster the out-
lines of shops, baths and two
once-luxurious houses, both
with exquisite mosaic floors.

At Conímbriga is one of the
largest houses discovered in
the western Roman empire.
This opulent villa, known as
the Casa de Cantaber, is built
around ornamental pools in
superb colonnaded gardens,

**Detail of a bedroom floor in
a house near the entrance**

with its own bath complex and
a sophisticated heating system.
Some of the fine mosaics in
the museum probably came
from this huge residence.

The Casa das Fontes, dating
from the first half of the 2nd
century, is under a protective
cover but walkways provide a
good view. Its pictorial mosaics
and fountains, rare survivals,
which give the house its name,
form a strong image of the
Roman taste for good living.
The city's pools, and the baths
and steam rooms of Trajan's
thermae, were fed by a spring
3.5 km (2 miles) away via an
aqueduct, mostly subterranean,
built in the time
of Augustus.

Official exca-
vation was begun
here in 1912, but
a considerable
part of the 13-ha
(32-acre) site has
yet to be fully ex-
plored, including
an amphitheatre
north of the city.
In the 3rd or early 4th century,
buildings were plundered for
stone as defensive walls were
hastily raised against Barbarian
hordes. In a successful assault
in AD 468, the Suevi burned
the city and murdered the inhabitants. Excavated skeletons
may date from this episode.

Just outside the ruins is an
informative museum which
explains the history and layout
of the site, and has exhibits
of Roman busts, mosaics and
coins alongside more ancient
Celtic artefacts. There is also
a restaurant and picnic site.

**View of the church of São Miguel
within the castle walls at Penela**

Penela ❿

Road map C3. 🏚 620. 🚌
🛈 Largo Marquesa dos Fornos de
Algodres (239-56 11 30). 🛍 Thu.

Pᴇɴᴇʟᴀ's ᴛʜɪᴄᴋsᴇᴛ **castle** was
built in 1087 by Sisinando,
governor of Coimbra, as part
of the line of defences of the
Mondego valley. Its squat
towers provide wonderful
views over the village and, to
the east, of the wooded Serra
da Lousã. The church within
the castle walls, **São Miguel**,
dates back to the 16th century.
Below, in Penela itself, **Santa
Eufémia**, dated 1551 above
its decorative doorway, has a
Roman capital used as a font.

Eɴᴠɪʀoɴs: Among walnut and
olive groves 5 km (3 miles) to
the west, is the tiny village of
Rabaçal, whose tasty cheese,
made with a mixture of sheep's
and goat's milk, is a regional
speciality *(see p146)*. Some
village women still mature the
cheese rounds in darkened
rooms in their homes.

Lousã ⓫

Road map C3. 🏚 9,000. 🚉 🚌
🛈 Câmara Municipal, Rua Dr João de
Cáceres (239-99 03 76). 🛍 Tue & Sat.

Tʜᴇ ᴘᴀᴘᴇʀ ꜰᴀᴄᴛoʀʏ at Lousã,
on the forested banks of
the River Arouce, was opened
in 1716 and is still working.
Skilled papermakers imported
from Italy and Germany by the
Marquês de Pombal *(see p52)*
brought prosperity, still evident
in the handsome 18th-century

The central garden of the Casa das Fontes in Conímbriga

The castle at Arouce, near Lousã, oddly defenceless in its deep valley

houses. Most elegant of these is the **Palácio dos Salazares**, a private home in Rua Viscondessa do Espinhal. Also notable is the **Misericórdia**, with a 1568 Renaissance portal, in Rua do Comércio.

ENVIRONS: Deep in a valley, 3 km (2 miles) south of Lousã, is the **Castelo de Arouce**. Legend says it was built in the 11th century by a King Arunce who took refuge in the valley when fleeing from raiders. Permission to visit the castle is available from the town hall. Near the castle are the three shrines of the **Santuário de Nossa Senhora da Piedade**.

A viewpoint on the tortuous road south towards Castanheira de Pêra gives a splendid view across the valley. A turning east leads up to **Alto do Trevim** which, at 1,204 m (3,950 ft), is the highest point in the Serra de Lousã.

Buçaco ⑫

See pp210–11.

Luso ⑬

Road map C3. 🏘 *3,000.* 🚌
🛈 *Rua Emídio Navarro (231-93 91 33).*
🛒 *Mon–Sat.*

IN THE 11TH CENTURY Luso was just a village linked to a monastery at Vacariça, but developed into a lively spa town in the 18th century as its hot-water springs became a focus for tourism. The thermal waters, which originate from a spring below the **Capela de São João**, are said to be of therapeutic value in the treatment of a wide range of conditions, from bad circulation and muscle tone to renal problems and rheumatism.

There are a number of grand, if somewhat faded, hotels here, and an elegant Art Nouveau lobby adorns the former casino, but the main reason for visiting the resort is to enjoy its spa facilities. An additional attraction of Luso is the proximity of the treasured national forest of Buçaco, which is a powerful presence above the town.

Taking the spa waters at the Fonte de São João, Luso

ENVIRONS: Between Luso and Curia, **Mealhada** is an attractive small town in the heart of a region famous for *leitão*, sucking pig *(see p146)*. This enormously popular dish is prominently advertised at numerous hotly competing restaurants in the area.

Arganil ⑭

Road map D3. 🏘 *3,000.* 🚌
🛈 *Avenida das Forças Armadas (235-20 48 23).* 🛒 *Thu.*

TRADITION SAYS that this was a Roman city called Argos. In the 12th century, Dona Teresa, the mother of Afonso Henriques *(see pp42–3)*, gave the town to the bishopric of Coimbra, whose incumbent also acquired the title of Conde de Arganil. Most of the town's architecture is unremarkable, but the church of **São Gens**, the Igreja Matriz in Rua de Visconde de Frias, dates back perhaps to the 14th century.

ENVIRONS: One of the most curious local sights is kept in the sanctuary of Mont'Alto, 3 km (2 miles) above the town. Here, the **Capela do Senhor da Ladeira** harbours the Menino Jesus, a Christ Child figure in a bicorne hat (part of a full wardrobe). He comes out for *festas* but the chapel key is otherwise available from the last house on the right.

Menino Jesus in Mont' Alto sanctuary, Arganil

THERMAL SPAS

In response to the Portuguese enthusiasm for thermal waters and health-orientated holidays, spa resorts have developed across the northern half of the country, with several of them in the Beiras, near Luso. All offer extensive sports facilities and a calm ambience as well as treatments for all the body's major systems. Most spas close for the winter, but Curia, 16 km (10 miles) northwest of Luso, is open all year for relaxation and treatments. Luso itself produces the country's best-known bottled mineral water.

Buçaco ⑫

Viewpoint of Cruz Alta

P ART ANCIENT WOODLAND, part arboretum, the National Forest of Buçaco is a magic place. As early as the 6th century it was a monastic retreat, and in 1628 the Carmelites built a house here, walling in the forest to keep the world at bay (women had already been banned by the pope in 1622). In their secluded forest the monks established contemplative walks, chapels – and trees. The trees, added to by Portuguese explorers, gained papal protection in 1632, and the 105 ha (260 acres) contain some 700 native and exotic species, including the venerable "Buçaco cedar". The peace of the forest was disturbed in 1810 as British and Portuguese troops fought the French on Buçaco ridge. In 1834 the monastery closed, but the forest endures, with its shady walks, hermits' grottoes and the astonishing Buçaco Palace Hotel at its centre.

★ Fonte Fria

This impressive cascade, fed b[y]
greatest of the forest's six spr[ings]
tumbles down to a magnolia[-]
fringed pool.

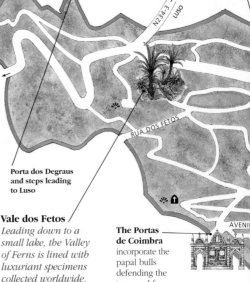

Porta dos Degraus and steps leading to Luso

Vale dos Fetos
Leading down to a small lake, the Valley of Ferns is lined with luxuriant specimens collected worldwide. The magnificent tree ferns give the valley a tropical air.

The Portas de Coimbra incorporate the papal bulls defending the trees and forbidding entry to women.

BUÇACO PALACE HOTEL

King Carlos, who commissioned this extravaganza in 1888, never lived to see his creation. His son, Manuel II, visited only briefly before his exile in 1910 *(see p55)* – he is said to have brought the French actress, Gaby Deslys, here for a romantic interlude. Its rebirth as a luxury hotel, serving its own renowned wines, was the inspiration of the royal chef and it became a fashionable rendezvous for socialites; in World War II it was also rumoured to be frequented by spies. It is now one of the great hotels of Portugal *(see p388)*.

Gaby Deslys, with whom Manuel II reputedly had a brief romance

KEY

▬▬ Wall

▪ ▪ ▪ Route of Via Sacra

🅿 Parking

🛉 Chapel

❄ Viewpoint

STAR SIGHTS

★ Buçaco Palace Hotel

★ Fonte Fria

Monastery

Only the cloisters, chapel and a few monks' cells of the Carmelite monastery remain. A plaque records that Wellington slept in one of the cork-lined cells.

VISITORS' CHECKLIST

Road map C3. 3 km (2 miles) SE of Luso. ⬛ ℹ️ *Luso (231-93 91 33).* **Monastery** ⬤ *Sat–Thu.* **Forest** ⬤ *daily.* 🚗 *for vehicles (May–Oct).* **Museu Militar** Almas do Encarnadouro. 📞 *231-93 93 10.* ⬤ *Tue–Sun.* ⬤ *1 Jan, Easter, 25 Dec.* 🚗 ♿ 🚗 *27 Sep: Anniversary of Battle of Buçaco.*

Porta da Rainha was made for Catherine of Bragança, but when her visit in 1693 was cancelled the gateway was sealed up for 11 years.

Museu Militar, devoted to the Peninsular War

Tasmanian eucalyptus (1876)

RUA DA RAINHA

N234

★ Buçaco Palace Hotel

Completed in 1907, the Neo-Manueline folly of a hunting lodge built by Luigi Manini includes murals and tiles by prominent artists. Azulejos in the hall feature scenes of the Battle of Buçaco.

The Monument to the Battle of Buçaco marks Wellington's victory on the ridge of Buçaco on 27 September 1810. As the nearby Museu Militar explains, this decisive battle halted the French march on Coimbra.

Cruz Alta, the forest's highest point, has glorious views as far as the sea.

Porta da Cruz Alta

The Buçaco cedar, now 26 m (85 ft) high, is believed to have been planted in 1644.

metres 250

yards 250

Via Sacra

Chapels containing life-size figures mark the Stations of the Cross along this winding pathway. They were installed by the Bishop of Coimbra in 1693.

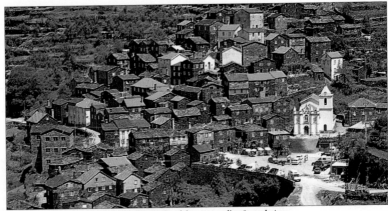

The village of Piodão, blending with the granite of the surrounding Serra de Açor

Piodão ⑮

Road map D3. 🏘 60. 🚌 to Coja 20 km (12 miles) away. 🛈 Arganil (235-20 48 23).

As its name suggests, the Serra de Açor, hills of the goshawk, is a place of bleak beauty, where solitary villages cling to precipitous terraces. Piodão, nestling in its valley, is the most striking of these dark schist and slate hamlets. Seemingly remote, Piodão was, until the late 19th century, on the main commercial route from Coimbra to Covilhã, but with newer roads the village was forgotten. With help from EU funds, it is now coming back to life: shops are opening, houses are being repainted with traditional blue trim, and in the main square the bright white **Igreja Matriz** stands out against the surrounding dark stone. Happily, Piodão still retains its old-world charm.

Oliveira do Hospital ⑯

Road map D3. 🏘 3,500. 🚌 🛈 Casa da Cultura, Rua do Colégio (238-609 269). ⊖ 2nd Mon of month.

These lands once belonged to the Knights Hospitallers, a gift in 1120 from the mother of Afonso Henriques. The 13th-century **Igreja Matriz** in Largo Ribeira do Amaral, houses a magnificent reminder of the era of these warrior monks. One of the founders of the

town, Domingues Joanes, lies in a large tomb surmounted by a charming equestrian statue.

Today, this lively industrial town is perfectly situated for exploring the valleys of the Mondego and the Alva.

Environs: At Lourosa, 12 km (7 miles) to the southwest, the 10th-century church of **São Pedro** reflects the changing fate of Portugal over the centuries. A cemetery excavated beneath the church dates from the Roman era; the porch is Visigothic, while inside are ten impressive Roman arches and an *ajimece* (Moorish window).

Caramulo ⑰

Road map C3. 🏘 1,700. 🚌 🛈 Avenida Jerónimo Lacerda (232-86 14 37).

In a grassy rolling serra west of Viseu, this small town was once, with its clear mountain air, a centre for sanatoria.

Interior of São Pedro at Lourosa, near Oliveira do Hospital

It is better known today for two very disparate museums in a single institutional block.

In the art collection of the **Museu do Caramulo**, the exhibits on show range across 16th-century Flemish tapestries, sculpture, porcelain, silver and ivory to Egyptian bronzes from 1580 to 900 BC. The paintings are as varied: from Portuguese primitives to the 20th century. Chagall and Dalí are represented, as is the Portuguese Maria Helena Vieira da Silva (1908–92). One of Picasso's haunting still lifes was donated by the artist in 1947.

The collection in the **Museu do Automóvel** is just as eclectic: a working 1899 Peugeot, Bugattis and Rolls-Royces, and a bullet-proof 1938 Mercedes-Benz ordered for Salazar when he was prime minister *(see pp56–7)* but never used.

🏛 **Museu do Caramulo (Fundação Abel de Lacerda) and Museu do Automóvel**
Caramulo. 📞 232-86 12 70. ◯ 10am–6pm daily. ● Easter, 24 & 25 Dec. 🖼

Environs: From the museum the road winds southwest up to two viewpoints and picnic spots in the Serra do Caramulo. About 4 km (2 miles) from Caramulo are the wild-flower pastures of **Cabeça da Neve**, at 970 m (3,200 ft). A little further on, signposted to the west, is the boulder-strewn upland of **Caramulinho**, rising to 1,074 m (3,524 ft). The views from here are magnificent.

Viseu ⑱

Road map D3. 🚶 *19,500.* 🚌
🛈 *Avenida Calouste Gulbenkian
(232-42 09 50).* 🚌 *Tue.*

A N ENTHRALLING old town is at the heart of this lively regional capital. Viseu has been a major northern crossroads since the time of the Romans and is the centre of the Dão wine-growing region *(see p29)*.

On a visit to Viseu it is hard to miss that this was the home town of one of Portugal's great 16th-century artists. The name of Grão Vasco graces a hotel, a museum, even a wine label.

On the western side of the old town is the striking 15th-century **Porta do Soar de Cima**, a remnant of the original walls. In the Rossio, the main square, the **Igreja dos Terceiros de São Francisco** (1773) has an Italianate façade and gilded interior. The 1887 town hall on the west side has a grand stairway and *azulejos* featuring the history of Viseu and its personalities. Just north is Rua Augusto Hilário, named after the originator of Coimbra-style *fado (see pp66–7)* who was born here.

The two-towered 17th-century façade of Viseu's cathedral

🏠 Sé

Largo da Sé. 📞 *232-42 29 84.*
🕙 *9am–noon, 2–7pm daily.* .

Viseu's cathedral still retains a few Romanesque features, but it has been altered over the centuries in a variety of styles which work together surprisingly well. The façade is a 17th-century replacement of a Manueline frontage that fell down in 1635. Inside, the vaulted roof is supported by 16th-century knotted ribs on 13th-century columns. In the

north chapel are fine *azulejos* from the 18th century, while those in the two-storey cloister date from a century earlier. The sacristy has a lavishly painted ceiling and early "carpet" tiles *(see p22)*. In the chancel, choir stalls in Brazilian jacaranda contrast with a startling modern altar, an inverted pyramid in polished granite and steel.

The Sé's treasury, housed in the chapterhouse, includes a 12th-century Gospel and a 13th-century Limoges coffer.

Facing the cathedral is the **Misericórdia** church, with its beautifully proportioned 18th-century Rococo façade; the interior is unexceptional.

The graceful Rococo façade of the church of the Misericórdia, Viseu

🏛 Museu de Grão Vasco

Largo da Sé. 📞 *232-42 20 49.*
🕙 *Tue–Sun.* ● *until Apr 2003.* 🎫

In the 16th-century former bishops' palace abutting the cathedral is the Museu de Grão Vasco, Viseu's "great Vasco". The paintings of Vasco Fernandes (c.1475–1540) and his fellow artists of the Viseu School are highly esteemed for their naturalism, background landscapes, drapery and attention to detail. Their treatment of light betrays the marked influence of Flemish painters.

On the upper floor of the three-storey museum are exhibited

the masterpieces that once adorned the chancel altarpiece in the cathedral. Predominant are Grão Vasco's monumental *St Peter* and, from a series of 14 panels on the life of Christ, *The Adoration of the Magi*. Painted in about 1503–5, it is memorable for the inclusion of a Brazilian Indian among those paying homage to the newborn Christ *(see p48)*. Some of the other panels are thought to be by fellow artists in the Viseu School.

Among other masterpieces hung here are works by Grão Vasco's great rival, Gaspar Vaz, including a *Last Supper*. On the lower floors are works by Portuguese artists from the 19th and 20th centuries, including the brilliant Columbano Bordalo Pinheiro.

St Peter (1503–5) by Vasco Fernandes in the Museu de Grão Vasco, Viseu

Sernancelhe ⑲

Road map D2. 🏛 *1,100.* 🚌
🛈 *Avenida das Tílias (254-595 103).*
🚌 *every other Thu.*

Small whitewashed houses
cluster around the granite
heart of this modest Beira
town which was established
on the banks of the Távora in
the 10th century. In the central
Praça da República stands the
Romanesque **Igreja Matriz**.
The granite statues in its façade
niches, survivors from the
12th century, flank a notable
arched portal embellished by
a semicircle of carved angels.
The pillory that stands across
the square is dated 1554.

The grandest house here is
the Baroque **Solar dos
Carvalhos** behind
the church. Long
and low, with
carved granite
portals against
whitewashed
walls, it is where
the local noble
family lived in
the 18th century.
It is still a private house.

Only a few stubs of castle
wall remain on the rocky outcrop overlooking the square,
but a small battlemented house
has been built into them.

Environs: In the Serra da
Lapa, which rises to the south
of Sernancelhe, stands a popular shrine known as the
**Santuário de Nossa
Senhora da Lapa**. The
story tells of a dumb
shepherd girl, Joana,
who found a statue of
the Virgin Mary on a
great boulder and took
it home. Irritated, her
mother threw it on the
fire, at which moment
the child miraculously
spoke: "Don't burn it,"
cried Joana. "It is the
Senhora da Lapa."

A chapel was built
to enshrine the boulder,
and the image, now
with a slightly scorched
face, looks down from
an ornamental recess.
The space below her
niche is packed with
images and offerings
left by pilgrims.

The main gateway into the old walled town of Trancoso

The castle at **Penedono** is captivating. Perched on rocks in
the middle of this small town
17 km (11 miles) northeast of
Sernancelhe, it has survived
since at least the 10th century.
The castle is mentioned
in the medieval tale of
a knight known as
O Magriço, who
went to England
with 11 other
knights to joust
in honour of 12
English ladies.
There is little to
see inside the
castle – if closed, the key is in
the store beside the *pelourinho*
(pillory), but there are splendid
views from the walls.

**Carved arch over the portal of
the Igreja Matriz, Sernancelhe**

🛉 **Santuário de Nossa
Senhora da Lapa**
Quintela da Lapa, 11 km (7 miles)
SW of Sernancelhe.
📞 *232-68 89 93.* ⭕ *daily.*

**The castle of Penedono, near Sernancelhe,
with its imposing medieval battlements**

Trancoso ⑳

Road map D2. 🏛 *6,000.* 🚌
🛈 *Avenida Herois de São Marcos
(271-81 11 47).* 🚌 *Fri.*

When King Dinis married
Isabel here in 1283 *(see
pp44–5)*, he gave her Trancoso
as a wedding gift. He was also
responsible for the impressive
walls that still encircle the town
and, in 1304, established here
the first unrestricted fair in Portugal. Left in peace after 1385,
the town became a lively commercial centre. Trancoso once
had a large Jewish population,
and in the old Judiaria, houses
survive with one broad and
one narrow door, separating
domestic life from commerce.

From the southern gate, Rua
da Corredoura leads to **São
Pedro**, restored after 1720. A
tombstone in the church commemorates Gonçalo Anes,
a local shoemaker who, in the
1580s, wrote the celebrated
Trovas under the name of
Bandarra. These prophesied
the return of the young King
Sebastião *(see p107)*.

Environs: Tumbledown ruins
above a humble village are all
that remain of the medieval
citadel of **Marialva**, 14 km
(9 miles) to the northeast of
Trancoso. Granite walls, fragments of stone carvings and
a striking 15th-century pillory
emanate an aura of lost grandeur. Probably founded by
Ferdinand of León and Castile
early in the 11th century and
fortified by Sancho I, it is not
known why Marialva fell into
ruin. No battle destroyed it
and it seems merely to have
been abandoned as townsfolk
moved to more fruitful lands.

SERRA CHEESE

Serra, made from the milk of ewes grazing in the Serra da Estrela *(see pp218–19)*, is Portugal's finest cheese. It is made in the winter – its success was once governed by the temperature of the women's hands as they worked in their cool granite kitchens – and traditionally the milk is coagulated with *flor do cardo*, thistle. Now the small factories producing the cheese, in rounds of 1.5–2 kg (about 3–5 lb), are certified to ensure quality and authenticity (fakes are not uncommon). At room temperature Serra becomes runny. The cheese is scooped out with a spoon through a hole cut into the top.

A shepherd with his flock on the slopes of the Serra da Estrela

Celorico da Beira ㉑

Road map D3. 🏠 *3,000.* 🚍 🚌
ℹ️ *Estrada Nacional 16 (271-74 21 09).*
🗓️ *Tue, Dec–May: alternate Fri.*

IN THE LEE OF the Serra da Estrela, the pastures around Celorico da Beira have long been a source of the region's famous Serra cheese. From December to May the cheese market in the Praça Municipal is a local attraction and every February Celorico holds a lively fair dedicated to cheeses.

Around Rua Fernão Pacheco, running from the main road up to the castle, is the old centre of Celorico, a cluster of granite houses with Manueline windows and Gothic doors. Of the 10th-century **castle**, battered by a long succession of frontier disputes with Spain, only a tower and the outer walls remain. Its stark silhouette is less dramatic at close quarters. The **Igreja Matriz**, restored in the 18th century, has a painted coffered ceiling. During the Peninsular War, the church served briefly as a makeshift hospital for the English forces.

Almeida ㉒

Road map E2. 🏠 *1,600.* 🚌
ℹ️ *Portas de São Francisco (271-57 42 04).* 🗓️ *8th day & last Sat of month.*

FORMIDABLE defences in the form of a 12-pointed star guard this small, delightfully preserved border town.

Almeida was recognized by Spain as Portuguese territory under the Alcañices Treaty on 12 September 1297, but this did not stop further incursions. The present Vauban-style stronghold *(see p297)* was designed in 1641 by Antoine Deville after Spain's Philip IV, in post-Restoration rage, destroyed the earlier defences protecting the town and its medieval castle.

From 1742 to 1743 Almeida was in Spanish hands again, and then during the Peninsular War was held in turn by the French under Masséna and the British under the Duke of Wellington. In 1810, a French shell lit a powder trail that destroyed the castle.

To breach the town's fortifications today, it is necessary to cross a bridge and pass through a tunnel. The underground **casamatas**, soldiers' barracks, can be visited and an armoury in the main gateway, the Portas de São Francisco, holds further mementoes of Almeida's military past. In the town itself are a 17th-century parish church and a **Misericórdia** church of a similar age, attached to one of Portugal's oldest almshouses. A walk around the grassy walls gives rewarding views of the town.

Almeida's complex fortifications, still discernible despite the incursion of grass and wild flowers

Border Castles Tour ㉓

Defending portugal's frontiers was a vital priority of the nation's early kings. The greatest period of castle-building was in the reign of King Dinis (1279–1325). All the shakily held border, Spanish incursions were frequent and loyalties divided. Castles were constantly being assaulted, besieged and rebuilt, and those that survived are a lasting reminder of this long period of dispute. Much of the terrain, especially in the Serra da Marofa, is bleak and rocky, but near Pinhel and beyond Castelo Mendo the scenic valley of the River Côa provides a dramatic backdrop.

Castelo Rodrigo ②
This tiny fortified village still has its encircling walls built by King Dinis in 1296. But the fine palace of its lord, the Spanish sympathizer Cristóvão de Moura, was burnt down at the Restoration in 1640 *(see pp50–51)*.

Figueira de Castelo Rodrigo ③
From the 18th century, Castelo Rodrigo was largely abandoned in favour of less isolated Figueira, now a flourishing little town known for its almond blossom. Just to the south, topped by a huge stone Christ the King, is the highest point of the Serra da Marofa, 977 m (3,205 ft).

Almeida ①
The town's star-shaped defences are a finely preserved example of the complex but effective style of fortifications developed by the French engineer, Vauban, in the 17th century *(see p297)*.

Pinhel ④
Part of the region's defences since Roman times, Pinhel formed the fulcrum for a network of fortresses, and in the early 14th century King Dinis built it up into an impressive citadel. Much of this ring of walls survives, as do two towers. Pinhel is nowadays noted for its wine.

Key

━━ Tour route
═══ Other roads
╍╍╍ International boundary
☀ Viewpoint

0 kilometres   10
0 miles   5

TIPS FOR DRIVERS

Length: 115 km (72 miles).
Stopping-off points: Most villages have cafés, and Pinhel and Almeida have restaurants.
Road conditions: The tour uses well-surfaced roads but short cuts are deceptive and are not recommended. (See also pp444–5.)

Map labels: VILA NOVA DE FOZ CÔA, SERRA DA MAROFA, Côa, Vale Verde, Aldeia Nova, Vilar Formoso, Fuentes de Oñoro, SALAMANCA, GUARDA, SABUGAL, Ribeira de Tourões, N221, N332, N340, N324, N16, IP5

Castelo Mendo ⑤
Beyond the main gate, guarded by two stone boars, little survives of the castle here, but the distant views make its role as a frontier fort easy to appreciate.

The soaring triple-aisled interior of Guarda's Gothic cathedral

Guarda ㉔

Road map D3. ㎘ 20,000. 🚂 🚌
🛈 *Rua Infante Dom Henrique (271-21 9 22).* 🗓 *1st & last Wed of month.*

SPREAD OVER a bleak hill on the northeast flank of the Serra da Estrela, Guarda is Portugal's highest city, at 1,056 m (3,465 ft). Founded in 1197 by Sancho I, the city's original role as frontier guard explains its name and its rather forbidding countenance. Some of its arcaded streets and squares are lively and interesting, but the great fortress-like **Sé**, with its flying buttresses, pinnacles and gargoyles, could never be described as lovely. Master architects who worked on the cathedral, begun in 1390 and completed in 1540, included Diogo Boitac (from 1504 to 1517) and the builders of Batalha *(see pp182–3).* The interior, by contrast, is light and graceful. The 100 carved figures high on the altarpiece in the chancel were worked by Jean de Rouen in 1552.

On display in the nearby **Museu de Guarda** are two floors of paintings, artefacts, archaeological discoveries and a section on the city's own poet, Augusto Gil (1873–1929).

From the cathedral square, Rua do Comércio leads down to the 17th-century **Misericórdia** church. Inside the ornamental portal are Baroque altars and pulpits. Just north of the cathedral, in the historic town centre, is the 18th-century church of **São Vicente**, which has 16 elaborate *azulejo* panels depicting the life of Christ.

Guarda used to support a thriving Jewish community and in Rua Dom Sancho I is a key shop that may once have served as a synagogue. History records that João I, on a visit to Guarda, was smitten by Inês Fernandes, the beautiful daughter of a Jewish shoemaker. From their liaison a son, Afonso, was born. In 1442 the title of first Duke of Bragança was bestowed on Afonso, and 200 years later his descendant would take the throne as João IV, first of the Bragança monarchs *(see p299).*

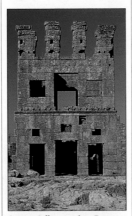

Cabral family crest in the chapel, Belmonte

🏛 **Museu de Guarda**
Rua Alves Roçadas 30. 🄲 271-21 34 60. 🄾 *Tue–Sun.* ● *public hols.* 🄳

Serra da Estrela ㉕

See pp218–19.

Belmonte ㉖

Road map D3. ㎘ 3,600. 🚂 🚌
🛈 *Castello de Belmont (275-91 14 88).* 🗓 *1st & 3rd Mon of month.*

BELMONTE was for generations the fiefdom of the Cabral family, a name associated with heroic exploits. Pedro Álvares Cabral, who in 1500 was the first navigator to land in Brazil, had forebears who fought at Ceuta *(see p48)* and Aljubarrota *(see p183).* Fernão, an earlier ancestor known as the Giant of the Beiras, was famed for his feats of strength. The family crest, incorporating a goat *(cabra)* as a play on words, can be seen in the castle and adjacent chapel. The **castle**, begun in 1266, retains its keep and, a later addition, an ornate Manueline window. The little church of **São Tiago** nearby has preserved its Romanesque simplicity: the frescoes above the altar and, in a tiny side chapel, a serene granite pietà date from the 13th century. Beside the church is the 15th-century **Capela dos Cabrais** which holds the Cabral family tombs.

On the opposite side of the village is the modern **Igreja da Sagrada Família** (1940). It is the repository for a treasured statue of Nossa Senhora da Esperança, which, according to tradition, accompanied Cabral on his voyage to Brazil.

ENVIRONS: Just northeast of Belmonte is a Roman tower, **Centum Cellas**, also called Torre de Colmeal. The role of this square, three-storeyed structure is uncertain and archaeologists' theories have suggested a range of functions from hostel or military base to mansion and temple.

Centum Cellas, a curious Roman landmark near Belmonte

Serra da Estrela 🌀

Haymaking near the town of Linhares

T HESE "STAR MOUNTAINS" are the highest range on mainland Portugal, with much of the Serra over 1,500 m (5,000 ft). The highest point rises to 1,993 m (6,539 ft) but is topped by a small stone tower – the Torre – to "stretch" it to 2,000 m. The exposed granite of the upper slopes is good for little but grazing sheep, and stone shepherds' huts form part of the landscape, their thatched roofs renewed each year after the harsh winter. Sheep have shaped the fortunes of the area, providing wool for a textile industry and supplying milk for Portugal's best-known cheese. A designated nature reserve, the Serra's long-distance paths and stunning flora attract walkers and nature enthusiasts, while a winter snowfall brings skiers to the slopes around Torre.

Cabeça do Velho

The granite of the mountain tops has been eroded into many weird shapes, such as this "old man's head" near Sabugueiro. It is matched by an "old woman's head" south of Seia.

Valezim

In Valezim are several old water mills of a type not often found in Portugal. Two of them are still used to grind grain.

Seia is one of the main entry points to the Parque Natural da Serra da Estrela.

Serra Cheese Shop

The best Serra cheese, prized for its rich flavour (see p215), is still made by hand. Farmers sell their produce at cheese fairs and at stalls or small shops such as this one near the summit of Torre.

Gou

Cabeça do Velho

Viseu

Seia

Alva

Sabugueiro

N339

Coimbra

Vide

Muro

Ribeira de Alvoco

Valezim

N231

Curr Ma

▲ Rodeio Grande

Penha dos Abutres

▲ Torre

Pe da S

N230

N231

Unhais da Serra

Alto da Pedrice

N230

N23

Penhas de Saúde once a health spa is now popula with skiers

Torre

Despite the unpredictability of snow, the slop below Torre are used f skiing, tobogganing o just fun in the snow.

STAR SIGHTS

★ **Zêzere Valley**

★ **Linhares**

★ Linhares
Guarded by the towers of its medieval castle, Linhares is like a living museum. The forum, from which medieval justice was dispensed, survives, as do many fine houses from its 15th-century heyday.

Visitors' Checklist

Road map D3. Praça da República 28, Seia (238-317 762); Covilhã (275-319 560); Gouveia (238-492 185); Manteigas (275-981 129). Covilhã, Guarda. to Covilhã, Seia & Guarda. Limited local service within park. Sat in most villages & towns. Feb: Carnaval & annual cheese fairs; Dec: Santa Luzia.

Key

- Major road
- Minor road
- Tourist information
- Viewpoint

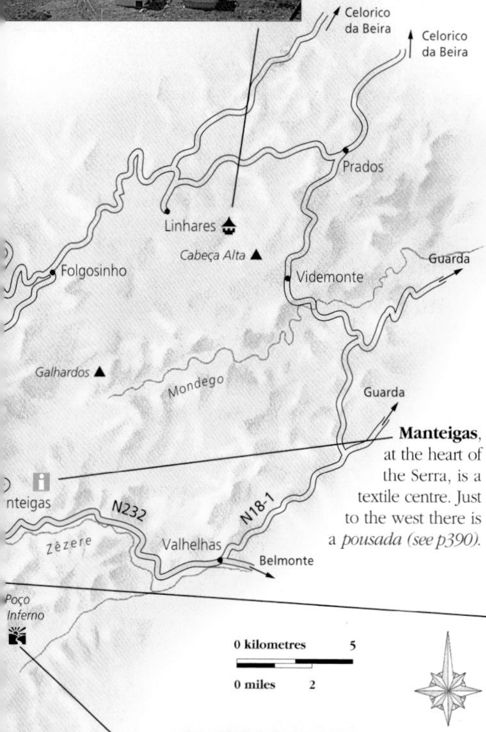
Celorico da Beira
Celorico da Beira
Prados
Linhares
Cabeça Alta
Folgosinho
Videmonte
Guarda
Galhardos
Mondego
Guarda
nteigas
N232
N18-1
Zêzere
Valhelhas
Belmonte
Poço Inferno
0 kilometres 5
0 miles 2

Manteigas, at the heart of the Serra, is a textile centre. Just to the west there is a *pousada* *(see p390)*.

★ Zêzere Valley
The Zêzere eventually joins the Tagus, but here, near its source, the young river flows through a classic glacier-cut valley. The golden broom growing here is used to thatch mountain huts.

Covilhã, the largest and liveliest town in the area, has a busy morning market. It is also known for its fine textiles woven from locally produced wool.

Poço do Inferno
This cascade in a gorge of the River Leandros is a spectacular sight, especially when it freezes in winter.

Sheepdog of the Serra

Intelligent, loyal and brave, the Serra da Estrela sheepdog embodies all the qualities required in this wild region. Its heavy coat, as shaggy as its charges, helps it survive the bitter high-altitude winters and in the past its strength was called upon to defend the flock from wolves. Pedigree Serra da Estrela dogs (reputedly with some wolf's blood introduced in their breeding) are raised at kennels near Gouveia and west of Manteigas.

Sabugal ❷

Road map E3. 🏠 *2,500.* 🚌
🈯 *Câmara Municipal, Praça da República (271-75 10 40).*
🅿 *1st Thu & 3rd Tue of month.*

In 1296, when this small town beside the River Côa was confirmed as Portuguese in the Treaty of Alcañices, the **castle** was refortified by the ever-industrious King Dinis *(see p44)*. Its imposing towered walls and unusual five-sided keep survive from this era, although the castle suffered in peacetime from villagers raiding it for building stone.

Peopled since prehistoric times, Sabugal still has part of its medieval walls, reinforced in the 17th century and now ringed by newer houses. In the Praça da República stands a granite **clocktower**, reconstructed in the 17th century.

ENVIRONS: Wrapped in its ring of walls, **Sortelha**, 20 km (12 miles) west, is enchanting. It sits on a granite outcrop and the views from the high keep of its gem of a 13th-century castle are stunning. In front of the arched castle entrance is a 16th-century pillory with an armillary sphere on top. In the tiny citadel are a school and stony lanes of granite houses, some discreetly converted into restaurants *(see p413)*.

The local fondness for bull-fights *(see pp144–5)* is reflected in names of nearby villages

The castle at Sabugal, with its distinctive five-sided keep

such as **Vila do Touro**. In a local variation, the *capeia*, bulls were taunted into charging into a huge fork of branches.

Penamacor ❷

Road map D3. 🏠 *3,200.* 🈯 🚌
🈯 *Rua 25 de Abril (277-39 43 16).*
🅿 *1st & 3rd Wed of month.*

Fought over by successive waves of Romans, Visigoths and Moors, this frontier town was fortified in the 12th century by Gualdim Pais, Master of the Knights Templar *(see pp184–5)*. Today the weather-beaten castle walls rise above a quiet town at the heart of hardy, sparsely inhabited country where the main attraction is the hunting of small game.

From the main square, the road up to the old town passes beside the former town hall,

built over a medieval archway. Beyond lie the restored **castle keep** and the 16th-century **Igreja da Misericórdia**, with an elegant Manueline portal capped by armillary spheres, the emblem of Manuel I.

ENVIRONS: Penamacor is the headquarters of the **Reserva Natural da Serra da Malcata**. These 20 sq km (8 sq miles) of forested wilderness shelter wolves, otters and, most importantly, are one of the last refuges of the Iberian lynx. Visitors should first call at the information centre for advice.

🔆 **Reserva Natural da Serra da Malcata**
🚌 *to Penamacor or Sabugal.* 🈯 *Rua dos Bombeiros Voluntários, Penamacor (277-39 44 67).* 📷 *by appt.*

Monsanto ❷

Road map E3. 🏠 *1,500.* 🚌
🈯 *Rua Marquês de Graciosa (800-265 265).* 🅿 *3rd Sat.*

An odd fame hit Monsanto in 1938 when it was voted "most Portuguese village in Portugal". The village is at one with the granite hillside on which it perches: its lanes blend into the grey rock, the houses squeezed between massive boulders. Tiny gardens sprout from the granite and dogs drink from granite bowls.

The ruined **castle** began as a *castro*, a Lusitanian fortified settlement, and suffered a long history of sieges and battles for its commanding position. It was finally destroyed by a 19th-century gunpowder

Monsanto's houses, dwarfed by immense granite boulders

explosion. Cars cannot venture beyond the village centre, but the view alone is worth the walk up to the ruined walls.

A story is told of how a long siege by the Moors drove the hungry villagers to a desperate ploy. They threw their last calf, full of their last grain, over the walls, a show of profligacy that convinced the Moors to give up. Each May there is a mock re-enactment of this victory amid much music and singing.

Idanha-a-Velha 30

Road map D3. 🏠 *90.* 🚌 ℹ️ *Rua da Sé (277-91 42 80).*

THIS MODEST HAMLET among the olive groves encapsulates the history of Portugal. Discreet signposts and explanations in Portuguese, French and English guide visitors round the landmarks of this fascinating living museum.

Idanha-a-Velha was, it is said, the birthplace of the Visigothic King Wamba, and had its own bishop until 1199. The present appearance of the **cathedral** comes from early 16th-century restoration, but in the echoing interior are stacked inscribed and sculpted Roman stones.

In the middle of the village stand several historic monuments: a 17th-century pillory and the Renaissance **Igreja Matriz**, while near an early 20th-century olive press is a ruined **Torre dos Templários**, a relic of the Templars. This order of religious knights held sway in Idanha until the 14th century *(see pp184–5).*

Statue-lined Stairway of the Apostles in the unusual Jardim Episcopal, Castelo Branco

Castelo Branco 31

Road map D4. 🏠 *35,000.* 🚊 🚌 ℹ️ *Alameda da Liberdade (272-33 03 39).* 🛍 *Mon.*

THIS HANDSOME, busy old city, overlooked by the vestiges of a Templar castle, is the most important in the Beira Baixa.

Much the greatest attraction is the extraordinary **Jardim Episcopal** beside the former bishops' palace. Created by Bishop João de Mendonça in the 18th century, the garden's layout is conventionally formal; its individuality lies in its dense population of statues. Baroque in style and often bizarre in character, stone saints and apostles line the box-edged paths, lions peer at their reflections in pools and monarchs stand guard along the balustrades – the hated kings of the 60-year Spanish rule *(see p50)* conspicuously half-size.

The 17th-century Paço Episcopal itself now houses the **Museu Francisco Tavares Proença Júnior**. Its wide-ranging collection includes archaeological finds, displays of 16th-century tapestries and Portuguese primitive art. Castelo Branco is also well known for its fine silk-embroidered bedspreads, called *colchas*, and examples of these are also exhibited in the museum.

In the mainly 18th-century Convento da Graça opposite there is a small **Museu de Arte Sacra** with a varied collection of religious art, including an ivory Christ. Beside the road back to the town centre stands a 15th-century cross known as the **Cruzeiro de São João**.

🌷 **Jardim Episcopal**
Rua Bartolomeu da Costa. ◯ *daily.* 🌀
🏛 **Museu Francisco Tavares Proença Júnior**
Rua Bartolomeu da Costa.
🕻 *272-34 42 77.* ◯ *10am–12:30pm, 2–5:30pm Tue–Sun.*
🏛 **Museu de Arte Sacra**
Rua Bartolomeu da Costa. 🕻 *272-34 44 54.* ◯ *9am–noon, 2–6pm Mon–Fri.* ● *public hols.* ♿

The historic little village of Idanha-a-Velha, among its olive groves beside the River Ponsul

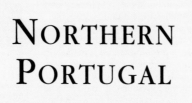

NORTHERN
PORTUGAL

INTRODUCING NORTHERN PORTUGAL 224-231
DOURO AND TRÁS-OS-MONTES 232-261
MINHO 262-281

Northern Portugal at a Glance

Portugal north of the River Douro is rural and unspoilt, yet offers splendid opportunities for cultural sightseeing, walking and water sports. Beyond the cultivated valley of the Douro and the fertile Minho rises the remote and romantically named Trás-os-Montes ("Behind the Mountains"), with its tracts of wilderness and tiny medieval townships. It could be said the nation was conceived between the Minho and the Douro, and historic cities such as Oporto, Bragança and Braga give fascinating insights into the country's past.

In the Parque Nacional da Peneda-Gerês scenery ranges *from dramatic forested valleys to flowery meadows. Local farmers store their grain in curious stone* espigueiros (see pp270–71).

Viana do Castelo, *at the mouth of the River Lima, is elegant and relaxed (see pp274–5). The stately buildings in the Praça da República, including the arcaded* Paços do Concelho (*the old town hall), reflect the town's wealthy past.*

MINHO
(See pp262–81)

Bom Jesus do Monte, *near Braga, attracts worshippers, penitents and tourists, who all come to climb 116 m (380 ft) up the Baroque staircase (see pp278–9). This is the Staircase of the Five Senses, with fountains depicting each of the senses.*

Douro Litoral

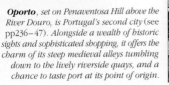

Oporto, *set on Penaventosa Hill above the River Douro, is Portugal's second city (see pp236–47). Alongside a wealth of historic sights and sophisticated shopping, it offers the charm of its steep medieval alleys tumbling down to the lively riverside quays, and a chance to taste port at its point of origin.*

◁ **Azulejos** on the Igreja do Carmo in Oporto, depicting the founding of the Carmelite Order

Casa de Mateus, familiar to many from the Mateus Rosé wine label, lies in the hills above the valley of the Douro. This Baroque solar, or manor house, is set in beautifully manicured formal gardens, its distinctive pinnacles rising above the orchards and vineyards that surround it (see pp254–5).

Bragança, capital of Trás-os-Montes, gave its name to Portugal's last and longest-ruling royal dynasty. The keep and walls of this remote citadel, founded in the 12th century, look out over the valley of the River Fervença (see pp258–9).

Trás-os-Montes

DOURO AND TRÁS-OS-MONTES
(See pp232–61)

Alto Douro

0 kilometres 25

0 miles 10

Port Country, as the scenic valley of the Upper Douro is commonly called, is the nursery of Portugal's port industry. A tour of a quinta, or wine estate, with its steeply terraced riverside vineyards, is highly recommended (see pp252–3).

The Festivals of the North

PORTUGUESE CITIES, towns and villages all have their own particular saints' days. These are primarily religious occasions, particularly in the Minho and across the devout north, but are also a chance to put aside the cares of life for a day or two. It is a popular maxim that a holy day is best celebrated by eating, drinking, dancing and merrymaking, as well as worshipping and giving thanks. The most solemn and spectacular celebrations of Holy Week, Semana Santa, can also be seen in the north, especially in Braga *(see pp276–7)*, Portugal's ecclesiastical capital.

Dressing up for Holy Week

Street procession during the Festa das Cruzes in Barcelos

A solemn moment as Easter candles are lit in Braga

EASTER

HOLY WEEK, culminating in Easter Sunday, is the major religious festival of the year. In Braga, processions snake round the city walls to the great cathedral, and every village has its own ceremonies.

The start of Holy Week is heralded by Palm Sunday, when branch-waving faithful line the streets to commemorate the entry of Christ into Jerusalem. Good Friday evening is palpably solemn, as innumerable processions follow the 14 Stations of the Cross, many believers doing public penance as they recall Christ's suffering. In some villages an effigy of the lifeless and bleeding Christ is carried through the streets.

On Easter Sunday, after an uplifting mass proclaiming the risen Christ, every parish priest processes around his village with a crucifix on a tall staff for parishioners to kiss the feet of Jesus. While the priest takes a customary glass of wine, his entourage ecstatically let off rockets. Families then traditionally lunch on roast kid *(cabrito)*.

After Easter, in early May, the passion of Christ is recalled in Barcelos *(see p273)*. Crosses are erected the length of a petal-strewn route for the **Festa das Cruzes**.

SÃO JOÃO

OPORTO'S celebration of São João *(23–24 Jun)* is one of Portugal's most exuberant festivals. It coincides with the summer solstice, and to celebrate, people eat, drink and dance all night, playfully hitting each other over the head with giant garlic-leeks (or sometimes, even more strangely, with squeaky plastic hammers). Bonfires are lit and a spectacular display of fireworks explodes over the Douro.

Wielding a São João hammer

COSTUME IN THE MINHO

Gold necklets

Embroidered apron pockets

Festivals are important vehicles for keeping alive tradition, particularly regional costume. These days, rock music and designer clothes are as much part of young people's life in Minho villages as elsewhere in western Europe, but traditional dress is worn with pride on days of celebration. The Minho's costume is the most colourful in Portugal, with exquisitely embroidered scarves and aprons in colours denoting village loyalties. Messages of love and friendship are stitched on to pockets, and bodices are half-lost under tiers of gold filigree.

A new tradition, which has become a part of São João over the last decade, is the annual regatta of the *barcos rabelos*, the boats in which port used to be shipped down the Douro *(see p252)*.

ROMARIAS

ANY KIND of celebration or party can be described as a *festa*, but one billed as a *romaria* implies a religious dimension. Most *festas* in the north are *romarias*; they begin with a special mass, then saints' statues are brought from the church to be paraded through the streets on litters. Blessings are dispensed in all directions – fire engines and ambulances frequently also getting the treatment – followed by a spraying with some Raposeira sparkling wine. Many *romarias* take place in the summer, and in August few days go by without a celebration. **Assumption Day** *(15 Aug)*

STICK DANCING

Stick dancers, or *pauliteiros*, can still be seen at village festivals in Trás-os-Montes. The dances are of ancient origin, probably associated with fertility rites, and the sticks may once have been swords. The most famous troupe comes from the village of Duas Igrejas, near Miranda do Douro *(see p260)*.

Dancers performing at a *festa*

Nossa Senhora da Agonia, Viana do Castelo

is fêted all over Portugal with dancing and music. *Gigantones*, grotesque giants of pre-Christian origin, join street processions and fireworks light the sky. A few days later, around 20 August, one of the year's most spectacular *romarias* takes place in Viana do Castelo *(see pp274–5)*. The festivities celebrating **Nossa Senhora da Agonia** include a bullfight and an afternoon devoted to a kaleidoscopic display of regional costume,

which may include more than a thousand participants. As a finale, fireworks are let off from the bridge over the River Lima to cascade down into the water as a fiery waterfall.

On the coast just to the west of Braga, villagers in São Bartolomeu do Mar mark the end of their *romaria* *(22–24 Aug)* by dipping their children in the sea, as a mock sacrifice to the waves.

Outlandish costumes and masks donned for the Dia dos Rapazes

CHRISTMAS AND WINTER

ON CHRISTMAS EVE, families gather to enjoy enormous quantities of *bacalhau* (salt cod) and mulled port, and to exchange presents, before attending midnight mass.

Between Christmas and Epiphany, Trás-os-Montes village boys dress in crazy, fringed suits to take part in the rite-of-passage **Dia dos Rapazes**. The Christmas season ends on **Dia de Reis** *(6 Jan)*, when the *bolo rei*, or "king cake", rich with crystallized fruit "jewels", is eaten *(see p33)*.

Comical giants leading an Assumption Day parade in Peso da Régua

The Story of Port

T HE "DISCOVERY" OF PORT dates from the 17th century, when
British merchants, keen to build up trade with Portugal,
doctored the wine of the Douro with brandy to stop it from
turning sour in transit. It was found that the stronger and
sweeter the wine, the better flavour it acquired. Over the
years, methods of maturing and blending were refined, and
continue today in the port lodges of Vila Nova de Gaia (see
p247). Croft was one of the first big shippers, followed by
other English and Scots firms, and much
of the port trade is still in British control.

Barco rabelo (see p250) fer
ing port down the Douro

THE PORT REGION

Port comes only from a de
cated region of the upper Dc
valley, stretching 100 km (62 mile
the Spanish border. Régua and Pinh
the main centres of production, but n
top-quality vineyards lie on estates or qu
in the harsh eastern terrain (see pp252–

STYLES OF PORT

A classic after-dinner drink, port is rich, full-bodied and high in alcohol.
The tawnies are lighter in taste and colour than ruby or vintage, but all
are blended from several wines, selected from scores of samples.

Vintage

The star of any
shipper's range is
made from wines of
a single vintage year,
from the best vine-
yards. Blended and
bottled after two
years in oak casks, vintage port is
then matured in tall black bottles.

LBV

LBV (Late Bo
Vintage) is w
a single year t.
has been matt
in wood for fo
to six years, be
being bottled n
for drinking. The label gives th
of vintage and when it was bo

Aged Tawny

This light port,
so-called because
it pales to an am-
ber colour as it
ages, is less full-
bodied than vintage or ruby ports.
The age on the label (10, 20, 30 or 40
years old) refers to the average age
of its blend of old and young wines.

Tawny

Less sw
and ligh
than rub
vintage p
tawny o
appeals for those very reasons.
blended from wines of differen
after ageing in wood, or may e
a clever mixture of red and w

Ruby

This full-bodied,
fruity port named
after its deep red
colour may be aged
in wood until ready
to drink. The younger
ones take no more
than three years. All are blended
from wines of various ages.

White

The two style
of white port -
and sweet – a
from the othe
they are drun
an aperitif, a
are at their best chilled. White
is made from a variety of grap
including white Malvasia.

...ecting grapes in tall wicker baskets for transport to the wineries

...w PORT IS MADE

...climax of the Douro farmers' year comes in late Septem-
...Bands of pickers from the outlying provinces congregate
in the Douro valley to harvest the
grapes. More than 40 varieties
are used in the making of port.

...ding the grapes *in stone
...s or* lagares *to extract the
... is a feature of very tradi-
...al quintas. Some shippers
...ve it adds a special quality.*

Fermentation *in cement or
steel tanks is a more common
method. Carbon dioxide builds
up within the tank, forcing the
fermenting must (juice from
the grapes) up a tube into an
open trough at the top. The gas
is released and the must sprays
back over the pips and skins, in
a process similar to treading.*

In the fortification *process,
the semi-fermented must is run
into a second vat where brandy
– actually grape spirit – is
added. This arrests the fermentation, leaving the wine sweet
from natural grape sugar.*

...usands of bottles *of
...ham's vintage port from
...7, one of the best years,
...it full maturation at the
...e in Vila Nova de Gaia.*

Most ports *apart from vintage
are matured in oak casks in
the port lodges. Once bottled,
they are ready for drinking
and do not require decanting.*

VINTAGE PORT

In years of outstand-
ing quality, shippers
may "declare" their
best wine as "vintage"
18 months after the har-
vest. It is bottled six months
later and begins its long, slow
maturation. Shippers usually
declare a "Vintage Year" about
three times per decade. The
minimum period for a good
vintage to mature is about
15 years, but the best ones
continue to improve indefi-
nitely. Always decant vintage
port before drinking it.

The following vintages are now ready to drink:

1960 Hard to find these days,
but soft, mellow and
mature if you do.

1963 A classic, full-bodied,
rich vintage.

1966 A high-quality, low-
yielding vintage; in
short supply, but
perhaps currently
at its peak.

1970 All-time great vintage;
magnificent now and
will go on improving.

1975 Comparatively thin,
unlikely to improve.

Vintages not ready for drinking yet:

1977 A superb vintage,
possibly a second
great from the 1970s.

1980 Initially viewed as
mediocre but some are
changing their minds.

1983 Full and powerful; may
turn out to be excellent.

1985 Bold and powerful;
delicious now but there
is no hurry to drink it.

1991 Declared by most
shippers, though a few
maintain the quality
was not high
enough.

1994 Expected to be
one of the best
vintages of the
20th century.

1997 Most recent
declaration;
good for long
term ageing.

Graham's 1994 vintage

Regional Food: Northern Portugal

Walnuts

THE LUSH MINHO IS CREDITED with the invention of many recipes which have been adopted nationally, the ubiquitous *caldo verde* soup being just one example. The coast is rich in fish, although salt cod *(bacalhau)* is actually imported, and lamprey and trout from the Minho's rivers are popular. Cumin, unusually, is used to spice dishes. The robust diet of Trás-os-Montes echoes the austere landscape: pork, both fresh and cured, features widely, and nuts and dried beans often add body to dishes. The local sweet tooth ensures the *pastelarias* have delicious pastries.

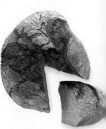

Broa *is a golden, close-textured maize bread with a thick, crunchy crust.*

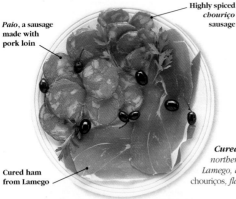

Paio, *a sausage made with pork loin*

Highly spiced *chouriço* sausage

Monte, *from Trás-os-Montes, is a smooth, creamy cheese made with cow's and ewe's milk.*

Cured ham from Lamego

Cured meats *play an important role in northern dishes. The best hams are from Lamego, and Trás-os-Montes produces fine* chouriços, *flavoured with paprika and often wine.*

Bola *is popular at Easter and for picnics. A rich bread dough is layered with a mixture of cured meats into a kind of pie.*

Pastéis de bacalhau *are a national addiction. These little salt-cod cakes are eaten cold as a snack or hot as a main dish.*

Caldo verde, *Portugal's most famous soup, gets its vibrant colour from its main ingredient:* couve galega, *a type of kale.*

Sopa de castanhas piladas, *a winter soup from Trás-os-Montes, is made with dried chestnuts, beans and rice.*

Bacalhau à Gomes de Sá *is a creation from Oporto of salt cod, potato and onion layers, topped with egg and olives.*

Truta de Barroso *uses local trout stuffed with ham and then fried in bacon fat. It is served with boiled potatoes.*

Feijoada, *popular throughout Portugal, is a stew of kidney or butter beans and cured meats, with many local variations.*

Vitela no espeto *is loin of veal barbecued (ideally on a spit), then sprinkled with oil and covered to draw out the juices.*

Rojões, *a widely popular and variable dish, uses cumin to spice pork which is then cooked in wine and garlic to a rich stew.*

Chouriço — Morcela

Pork

Chicken — Beef

Cozido à portuguesa *is a national dish with its origins in Trás-os-Montes, where it is a Carnaval speciality. A variety of meats, sausages and vegetables are served in their own broth.*

Morcela

Farinheira

***These sausages** are two of the many types of cured meats used in dishes such as* cozido à portuguesa. Farinheira *is made from pork, wine and flour, while* morcela *is a well-seasoned blood sausage. It is good sliced and fried or barbecued.*

Torta de Viana *is a sponge roll with a sweetened egg filling.*

Toucinho do céu *is a rich almond and cinnamon cake; it means "bacon from heaven".*

Papos de anjo *(angel's breasts) take their curious name from their delicate shape.*

Sopa dourada, *sponge cake under a blanket of ground almonds and egg yolk, was created in Viana do Castelo.*

Cakes *fulfil the Portuguese passion for sweet things. Northern specialities are rich and velvety smooth, addictively sugary, and often flavoured with cinnamon.*

Pudim Abade de Priscos, *named after the abbot who invented it, is flavoured with port, spices and lemon.*

DRINKS

Northern grapes also produce *baga-ceira*, a clear distillation of the remains of wine pressing, and Portuguese spirit, *aguardente*. The region has many spa towns, such as Pedras Salgadas, that provide excellent mineral waters.

Mineral water from Pedras Salgadas

Aguar-dente

DOURO AND TRÁS-OS-MONTES

O N ITS WAY TO THE ATLANTIC, *the Douro or "Golden River" weaves its scenic path through deep-cleft gorges, terraced with thousands of vineyards, to the historic city of Oporto, home of port. To the northeast, the high plateaus and mountain ranges of Trás-os-Montes, "Behind the Mountains", form Portugal's wildest region.*

As early as the 9th century BC, Phoenician merchants arrived in the Douro estuary to trade. The Romans later developed the settlements of Portus and Cale on either side of the river, and the names subsequently united, as Portucale, to denote the region between the Minho and Douro rivers. This was the nucleus of the kingdom of Portugal *(see pp42–3).* The estuary and coastal strip, or Douro Litoral, is now a mix of fishing ports, beach resorts and industrial zones, while Portus, at the river's mouth, became Oporto, the regional capital and Portugal's second city.

Rich from centuries of trade, cosmopolitan Oporto is at once modern and steeped in the past, its waterfront and higgledy-piggledy streets a delight to explore. From its hillside, Oporto looks across the Douro to the lodges which nurture the precious wine to which the city gave its name: port.

The upper reaches of the river are devoted to the cultivation of grapes for port, the landscape shaped by endless vineyards and wine estates *(quintas).*

In contrast with the thriving Douro valley, Trás-os-Montes is remote and untamed, a refuge in the past of religious and political exiles. The hard life and lack of opportunity to better it have depopulated the land; those who remain till the fields and herd their flocks in the unforgiving climate, according to the rhythm of the seasons.

The rural north clings closely to tradition and local *festas* are some of the country's most colourful *(see pp226–7).* Outside influences are beginning to make an impact on Trás-os-Montes, but for the visitor it remains a land of quiet stone villages amid fields of rye and moorland, where the wild Parque Natural de Montesinho stretches from Bragança to the Spanish border.

Terraced vineyards covering the hillsides between Pinhão and Alijó, in the valley of the Upper Douro

◁ Oporto's Barredo district, where houses are squeezed into the steep maze of ancient alleys

Exploring the Douro and Trás-os-Montes

OPORTO ITSELF IS SO FULL OF INTEREST that many visitors venture no further. But to follow the Douro upstream is to discover a world of neat terraced vineyards and prosperous *quintas* all dedicated to producing wine and port. Oporto apart, either Peso da Régua or the pilgrimage town of Lamego would make a convenient base from which to explore the area.

Trás-os-Montes is Portugal's poorest and least-known region. Its isolated capital, Bragança, is full of historic associations, and lies on the edge of the wild terrain of the Montesinho reserve. Between here and Chaves is spectacular country seldom visited by tourists.

Rocky outcrops of the Parque Natural do Alvão

SIGHTS AT A GLANCE

Amarante ❹
Bragança pp258–9 ⓱
Casa de Mateus pp254–5 ❿
Chaves ⓮
Cinfães ❺
Freixo de Espada à Cinta ㉒
Lamego ❽
Mesão Frio ❻
Miranda do Douro ⓳
Mirandela ⓰
Mogadouro ⓴
Murça ⓯
Oporto pp236–47 ❶

Parque Natural do Alvão ⓬
Parque Natural de Montesinho ⓲
Penafiel ❸
Peso da Régua ❼
Santo Tirso ❷
Serra do Barroso ⓭
Torre de Moncorvo ㉑
Vila Real ⓫

Tours
Port Country Tour pp252–3 ❾

Oporto's quayside, the Cais da Ribeira, in the early morning

KEY

▨	Motorway
▬	Major road
▭	Minor road
▭	Scenic route
⌐	River
☼	Viewpoint

Port country near Pinhão, where vineyards clothe the banks of the Douro

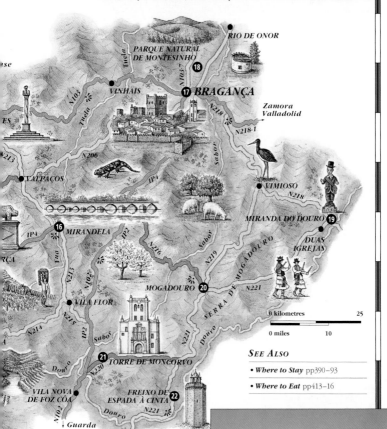

The Sabor near Bragança, on the southern edge of the Parque Natural de Montesinho

Map labels

RIO DE ONOR

PARQUE NATURAL
DE MONTESINHO

18

VINHAIS

17 BRAGANÇA

Zamora
Valladolid

N218

N218-1

TALPAÇOS

N206

IP4

VIMIOSO
N218

MIRANDA DO DOURO **19**

16 MIRANDELA

DUAS
IGREJAS

N216

N219

MOGADOURO **20**

N221

SERRA DE MOGADOURO

VILA FLOR

N215

SERRA DE MOGADOURO

0 kilometres   25

0 miles   10

21 TORRE DE MONCORVO

SEE ALSO

• *Where to Stay* pp390–93

• *Where to Eat* pp413–16

VILA NOVA
DE FOZ CÔA

FREIXO DE
ESPADA À CINTA **22**

Guarda

N221

GETTING AROUND

With the frenetic tempo of traffic in Oporto, it is best to negotiate the inner city by bus, taxi or on foot. Boat trips from Oporto are a good way to see the varied Douro landscape at a relaxed pace. Trains link Oporto to the major towns of the north and also run along the Douro valley. Services are less frequent beyond Peso da Régua, but a trip alongside the Douro is highly recommended. In Trás-os-Montes, public transport is minimal and driving is the most convenient way to explore this remote region, especially now the IP4 links Vila Real and Bragança. However, the state of repair of many minor roads leaves a lot to be desired.

Oporto ❶

E VER SINCE THE ROMANS built a fort here, where their trading route crossed the Douro, Oporto has prospered from commerce. Quick to expel the Moors in the 11th century and to profit from provisioning crusaders en route to the Holy Land, resourceful Oporto took advantage of the wealth generated by Portugal's maritime discoveries in the 15th and 16th centuries. Later, the wine

Lion and eagle statue, Rotunda da Boavista

trade with Britain compensated for the loss of the lucrative spice trade. Still a thriving industrial centre and the country's second largest city, Oporto, known locally as Porto, blends industry with charm. In 2001 the city was the European Capital of Culture, and hosted an array of events throughout the year.

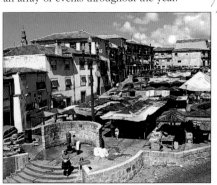

Market stalls set up in the shadow of the cathedral

The Cathedral District

Oporto's cathedral *(see p240)* crowns the city's upper level and in the surrounding streets are a variety of monuments to the city's past, including the

Renaissance church of Santa Clara *(see p239)* and the turn-of-the-century railway station of São Bento *(see p239)*, alongside bustling street markets.

Beneath the towering cathedral lies the crowded Barredo, a quarter seemingly unchanged since medieval days, where balconied houses cling to each other and to the vertiginous hillside, forming a maze of ancient alleys; some are no more than outside staircases.

Ribeira

This riverside quarter is a warren of narrow, twisting streets and shadowy arcades. Behind brightly tiled or pastel-painted façades, many in faded glory, a working population earns its living, hangs out the washing, chats and mixes in lively street scenes. Restoration of this atmospheric district is attracting a growing number of restaurants and nightclubs.

Washing hanging out to dry in a typical street in the Ribeira district

Cordoaria

The Cordoaria gardens, popular with students at the nearby university, lie in the lee of the Torre dos Clérigos *(see p241)*. The steep streets around are full of interesting shops.

A shop in the Cordoaria area specializing in *bacalhau* (salt cod

Looking north up the Avenida dos Aliados to the Câmara Municipal

KEY

	Cathedral District *pp238–9*
	Railway station
	Main terminal for coaches
	River boat service
	Parking
	Tourist information
	Church

VISITORS' CHECKLIST

Map C2. 300,000.
Francisco Sá Carneiro 10 km
(6 miles) N (22-941 31 41).
National & International:
Campanhã (22-536 41 41 for
timetable information). Regional:
São Bento. Rua Alexandre
Herculano; Praça da Galiza;
Campo 24 de Agosto; Praçeta
Régulo Megoanha. Rua Clube
dos Fenianos 25 (22-339 34 72);
Rua Infante Dom Henrique 63
(22-200 97 70). 2nd half of
Jun: Festas da Cidade.
www. portoturismo.pt

Central and Baixa

The civic centre of Oporto ranges along the Avenida dos Aliados, leading up to the modern Câmara Municipal, or town hall. Along this broad double avenue are to be found the city's banks and offices, and thriving outdoor cafés. To the east, the Baixa or "lower level" district attracts shoppers, especially to the fashionable leather and jewellery shops in and around the pedestrianized Rua de Santa Catarina and the parallel Rua Sá da Bandeira. Between them lies the two-tier covered Bolhão market. Noisy and exuberant, it provides an entertaining view of Oporto daily life. Everything can be bought here, from fresh fruit and vegetables to household goods and pets.

Boavista

The busy traffic artery of the Avenida da Boavista is lined with hotels, residential blocks and shops. In the centre of the Rotunda da Boavista, as Praça de Mouzinho de Albuquerque is known locally, a statue of a jaunty lion (the Luso-British forces) crushing an eagle (the French) marks the victory in the Peninsular War. South of the rotunda is one of the best shopping areas in the city.

OPORTO CITY CENTRE

Casa-Museu Guerra Junqueiro ⑭
Feitoria Inglesa ⑫
Igreja do Carmo ⑤
Igreja dos Clérigos ⑥
Igreja dos Congregados ⑦
Igreja da Misericórdia ⑧
Igreja Românica ①
Jardim do Palácio de Cristal ③
Museu de Etnografia e História ⑨
Museu Romântico ②
Museu Soares dos Reis ④
Palácio da Bolsa ⑩
Ponte de Dom Luís I ⑯
Santa Clara ⑮
São Francisco ⑪
Sé ⑬

Fresh fruit and vegetables in the colourful Bolhão market

Street-by-Street: Oporto's Cathedral District

ARCHAEOLOGICAL EXCAVATIONS show that Penaventosa Hill, now the site of Oporto's cathedral, or Sé, was inhabited as early as 3,000 years ago. In its elevated position, the cathedral is a useful landmark and its terrace provides an excellent orientation point. The broad Avenida de Vímara Peres, named after the military hero who expelled the Moors from the city in AD 868, sweeps south past the huddle of steep alleys and stairways of the Barredo. The view to the north is towards the extraordinarily embellished São Bento station and the busy commercial heart of the city.

Rua das Flores
Behind the traditional shop-fronts in the Street of Flowers are many of the city's best jewellers and goldsmiths.

Street markets near the Sé offer fresh fish, fruit and vegetables alongside household goods, bric-a-brac and souvenirs.

RUA DAS F

R. MOUZINHO D.

RUA ESCURA

CALÇADA DE VANDO

TERREIRO DA SÉ

RUA DE DOM HUGO

Terreiro da Sé
This broad open terrace offers a wonderful panorama of the city. In one corner stands a Manueline pillory, complete with hooks.

Former bishops' palace

★ Sé
Although imposing and perhaps a little forbidding, Oporto's cathedral contains many small-scale treasures. This 17th-century gilded painting of the Last Supper is in the Capela de São Vicente (see p240).

The Casa-Museu Guerra Junqueiro is a charming museum in a house that once belonged to the 19th-century poet *(see p240)*.

Ponte de Dom Luís I

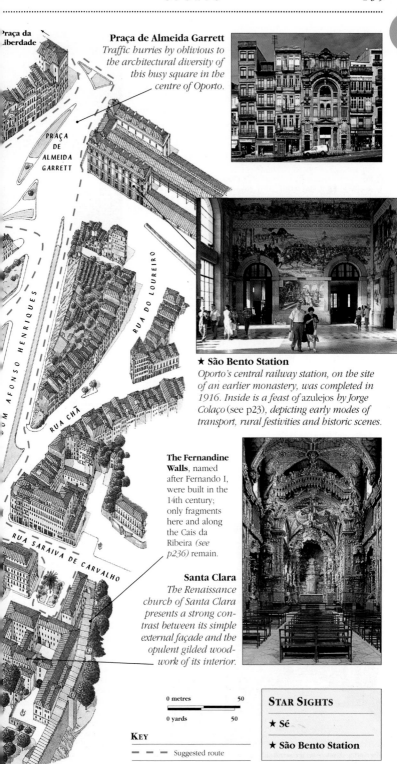

Praça de Almeida Garrett
Traffic hurries by oblivious to the architectural diversity of this busy square in the centre of Oporto.

★ São Bento Station
Oporto's central railway station, on the site of an earlier monastery, was completed in 1916. Inside is a feast of azulejos by Jorge Colaço (see p23), depicting early modes of transport, rural festivities and historic scenes.

The Fernandine Walls, named after Fernando I, were built in the 14th century; only fragments here and along the Cais da Ribeira *(see p236)* remain.

Santa Clara
The Renaissance church of Santa Clara presents a strong contrast between its simple external façade and the opulent gilded woodwork of its interior.

0 metres 50
0 yards 50

KEY

– – – Suggested route

STAR SIGHTS

★ Sé

★ São Bento Station

Exploring Oporto

THROUGHOUT OPORTO THERE IS EVIDENCE of the wealth that flowed into the city from the 15th century onwards. Trade in the commodities from Portugal's newly claimed lands *(see pp48–9)* brought Brazilian gold and exotic woods to embellish Oporto's churches, and prosperous merchants spent prodigiously on paintings and *azulejos*. The extravagant stock exchange, the Palácio da Bolsa, and the exclusive Feitoria Inglesa are later reminders of the city's continued importance as a trading centre.

⛪ Sé
Terreiro da Sé. **(** 22-205 9028.
○ 9am–12:30pm, 2:30–7pm daily.
cloisters ○ Mon–Sat. 🖼
Built as a fortress church in the 12th and 13th centuries, the cathedral has since been so modified that it lacks a unified style. The only noteworthy survival from the 13th century is the beautiful rose window in the west front. In the small chapel to the left of the chancel is a silver retable of dazzling workmanship, saved from invading French troops in 1809 by means of a hastily raised plaster wall. The south transept gives access to the 14th-century cloisters and the Capela de São Vicente. Niccolò Nasoni's graceful 18th-century staircase leads to the upper levels. Here, vibrant *azulejo* panels depict the life of the Virgin and Ovid's *Metamorphoses*, and there is a splendid panorama of the city.

Portuguese water jug, Museu Guerra Junqueiro

🏛 Casa-Museu Guerra Junqueiro
Rua de Dom Hugo 32. **(** 22-205 3644. **○** Tue–Sun. **●** public hols. 🖼
The former home of the poet and fiery Republican activist, Guerra Junqueiro (1850–1923), is an 18th-century Baroque gem. From the tranquil courtyard, visitors enter the poet's private collection, which ranges from Portuguese furniture and rare ceramics to Flemish tapestries and a remarkable set of English alabaster sculptures. On elegant tables in the Dom João V Room there is a colourful parade of Chinese dogs.

🏛 Feitoria Inglesa
Rua do Infante Dom Henrique 8.
(22-339 2980.
Closed to the public unless by invitation from a member, the "English factory" is the headquarters of the port-shippers' British Association. It was built to the design of a Robert Adam town house in 1790. A sweeping staircase leads up to the Map Room and a grand ballroom. This exclusive, male domain invited its first ladies to dinner in 1843.

🏛 Palácio da Bolsa
Rua Ferreira Borges.
(22-339 9000.
○ 9am–1pm, 2pm–6pm daily. **●** public hols. 🖼
🎦 compulsory.
Where the monastery of São Francisco once stood, the city's merchants built the stock exchange, or Bolsa, in 1842. The Tribunal do Comércio, where Oporto's mercantile

The magnificently gilded Arabian Room in Oporto's Palácio da Bolsa

law was upheld, is full of historic interest, and has a small adjoining picture gallery. But the glittering highlight is the Arabian Room. This galleried salon, its convoluted blue and gold arabesques inspired by Granada's Alhambra, makes a setting fit for Scheherazade.

🏛 Museu de Etnografia e História
Largo de São João Novo 11.
● for restoration.
Housed in an imposing 18th-century palace, the museum covers the life and customs of the Douro. As well as archaeological discoveries and exhibits of local ceramics, there are displays of rural costumes, animal traps, coins and curiosities such as the city's first lift (1910). Adding to the interest of this eclectic collection are reconstructions of an old wine cellar and a weaver's workshop.

⛪ Casa da Misericórdia
Rua das Flores 15. **(** 22-207 4710.
○ Mon–Sat. **●** public hols. 🖾
This religious hospice, alongside its imposing church, was founded in the 16th century. Its most precious possession is the masterful *Fons Vitae* (Fountain of Life), donated by Manuel I in about 1520. The artist's identity remains unproven, but Van der Weyden and Holbein have both been suggested. The picture shows the king with his family and nobles kneeling before the crucified Christ.

The Gothic cloisters on the south side of the Sé

SÃO FRANCISCO'S TREE OF JESSE

Illustrating biblical episodes, either in stained-glass windows or as elaborate carvings, was a common form of "Bible teaching" before literacy became widespread. A popular subject was Christ's genealogy, showing his descent from the kings of Judah and Israel. This was commonly rendered as an actual tree, tracing the family line back through Joseph to the father of King David, Jesse of Bethlehem.

São Francisco's Tree, in gilded and painted wood, was carved between 1718 and 1721 by Filipe da Silva and António Gomes. Its sinuous branches and trunk, sprouting from a reclining Jesse, support a dozen expressive figures, culminating in Christ flanked by His mother, Mary, and St Joseph.

Virgin Mary

Jesus Christ

Joseph

Solomon, who succeeded his father, David, was famed for his wisdom and for the building of the Temple in Jerusalem.

Jesse is shown with the roots of the Tree springing from his loins. His youngest son was David, the slayer of Goliath, who became king of Israel and Judah.

King David, identified by his harp

🔒 São Francisco

Rua do Infante D.Henrique. **☎** 22-206 2100. ◯ 9am–6pm daily.
🏛 Catacombs included.

Construction of São Francisco began in the 14th century, but it is the 18th-century interior that amazes visitors. Over 200 kg (450 lb) of gold encrusting the high altar, columns and pillars is wrought into cherubs, garlands and cavorting animals, reaching a crescendo with the Tree of Jesse on the north wall. A tour includes the catacombs and treasures from the church's monastery, destroyed in 1832.

🔒 Igreja dos Congregados

Rua da Sá Bandeira ll. **☎** 22-200 29 48. ◯ daily. ● public hols

The modern tiles clothing the façade of this 17th-century church are by Jorge Colaço (see p23). They depict scenes from the life of St Antony, and provide a dignified presence amid the traffic that clogs this part of the city.

🔒 Igreja dos Clérigos

Rua São Filipe Néri. **☎** 22-200 17 29. ◯ Thu–Tue.
Tower ◯ daily. 🏛

This hilltop ensemble of church and tower is an unmistakable landmark. Built in the 18th century by Niccolò Nasoni, the church's oval interior was the first in Portugal.

The soaring Torre dos Clérigos with which the architect complemented his design is, at 75 m (246 ft), still one of the tallest buildings in Portugal. The dizzying 240-step climb is worth it for the superb views of the river, the coastline and the Douro valley.

São Francisco's extravagant interior

Torre dos Clérigos, Oporto's landmark and panoramic viewpoint

Detail of the *azulejo* panel on the side wall of the Igreja do Carmo

🔒 Igreja do Carmo

Rua do Carmo. 📞 *22-207 8400.*
⭘ *daily.* ♿

This characteristic example of Portuguese Baroque architecture was constructed by José Figueiredo Seixas between 1750 and 1768. Its most notable feature is the immense *azulejo* panel covering one outside wall. Designed by Silvestro Silvestri, it depicts the legendary founding of the Carmelite order on Mount Carmel.

The earlier Igreja das Carmelitas next door was completed in 1628 in a combination of Classical and Baroque styles. It is now part of a barracks.

🏛 Museu Soares dos Reis

Rua Dom Manuel II. 📞 *22-339 37 70.*
⭘ *Tue–Sun.* ⬤ *public hols.* ♿

The elegant Carrancas Palace, built in the 18th century, has been a Jewish textile workshop, a royal abode and, in the Peninsular War, a military headquarters. In 1809 Oporto was in French hands, and Marshal Soult and his troops were quartered here. They were ousted in a surprise attack by Arthur Wellesley, later Duke of Wellington, who then calmly installed himself at the marshal's dinner table.

Today, the palace provides an appropriate setting for an outstanding museum, named after António Soares dos Reis, the country's leading 19th-century sculptor. Pride of place goes to the display of Portuguese art. This includes paintings by the 16th-century master, Frey Carlos, and the Impressionist, Henrique Pousão. Also hung here are landscapes of Oporto by the French artist, Jean Pillement (1728–1808). The star sculpture exhibit, *O Desterrado* (The Exile), is Soares dos Reis's own marvel of pensive tension in marble, completed in 1874. Further sections display

O Desterrado
Soares dos R

A River View of Oporto

FLOWING OVER 927 km (576 miles) from its source in Spain to the Atlantic, the Douro has been linked with the fortunes of Oporto since time immemorial. There is an unsubstantiated story that Henry the Navigator, patron of Portuguese explorers, *(see p49),* was born in the waterfront Casa do Infante. The days are long since gone when ships laden with port or goods from overseas would moor here, but the river continues to be a focal point of the city. A river cruise is a chance to appreciate Oporto from a different viewpoint.

Most river-boat operators are based in the shadow of the swooping curve of the splendid two-tier Ponte de Dom Luís I, built in 1886 by an assistant of Gustave Eiffel, to link the city to Vila Nova de Gaia on the southern bank. The city is in the early stages of constructing a metro system which will use the upper level of the Dom Luís I bridge. A new bridge is also being built for cars. The bridge and metro are unlikely to open before 2003.

Vila Nova de Gaia is home of the port lodges *(see p247).*

Ponte da Arrábida

Quayside of the Cais da Estiva

ortuguese pottery, Limoges
namels, porcelain and deco-
ative art. Historical exhibits
n the museum include an
ppealing 15th-century silver
ust of São Pantaleão, patron
aint of Oporto, and a sword
vhich was once owned by
ne first king of Portugal.

Igreja Románica

argo do Priorado. 22-200 0635.
phone to check.

onstructed in Romanesque
tyle in the 12th century, this
lain little church is thought to
e the oldest in the city. It is
aid to have been built on the
ite where Theodomir, the King
f the Suevi (a Germanic tribe
vho occupied the area), was
onverted to Christianity in the
th century by Saint Martin.
he church stands next to the
nodern Igreja de Cedofeita.

Museu Romântico

ua de Entre-Quintas 220.
22-609 11 31. Tue–Sun.
public hols.

he Quinta da Macieirinha was
riefly the residence of the
bdicated King Carlo Alberto
f Sardinia (1798–1849), who
ved here for the final two
nonths of his life. In 1972 the
pper floor of the mansion

**Temporary exhibits in the billiards
room of the Museu Romântico**

was converted into a museum.
The well-proportioned rooms
looking out over the river display to advantage delicately
finished French, German and
Portuguese furniture, as well
as rugs, ceramics and miscel-
laneous exhibits. Among the
oil paintings and watercolours
displayed here are
portraits of Baron
Forrester *(see p252)*
and Almeida Garrett,
the great Portuguese
Romantic poet, play-
wright and author.

On the ground
floor of the Quinta
da Macieirinha, the
Port Wine Institute
operates the Solar
do Vinho do Porto.
In this unexpected
bar it is possible to

choose from a tasting list of
over 150 varieties of port,
then relax in the secluded
garden and enjoy the view
across the Douro.

Jardim do Palácio de Cristal

Rua Dom Manuel II. daily.

Inspired by the Crystal Palace
of London's Great Exhibition
in 1851, Oporto's own crystal
palace was begun in 1861. The
steel and glass structure of the
original was replaced in the
1950s by the Sports Pavilion,
an ungainly shape dubbed
"the half-orange" by local wits.
Concerts are occasionally held
here and the leisure gardens
around the dome are enlivened
by a fair at *festa* time.

Cyclists in the Jardim do Palácio de Cristal

ais da Ribeira is one
f the quays at which
ver boats moor.

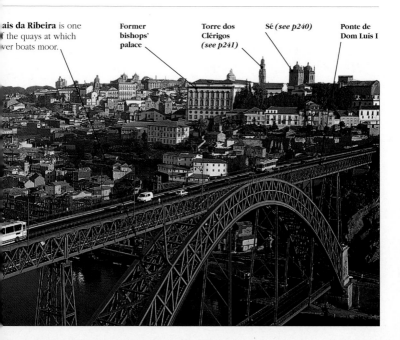

Former
bishops'
palace

Torre dos
Clérigos
(see p241)

Sé *(see p240)*

Ponte de
Dom Luís I

Oporto: Further Afield

AWAY FROM THE CITY CENTRE, Oporto has many additional places of interest. Crossing the Ponte de Dom Luís I brings you to Vila Nova de Gaia, the home of port, and the Mosteiro da Serra do Pilar, with one of the finest views of the old city. In the northern and western suburbs are several fascinating attractions, from the great church of the Hospitallers at Leça do Bailio, north of Oporto, to the latest developments in Portuguese art exhibited in the palatial Art Deco setting of the Casa de Serralves.

Along the coast, beyond the river-mouth castle at Foz do Douro, lies Matosinhos which, despite its industrial port, is renowned for its seafood. The beaches, such as Espinho, are the main draw along the coast south of Oporto.

A tram, once such a feature of Oporto, in the Museu do Carro Eléctrico

Mosteiro da Serra do Pilar

Serra do Pilar. ☎ 22-375 22 98. ○ Jun–Sep (cloisters by appt only).

It is a steep walk up to this circular 16th-century church, but worth it. From the terrace, the future Duke of Wellington planned his surprise attack on the French in 1809. It is easy to see the advantage gained, for the panoramic view takes in the port lodges below, the sweep of the River Douro and the old city on the far side.

Museu do Carro Eléctrico

Alameda Basílio Teles 51. ☎ 22-507 1000. ○ Tue–Sun.

Trams, once the backbone of the city's transport system, have been trundled into retirement, but the tram museum keeps alive their memory. Among the gleaming beauties preserved here are No. 22, introduced in 1895 as the first electric tram on the Iberian Peninsula, and No. 8, dating from 1872, which relied on mules for traction.

Special excursions are run for a substantial charge but you can enjoy a similar experience on the No. 18, Oporto's last tram, which leaves from near the museum, looping north to end at Boavista (see pp236–7).

Fundação de Serralves

Rua Dom João de Castro. ☎ 22-615 6500. ○ Tue–Fri (pm), Sat & Sun. ● 1 Jan, 25 Dec.

The clean Art Deco lines of the 1930s Casa de Serralves, surrounded by its magnificent garden, provide the perfect setting for displaying contemporary art. Regularly changing exhibitions by the foundation aim to offer an insight into the modern developments in Portuguese art, including trends in sculpture and architecture.

Casa-Museu Fernando de Castro

Rua Costa Cabral 716. ○ by appt only. ☎ 22-339 3770.

The former residence of the businessman, collector and poet, Fernando de Castro (1888–1950), was donated to the state by his sister in 1951. His collection ranges from religious sculpture saved from disbanded churches to works by modern artists, and includes a painting of the infant Jesus attributed to Josefa de Óbidos (see p51). Also of special interest are figurines from the 19th and 20th centuries by Teixeira Lopes, both father and son.

ENVIRONS: Forts around the river mouth, such as **Castelo da Foz** at Foz do Douro and **Castelo do Queijo** just to the north, are reminders that for centuries the coast and ships were under constant threat from the Spanish and pirates.

The church of **Bom Jesus**, near Matosinhos, was reconstructed by Niccolò Nasoni in the 18th century. Each June, pilgrims come here to honour a wooden statue of Christ. Found on the beach in the 10th century, it was allegedly carved by the disciple Nicodemus.

The 14th-century fortified **Igreja do Mosteiro** at Leça do Bailio, 8 km (5 miles) north of Oporto, was Portugal's first headquarters of the Order of Hospitallers. The church is graced with elegant Gothic arches, finely sculpted capitals and a splendid rose window.

The Art Deco Casa de Serralves, a forum for modern art

◁ **Barcos rabelos** moored beside the quay at Vila Nova de Gaia

Vila Nova de Gaia

AFONSO III, IN DISPUTE with the Bishop of Oporto over shipping tolls, established a rival port at Vila Nova de Gaia. In 1253, they reluctantly agreed to share the levies. Today the heart of Vila Nova de Gaia is devoted mostly to the maturation and shipping of port *(see pp252–3)*. Although the regulation that port could be made only in Vila Nova de Gaia was relaxed in 1987, this is still very much the centre of production. Every alley is lined with the lodges or *armazéns* (there are no cellars here) in which port is blended and aged.

Taylor's port

Guided tours *are a chance to see how port is made* (see pp228–9) *and often end with a tasting to demonstrate the different styles.*

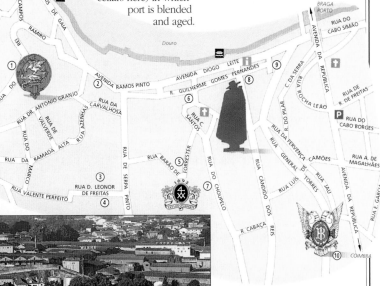

The port lodges *dominate Vila Nova de Gaia. Over 50 port companies are based in these narrow streets, ageing and blending most of the world's supply of port beneath a sea of red roofs emblazoned with world-famous names.*

PORT LODGES

Barros ④	Graham ①
Borges ⑩	Ramos Pinto ⑥
Cálem ⑨	Sandeman ⑧
Cockburn ③	Taylor ⑦
Ferreira ②	Vasconcelos ⑤

KEY

🚢	Boat trips
🅿	Parking
ℹ	Tourist information
✝	Church

0 metres   250
0 yards   250

VISITING THE LODGES

Joining a tour: Lodges listed here are among those offering tours. Booking is not usually necessary, but contact a lodge beforehand to confirm times; the tourist office at Avenida Diogo Leite 242 (22-379 0994) can supply addresses and telephone numbers.
Opening times: Variable. Usually Mon–Fri; some also at weekends. Most close on public holidays.

The former monastery of São Bento at Santo Tirso, now a college

Santo Tirso ❷

Road map C2. 🏘 *12,000.* 🚉 🚌
ℹ *Praça 25 de Abril (252-830 411).*
🛒 *Mon.*

SANTO TIRSO, a major textile centre, lies beside the River Ave. The town's most notable building is the former monastery of **São Bento**. Founded by the Benedictines in the 8th century, the monastery was later rebuilt, then modified in the 17th century. The pairs of columns in the 14th-century Gothic cloister are graced with richly carved capitals.

The monastery is now an agricultural college, but houses the **Museu Abade Pedrosa**, featuring local archaeological finds, including stone axes, bronze armlets and ceramics.

🏛 Museu Abade Pedrosa
Rua Unisco Godiniz. 📞 *252-83 04 00.* ☐ *Tue–Sun.* ● *public hols.*

The sanctuary of Nossa Senhora da Piedade in Penafiel

ENVIRONS: At Roriz, 13 km (8 miles) east of Santo Tirso, the Romanesque church of **São Pedro** perches above the Vizela valley. A date of 1228 is carved in the porch, although there are claims that a church may have stood here as early as the 8th century. Above the portal is a fine rose window. Set apart from the church are an attractive belltower and the ruins of the monastic cloister.

Sanfins de Ferreira, 5 km (3 miles) further east, is the hilltop site of a *citânia*, an Iron Age citadel, probably inhabited from around the 6th century BC. Traces remain of a triple ring of defensive walls around about 100 huts, and there is also a small museum on the site. The guard next door will let you in on public holidays.

⋔ Sanfins de Ferreira
Sanfins, signposted off N209.
📞 *255-86 20 29.* ☐ *by appt only.*

Penafiel ❸

Road map C2. 🏘 *8,000.* 🚌
ℹ *Avenida Sacadura Cabral 90 (255-71 25 61).* 🛒 *10 & 20 of month.*

THE GRANITE TOWN of Penafiel stands on a hilltop above the River Sousa. Apart from an elegant Renaissance-style **Igreja Matriz**, there is also a sanctuary, **Nossa Senhora da Piedade**, built in 1908 in a curious medley of Neo-Gothic and Byzantine styles. Penafiel is chiefly known, however, as the regional centre for *vinho verde* production *(see pp28–9)*.

ENVIRONS: One of the region's foremost estates producing *vinho verde* is the picturesque **Quinta da Aveleda**, which lies just north of Penafiel.

Boelhe, around 17 km (11 miles) south of Penafiel, merits a detour for the 12th-century church of São Gens. Only 10 m (33 ft) high, and a mere 7 m (23 ft) in width and length, it is claimed to be the smallest Romanesque church in the country. Its simple design enhances the aesthetic appeal.

In the 13th-century church of São Salvador at **Paço de Sousa**, 8 km (5 miles) southwest of Penafiel, is the tomb of Egas Moniz. A figure of legendary loyalty, he was counsellor to Afonso Henriques (1139–85), the first king of Portugal.

🍷 Quinta da Aveleda
Signposted from N115. 📞 *255-71 10 41.* ☐ *Mon–Fri.* ● *public hols.*
🅿 🚫 🎟 *compulsory.*

The tiny church of São Gens at Boelhe, south of Penafiel

Amarante ❹

Road map D2. 🏘 *10,000.* 🚉 🚌
ℹ *Alameda Teixeira de Pascoães (255-420 200).* 🛒 *Wed & Sat.*

THE PRETTY, RIVERSIDE town of Amarante is one of the gems of northern Portugal. Rows of 17th-century mansions with brightly painted wooden balconies line Amarante's narrow streets, and restaurants seat diners on terraces overhanging the river. The origins of the town are uncertain but the first settlement here was probably around 360 BC. Much of the town was burnt down in 1809, after a two-week siege by the French forces under Marshal Soult.

A recurring name in Amarante is that of São Gonçalo, a very popular saint born at the end of the 12th century. There are many stories of the dancing and festivities he organized to keep ladies from temptation by finding them husbands, and he has become associated with matchmaking and fertility. On the first weekend in June, the Festa de São Gonçalo begins with prayers for a marriage partner, followed by dancing, music and the giving of phallic-shaped São Gonçalo cakes.

When the old Roman bridge across the Tâmega collapsed during floods in the 13th century, it was São Gonçalo who was credited with replacing it. The present Ponte de São Gonçalo crosses to the 16th-century **Mosteiro de São Gonçalo**, where his memory lives on. In the chapel to the left of the chancel, the image on his tomb has been eroded through the embraces of thousands of devotees in search of his intercession.

The **Museu Amadeo de Sousa-Cardoso** is housed in the old monastery cloister next to the church. One of the exhibits describes a fertility cult that predates even São Gonçalo. The *diabo* and *diaba* are a pair of bawdy devils carved in black wood, and are 19th-century replacements for a more ancient duo destroyed in

The Ponte de São Gonçalo across the Tâmega at Amarante

the Peninsular War. They gradually became the focus of a type of local fertility rite, and were threatened with burning by an outraged bishop of Braga; the *diabo* was "castrated" instead.

The museum's other prized possession is the collection of Cubist works by the artist after whom the museum is named. Amadeo de Sousa-Cardoso (1887–1918), one of Portugal's leading 20th-century artists, was a native of Amarante.

🏛 Mosteiro de São Gonçalo
Praça da República.
📞 255-42 20 50. ⏱ daily.

🏛 Museu Amadeo de Sousa-Cardoso
Alameda Teixeira de Pascoães.
📞 255-420 233. ⏱ Tue–Sun.
⏺ public hols.

Cinfães ❺

Road map D2. 🏘 4,000. 🚌
ℹ Rua Dr Flavio Resende 43 (255-561 768). 🗓 10 & 26 of month.

CINFÃES LIES just above the Douro, tucked below the foothills of the Serra de Montemuro whose peaks rise over 1,000 m (3,300 ft). The town is a gateway to Lamego and the Upper Douro to the east *(see pp252–3)* and is surrounded by verdant scenery. Cinfães itself is an agricultural centre and local handicrafts include weaving, lacework, basketry, and the production of miniature *rabelos*, the boats that used to ship port down the river to Oporto *(see p250)*.

ENVIRONS: Around 16 km (10 miles) west of the town, at Tarouquela, is the 12th-century church of **Santa Maria Maior**. Romanesque columns flank the portal, while later additions include the 14th-century Gothic mausoleum beside the chancel.

In the village of **Cárquere**, between Cinfães and Lamego, stands another church dedicated to the Virgin Mary. Legend tells how the sickly young Afonso Henriques, future king of Portugal, was healed at Cárquere by his devoted aide, Egas Moniz. In about 1110, guided by a dream, Moniz unearthed a buried statue of the Virgin and built a church for her. Miraculously, his young charge was cured overnight. The present church dates from the 14th or 15th century, but the finest of its treasures is a minute ivory carving of the Virgin, of unknown date.

The 12th-century church of Nossa Senhora de Cárquere, near Cinfães

Painted ceiling panels in São Nicolau, Mesão Frio's Igreja Matriz

Mesão Frio **❻**

Road map D2. 🏠 700. 🚌
🚹 Avenida José Maria Alpoim
(254-89 01 00). 🚂 Fri.

THIS SCENIC GATEWAY to the
port wine-growing region
enjoys a fine setting above the
River Douro. Around it, the
majestic tiers of the Serra do
Marão rise to form a natural
climatic shield for the vineyards
to the east. Mesão Frio itself is
known for its wickerwork and
a culinary speciality, *falachas*
or chestnut cakes.

The Igreja Matriz of **São
Nicolau** was rebuilt in 1877,
but has fortunately retained its
magnificent late 16th-century
ceiling panels, each one featuring an individual portrait of
a saint. The tourist office and
town hall are housed in the
18th-century **cloisters** of a
former Franciscan monastery.

On the western edge of the
town, the lavish Baroque **Casa
da Rede** can be seen from the
roadside, but not visited.

Peso da Régua **❼**

Road map D2. 🏠 5,500. 🚆 🚌
🚹 Rua da Ferreirinha (254-31 28 46).
🚂 Wed.

DEVELOPED from the villages
of Peso and Régua in the
18th century, Peso da Régua
is the major hub for rail and
road connections in the region.

In 1756, Régua, as the town
is invariably called, was chosen
by the Marquês de Pombal as
the centre of the demarcated
region for port production.
From here, *rabelos*, the traditional wooden sailing ships,
transported the barrels of port
through hazardous gorges to
Vila Nova de Gaia *(see p247)*.
They continued to ply the
river even after the advent of
the Douro railway in the 1880s
offered a faster and safer means
of transport. Régua suffered
frequently in the past
from severe floods,
and these are still a
threat, although they
have lessened since
dams were built
across the Douro in
the 1970s and 1980s.

Visitors to Régua
usually pause only
briefly on their way
to explore the "port
country" *(see pp252–3)*, but it
is worth seeking out the **Casa
do Douro**, the administrative
headquarters of the Port Wine
Institute. Its modern stained-
glass windows, created by Lino
António, vividly depict the history and production of port.
Also displayed is a fine map of
the Douro valley drawn in the
mid-19th century by Baron
Forrester *(see p252)*.

🏛 **Casa do Douro**
Rua dos Camilos. 📞 254-32 08 11.
🕐 Mon–Fri. ⬤ public hols.

ENVIRONS: In the surrounding
countryside are some beautiful *quintas*, the country estates
where port is produced. One
of the nearest to Régua is the
attractive **Quinta da Pacheca**
at Cambres, 4 km (2 miles) to
the southwest. The **Enoteca
de Granjão**, in a village on
the road to Mesão Frio, will
organize visits to this and other
port lodges, and can collect
visitors from hotels or the
bus or train station in Régua.

🍷 **Enoteca de Granjão**
Granjão (on N108). 📞 254-32 27 88.
🕐 10am–7pm daily. ⬤ public hols.

**Stained-glass window of the Casa do Douro,
Peso da Régua, showing loaded *rabelos***

Lamego **❽**

Road map D2. 🏠 12,000. 🚌
🚹 Avenida Visconde Guedes Teixeira
(254-61 20 05). 🚂 Thu.

AN ATTRACTIVE TOWN within
the demarcated port area,
Lamego also produces wines,
including Raposeira, Portugal's
premier sparkling wine. This
fertile region is also known for
its fruit and choice hams.

In its more illustrious past,
Lamego claims to have been
host in 1143 to the first *cortes*,
or national assembly, to recog-
nize Afonso Henriques as first
king of Portugal. The town's
later economic decline was
halted in the 16th century,
when it turned to wine and
textile production, and handsome Baroque mansions from
this prosperous period are still
a feature of the town. Today,
the main focus of Lamego is
as a pilgrimage town.

Vineyards on the slopes of the Serra do Marão around Mesão Frio

The grand staircase leading up to Nossa Senhora dos Remédios, Lamego

🔒 Nossa Senhora dos Remédios

Monte de Santo Estêvão. ◯ *daily.*

A small hilltop chapel, originally dedicated in 1391 to St Stephen, became the focus of pilgrims devoted to the Virgin, and in 1761 Nossa Senhora dos Remédios was built on the spectacular site. The church is reached via an awe-inspiring double stairway, similar to Braga's even larger Bom Jesus *(see pp278–9)*. Its 686 steps and nine terraces, embellished with *azulejos* and urns, rise to the Pátio dos Reis, a circle of noble granite figures beneath the twin-towered church. The church itself is of marginal interest, but there is a well-earned view across the town to the Douro and its tributaries.

In early September pilgrims arrive in their thousands for Lamego's Romaria de Nossa Senhora dos Remédios *(see p32)*, many of them climbing the steps on their knees.

🔒 Sé

Largo da Sé. 📞 254-612 766. ◯ *daily.*

Lamego's Gothic cathedral, founded in 1129, retains its original square tower, while the rest of the architecture reflects modifications between the 16th and 18th centuries, including a Renaissance cloister with a dozen arches.

🏛 Museu de Lamego

Largo de Camões. 📞 254-600 230. ◯ *Tue–Sun.* ● *public hols.* 📷

One of the country's best local museums is housed in the former bishops' palace. Pride of place goes to the strikingly original *Criação dos Animais* (Creation of the Animals), part of a series of masterly altar panels attributed to the great 16th-century Portuguese artist, Grão Vasco *(see p213)*. Finely worked 16th-century Flemish tapestries include a vividly detailed life of Oedipus.

ENVIRONS: At the foot of the valley 4 km (2 miles) east, the **Capela de São Pedro de Balsemão** is said to be the oldest church in Portugal. Although much modified, the 7th-century sanctuary, of Visigothic origins, remains. Here, in an ornate tomb, lies Afonso Pires, a 14th-century bishop of Oporto. A statue of Nossa Senhora do Ó, the pregnant Virgin, is from the 15th century.

The 12th-century monastery of **São João de Tarouca**, the first Cistercian house in Portugal, lies 16 km (10 miles) south of Lamego. The interior of the church has many fine 18th-century *azulejo* panels, notably those in the chancel depicting the founding of the monastery, and in the sacristy, where none of the 4,709 tiles has the same design. The church also contains a remarkable *St Peter* by Grão Vasco. The Count of Barcelos, bastard son of King Dinis, is buried here, his tomb adorned with vigorous scenes of a boar hunt.

Just to the northeast, **Ucanha** is famed for its fortified tollgate and bridge, imposing survivals from the 12th century.

🔒 São João de Tarouca

Signposted from N226. ◯ *Tue–Sun.* ● *3rd weekend of month.* ♿

The monastery church of São João de Tarouca in its peaceful setting

Port Country Tour ⑨

Bottles of Graham's port

THE BARRELS OF PORT maturing in the port lodges of Vila Nova de Gaia *(see p247)* begin their life here, on the wine estates *(quintas)* of the Upper Douro *(see pp228–9)*. Centuries of toil on the poor schist have created thousands of terraces along the steep river banks, many no wider than a person's outstretched arms. An EU-funded programme to dynamite and bulldoze tractor access to the terraces is labour saving, but set to change the face of the land. Many traditional *quintas*, including those indicated on the map, welcome visitors. Early autumn is the most rewarding time to tour; workers sing as they pick, and celebrate a successful *vindima* or harvest.

The village and vineyards of Vale de Mendiz just before sunset

Peso da Régua ①
Régua's role as an administrative centre for port and, later, for the wines of the region, goes back to 1756. The *rabelos* moored here are a reminder of how port used to be transported down to the lodges of Vila Nova de Gaia.

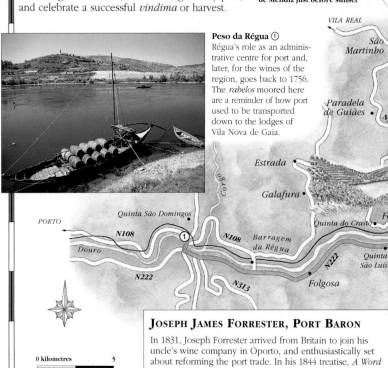

KEY

▰▰▰	Tour route
---	Other roads
—	Railway
❃	Viewpoint

0 kilometres 5

0 miles 3

JOSEPH JAMES FORRESTER, PORT BARON

In 1831, Joseph Forrester arrived from Britain to join his uncle's wine company in Oporto, and enthusiastically set about reforming the port trade. In his 1844 treatise, *A Word or Two on Port*, he waged war on shippers who adulterated the wine. He also studied the vine blight, *Oidium tuckeri*, drew up remarkably detailed maps of the Douro valley and found time to become a talented watercolourist. His contribution was such that in 1855 Pedro V bestowed on him the title of Barão. In 1862, Forrester's boat capsized at Cachão de Valeira. Dragged down by his moneybelt, he drowned, but the ladies in his company survived, buoyed up by their crinolines.

Pinhão ②

Many of the most famous names in port production have *quintas* close to this small town. Its railway station is decorated with 24 dazzling *azulejo* panels depicting local scenes and folk culture.

TIPS FOR DRIVERS

Tour length: 125 km (78 miles). Beyond Pinhão, steep, narrow roads can make the going slow.
Stopping-off points: The drive beside the Douro has several fine viewpoints. Alijó, Régua and Sabrosa make good overnight stops (see pp390–93) and many quintas offer tours and port-tasting. (See also pp444–5.)

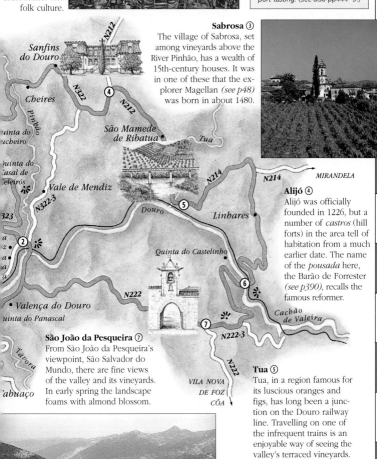

Sabrosa ③

The village of Sabrosa, set among vineyards above the River Pinhão, has a wealth of 15th-century houses. It was in one of these that the explorer Magellan *(see p48)* was born in about 1480.

Alijó ④

Alijó was officially founded in 1226, but a number of *castros* (hill forts) in the area tell of habitation from a much earlier date. The name of the *pousada* here, the Barão de Forrester *(see p390)*, recalls the famous reformer.

São João da Pesqueira ⑦

From São João da Pesqueira's viewpoint, São Salvador do Mundo, there are fine views of the valley and its vineyards. In early spring the landscape foams with almond blossom.

Tua ⑤

Tua, in a region famous for its luscious oranges and figs, has long been a junction on the Douro railway line. Travelling on one of the infrequent trains is an enjoyable way of seeing the valley's terraced vineyards.

Barragem de Valeira ⑥

Until the end of the 18th century the Douro was unnavigable beyond Cachão de Valeira. Even when engineers had bypassed the worst of the rapids, this stretch of water remained treacherous – it was here that Baron Forrester met his death – until the water was tamed by the Valeira dam in 1976.

Casa de Mateus ⑩

English 17th-century cupboard in the Tea Salon

T HE SPLENDID MANOR HOUSE, or *solar*, depicted on the labels of Mateus Rosé *(see p28)* epitomizes the flamboyance of Baroque architecture in Portugal. It was built in the early 18th century, probably by Niccolò Nasoni, for António José Botelho Mourão, among whose titles was 3rd Morgado de Mateus. His descendants still live here, but visitors can tour the gardens and part of the house, and buy the estate's produce (but not Mateus wine, which is a separate concern).

The wood-panelled library, repository of many valuable works

The Manor House

Inside and out, the Casa de Mateus was conceived to present carefully created vistas and series of mirror images. A formal pool added in the 1930s continues this spirit of harmonious repetition, reflecting the main façade and its two wings.

Tours start in the first-floor entrance salon, a well-proportioned room graced by a pair of sedan chairs and with a magnificent wooden ceiling featuring family coats of arms. Doorcases and ceilings throughout the house are of richly carved chestnut. The Tea Salon has a 17th-century William and Mary cupboard and

Coat of arms on the entrance hall ceiling

matching longcase clock from England, while the Salon of the Four Seasons gets its name from the large 18th-century paintings on its walls. Many of the paintings in the house were contributed by the 4th Morgado's uncle, an archdeacon in Rome who was also responsible for the original gardens. The library, remodelled in the mid-20th century, contains volumes dating back to the 16th century, but the rarest book is in the small museum: an 1817 copy of *Os Lusíadas (see p188)*, with engravings by leading artists. It is one of a

limited edition produced by the colourful diplomat grandson of the 3rd Morgado (his tomb is in the family chapel beside the house). Also on display in the museum is family correspondence with famous figures of the era, including Frederick the Great and Wellington.

The Gardens

Beneath the entrance staircase a dark passageway leads between the stables to an inner courtyard and out to the formal gardens on the far side of the house. Little remains of the original gardens planted by the horticultural archdeacon, and the present gardens were laid out in the 1930s and 1940s. The style, however, is of an earlier, romantic era and the complex parterres and formal beds edged with tightly clipped dwarf box hedges form a living tapestry which

The principal façade of the Casa de Mateus, its pinnacled symmetry reflected in a rectangular pool

VISITORS' CHECKLIST

Road map D2. Mateus, 3 km
(2 miles) NE of Vila Real. **(** 259-
32 31 21. **R** to Vila Real.
O Mar–Oct: 9am–1pm, 2–6pm
(Jun–Sep: 7pm) daily; Nov–Feb:
10am–1pm, 2–5pm daily. **●** 25
Dec. **⚑ ⓞ** gardens only.
⚑ compulsory in house. **⚐ ⚑**
♫ Jul–Sep: Encontros de Música.

mmaculate box-edged flower beds
n the Casa de Mateus gardens

eflects perfectly the ornate
ymmetry of the house. In
vinter the grand old camellias,
elics from the 19th century,
re a highlight of the gardens,
ut for most visitors the lasting
nemory is of the vast cedar
unnel, greatest among the
nany pieces of topiary here.
    Beyond the formal gardens
e the well-ordered orchards
nd fields of the estate.

THE CEDAR TUNNEL

This celebrated feature in
the Casa de Mateus garden
was formed from cedars
planted in 1941. It is 35 m
(115 ft) long and 7.5 m
(25 ft) high, the tight-knit
greenery providing an aromatic walk in summer. To
keep it in shape, gardeners
have to scale specially
fashioned outsize ladders.

Vila Real ⑪

Road map D2. **▨** 14,000. **R** 🚌
🛈 Avenida Carvalho Araújo 94 (259-
32 28 19). **🚌** Tue & Fri.

PERCHED OVER a gorge cut by
the confluence of the Cabril
and Corgo rivers, Vila Real is
a busy commercial centre. As
the communications hub of
the Upper Douro, it makes a
convenient starting point from
which to explore the valley of
the Douro to the south and the
Parque Natural do Alvão to the
northwest. Vila Real also has
a motor-racing circuit, which
hosts major events each year
during June and July.
    Midway along the broad
main street, Avenida Carvalho
Araújo, is the 15th-century
Sé. This fine Gothic cathedral
was originally the church of
a Dominican friary. The other
monastic buildings burnt down
in suspicious circumstances in
the mid-19th century.
    At the southern end of the
avenue, a plaque on the wall at
No. 19 marks the birthplace of
Diogo Cão, the explorer who
discovered the mouth of the
Congo in 1482 (see pp48–9).
    The **Igreja dos Clérigos**, in
nearby Rua dos Combatentes
da Grande Guerra Portela, is
also known as Capela Nova.
It presents a pleasing Baroque
façade attributed to Niccolò
Nasoni and an interior of fine
blue and white azulejos.

ENVIRONS: The small village
of **Bisalhães**, 6 km (4 miles)
to the west, is famed for its
boldly designed black pottery
(see p25). Examples can be

seen displayed for sale at the
annual Festa de São Pedro,
celebrated in Vila Real each
year on 28–9 June. Also seen
at this time is the fine linen
from nearby Agarez.

Parque Natural do Alvão ⑫

Road map D1. 🚌 to Ermelo via
Campeã. **🛈** Praceta do Tronco, Cruz
das Almas, Vila Real (259-32 41 38).

The scenic Parque Natural do Alvão

WITHIN THE 72 sq km (28 sq
miles) of the nature re-
serve between the Corgo and
Tâmega rivers, the scenery
ranges from verdant, cultivated
lowlands to bleak heights that
reach 1,339 m (4,393 ft) at
Alto das Caravelas. Despite
hunters and habitat encroach-
ment, hawks, dippers and
otters can still be spotted. Between the picturesque hamlets
of **Ermelo** and **Lamas de Olo**,
where maize is still kept in
espigueiros (see p271), the Olo
drops in a spectacular cascade,
the **Fisgas de Ermelo**. From
Alto do Velão, just southwest
of the park, are splendid views
west over the Tâmega valley.

Vila Real seen across the deep gorge of the Corgo and Cabril rivers

A farmer and his grazing ox near Carvalhelhos, Serra do Barroso

Serra do Barroso ⓭

Road map D1. 🚌 to Montalegre or Boticas. ℹ️ Praça do Município, Montalegre (276-51 02 00).

JUST SOUTHEAST of the Parque Nacional da Peneda-Gerês (see pp270–71) is the wild and remote Serra do Barroso. The landscape of heathery hill-sides is split by the immense Barragem do Alto Rabagão, the largest of many reservoirs in the area created by the damming of rivers for hydro-electric power. Water is a main-stay of the local economy: a high rainfall enables farmers to eke out an existence on the poor soil, and the artificial lakes attract fishing and water-sports enthusiasts. The source of one of the country's most popular bottled mineral waters is at **Carvalhelhos**.

The village of **Boticas** near-by produces a beverage with a more original claim to fame. In 1809, the locals buried their wine rather than have it fall into the hands of the invading French. When the enemy de-parted, the wine was retrieved and found to have improved. The bottles were colloquially termed *mortos* ("dead"), hence the name of the wine – *vinho dos mortos*. The practice con-tinues and bottles are usually buried for up to two years.

The area's principal town is **Montalegre**, on a plateau to the north. Its most notable feature is the imposing keep, 27 m (88 ft) high, of the ruined 14th-century castle.

Oxen are bred in the Serra, and inter-village *chegas dos bois* (ox fights) are a popular pastime. The contest is usually decided within half an hour, when the weaker ox takes to its heels – champions are fêted by hordes of adoring fans.

Chaves ⓮

Road map D1. 🏛️ 18,000. 🚌 ℹ️ Terreiro da Cavalaria (276-34 06 61). 🌐 www.rt-atb.pt 🗓️ Wed.

BESIDE THE UPPER REACHES of the Tâmega stands historic Chaves, attractively sited in the middle of a fertile plain.

Thermal springs and nearby gold deposits encouraged the Romans to establish Aquae Flaviae here in AD 78. Its stra-tegic position led to successive invasion and occupation by the Suevi, Visigoths and Moors, before the Portuguese gained final possession in 1160. The name Chaves ("keys") is often associated with the keys of the north awarded to Nuno Álvares Pereira, hero of Aljubarrota (see p183). A likelier but more pedestrian explanation is that Chaves is simply a corruption of the Latin "Flaviae".

Today Chaves is renowned for its spa and historic centre, and for its smoked hams. A curiosity of the north, the dis-tinctive black pottery (see p25), is made in nearby Nantes.

The old town focuses on the Praça de Camões. The 14th-century **keep** overlooking this pleasant medieval square is all that remains of the castle given to Nuno Álvares Pereira by João I. On the south side of the square stands the **Igreja Matriz** with its fine Roman-esque portal. The Baroque

Tiled and gilded Misericórdia church at Chaves

Misericórdia church opposite has an exquisite interior lined with 18th-century *azulejos*. Attributed to Policarpo de Oliveira Bernardes (see p22), the huge panels depict scenes from the New Testament.

The 14th-century keep of Chaves castle, set in formal gardens

🏛️ **Museu Militar and Museu da Região Flaviense**
Praça de Camões. 📞 276-34 05 00. ⏰ Tue–Fri, Sat & Sun pm. ● public hols. 🎟️ joint ticket.
Within the castle keep is a small military museum, where suits of armour, uniforms and associated regalia are on dis-play. Also exhibited are military memorabilia from the city's defence against the attack by Royalists from Spain in 1912.

In the flower-filled garden surrounding the keep are a few archaeological finds from Chaves's long history, but most are to be found in the Museu da Região Flaviense behind the keep. Here, in the Paço dos Duques de Bragança, are dis-played a variety of local archaeological discoveries. Items of interest include sou-venirs of the Roman occupation, such as milestones and coins, alongside an oxcart and a straw mantle of the type worn by shepherds for protection in the rain or the hot sun.

⊞ Ponte Romana

The 16-arch Roman bridge across the Tâmega was completed around AD 100, at the time of the Emperor Trajan. Its construction brought added importance to Chaves as a staging post on the route between Braga and Astorga (in northwestern Spain). On the bridge are Roman milestones which record that funds to build it were raised locally.

⊞ Thermal springs

Largo Tito Flávio Vespasiano.
📞 276-33 24 45. ⏲ daily. ♿
A few minutes on foot from the city centre is one of the hottest springs in Europe. Water here bubbles up at a temperature of 73°C (163°F) and the spa's facilities attract both holiday-makers and patients seeking treatment *(see p209)*. Chaves water is recommended for the treatment of ailments as diverse as rheumatism, kidney dysfunction and hypertension.

The huge cleft Pedra Bolideira near Chaves

Environs: Close to the village of Soutelo, 4 km (2 miles) northwest of Chaves (the route is signposted), is the strange **Outeiro Machado Boulder**. It measures 50 m (165 ft) in length and is covered with mysterious hieroglyphs and symbols of unknown meaning. These may be Celtic in origin.

Another gigantic boulder, the **Pedra Bolideira**, lies near Bolideira, 16 km (10 miles) east of Chaves. Split in two, the massive larger section balances lightly, needing only a gentle push to rock it to and fro.

The spa town of **Vidago**, 17 km (11 miles) southwest of Chaves, is well known for its therapeutic water. The Vidago Palace Hotel *(see p393)*, once the haunt of royalty, has been renovated in recent years, but retains the regal charm of its park, lakes and pump room.

Murça's Misericórdia chapel, with its vine-embellished pillars

Murça ⑮

Road map D2. 🏠 *3,000*. 🚌
ℹ️ *Alameda do Paço (259-51 15 08).*
📅 *13 & 28 of month.*

THE MARKET TOWN of Murça is famed for its honey, goat's cheese and sausage. Its major attraction, and the focal point of the garden in the main square, is its **porca**, an Iron Age granite pig with a substantial girth of 2.8 m (9 ft) *(see p40)*. The role of *berrões*, as beasts such as these are called, is enigmatic, but they may have been linked to fertility cults. Smaller versions survive in Bragança, Chaves and elsewhere. In more recent times the Murça *porca* has been pressed into service at elections, when the winning political parties would paint her in their colours.

The **Misericórdia** chapel on the main street is notable for its early Baroque façade, attractively ornamented with designs of vines and grapes.

Mirandela ⑯

Road map D1. 🏠 *8,000*. 🚆 🚌
ℹ️ *Praça do Mercado (278-20 02 72).*
📅 *3, 14 & 25 of month.*

MIRANDELA, at the end of the Tua narrow-gauge railway line, has pretty gardens running down to the River Tua and an elegant Roman bridge with 20 asymmetrical arches. Built for the deployment of troops and to aid the transport of ore from local mines, it was rebuilt in the 16th century and is now for pedestrians only.

Displayed in the **Museu Municipal Armindo Teixeira Lopes** are sculpture, prints and paintings, including views of Lisbon and Mirandela by the local 20th-century artist after whom the museum is named.

The 17th-century **town hall** once belonged to the Távoras, but the family was accused of attempted regicide in 1759 and all trace of them was erased.

⚖ Museu Municipal Armindo Teixeira Lopes

Rua Coronel Sarmento Pimentel.
📞 278-26 57 68. ⏲ Mon–Fri; Sat & Sun pm. ⏺ public hols.

Environs: In a pretty valley 15 km (9 miles) northeast of Mirandela lies **Romeu**. Its **Museu das Curiosidades**, as the name implies, is a hotch-potch of exhibits from the turn of the century onwards. The collection of the local Menéres family, it includes Model-T Fords, musical boxes and early photographic equipment. Next door is the famed Maria Rita restaurant *(see p415)*.

⚖ Museu das Curiosidades

Jerusalém do Romeu. ⏲ noon–4pm Tue–Sun. ⏺ public hols. 📷

The River Tua at Mirandela, with its Roman bridge and waterside parks

Bragança: the Citadel ⑰

THIS STRATEGIC HILLTOP was the site of a succession of forts before Fernão Mendes, brother-in-law to King Afonso Henriques, built a walled citadel here in 1130. Like several predecessors, it was named Brigantia. Within the walls still stand Sancho I's castle, built in 1187, with its watchtowers and dungeons, and the pentagonal 12th-century Domus Municipalis beside the church of Santa Maria.

The town gave its name to Portugal's final royal dynasty, descended from an illegitimate son of João I who was created first Duke of Bragança in 1442 *(see p299)*.

Bragança's walled citadel on its isolated hilltop

The Museu Militar in the robust Gothic keep includes memorabilia from the Africa campaigns (1895) of a local regiment. The keep is 33 m (108 ft) high.

The medieval pillory has the appearance of skewering a hapless *porca*, an ancient stone pig *(see p40)*, to the pedestal.

★ Castle
The castle's Torre da Princesa, scene of many tragic tales, was refuge to Dona Sancha, unhappy wife of Fernão Mendes, and prison to other mistreated wives.

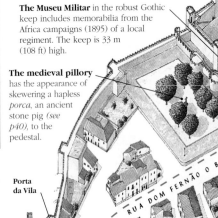

Porta da Traição

Porta da Vila

RUA DOM FERNÃO O BRAVO

To town ←

Porta de Santo António

Santa Maria
The church's elaborately carved portal dates from its 18th-century restoration.

★ Domus Municipalis
This, the only surviving example of Romanesque civic architecture in Portugal, served as a hall where the homens boms ("good men") settled disputes. Below was the town's cistern.

STAR SIGHTS

★ Castle

★ Domus Municipalis

VISITORS' CHECKLIST

Road map E1. 🏘 *35,000.*
🚌 *Agência de Viagens e Turismo
Sanvitura, Avenida João da Cruz.*
🅸 *Avenida Cidade de Zamora
(273-38 12 73).* 🗓 *3, 12 & 21
of month.* 📅 *mid-Aug: Nossa
Senhora das Graças.* **Castle** and
Museu Militar 📞 *273-322 378.*
🕐 *Fri–Wed.* ⬤ *public hols.* 🚫

KEY

– – – Suggested route

0 metres　　　　50
0 yards　　　　　50

Porta do Sol

Museu Abade de Baçal gardens, where archaeological finds are displayed

Beyond the Citadel

By the 15th century, Bragança had expanded west along the banks of the River Fervença. The Jewish quarter in Rua dos Fornos survives from this era, when Jews from North Africa and Spain settled here and founded the silk industry.

Despite its royal links, the town never overcame its isolation, the Bragança monarchs preferring Vila Viçosa *(see pp298–9).* Only now are the investments of returning emigrants and the completion of the Oporto-Spain motorway reviving trade. A new cathedral "for the millennium" was inaugurated in 1996, another indicator of the city's rebirth. Near the modest old cathedral in the town centre is a lively covered market where delicacies such as smoked hams and *alheiras* (chicken sausages) are sold.

🏛 Museu Abade de Baçal

Rua Abílio Beça 27. 📞 *273-33 15 95.*
🕐 *Tue–Sun.* ⬤ *public hols.* 🚫
The Abbot of Baçal (1865–1947) was a prodigious scholar whose definitive researches into the region's history and customs, including its Jewish connections, were published in 11 volumes. Bragança's museum is named after him.

Highlights among the paintings are *The Martyrdom of St Ignatius,* an unsigned triptych of the 16th century, and watercolours by Aurélia de Sousa (1865–1922), including her impressionist *A Sombra* (In the Shade). In another section are displayed colourful *pauliteiros* costumes *(see p227)* and gruesome instruments of torture.

In the garden are a variety of archaeological discoveries including *porcas* and tablets with Luso-Roman inscriptions.

🏠 São Bento

Rua de São Francisco.
🕐 *variable hours.* ♿
Founded in 1590 by Bishop António Pinheiro, São Bento has two startlingly contrasting ceilings: a splendid canopy of Moorish-influenced geometric carving in the chancel, and a richly coloured 18th-century trompe l'oeil over the nave.

🏠 São Vicente

Largo do Principal. 🕐 *variable hours.*
The secret wedding between Inês de Castro and Dom Pedro is reputed to have taken place here in 1354 *(see p179).* The original 13th-century church was reconstructed in the 17th century with the addition of a great deal of sumptuous giltwork. The *azulejo* panel to the right of the main door depicts General Sepúlveda exhorting the citizens of Bragança to free themselves from French occupation in 1809.

Street in the old Jewish quarter, sloping steeply down to the river

Houses within the Citadel
Bragança had outgrown the citadel by the 15th century, but streets of small houses still cluster within the walls.

The sparsely inhabited landscape of the Parque Natural de Montesinho

Parque Natural de Montesinho ⑱

Road map E1. 🚌 *to Rio de Onor & Vinhais.* 🛈 *Bairro Salvador Nunes Teixeira 5, Bragança (273-381 234).*

ONE OF THE WILDEST areas in Europe, the reserve covers 70,000 ha (175,000 acres) between Bragança and the border with Spain. The region, understandably, is known as Terra Fria (Cold Land). Bleak mountains rise to 1,481 m (4,859 ft) above heather and broom, descending to oak forests and valleys of alder and willow.

Spectacular views of the park can be enjoyed from **Vinhais**, on its southern fringe, and the wilderness attracts walkers and riders – mountain bikes and horses can be hired locally.

The population clusters in farming communities on the lowlands, leaving much of the Serra an undisturbed habitat for rare species such as wolves and golden eagles, as well as boars, otters and falcons.

Little changed from medieval times, villages such as **França** and **Montesinho** are typical in their stone houses, wooden balconies and cobbled streets. Ancient practices such as herbal cures and reverence for the supernatural linger, and ties are communal rather than national: in **Rio de Onor** Spanish and Portuguese have been welded into a unique dialect, Rionorês.

Farm parlour, Museu da Terra de Miranda

Miranda do Douro ⑲

Road map E1. 🏠 *3,000.* 🚌 🛈 *Largo do Menino Jesus da Cartolinha (273-43 11 32).* 🛒 *1st of month.*

THIS MEDIEVAL OUTPOST stands on top of the Douro gorge, which here forms an abrupt border with Spain. Its key position and the establishment of a bishopric here in 1545 paved the way for the town's development into the cultural and religious centre of Trás-os-Montes. But in 1762, during the Seven Years' War against France and Spain, the powder store exploded, claiming 400 lives and destroying the castle (only the keep remains). This mishap, compounded by the transfer of the bishopric to Bragança, led the town into a deep economic decline, only recently halted by new trade links with the coast and Spain.

The lovely twin-towered **Sé** was founded in the 16th century. The graceful woodcarvings of the chancel retable depict, among other themes, the Apostles and the Virgin attended by angels. But the cathedral's most original feature is a wooden figure of the Boy Jesus in the south transept. The Menino Jesus da Cartolinha represents a boy who, legend tells, appeared during a Spanish siege in 1711 to rally the demoralized Portuguese to miraculous victory. Devotees dressed the statue in 17th-century costume and later gave him a top hat *(cartolinha)*.

The excellent **Museu da Terra de Miranda** houses an eclectic display of archaeological finds, folk costume, a reconstruction of a Mirandês farmhouse parlour and curious rural devices such as an inflated pig's-bladder cosh.

🏛 Museu da Terra de Miranda

Largo Dom João III. 📞 *273-43 11 64.* 🕐 *Tue–Sat & Sun am.* ⬤ *public hols.* 🏷

ENVIRONS: Just southwest of Miranda, the village of **Duas Igrejas** is famed for its stick dancers, or *pauliteiros*, who perform at local festivals and overseas *(see p227)*. The tradition is in decline, but for the Festa de Santa Bárbara, on the third Sunday in August, the dancers don their distinctive black and white costumes and are accompanied in their energetic display by drums and *gaita de foles* (bagpipes).

A distinctive *pombal* or dovecote still found around Montesinho

THE DOVECOTES OF MONTESINHO

Doves supply not only food, but also droppings, which are highly prized as fertilizer. In this part of Trás-os-Montes the traditional horseshoe-shaped dovecote or *pombal* is still a familiar sight, although many are now disused. The birds nest in rough cells inside the whitewashed schist walls and enter and leave through gaps in the tile or slate roof. They are fed via a small raised door at the front of the *pombal*.

The church and town of Mogadouro, viewed from beside the ruins of its 13th-century castle

Mogadouro ⓴

Road map E2. 🏃 *3,000.* 🚌
🚹 *Largo Santo Cristo (279-343 756).*

APART FROM the hilltop tower, little remains of the great castle founded here by King Dinis and presented to the Templars in 1297. From the top there are fine views over the drowsy little market town known for its handicrafts, particularly leather goods, and articles of silk, linen and wool.

Mogadouro's 16th-century **Igreja Matriz** features a 17th-century tower, while lavishly gilded retables from the 18th century decorate the altars.

Torre de Moncorvo ㉑

Road map E2. 🏃 *2,500.* 🚌
🚹 *Rua Manuel Seixas (279-25 22 89).*
📅 *8 & 23 of month.*

FAMED FOR the white mantle of almond blossom that fleetingly covers the valleys in early spring (egg-shaped *amêndoas cobertas*, sugared almonds, are an Easter treat), Moncorvo also offers an atmospheric stroll through its maze of medieval streets. Its name is variously attributed to a local nobleman, Mendo Curvo, or perhaps to his raven *(corvo)*.

The ponderous 16th-century **Igreja Matriz**, the largest in Trás-os-Montes, boasts a 17th-century altarpiece depicting scenes from the life of Christ.

ENVIRONS: The fate of the Côa valley, south of Moncorvo, was finally decided in 1996 when plans for a dam were dropped to preserve the world's largest collection of open-air Stone Age engravings. The rock art, first discovered in 1933 and estimated to be 20,000 years old, features bulls, horses, fish and a naked man, the Homem de Pisco. Visitor facilities in the 20-km (12-mile) long **Parque Arqueológico do Vale do Côa** are still being improved but tours can be arranged in Vila Nova de Foz Côa.

🏛 Parque Arqueológico do Vale do Côa
Avenida Gago Coutinho 19a, Vila Nova de Foz Côa. ☎ *279-768 260.* ⏰ *by appt only.* ⬤ *public hols.* 📷 ✦

Rich interior of the Igreja Matriz at Freixo

Freixo de Espada à Cinta ㉒

Road map E2. 🏃 *2,300.* 🚌
🚹 *Avenida do Emigrante (279-65 34 80).* ⬤ *5th of every month.*

SEVERAL STORIES try to explain the curious name of this remote border town. "Ash tree of the girt sword" may derive from the arms of a Spanish nobleman, or a Visigoth called Espadacinta, or from a tale that, when founding the town in the 14th century, King Dinis strapped his sword to an ash.

Dominating the skyline is the heptagonal **Torre do Galo**, a relic from the 14th-century defences. Views from the top are splendid, especially in spring when the almond blossom attracts a great many tourists. A newer cultivation is that of silkworms, revival of an 18th-century industry.

The intricate 16th-century portal of the **Igreja Matriz** leads into a splendid small-scale version of Belém's Mosteiro dos Jerónimos *(see pp106–7)*. Panels of the altarpiece, attributed to Grão Vasco *(see p213)*, include a fine *Annunciation*.

♣ Torre do Galo
Praça Jorge Álvares. ⏰ *Tue–Fri.* ⬤ *public hols.*

MINHO

....

KNOWN AS THE BIRTHPLACE *of the nation, the Minho has two of Portugal's most historic cities: its first capital, Guimarães, and Braga, the country's main religious centre. Life in the province is still firmly rooted in tradition. Agriculture thrives thanks to abundant rainfall that makes this the greenest area in Portugal.*

The province of Minho occupies land between the River Douro in the south and the River Minho in the north. Fortified hilltop stone forts *(castros)* remain as evidence of the Neolithic history of the region. When Celtic peoples migrated into the area in the first millennium BC, these sites developed into *citânias* (settlements) such as Briteiros.

During the 2nd century BC, advancing Roman legions conquered the land, introduced vine-growing techniques and constructed a network of roads. Roman milestones are still visible in Peneda-Gerês National Park. When Christianity became the official religion of the Roman empire in the 4th century AD, Braga became an important religious centre, a position it holds to this day. The Suevi swept aside the Romans in the 5th century, followed by the Visigoths, who were ousted in turn by the Moorish invasion of 711. The Minho was won back from the Moors in the 9th century. The region rose to prominence in the 12th century under Afonso Henriques *(see pp42–3)*, who proclaimed himself the first king of Portugal and chose Guimarães as his capital.

The Minho's fertile farms and estates have been handed down within families for centuries, each heir traditionally receiving a share of the land. This custom results in plots of land too small to support their owners, many of whom emigrate in search of work. The economy of the Minho, under pressure from high local unemployment, concentrates on medium-scale industry around Braga and Guimarães. Agriculture in the valleys includes production of the area's distinctive *vinhos verdes* or "green wines". Despite the growth of tourism, the Minho has maintained its strong folk traditions. Carnivals and street markets pervade everyday life and ox-drawn carts are still in use.

Cows being herded across a bridge near the Brejoeira Palace, south of Monção

◁ The sanctuary of Nossa Senhora da Peneda, in the Parque Nacional da Peneda-Gerês

Exploring the Minho

I N THE SOUTH of the Minho lie Braga and Guimarães, the two major cities of the region, both rich in historic sights. From Braga, the Baroque splendour of Bom Jesus or the ruins of Citânia de Briteiros, the country's largest Iron Age site, are within easy reach. Between Braga and the coast lies Barcelos, the ceramics centre of the region, famed for its weekly market. Travelling north, the pretty town of Viana do Castelo is a useful base from which to explore the coast. Turning inland again, the picturesque market town of Ponte de Lima, beside the River Lima, is one of many places in the Minho that provide accommodation in traditional manor houses. In the north of the Minho, the River Minho forms the border with Spain. Along the river, fortified towns offer magnificent views into Spain. To the northeast, walkers and wildlife enthusiasts should not miss the dramatic mountain ranges of the Parque Nacional da Peneda-Gerês.

Foal grazing in the Parque Nacional da Peneda-Gerês

SEE ALSO

- *Where to Stay* pp393–4
- *Where to Eat* pp416–17

Manueline portal on the 16th-century parish church, Vila do Conde

MONÇÃO ❸

Vigo
Pontevedra

❷ VALENÇA DO MINHO

N13

VILA NOVA DE
CERVEIRA

N303

PAREDES DE COURA

Minho

❶ CAMINHA

N305

N201

N306

ARCOS DE VALD

PONTE DA

BRAVÃ

VILA PRAIA
DE ÂNCORA

❻ PONTE DE LIMA

N202

❼

Lima

VIANA DO CASTELO

N13

N204

N201

N103

Cávado

ESPOSENDE

❾

BARCELOS

BR

N13

N205

N206

VILA NOV
FAMALIC

PÓVOA DE
VARZIM

❽ VILA DO CONDE

Ave

Por

Porto

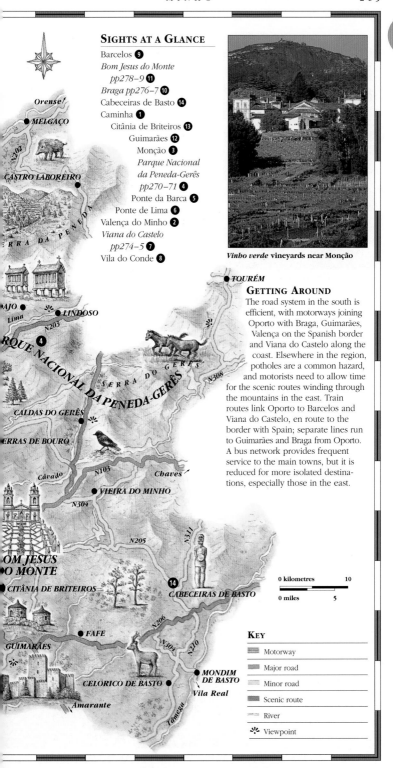

SIGHTS AT A GLANCE

Barcelos **9**
Bom Jesus do Monte
pp278–9 **11**
Braga pp276–7 **10**
Cabeceiras de Basto **14**
Caminha **1**
Citânia de Briteiros **13**
Guimarães **12**
Monção **3**
Parque Nacional
da Peneda-Gerês
pp270–71 **4**
Ponte da Barca **5**
Ponte de Lima **6**
Valença do Minho **2**
Viana do Castelo
pp274–5 **7**
Vila do Conde **8**

Vinho verde **vineyards near Monção**

GETTING AROUND

The road system in the south is
efficient, with motorways joining
Oporto with Braga, Guimarães,
Valença on the Spanish border
and Viana do Castelo along the
coast. Elsewhere in the region,
potholes are a common hazard,
and motorists need to allow time
for the scenic routes winding through
the mountains in the east. Train
routes link Oporto to Barcelos and
Viana do Castelo, en route to the
border with Spain; separate lines run
to Guimarães and Braga from Oporto.
A bus network provides frequent
service to the main towns, but it is
reduced for more isolated destinations, especially those in the east.

0 kilometres	10
0 miles	5

KEY

▬▬ Motorway

▬▬ Major road

▬▬ Minor road

▬▬ Scenic route

═ ═ River

☀ Viewpoint

Popular cafés in Praça do Conselheiro Silva Torres, Caminha's attractive main square

Caminha ❶

Road Map C1. 🏠 *2,000.* 🚊 🚉 🚌
ℹ️ *Rua Ricardo Joaquim de Sousa (258-92 19 52).* 🗓️ *Wed.*

THIS ANCIENT FORTRESS town perches beside the Minho with fine views across the river to Spain. Occupied in Celtic and Roman times for its strategic position, Caminha developed into a major port until the diversion of its trade to Viana do Castelo in the 16th century. Today it is a small port, with a daily ferry connection to A Guarda in Spain.

On the main square is the 15th-century **Torre do Relógio** clock tower, once a gateway in the medieval defensive walls, and the 17th-century **Paços do Concelho** with its attractive loggia supported by pillars. Cross to the other side of the square, past the Renaissance fountain, to admire the seven Manueline windows on the upper storey of the **Solar dos Pitas** mansion (15th century).

The Rua Ricardo Joaquim de Sousa leads to the Gothic **Igreja Matriz**. Begun in the late 15th century, it has a superb inlaid ceiling of panels carved in Mudéjar (Moorish) style. Renaissance carvings above the side doors depict the Apostles, the Virgin, and several figures in daring poses, including one man with his posterior bared towards Spain.

ENVIRONS: Foz do Minho, the mouth of the Minho, lies 5 km (3 miles) southwest of town. From here local fishermen will take groups (by prior arrangement) to the ruined island fortress of **Forte da Ínsua**.

The small walled town of **Vila Nova de Cerveira**, 12 km (7 miles) northeast of Caminha on the road to Valença, has a 16th-century castle, refurbished as the luxurious Pousada Dom Dinis (*see p394*). The tranquil atmosphere is ideal for a stroll in narrow streets lined with 17th- and 18th-century mansions, or along the riverfront, where a car ferry runs to the Spanish town of Goián.

Valença do Minho ❷

Road Map C1. 🏠 *3,000.* 🚉 🚌
ℹ️ *Avenida de Espanha (251-823 329).* 🗓️ *Wed.*

SET IN A COMMANDING position on a hilltop overlooking the River Minho, Valença is an attractive border town with an old quarter set in the narrow confines of two double-walled forts, shaped like crowns and linked by a causeway. During the reign of Sancho I (1185–1211), the town was named *Contrasta*, due to its position facing the Spanish town of Tui.

The **forts** date from the 17th and 18th centuries and were designed according to the principles of the French architect, Vauban. There are fine views from the ramparts across the river into Galicia. Although the town was briefly captured by Napoleonic troops in 1807, its formidable bastions resisted subsequent shelling and attacks from across the river in 1809.

Lining the cobbled alleys of the old quarter are shops full of linen, wickerwork, pottery and handicrafts to tempt the thousands of Spanish visitors who stroll across the bridge to shop. South of the ramparts is the newer part of town.

In Praça de São Teotónio, **Casa do Eirado** (1448) boasts a crenellated roof and late Gothic window, adorned with the builder's signature. The 18th-century **Casa do Poço** presents symmetrical windows and wrought-iron balconies.

A quiet sunlit corner in the old quarter of Valença do Minho

ENVIRONS: The **Convento de Ganfei**, 5 km (3 miles) east of Valença on the N101, was reconstructed in the 11th century by a Norman priest. It retains pleasing Romanesque features, including ornamental animal and plant motifs and vestiges of medieval frescoes. To visit the chapel, ask for the key at the house opposite.

Part of the walls and ramparts surrounding Valença do Minho

Monção ❸

Road Map C1. 🏛 *2,500.* 🚌
🛈 Praça Deu-la-Deu (251-65 27 57).
🗓 Thu.

A REMOTE and charming town,
Monção once formed part
of the string of fortified border
posts standing sentinel on the
river Minho. Both the town's
main squares are lined with old
houses, and decorated with
chestnut trees, flowerbeds and
mosaic paths.

The 13th-century **Igreja
Matriz** in Rua João de Pinho
boasts an outstanding Roma-
esque doorway of sculpted
canthus flowers. Inside, to
the right of the transept is the
cenotaph of the valiant Deu-
-Deu Martins, the town's
heroine, erected in 1679 by
a descendant. A leafy avenue
east of the town leads to the
hot mineral springs used for
the treatment of rheumatism.
A colourful element in the
June Corpus Christi festival is
the Festa da Coca, when
St George engages the dragon
(*coca*) in comic ritual combat
before giving the final blow.

ENVIRONS: The countryside
around Monção produces excellent *vinho verde (see p29)*;
one of the best-known estates
is the privately owned Neo-
classical Palácio de Brejoeira,
5 km (3 miles) south of town.
About 5 km (3 miles) southeast of Monção, the monastery
of **São João de Longos Vales**
was built in Romanesque style

Bridge across the Lima at Ponte da Barca, with the town behind

in the 12th century. The exterior capitals and interior apse
have fantastical sculpted figures, including serpents and
monkeys. Visits are arranged
by the tourist office in Monção.

The town of **Melgaço,** 24 km
(15 miles) east of Monção provides a useful gateway to the
Peneda-Gerês National Park.

Parque Nacional da Peneda-Gerês ❹

See pp270–71.

Ponte da Barca ❺

Road Map C1. 🏛 *2,000.* 🚌
🛈 Largo da Misericórdia 11 (258-45
28 99). 🛒 every other Wed.

THE TOWN of Ponte da Barca
derives its name from the
graceful 15th-century bridge
that replaced the boat once
used to ferry pilgrims across
the River Lima (*ponte* means

bridge, and *barca* means boat).
A stroll through the tranquil
town centre leads past the pillory (crowned with sphere and
pyramid), the graceful arcades
and noble mansions from the
16th and 17th centuries. The
Jardim dos Poetas (Poets'
Garden) and riverside parks
are ideal for picnics, and the
huge open-air market along
the river is well worth a visit.

Carved relief on the tympanum of
the small parish church at Bravães

ENVIRONS: Some of Portugal's
finest Romanesque carvings
are on the 13th-century church
at **Bravães**, 4 km (2 miles)
west of Ponte da Barca. Sculpted monkeys, oxen, and birds
of prey decorate the columns
of its main portal; the tympanum shows Christ in majesty
flanked by two angels.

The town of **Arcos de
Valdevez**, 5 km (3 miles) north
of Ponte da Barca, nestles by
the banks of the River Vez and
lies within convenient reach of
Peneda-Gerês National Park.
The impressive church of
Nossa Senhora da Lapa was
built in 1767 by André Soares.
This Baroque showpiece has
an oval exterior, yet transforms
the interior into an octagon.

Hiking enthusiasts should
ask the tourist office for directions to follow the circuit of
elevated viewpoints and local
villages from the hamlet of
São Miguel, 11 km (7 miles)
east of Ponte da Barca.

DEU-LA-DEU MARTINS

In 1368, when a Spanish army had besieged Monção to the
verge of starvation, Deu-la-Deu Martins used the last of
the town's flour to bake rolls that she flung over the walls
to the Spaniards, with taunts that there were plenty more

The heroic Deu-la-Deu Martins
on Monção's coat of arms

to throw at them. Thinking
their time was being wasted in
a futile siege, the troops soon
withdrew. In gratitude for
saving the town, Deu-la-Deu
(the name means "God gave
her") is remembered on the
town's coat of arms, where
she is shown with a loaf of
bread in each hand. *Pãezinhos*
(bread rolls) *de Deu-la-Deu*
used to be baked to honour
her memory, but the tradition
is no longer followed.

Vinho verde **vineyards near Monção** ▷

Parque Nacional da Peneda-Gerês ❹

Broom in Peneda Mountains

Pᴇɴᴇᴅᴀ-ɢᴇʀᴇ̂s National Park, one of Portugal's greatest natural attractions, stretches from the Gerês Mountains in the south to the Peneda range and the Spanish border in the north. Established in 1971, it extends over about 700 sq km (270 sq miles) of wild, dramatic scenery, with windswept peaks and wooded valleys of oak, pine and yew. It also hosts rare wolves and golden eagles among its rich variety of fauna. In the park's villages, everyday life remains firmly rooted in tradition.

Lamas de Mouro, at the northern entrance to the park, serves as an information centre and offers accommodation.

Castro Laboreiro is best known for the breed of sheepdog to which it gives its name. The ruins of a medieval castle can be seen in the village.

★ Nossa Senhora da Peneda
Surrounded by massive rocks, this elaborate sanctuary is a replica of Bom Jesus (see pp278–9). The site is visited in early September by pilgrims from all over the region.

Castelo Lindoso, in the frontier village of Lindoso, is a fine 13th-century castle which has now been renovated to house an art gallery.

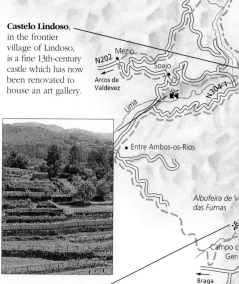

Soajo
The traditional village of Soajo, surrounded by ter-raced hillsides, is known for its collection of espigueiros. The village's local festival takes place in the middle of August.

Vilarinho das Furnas
Beautifully set in a rocky landscape, the Vilarinho das Furnas reservoir was formed by the damming of the River Homem. The reservoir is good for swimming as well as hikes along its shores.

Caldas do Gerês, known since Roman times for its spa, now serves as an information centre and base for ex-cursions from the centre of the park.

Pitões das Júnias Monastery
Dating to 1147, the picturesque ruins of this mon-
astery lie approximately 3 km (2 miles) south of
the road leading into Pitões das Júnias village.

VISITORS' CHECKLIST

Road map C1. 🚌 *from Braga*
to Caldas do Gerês; from Arcos
de Valdevez to Soajo & Lindoso;
from Melgaço to Castro Laboreiro
& Lamas de Mouro. 🛈 *Caldas*
do Gerês: on main road (253-39
01 10); Lamas do Mouro: next to
camp site; Arcos de Valdevez: Rua
Padre Manuel Himalaia (258-515
338). Information on camp sites,
hiking & pony trekking is available
at these offices and at Montalegre
(see p256). **Castelo Lindoso** ⬜
Tue–Sun. ⬛ *public hols.* 🏷

Inverneiras in Sedra
Migration during the
summer from these
solidly built winter
houses to brandas,
stone shelters high
in the mountains,
is still practised
in some villages.

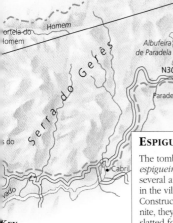

Tourém

🏠
Pitões das
Júnias
☡

★ Roman Road
Sections of the old Roman
road that ran from Braga
to Astorga in Spain, can
still be seen at points along
the Homem river valley.

orfela do
Homem

Homem

Outeiro   Montalegre

Albufeira
de Paradela

N308

Paradela

Serra do Gerês

s do

Cabril

ado

STAR SIGHTS

★ Nossa Senhora
da Peneda

★ Roman Road

ESPIGUEIROS

The tomb-like architecture of
espigueiros (granaries) appears in
several areas of the park, especially
in the villages of Lindoso and Soajo.
Constructed either of wood or granite, they are raised on columns and
slatted for ventilation. The design
keeps grain and maize at the right
humidity as well as off the ground,
out of reach of hens and rodents.
Topped with an ornamental
cross or pyramid, the design of
espigueiros has scarcely changed
since the 18th and 19th centuries.

Granite *espigueiro*, Lindoso

KEY

═══	Road
─ ─	Long-distance footpath
─ ∙ ─	National boundary
🛈	Tourist information
☡	Viewpoint

Ponte de Lima ❻

Road Map C1. ![icon] *3,200.* ![icon]
ℹ️ *Praça da República (258-94 23 35).*
🔄 *every other Mon.*

THIS ATTRACTIVE riverside
town takes its name from
the ancient bridge over the
River Lima. During the Middle
Ages, the town played a pivotal role in the defence of the
Minho against the Moors.

The Roman **bridge** has only
five of its original stone arches;
the rest were rebuilt or restored
in the 14th and 15th centuries.
The 15th-century church of
Santo António now houses the
Museu dos Terceiros, a museum of sacred art. The **Museu
Rural** has antique farming
equipment, an authentic
regional kitchen and gardens.

The remaining medieval
fortifications of Ponte de
Lima include the 15th-
century **Palácio dos
Marqueses de Ponte
de Lima**.

The town's market,
a tradition dating back
to 1125, takes place
on the river's wide and
sandy left bank. In mid-
September crowds gather
in the town to celebrate
the *Feiras Novas* (new
fairs), a combined
religious festival and
folkloric market.

🏛️ **Museu Rural**
Largo da Arnado. 📞 258-900 414.
🕐 2–6pm Tue–Sun. ⬤ public hols.

Viana do Castelo ❼

See pp274–5.

Former dormitory of the Mosteiro de Santa Clara, Vila do Conde

Vila do Conde ❽

Road map C2. ![icon] *21,000.* ![icon] ![icon]
ℹ️ *Rua 25 de Abril (252-24 84 73).*
🔄 *Fri.*

THE SMALL TOWN of Vila
do Conde enjoyed its
boom years as a ship-
building centre in the
Age of Discovery *(see
pp46–7)*; today it is
a quiet fishing port.

By the river, in the
historic centre, the main
attraction is the **Mosteiro
de Santa Clara**, founded
in 1318. The principal
dormitory building,
dating from the 18th
century, is now a
correctional institu-
tion for teenagers.
The church and cloisters, however, are open to the public.
The Gothic church has Renaissance additions and contains
the tombs of the nunnery's
founders, Dom Afonso Sanches
(son of King Dinis) and his
wife Dona Teresa Martins. By

**Stone carving of
a musician, Museu
dos Terceiros**

the Mosteiro de Santa Clara
are parts of the imposing 5-km
(3-mile) **aqueduct**, built in
1705–14, with 999 arches.

At the heart of the historic
centre is Praça Vasco da Gama,
with an unusual pillory in the
shape of an arm with thrusting
sword – a vivid warning to
potential wrongdoers. Bordering the square by the pillory is
the 16th-century **Igreja Matriz**,
notable for its wonderfully
ornate Manueline portico,
attributed to João de Castilho.

The town is a centre for lace-
making (bone lace or *rendas
de bilros*). Visitors can buy
samples and see the skills at
the **Escola de Rendas** (lace-
making school). The same
building also houses the Museu
de Rendas (lace museum).

🔓 **Mosteiro de Santa Clara**
Largo Dom Afonso Sanches. 📞 252-
63 10 16. 🕐 Mon–Fri. ⬤ public hols.

🏛️ **Escola de Rendas**
Rua de São Bento 70. 📞 252-248
470. 🕐 mid Jun–Sep: daily; Oct–
mid-Jun: Mon–Fri. ⬤ public hols.

ENVIRONS: The town of **Póvoa
de Varzim**, 3 km (2 miles)
north of Vila do Conde, is a
resort with sandy beaches,
amusements and nightlife.

In the village of Rates, 10 km
(6 miles) northeast, the 13th-
century church of **São Pedro
de Rates** boasts a portal surmounted by gracefully sculpted
statues of saints, and a rose
window. Its nearby counterpart
at Rio Mau, the church of **São
Cristóvão de Rio Mau**, was
finished in 1151. Above the
door is a bishop (possibly St
Augustine) flanked by helpers.

Ponte de Lima's Roman bridge, leading to the church of Santo António

THE LEGEND OF THE BARCELOS COCK

A Galician pilgrim, as he was leaving Barcelos en route to Santiago de Compostela, was accused of stealing silver from a landowner, and sentenced to death by hanging. As a final plea to save himself, the prisoner requested a meeting with the judge, who was about to tuck into a meal of roast cockerel. The Galician vowed that as proof of his innocence the cockerel would stand up on the plate and crow.

The judge pushed aside his meal and ignored the plea. But as the prisoner was hanged, the cockerel stood up and crowed. The judge, realizing his mistake, hurried to the gallows and found that the Galician had miraculously survived thanks to a loose knot. According to legend, the Galician returned years later to carve the Cruzeiro do Senhor do Galo, now housed in the Museu Arqueológico in Barcelos.

Traditional Barcelos cock

River Cávado. The privately owned **Solar dos Pinheiros** is an attractive mansion on Rua Duques de Bragança, built in 1448. The sculpted figure plucking his beard on the south tower is known as Barbadão, the "bearded one". So incensed was this Jew when his daughter bore a child to a gentile (King João I) that he vowed never to shave again, hence his nickname.

A rich Gothic pillory stands in front of the ruined Counts' Palace or Paço dos Condes, destroyed by the earthquake of 1755. The ruins provide an open-air setting for the **Museu Arqueológico**, which displays stone crosses, sculpted blazons, sarcophagi, and its famous exhibit, the Cruzeiro do Senhor do Galo, a cross paying tribute to the Barcelos cock legend. Next to the palace, the **Igreja Matriz** is Romanesque with Gothic influences, and dates from the 13th century. There are 18th-century *azulejos* inside as well as an impressive rose window. The nearby **Museu de Olaria** illustrates the history of ceramics in the region.

🏛 **Museu Arqueológico**
Largo do Município. 253-82 47 41. ⬤ *daily.*

🏛 **Museu de Olaria**
Rua Cónego J. Gaiolas. 253-82 47 41. ⬤ *Tue–Sun.* ⬤ *1 Jan, Easter, 15 Aug, 1 Nov, 25 & 26 Dec.* 🌀 &

Azulejos **of St Benedict's miracle of the sickle, Nossa Senhora do Terço**

Barcelos ❾

Road map C1. 🏠 *10,000.* 🚉 🚌
ℹ️ *Torre de Menagem, Largo da Porta Nova, (253-81 18 82).* ⬤ *Thu.*

A PLEASANT riverside town, Barcelos is famed as the country's leading ceramics and crafts market and the source of the legendary cock that has become Portugal's national symbol. From its origins as a settlement in Roman times, the town of Barcelos developed into a flourishing agricultural centre and achieved political importance during the 15th century as the seat of the First Duke of Bragança. The town's star attraction is the Feira de Barcelos, a huge weekly market held on Campo da República. Anything from clothes to livestock can be bought here. Pottery enthusiasts can browse amongst bright designs including pagan figurines and the famous clay cockerels.

North of the square stands **Nossa Senhora do Terço**, the 18th-century church of a former Benedictine nunnery. In contrast to its plain exterior, the interior is beautifully decorated with panels of *azulejos* illustrating St Benedict's life.

In the southwest corner of the square, a graceful cupola crowns the **Igreja do Senhor da Cruz**, built around 1705 on the site where two centuries earlier João Pires, a cobbler, had a miraculous vision of a cross etched into the ground. The Festa das Cruzes (festival of crosses), the town's most spectacular event, is held at the beginning of May to celebrate the vision. During the celebrations thousands of flowers are laid on the streets to welcome a procession to the church, and events include magnificent displays of local folk costumes, dancing and fireworks.

The other historic attractions in the town are clustered together in a tranquil setting beside the 15th-century granite bridge that crosses over the

16th-century pillory on terrace overlooking the River Cávado at Barcelos

Street-by-Street: Viana do Castelo ❼

V IANA DO CASTELO lies in a beautiful setting on the Lima estuary. During the 15th century, the town gained prominence as a fishing centre and provided ships and seafarers for the great maritime discoveries of the 16th century *(see pp48–9)*. From here João Velho set off to explore the Congo, and João Álvares Fagundes charted the rich fishing grounds of Newfoundland. Wealth derived from trade with Europe and Brazil funded the town's many opulent mansions built in Manueline, Renaissance and Baroque styles. Today the main interest lies in the winding streets and intimate squares of the city centre, easily explored on foot.

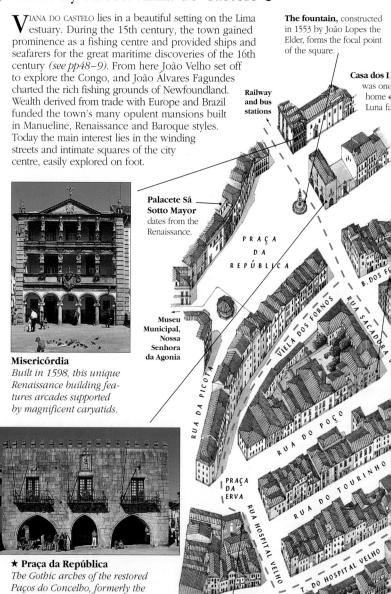

The fountain, constructed in 1553 by João Lopes the Elder, forms the focal point of the square.

Casa dos I
was on
home
Luna fa

Railway and bus stations

Palacete Sá Sotto Mayor dates from the Renaissance.

PRAÇA DA REPÚBLICA

Museu Municipal, Nossa Senhora da Agonia

Misericórdia
Built in 1598, this unique Renaissance building features arcades supported by magnificent caryatids.

RUA DA PICOTA

VIELA DOS FORNOS

RUA SACADORA

B. DOS F

RUA DO POÇO

RUA DO TOURINHO

PRAÇA DA ERVA

RUA HOSPITAL VELHO

T. DO HOSPITAL VELHO

VIELA DA PARENTA

★ Praça da República
The Gothic arches of the restored Paços do Concelho, formerly the town hall, dominate the head of Viana's main square. Manueline motifs include the arms of João III.

STAR SIGHTS

★ **Igreja Matriz**

★ **Praça da República**

The Hospital Velho
was originally a pilgrims' hospice. It now houses the Alto Minho tourist office.

KEY

– – – Suggested route

| 0 metres | 50 |
| 0 yards | 50 |

VISITORS' CHECKLIST

Road Map C1. 👥 25,000.
🚉 Largo da Estação.
🚌 Avenida Capitão Gaspar de
Castro. 🛈 Edifício do Hospital
Velho (258-82 26 20).
📅 Fri. 🎉 2nd Sun in May:
Festa das Rosas; mid-Aug:
Romaria de Nossa Senhora
da Agonia.

The fountain in Praça da República, the centre of daily life in Viana

Casa da Praça, a magni-
ficent Baroque mansion

Casa de João Velho
is a 15th-century
house, said to
have belonged
to the town's
most famous
navigator.

GAGO COUTINHO

T. DOS CLÉRIGOS

V. DO SEQUEIRO

★ **Igreja Matriz**
*The arch surrounding the
west door of Viana's 15th-
century, fortress-like parish
church is adorned with
Gothic reliefs of the apostles.*

Exploring Viana do Castelo
Both a busy fishing port and
holiday resort, Viana is overlooked by the peak of Monte
de Santa Luzia. The town is
the capital of Minho folk culture, playing host to lively
festivals and supporting a
thriving handicrafts industry.

🏛 Museu Municipal
Largo de São Domingos. 📞 258-82
03 77. 🕐 Tue–Sun. ⬤ public hols.
📷 ♿ new wing only.
Viana's Museu Municipal
is housed in the 18th-
century Palacete dos
Barbosas Maciéis
and has an excellent
collection of rare
ceramics, furniture,
archaeological
finds and paintings.
In one of the upstairs
rooms, the walls are
tiled with animated
allegorical depictions
of the continents,
while the chapel is
lined with tiles signed
by the 18th-century
artist Policarpo de
Oliveira Bernardes,
(see p22). Among
the exhibits are a
17th-century Indo-
Portuguese cabinet
magnificently deco-
rated with inlaid ivory, and
pieces of Oporto faïence from
the Massarelos district, embellished with fine brushwork.

**Early 19th-
century ceramic,
Museu Municipal**

🛐 Nossa Senhora da Agonia
Campo de Nossa Senhora da Agonia.
📞 258-824 067. 🕐 daily. ♿
Northwest of the centre, the
mid-18th century chapel of
Nossa Senhora da Agonia
houses a statue of Our Lady of

Sorrows *(agonia)*. The chapel,
with façade and altar designed
by André Soares, draws enormous crowds for the *romaria*
of Nossa Senhora da Agonia,
a three-day festival held each
year in the month of August
(see p227). The statue is carried in procession through the
town amid much feasting and
carnival celebration.

ENVIRONS: In order to enjoy
exceptional views, take the
zig-zag road to **Monte
de Santa Luzia**, 5 km
(3 miles) north of the
town centre. (A funicular
runs on winter weekends
from the station.) The
basilica, completed in
1926 and modelled on
the Sacré Coeur in Paris,
is a pilgrimage site with
little aesthetic appeal.
The steep climb, how-
ever, is well rewarded
by the superb views from
the top of the dome. Be-
hind the church you can
wander along woodland
paths or visit the
Pousada de Santa Luzia
(see p394). From the
pousada it is a short
walk to the top of the
hill, where there are
traces of a Celtiberian
settlement *(citânia)*.
The excellent beach of
Praia do Cabedelo lies to
the south of the town. The
beach is accessible by road
via the bridge or by a five-
minute ferry crossing from
the riverside dock on Avenida
dos Combatentes da Grande
Guerra. To the north lies **Vila
Praia de Âncora**, another
popular beach resort.

Braga ⓾

CHURCHES, GRAND 18TH-CENTURY HOUSES and pretty gardens provide the focus for the charm and interest of Braga's centre, once past the urban development on the city outskirts.

Known in Roman times as Bracara Augusta, Braga has a long history as a religious and commercial centre. In the 12th century, it became the seat of Portugal's archbishops, and the country's religious capital. The city lost some influence in the 19th century, but today continues as the ecclesiastical capital of Portugal and main city of the Minho.

Not surprisingly, Braga hosts some of Portugal's most colourful religious festivals. Semana Santa (Holy Week) is celebrated with dramatic, solemn processions, while the lively festival of São João in June sees dancing, fairs and fireworks.

Symbol of the city, Our Lady of the Milk

The west façade of the Sé, with its 15th-century galilee, or porch

Exploring Braga
The compact historic centre borders **Praça da República**, the central square. Within the square stands the 14th-century **Torre de Menagem**, all that remains of the city's original fortifications. A short walk leads to Rua do Souto, a narrow pedestrian street lined with elegant shops and cafés, including the **Café Brasileira**, furnished in 19th-century salon style. Towards the end of the road stands the impressive **Sé**, the cathedral of Braga. Other churches worth a visit include the small, 16th-century **Capela dos Coimbras**, and the 17th-century Baroque **Santa Cruz**. Many of the finest mansions in Braga also date from the Baroque period, such as the **Palácio do Raio** and the **Câmara Municipal** (the town hall). Both buildings are attributed to the 18th-century architect André Soares da Silva.

The blue-tiled façade of the Palácio do Raio, also known as the Casa do Mexicano

🔒 Sé
Rossio da Sé. ◯ *daily.*
Museu de Arte Sacra 📞 *253-26 33 17.* ◯ *daily.* 🔲
Braga's cathedral was begun in the 12th century, when Henry of Burgundy decided to build on the site of an older church, destroyed in the 6th century. Since then the building has seen many changes, including the addition of a graceful galilee (porch) in the late 15th century. The church

now exhibits a range of styles from Romanesque to Baroque. Outstanding features include the chapel to the right, just inside the west door, housing the ornate 15th-century tomb of the first-born son of João I (*see pp46–7*), Dom Afonso, who died in childhood. Also of interest are the upper choir

with its elaborately carved wooden stalls, and the ornate, gilded, Baroque organ cases.

The cathedral also houses the Treasury or **Museu de Arte Sacra**, which contains a rich collection of ecclesiastical treasures as well as, statues, carvings and *azulejo* tiles.

Several chapels can be seen in the courtyard and cloister. The Capela dos Reis houses the tombs of the founders, Henry of Burgundy and his wife Dona Teresa, as well as the preserved body of the 14th-century archbishop Dom Lourenço Vicente.

From Rua de São João you can admire a statue of Nossa Senhora do Leite (Our Lady of the Milk), symbol of the city of Braga, sheltered under an ornate Gothic canopy.

🏛 Antigo Paço Episcopal
Praça Municipal. 📞 *253-61 22 34.*
Library ◯ *Mon–Fri.*
Near the Sé is the former archbishops' palace. The façades date from the 14th, 17th and 18th centuries, but

The Jardim de Santa Bárbara by the walls of the Antigo Paço Episcopal

major fire destroyed the interior in the 18th century. The palace is now used as a library and archives. Beside it are the immaculate gardens of the Jardim de Santa Bárbara.

⛪ Palácio dos Biscainhos

Rua dos Biscainhos. [253-20 46 50. ☐ Tue–Sun. ⓘ

To the west of the city centre is the Palácio dos Biscainhos. Built in the 16th century and modified over the centuries, this imposing aristocratic mansion features ornate, terraced gardens and grand salons with lavish stucco ceilings. It now houses the city's Museu Etnográfico e Artístico

(Ethnography and Arts Museum) with displays of foreign and Portuguese furniture. An unusual detail is the ribbed, paved ground floor, designed to allow carriages inside the building to deposit guests and drive on to the stables beyond.

ENVIRONS: The attractively simple chapel of **São Frutuoso de Montélios**, 3.5 km (2 miles) northwest of Braga, is one of the very few remaining examples of pre-Romanesque architecture to be found in Portugal. Built around the 7th century, it was destroyed by the Moors and rebuilt in the 11th century.

VISITORS' CHECKLIST

Road map C1. 🚋 160,000.
🚉 Largo da Estação. 🚌 Praça da Galiza. 🛈 Praça da República 1 (253-26 25 50). 🚐 Tue. 🎉 Holy Week (week before Easter); 23–24 Jun: Festa de São João.

West of Braga, 4 km (2.5 miles) from the centre and on the road to Barcelos, is the former Benedictine **Mosteiro de Tibães**. Dating back to the 11th century, this magnificent architectural complex with its gardens and cloisters, was rebuilt in the 19th century and is being refurbished to house a historical centre.

At Falperra, 6 km (4 miles) southeast of Braga, stands the church of **Santa Maria Madalena**. Designed by André Soares da Silva in 1750, it is known for its ornate exterior, perhaps the country's finest expression of the Rococo.

⛪ São Frutuoso de Montélios

Av. São Frutuoso. ☐ times subject to change, check with Braga tourist office (253-26 25 50).

🏛 Mosteiro de Tibães

Lugar de Tibães. [253-62 26 70. ☐ Tue–Sun. ⓘ to museum. ♿

Interior of the old coach stable at the Palácio dos Biscainhos

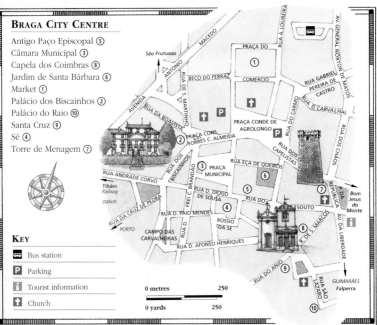

BRAGA CITY CENTRE

Antigo Paço Episcopal ⑤
Câmara Municipal ③
Capela dos Coimbras ⑧
Jardim de Santa Bárbara ⑥
Market ①
Palácio dos Biscainhos ②
Palácio do Raio ⑩
Santa Cruz ⑨
Sé ④
Torre de Menagem ⑦

KEY

🚌	Bus station
🅿	Parking
🛈	Tourist information
⛪	Church

0 metres 250
0 yards 250

Bom Jesus do Monte ⓫

Fountain on Staircase of the Three Virtues

O N A FORESTED SLOPE east of Braga stands Portugal's most spectacular religious sanctuary. In 1722 the Archbishop of Braga devised the giant Baroque Escadaria (stairway) of Bom Jesus as the approach to a small existing shrine. The stairway and the church of Bom Jesus were completed by Carlos Amarante in 1811. The lower section features a steep Sacred Way with chapels showing the 14 Stations of the Cross, the scenes leading up to Christ's crucifixion. The Escadório dos Cinco Sentidos, in the middle section, depicts the five senses with ingenious wall-fountains and statues of biblical, mythological and symbolic figures. This is followed by the similarly allegorical Staircase of the Three Virtues.

At the summit, an esplanade provides superb views and access to the church. Close by are several hotels, a café and a boating lake hidden among the trees. Both a pilgrimage site and tourist attraction, the sanctuary attracts large festive crowds at weekends.

★ Escadaria
The staircase is built of granite accentuated by whitewashed walls. The steps represent an upward spiritual journey.

Chapel of the Crucifixion

Chapel of Jesus before Pilate

Chapel of the Road to Calvary

Chapel of the Flagellation

Chapel of the Kiss of Judas

Chapel of Darkness

Chapel of Christ's Agony in the Garden

Chapel of the Last Supper

Entrance Portico
At the foot of the giant stairway stands a portico bearing the coat of arms of Dom Rodrigo de Moura Teles, the archbishop who commissioned the work.

★ Funicular Railway
The funicular (elevador) dates back to 1882. Hydraulically operated, it makes the ascent to the terrace beside the church in three minutes.

e Hotel do Elevador
e p393) stands
ar the top of
funicular.

Hotel do Parque

Pelican
fountain

VISITORS' CHECKLIST

Road map C1. 5 km (3 miles) E of
Braga. 253-67 66 36.
funicular to the top. daily.
daily.

**The church of
Bom Jesus** was
built on the site
of a 15th-century
sanctuary. In front
of it stand eight
statues of people
who condemned
Christ, including
Herod and Pilate.

**Chapel of the
Descent from the Cross**
*Each chapel has a tableau
of life-size terracotta
figures in a scene
from Christ's
last journey.*

**On the Staircase of
the Five Senses** are five
fountains, each representing
a bodily sense: sight, hearing,
smell, taste and touch.

**Statues,
symbols and
inscriptions**
elaborate on
the theme of
the senses.

**Staircase of
the Three Virtues**
*The final stretch of
staircase represents
the gaining of Faith,
Hope and Charity,
symbolized by foun-
tains and various
allegorical figures.*

**Chapel
of Simon
the Cyrenian**

**Chapel of the
Crown of Thorns**

**Fountain of the Five
Wounds of Christ**
*The fountains positioned
at various points on the
long ascent symbolize
the water of life and puri-
fication of the body and
spirit. In the fountain at
the foot of the Staircase
of the Five Senses, water
spills from the five bezants
on the Portuguese coat of
arms, a symbolic refer-
ence to Christ's wounds.*

| 0 metres | 25 |
| 0 yards | 25 |

STAR FEATURES

★ **Escadaria**

★ **Funicular Railway**

Guimarães ⑫

FRAMED BY GENTLY RISING HILLS, the town of Guimarães is celebrated as the birthplace of the nation. When Afonso Henriques proclaimed himself king of Portugal in 1139 *(see pp42–3)*, he chose Guimarães as his capital, and the distinctive outline of its proud castle appears on the Portuguese coat of arms. In the well-preserved city centre, the narrow streets of the medieval quarter are ideal for exploration on foot. The cobbled Rua de Santa Maria, lined with old town houses embellished with ornate statuary, leads up from the main square, the Largo da Oliveira, past the Paço dos Duques to the castle. To feel the hustle and bustle of the Middle Ages, visit the town in the first week of August for the Festas Gualterianas, a festival of medieval art and costume.

Baroque candle-holder, Paço dos Duques

♜ Castelo de São Miguel

Rua Conde Dom Henrique. **[** 253-41 22 73. ◻ *daily.* ● *1 Jan, Easter, 1 May, 25 Dec.* 🖼

The castle's huge square keep, encircled by eight crenellated towers, dominates the skyline. First built to deter attacks by Moors and Normans in the 10th century, it was extended by Henry of Burgundy two centuries later and, according to tradition, was the birthplace of Portugal's first king, Afonso Henriques. The font where he was reputedly baptized is kept in the tiny Romanesque church of **São Miguel**, situated at the western end of the castle.

⚜ Paço dos Duques

Rua Conde Dom Henrique. **[** 253-41 22 73. ◻ *daily.* ● *1 Jan, Easter, 1 May, 25 Dec.* 🖼

Constructed in the 15th century by Dom Afonso (first Duke of Bragança), the Burgundian

style of the Paço dos Duques reflects Dom Afonso's taste acquired on his travels through Europe. The palace fell into disuse when the Bragança family moved to Vila Viçosa *(see pp298–9)*. In 1933, under the Salazar dictatorship *(see pp56–7)*, it was renovated as an official residence for the president.

On view in a small museum inside the palace, are lavish displays of Persian rugs, Flemish tapestries and paintings, such as the impressive *O Coreiro Pascal* (Paschal Lamb) by Josefa de Óbidos *(see p51)*. Paying unusual homage to the nation's maritime exploits, the chestnut ceiling in the banqueting hall imitates the upturned hull of a Portuguese caravel.

🏛 Museu de Alberto Sampaio

Rua Alfredo Guimarães. **[** 253-423 910. ◻ *Tue–Sun.* ● *1 Jan, Easter, 1 May, 25 Dec.* 🖼

This museum, housed in the beautiful Romanesque cloister and adjoining rooms of Nossa Senhora da Oliveira, displays some outstanding religious art, *azulejos* and ceramics, all from local churches.

The star exhibits, donated to the church by João I, are his tunic worn at the battle of Aljubarrota in 1385 *(see p183)*, and a 14th-century silver altarpiece, comprising a triptych of the Visitation, Annunciation and Nativity, reportedly taken from the defeated Spanish king. The Santa Clara room contains gilt carving, the work of local craftsmen, taken from the former convent of Santa Clara, now the town hall.

Largo da Oliveira, centre of old Guimarães

⛪ Nossa Senhora da Oliveira

Largo da Oliveira. **[** 253-41 61 44. ◻ *daily.*

This former monastery lies on the square's east side. Founded by Afonso Henriques, the church was restored by João I in gratitude to Our Lady of the Olive Tree for his victory at Aljubarrota *(see p183)*. The Manueline tower is from 1515.

In front of it is the Padrão do Salado, a 14th-century Gothic shrine housing a cross. It commemorates the legend of how the church and square acquired their name. An olive tree was transplanted here to supply the altar lamp with oil, but it withered. In 1342, the merchant Pedro Esteves placed the cross on it, whereupon the tree flourished. The tree that stands in the square today dates only from 1985.

The massive battlements surrounding the keep of Castelo de São Miguel

VISITORS' CHECKLIST

Road map C1. 🚍 60,000.
🚉 Avenida Dom João IV.
🚌 Alameda Mariano Felgueiras.
🛈 Praça de São Tiago (253-518
394). 🛍 Fri. 🎪 first weekend
in Aug: Festas Gualterianas.

🏛 Museu Martins Sarmento

Rua Paio Galvão. 🕻 253-41 59 69.
◯ Tue–Sun. ⬤ public hols. 🎫
Named after the archaeologist
who excavated major Iron
Age sites in the north, notably
Citânia de Briteiros, the museum is housed in the Gothic
cloister of the 14th-century
convent of São Domingos. Specializing in finds from these
sites, some dating to the Stone
Age, the museum contains
a wealth of archaeological,
ethnological and numismatic
exhibits. These include a rare
pair of Lusitanian granite
warriors, a bronze votive oxcart, and the Pedras Formosas,
two stone slabs inscribed with
human figures. The most striking exhibit is the Colossus of
Pedralva, a stone figure that
stands 3 m (10 ft) tall.

🏠 São Francisco

Largo de São Francisco. 🕻 253-51
79 26. ◯ Tue–Sun. ⬤ public hols.
Built in 1400 in Gothic style,
the elegant church of São Francisco was reconstructed in the
18th century. The interior of
the church boasts a chancel
covered in magnificent 18th-
century azulejos with scenes
from the life of St Antony.

ENVIRONS: The former monastery of **Santa Marinha da
Costa** is one of Portugal's top
pousadas (see p379). It stands
5 km (3 miles) southeast of
Guimarães, and was founded
in 1154. The gardens and
chapel are open to the public.

Renaissance stone fountain at Santa
Marinha da Costa monastery

Reconstructed huts at the Iron Age site of Citânia de Briteiros

Citânia de Briteiros ⑬

Road map C1. 15 km (9 miles) N of
Guimarães, off N101. 🕻 253-41 59
69. 🚌 from Guimarães & Braga.
◯ Apr–Sep: 9am–7pm daily;
Oct–Mar: 9am–6pm daily. 🎫

THE IRON AGE settlement
of Citânia de Briteiros
is one of Portugal's most
impressive archaeolo-
gical sites. Excavated by
Martins Sarmento (1833–
99), who devoted his life
to the study of Iron Age
sites, are the foundations
of 150 stone dwellings,
a number of which have
since been reconstructed.
From about the 4th
century BC to the
4th century AD, the
site was inhabited by
Celtiberians, but was
most probably under
Roman rule from c.20
BC. A network of
paths leads visitors
past paved streets,
subterranean cisterns,
sewers and water supply ducts.
The Museu Martins Sarmento
in Guimarães displays various
excavated artefacts.

*The basto statue
of Cabeceiras
de Basto*

Cabeceiras de Basto ⑭

Road map D1. 🚍 17,000. 🚌
🛈 Paços do Concelho, Praça da
República (253-66 91 00). 🛍 Mon.

THE TERRAS DE BASTO, once
a region of refuge from
Moorish invasion, lie east of
Guimarães among mountains
and forests. Statues known as
bastos, believed to represent
Celtic warriors, are found in
various parts of the Terras de
Basto where they served as
territorial markers. In the main
town, Cabeceiras de Basto,
the prime attraction is the
Baroque **Mosteiro de
Refojos**, with its splendid
dome 33 m (108 ft) high,
surrounded by statues of
the Apostles, and sur-
mounted by a statue of
the archangel Michael.
The town also owns the
best of the basto statues,
albeit with a French
head; it was changed by
troops as a joke during
the Napoleonic Wars.

ENVIRONS: The fine
hiking country of
the Terras de Basto,
carpeted with flowers
in spring, has other
villages worth visiting.
Mondim de Basto,
overlooking the River
Tâmega some 25 km
(15 miles) south of
Cabeceiras, is a convenient
base for climbing **Monte
Farinha** which, at 966 m
(3,169 ft) is the highest peak
in the region. Then climb the
steps to the top of the church
of Nossa Senhora da Graça on
the summit, for splendid views.
Over the Tâmega, the village
of **Celorico de Basto** has a
small castle and several manor
houses in the surrounding area.
Most are private but some,
such as the **Casa do Campo**
(see p393), are part of the
Turismo de Habitação scheme
(see p376) and take in guests.

SOUTHERN PORTUGAL

INTRODUCING SOUTHERN PORTUGAL 284-289

ALENTEJO 290-313

ALGARVE 314-331

Southern Portugal at a Glance

SOUTH OF THE TAGUS the vast wheatfields and parched plains of the Alentejo stretch almost uninterrupted to the horizon. There is a rich legacy of early civilization here, dating back to prehistory, but visitors to Elvas, Beja or even the World Heritage city of Évora will usually be untroubled by mass tourism – until reaching the southern coast. Many visitors know nothing of Portugal except the tourist playground of the Algarve, yet it is least typical of the country. The sandy beaches are a year-round attraction but the historic town centres such as Faro, and the quieter hinterland, are well worth exploring.

***Évora**, the Alentejo's historic university city, has monuments dating back to the Roman era. Gleaming white arcades and balconies of finely wrought ironwork are reminders that for over 450 years, until 1165, Évora was inhabited by the Moors (see pp302–5).*

***Beja** flourished under the Moors and its museum is housed in a former convent resplendent with Hispano-Arab tiles, such as these in the chapter-house (see p311).*

Baixo Alentejo

ALGARVE
(See pp314–31)

0 kilometres	25
0 miles	10

***Lagos**, principal town of the western Algarve, is flanked by inviting cove beaches, such as Praia de Dona Ana, which make it easy to understand why sunseekers flock here (see pp320–21).*

◁ **Sandy beach and calm waters at the popular resort of Albufeira**

Alto Alentejo

Marvão, *within a stone's throw of the Spanish border, sits like a miniature fortress high in the Serra de São Mamede. The granite walls which protect the tiny town merge imperceptibly with the rock and have kept Marvão safe through centuries of dispute (see p294).*

Elvas *has some of the best-preserved fortifications in Europe (see p297). At the centre of the walled old town lies the Praça da República, where Elvas's former cathedral looks out over the square's striking geometric mosaics.*

ALENTEJO
(See pp290–313)

Vila Viçosa *was chosen in the 15th century as the seat of the dukes of Bragança. Here they built their vast Paço Ducal (see pp298–9), in front of which stands a bronze equestrian statue of the 8th Duke, who became King João IV in 1640.*

Faro, *the gateway to the Algarve thanks to its international airport, is nevertheless bypassed by many visitors. Much was destroyed by the 1755 earthquake, but the town has retained a quiet historic centre beside the harbour. In spring the streets and squares are scented with the sweetness of orange blossom (see pp326–8).*

The Beaches of the Algarve

FACING NORTH AFRICA to the south, and exposed to the force of the Atlantic in the west, the Algarve has a varied coastline. The Barlavento (windward side) includes the west coast and the south coast almost as far as Faro. Beaches around the promontory of Sagres are backed by soaring cliffs and on the west coast many beaches are deserted. The sea here is colder and rougher than the south coast, with dangerous currents. Between Sagres and Lagos is the start of a series of beautiful sandy coves, punctuated with grottoes, overlooked by tightly packed holiday resorts. East of Faro, the Sotavento (leeward side) has long, sandy beaches washed by warm, calm water.

Sunbathing on the beach

Arrifana ①
The gracefully curving beach of Arrifana is one of the most stunning on the west coast. Sheltered below high cliffs, the approach by road offers dramatic views *(see p318)*.

Beliche ③
Despite being at the "world's end", Beliche is sheltered by Cabo de São Vicente. The sandy beach is backed by fascinating caves and rock formations *(see p320)*.

Castelejo ②
This long, deserted beach of soft sand can only be reached via a dirt road by bicycle, car or jeep. Its remote location, however, ensures peace and quiet *(see p319)*.

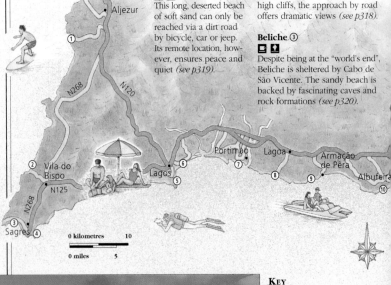

KEY
━━━ Motorway
━━━ Major road
━━━ Minor road

For key to symbols see back flap

Martinhal ④
Martinhal is a wide, sheltered expanse of sand east of Sagres. The area is popular for water sports of all kinds, and the beach boasts an aquatic school with parasailing, water-skiing and windsurfing *(see p320)*.

Dona Ana ⑤

A tiny cove on the way to Ponta da Piedade, Dona Ana is one of the prettiest beaches in the Algarve, although crowded during the summer. A boat trip to see nearby caves and grottoes is highly recommended *(see p321)*.

Meia Praia ⑥

A vast expanse of sand stretching for 4 km (2 miles), the sheltered Meia Praia is the longest beach in the Algarve. Easily reached by road, there is also a boat trip from Lagos during the summer months *(see p321)*.

Praia da Rocha ⑦

Framed by ochre cliffs and lapped by calm water, this spacious beach is justifiably famous – and crowded in high season. Water sports can be practised here in a gentler sea than the extreme southwest and visitors are well catered for *(see p322)*.

Ilha de Tavira ⑪

In summer, boats go from Quatro Águas to the sandy Ilha de Tavira. The beach facing the coast has calm water, whereas the beaches on the ocean side, that run the length of the island, offer good swimming and windsurfing *(see p330)*.

Carvoeiro ⑧

Carvoeiro is a fishing village with a diminutive cove. The whole area is great for cove beaches, and a boat trip or a walk along the cliff will take you to spectacular sandy beaches with excellent swimming and snorkelling.

Monte Gordo ⑫

The warm water and balmy climate, combined with vast stretches of clean sand backed by pine woods, make Monte Gordo a very popular resort.

Senhora da Rocha ⑨

Senhora da Rocha, named after a small chapel on its eastern promontory, is actually three small, sheltered beaches. Typical of this part of the coast, these half-moons of sand tucked below eroded yellow cliffs are reached via steep steps.

São Rafael ⑩

The small, popular beach of São Rafael offers soft sand and shallow water, with spectacular caves and eroded rock formations to explore. For those without a car, it is a steep walk down from the bus stop on the main road *(see p323)*.

Regional Food: Southern Portugal

THE TUNA AND SARDINES on offer in the Algarve are unrivalled, but every type of seafood, from cod to clams, is excellent. Inland, fish is replaced by goat, lamb and, above all, acorn-fed pigs, cooked into delicious stews with local wine. A feature of southern cooking is the *cataplana*, a kind of tightly sealed wok in which the food steams in its own juice. Bread is enjoyed, not just as a snack, but to soak up the herby juices in fish and meat dishes *(ensopados)*. Almonds, oranges, figs and olives grow in abundance throughout the south.

Peppers

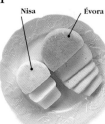

Ewe's milk cheeses *come from all over the Alentejo. Among the best are Évora and the piquant Nisa.*

Nisa   Évora

Spicy **linguiça**

Presunto **pata negra**

Chouriço

Salpicão, made with pork loin

Empadas (chicken pies)

Pão alentejano, *the peasant loaf of the Alentejo, is served at most meals and used in many bread-based dishes.*

Pork *is used in many guises in the Alentejo, t produces sausages and smoked hams (presuno) delicious variety. Chicken pies are a speciality of Évor*

Sopa alentejana, *fragrant with garlic, coriander and olive oil, is a bread-based soup topped with a poached egg.*

Gaspacho, *always served cold, is a garlic-laden tomato soup, incorporating cucumber, sweet peppers and olive oil.*

Salada mista *usually means a simple salad of lettuce leaves, tomatoes and onions dressed with olive oil and vinegar.*

Atum de cebolada, *from the Algarve, is a fresh tuna steak which is cooked on a bed of onions with tomato sauce.*

Sardinhas assadas, *charcoal-grilled sardines, are a seaside tradition – a feast in summer when they are at their best.*

Lulas cheias *are succulent squid stuffed with cured meats and rice, then cooked in a onion and tomato mixture.*

Caldeirada *is a stew made with a variety of fish layered with potato. It is extremely popular all along the coast.*

Porco à alentejana, *a curious marriage of pork and clams, is usually cooked in a* cataplana, *which seals in the flavours.*

Borrego ensopado, *an everyday favourite in the Alentejo, is a stew of young lamb served on bread to mop up the gravy.*

Coelho em vinho *is an Alentejan recipe for rabbit, a meat popular all over Portugal. This version is cooked in wine.*

Cabrito assado *is a small kid, roasted whole, with a covering of paprika, garlic, wine and lard to keep it moist.*

Olive oil (azeite) *enriches dishes from gaspacho to salads.*

Bolo podre **("rotten cake"), a dark, spiced honey cake**

Selection of marzipan *doces de amêndoa*

Figos cheios, **figs studded with almonds**

Queijada, **a cheesecake from the Alentejo**

Ameixas de Elvas, **the preserved greengages known as Elvas plums**

Almonds

Dried figs

Sweetmeats in the south reflect the rich harvest of figs and almonds from the Algarve, fashioned into mouthwatering honeyed treats.

FRUIT

As well as the ubiquitous grape, the climate favours greengages, apricots and citrus fruits. Mild winters help the Algarve grow the best figs, oranges and strawberries in the country.

Oranges

Grapes

LIQUEURS

The south's best wines are from the Alentejo *(see pp28–9)*, but the Algarve has two local liqueurs: the bitter-almond *amarguinha*, splendid on ice, and *medronheira*, made from the pretty fruit of the strawberry tree *(Arbutus unedo).*

Amarguinha, an almond liqueur

Medronheira sweetened with honey

ALENTEJO

T HE SUN-BAKED ALENTEJO *occupies nearly one-third of Portugal, stretching all the way from the Tagus south to the Algarve. Its vast rolling plains, golden with wheat or silver with olive trees, its whitewashed villages, megaliths and castles, and above all the space and tranquillity, are the Alentejo's great attractions for visitors.*

Stone circles, dolmens and other relics of Stone Age life pepper the Alentejan plain, particularly around Évora, a historical gem of a city at the region's geographical centre.

Évora, like Beja, Vidigueira and other towns, was founded by the Romans, who valued this land beyond the Tagus – *além Tejo* – for its wheatfields. Introducing irrigation systems to overcome the soil's aridity, they established enormous farms to grow grain for the empire. Worked by peasant farmers, these huge estates, or *latifúndios*, still exist, some of them now being run as co-operatives.

Grain apart, the vast plains yield cork from the bark of cork oaks and olives – Elvas is prized for these as well as its candied greengages *(see p289)*. Vineyards around Reguengos and Vidigueira have long produced powerful wines, and the Alentejo has a number of demarcated wine regions *(see pp28–9)*. Since 1986, Portugal's membership of the European Union has increased the rate of investment and modernization, although the region is still sparsely populated, supporting only ten per cent of the population. Land tenure has always been a concern here, and communism has a strong appeal – the Alentejans were solid supporters of the 1974 revolution *(see p57)*.

Many towns and villages, especially in the south, carry echoes of the long Moorish occupation in the cube-like white houses, while to the north and east the plains give way to a rocky terrain of fortified villages and scrubland grazed by flocks of sheep.

Portuguese from other regions mock the amiable *alentejanos* for their slow ways, but they are widely admired for their singing and their handicrafts.

An Alentejan house in Odemira, with the traditional blue trim typical of the region

◁ Cork oaks and olive trees breaking up the wheatfields of the Alentejo plains

Exploring the Alentejo

THE ANCIENT CITY of Évora, with its exceptional historic centre and location in the heart of the Alentejo, is an obvious starting point for exploring this varied and beautiful region.

To the northeast lie the white towns of Estremoz and Vila Viçosa, where local marble has been used in the construction of some fabulous façades, and Alter do Chão, home of Portugal's royal horse, the Alter Real. Nearer the formerly-disputed Spanish frontier, towns and villages still shelter within massive fortifications, while travelling south the legacy of the Moors becomes ever more apparent; Beja and Mértola, especially, are full of Moorish history.

On the west coast there are some lovely beaches, with many stretches still relatively untouched by tourism.

The cromlech of Almendres, one of many prehistoric sites around Évora

SIGHTS AT A GLANCE

Alandroal ⑩
Alter do Chão ⑥
Arraiolos ⑭
Beja ㉓
Campo Maior ⑦
Castelo de Vide ④
Crato ⑤
Elvas ⑧
Estremoz ⑫
Évora pp302–5 ⑯
Évoramonte ⑬
Marvão ②
Mértola ㉘
Monsaraz ⑱
Montemor-o-Novo ⑮

Moura ㉑
Portalegre ③
Redondo ⑪
Santiago do Cacém ㉔
Serpa ㉒
Serra de São Mamede ①
Sines ㉕
Viana do Alentejo ⑲
Vidigueira ⑳
Vila Nova de Milfontes ㉖
Vila Viçosa pp298–9 ⑨
Zambujeira do Mar ㉗

Tours
Megaliths Tour ⑰

The fertile farmland and orchards of the northern Alentejo, seen from Estremoz

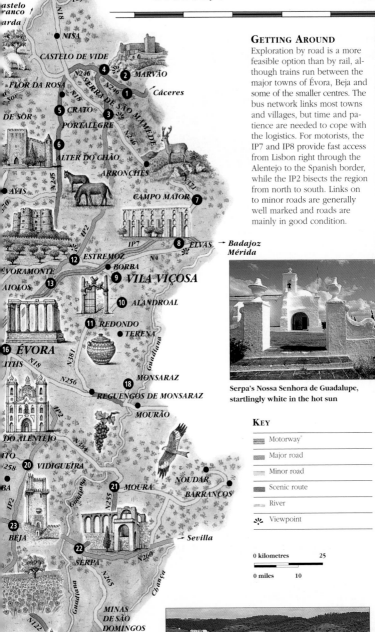

GETTING AROUND

Exploration by road is a more feasible option than by rail, although trains run between the major towns of Évora, Beja and some of the smaller centres. The bus network links most towns and villages, but time and patience are needed to cope with the logistics. For motorists, the IP7 and IP8 provide fast access from Lisbon right through the Alentejo to the Spanish border, while the IP2 bisects the region from north to south. Links on to minor roads are generally well marked and roads are mainly in good condition.

Serpa's Nossa Senhora de Guadalupe, startlingly white in the hot sun

KEY

▰▰▰	Motorway
▬▬▬	Major road
───	Minor road
▬▬▬	Scenic route
≈≈≈	River
☼	Viewpoint

0 kilometres 25

0 miles 10

A sea of wheat surrounding a farmhouse near Moura

Serra de São Mamede ❶

Road map D4. 🚌 to Portalegre.
🛈 Portalegre.

THE DIVERSE GEOLOGY and capricious climate of this remote range, caught between the Atlantic and the Mediterranean, encourage a fascinating range of flora and fauna. In 1989, 320 sq km (120 sq miles) of the Serra were designated a *parque natural*, and griffon vultures and Bonelli's eagles soar overhead. Red deer, wild boar and the cat-like genet live among the sweet chestnut trees and holm oaks, and streams attract otters and amphibians, such as the Iberian midwife toad. The reserve is also home to one of the largest colonies of bats in Europe.

The Serra's apparent emptiness is deceptive: megaliths suggest that it was settled in prehistoric times, and in the south of the reserve, rock paintings survive in the Serra de Cavaleiros and Serra de Louções. Below Marvão is the Roman town of Amaia (São Salvador de Aramenha), and the Roman network of roads still winds among the trim white villages, offering grand views at every curve.

From Portalegre, the road climbs for 15 km (9 miles) to the Pico de São Mamede at 1,025 m (3,363 ft). A minor road leads south to Alegrete, a fortified village crowned by its ruined 14th-century castle.

Sheep in the summer pastures of the Serra de São Mamede

Marvão ❷

Road map D4. 🚶 270. 🚊 🚌
🛈 Largo de Santa Maria (245-99 38 86). 🛒 Thu.

THIS SERENE MEDIEVAL hamlet is dramatically set at 862 m (2,828 ft) on a spectacular escarpment facing Spain. Its 13th-century walls and 17th-century buttresses blend seamlessly into the granite of the mountains, making it an impregnable stronghold. The Romans, who called the outcrop Herminius Minor, were followed by the Moors – the name may have come from Marvan, a Moorish leader – whom the Christians evicted with difficulty only in 1166.

The walls completely enclose the little collection of whitewashed houses, a *pousada* (*see p395*) and the 15th-century **Igreja Matriz**. Rua do Espírito Santo leads past the former governor's house (now a bank) with its 17th-century iron balcony, and a Baroque fountain, up towards the **castle**.

Built by King Dinis in about 1299, the castle dominates the village. Its walls enclose two cisterns, a museum displaying historic weapons and a keep. The castle offers spectacular views south and west towards the Serra de São Mamede and east to the Spanish frontier.

The **Museu Municipal**, in the former church of Santa Maria, retains the main altar, and has an interesting exhibition of traditional remedies and local archaeological finds dating from Palaeolithic to Roman times.

🏛 **Museu Municipal**
Largo de Santa Maria. 🕻 245-909 132. 🔲 daily. ⬤ 25 Dec. 🎟

Portalegre ❸

Road map D4. 🚶 15,000. 🚊 🚌
🛈 Rossio (245-331 359). 🛒 Wed & Sat (food); 2nd Wed of month (clothes). 🆆 www.rtsm.pt

STRATEGICALLY POSITIONED on a low plateau of the Serra de São Mamede amid fertile country, Portalegre is of Roman origin. Fortified by King Dinis (*see pp44–5*), it acquired city status in 1550.

Textile, tapestry and silk industries brought prosperity in the 16th and 17th centuries, reflected in the city's fine Renaissance and Baroque mansions. These are to be

Looking out over the plain from the heights of Marvão's castle

found along Rua 19 de Junho, the main street of the old town. Near the new town's central square, the Rossio, a former Jesuit monastery is now the only tapestry factory still in use. Cork production is also a tradition here, and the tall chimneys of cork factories on the edge of the city indicate a continuing industry.

Uphill lies the cathedral or **Sé**. Built in 1556, it acquired its Baroque façade and twin pinnacles in the 18th century. The late Renaissance interior has paintings by anonymous Portuguese artists and a sacristy lined with striking *azulejo* panels. These blue and white tile pictures, dating from the first years of the 17th century, depict scenes from the life of the Virgin Mary and the flight of the Holy Family into Egypt.

In an adjacent 18th-century mansion is the small **Museu Municipal**, where the eclectic collection on display ranges from religious art to Portuguese ceramics.

The home of José Régio (1901–69), the eminent Portuguese poet and dramatist, is near the Praça da República. Now the **Museu José Régio**, it contains some fascinating folk art objects in a variety of media as well as his collection of crucifixes and a recreated Alentejan kitchen.

Folk crucifix, Museu José Régio, Portalegre

🏛 **Museu Municipal**
Rua José Maria da Rosa.
📞 245-300 120. ⏰ Wed–Mon. 🖼

🏛 **Museu José Régio**
Rua José Régio. 📞 245-203 625.
⏰ Tue–Sun. 🖼

Castelo de Vide ❹

Road map D4. 🏘 *3,000.* 🚉 🚌
ℹ *Rua Bartolomeu A. da Santa 81 (245-901 361).* 🛍 *Fri (clothes).*

SPRAWLED ON a green slope of the Serra de São Mamede, this pretty spa town enjoyed by the Romans has worn well. It is fringed by modern development but the lower town, around Praça Dom Pedro V, retains its Baroque church of **Santa Maria**, the 18th-century town hall and pillory, and handsome mansions from the same era. In the Largo Frederico Laranjo is one of several sources of the town's curative waters: the **Fonte da Vila**, a carved stone fountain with a pillared canopy. Just above is the maze-like **Judiaria**, where small white houses sprout vivid pots of geraniums. Its cobbled alleys conceal a 13th-century **synagogue** and are lined with fine Gothic doorways. The town's oldest chapel, the 13th-century **Salvador do Mundo** on the Estrada de Circunvalação, has a much admired *Flight into Egypt* by an unknown 18th-century artist.

In the upper town, the tiny **Nossa Senhora da Alegria** offers a feast of 17th-century polychrome floral tiles. It stands within the walls of the **castle** that gave the town its name. This was rebuilt in 1310 by King Dinis, who negotiated here to marry Isabel of Aragon. Much of the castle was lost in an explosion in 1705.

Red-tiled roofs of Castelo de Vide

Crato ❺

Road map D4. 🏘 *2,000.* 🚉 🚌
ℹ *as for Portalegre (245-331 359).* 🛍 *3rd Thu of month.*

MODEST HOUSES under outsize chimneys give no hint of Crato's past eminence. Part of a gift from Sancho II to the powerful crusading Order of Hospitallers, Crato was the Order's headquarters by 1350. Its prestige was such that Manuel I and João III were both married here, and João III's nephew was Grand Prior.

In 1662, invading Spanish forces sacked and burned the town, a catastrophe from which it never recovered. The Hospitallers' **castle** remains, in ruins, and in the Praça do Município the 15th-century **Varanda do Grão-Prior** marks the entrance to what was the Grand Prior's residence.

Rua de Santa Maria leads, via an avenue of orange trees, to the **Igreja Matriz**, much altered since its 13th-century origins. In the chancel, 18th-century *azulejos* depict fishing, hunting and travelling scenes.

ENVIRONS: Just north of Crato are the imposing monastery and church of **Flor da Rosa**. Built in 1356 by the Grand Prior of Crato, father of Nuno Álvares Pereira *(see p183)*, the monastery was restored and in 1995 opened as a *pousada (see p395)*. A tapestry in the dining room shows the monastery surrounded by pine forests, as it was until the 20th century.

The crenellated monastery, now a *pousada*, of Flor da Rosa, near Crato

Alter do Chão ❻

Road map D4. 🏛 *2,700.* 🚍
🛈 *Palácio do Álamo, Largo Barreto Caldeira (245-61 00 04).*
🗓 *1st Thu of month.*

THE ROMANS founded Elteri (or Eltori) in 204 BC, but razed it under the Emperor Hadrian after the inhabitants were accused of disloyalty. The town was re-established in the 13th century.

Dominating the town centre is the five-towered **castle** with a Gothic portal built in 1359 by Pedro I. Its forbidding walls contrast with the flower-filled market square, the Largo Doze Melhores de Alter, at its feet.

Several streets northwest of the castle are graced by fine Baroque town houses, many trimmed with yellow paintwork in typical Alentejan style. The elegant 18th-century **Palácio do Álamo**, which houses the tourist office, also serves as an art gallery and library.

♣ Castle

Largo Barreto Caldeira. 🔓 *Jun–Sep: variable hours.* ⬤ *until further notice.*

ENVIRONS: Alter is best known for the **Coudelaria de Alter**, founded in 1748 to breed the Alter Real. The stud extends to 300 ha (740 acres) around attractive stables painted in the royal livery of white and ochre.

Spanning the Seda 12 km (7 miles) west along the N369 is the robust six-arched **Ponte de Vila Formosa**. This bridge carried the Roman road from Lisbon to Mérida in Spain.

Ⓤ Coudelaria de Alter

3 km (2 miles) NW of town. 📞 *245-61 00 60.* 🔓 *Tue–Sun.* 📷 ♿

Campo Maior's macabre but compelling Capela dos Ossos

Campo Maior ❼

Road map E5. 🏛 *8,500.* 🚍
🛈 *Rua Major Talaya 104 (268-68 89 36).* 🗓 *2nd Sat of month.*

ACCORDING TO LEGEND, this town got its name when three families settled in *campo maior*, the "bigger field". King Dinis fortified the town in 1310 and the monumental Porta da Vila was added in 1646.

Disaster struck in 1732 when a gunpowder magazine, ignited by lightning, destroyed the citadel and killed 1,500 people. It seems likely that after a decent period, the victims provided the material for the morbid **Capela dos Ossos**, entirely faced in human bones. Dated 1766, it bears an inscription on mortality spelt out in collar bones.

Each September the streets are dressed with paper flowers for the joyful Festa das Flores.

🏛 Capela dos Ossos

Largo do Regala. 📞 *268-686 168.*
🔓 *daily (if closed, ask priest to open).*

Elvas ❽

Road map D5. 🏛 *15,000.* 🚇 🚍
🛈 *Praça da República (268-62 22 36).*
🗓 *2nd & 4th Mon of the month.*

ONLY 12 KM (7 miles) from the Spanish border, Elvas feels like a frontier town. The sprawl of modern Elvas caters for busy cross-border traffic, but the old town's fortifications are among the best preserved in Europe. Within the walls a few architectural features and many of the street names are reminders that for 500 years the town was in Moorish hands.

Elvas was liberated from the Moors in 1230, but for another 600 years its fate was to swing between periodic attacks from Spain and the witnessing of numerous peace treaties.

Despite its dramatic history, Elvas is nowadays associated in Portuguese minds with Elvas plums *(see p289)*.

Summer roses brightening an Elvas street

ALTER REAL: HORSE OF KINGS

Most Lusitano horses – Portugal's national breed – are grey, but those called Alter Real ("real" means royal) are purebred bay or brown. King José (1750–77), who yearned for a quality Portuguese horse, imported a stock of Andalusian mares, from which the gracious, nimble Alter Real was bred. The equestrian statue in Lisbon's Praça do Comércio *(see p65)* is of José astride his beloved Alter, Gentil. The stud prospered until the Napoleonic Wars (1807–15), when horse stealing and erratic breeding sent the Alter into decline. By 1930, the royal horse was practically extinct, but years of dedication have ultimately revived this classic breed.

THE FORTIFICATIONS OF ELVAS

A walk around the top of the battlements gives a fine view of the old town and a vantage point from which to appreciate the ingenious design of the fortifications. Using the principles of the French military architect, the Marquis de Vauban, a series of pentagonal bastions and free-standing angled ravelins form a multi-faceted star, protecting the walls from every angle. What survives dates mostly from the 17th century, when the defences held off Spanish troops in the War of Independence *(see pp50–51)*. Elvas also served as Wellington's base to besiege Badajoz across the Guadiana.

Two surviving satellite forts indicate the strategic importance of Elvas: just to the southeast lies **Forte de Santa Luzia** (1641–87), and 2 km (1 mile) to the north is the 18th-century **Forte de Graça**, which is still a military post.

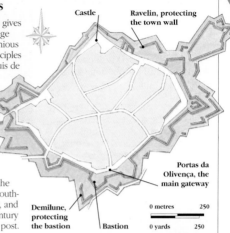

Castle

Ravelin, protecting the town wall

Portas da Olivença, the main gateway

Demilune, protecting the bastion

Bastion

0 metres 250
0 yards 250

♠ Castle
Parada do Castelo. ○ *daily.*
Romano-Moorish in origin, the castle which crowns the steep Elvas streets was rebuilt for Sancho II in 1226. It has been subjected to further remodelling over the years, principally by King Dinis and then in the late 15th century under João II, whose arms, which incorporate a pelican, can be seen above the entrance. The great keep was erected in 1488. Until the end of the 16th century the castle was used as the residence of the mayors of Elvas.

♠ Nossa Senhora da Assunção
Praça da República. 🕿 268-62 59 97. ○ *Mon–Fri.* &
Until 1882, this was the cathedral of Elvas. Built in the early 16th century, its architect was Francisco de Arruda, who also designed the town's impressive aqueduct. His Manueline south portal survives, but much of the church has been modified. The *azulejos* in the nave date from the early 17th century.

🏛 Museu Arqueológico and Biblioteca
Largo do Colégio. 🕿 268-62 24 02. ○ *Tue–Sun (library: Mon–Sat).* ● 1 Jan, Easter, 25 Dec. 🈺 *to museum.*
The archaeological museum's cool rooms display a collection which ranges from Roman water pots to prehistoric artefacts. The building in which the museum has been installed

since 1880 is a former Jesuit college. The associated library, which is entered by a quaint tiled porch, contains more than 50,000 books, including a number of rare early works.

♠ Nossa Senhora dos Aflitos
Largo do Pelourinho. ○ *Tue–Sun.*
The plain exterior belies the wealth within the walls of this little 16th-century church. The octagonal floor plan originates from the layout of an earlier Templar church, but its appeal is in the fine marble columns and spectacular yellow and blue *azulejos* added in the 17th century. These line the walls and reach up into the cupola.

Just behind the church is the archway of the Arab Porta da Alcáçova, a vestige of Elvas's Moorish fortifications. In the

Largo de Santa Clara, with its ornate pillory

adjacent Largo de Santa Clara is a pillory, carved in typically exuberant Manueline style *(see pp20–21)* and still armed with its hooks.

The arches of the great aqueduct

♠ Aqueduto da Amoreira
Until the 16th century the only source of drinking water in Elvas was the Alcalá well in the west of the town. When this began to fail, alarmed citizens conceived the notion of an aqueduct to bring water from the spring at Amoreira, some 8 km (5 miles) away. Work, begun in 1498, was not finished until 1622. The great round buttresses and arches of architect Francisco de Arruda march across the valley and still deliver water to the fountain in the Largo da Misericórdia. The aqueduct has a total of 843 arches in up to five tiers and in places towers to over 30 m (100 ft).

Vila Viçosa: Paço Ducal

THE DUKES OF BRAGANÇA owned vast estates, but the lavish palace at Vila Viçosa, begun by Dom Jaime in 1501, became their favoured residence.

When the 8th Duke became king in 1640, many of the furnishings accompanied him to Lisbon, but the long suite of first-floor rooms is still splendid, from the Sala de Cabra-Cega, where royal parties played blind man's buff, to the heroic Sala de Hércules. More intimate are the rooms of King Carlos and his wife, which are much as he left them the day before his assassination in 1908.

Chapel
*Despite later additio[n]
the chapel has retain[ed]
its coffered ceiling a[nd]
other features from t[he]
early 16th century. [It]
was here, on 3 Decem[ber] 1640, that the 8t[h]
Duke learnt that he
was to become king*

Dining room

First floor —

The vast kitchen, which once regularly fed several hundred people, gleams with over 600 copper pots and pans, some large enough to bathe in.

Sala de Cabra-Cega

★ **Sala dos Duques**
Lining the ceiling of the Room of the Dukes are portraits of all the dukes of Bragança by the Italian Domenico Dupra (1689–1770), commissioned by João V. On the walls are Brussels tapestries of scenes from the life of Achilles.

The armouries, in a series of vaulted rooms, display swords, crossbows, halberds and suits of armour.

Ground floor

The libra[ry]
is contained [in]
several rooms a[nd]
includes precious e[arly]
works collected by K[ing]
Manuel II in exile (*see p5[?]*)

Formal Gardens
The Jardim da Duquesa and the Jardim do Bosque are partly enclosed by palace walls, but can be seen from the dining-room windows. Their geometric formality reflects the palace's architectural style.

Entrance

STAR FEATURE

★ **Sala dos Duques**

VISITORS' CHECKLIST

Terreiro do Paço. 268-980 659. 9am–1pm, 2:30–5:30pm daily. (Last admission at 4:30pm.) 1 Jan, Easter, 25 Dec, 1 May. compulsory.

KEY TO FLOORPLAN

- Royal rooms
- Library
- Chapel
- Armouries
- Kitchen
- Treasury
- Public areas

PALACE GUIDE

Guided tours, which last about an hour, take in the royal rooms ranged along the first floor and ground-floor areas such as the kitchen and the treasury. Entry to the coach museum, on the north side of the palace, and armoury is by separate tickets. From time to time areas may be closed for restoration and rooms can be shut off without notice.

Vila Viçosa 9

Road map D5. 10,000. Praça da República (268-88 11 01). Wed.

After the expulsion of the Moors in 1226, this hillside town was named Val Viçosa – "fertile valley". In the 15th century it became the country seat of the dukes of Bragança, and when the 8th Duke became King João IV, Vila Viçosa was expanded to meet the needs of nobles and visiting ministers. Substantial houses, built from the local white marble, in streets lined with orange trees, reflect its prosperous royal past.

The town is full of reminders of the Braganças. Dominating the west side of the Terreiro do Paço is the long façade of the **Paço Ducal**, which stretches for 110 m (360 ft). Visitors to the palace emerge through the **Porta do Nó**, a marble and schist gateway formed into the knot symbol of the Braganças.

In the centre of the square a statue of João IV on horseback looks across to the **Igreja dos Agostinhos** (not open to the public). Founded in 1267 but rebuilt in the 17th century, the church was intended as the last resting place of the dukes, but despite their affection for Vila Viçosa, most Bragança monarchs are buried in Lisbon, at São Vicente de Fora *(see p72)*.

View from the castle at Vila Viçosa, looking towards the Paço Ducal

In the Renaissance **Convento das Chagas**, on the south side of the square, are the tombs of the Bragança wives. Founded by the 4th Duke's second wife in 1530, the convent is being converted to a *pousada*.

Alongside the Paço Ducal, an 18-km (11-mile) wall rings the **tapada real**, or royal chase. Uphill from the Terreiro do Paço is the **castle**, where an exhibition explains the history of the hunt. The castle, built by King Dinis, was the Braganças' residence from 1461 until the Paço Ducal became habitable.

In the nearby 14th-century church of **Nossa Senhora da Conceição** stands a Gothic image of the Virgin, said to be from England. During the 1646 *cortes* João IV crowned her as patron saint of Portugal, after which no Portuguese monarch ever wore a crown.

♣ Castle
Avenida Duques de Bragança. 268-980 128. Tue–Sun. public hols.

THE ROYAL HOUSE OF BRAGANÇA

Catherine, born at Vila Viçosa in 1638

Afonso, illegitimate son of João I, was created Duke of Bragança in 1442, first of an influential but bloodstained dynasty. Fernando, the 3rd Duke, was executed in 1483 by his cousin, João II, who feared his power. Jaime, the unstable 4th Duke, locked up his wife in Bragança castle *(see p258)*, then killed her at Vila Viçosa. It was Dom Jaime who initiated the building of the palace at Vila Viçosa, an ambitious work embellished by later dukes to reflect their aspirations and affluence. The 8th Duke only reluctantly relinquished a life of music and hunting here to take up the throne *(see p50)*.

The Braganças ruled Portugal for 270 years, accumulating wealth and forging alliances (João IV's daughter, Catherine, married Charles II of England), but inbreeding enfeebled the bloodline *(see p165)*. The last monarch, Manuel II, fled to exile in 1910, two years after his father and brother were shot by Republicans. The present duke farms quietly near Viseu.

The Porta do Nó, its carved knots the symbol of the Braganças

Alandroal, surrounded by groves of cork oaks

Alandroal ⑩

Road map D5. 🏚 *2,100.* 🚍
🛈 *Largo da Misericordia (268-440 040).* 🏛 *Wed.*

THE LOW-LYING little town of Alandroal, wrapped tidily around its **castle** ruins, was built by the Knights of Avis, who settled here from 1220. Little remains inside, but a surviving inscription shows it was completed in 1298. The **Igreja Matriz** within its walls dates from the 16th century.

The **Misericórdia** church near the castle walls contains beautiful *azulejos* reputed to be the work of Policarpo de Oliveira Bernardes (1695–1778).

ENVIRONS: Terena, 10 km (6 miles) south of Alandroal, is well known for its pottery. The 14th-century sanctuary of **Nossa Senhora de Boa Nova** has frescoes covering its walls and ceiling; dating from 1706, these depict saints and Portuguese kings. For access ask at the house opposite the church.

MARBLE: ALENTEJO'S WHITE GOLD

Portugal is the world's second largest exporter of marble, and even Italy, the biggest producer, buys Portugal's quality stone. Around 90 per cent – over 500,000 tonnes a year – is quarried around Estremoz. The marble from Estremoz and nearby Borba is white or pink, while the quarries at Viana do

Quarrymen near Estremoz, working on elephantine blocks of prized marble

Alentejo yield green stone. Marble has been used for construction since Roman times and in towns such as Évora *(see pp302–5)* and Vila Viçosa *(see pp298–9)*, palaces and humble doorsteps alike gleam with the stone often referred to as Portugal's "white gold".

Redondo ⑪

Road map D5. 🏚 *3,600.* 🚍
🛈 *Praça da República (266-989 21C*
🏛 *2nd Thu of month.*

THE CENTRE OF ONE of the Alentejo's wine regions *(see p29)*, medieval Redondo is also renowned for its pottery. Whole families work to produce Roman-style water jugs, casseroles and bowls painted with humorous folk-art motifs *(see p25)*. These are sold from the tiny white houses leading up to the ruins of the **castle** founded by King Dinis.

ENVIRONS: The **Convento de São Paulo** in the Serra de Ossa, 10 km (6 miles) north, was built in 1376; Catherine of Bragança stayed here on her return home in 1692 after the death of her husband, King Charles II of England. It is now a luxury hotel *(see p396)*, but retains its wonderful 16th- to 18th-century *azulejos*.

Estremoz ⑫

Road map D5. 🏚 *8,000.* 🚍
🛈 *Praça da República 26 (268-33 35 41).* 🏛 *Sat.*

A KEY STRONGHOLD in the War of Restoration *(see p50)* and then in the War of the Two Brothers *(see p54)*, Estremoz looks out from its hilltop over groves of gnarled olive trees.

The medieval upper town, set within stout ramparts, is dominated by a 13th-century marble keep, rising to 27 m (89 ft). This is the **Torre das Três Coroas**, the Tower of the Three Crowns, recalling the kings (Sancho II, Afonso III and Dinis) in whose reigns it was built. The adjoining castle and palace complex, built for Dona Isabel, is now restored as a *pousada (see p395)*. The saintly Isabel *(see p45)*, wife of King Dinis, died here in 1336 and the **Capela da Rainha Santa** dedicated to her is lined with *azulejos* recording her life.

Today the bustling weekly market in the Rossio, the main square in the lower town, is a reflection of local farming life. Across the square are the remains of King Dinis's once-fine palace and the town's **Museu Municipal**, with a display of archaeological finds, restored living rooms and a parade of *bonecos*, the charming pottery figurines for which Estremoz is famous *(see p25)*.

🏛 Museu Municipal
Largo Dom Dinis. 📞 268-33 92 00. ⭘ *Tue–Sun.* ⬤ *public hols.* ⬛
⛪ Capela da Rainha Santa
Largo Dom Dinis. (Entrance through adjacent Design Gallery.) ⭘ *Design Gallery staff will open on request.*

Évoramonte ⑬

Road map D5. 🏠 *1,000.* 🚌 📋 *Junta de Freguesia (268-95 91 51).*

Stone "rope" embellishing the castle walls at Évoramonte

ABOVE THE DOORWAY of No. 41, along Évoramonte's single street, is a historic plaque. It records that here, on 26 May 1834, Dom Miguel ceded the throne, ending the conflict with his older brother *(see p54)*.

Évoramonte's eye-catching **castle**, its walls bound by bold stone "ropes", largely replaced an earlier castle that fell in an earthquake in 1531. The 16th-century walls, however, have been controversially "restored" with concrete. An exhibition explains the castle's history.

⛪ Castle
⭘ *Wed–Mon.* ⬤ *public hols.* ⬛

Arraiolos ⑭

Road map D5. 🏠 *2,400.* 🚌 📋 *Praça Lima e Brito (266-490 240).* 🏷 *Sat (food), 1st Sat of month (general).*

THE FOUNDATION of Arraiolos is attributed either to Celts or perhaps to local tribes in about 300 BC. Its 14th-century **castle** seems overwhelmed

by the town walls and looming 16th-century **Igreja do Salvador**. Typically, houses in Arraiolos are low and white, with a blue trim to ward off the devil.

The principal sight in Arraiolos, however, is of women stitching at their bright wool rugs in the shadowy rooms behind the main street. Carpets have been woven in Arraiolos since the 13th century and decorate countless manor houses and palaces throughout Portugal. The craft may have begun with the Moors, but floral designs of the 18th century are thought to be the finest. At the many carpet shops here it is also possible to see a range of contemporary designs with their bright colours and less elaborate patterns.

ENVIRONS: At **Pavia**, 18 km (11 miles) to the north, is the startling sight of a tiny chapel built into a dolmen. It is signposted as Anta de São Dinis; if closed, ask at the café nearby.

Montemor-o-Novo ⑮

Road map C5. 🏠 *7,000.* 🚌 📋 *Largo Calouste Gulbenkian (266-898 103).* 🏷 *2nd Sat of month.*

MONTEMOR WAS fortified by the Romans and then by the Moors – the Arab warrior Al-Mansur is remembered in the name of the nearby River

The view down the nave of the Igreja Matriz in Montemor-o-Novo

Almançor. The town, regained from the Moors in the reign of Sancho I, was awarded its first charter in 1203. The **castle**, rebuilt in the late 13th century, is now a ruin crowning the hill.

Montemor's 17th-century **Igreja Matriz** stands in Largo São João de Deus, named after the saint who was born nearby in 1495. The Order of Brothers Hospitallers that St John of God founded evolved from his care for the sick, especially foundlings and prisoners.

A former convent in the upper town is now the **Museu de Arqueologia**. As well as local archaeological finds, there are numerous agricultural exhibits, from old farm pumps to implements for carving cork.

🏛 Museu de Arqueologia
Convento de São Domingos, Largo Professor Dr Banha de Andrade. 📞 *266-890 235.* ⭘ *Tue–Sun.* ⬤ *1 Jan, 25 Dec.* ⬛ ♿

Arraiolos, crowned by its castle and the Igreja do Salvador

Street-by-Street: Évora ⑯

RISING OUT OF the Alentejan plain is the enchanting walled city of Évora. The town rose to prominence under the Romans and flourished throughout the Middle Ages as a centre of learning and the arts. It was a popular residence of Portuguese kings, but fell out of favour after Spain's annexation of Portugal in 1580. Its influence waned further when the Jesuit university closed in the 18th century. Students once again throng Évora's streets, joined by visitors who come to discover its many historical sites and enjoy the atmosphere of the old town. The city's historic legacy was officially recognized in 1986, when UNESCO declared Évora a World Heritage Site.

★ Roman Tem
Popularly belie
to have been de
cated to the gode
Diana, this temp
was erected in t
2nd or 3rd cent
AD. It was used
armoury, theatr
and slaughterho
before being
rescued in
1870.

Rua 5 de Outubro
The shops along this street sell curios and handicrafts, from painted chairs to carved cork.

| 0 metres | 50 |
| 0 yards | 50 |

KEY

— — — Suggested route

RUA DO SALVADOR

RUA DE DONA ISABEL

RUA DAS CASAS PINTADAS

PRAÇA DO SERTÓRIO

RUA DE VASCO DA G

RUA JOÃO DE DEUS

RUA NOVA

RUA S DE OUT

PRAÇA DO GIRALDO

Tourist information

RUA DA REPÚBLICA

Praça do Giraldo
The fountain in Évora's main square was erected in 1571. Its marble predecessor received the first water delivered by the town's aqueduct (see p305).

STAR SIGHTS
★ Sé
★ Roman Temple
★ Museu de Évora

To railwa and b statio

Convento dos Lóios

This 15th-century monastery is now a luxurious pousada, where guests sleep in cells and dine in the cloisters (see p395). The convent's white-fronted church, known as Os Lóios or São João Evangelista, contains some remarkable 18th-century azulejos.

VISITORS' CHECKLIST

Map D5. 👥 55,000. 🚉 Largo da Estação. 🚌 Estrada de Lisboa. ℹ Praça do Giraldo (266-702 671). 🛒 Sat & 2nd Tue of month. 🎉 Jun: Festa de São João; end Sep in odd years: Évora, os Povos e as Artes (biennial arts festival).

Old University
(see p304)

Roman walls

★ **Museu de Évora**
The city's museum (see p304) includes works by artists who painted in Évora, such as the early 16th-century Two Bishop-Saints by the Master of Sardoal.

Casa de Garcia de Resende

The house of the Renaissance poet and diplomat, Garcia de Resende (1470–1536), is distinguished by a remarkable Manueline window.

★ **Sé**
Évora's cathedral (see p304), which took over 50 years to complete, has the look of a fortress about it. The portal is flanked by a pair of unmatched towers.

Largo do Marquês de Marialva

The Igreja da Misericórdia is noted for its panels of early 18th-century azulejos (see p22).

Nossa Senhora da Graça

Above the Palladian façade of this 16th-century church loom four muscular figures supporting globes. They are quaintly nicknamed Os Meninos, "the children".

Exploring Évora

SQUEEZED WITHIN ROMAN, medieval and 17th-century walls, Évora's web of streets is an architectural and cultural cornucopia. From the forbidding cathedral, a stroll down past the craft shops of Rua 5 de Outubro leads to Praça do Giraldo, the city's lively main square, whose arcades are a reminder of Moorish influence. Évora's religious dedication is reflected in the number and variety of its churches – over 20 churches and monasteries, including a grisly chapel of bones. On a happier note, Évora's restaurants are excellent and the pleasure of wandering the historic streets is enhanced by evocative names such as Alley of the Unshaven Man and Street of the Countess's Tailor.

Azulejos at the Old University, depicting Aristotle teaching Alexander

� Sé
Largo do Marquês de Marialva.
☎ 266-759 330. ○ daily (museum Tue – Sun). ▓ to cloister & museum.

Begun in 1186 and consecrated in 1204, the granite cathedral of Santa Maria was completed by 1250. Romanesque melds with Gothic in this castle-like cathedral whose towers, one turreted, one topped by a blue cone, give the façade an odd asymmetry. Flanking the portal between them are superb 14th-century sculpted Apostles. The 18th-century high altar and marble chancel are by JF Ludwig, the architect of the monastery at Mafra *(see pp52–3)*. A Renaissance portal in the north transept is by Nicolau Chanterène. In the cloisters, which date from about 1325, statues of the Evangelists stand watch at each corner.

A glittering treasury houses sacred art. The most intriguing exhibit here is a 13th-century ivory Virgin whose body opens out to become a triptych of tiny carved scenes: her life in nine episodes.

🏛 Museu de Évora
Largo do Conde de Vila Flor.
☎ 266-702 604. ○ Tue–Sun.
● some public hols. ▓

This 16th-century palace, once the residence of governors and bishops, is now the regional museum. Évora's long history is represented here, from Roman columns to modern sculpture in creamy local marble. A beautiful Moorish window came from the old town hall, and a stone frieze probably from the Roman temple. Notable upstairs are *The Life of the Virgin*, a 16th-century

Carved figures of the Apostles decorating the Gothic entrance to the Sé

Flemish polyptych in 13 panels and works by the Portuguese painter known as the Master of Sardoal, especially his *Two Bishop-Saints* and a *Nativity*.

⚲ University
Largo dos Colegiais. **☎** 266-740 800.
○ daily. ● public hols.

With the establishment of the Jesuits' Colégio do Espírito Santo, Évora, already noted for its architecture and sacred art, became a seat of learning. The school, which was inaugurated in 1559 by Cardinal Henrique, brother of João III, flourished for 200 years, but was closed in 1759 when the reforming Marquês de Pombal banished the Jesuits *(see p53)*.

Today part of the University of Évora, the school still has a graceful cloister and notable *azulejos* – in the classrooms they depict suitably studious themes such as Plato lecturing to disciples (1744–9). The 18th-century Baroque chapel, now the Sala dos Actos, is used for graduation ceremonies.

⚲ Praça do Giraldo
Évora's bustling main square is bounded along its eastern side by a series of graceful Moorish arcades. The name Giraldo, some say, stems from Geraldo Sem-Pavor (the Fearless), an outlaw who in 1165 ousted the Moors for King Afonso Henriques.

The square has witnessed some bloody acts: João II watched the beheading of his brother-in-law, the Duke of Bragança, here in 1483, and it was the site in 1573 of an Inquisitional burning. Today, it is a favourite meeting-place, especially on market days.

⚵ São Francisco
Praça 1° de Maio. **☎** 266-704 521.
○ daily. ▓ to Capela dos Ossos.

The principal fascination of this 15th-century church is its Capela dos Ossos. This gruesome chapel of bones was created in the 17th century from the remains of 5,000 monks. Two leathery corpses, one of a child, dangle from a chain, and a mordant reminder at the entrance reads: *Nós ossos que aqui estamos, pelos vossos esperamos* (We bones that are here await yours).

Largo da Porta de Moura, with its striking Renaissance fountain

♯ Largo da Porta de Moura

The western entrance to this square is guarded by the vestiges of a Moorish gateway. Both the domed Casa Soure and the double arches of the belvedere on Casa Cordovil at the opposite end, show the Arab influence on architecture in Évora. The central fountain, looking like some futuristic orb, surprisingly dates back to 1556. Just south of the square, the portal of the Convento do Carmo features the knot symbol, denoting it once belonged to the Braganças (see p299).

♣ Jardim Público

⬛ daily. ♿

On the southern edge of the old town, Évora's public gardens are set out on the site of the grandiose Palácio de Dom Manuel, built for Afonso V (1438–81) and embellished by successive kings. It was the venue for grand banquets and ceremonies but fell into disrepair and finally disappeared in 1895. All that remains is the graceful Galeria das Damas, a 20th-century reconstruction of a walkway and pavilion built for Manuel I (1495–1521).

♠ Walls

The fortifications that have protected Évora down the centuries form two incomplete concentric circles. The inner ring, of which only fragments are discernible, is Roman, from perhaps as early as the 1st century AD, with Moorish and medieval additions – the two stubby towers that give the Largo da Porta de Moura its name mark an Arab gate.

In the 14th century, new walls were built to encompass the growing town. Completed under Fernando I, these had 40 towers and ten gates, including the Porta de Alconchel, which still faces the Lisbon road.

When João IV was defiantly declared king in 1640 (see p50), major fortifications were erected on this outer ring in anticipation of Spanish attack, and it is these 17th-century walls which are most evident today. The fear of attack was not unfounded, and the walls withstood much battering from the besieging Spanish in 1663.

Surviving arches of Évora's 16th-century aqueduct

♙ Aqueduto da Água de Prata

Évora's aqueduct, evocatively called "of the silver water", was built between 1531 and 1537 by the town's own eminent architect, Francisco de Arruda. The construction was regarded with wonder, and is even described in *Os Lusíadas*, the epic by Luís de Camões (see p188). It originally carried water as far as the Praça do Giraldo. Like the walls, it was damaged in the 17th century during the Restoration War with Spain, but a surviving stretch, some 9 km (5 miles) long, can still be seen approaching from the northwest: there is a good view of it from Rua Cândido dos Reis.

THE ROMANS IN THE ALENTEJO

Once the Romans gained dominance over Lusitania (see pp40–41), they turned the Alentejo into a vast wheatfield: their very name for the principal town – Ebora Cerealis (Évora) – reflects the importance of the region's grain supply. *Latifúndios*, large farms instigated by the Romans, survive to this day, as do Roman open-cast copper and iron mines. Local marble was used in the construction of the finest villas, and Roman remains are to be found scattered throughout the region, particularly in Évora and Beja (see p311) and in more isolated sites such as São Cucufate, near Vidigueira (see p310) and Miróbriga, near Santiago do Cacém (see p312).

Roman bridge over the Odivelas, near Vidigueira

Megaliths Tour ⑰

ARCHAEOLOGISTS DATE the *pedras talhas*, hewn stones, near Évora to between 4000 and 2000 BC. Their symbolism remains mysterious. Dolmens are thought to be where Neolithic communities buried their dead, together with their possessions – more than 130 have been found in the region. Tall phallic menhirs jutting from olive groves immediately suggest fertility rites, while cromlechs, carved stones standing in regulated groups, probably had religious significance. This tour includes examples of each; more can be found further east, near Monsaraz, and the museum in Montemoro-Novo *(see p301)* has finds related to the area.

Menhir of Almendres ②
Standing 2.5 m (8 ft) tall, this solitary stone is located away from the cromlech, in an olive grove behind a row of tall Cooperativa Agrícola storage bins.

Cromlech of Almendres ③
This oval, made up of 95 elliptical stones, is believed to have been a temple dedicated to a solar cult. The route to the cromlech is signposted from the N114.

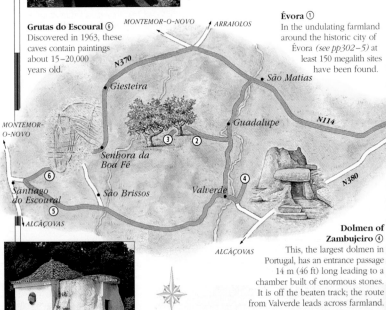

Grutas do Escoural ⑥
Discovered in 1963, these caves contain paintings about 15–20,000 years old.

Évora ①
In the undulating farmland around the historic city of Évora *(see pp302–5)* at least 150 megalith sites have been found.

Dolmen of Zambujeiro ④
This, the largest dolmen in Portugal, has an entrance passage 14 m (46 ft) long leading to a chamber built of enormous stones. It is off the beaten track; the route from Valverde leads across farmland.

Dolmen-chapel of São Brissos ⑤
Beyond the hamlet of Brissos, this tiny chapel has been created from an *anta* or dolmen. Another is to be found at Pavia *(see p301)*.

KEY

▬▬ Tour route
═══ Other roads

0 kilometres   5
0 miles   3

TIPS FOR DRIVERS

Tour length: 80 km (50 miles).
Access to sites: The only guarded site is Escoural. The caves are closed at lunchtime, on Mondays and at some other times. Access roads to the sites are often no more than tracks, and signposting can be erratic. *(See pp444–5.)*

Riding through the narrow streets of Monsaraz on the day of a bullfight

Monsaraz ⑱

Road map D5. 👥 *150*. 🚌
ℹ️ *Largo Dom Nuno Álvares Pereira 5
(266-557 136).*

THE TINY MEDIEVAL walled
town of Monsaraz perches
above the River Guadiana on
the frontier with Spain. Now a
pretty backwater, it has known
more turbulent times. Regained
from the Moors in 1167 by the
intrepid adventurer Geraldo
Sem-Pavor (the Fearless), the
town was handed over to the
militant Knights Templar. Its
frontier position continued to
expose it to Spanish attack, but
in 1381 assault came from an
unexpected quarter. Troops of
the Earl of Cambridge, Portugal's ally, were enraged by lack
of pay and the annulment of
the earl's betrothal to Fernando
's daughter, and unleashed
their wrath on Monsaraz.

Principal access to the town
is through the massive Porta
da Vila. Rua Direita, the main
street, leads up to the **castle**,
built by Afonso III and Dinis
in the 13th century as part of
the border defences, it was
reinforced in the 17th century.
The keep commands glorious
views in all directions and at
its foot is the garrison courtyard which today serves on
occasion as a bullring.

The 16th-century **Igreja
Matriz** in Rua Direita is worth
visiting for its tall gilded altars
and painted pillars. The 17th-
and 18th-century houses along
here display coats of arms. In

the Gothic Paços da Audiência,
now the **Museu de Arte Sacra,**
is a collection of vestments,
religious books and sculpture.
Its earlier role as a law court is
reflected in an unusual secular
fresco: *O Bom e o Mau Juiz*
(The Good and Bad Judge).

🏛 Museu de Arte Sacra
Largo Dom Nuno Álvares Pereira.
🕘 *9am–6pm daily.* 🎫

ENVIRONS: Surrounded by
vineyards, **Reguengos de
Monsaraz**, 16 km (10 miles)
west, lies at the heart of one
of the region's demarcated
wine areas *(see p29)*. Its 19th-
century church, Santo António,
was built in flamboyant Neo-
Gothic style by the
architect of Lisbon's
bullring *(see p120)*.

A number of striking
megaliths are found
near Monsaraz. The
spectacular **Menhir of
Outeiro**, 5.6 m (18 ft)
tall, and the strangely
inscribed **Menhir of
Bulhôa** are signposted
in Telheiro, just north
of Monsaraz. About
4 km (2 miles) south
is the **Cromlech of
Xerez**, a menhir in a
square of lesser stones.

Mourão, some 8 km
(5 miles) further on, is
noted for the huge
pepperpot chimneys
on its tiny houses. The
town's 14th-century
castle looks out over
the River Guadiana.

Viana do Alentejo ⑲

Road map D6. 👥 *3,500*. 🚌
ℹ️ *Praça da República (266-95 31
06).* 🛒 *2nd & last Thu of month.*

THE NATURAL SPRINGS of Viana
do Alentejo have offered
an abundant water source in
the Alentejo's dry heartland
since Roman times. Its **castle**,
begun in 1313, was built to
the design of King Dinis, the
height of the outer wall exactly
calculated to protect soldiers
from attacking lancers. The
unusual cylindrical towers
show a Moorish influence and
much of the later remodelling
dates from João II, who held
a *cortes* here in 1481–2.

Mirroring the castle walls are
the crenellations and pinnacles
of the adjacent 16th-century
Igreja Matriz. The highly
carved Manueline entrance to
this splendid fortified church
leads into a majestic triple-
naved interior.

Ten minutes' walk east of
the town stands the vast pilgrimage church of **Nossa
Senhora de Aires**, rebuilt in
the 1700s. Inside, the chancel's
golden canopy contrasts with
pilgrims' humble ex votos.

ENVIRONS: The Moorish-style
castle at **Alvito**, 10 km (6 miles)
south of Viana, was built in
1482 for the newly ennobled
Barão de Alvito; it now operates as a *pousada (see p395)*.

The low roofs and distinctive pepperpot
chimneys of Mourão, near Monsaraz

A bullfight in the shadow of the 13th-century keep of Monsaraz castle ▷

The vineyards around Vidigueira caught in the evening light

Vidigueira ⑳

Road map D6. 🏛 *2,800*. ▭
🛈 *Piscinas Municipais (284-436 564)*.
🎪 *2nd Sat of month.*

Fine wines from Vidigueira make it a leading centre of wine production in the Alentejo. Less well known is the fact that the explorer Vasco da Gama was Conde de Vidigueira. His remains, now in the Mosteiro dos Jerónimos *(see pp106–7)*, lay from 1539 to 1898 in the Convento do Carmo, now private property. A mediocre statue of the town's most famous son stands in the flowery square named after him. The main features of this unpretentious little town are a **Misericórdia** church dated 1620, and a clocktower from Vasco da Gama's time.

ENVIRONS: One of Portugal's most notable Roman sites, **São Cucufate**, named after a later monastery, lies 4 km (2 miles) west. The vaulting belonged to a 4th-century villa, but excavations have revealed the baths of a 2nd-century house, whose wine presses, reservoir and temple indicate a sumptuous Roman residence.

Moura ㉑

Road map D6. 🏛 *12,000*. ▭
🛈 *Largo de Santa Clara (285-25 13 75)*. 🎪 *1st Sat of month.*

Legend mingles with history in this quiet town among oak and olive trees. Salúquia, daughter of a Moorish governor is said to have thrown herself from the castle tower on learning that her lover had been killed. From this tragedy the town acquired its name – Moura, the Moorish girl. The town's old Moorish quarter is an area of narrow streets and low, whitewashed houses.

Even after the Reconquest in the 12th century, Moura's frontier position left it open to attack. A siege in 1657, during the War of Restoration *(see pp50–51)*, levelled much of it. The 13th-century **castle** survived, only to be blown up by the Spanish in 1707 – just a skeletal keep and wall remain.

Nossa Senhora do Carmo, near the castle, was founded in 1251, the first Carmelite convent in the country. Its two-storey cloister shows Gothic and Renaissance influence and the chancel ceiling frescoes are early 18th century.

View over Moura's quaint Moorish quarter

Serpa ㉒

Road map D6. 🏛 *4,800*. ▭
🛈 *Largo Dom Jorge de Melo 2–3 (284-54 47 27)*. 🎪 *last Tue of month.*

After peaceful vistas of olive trees, Serpa's stout walls, topped by an arched aqueduct, come as a surprise. Beside the monumental **Porta de Beja** is a *nora*, or Arab water wheel. Won from the Moors in 1232, Serpa successfully resisted foreign control until a brief Spanish occupation in 1707.

Today, Serpa is a quiet agricultural town that produces an esteemed ewe's-milk cheese. Pleasing squares and streets of houses that dazzle with the brilliance of their whitewash are overlooked by a **castle** of Moorish origin, rebuilt by King Dinis in the late 13th century. The **Convento de Santo António** in Rua da Ladeira was founded in the 15th century and is noted for its flamboyant 18th-century *azulejos*.

Serpa's great Porta de Beja

ENVIRONS: Serpa is just 35 km (22 miles) from the Spanish border. The Moors, and later Spain, fought for control of the region, which was finally ceded to Portugal in 1295. Continued disputes have left the legacy of a chain of watchtowers and a peppering of fortresses across these hills. One of the most remote, the deserted fort at **Noudar**, was built in 1346, but even in this isolated corner, evidence of pre-Roman habitation has been uncovered.

On the border at **Barrancos** an incomprehensible mix of Spanish and Portuguese is spoken. A speciality here is *pata negra* (black trotter), a ham from the local black pigs

LOVE LETTERS OF A HEARTSICK NUN

Mariana's window

Lettres Portugaises, published in French in 1669, are celebrated for their lyric beauty. They are the poignant letters of a nun whose French lover deserted her: she was Mariana Alcoforado, born in Beja in 1640; he was the Comte de Saint-Léger, later Marquis de Chamilly, fighting in the Restoration wars with Spain. The true authorship of the five letters may be in doubt, but the story of the lovelorn nun endures – Matisse even painted her imaginary portrait. Sentimental visitors to the convent of Nossa Senhora da Conceição (now the Museu Regional) in Beja still sigh over "Mariana's window".

Beja ㉓

Road map D6. 🏘 *18,000.* 🚆 🚌 🚏 *Rua Capitão João Francisco de Sousa 25 (284-31 19 13).* 🛍 *1st & 3rd Mon of month.*

CAPITAL OF the Baixo (lower) Alentejo, Beja is a city of historic and social importance. It is also a major centre for the production of wheat, olives and cork, which are grown on the Bejan plains and provide the city's lifeblood.

The town became a regional capital under Julius Caesar, who called it Pax Julia after the peace made here with the Lusitani *(see p40)*. The Praça da República marks the site of the Roman forum. The Moors arrived in AD 711, giving it its present name and a lively, poetic culture until they were forced out in 1162.

More recently, Beja has been the scene of struggles against oppressive regimes. In 1808, occupying French troops massacred the inhabitants and sacked the city, and in 1962, during the Salazar regime *(see pp56–7)*, General Delgado led an unsuccessful uprising here.

Beja's old town, an area of narrow, often cobbled, streets, stretches from the castle keep southeast to the 13th-century convent of São Francisco, now a superb *pousada (see p395)*.

🏛 Museu Regional Rainha Dona Leonor

Largo da Conceição. 🕿 *284-32 33 51.* 🕙 *Tue–Sun.* ⬤ *public hols.* 🎫
In the heart of the old town, the former Convento de Nossa Senhora da Conceição houses the regional museum. A little marble ossuary near the entrance contains the bones of the convent's first abbess. Exhibits are mostly paintings and coats of arms, but the building itself is a remarkable blend of architectural styles, with a Gothic church portal, Manueline windows and a dazzling Baroque chapel. Its *azulejos* are especially beautiful, the most notable being the Hispanic-Arab tiles in the chapterhouse and the early 16th-century examples in the cloister. Upstairs is a section on local archaeology and the romantic "Mariana's window".

⚜ Torre de Menagem

Largo do Lidador. 🕿 *284-31 18 00.* 🕙 *Tue–Sun.* ⬤ *public hols.* 🎫
The unmistakable landmark of the castle keep marks the northwest limit of the old quarter. This work of King Dinis in the late 13th century towers 36 m (118 ft) high. The 183-step climb up through its three storeys provides a rewarding panorama from the top.

Beja's landmark castle keep

🏛 Museu Visigótico

Largo de Santo Amaro. 🕿 *284-323 351.* 🕙 *Tue–Sun.* ⬤ *public hols.* 🎫 *joint ticket with Museu Regional.*
Just beyond the castle keep stands Beja's oldest church, Santo Amaro, its columns surviving from its Visigothic origins. Appropriately, the church now serves as an exhibition area for the Museu Regional's collection of relics from this early but important period of Portugal's history.

ENVIRONS: The remains of the luxurious **Roman villa** at Pisões, 10 km (6 miles) southwest of Beja, date from the 1st century AD. Excavation is far from complete, but extensive floor mosaics and fragments of decorated walls, baths, a bathing pool and hypocaust have been uncovered.

⌂ Roman villa

Herdade de Almocreva, Estrada de Aljustrel (follow signs). 🕙 *Tue–Sun.*

Chapterhouse of the former convent, now Beja's Museu Regional

Igreja Matriz, Santiago do Cacém

Santiago do Cacém ②④

Road map C6. 🏛 6,000. 🚌
🛈 Largo do Mercado (269-82 66 96).
🗓 2nd Mon of month.

Santiago do Cacém's Moorish castle was rebuilt in 1157 by the Templars (see pp184–5). Its walls, which enclose the cemetery of the adjacent 13th-century **Igreja Matriz**, afford panoramic views of the Serra de Grândola to the northeast. The attractive main square is enhanced by the elegant 18th-century mansions built by rich landowners who came here to escape the heat of the plains.

The **Museu Municipal** still retains some cells from its days as a Salazarist prison (see p56). Exhibits here include Roman finds from nearby Miróbriga.

🏛 Museu Municipal

Largo do Município. 📞 269-82 73 75.
🕐 Tue–Fri, Sat & Sun (pm only).
⬤ public hols.

ENVIRONS: On a hill just to the east of Santiago do Cacém lies the site of the Roman city of **Miróbriga**. Excavations, still in progress, have uncovered a forum, two temples, thermal baths and a circus which had seating for 25,000 spectators.

🏛 Miróbriga

Signposted off N121. 📞 269-825 148.
🕐 Tue–Sun. ⬤ public hols. 🖼

Sines ②⑤

Road map C6. 🏛 9,300. 🚢 🚌
🛈 Castelo de Sines (269-63 44 72).
🗓 1st Thu of month.

The birthplace of Vasco da Gama (see p108) is now a major industrial port and tanker terminal ringed with refinery pipelines. Once past this heavy industrial zone visitors reach the old town with its popular sandy beach, but it is not always possible to escape the haze of pollution.

A prominent landmark above the beach is the modest medieval **castle**, restored in the 16th century by King Manuel. It was here that Vasco da Gama, son of the *alcaide-mor*, or mayor, is reputed to have been born in 1469, and a museum dedicated to the great navigator is to be housed in the castle keep. A modern statue of Vasco da Gama stands looking out over the bay.

The **Museu Arqueológico** in the town displays striking jewellery, perhaps Phoenician, found on a nearby estate.

🏛 Museu Arqueológico

Rua Francisco Luís Lopes 38. 📞 269-63 23 30. 🕐 Tue–Sun. ⬤ public hols.

ENVIRONS: North and south of Sines are attractive beaches. About 10 km (6 miles) south, **Porto Covo** is a picturesque village with an old fort above a cove beach. A little further to the south and a short boat ride offshore is the low hump of **Ilha do Pessegueiro**, Peach Tree Island. Treeless and windswept, with the ruins of a fort, the little island is rather less romantic than it sounds.

More appealing are two sea-blue lagoons, **Lagoa de Santo André** and **Lagoa de Melides**, set in a long stretch of sandy coast about 20 km (12 miles) north of Sines. The lagoons attract a commune of campers, but vast open spaces remain for seekers of privacy.

Whitewashed houses with the traditional blue trim at Porto Covo, south of Sines

Vila Nova de Milfontes ②⑥

Road map C6. 🏛 3,200. 🚌 🛈 Rua António Mantas (283-996 599). 🗓 2nd & 4th Sat of month in Brenheiras.

One of the loveliest places on Portugal's west coast is where the River Mira meets the sea. The popular resort of Vila Nova de Milfontes, on the sleepy estuary, is low-key and unassuming, but offers many places to stay. Its small castle overlooking the bay once defended the coast from pirates, and is now a hotel. In contrast to the quiet river are the pretty beaches with their crashing waves, a major summer attraction, especially with surfers.

ENVIRONS: To the south about 10 km (6 miles) is the unspoilt beach of **Almograve**, backed by impressive cliffs.

The calm, sunny face of the sandy coast near Vila Nova de Milfontes

Zambujeira do Mar ㉗

Road map C7. 🏠 *1,000.* 🚌
ℹ️ *Rua Miramar (283-96 11 44).*

A NARROW STRIP of sheltered
land divides the plains of
the Alentejo from the bracing
Atlantic. Here lies the solitary
village of Zambujeira do Mar,
the whiteness of its gorgeous
beach enhanced by the dark
backdrop of high basalt cliffs.
Traditionally, families come
here for Sunday beach outings,
joined nowadays by campers
and more adventurous tourists.

Mértola ㉘

Road map D6. 🏠 *1,200.* 🚌
ℹ️ *Rua Alonso Gomes 18 (286-61 25
73).* 🎪 *1st Thu of month.*

P RETTY, WHITEWASHED Mértola
is of great historical interest.
The whole of this small town
is a *vila museu*, a museum site,
with discoveries from different
eras exhibited in *núcleos*, or
areas where a concentration of
treasures from that period can
be found. The tourist office
has details of each *núcleo*.

Mértola's origins date back to
the Phoenicians, who created
a thriving inland port here on
the Guadiana, later enjoyed by
the Romans and the Moors.
Roman artefacts can be seen

Mértola's unusual Moorish-style church, high above the River Guadiana

at the **Núcleo Romano**, based
at an excavation beneath the
municipal council buildings.

The post-Roman period in
Mértola is on display in the
Núcleo Visigótico and in an
early Christian **basilica** whose
ruins adjoin the Roman road to
Beja *(see p.311)*. The influence
bequeathed by several centuries of Moorish domination
is seen in Mértola's **Núcleo
Islâmico** which houses one of

the country's best collections
of Portuguese Islamic art, and
includes ceramics, coins and
jewellery. The **Igreja Matriz**
below the Moorish walls was
formerly a mosque, unique in
Portugal for being so little
altered. Among surviving Arab
features are the five-nave layout, four horseshoe arches and
a *mihrab* or prayer niche.

Overlooking the town is the
crumbling hilltop **castle**, with
its keep of 1292, offering lovely
views of the river valley.

ENVIRONS: The copper mines
at **Minas de São Domingos**,
16 km (10 miles) to the east,
were the main employer in the
area from 1858 to 1965, when
the vein was exhausted. An
English company ran the mine
under the harshest conditions,
with miners' families living in
one windowless room. The
village's population has now
fallen from 6,000 to 800, and
the ghost-town atmosphere is
relieved only by a reservoir
and surrounding lush greenery.

Around Mértola, 600 sq km
(230 sq miles) of the wild
Guadiana valley is a newly
designated **Parque Natural**,
home to the black stork, the
azure-winged magpie and
raptors such as the red kite.

THE VERSATILITY OF CORK

Groves of evergreen cork oak *(Quercus suber)* provide the
Alentejo with welcome shade and a thriving industry. It was
Dom Pérignon, the wine-making monk, who in the 17th century revived the use of cork
as a tasteless, odourless seal
for wine. Portugal, the world's
largest cork producer, has almost 7,000 sq km (2,700 sq
miles) under cultivation and
turns out some 30 million
corks a day. In rural areas,
this versatile bark is fashioned
into waterproof, heatproof
food containers and these
decorated boxes are a traditional craft of the Alentejo.

Harvesting cork is a skilled
task. Mature trees, stripped in
summer every ten years or so,
reveal a raw red undercoat
until their new bark grows.

**The glowing red of a stripped
tree in an Alentejan cork grove**

ALGARVE

ENCLOSED BY RANGES OF HILLS *to the north, the Algarve has a climate, culture and scenery very different from the rest of Portugal. Its stunning coastline and year-round mild weather, maintained by warm sea and air currents from nearby North Africa, make it one of the most popular holiday destinations in southern Europe.*

The Algarve's fertile soil and strategic headlands and rivers have attracted visitors since the time of the Phoenicians. Five centuries of Arab rule, from AD 711, left a legacy that is still visible in the region's architecture, lattice chimneys, *azulejos*, orange groves and almond trees. Place names beginning with Al are also of Moorish origin; Al-Gharb ("the West") denoted the western edge of the Islamic empire.

When the Algarve was reclaimed by the Christians in 1249, the Portuguese rulers designated themselves kings "of Portugal and of the Algarves", emphasizing the region's separateness from the rest of the country. It was the Algarve, however, that shot Portugal to prominence in the 15th century, when Henry the Navigator *(see p49)* is said to have set up a school of navigation at Sagres, and launched the age of exploration from these southern shores.

The earthquake of 1755 *(see pp62–3)* had its epicentre just south of Lagos, then the region's capital. Virtually all the towns and villages were destroyed or badly damaged, which explains why very few buildings in the region predate this period.

Since the 1960s, when Faro airport was opened, international tourism has replaced agriculture and fishing as the region's main industry. A few stretches of the southwestern seashore are now cluttered with high-rise complexes catering for the yearly influx of tourists. However, the whole western seaboard exposed to the Atlantic and the lagoons east of Faro have been barely touched by development. Trips inland, to the pretty whitewashed village of Alte or the border town of Alcoutim in the east, provide a welcome reminder that, in places, the Algarve's rural way of life continues virtually uninterrupted.

Colourful ceramic plates for sale outside a local craft shop in Alte

◁ **Strolling along the sandy Praia da Rocha near Portimão**

Exploring the Algarve

THE ALGARVE IS A DELIGHT to visit all year round. In summer, the coast between Faro and Lagos attracts thousands of visitors; but even near popular resorts such as Albufeira and Portimão it is possible to escape the crowds. Though often bypassed, Faro itself is well worth a visit. Picturesque Tavira is an ideal centre for the lagoons of the eastern Algarve, while from Lagos you can reach the beaches on the rugged southwest coast. Inland, the hillside villages are peaceful, with lush vegetation, both wild and cultivated. The wooded Serra de Monchique is an area of outstanding beauty offering lovely walks.

Wooded slopes around the vast lake created by the Bravura dam, north of Lagos

Odemira
ODECEIXE

Beja
Ourique

Ribeira de Seixe

MONCHIQUE ③

① ALJEZUR
N267
SERRA DE MONCHIQUE
②

CALDAS DE MONCHIQUE
N266

CARRAPATEIRA

Barragem da Bravura

⑩ SILVES
N269

N125
ALVOR ⑧
Arade
⑨ PORTIMÃO
N125
ALB

SERRA DO ESPINHAÇO DE CÃO

④ VILA DO BISPO
N125
⑦ LAGOS
PONTA DA PIEDADE

⑤ CABO DE SÃO VICENTE

⑥ SAGRES

KEY

	Motorway
	Major road
	Minor road
	Scenic route
	River
☀	Viewpoint

Brightly painted fishing boats in the harbour at Sagres

f the delightful sandy coves near Albufeira

SIGHTS AT A GLANCE

Albufeira ⑪
Alcoutim ㉓
Aljezur ①
Almancil ⑭
Alte ⑫
Alvor ⑧
Cabo de São Vicente ⑤
Cacela Velha ㉑
Castro Marim ㉒
Estoi ⑯
Faro pp326–8 ⑰
Lagos ⑦
Loulé ⑮

Monchique ③
Olhão ⑱
Parque Natural
  da Ria Formosa ⑲
Portimão ⑨
Sagres ⑥
Serra de
  Monchique ②
Silves ⑩
Tavira ⑳
Vila do Bispo ④
Vilamoura ⑬

GETTING AROUND

The IP1 is a toll-free motorway from Albufeira to Spain and has relieved the N125, which can become congested in summer. Roads branch off to beaches, coastal towns and inland villages.

A frequent but slow rail service connects the main towns, but stations are sometimes far from the centre. Reliable buses link coastal resorts and inland towns, though progress can be slow.

0 kilometres   10

0 miles   5

SEE ALSO

• *Where to Stay* pp396–9

• *Where to Eat* pp418–21

Whitewashed house and lattice-work chimney in Cacela Velha

Commanding view of the countryside from Aljezur's Moorish castle

Aljezur ❶

Road map 7C. 👥 *2,500.* 🚌
ℹ *Largo do Mercado (282-99 82 29).*
📅 *3rd Mon of month.*

T HE SMALL VILLAGE of Aljezur is overlooked by a 10th-century **Moorish castle**, reached via the old quarter. Although now in ruins, a cistern and towers remain, and there are splendid views towards the Serra de Monchique.

Aljezur's **Igreja Matriz**, much rebuilt after the earthquake of 1755 (*see pp62–3*), has a fine Neo-Classical altarpiece. Dating from about 1809, it was probably executed in the workshop of José da Costa of Faro.

ENVIRONS: From Aljezur, the wild and deserted beaches of the Algarve's west coast are easily explored, although a car

is essential. Open to the strong currents of the Atlantic, **Praia de Arrifana** 10 km (6 miles) southwest, and **Praia de Monte Clérigo**, 8 km (5 miles) northwest, are sandy, sweeping beaches backed by cliffs. On the Alentejo border, **Praia de Odeceixe** is a sheltered cove that is popular with surfers.

Serra de Monchique ❷

Road map 7C. 🚌 *Monchique.*
ℹ *Monchique.*

P ROVIDING SHELTER from the north, this volcanic mountain range helps to ensure the mild southern climate of the Algarve. The highest point is **Fóia** at 902 m (2,959 ft). This, however, is less pleasantly wooded than **Picota**, which, at 773 m (2,536 ft), is the second highest peak. An impressive 4-km (2-mile) walk to this peak from Monchique passes among chestnut trees and fields of wild flowers. A spectacular panorama sweeps down to the Ponta de Sagres (*see p320*) and there are stunning views of the rest of the range. Whether you explore the Serra on foot or by car, there is a wonderful variety of vegetation to enjoy with rhododendron, mimosa, chestnut, pine, cork oak and patches of terraced fertile land in the valleys.

The mountains of the Serra de Monchique rising above meadows of wild flowers

Monchique ❸

Road map 7C. 👥 *7,000.* 🚌
ℹ *Largo dos Chorões (282-91 11 89).*
📅 *2nd Fri of month.*

Manueline portal of the Igreja Matriz in Monchique

T HE SMALL market town of Monchique is primarily famous for its altitude, 458 m (1,500 ft), and consequently spectacular views. It is also known for its wooden handicrafts, particularly the folding chairs which are believed to date back to Roman times.

The 16th-century **Igreja Matriz**, on the cobbled Rua da Igreja behind the main square, has an impressive Manueline doorway whose knotted columns end in unusual pinnacles. Above the town is the ruined monastery of **Nossa Senhora do Desterro**. This Franciscan house, founded in 1632 by Dom Pero da Silva, is now only a shell but it is worth visiting for the stunning views across to the peak of Picota.

ENVIRONS: A delightful, tiny spa, 6 km (4 miles) south, **Caldas de Monchique** is set in the foothills of the Serra in peaceful wooded surroundings.

The hot, curative waters have attracted the ailing since Roman times, and even though João II died soon after taking them in 1495, their reputation has remained undiminished. In the summer, people come to be treated for skin, digestive and rheumatic complaints. As well as the wholesome spring water, the bars here offer the local firewater, *medronheira*.

The shady main square has a large, attractive handicraft centre and there are some pretty walks in the woods.

Vila do Bispo ❹

Road map 7C. 🏛 *7,000.* 🚌
ℹ️ *Sagres (282-624 873).* 🗓 *1st Thu of month.*

THE GRAND NAME of "The Bishop's Town" today refers to a peaceful village, rather remote in feel, which makes the crowds of central Algarve seem very far away. It acquired its name in the 17th century when it was donated to the see of Faro. The town's parish church, **Nossa Senhora da Conceição**, has a delightful interior decorated with 18th-century *azulejos* from the floor up to the wooden, painted ceiling, and a Baroque altarpiece dating from 1715.

ENVIRONS: The beaches in the area are remote and unspoiled. **Praia do Castelejo**, 5 km (3 miles) to the west, is accessible by a dirt road that

Baroque altarpiece inside Nossa Senhora da Conceição, Vila do Bispo

Promontory of Cabo de São Vicente jutting into the Atlantic Ocean

winds up from the village over moorland. The beach, set at the foot of steep cliffs, is large, sandy and surf-fringed. The intrepid can turn off this track for the 6 km (4 miles) journey to **Torre de Aspa**, an obelisk at 156 m (512 ft) marking the spot for spectacular views over the ocean. The road is quite rough, so it is advisable to walk the last 2 km (1 mile).

Cabo de São Vicente ❺

Road map 7C. 🚌 *to Sagres then taxi.* ℹ️ *Sagres (282-624 873).*

IN THE MIDDLE AGES, this windblown cape at the extreme southwest of Europe was believed to be the end of the world. The Romans called it the *Promontorium Sacrum* (Sacred Promontory), and today, with its 60-m (200-ft) cliffs fronting the Atlantic, it still presents a most awe-inspiring aspect. The ocean waves have created long, sandy beaches and carved deep caves into the cliffs.

Since the 15th century, Cabo de São Vicente has been an important reference point for shipping, and its present lighthouse has a 95-km (60-mile) range, said to be the most powerful in Europe. For even longer it has had religious associations, and its name arises from the legend that the body of St Vincent was washed ashore here in the 4th century. Prince Henry the Navigator *(see p49)* was also reputed to have lived here, but, if so, all traces of his Vila do Infante have disappeared. A number

of important naval battles have taken place off the Cape, including the defeat of a Spanish fleet in 1797 by the British admirals Jervis and Nelson.

Since 1988 the coast from Sines in the north to Burgau in the east has been made a nature reserve, providing important nesting grounds for Bonelli's eagle, kestrel, white stork, heron and numerous other bird species. There is also a colony of sea otters.

Clump of scented thyme near Cabo de São Vicente

FLOWERS OF THE WESTERN ALGARVE

The remote headlands of Cabo de São Vicente and Sagres are renowned in botanical circles for their flowers, which put on a strikingly colourful and aromatic display from February to May. The climate, underlying rock and comparative isolation of these headlands have given an intriguing, stunted appearance to the local vegetation. There is a great array of different species, including cistuses, squills, an endemic sea pink, junipers, lavenders, narcissi, milk-vetches and many other magnificent plants.

The enormous Rosa dos Ventos wind compass on Ponta de Sagres

Sagres ❻

Road map 7C. 🏛 3,500. 🚍
ℹ️ Rua Comandante Matoso (282-62 48 73). 🎪 1st Fri of month.

THE SMALL TOWN of Sagres has little to offer except a picturesque harbour. Essentially it is a good base from which to explore the superb beaches (see p286) and isolated peninsula west of the town. Henry the Navigator (see p49) built a fortress on this windswept promontory and, according to tradition, a school of navigation and a shipyard. From here he realized his dream "to see what lay beyond the Canaries and Cape Bojador … and attempt the discovery of things hidden from men". From 1419–60, he poured his energy and the revenues of the Order of Christ (see p185), of which he was master, into building caravels and sending his fear-stricken sailors into unknown waters.

In 1434 Gil Eanes of Lagos was the first sailor to round the dreaded Cape Bojador, in the region of Western Sahara. With this feat, the west coast of Africa was opened up for exploration (see pp48–9) and Portugal poised for expansion.

Little remains of Prince Henry's original fortress: the walls that can be seen today are part of a 17th-century fort. Still visible is the giant pebble wind compass, the **Rosa dos Ventos**, 43 m (141 ft) in diameter, said to have been used by Henry. The simple chapel of **Nossa Senhora da Graça** was also built by him. The whole site, looking across to Cabo de São Vicente and out towards the open Atlantic, is exhilarating and atmospheric.

ENVIRONS: The town is also within easy reach of many superb beaches. Some, such as **Telheiro**, 9 km (5 miles) west of Sagres, and **Ponta Ruiva** 2 km (1 mile) further up the west coast, are only accessible by car. Nearer to Sagres, **Beliche** is surprisingly sheltered, **Tonel**, on the tip of the promontory, has wonderful surf and **Martinhal**, 1 km (half a mile) east, has a watersports school offering water-skiing, surfing and wind surfing.

São Gonçalo in Santa Maria, Lagos

Lagos ❼

Road map 7C. 🏛 20,000. 🚉 🚍
ℹ️ Sítio de São João (282-76 30 31). 🎪 1st Sat of month.

SET ON ONE of the largest bays in the Algarve, Lagos is an attractive, bustling town. In the 8th century it was conquered by the Arabs, who left

Moorish archway leading onto Avenida dos Descobrimentos, Lagos

behind fortifications that were extended in the 16th century. A well-preserved section and archway can be seen near Rua do Castelo dos Governadores where there is a monument to the navigator Gil Eanes.

The discoveries of the 15th century (see pp48–9), pioneered by Henry the Navigator whose statue gazes scowlingly out to sea, turned Lagos into an important naval centre. At the same time a most deplorable period of history began, with the first slaves brought back from the Sahara in 1441 by Henry's explorer Nuno Tristão. The site of the first **slave market** in Europe is marked by a plaque under the arcades on Rua da Senhora da Graça.

The city was the capital of the Algarve from 1576–1756. Extensive damage was caused by the earthquake of 1755 (see pp62–3), so that today the centre consists primarily of pretty 18th- and 19th-century buildings. The citizens of Lagos continue to make their living from fishing, which helps the town to retain a character independent of the tourist trade.

The smart new marina on the east side of town provides the first safe anchorage on the south coast for boats coming in from the Atlantic.

⚓ Forte Ponta da Bandeira
Avenida dos Descobrimentos.
📞 282-76 14 10. 🕐 Tue–Sun.
⬤ public hols. 🎟
On the seafront stands the 17th-century fortress which defended the entrance to the harbour. Its imposing ramparts afford far-reaching views over the town and the bay.

⛪ Santa Maria
Praça Infante Dom Henrique.
📞 282-76 27 23. 🕐 daily. ♿
The parish church of Lagos originated in the 16th century, and still retains a Renaissance doorway. Of local interest is a statue of São Gonçalo of Lagos, a fisherman's son born in 1360 who became an Augustinian monk, preacher and composer of religious music.

Santo António

Rua General Alberto Silveira. 282-76 23 01. Tue–Sun. public hols.

This 18th-century church is an Algarvian jewel. The lower section of the walls is covered in blue and white *azulejos*, the rest in carved, gilded and painted woodwork, an inspirational and riotous example of Baroque carving. Cherubs, beasts, flowers and scenes of hunting and fishing, surround eight panel paintings of miracles performed by St Antony.

A statue of the saint stands above the altar, surrounded by gilded pillars and arches adorned with angels and vines. St Antony was patron and honorary colonel-in-chief of the local regiment and, according to tradition, this statue accompanied it on various campaigns during the Peninsular War (1807–11) *(see p54)*.

Near the altar is the grave of Hugh Beatty, an Irish colonel who commanded the Lagos regiment during the 17th-century wars with Spain. He died here in 1709 and his motto "Non vi sed arte" (Not with force but with skill) adorns the tomb.

☼ Museu Regional

Rua General Alberto Silveira. 282-76 23 01. Tue–Sun. public hols.

Next door to the church of Santo António, an eclectic ethnographic museum displays local handicrafts and artefacts, traditional costumes and – most oddly – pickled creatures, including animal freaks such as an eight-legged goat kid. The custodian provides an informal guided tour.

Ochre sandstone rocks on the sheltered beach of Praia de Dona Ana, Lagos

ENVIRONS: The promontory, called the **Ponta da Piedade**, sheltering the bay of Lagos to the south has a series of wonderful rock formations, caves and calm, transparent waters. Accessible by road and sea, and most spectacular at sunset, this area is not to be missed. The prettiest beach is **Praia de Dona Ana**, 25 minutes' walk from the centre of town, but **Praia do Camilo**, further round to the tip of the promontory, may be less crowded. The long **Meia Praia** stretches for 4 km (2 miles) east of Lagos; a regular bus service leaves from the centre of town.

A 10-km (6-mile) drive due north of Lagos leads to the huge **Barragem de Bravura** reservoir. It is peaceful and especially picturesque seen from a viewpoint high up.

Alvor ❽

Road map 7C. 7,000. Rua Dr. Afonso Costa, 51 (282-45 75 23). 2nd Tue of month.

THIS PRETTY FISHING town of white houses is popular with holiday-makers, but in low season retains its charm. It was a Roman port, and later the Moorish town of Al-Bur. By the 16th century it was again a prosperous town, but it suffered much damage in the earthquake of 1755. The town was rebuilt with stone from the Moorish castle, so little of that fortress remains.

At the top of the town the 16th-century church, **Divino Salvador**, has a Manueline portal, carved with foliage, lions and dragons. The outermost arch is an octopus tentacle.

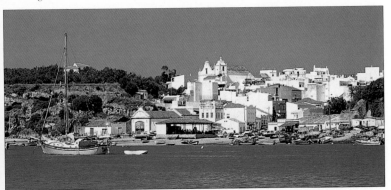
Church of Divino Salvador overlooking the whitewashed houses and the harbour at Alvor

Nossa Senhora da Conceição, Portimão

Portimão **9**

Road map 7C. **40,000.** 🚆 🚌
🛈 Avenida Zeca Afonso (282-41 91
31). 🛒 1st Mon of month.

O NE OF THE LARGEST towns in
the Algarve, Portimão is
not renowned for its beauty
but has plenty of character and
a long history as a port. The
Romans settled here, attracted
by the natural harbour on the
wide estuary of the Rio Arade.

While Portimão's outskirts
are modern and sprawling,
its town centre dates from the
18th century and has excellent
shopping facilities as well as
a large, bustling market.

The centre lies around the
pedestrianized **Rua Vasco da
Gama**, with numerous shops
specializing in leather goods.
Along Rua Diogo Tomé, the
church of **Nossa Senhora da
Conceição** occupies a low
hill. Rebuilt after the earthquake of 1755 (see pp62–3),
its 14th-century origins are still
visible in the portico with its
carved capitals. Inside, there

are 17th- and 18th-
century azulejo panels.
In Largo 1° de Dezem-
bro there are benches
adorned with brightly
coloured 19th-century
tiles. The waterfront is
always lively and res-
taurants serve fresh
sardines and sea bass.

ENVIRONS: Just 3 km
(2 miles) south lies
Portimão's touristic
neighbour, **Praia da
Rocha**, a series of
sandy coves amongst protruding red and ochre rocks. At its
east end is the **Fortaleza de
Santa Catarina**, a castle built
in the 16th century to protect
Portimão and Silves. From here
there is a superb view of the
lovely, sweeping beach backed
by 70-m (230-ft) cliffs, and
overlooked by a swathe of
high-rise hotels. These are
multiplying, and visitors will
find themselves fighting for
space in high season.

Silves **10**

Road map 7C. **10,000.** 🚆 🚌
🛈 Rua 25 de Abril 26–28 (282-44
22 55). 🛒 3rd Mon of month.

S ILVES'S COMMANDING position
made it the ideal fortified
settlement. The Romans built
a castle here, but it was under
the Arabs that the city flourished, becoming the Moorish
capital, Xelb. In the mid-12th
century the Arab geographer
Idrisi praised its beauty and
its "delicious, magnificent" figs.

Silves was renowned as a
centre of culture in Moorish
Al-Gharb, home of poets,
orators and historians until
the Knights of Santiago (see
pp42–3) took the city in 1242.

Until the 15th century, when
the River Arade silted up, Silves
was a prosperous port. Today,
the city's economy is largely
based on oranges and lemons,
grown to picturesque effect
in the surrounding orchards.
Above the town, the red walls
of the impressive castle stand
out against the skyline.

Quiet cobbled street in Silves

⌂ Castle
Castelo de Silves. 🕿 282-44 56 24.
🔾 daily. 🖼 🛇
The red sandstone castle dates
back mainly to Moorish times,
though it has done duty as a
Christian fortress and, more
recently, a gaol. It was the site
of the Palace of the Verandahs,
abode of Al-Mu'tamid from
1053 when he was ruler of
Seville and Wali of Al-Gharb.

There are superb views of
the town and countryside from
the massive, polygonal ramparts. Inside, there are the
impressive vaulted Moorish
**Cisterna da Moura
Encantada** (Cistern of the
Enchanted Moorish Girl).

The castle and town of Silves rising above a fertile valley of orange groves

🔒 Sé

Largo da Sé. ☐ *daily.* ⬤ *public hols.*
Built on the site of a mosque,
the cathedral dates from the
13th century, but has been
much altered over the years.
In the chancel, light falls from
lovely double windows with
stained-glass borders, on a jas-
per statue of Nossa Senhora
da Conceição, believed to date
from the 14th century.

Opposite the Sé, the 16th-
century **Misericórdia** church
has a Manueline side door and
a Renaissance altarpiece.

🏛 Museu Arqueológico

Rua das Portas de Loulé. 📞 *282-44
48 32.* ☐ *Tue–Sun.* 📷
Situated down the hill from
the cathedral, the Municipal
Museum was opened in 1990.
Its exhibits include Stone and
Iron Age tools, sculpted Roman
capitals, surgical instruments
from the 5th–7th centuries, a
13th-century anchor and items
of 18th-century ceramics. The
museum is built around its
star exhibit, a large Arab
well-cistern of about the
12th century that was
uncovered here in
1980. The staircase
built into the structure
descends 15 m (49 ft) to
the bottom of the well.

ENVIRONS: One kilometre
(half a mile) east of Silves
is the **Cruz de Portugal**,
an ornate 16th-century
granite cross. This may have
been given to the city by
Manuel I, when João II's
body was transferred   *Silves's Cruz*
from Silves Cathedral to   *de Portugal*
Batalha *(see pp182–3)*.
The faces are intricately carved
with the Crucifixion and the
Descent from the Cross.

Albufeira ⓫

Road map 7C. 🏠 *20,000.* 🚉 🚌
🅷 *Rua 5 de Outubro (289-58 52 79).*
🗓 *1st & 3rd Tue of month.*

Iᴛ ɪs ʜᴀʀᴅʟʏ surprising that
this charming fishing town
of whitewashed houses, overlooking a sheltered beach, has
become the tourist capital of
the Algarve. The Romans liked
it too, and built a castle here.
For the Arabs it was Al-Buhar

Colourful fishing boats on the beach at Albufeira

(The Castle on the Sea), and
under them it prospered from
trade with North Africa. The
Knights of Santiago *(see p43)*
took it in the 13th century,
but the consequent loss of
trade almost ruined it. In
1833 it was set on fire by
supporters of Dom
Miguel during the
War of the Two
Brothers *(see p54)*.
Much of the town centre
is pedestrianized, including the oldest part around
Rua da Igreja Velha where
some of the buildings still
have original Moorish
arches. The church of **São
Sebastião**, on Praça Miguel
Bombarda, has a Manueline
doorway. Rua 5 de Outubro
leads through a tunnel
to the beach, east of
which is the **Praia dos
Barcos** where the fishermen
ply their trade. From **Praia de
São Rafael**, 2 km (1 mile) west
of Albufeira, to **Praia da Oura**
due east, the area is punctuated by small sandy coves set
between eroded ochre rocks.

Alte ⓬

Road map 7C. 🏠 *500.* 🚉 🚌
🅷 *Estrada da Ponte 17 (289-478
666).* 🗓 *3rd Thu of month.*

Pᴇʀᴄʜᴇᴅ ᴏɴ ᴀ ʜɪʟʟ, Alte is one
of the prettiest villages of
the Algarve. The approach
from the east along the N124

is the most picturesque, with
sweeping views of rolling hills.
The focus of this steep, white
village is the 16th-century
Nossa Senhora da Assunção,
which has a Manueline doorway and baptismal fonts, and
a fine gilded altarpiece celebrating the Assumption. The
chapel of São Sebastião has
beautiful, rare 16th-century
Sevillian *azulejos*.

About ten minutes' walk
from the church, and clearly
marked, is the River Alte, over-
hung with trees, and a water
source known as the **Fonte
Grande**. This leafy setting is
ideal for picnicking. On the
steep slopes, about 700 m (half
a mile) from the village is a
mill (converted into a restaurant) and a 5-m (16-ft) high
waterfall, **Queda do Vigário**.

**One of many filigree chimneys
that adorn the rooftops of Alte**

Vilamoura ⑬

Road map C7. 🏛 *9,000.* 🚌
ℹ️ *Praça do Mar, Quarteira (289-389 209).*

THE COAST between Faro and Lagos has effectively become a strip of villa complexes and high-rise hotels. Vilamoura is a prime example of this kind of development and is set to become Europe's largest leisure complex. Its 1,600 ha (4,000 acres) encompass four golf courses, tennis courts, a riding school, fishing and shooting facilities, and indoor and outdoor sports complexes. There is even a small landing strip. Its hotels and apartment blocks are still on the rise, and the already well-established complex is still under construction.

The focal point is the large **marina**, which bristles with powerboats and is fronted by restaurants, cafés and shops. It makes a diverting excursion, attracting many Portuguese visitors, including Lisbon's jet set. Due east is the crowded **Praia da Marina**. You can also visit the nearby Roman ruins of **Cerro da Vila**, which date from the 1st century AD and include a bath complex and a house with mosaics depicting fish.

🏛 **Cerro da Vila**
Avenida Cerro da Vila. 📞 *289-312 153 (museum).* 🕐 *daily.* 📷 ♿

Luxury yachts and powerboats moored at the smart marina at Vilamoura

18th-century tile panels and gilded altar in São Lourenço, Almancil

Almancil ⑭

Road map D7. 🏛 *2,000.* 🚉 🚌
ℹ️ *Loulé.* 🔄 *1st & 4th Sun of month, antiques 2nd Sun.*

OUTSIDE the undistinguished village of Almancil lies one of the Algarve's gems, the 18th-century **Igreja Matriz de São Lourenço**. Its interior is an outstanding masterpiece of decoration in *azulejo* panels. The church was commissioned by local inhabitants in gratitude to St Laurence, who answered their prayers for water.

The copious blue and white tiles were probably designed by master craftsmen in Lisbon and shipped down. They cover the cupola, the walls of the chancel, nave, and nave vault, to stunning effect. The wall panels depict episodes from the life of St Laurence; on one side of the altar the saint is shown healing two blind men, and on the other, giving money to the poor. The nave arches show the saint conversing with Pope Sixtus II; arguing for his Christian belief with the Roman Emperor Valerian; and refusing to give up his faith. The story culminates in his martyrdom. In the last panel on the right, in which the saint is placed on a gridiron to be burned, an angel comforts him. The nave vault depicts the *Coronation of St Laurence*,

and the cupola has decorative, *trompe-l'oeil* effects of exceptional quality. The last tiles were put in place in 1730.

The altarpiece, dated around 1735, was the work of Manuel Martins and was gilded by leading local painters. Astonishingly, the 1755 earthquake (*see pp62–3*) only dislodged five tiles from the vault.

St Laurence's feast day is celebrated on 10 August. In the 18th century, worshippers would flock to the church, "not only due to their devotion to St Laurence, but also for the grandeur of his feast … and for the dancing and singing of all those present."

Loulé ⑮

Road map D7. 🏛 *20,000.* 🚉 🚌
ℹ️ *Edifício do Castelo (289-46 39 00).* 🔄 *Sat.*

LOULÉ IS AN ATTRACTIVE market town and thriving craft centre. Its Moorish origins are still visible in the belltower of the church of São Clemente. The **castle**, on the north side of town, is also Moorish in origin, rebuilt in the 13th century. Remnants of the walls behind the castle afford an overview of the town and the many pretty filigree chimneys, typical of the Algarve.

The heart of the town lies immediately south of Praça da República and encompasses the busy, pink-domed market. On Saturdays the area is particularly lively when gypsies run a simultaneous outdoor

market. From Rua 9 de Abril
to the Igreja Matriz you can
watch handicraft workers
carving wood, weaving
hats, making lace, deco-
rating horse tackle and
painting pottery and tiles.

The 13th-century **São
Clemente**, on Largo da
Silva, was badly damaged
in three earthquakes,
the last in 1969, but its
triple nave, defined by
Gothic arches, has been
conserved. There are two
beautiful side chapels
dating from the early
16th century. The Capela
de Nossa Senhora da
Consolação is decorated
from floor to vault with
superb blue and white
azulejo panels, while the
Capela de São Brás, has a
Manueline arch and a blue
and gold Baroque altarpiece.

Other churches of note are
the **Igreja da Misericórdia**,
on Avenida Marçal Pacheco,
which has a Manueline doorway, and the chapel of **Nossa
Senhora da Conceição**, close
to Praça da República. Here,
the Baroque altarpiece (1745)
by Miguel Nobre of Faro is
complemented by scenes in
blue and white *azulejos*.

ENVIRONS: The 16th-century,
hilltop chapel of **Nossa
Senhora da Piedade**, adorned
with *azulejo* panels, lies 2 km
(1 mile) west of Loulé. Behind
it stands a modern white
church of the same name built
to replace the old chapel but
which never became a popular place of worship. The spot
also affords spectacular views.

Colourful tiled fountain on the terrace
of the Patamar da Casa do Presépio, Estoi

Estoi 🔞

Road map D7. 👥 *4,300*. 🚉
ℹ️ *Faro (289-800 400).* 🔄 *daily.*

THE QUIET VILLAGE of Estoi
has two notable sights,
separated by a short distance
and about 1,800 years. Just off
the main square is the **Palácio
de Estoi**, an unashamedly
pretty Rococo pastiche, unique
to the region. The palace was
the brainchild of a local nobleman, who died soon after
work was begun in the mid-
1840s. Another wealthy local
later acquired the place, and
completed it in 1909. For the
vast amount of money and
energy he expended on his
new home, he was made
Viscount of Estoi. The work
was supervised by the architect

Domingos da Silva Meira,
whose interest in sculpture
is evident everywhere.

The palace now belongs
to Faro Council, and its
interior – a feast of pastel
and stucco – is slowly
being restored.

🌿 Palace gardens
Rua do Jardim. 📞 *289-991 620.*
🕐 *Tue–Sat.* ⬤ *public hols.* ♿
Dotted with orange trees
and palms, the gardens
are well worth visiting and
continue the joyful Rococo
spirit of the palace. The
lower terrace features a
blue and white tiled pavilion, the Casa da Cascata,
inside which is a copy of
Canova's *Three Graces*.
The main walled terrace
above, the Patamar da
Casa do Presépio, has a
large pavilion with stained-
glass windows, fountains
adorned with nymphs and
niches covered in charming
pastoral scenes in *azulejos*.

Detail of fish mosaic in the baths
of the Roman ruins at Milreu

🏛 Milreu
N2-6. 🕐 *Tue–Sun.* ⬤ *public hols.*
A ten-minute walk downhill
from the other end of the main
square leads to Estoi's second
sight: the Roman complex of
Milreu, which dates from the
1st or 2nd century AD. The
buildings probably began as
a large farmhouse that was
converted in the 3rd century
into a luxurious villa, built
around a central courtyard.

Ebullient fish mosaics still
adorn the baths, alongside
the living quarters, but most
portable archaeological finds
are now housed in Faro's
Museu Municipal *(see p327)*.
The importance of the villa,
which may have belonged to
a wealthy patrician, is indicated
by the remains of a temple
overlooking the site. This was
converted into a Christian
basilica in the 5th century.

Pink Rococo façade of the Palácio de Estoi

Faro ⑰

CAPITAL OF THE ALGARVE since 1756, Faro has been reborn several times over the centuries – following invasion, fire and earthquake. A prehistoric fishing village, it became an important port and administrative centre under the Romans, who named it Ossonoba. Captured from the Moors in 1249 by Afonso III, Faro prospered until 1596, when it was sacked and burned by the Earl of Essex, favourite of Elizabeth I of England. A new city rose from the ashes, only to be badly damaged in the earthquake of 1755 *(see pp62–3).* Although vestiges of the ancient city walls are still standing, the finest buildings date mainly from the late 18th and 19th centuries.

Azulejo **crucifix in exterior chapel of Nossa Senhora do Pé da Cruz**

Statue of Dom Francisco Gomes do Avelar in Largo da Sé

Exploring the Old City

The centre of Faro is attractive and easily explored on foot. It fans out from the small harbour to encompass the compact Old City to the southeast. Partly encircled by ancient walls, this is reached via the

Arco da Vila. The arch was built on the site of a medieval castle gate in the 19th century for the bishop, Dom Francisco Gomes do Avelar, who had taken it upon himself to redesign the city in decline. The portico is originally Moorish, and a statue of St Thomas Aquinas, patron saint of Faro, surveys the scene. At the heart of the Old City, the Largo da Sé is a peaceful square, lined with orange trees and flanked by the elegant 18th-century seminary and **Paço Episcopal** (bishops' palace), still in use and closed to the public. Just outside the walls, through another archway of Moorish origin, the Arco do Repouso, is the 18th-century church of **São Francisco**, impressively decorated with tiled scenes of the life of St Francis. Further north is the 17th-century **Nossa Senhora do Pé da Cruz** with

fanciful oil panels of stories from Genesis, such as the creation of the sun and stars. At the rear is an interesting exterior chapel or *bumilbadero.*

🔒 Sé

Largo da Sé. 🄲 289-80 66 32.
🄾 daily. 🄾 until further notice.
The first Christian church here, built on the site of a mosque, was all but destroyed in the attack by the English in 1596. The base of the belltower, its medieval doorway and two chapels survived, and long-term reconstruction resulted in a mixture of Renaissance and Baroque styles.

By the 1640s a grander building had emerged which included a chancel decorated with *azulejos* and the Capela

Orange trees in front of the 18th-century bishops' palace along the Largo da Sé

de Nossa Senhora dos Prazeres, decorated with ornate gilded woodcarving. One of the cathedral's most dashing and eccentric features is the large 18th-century organ decorated with Chinese motifs. Its range includes an echoing horn and a nightingale's song, and it has often been used by leading European organists.

⌂ Museu Municipal

Largo Dom Afonso III. [289-82 20 42.] Mon–Fri. ⬤ public hols. ✎
Since 1973 the Municipal Museum has been housed in the former convent of Nossa Senhora da Assunção, founded for the Poor Clares by Dona Leonor, sister of Manuel I. Her emblem, a fishing net, adorns the portico.

A variety of local archaeological finds are displayed in the museum, partly in the lovely two-storey Renaissance cloister built by Afonso Pires in 1540. The collection contains Roman,

17th-century chancel of Faro's Sé

medieval and Manueline stone carvings and statuary. However, the most attractive exhibit is a huge, Roman floor mosaic featuring a magnificently executed head of the god Neptune (3rd century AD), found near the railway station.

VISITORS' CHECKLIST

Road map D7. ⛪ 40,000. ✈ 5 km (3 miles) SW. ☒ Largo da Estação. ⬛ Avenida da República. ℹ Avenida 5 Outubro (289-800 400). ⬤ daily. ✎ 7 Sep: Dia da Cidade.

⌂ Museu Marítimo

Rua da Comunidade Lusiada.
[289-80 36 01.] Mon–Fri (pm). ⬤ public hols. ✎
The Museu Marítimo is housed in part of the harbour master's building on the waterfront. Its small and curious collection of maritime exhibits centres on models of boats from the Age of Discovery *(see pp46–9)* onwards, including the square-rigged *nau*, prototype of the galleon. One example is Vasco da Gama's *São Gabriel*, the flagship on his voyage to India in 1498. There are also displays of traditional fishing methods from the Algarve.

FARO CITY CENTRE

Arco da Vila ⑤
Igreja do Carmo ①
Museu Etnográfico ⑩
Museu Marítimo ④
Museu Municipal ⑧
Paço Episcopal ⑥
Palácio Bivarin ③
São Francisco ⑨
São Pedro ②
Sé ⑦

KEY

🚉 Railway station

🚌 Bus station

🅿 Parking

ℹ Tourist information

✝ Church

— Railway line

▦ City walls

0 metres 250
0 yards 250

Exploring Faro

The lively centre of Faro along Rua de Santo António is a stylish, pedestrianized area full of shops, bars and restaurants. Between here and the Largo do Carmo are some fine 18th-century buildings, such as the **Palácio Bivarin**. The early morning market on Largo de Sá Carneiro, to the north, offers fresh produce, clothing and local crafts. From here, a brisk walk uphill to the **Ermida de Santo António do Alto** brings a panorama of Faro with the sea and saltpans to the south.

🏛 Museu Etnográfico

Praça da Liberdade 2. **(** 289-827 610. ◯ *Mon–Fri.* ● *public hols.* 🖼 📷
The Ethnographic Museum takes a nostalgic look at the Algarve's traditional way of life showing ceramics, looms and decorative horse tackle. Old photographs document peasant farming techniques, with their heavy reliance on manpower, donkeys and oxen. The most charming exhibit is the cart used by the last waterseller in Olhão, in operation until 1974.

Imposing twin-towered façade of the Baroque Igreja do Carmo

🔒 Igreja do Carmo

Largo do Carmo. **(** 289-82 44 90. ◯ *Mon–Fri.* ● *to Capela dos Ossos.*
The impressive façade of this church was begun in 1713. Inside, the decoration is Baroque run wild, with every scroll and barley-sugar twist covered in precious Brazilian gold leaf.

In sombre contrast, the Capela dos Ossos (Chapel of Bones), built in 1816, has walls lined with skulls and large bones taken from the friars' cemetery. It is a stark reminder of the transience of human life.

Sumptuous Baroque decoration of the main altarpiece in São Pedro

🔒 São Pedro

Largo de São Pedro. **(** 289-80 54 73. ◯ *daily.*
The parish church of Faro is dedicated to St Peter, patron saint of fishermen. Though restored with Italianate columns after the earthquake of 1755, much original Baroque decoration has survived, including the main altarpiece (1689).

Highlights include the chapel of the Santíssimo Sacramento, with a dazzling altarpiece (c.1745) featuring a bas-relief of the Last Supper, and a sculpture of St Anne teaching the young Virgin Mary to read. The altar of the Capela das Almas is surrounded by stunning *azulejos* (c.1730) showing the Virgin and other saints pulling souls out of purgatory.

✝ Cemitério dos Judeus

Estrada da Penha. **(** 282-41 67 10. ◯ *Mon–Fri (am).* ● *public hols.* ♿
At the far northeast corner of town is the Jewish cemetery, created for the Jewish community brought here in the 18th century by the Marquês de Pombal *(see pp52–3)* to revitalize the economy. The cemetery is laid out in the traditional Sephardic way with children buried nearest the entrance, women in the centre and men at the back. It served from 1838 until 1932, during which time 60 families prospered in the area then gradually moved away so that there is no Jewish community in Faro today.

Olhão ⑱

Road map D7. 🚗 *15,000.* 🚲 🚌 ℹ *Largo da Lagoa (289-71 39 36).* 🐟 *daily (fish); Sat (general).*

OLHÃO HAS BEEN involved in fishing since the Middle Ages, and today is one of the largest fishing ports and tuna and sardine canning centres in the Algarve. In 1808 the village was elevated to the status of town, after 17 of its fishermen crossed the Atlantic Ocean without charts, expressly to bring the exiled King João VI, in Rio de Janeiro, the news that Napoleon's troops had been forced out of the country.

Olhão's square, whitewashed houses with their flat roof terraces and box-like chimneys are reminiscent of Moorish architecture. The best view is from the top of the belltower of the parish church, **Nossa Senhora do Rosário**, on Praça da Restauração, built between 1681 and 1698 with donations from the local fishermen. The custodian lets visitors through the locked door leading from the nave. In 1758 the parish priest remarked on the fishermen's great devotion to "Our Lady of the Rosary in their grief and danger at sea, especially in summertime when North African pirates often sail off this coast." At the rear of the church is the external chapel of **Nossa Senhora dos Aflitos**, where women pray for their men's safety in stormy weather.

The narrow, pedestrianized streets of the old town wind down from here to the waterfront, lined with shops and also the scene of

Whitewashed chapel of Nossa Senhora dos Aflitos behind the parish church in Olhão

The wide lagoon of the Parque Natural da Ria Formosa

one of the region's most lively and picturesque markets. The noisy covered fish market sells the catch that has come in that morning, while on Saturdays outside stalls line the quay, with local farmers selling other produce such as fruit, nuts, honey and live chickens.

Shop selling local basketware in Olhão

ENVIRONS: At the eastern end of the quay, beyond the market, boats take you out to the islands of **Armona** (15 min), **Culatra** (30 min) and **Farol** (45 min). These flat, narrow bars of sand provide shelter to the town, and excellent sandy beaches for visitors, particularly on the ocean side. The islands are part of the Parque Natural da Ria Formosa.

Parque Natural da Ria Formosa ⑲

Road map D7. 🛈 *Quinta de Marim, Marim (289-70 41 34).* 🚌 *along N125.* ⛴ *from Faro, Olhão & Tavira.*

STRETCHING from Praia de Faro to Cacela Velha *(see p331)*, the Ria Formosa Nature Reserve follows 60 km (37 miles) of coastline. It was created in 1987 to protect the valuable ecosystem of this area, which was under serious threat from uncontrolled building, sand

extraction and pollution, all by-products of the massive rise in tourism. The lagoon area of marshes, saltpans, islets and channels is sheltered from the open sea by a chain of barrier islands – actually sand dunes above sea level. Inlets between the islands allow the tide to ebb and flow into the lagoon.

The lagoon waters are warm and highly nutritious, and therefore rich in shellfish, such as oysters, cockles and clams. These are also bred here and make up 80 per cent of the nation's mollusc exports. The fish life and warm climate attract numerous wildfowl and waders, and snakes, toads and chameleons also live here. Apart from fish and shellfish farming and salt panning, all other human activities which might encroach on the park's ecosystem are strictly controlled or forbidden.

Quinta de Marim, about 3 km (2 miles) east of Olhão, is an environmental education centre. Its 60 ha (148 acres) of dune and pinewoods are home to various sights, including a restored farmhouse, a tidal mill, a centre for injured birds, as well as exhibitions and aquariums. The web-footed Portuguese water dog, once much used by fishermen, has been bred back from near-extinction here. At the eastern end of the park are Roman tanks where fish was salted before being exported to the empire.

✗ Quinta de Marim
Marim. 🛈 289-70 41 34. ◯ *daily.* ● *1 Jan, 25 Dec.* 🖾 🖈 🛆

WATER BIRDS OF THE RIA FORMOSA

The Ria Formosa is an important area for breeding wetland birds such as cattle egrets, red-crested pochard and purple herons. On drier areas of land, both pratincoles and Kentish plovers can be found. Some northern European species, such as the wigeon and dunlin, winter here, and it is a stopover for migrant birds en route to Africa. Among the resident species is the rare purple gallinule, symbol of the park.

Cattle egrets *feed among cattle and are often seen perched on their backs pecking off insects and flies.*

The purple gallinule *is a dark-coloured relative of the moorhen. It can run fairly fast on its extremely long legs but is a poor flier.*

The red-crested pochard *is a brightly coloured duck originally from central Europe.*

Houses with four-sided roofs, "Telhados de Quatro Águas", along the river Gilão in Tavira

Tavira ⑳

Road map D7. 🏙 10,000. 🚃 🚌
ℹ️ Rua da Galeria 9 (281-32 25 11).
📅 3rd Sat of month.

THE PRETTY TOWN of Tavira, full of historic churches and fine mansions with filigree balconies, lies along both sides of the Gilão river, linked by a **bridge** of Roman origin. This was part of the coastal Roman road between Castro Marim and Faro *(see pp326–8)*.

Tavira's early ascendancy began with the Moors, who saw it as one of their most important settlements in the Algarve, along with Silves and Faro. It was conquered in 1242 by Dom Paio Peres Correia, who was outraged at the murder of seven of his knights by the Moors during a truce. The proximity of Tavira to the coast of Morocco ensured its importance, formally recognized in 1282 by King Dinis who gave its seamen equal rights with those of Lisbon. The town became an ideal base for the control of piracy and the support of Portuguese positions in North Africa.

Tavira flourished until the 16th century, after which a slow decline set in, aggravated by a severe plague (1645–6) and the silting up of the harbour. Fishing for tuna became a major enterprise, but since the shoals have moved away, the town now accommodates tourists, without compromising either its looks or atmosphere.

The best view of the town is from the walls of the **Moorish castle** in the old Arab centre on top of the hill. From here the four-sided "Telhados de Quatro Águas" (roofs of four waters) that line Rua da Liberdade are clearly visible. An architectural feature that seems to have originated in Tavira, these pyramid-like roofs possibly evolved to allow the sudden torrential rain of the Algarve to run off easily. From the castle walls, the nearby clock tower of the church of **Santa Maria do Castelo** also acts as a landmark. The church itself occupies the site of what was once the biggest mosque in the Algarve. Its façade retains a Gothic doorway and

Beach on Ilha de Tavira, one of the many islands off the Algarve's eastern coast

windows, and its interior, restored in the 19th century, houses the tombs of Dom Paio Peres Correia and his seven knights. Santa Maria do Castelo and **Igreja da Misericórdia** are the only two of Tavira's 21 churches to be open outside service hours. Below the castle, the arcaded convent of **Nossa Senhora da Graça** was built in 1569 for the Order of St Augustine.

Renaissance architecture was pioneered in the town by André Pilarte, and can be seen on the way up to the castle, in the Igreja da Misericórdia (1541–51), with its lovely doorway topped by saints Peter and Paul, and in the nearby **Palácio da Galeria** (open for temporary exhibitions). Rua da Liberdade and Rua José Pires Padinha have a sprinkling of 16th-century houses. The river embankments are graced by 18th-century mansions, in particular along the east bank next to the Roman bridge. A stroll along Rua do Cais takes you to the old market building.

♣ Moorish castle
Alto de Santa Maria. ⏲ daily. ♿

ENVIRONS: The sandy, offshore **Ilha de Tavira**, 11 km long by 500 m wide (7 miles by 550 yards), provides excellent swimming. In the summer it is a popular resort reached by ferry from Quatro Águas, 2 km (1 mile) southeast of Tavira. The area, part of the Ria Formosa nature park *(see p329)*, is popular for bird-watching.

Cacela Velha ㉑

Road map D7. 🚶 50. ℹ️ Junta de Vila Nova de Cacela (281-95 12 28).

THIS HAMLET perches on a cliff overlooking the sea, reached via a landscape of fields and olive trees. It is uniquely pretty, and bypassed by tourism, with a peaceful, self-contained air. Immaculate blue and white fishermen's houses cluster around the remains of a fort and a whitewashed 18th-century church.

On the beach, which is sheltered by a long spit of sand, fishing boats are dotted about. The Phoenicians and later the Moors adopted this protected, attractive site until it was taken over by the Knights of Santiago in 1240 (see p43).

Blue and white houses, Cacela Velha

Castro Marim ㉒

Road map D7. 🚶 4,000. 🚌 ℹ️ Rua Jose Alves Moreira 2–4 (281-53 12 32).

CASTRO MARIM has attracted "visitors" since ancient times. The Phoenicians, Greeks and Romans all made use of its commanding location above the River Guadiana. It was the gateway to the Moorish Al-Gharb, and later, successive Christian kings granted it privileges in order to expand the population and ensure its strategic value. For centuries it became a sanctuary for fugitives from the Inquisition (see p51). The **castle** with round turrets above the town is of Moorish origin, the outlying walls a 13th-century addition.

Moorish castle and the abandoned Misericórdia church, Castro Marim

ENVIRONS: The town was also a centre for salt production and the surrounding *salinas* are now home to valuable wildlife in the **Reserva Natural do Sapal**, established in 1975. Extending for 2,090 ha (5,160 acres) south of the town, this is a damp area of marshes and saltpans with a large variety of bird species including flamingos, white storks, and black-winged stilts, symbol of the reserve. Group tours may be booked on 281-510 680.

Alcoutim ㉓

Road map D7. 🚶 1,300. 🚌 ℹ️ Rua 1° de maio (281-54 61 79).

THE TINY, GEM-LIKE, unspoilt village of Alcoutim lies 15 km (9 miles) from the border with the Alentejo, and on the natural border with Spain, the River Guadiana. The drive there along the N122-2, a rough, winding road which sometimes runs alongside the Guadiana, provides stunning views of the countryside and across the river to Spain.

The size of Alcoutim belies its history. As a strategic location and river port, it was seized on by the Phoenicians, Greeks, Romans and, of course, the Moors who stayed until the reconquest in 1240. Here, in 1371, on flower-decked boats midway between Alcoutim and its Spanish counterpart, Sanlúcar de Guadiana, King Fernando I of Portugal signed the peace of Alcoutim with Enrique II of Castile. By the late 17th century, when its political importance had waned, the town had acquired a new reputation – for smuggling tobacco and snuff from Spain.

The walls of the 14th-century **castle** give an excellent view over the small village and its idyllic setting. Near the main square, by the river, is the refreshingly simple 16th-century church of **San Salvador**.

ENVIRONS: Visitors can take a scenic trip 15 km (9 miles) downriver to **Foz de Odeleite** by fishing boat from the jetty. The boat passes orchards and orange groves and, at Álamo, there is a Roman dam.

View from Alcoutim across the Guadiana to Sanlúcar in Spain

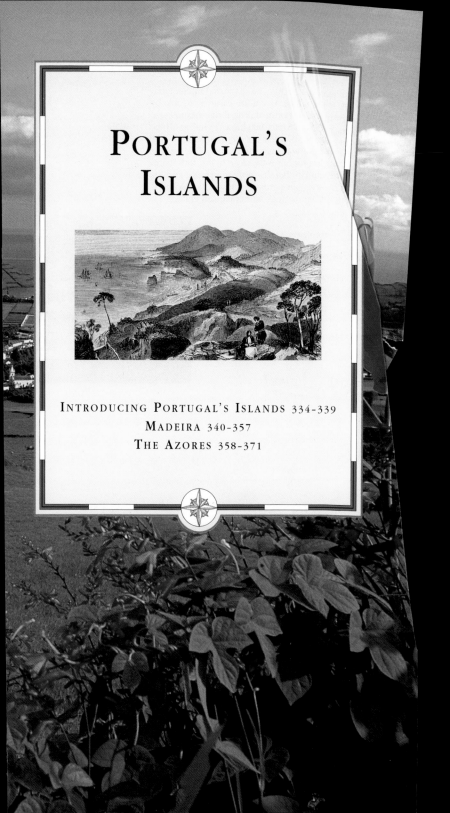

PORTUGAL'S ISLANDS

INTRODUCING PORTUGAL'S ISLANDS 334-339
MADEIRA 340-357
THE AZORES 358-371

Portugal's Islands at a Glance

ONCE REMOTE OUTPOSTS of a maritime empire, today Madeira and the Azores are easily accessible by air from mainland Portugal. The fertile islands of Madeira and Porto Santo, 600 km (375 miles) off the African coast, are popular holiday destinations, with subtropical flora and high mountains. The Azorean archipelago lies further west, close to the Mid-Atlantic Ridge. The climate here is more temperate and the active volcanoes have created a fascinating scenery of moon-like landscapes and collapsed craters.

THE AZORES

MADEIRA

__Terceira__ is a relatively flat island famous for its bull-running festivals, the "tourada à corda". On the southern coast, the twin-towered church of São Mateus, built at the turn of the century, overlooks the harbour of São Mateus.

THE AZORES
(See pp358–71)

Graciosa

São Jorge

Faial   Pico

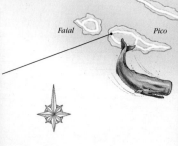

__Pico__ is the summit of a steep volcano protruding from the sea. On the lower slopes of the mountain that fall towards the sea, the fields are crisscrossed with a patchwork of dry-stone walls made from black volcanic basalt.

◁ **Fertile pastures sloping down to volcanic cones and the sea on the Azorean island of Faial**

ADEIRA
(see pp340–57)

Funchal is the capital of Madeira, famous for its flowers. Exotic blooms are sold along the main street, Avenida Arriaga, which is lined with tall jacaranda trees.

Porto Santo

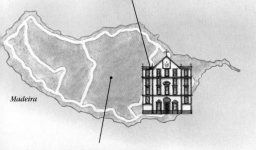

Madeira

Ilhas Desertas

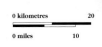

| 0 kilometres | 20 |
| 0 miles | 10 |

Pico Ruivo, at 1,861 m (6,105 ft), is the highest point on the island of Madeira. Its slopes, covered in giant heather, offer stunning views.

Terceira

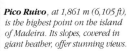

| 0 kilometres | 50 |
| 0 miles | 25 |

São Miguel

São Miguel is popular for its therapeutic spa treatments in hot pools of mineral water. At Caldeira das Furnas, in the east of the island, steaming mud springs bubble from the ground.

Santa Maria

The Landscape and Flowers of Madeira

MADEIRA HAS A MILD, moist climate which promotes a rich cover of vegetation. At first glance, the flowers and foliage appear to harmonize with the environment. The well-travelled botanist, however, will soon become aware of the strange assortment of flowers from around the world. For example, over the past few centuries, many flowers from South Africa's Cape region and exotic blooms from South America have been introduced, which now thrive alongside indigenous plants.

Pride of Madeira

MADEIRA'S GARDENS

The sub-tropical climate and m of indigenous and imported p combine to produce gardens are the envy of hor culturalists all ove world. Gardens su the Botanical Garde Funchal *(see p346* awash with colou year. Here are some of most striking plants that be found in Madeira's garc

Magnolia in bloom

AROUND THE COAST

In many coastal areas the cliffs are spectacular, such as this stretch at Ponta de São Lourenço *(see p350)*. A rich and varied flora, both native and introduced, can be found along Madeira's coast despite the dry and stony habitat.

Hottentot fig is a coastal, ground-cover plant originating from South Africa.

Lampranthus spectabilis *is a South African plant which flowers on the coast between May and July.*

Canary Island date palms are a familiar sight, especially along the sunny south coast.

AGRICULTURAL AND WAYSIDE GROUND

An irrigation system using man-made chan called *levadas*, such as this one near Curra Freiras *(see p354)*, allows the islanders to cu many otherwise unpromising areas. The ma of agricultural land are often rich with flov

Mimosa trees *grou especially well in woc parts of Madeira, wh they bloom in winter*

Parrot's Beak *is a large, striking flower that appears in March and April.*

Hibiscus syriacus, *from the Far East, flowers be- tween June and October.*

Lady's slipper orchids come in a variety of colours and are great favourites among Madeira's more serious gardeners.

Cymbidium orchids from Southeast Asia thrive when they are grown in sheltered sites and in partial shade.

Coral trees *...ate from south-...razil, and on ...ira flower ...en Jan-...and ...b.*

Camellia thrives in partial shade and grows to the size of a small tree.

Protea cynaroides comes from South Africa where it is known as the Cape artichoke or king protea.

...H GROUND

...iews from the summit of Pico Ruivo, the ...'s highest point *(see p354)*, are spectacular. ...land areas, the vegetation harbours a higher ...ortion of native species than in the lowlands.

TERRACED PLANTATIONS

Plantations, such as this one growing bananas near Calheta *(see p356)*, are made by digging terraces into the hillside. A wide range of crops are grown, for home consumption and export.

Isoplexis sceptrum, known as the yellow foxglove, is a flowering shrub native to Madeira.

Sweet chestnuts grow well in Madeira and produce an abundant autumn harvest.

Pawpaws produce fruit all year round. The plant originates from South America.

Broom flowers are colourful and popular with pollinating insects.

Prickly juniper is a hardy, spiny evergreen shrub covered in tough red berries.

Sword aloe has spiky leaves which provide a good physical barrier around plantations.

The Azores: Volcanic Islands Rising from the Ocean Bed

S ITUATED ON EITHER SIDE of the Mid-Atlantic Ridge, the
Azores are a result of 20 million years of volcanic
activity. As the plates of the earth's crust pull apart,
volcanic eruptions form a giant ridge of mountains
beneath the Atlantic. In places, the ridge is buckled
and cut by perpendicular fractures, known as transform
faults. Molten rock (magma) has been forced through
these faults to form the Azores. These islands, among
the youngest on earth, emerged above the waves
less than five million years ago. Their
striking landscape tells of their volcanic past and is still shaped
by volcanic activity today.

The Mid-Atlantic Ridge *is a line*
submarine volcanoes that runs
whole length of the Atlantic Oce

Terceira lies directly
a major transform

Corvo

Graciosa

Flores

**Transform
fault**

**The Mid-
Atlantic Ridge**
marks the join where
the African, Eurasian
and American plates
of the earth's crust are
being pulled apart.

Faial

Pico

São Jorge

A mantle plume is a mass of
partially molten mantle that
has welled upwards, pooling
beneath the rocky lithosphere.
The magma it produces seeks
fissures through which to erupt.

São Miguel has several
spectacular water-filled
calderas and hot springs.

Santa Maria

VOLCANIC RESOURCES
OF THE AZORES

The dramatic formation of the
Azores has left the islands with
abundant natural resources. Hot
springs, strong building materials
and, eventually, fertile soil, are
all the result of the ongoing volcanic activity. A wet, temperate
climate gradually breaks down
the volcanic rocks into fertile
soils. Older soils support luxuriant vegetation and are excellent
for arable farming, but younger
soils, like those found on Pico,
support little agriculture yet.

These stone cottages *on Pico,*
like many on the islands, make
use of the plentiful basalt rock
as a durable building material.

Furnas, on São Migue
an area of sulphur and
mud springs used for ba
and for medicinal purpo

...g high above the clouds, the still-active ...nic peak of Pico Alto dominates the island of ... which is itself the top of a giant underwater ...no. At 2,350 m (7,700 ft) above sea level, Pico ...s the highest peak in the whole of Portugal.

GEOLOGY OF THE AZORES

...Azores lie along transform fault lines, cracks ... earth's crust which cross the Mid-Atlantic ... These faults are weak points through ...h magma can rise. Successive volcanic erup-...ons have formed hundreds of undersea mountains on either side of the ridge. The highest peaks of these mountains are the nine islands of the Azores. Their emergence above the sea has been aided by the swelling of the mantle plume beneath the ocean crust, which lifts the sea floor closer to the surface of the sea.

Thin ocean crust

Atlantic Ocean

The upper mantle is a layer of dense rock. With the crust above, it forms the lithosphere, a series of semi-rigid moving plates.

The lower mantle, or asthenosphere, is a deep layer of partially molten rock that surrounds the earth's core.

...lt lava blocks used for dry-stone walls provide ...r for vines and protect against soil erosion on ...Volcanic soil here is of relatively recent for-...on and suitable for few crops except grapes.

THE FORMATION OF A CALDERA

A caldera is a large crater that forms during or after a volcanic eruption, when the roof of the magma chamber collapses under the weight of the volcano's cone. Water collecting in the natural bowl of a caldera can form a crater lake.

Caldeira das Sete Cidades on the island of São Miguel

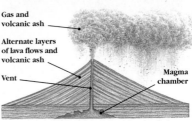

Gas and volcanic ash

Alternate layers of lava flows and volcanic ash

Vent

Magma chamber

In an active volcano, the magma chamber below the cone is full of molten rock. As pressure forces this magma up through the volcano's vent, it is expelled to the surface as a volcanic eruption.

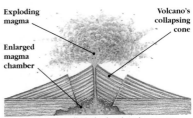

Exploding magma

Volcano's collapsing cone

Enlarged magma chamber

As magma is expelled, the level in the magma chamber drops. This may cause the volcano's cone to collapse under its own weight, leaving behind the characteristic bowl-shaped crater, or caldera.

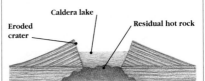

Caldera lake

Eroded crater

Residual hot rock

After the volcano has died down and is eroded, the caldera can fill with water and form a lake. Residual hot rock near the magma chamber may continue to heat the surrounding ground water.

MADEIRA

....

MADEIRA IS A GREEN, SUBTROPICAL *paradise of volcanic origin, its soils formed from lava and ash, completely different in character from the Portuguese mainland. Blessed with an equable daytime temperature that varies only by a few degrees either side of 20° C (68° F), the island has an all-year-round appeal.*

Madeira is a mere dot in the Atlantic Ocean, 608 km (378 miles) from Morocco, and nearly 1,000 km (621 miles) from Lisbon. Despite this, Madeira and Porto Santo appear on a Genoese map of 1351, so there is no doubt that sailors had long known about the islands. They remained unclaimed, however, until 1418 when João Gonçalves Zarco was blown out into the Atlantic by violent storms while exploring the coast of Africa. Zarco counted his blessings at having found safe harbour in Porto Santo, set up the Portuguese flag and returned to Lisbon. A year later he returned on a voyage of discovery sponsored by Henry the Navigator *(see p49)*. Early in 1420, after a winter on Porto Santo, he set sail for the mist-shrouded land on the horizon. He found a beautiful, thickly wooded island (*madeira* means wood), with abundant fresh water.

The bird-of-paradise flower (*Strelitzia reginae*)

Within seven years the island had attracted a pioneer colony and the early settlers exploited the fertile soil and warm climate to grow sugar cane. The islanders grew rich on this "white gold", and slaves were brought in to work the land and create the terraced fields and irrigation channels (*levadas*) that still cling to the steep hillsides. Today, despite the gradients, Madeirans make use of every spare patch of land, and wine, bananas and exotic flowers form the backbone of the economy.

In the late 19th century, Madeira became a popular winter holiday spot for northern Europeans. The start of commercial flights in 1964 introduced the rest of the world to its charms. Today Madeira appeals to keen walkers, plant lovers and sun seekers, although it lacks the sandy beaches of its sister island, Porto Santo.

Triangular-shaped houses, typical of the town of Santana on the north coast of Madeira

◁ Footpath winding through the spectacular mountain scenery of Pico do Arieiro

Exploring Madeira

Funchal is the island's capital and the only town of any size. This is where most of the museums and historic buildings are to be found, as well as the best hotels, restaurants and shops. Most of Madeira's agricultural crops are grown along the sunny, prosperous south coast. The cooler, wetter north side has fewer settlements and more cattle. Many parts of the mountainous and volcanic interior remain wild, and some are accessible only on foot. Pico Ruivo, the highest peak on the island, is a favourite destination for walkers.

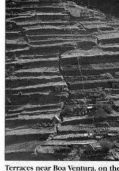

Terraces near Boa Ventura, on the road from Santana to São Vicente

15 PORTO MONIZ

ACHADAS DA CRUZ

PONTA DELGADA

SEIXAL

Ribeira da Janela

R101

PONTA DO PARGO

R101

R101

SÃO VICENTE **14**

B VENTU

RABAÇAL WALKS

Ribeira de São Vicente

R201 **13**

RABAÇAL

12

PAÚL DA SERRA

PRAZERES

R222

SERRA DE AGUA

CURRAL DAS FRE

16 CALHETA

R209

R104

0 kilometres 5

0 miles 3

R101

ESTREITO DE CÂMARA DE LOBOS

PONTA DO SOL

RIBEIRA BRAVA **17**

CABO GIRÃO R101

CÂMARA DE LOBOS

Early morning view across the rooftops of Funchal, with the mountainous interior beyond

GETTING AROUND

Madeira's new international airport, Santa Catarina, is at Santa Cruz, 18 km (11 miles) northeast of Funchal. Buses operate to all corners of the island from Funchal but are not geared to tourists. Taxis can be used, but for flexibility car hire is best. From north to south the island is 19 km (12 miles) wide and from east to west just 56 km (35 miles) long. Even so, travelling times are magnified by the mountainous terrain. To reach the nearby island of Porto Santo, you can either fly from Santa Cruz or take the ferry from Funchal to Porto de Abrigo (near Vila Baleira). *(See also pp444–5.)*

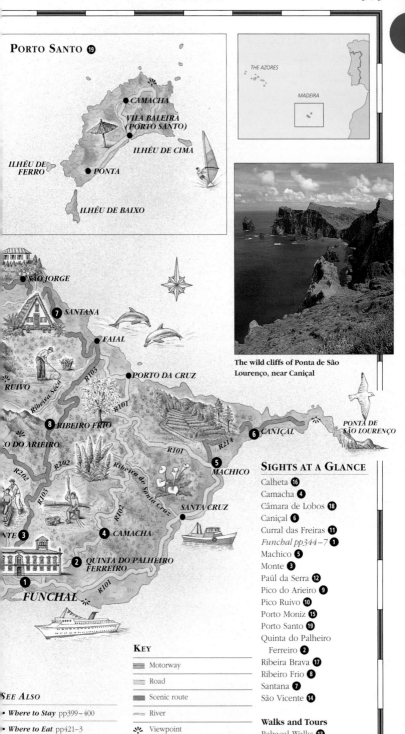

The wild cliffs of Ponta de São Lourenço, near Caniçal

SIGHTS AT A GLANCE

Calheta ⑯
Camacha ④
Câmara de Lobos ⑱
Caniçal ⑥
Curral das Freiras ⑪
Funchal pp344–7 ①
Machico ⑤
Monte ③
Paúl da Serra ⑫
Pico do Arieiro ⑨
Pico Ruivo ⑩
Porto Moniz ⑮
Porto Santo ⑲
Quinta do Palheiro
 Ferreiro ②
Ribeira Brava ⑰
Ribeiro Frio ⑧
Santana ⑦
São Vicente ⑭

Walks and Tours
Rabaçal Walks ⑬

KEY

Motorway
Road
Scenic route
River
Viewpoint

SEE ALSO

• *Where to Stay* pp399–400
• *Where to Eat* pp421–3

Street-by-Street: Funchal ●

Tiling on Palácio do
Governo Regional,
Avenida M. Arriaga

THE DEEP NATURAL HARBOUR of Madeira's capital, Funchal, attracted early settlers in the 15th century. The historic core of the capital still overlooks the harbour and boasts fine government buildings and stately 18th-century houses with shady courtyards, iron balconies and carved black basalt doorways. Visitors have justly called Funchal a "little Lisbon" because of the town's steep cobbled streets and overall air of grandeur.

The Igreja do Colégio
(Collegiate Church) was fou...
by the Jesuits in 1574. The ...
exterior contrasts with the ...
decorated high altar, frame...
carved; gilded wood (1641–...

Rua da Carreira
and Rua do Surdo
have preserved many
of their original elegant
balconied houses.

São Pedro church

The Museu
Municipal
houses an
aquarium and
is a favourite
with children.

RUA DAS PRETAS

RUA DO SURDO

RUA DA CARREIRA

RUA S. FRANCISCO

AVENIDA M. ARRI...

RUA DAS FONTES

Adegas de São
Francisco *(see p347)*

The monument to
João Gonçalves Zarco,
the man who claimed
Madeira for Portugal, was
created by the sculptor
Francisco Franco in 1927.

Toyota Showroom
The building's exterior is
decorated with 20th-century
tiles depicting various Madeiran
scenes including the famous
Monte toboggan (see p348).

The Palácio de São Lourenço
is a 16th-century fortress housing
Madeira's military headquarters.

0 metres 50

0 yards 50

Yacht Marina
Lined with seafood restaurants,
the yacht marina on Avenida
do Mar is ideal for an evening
stroll. The sea wall around the
marina offers good views.

Avenida
do Mar

STAR SIGHTS

★ **Sé**

★ **Praça do Município**

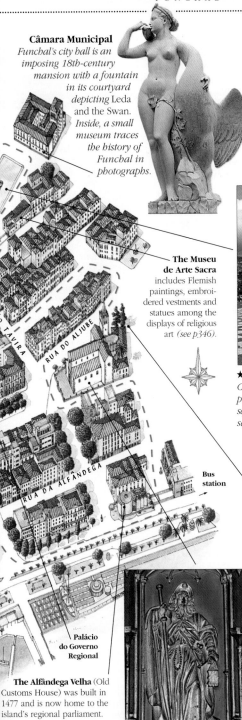

Câmara Municipal
Funchal's city hall is an imposing 18th-century mansion with a fountain in its courtyard depicting Leda and the Swan. *Inside, a small museum traces the history of Funchal in photographs.*

The Museu de Arte Sacra includes Flemish paintings, embroidered vestments and statues among the displays of religious art *(see p346).*

Bus station

Palácio do Governo Regional

The Alfândega Velha (Old Customs House) was built in 1477 and is now home to the island's regional parliament.

KEY

– – – Suggested route

VISITORS' CHECKLIST

🏙 120,000. ✈ Santa Catarina 18 km (11 miles) NE. ⛴ Porto do Funchal. 🚌 Avenida do Mar. ℹ Avenida Arriaga 16 (291-225 658). 🛒 Mon–Sat. 🎉 Apr/May: Flower Festival; mid-Sep: Wine Festival; 31 Dec: Firework display. **Museu Municipal** Rua da Mouraria 31. 📞 291-229 761. ⏰ Tue–Sun. ⬤ 25 Dec, 1 Jan. ♿

★ Praça do Município
Contrasting black and white stones pave the attractive municipal square. On the northeast side of the square is the Câmara Municipal.

Rua do Aljube
Alongside the Sé, flower sellers in traditional costumes offer a colourful array of exotic flowers.

★ Sé
São Tiago (St James) is one of many gilded figures that adorn the wonderfully carved wooden choir stalls in Funchal's 15th-century cathedral (see p346).

Exploring Funchal

Funchal has three main areas: to the west lies the so-called "tourist zone" where all the major hotels are located; to the east is the Zona Velha, the Old Town, a warren of former fishermen's houses, some now turned into lively restaurants. The central downtown area *(see pp344–5)* is characterized by its historic buildings and smart shops. Linking all three areas is the Avenida do Mar, the harbourside promenade. Funchal is also divided by three rivers, though these flow along concrete channels and are virtually hidden from view by trellises covered with scarlet and purple bougainvillea.

Carved Manueline-style lions in the garden at Quinta das Cruzes

🛡 Sé

Largo da Sé. 📞 *291-22 81 55.*
⭘ *daily.*

The cathedral is one of the few buildings in Madeira to have survived virtually untouched since the early days of the island's colonization. In the 1490s, King Manuel I *(see pp46–9)* sent the architect Pêro Anes from the mainland to work on the design of the colony's cathedral. The Sé was finally completed in 1514.

The highlights are the ceiling and the choir stalls, though neither is easy to see in the dark interior. The ceiling of inlaid wood is best seen from the south transept, where enough light filters in to illuminate the intricate patterning. The choir stalls depict saints, prophets and apostles in 16th-century costume. Aspects of Madeiran life feature in the decorative details of the armrests and seats: one cherub carries a bunch of bananas, another a goatskin full of wine.

Clock tower of Funchal's Sé

🏛 Museu de Arte Sacra

Rua do Bispo 21. 📞 *291-22 89 00.*
⭘ *Tue–Sat & Sun am.* ● *public hols.* 🖼

Madeiran merchants, who grew rich on the profitable sugar trade, sought to secure their salvation by commissioning paintings, statues, embroidered vestments and illuminated hymn books for their local churches. Hundreds of examples now fill this museum which is housed in the former bishops' palace, a building dating from 1600. There are some masterpieces in the collection, including the late-Gothic processional cross donated by King Manuel I, and religious paintings by major Flemish artists of the 15th and 16th centuries. Some works include portraits of the dignitaries who commissioned them. *Saints Philip and James* is a 16th-century painting showing Simão Gonçalves de Câmara, Zarco's *(see p341)* grandson.

🏛 Quinta das Cruzes

Calçada do Pico 1. 📞 *291-74 13 88.*
⭘ *Tue–Sun.* ● *public hols.* 🖼

It is said that Zarco, the man who claimed Madeira for Portugal *(see p341)*, built his house where the Quinta das Cruzes now stands. The elegant 19th-century mansion is now the Museum of Decorative Arts, furnished as a wealthy merchant's house with Indian silk wall hangings, Regency sideboards and oriental carpets. In the basement is furniture made from mahogany packing cases used in the 17th century for shipping sugar, and turned into chests and cupboards when the sugar trade died.

The garden is dotted with ancient tombstones and architectural fragments. These include two window frames from 1507 carved with rope motifs, acrobatic figures and man-eating lions in a Madeiran version of the Manueline style of architecture *(see pp20–21)*.

🛡 Convento de Santa Clara

Calçada de Santa Clara. 📞 *291-74 26 02.* ⭘ *daily (ring doorbell).*

Opposite Quinta das Cruzes is the Convento de Santa Clara, founded in 1496 by João Gonçalves de Câmara, one of Zarco's grandsons. Zarco himself is buried under the high altar, and Martim Mendes Vasconcelos, his son-in-law, has a tomb at the rear of the church. Precious 17th-century *azulejo* tiles cover the walls.

🌿 Jardim Botânico

Quinta do Bom Sucesso, Caminho do Meio. ⭘ *daily.* ● *25 Dec.* 🖼

Opened to the public in 1960, the Botanical Gardens display plants from all over the world. Desert cacti, rainforest orchids and South African proteas grow here as well as native Madeiran dragon trees. There are contrasting sections: formal areas of bedding plants, quiet carp ponds and wild wooded parts.

The intricately patterned formal gardens of the Jardim Botânico

♀ Adegas de São Francisco

Avenida Arriaga 28. **☎** *291-74 01 10.* ◻ *Mon – Fri, Sat am.* ◐ *public hols.* ▨ ☑ *compulsory.*

In the cobbled courtyards of the St Francis wine lodge, visitors are greeted by the scents of ancient wood and Madeira. Some of the buildings in this maze of coopers' yards, wine vaults and sampling rooms go back to the 17th century when the site was part of Funchal's Franciscan friary. It is possible to sample wines made on the premises more than 150 years ago as well as more recent (and cheaper) vintages. Included in the guided tour is a visit to the warming rooms where Madeira is "cooked" by hot water pipes *(see p349).*

Tasting Madeira wine at the Adegas de São Francisco

⊜ Mercado dos Lavradores

Rua Dr Fernão Ornelas. **☎** *291-22 25 84.* ◻ *Mon – Sat.* ◐ *public hols.*

The Mercado dos Lavradores is where flower growers, basket weavers, farmers and fishermen from all over Madeira bring their products to market. The covered market building, situated on three floors around an open courtyard, is full of the colour and bustle of island life. Stall-holders offer slices of mango or custard fruit to prove that theirs are the sweetest and best. In the basement, marble tables are draped with great slabs of tuna and black-skinned scabbard fish with huge eyes and razor-sharp teeth.

On Fridays the market spills out into the back streets of the Zona Velha (Old Town), the former fishermen's quarter and now an area of small shops

House and gardens of the Quinta do Palheiro Ferreiro

and lively pavement cafés and bars. The simple, single-storey dwellings situated at the pedestrianized eastern end of Rua Dom Carlos I, are said to date from the 15th century. The little Corpo Santo chapel was built by 16th-century fishermen in honour of their patron, St Peter, and is said to be the oldest such building in Funchal.

⚓ Fortaleza de São Tiago

Rua do Portão de São Tiago. **☎** *291-22 64 56.* **Museum** ◻ *Tue – Sun.* ◐ *public hols.* ▨

Along the seafront is the newly restored Fortaleza de São Tiago, built in 1614, with additions dating from 1767. The fortress, with its maze of passages and staircases, commands extensive views over Funchal and houses a Museum of Contemporary Art.

Quinta do Palheiro Ferreiro ❷

Palheiro Ferreiro. **☎** *291-793 044.* ▦ ◻ *9am – 12:30pm Mon – Fri.* ◐ *1 Jan, Easter, 1 May, 25 Dec.* ▨

T HE QUINTA DO PALHEIRO Ferreiro is Madeira's finest garden and a place of pilgrimage for flower-loving visitors. A French landscape architect laid out the gardens in the 18th century for the wealthy Count of Carvalhal, who built the elegant mansion (not open to visitors) overlooking the garden and the little Baroque chapel in the garden itself.

The estate was acquired in 1885 by the long-established Anglo-Madeiran Blandy family, hence its English name: Blandy's Gardens. New species were introduced from South Africa, China and Australia, resulting in a garden that combines the clipped formality of late 18th-century layout with the profusion of English-style herbaceous borders, plus the combination of tropical and temperate climate varieties.

Quite apart from its horticultural interest, the garden is a peaceful wildlife haven, full of beauty and contrast as you pass from the formality of the Ladies' Garden to the tropical wilderness of the ravine ominously signposted "Inferno" (Hell).

Fishmonger chopping tuna into huge steaks in the basement of Funchal's Mercado dos Lavradores

The contrasting façade of Nossa Senhora do Monte, created by basalt against whitewash

Monte ❸

🏠 10,000. 🚏 ℹ️ Caminho de Ferro 182, Junta da Freguesia (291-78 25 55).

MONTE HAS BEEN a favourite destination for visitors to Madeira since the late 19th century, when a rack and pinion railway was built to haul cruise liner passengers up the hillside from Funchal. Coming down they would take the famous **Monte toboggan** ride. The railway closed in 1939, but the station and a viaduct survive, now forming part of the luxuriant **Jardim do Monte** public gardens. It is a short stroll through the gardens to the church of **Nossa Senhora do Monte**, whose twin-towered façade looks down on the island's capital. The present church was built in 1818 on the site of a chapel built in 1470 by Adam Gonçalves Ferreira (Adam and his twin sister Eve were the first children to be born on Madeira).

The Virgin of Monte is Madeira's patron saint and this church is the focal point of the pilgrimage that takes place annually on 15 August (the Feast of the Assumption) when penitents climb the church's 74 steps on their knees. The object of their worship is a tiny statue of the Virgin kept in a silver tabernacle on the high altar. Devout Madeirans believe that the Virgin herself gave this statue to a Madeiran shepherd girl in the 15th century.

Left of the nave is a chapel housing a mortuary chest. This contains the remains of the last Hapsburg Emperor, Karl I, who was crowned in 1916 but deposed in 1918. He sought exile in Madeira but died of pneumonia in 1922, aged only 35.

Toboggan drivers in straw hats wait for passengers every day on the corner of Caminho do Monte, and they run (for a fee) to Livramento and on to Funchal. From the church steps, past the drivers' corner, a left turn signposted "Old Monte Gardens" leads to the entrance of the **Monte Palace Gardens**. These superb gardens, laid out in 1894, will delight children with their maze of pathways and bridges, follies, fountains, cascades and tame black swans. The gardens extend for 7 ha (17 acres) down a lushly planted valley with areas devoted to Madeiran flora, South African proteas, plants from Japan and China, azaleas, camellias and orchids.

🌿 **Monte Palace Gardens**
Caminho do Monte 174.
📞 291-78 23 39. ⬜ Mon – Sat. 🈵

One of the skilled wicker workers of Camacha constructing a table

Camacha ❹

🏠 9,000. 🚏 ℹ️ Junta da Freguesia, Urbanização dos Casais de Além (291-92 24 66).

MOST OF THE wicker products sold in Funchal are made in and around Camacha, and the sole attraction in this otherwise sleepy village is a large shop packed with everything wicker, from picture frames, bedsteads and cradles to peacock-backed armchairs. It is often possible to see weavers at work, bending the pliant stripped willow round a frame to produce a linen basket or plant-pot container. A Noah's Ark full of paired animals is displayed on the middle floor, along with a full-sailed galleon, as an advertisement of the local wicker weavers' skills.

THE MONTE TOBOGGAN

Sliding in a wicker basket mounted on wooden runners, it is possible to cover the 4-km (2-mile) descent from Monte to Funchal in 20 minutes. The trip is made by thousands every year, fascinated by the experience of travelling at speed down a public highway on a wooden sled. Ernest Hemingway once described it as "exhilarating". A cushioned seat softens the ride and passengers are in the safe hands of the toboggan drivers, who push and steer from the rear, using their rubber-soled boots as brakes. Madeiran tobogganing was invented as a form of passenger transport around 1850.

The famous Monte toboggan ride

Madeira Wine

Wicker-covered Madeira bottle

From the middle of the 16th century, ships stopping at Madeira would take on barrels of local wine, which helped sailors to avoid scurvy because of its vitamin and mineral content. It was found that the wine tasted better at the end of an equatorial voyage, and so people started sending Madeira on long voyages to be heated by the tropical sun. By the 18th century, a simpler, artificial means of heating the wine had been developed. This process, known as *estufagem*, is still used today. The Madeira is "cooked" for six months using the heat of the sun, assisted by hot water pipes. A Madeira will typically spend six months at temperatures of 40–50°C (104–122°F) before it is fortified with brandy. Today, the four main "noble" varieties of grape used to make the wine are frequently blended with other types of grape such as the red negra mole.

Making barrels for Madeira, Funchal

THE FOUR TYPES OF MADEIRA

Sercial is made from white grapes grown at about 800 m (2,600 ft). It is an amber-coloured dry wine drunk as an aperitif, with soup or as an accompaniment to fish, and is best served lightly chilled. A good-quality Sercial is aged for at least eight years.

Verdelho grapes are white, grown at 400–600 m (1,300–2,000 ft), and make a medium-dry tawny wine for drinking with meat. Sweeter than Sercial, Verdelho goes well with a slice of Madeira cake (invented by the English for just this purpose).

The barrels in the Adegas de São Francisco (see p347), where Madeira is warmed, need frequent repair as do the wooden floors that bear their huge weight.

Bual is a dark, rich and nutty wine made from white grapes grown on terraces below 400 m (1,300 ft). It is a medium-sweet wine that can be served as an alternative to port. It makes an excellent accompaniment to cheeses and dessert.

Malmsey, the most celebrated Madeira, is made from Malvasia grapes grown in sunny vineyards backed by cliffs, where the heat absorbed by the rock by day warms the grapes by night. The result is a rich dark wine drunk as an after-dinner digestive.

These casks of Verdelho are being aged after the addition of brandy to the wine. Vintage wine must spend at least 20 years in the cask and two in the bottle.

Vintage Madeira from every decade as far back as the mid-19th century is still available for sale. The oldest surviving bottle of Madeira dates from 1772.

Machico ❺

🏠 22,000. 🚉 🛈 Forte do Amparo, Rua da Nossa Senhora (291-96 22 89). 🐟 Mon–Fri (fish).

LEGEND HAS IT that Machico was named after Robert Machim, a merchant from Bristol, who eloped with the aristo-cratic Anne of Hertford and set sail for Portugal. Caught in a storm and shipwrecked on Madeira, the two lovers died from exposure and were buried. The rest of the crew repaired the boat and sailed to Lisbon, where their story inspired Prince Henry the Navigator (see p49) to send João Gonçalves Zarco (see p341) in search of this mysterious wooded island.

Machico has been Madeira's second most important town since the first settlements, when the island was divided into two captaincies: Zarco ruled the west from Funchal whilst his fellow navigator, Tristão Vaz Teixeira, ruled the east from Machico. However, Funchal's superior location and harbour soon ensured that it

developed as the capital of Madeira while Machico became a sleepy agricultural town.

The **Igreja Matriz** on Largo do Município, Machico's main square, dates from the 15th century. Above the high altar is a statue of the Virgin Mary, donated by Manuel I (see pp46–9), as were the three marble pillars used in the construction of the Gothic south por-tal. Inside, there is a fine example of Manueline-style stone masonry in the Capela de São João Baptista, whose arch shows Teixeira's coat of arms, with a phoenix rising from the flames.

Across the River Machico, on Largo dos Milagres, is the **Capela dos Milagres** (Chapel of the Miracles). The present structure dates from 1815, but it stands on the site of Madeira's first church, where Robert Machim and Anne of Hertford are supposedly buried. The earlier church of 1420 was destroyed in a flood in 1803, but the 15th-century crucifix was found floating out at sea. Machico celebrates the return of its cross with a procession every year on 8 October.

Main altar in the Capela dos Milagres, Machico

View from Ponta de São Lourenço promontory, east of Caniçal

Caniçal ❻

🏠 5,000. 🚉 🛈 Rua da Nossa Senhora (291-96 22 89).

CANIÇAL WAS ONCE the centre of Madeira's whaling in-dustry: the whaling scenes for John Huston's film version of Moby Dick (1956) were shot here. Whaling only ceased in June 1981, and since then the waters around Madeira have been declared a marine mam-mal sanctuary, where the kill-ing of whales, dolphins and seals is forbidden. Local fisher-men who once hunted whales now work with the Society for the Protection of Sea Mammals helping marine biologists understand whale migrations.

The old whaling company's office is now the **Museu da Baleia** (Whaling Museum). It shows a 45-minute video on whale hunting with commen-taries by retired fishermen.

Caniçal is still a busy fishing port, and the stony beach is used by tuna fishermen to repair their colourful boats.

🏛 Museu da Baleia
Largo Manuel Alves. 🗂 291-96 14 07 🕒 Tue–Sun. 🚫 public hols. 🎫 🛊

ENVIRONS: The easternmost tip of Madeira, the **Ponta de São Lourenço**, is characterized by dramatic wave-battered cliffs plunging 180 m (590 ft) to the Atlantic. Walkers are attracted by footpaths which meander from one clifftop to another, with wild flowers growing in sheltered hollows. The treeless landscape contrasts totally with the island's wooded interior.

On the road from Caniçal to Ponta de São Lourenço, look out for the signpost to the bay of **Prainha**, Madeira's only naturally sandy beach.

Fishing boats hauled up on the beach at Caniçal

Santana ❼

🏚 10,500. 🚌 📖 *Câmara Municipal, Sítio do Serrado (291-57 29 92).*

Sᴀɴᴛᴀɴᴀ (named after St Anne, mother of the Virgin) has more than 100 thatched triangular houses, several of which, restored and brightly painted, can be visited by the public. The hillsides above the broad valley in which Santana sits are also dotted with triangular thatched byres, where cows are tethered to stop them from wandering along narrow terrace paths and harming themselves or crops.

The valley is intensively farmed both for fruit and vegetables, and osiers, the willow branches that are the raw material for the wicker workers of Camacha *(see p348).*

Ribeiro Frio ❽

🏚 45. 🚌 *from Funchal.*

Bridge across a *levada* **on the walk from Ribeiro Frio to Balcões**

Rɪʙᴇɪʀᴏ Fʀɪᴏ is a pretty spot consisting of a couple of restaurants, a shop and a trout farm, fed by the "cold stream" after which the place is named.

Surrounding the trout farm is an attractive garden full of native trees and shrubs. This is the starting point for two of the island's best *levada* walks *(see p355).* The 12-km (7-mile) path signposted to **Portela** (on the right heading downhill past the restaurants) passes through dramatic mountain scenery but is best left to experienced walkers because of the long tunnels and steep drops in places. Far easier is

Sunrise over the mountains, seen from Pico do Arieiro

the 20-minute walk on the left (going downhill) signposted to **Balcões** (Balconies). This viewpoint gives panoramic views across the valley of the River Ametade to Penha de Águia (Eagle Rock), the sheer-sided hill that projects from Madeira's northern coast.

Pico do Arieiro ❾

🚌 *to Camacha, then taxi.* **Pousada do Pico do Arieiro** 🕻 *291-23 01 10 (reservations: 291-70 20 30).*

Fʀᴏᴍ ғᴜɴᴄʜᴀʟ it is about a 30-minute drive up the Pico do Arieiro, Madeira's third highest mountain at 1,810 m

(5,938 ft). The route leads through steep hillsides cloaked in fragrant eucalyptus and bay laurel. At around 900 m (2,950 ft), you will often meet the cloudline and pass for a few minutes through swirling mists and possibly rain, before emerging into a sunlit landscape of volcanic rocks. At the top, the view is of clouds in the valleys and dramatic mountain ridges with knife-edge peaks. Just visible on a clear day is Pico Ruivo *(see p354),* connected to Pico do Arieiro by a 10-km (6-mile) path. The Pousada do Pico do Arieiro guesthouse on the mountaintop allows walkers to see a spectacular sunrise.

Tʜᴇ Tʀɪᴀɴɢᴜʟᴀʀ Hᴏᴜsᴇs ᴏғ Sᴀɴᴛᴀɴᴀ

Simply constructed from two A-shaped timber frames, with a wood-panelled interior and thatched roof, these triangular houses are unique to Madeira. They are first mentioned in the 16th century, but most of the surviving examples are no more than 100 years old. Today their doors and windows are often painted a cheerful red, yellow or blue. In the warm year-round climate of Madeira, cooking and eating take place out of doors, and the toilets are placed well away from the house. To the inhabitants, therefore, the triangular houses serve principally as shelter from the rain and for sleeping in. The interior is deceptively spacious, with a living area downstairs and sleeping space up in the loft.

Panoramic view of the mountains from the Pico Ruivo summit

Pico Ruivo ❿

🚌 to Santana or Faial, then taxi to Achada do Teixeira, then walk.

MADEIRA'S HIGHEST mountain at 1,861 m (6,105 ft), Pico Ruivo is only accessible on foot. The easiest way to scale its heights is via a well signposted footpath which begins at the village of Achada do Teixeira and leads visitors on a 45-minute walk to the top.

Alternatively, follow the walk from the top of Pico do Arieiro *(see p351)* along one of the island's most spectacular footpaths. Awe-inspiring mountain scenery and glorious views can be enjoyed all along the 10-km (6-mile) walk. This takes two to three hours and is really only suitable for experienced, well-equipped walkers. Vertigo sufferers should not attempt the path, as it involves negotiating narrow ridges with sheer drops on either side.

Curral das Freiras ⓫

🏠 3,000. 🚌 🚹 Câmara de Lobos (291-94 34 70).

CURRAL DAS FREIRAS means "Nuns' Refuge" and the name refers to the nuns of the Santa Clara convent who fled to this idyllic spot when pirates attacked Funchal in 1566. The nuns have left now, but the village remains. Visitors first glimpse Curral das Freiras from a viewpoint known as the **Eira do Serrado**, perched some 800 m (2,625 ft) above the scattered village.

The valley is surrounded on all sides by jagged mountain peaks. Until 1959 the only access to the village was by a steep zig-zagging path, but road tunnels now make the journey much easier and allow local people to transport their produce to the capital. Television arrived in 1986.

The sweet chestnuts that grow in profusion around the village are turned into sweet chestnut bread, best eaten still warm from the oven, and *licor de castanha*, a chestnut-flavoured liqueur. Both can be sampled in local bars.

Paúl da Serra ⓬

🚌 to Canhas, then taxi.

Sheep grazing on the wide plateau of Paúl da Serra, east of Rabaçal

THE PAÚL DA SERRA (literally "high moorland") is a large, boggy plateau, 17 km (11 miles) in length and 6 km (4 miles) in width. The plain contrasts dramatically with the jagged mountains that characterize the rest of Madeira.

Electricity for the north of the island is generated here by wind turbines. Only gorse and grass grow on the thin soil, and the sponge-like volcanic substrata act as a natural reservoir for rainfall. Water filters through the rock to emerge as springs which then feed the island's *levada* system.

THE LEVADAS OF MADEIRA

Madeira possesses a unique irrigation system that enables the plentiful rainfall of the north of the island to be distributed to the dry, sunny south. Rainfall is stored in reservoirs and lakes, or channelled from natural springs, and fed into

Levada do Risco, one of many walking routes across Madeira

the network of *levadas* that ring the island. These narrow channels carry water long distances to banana groves, vineyards and market gardens. Altogether there are 2,150 km (1,335 miles) of canals, some dating back to the 1500s. Maintenance paths run alongside the *levadas*, providing a network of footpaths reaching into remote parts of the island inaccessible by road.

◁ **Terraced hillsides around the village of Curral das Freiras**

Rabaçal Walks ⑬

REACHED DOWN a single-track road from the Paúl da Serra plateau, Rabaçal is the starting point for two, equally magical, *levada* walks. One is a simple 30-minute, there-and-back stroll to the Risco waterfall, while the other is a more demanding two- to three-hour walk to the beauty spot known as Vinte e Cinco Fontes (25 Springs).

TIPS FOR WALKERS

Length: These two walks can be combined to create a circular route of 8 km (5 miles), taking around three and a half hours.
Note: The levadas can be slippery and sometimes very narrow. In places the path is only 30 cm (1 ft) wide, but the channel runs at waist height and you can hold on.

Levada da Rocha Vermelha ⑥
Wild, mountainous terrain forms the backdrop to the steep path down to the lower *levada*.

25 Fontes ⑤
A 30-minute walk brings you to a mossy, fern-hung area with a main cascade and many smaller ones.

Ribeira da Janela ④
Cross the bridge and then tackle the steep uphill climb on the left.

Levada da Rocha Vermelha

Levada Nova do Rabaçal

Levada Nova do Rabaçal

Levada das 25 Fontes

Ribeira da Janela

Levada do Risco

Levada das 25 Fontes

Levada do Risco

P

PAÚL DA SERRA

Rabaçal ①
The starting point of the walk has a car park and government rest house with picnic tables and views down the secluded valley. Follow the signposted path down to the right to meet the Levada do Risco.

Risco Waterfall ③
At this magnificent spot, a torrent of water cascades from the rocky heights down into the green depths of the Risco valley far below.

KEY

- - - Walk route

═══ Road

═══ River

─── Levada

P Parking

Levada do Risco ②
The course of the *levada*, which leads to the waterfall, is shaded by tree heathers draped with hair-like lichens.

0 metres		250
0 yards		250

Simple stone font in the attractively tiled baptistry of the Igreja Matriz in São Vicente

São Vicente ⓮

🏘 8,000. 🚌 ℹ Câmara Municipal, Vila de São Vicente (291-84 21 35).

THE AGRICULTURAL town of São Vicente has grown prosperous over the years by tempting travellers to break their journeys here as they explore Madeira's northern coast.

To see how the village looked before development began, visit the **Igreja Matriz** (originally built in the 17th century), and look at the painting on the ceiling of St Vincent blessing the town. St Vincent appears again over the elaborately carved and gilded main altar, this time blessing a ship.

Around the church, cobbled traffic-free streets are lined with boutiques, bars and shops selling sweet cakes, including the popular Madeiran speciality *bolo de mel*, the so-called "honey cake" (actually made with molasses and fruit).

São Vicente marks the starting point of the coastal road northwest to Porto Moniz, one of the island's most exhilarating drives. The road, little more than a ledge cut into the sheer cliffs, sometimes passes through tunnels, sometimes through waterfalls. The 19-km (12-mile) road took 16 years to build without the aid of machinery.

The only village along this lonely road is **Seixal**. Despite the Atlantic storms that can batter the island's northern coast, Seixal occupies a remarkably sheltered spot where vineyards cling to the hillside terraces, producing excellent wine.

Porto Moniz ⓯

🏘 4,000. 🚌 ℹ Porto, Vila Porto Moniz (291-85 25 94).

ALTHOUGH IT IS only 75 km (47 miles) from Funchal, visitors arriving in Porto Moniz feel a great sense of achievement after the long journey to this remote coastal village, on the northwest tip of Madeira.

Porto Moniz is surrounded by a patchwork pattern of tiny fields. The fields are protected by fences made from tree heather and dried bracken, a necessary precaution against the heavy, salt-laden air that blows in off the Atlantic.

Apart from its picturesque charm, the main attraction at Porto Moniz is the series of natural rock pools joined by concrete paths on the foreshore, where you can paddle or immerse yourself in sunwarmed water while being showered by spray as waves break against the nearby rocks.

Calheta ⓰

🏘 3,500. 🚌 ℹ Câmara Municipal, Vila da Calheta (291-82 25 39).

Bananas, a prolific crop in Calheta

CALHETA STANDS among flourishing vineyards and banana plantations. It is also at the centre of what little sugar-cane production survives on Madeira, and the sweet smell of cane syrup being extracted and turned into rum hangs around the village from the **factory** (visitors are welcome; the best time is March to April).

The **Igreja Matriz** looks unpromisingly modern but it dates from 1430 and contains a large ebony and silver tabernacle donated by Manuel I *(see pp46–7)*. There is also a fine wooden ceiling.

🔔 **Factory**
Vila da Calheta. 📞 291-82 22 64.
🔲 daily.

ENVIRONS: About 2 km (1 mile) east of Calheta, at **Loreto**, the 15th-century chapel has a Manueline south portal and geometrically patterned ceiling. Outside Estreito da Calheta, 3 km (2 miles) northwest of Calheta, is **Lombo dos Reis**. Here the Capela dos Reis Magos (Chapel of the Three Kings) has a lively 16th-century Flemish altar carving of the *Adoration of the Magi*.

The warm, natural rock pools at Porto Moniz

Part of Porto Santo's splendid sandy beach

Ribeira Brava ⑰

🏠 *13,500.* 🚌 **ℹ** *Forte de São
Bento (291-95 16 75).* 🛒 *daily.*

R IBEIRA BRAVA is a small,
attractive resort town,
situated on the sunny
south coast of Madeira.
It has a pebble beach
and a fishing harbour,
which is reached
through a tunnel to the
east of the main town.

Overlooking the
principal square, **São
Bento** remains one
of the most unspoiled
churches on Madeira.
Despite restoration
and reconstruction,   **São Bento's clock**
several of its 16th-   **tower, Ribeira Brava**
century features are still intact.
These include a stone-carved
font and ornate pulpit decorated with wild beasts such as
wolves, the Flemish painting of
the *Nativity* in the side chapel,
and the wooden statue of the
Virgin over the main altar. The
church's clock tower has a
beautifully tiled roof.

This is one of Madeira's main
centres for catching scabbard
fish *(peixe espada)*, which
feature on every Madeiran
menu. Long lines are baited
with octopus to catch these
unusual fish that dwell
at depths of 800 m
(2,600 ft). The fisher-
men live in single-
storey dwellings
along the harbour
front, and their tiny
chapel dates from
the 15th century, but
was rebuilt in 1723.
The chapel is dedi-
cated to St Nicholas,
the patron saint of
seafarers, and is de-
corated with scenes
from the saint's life,
as well as vivid portrayals of
drownings and shipwrecks.

ENVIRONS: The second highest
sea cliff in Europe is **Cabo
Girão**, located 10 km (6 miles)
west of Câmara de Lobos. It
peaks at a dramatic 589 m
(1,932 ft) above sea level.

Câmara de Lobos ⑱

🏠 *15,000.* 🚌 **ℹ** *Câmara Municipal,
Largo da República (291-94 34 70).*
🛒 *Mon–Sat.*

V ISITORS TO this pretty fishing
village are not allowed to
forget that it was several times
painted by Winston Churchill,
who often visited Madeira in
the 1950s. Bars and restaurants
are named in his honour and
a plaque marks the spot on the
main road, east of the harbour,
where the great statesman set
up his easels. The town has
not changed greatly since then.

Porto Santo ⑲

🏠 *5,000.* ✈ 🚢 **ℹ** *Avenida
Henrique Vieira de Castro, Vila Baleira
(291-98 23 61).* 🛒 *Mon–Sat, Sun am.*

P ORTO SANTO, the island that
lies 37 km (23 miles) to the
northeast of Madeira, is glimp-
sed by visitors as they fly in to
Madeira's airport. A rough sea
journey by ferry leaves from
Madeira's harbour in Funchal
for Porto de Abrigo, near Vila
Baleira, Porto Santo's capital.
You can also fly to the island
by helicopter or scheduled
TAP (Air Portugal) flight.

Madeirans like to visit their
sister island for the one thing
that their own island lacks:
a sandy beach that runs for
9 km (6 miles) along the entire
south coast of the island. The
beach and the surrounding
seas are ideal for all sorts of
water sports, from windsurfing
and snorkelling to yachting
and deep-sea diving.

The one historic site of
note on the island is the **Casa
de Colombo** (house of Christopher Columbus), located
behind Nossa Senhora da
Piedade in Vila Baleira. The
house is built from rough stone
and was restored for the 500th
anniversary of his landing in
America. It contains an account
of what is known of Columbus's life, along with maps,
paintings and engravings.

🏛 **Casa de Colombo**
Travessa da Sacristia, Vila Baleira.
ℂ *291-98 34 05.* 🕐 *Tue–Fri,
Sat & Sun am.*

CHRISTOPHER COLUMBUS ON PORTO SANTO

Historical records vouch for the fact
that Christopher Columbus came to
Madeira in 1478, probably as an
agent for sugar merchants in his
native Italian town of Genoa.
He went to Porto Santo to meet
Bartolomeu Perestrelo, also
from Genoa and the island's
governor. There he met Filipa
Moniz, Perestrelo's daughter.
The two were married in 1479,
but Filipa died soon after
giving birth to their son. Nothing
else is known about Columbus's
visit to the island, though this
has not prevented local people
from identifying his house.

**Christopher Colombus by
Ridolfo Ghirlandaio (1483–1561)**

THE AZORES

F AR OUT IN THE ATLANTIC, *1,300 km (800 miles) west of Portugal's mainland, the nine islands of the Azores are known for their spectacular volcanic scenery, abundant flora and peaceful way of life. Once wild and remote, they are now a popular destination for travellers who enjoy walking, sailing and getting away from it all.*

Santa Maria was the first island discovered by the Portuguese in 1427. The archipelago was named after the buzzards the early explorers saw flying overhead and mistook for goshawks *(açores)*. The islands were settled during the 15th and 16th centuries by colonists from Portugal and Flanders who introduced cattle, maize and vines.

Império chapel on Pico

The Azores have profited from their far-flung position in the Atlantic. Between 1580 and 1640, when Portugal came under Spanish rule *(see pp50–51)*, the ports of Angra do Heroísmo on Terceira and Ponta Delgada on São Miguel prospered from the trade with the New World. In the 19th century the islands were a regular port of call for American whaling ships. During the 20th century they have benefited from their use as stations for transatlantic cable companies, meteorological observatories and military air bases.

Today the majority of islanders are involved in either dairy farming or tuna fishing, and close links are maintained with both mainland Portugal and the sizeable communities of emigrant Azoreans in the United States and Canada. Many emigrants return to their native island for the traditional annual festivals, such as the *festas* of the Holy Spirit, celebrated in the colourful *impérios*. With few beaches, a capricious, often wet climate and no large-scale resorts, the Azores have escaped mass tourism. Most travellers come here to explore the green mountains embroidered with blue hydrangeas and relax in quiet ports adorned with cobbled streets and elegant Baroque churches. Once a brave new world of pioneer communities, the Azores are now an autonomous region of Portugal and an exotic corner of the European Union, where life remains refreshingly civil and unhurried.

Small fishing boats on the quayside at Lajes on the southern coast of Pico

◁ Terceira's walled pastures sloping down to the sea with the two small Ilhéus das Cabras in the distance

Exploring the Azores

THE ISLANDS OF THE AZORES are spread 650 km (400 miles) apart and fall into three distinct groups. In the east lie Santa Maria and São Miguel, the largest island and home to the regional capital, Ponta Delgada. The main towns in the central group of five islands are Horta on Faial, a popular stop-over port for boats crossing the Atlantic, and Angra do Heroísmo on Terceira, a charming, historic town. From here visitors can travel to the other islands of São Jorge, Graciosa and Pico, the last dominated by a towering volcanic peak 2,350 m (7,700 ft) high. Further west lie the remote, weather-beaten islands of Flores and Corvo.

Transatlantic sailing boat moored in Faial's fine marina at Horta

⑨ CORVO
● Vila Nova do Corvo

⑧ FLORES
R1-2
● Santa Cruz das Flores
R1-2
● Lajes

Santa Cruz da Graciosa

R1-1 ● Praia
④ GRACIOSA

SIGHTS AT A GLANCE

Corvo ⑨
Faial ⑦
Flores ⑧
Graciosa ④
Pico ⑥
Santa Maria ②
São Jorge ⑤
São Miguel pp362–3 ①
Terceira ③

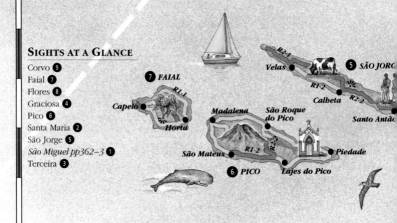

⑦ FAIAL
R1-1
Capelo ●
● Horta

Velas ●
R2-1
⑤ SÃO JORGE
R1-2
Calbeta ●
R2-2
Santo Antão

Madalena ●
São Roque do Pico ●
São Mateus ● R1-2
R2-1
● Piedade
⑥ PICO
Lajes do Pico ●

Walking among Pico's black volcanic lava rock

0 kilometres   25

0 miles   10

KEY

▬ Road

▬ Scenic route

❋ Viewpoint

SEE ALSO

• *Where to Stay* pp400–1

• *Where to Eat* p423

GETTING AROUND

São Miguel, Faial and Terceira have international airports and the local airline, SATA, has internal flights between all the islands. Ferry services connect the five central islands several times a week in summer. There is a daily summer service between Flores and Corvo but no service between Santa Maria and São Miguel. All ferry services are subject to the weather. Bus services on the islands are designed for the locals and therefore not very useful for tourists. Car hire is more convenient and available on all islands except Corvo. *(See also p447.)*

③ TERCEIRA

Biscoitos

Praia da Vitória

Santa Bárbara

São Mateus

Angra do Heroísmo

Angra do Heroísmo, capital of Terceira

R1-1

Ribeira Grande

Porto Formoso

R1-1

Sete Cidades

R6-2

Furnas

Lagoa

Ponta Delgada

Vila Franca do Campo

Povoação

R1-1

① SÃO MIGUEL

Ponta Delgada's elegant waterfront, São Miguel

② SANTA MARIA

Anjos

Santa Bárbara

Vila do Porto

São Miguel ●

WITH ITS HISTORIC maritime capital, rich green fields and dramatic volcanic scenery, this *ilha verde* (green island) provides a rewarding introduction to the Azores. The largest and most populated of the archipelago's nine main islands, São Miguel is 65 km (40 miles) long and was originally two separate islands. The capital, Ponta Delgada, is a good base from which to make day tours of the rugged coast or visit the volcanic crater lakes and steaming thermal springs in the interior of the island.

The 18th-century city gates leading onto Ponta Delgada's central square

Ponta Delgada

Lined with many impressive churches, convents and trim white houses, the cobbled streets of the Azorean capital recall the wealthy days when the port was a crucial staging post between Europe and the New World *(see pp48–9)*. Its hub is the arcaded Praça de Gonçalo Velho Cabral, named after the first governor of the island in 1444, which looks out onto the seafront. It is dominated by three imposing arches, dating from 1783, that once marked the entrance to the city. To the north, in Largo da Matriz, stands the parish church of **São Sebastião**. Founded in 1533 it has a graceful Manueline portal intricately carved in limestone. The sacristy is decorated with *azulejo* panels and beautiful 17th-century furniture made of jacaranda wood from Brazil.

A short walk west lies the Praça 5 de Outubro, a shaded, tree-lined square overlooked by the **Forte de São Brás**. This Renaissance fortress, built on a spur overlooking the sea, was greatly restored in the 19th century. Also on the square, the immense **Convento da Esperança** becomes the focus of intense festivities when the city celebrates the festival of Santo Cristo dos Milagres on the fifth Sunday after Easter. A statue of Christ, wearing a red robe decorated with sumptuous diamond and gold ornaments, leads the procession through the streets. The statue can be seen in the lower church along with other religious treasures, including reliquaries, monstrances and precious jewels. Colourful tiles, dating from the 18th century, by António de Oliveira Bernardes *(see p22)* decorate the choir.

The principal museum in the Azores, the **Museu Carlos Machado**, occupies the former monastery of Santo André. Its exhibits reflect the fishing and farming industries that have ruled life on the islands. Of particular interest are the paintings by Domingos Rebelo (1891–1975) showing scenes of Azorean life. The natural history wing is packed with an encyclopedic array of stuffed animals, varnished fish, skeletons and a large relief model of the island.

🏛 **Museu Carlos Machado**
Rua João Moreira. **[** 296-283 814.
◯ Tue–Sun. **●** public hols. **▨**

West of the Island

The northwest of São Miguel is punctured by a giant volcanic crater, **Caldeira das Sete Cidades**, with a 12-km (7-mile) circumference. In places its sheer walls drop like green curtains for 300 m (1,000 ft). When not obscured by cloud, the crater is best seen from the viewpoint of **Vista do Rei** from where a walk leads west around its rim. The crater floor contains the small village of Sete Cidades and three dark green lakes separated by a thin strip of land. The crater is believed to have been formed in the 1440s when an eruption destroyed the volcanic peak that had formed the western part of the island. In contrast to the lush vegetation that covers the crater now, the first settlers described the area as a burnt-out shell.

The main town on the north coast, **Ribeira Grande** has a small **Casa da Cultura** (cultural centre) housed in the restored 17th-century Solar de São Vicente. *Azulejos* from the 16th to 20th century are on display and in other rooms the crafts and rural lifestyle of the islanders are recorded, including a period barber's shop rescued from Ponta Delgada.

🏛 **Casa da Cultura**
Rua São Vicente Ferreira 10, Ribeira Grande. **[** 296-47 21 18. **◯** Mon–Fri. **●** public hols. **Donation.** **▯**

KEY

▭▭	Main road
▭▭	Other road
�►ᄠ	Viewpoint

Turquoise waters of the crater lake, Lagoa do Fogo

VISITORS' CHECKLIST

125,000. 3 km (2 miles) W of Ponta Delgada. Avenida Infante Dom Henrique, Ponta Delgada. Avenida Infante Dom Henrique, Ponta Delgada (296-28 57 43). 5th Sun after Easter: Santo Cristo dos Milagres (Ponta Delgada); Festas do Espírito Santo (see p366); 29 Jun: São Pedro Cavalcade (Ribeira Grande).

East of the Island

The **Lagoa do Fogo**, "Lake of Fire", was formed in the island's central mountains by a volcanic eruption in 1563. On sunny days its remote sandy beach is a tranquil picnic spot.

Further east, the spa resort of **Furnas** is the perfect place to admire the geothermal activity taking place beneath the surface of the Azores (see pp338–9). Scattered around the town are the **Caldeiras das Furnas** where visitors will see the steaming geysers and hot bubbling springs that provide the therapeutic mud and mineral water used for the spa's treatments. In the 18th century, Thomas Hickling, a prosperous merchant from Boston, laid out gardens in Furnas which have now grown into the glorious **Parque Terra Nostra**. Covering 12 ha (30 acres), the gardens have a rich collection of mature trees and plants, including hibiscus and hydrangeas, as well as a bizarre swimming pool with warm, mustard-coloured water.

The volcanic ground on the northern shores of the **Lagoa das Furnas**, 4 km (2 miles) south, is so hot the islanders come here to cook *cozido* (see p231). The rich meat and vegetable stew is placed underground in a huge pot, where it simmers for five hours.

The far east of São Miguel is a quiet, staggeringly beautiful area of deep valleys. Two immaculately kept viewpoints, **Miradouro do Sossego** and **Miradouro da Madrugada**, have splendid gardens – the latter is a favourite spot for watching the sunrise.

Caldeiras das Furnas

Off R1-1. 296-549 000. daily.

Pristine gardens and picnic area of the Miradouro da Madrugada

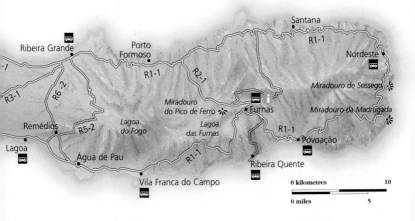

The wide bay of São Lourenço on Santa Maria

Santa Maria ❷

🏠 6,000. ✈ 3 km (2 miles) NW of Vila do Porto. ⛴ Vila do Porto. 🚌 Rua Dr Luis Bettencourt, Vila do Porto. ℹ Aeroporto de Santa Maria, Vila do Porto (296-886 355). 📅 Festas do Espírito Santo (see p366); 15 Aug: Nossa Senhora da Assunção (Vila do Porto).

Lying 55 km (34 miles) south of São Miguel, Santa Maria was the first island in the archipelago to be discovered by the Portuguese around 1427. Though only 18 km (11 miles) long, it has great scenic variety and boasts sandy beaches, tranquil countryside and the warmest climate in the Azores.

Nossa Senhora da Purificação studded with black basalt in Santo Espírito, Santa Maria

The island's capital, **Vila do Porto**, is on the south coast and consists of a long main street that runs down to a small harbour. The west of the island is a dry, flat plateau with a vast airstrip built in World War II. To the north lies the fishing town of **Anjos**, where a statue commemorates a visit made by Christopher Columbus in 1493 on his return from discovering the New World. Next to it, the small, whitewashed chapel of **Mãe de Deus** is the oldest in the Azores.

The highest point of Santa Maria is the central **Pico Alto**, 590 m (1,935 ft) above sea level, which on a clear day offers fine views over the green and hilly east side of the island. Towards the east coast, the village of **Santo Espírito** is worth visiting for the white Baroque façade of its church of Nossa Senhora da Purificação adorned with black lava decoration, while the vine-covered half-crater of **Baía de São Lourenço**, north of here, is a delightful summer beach resort.

Terceira ❸

🏠 60,000. ✈ 3 km (2 miles) NW of Praia da Vitória. ⛴ Angra Alvaro Martins Homem. 🚌 Avenida 1º de Maio, Angra do Heroísmo. ℹ Rua Direita 72, Angra do Heroísmo (295-213 393). 📅 Festas do Espírito Santo (see p366); last 2 weeks in Jun: Festas de São João.

Terceira, meaning "third" in Portuguese, is so named because it was the third island to be discovered, in 1427. It is the most developed of the five central islands – a result in part of the large American-run airbase that has been operating at Lajes since World War II. Terceira is famous for its unusual form of bull-running, known as the *tourada à corda* (bullfight with a rope), which takes place from spring to autumn. A bull is let loose in the street and taunted while tied to a rope held tight by teams of men. It is also renowned for the brightly painted chapels devoted to the cult of the Holy Spirit *(see p366)*. Terceira's interior is predominantly green pastureland, while the coast has barren areas of black lava.

Taunting a bull with umbrellas during a *tourada à corda*, Terceira

Angra do Heroísmo

This attractive and historic large town was declared a UNESCO World Heritage site in 1983, in recognition of the strategic role the port has played in the Atlantic. For over three centuries the town was a stopover point on the routes between Europe, America and Africa. It was late in 1499 that Vasco da Gama *(see p108)* buried his brother Paulo after their pioneering journey to India, and in the early 17th century its harbour glittered with Spanish fleets returning laden with treasure

The 16th-century Sé (cathedral) at the centre of Terceira's capital, Angra do Heroísmo

from the Americas. Maria II gave the town its name for the bravery *(heroísmo)* it demonstrated during the struggles for Liberalism in the early 19th century *(see pp54–5)*. Despite the severe damage caused by an earthquake in 1980, the city's wealthy past is reflected in the pretty streets lined with monumental churches and balconied houses.

The most spectacular view of the harbour is from **Monte Brasil**, a volcanic crater on the western side of the bay. Beside this popular picnic spot stands the fort, **Castelo de São João Baptista**, built during Spain's annexation of Portugal *(see pp50–51)* as a treasure store, and still in military use. A second rewarding viewpoint is from the **Alto da Memória** at the south end of Rua São João de Deus, from where the twin towers of the 16th-century **Sé** (restored after a fire in 1983) are easily seen. A path leads down into the **Jardim Municipal**, the city's restful public gardens. These once formed part of the 15th-century Convento de São Francisco which now houses the **Museu de Angra do Heroísmo**. The museum's exhibits reflect the history of the Azores and the city and include armour, maps, paintings and sculptures.

Wooden John the Baptist, Museu de Angra

🏛 **Museu de Angra do Heroísmo**
Ladeira de São Francisco. **[** 295-21 31 47. **○** Tue–Sun (Sat & Sun pm only). **&**

Around the Island
Terceira is a large, oval-shaped island with a gentle green interior of forested hills and farmland. Its centre bears witness to its volcanic origins: the **Caldeira de Guilherme Moniz** is an eroded crater 3 km (2 miles) wide, the largest in the Azores. Nearby, the **Algar do Carvão** is a dramatic volcanic blast-hole, thick with dripping moss where visitors can tour an enormous subterranean cave. West of here, the **Furnas do Enxofre** are hot steaming geysers where the heavy sulphur vapours crystallize into brightly coloured formations.

Two viewpoints overlooking the island can be reached by car: in the west, a road bordered with blue hydrangeas winds up through the **Serra de Santa Bárbara** to a vast lonely crater at 1,022 m (3,353 ft), while the eastern **Serra do Cume**, at 545 m (1,788 ft), overlooks the airport and **Praia da Vitória**. This port has a large bay with a sandy beach. Its name pays tribute to a famous victory in 1581 when the Spanish attempted to seize the island at Baía da Salga, 10 km (6 miles) south, and were thwarted by the release of a herd of cattle onto the shore.

On the north coast, **Biscoitos** (which means biscuits) takes its name from the rubble of biscuit-like lava spread along the shore. Exhilarating swimming pools, popular in the summer, have been created amongst the rocks. The area is also known for its wine, and the land is covered in a chessboard of stone-walled pens *(curraletas)* built to shelter vines. The friendly **Museu do Vinho** explains the simple production methods used to produce the rich *verdelho* wine that was once exported to the Russian court, and provides an opportunity to taste and purchase today's vintages.

🏛 **Algar do Carvão**
Off R5-2. **[** 295-21 29 92. **○** 3–5pm daily (Oct–Mar: on request). **&**

🏛 **Museu do Vinho**
Canada do Caldeiro, Biscoitos. **[** 295-908404. **○** daily. **●** 1 Jan, 25 Dec.

Patchwork of stone-walled fields in the northeast of Terceira, near Praia da Vitória

The Holy Spirit Festivals

FESTIVALS ARE A VIBRANT feature of life in the Azores and have helped foster the deep sense of community that is a hallmark of the islands' culture. Emigrants and relatives from North America and mainland Portugal often return to their native island to celebrate the most popular *festas*.

The islands' most traditional festivals are associated with the Holy Spirit *(Festas do Espírito Santo)*. Brought to the Azores by the first Portuguese settlers, who called upon the Holy Spirit to

A girl wearing the emperor's crown

protect them against natural disasters, the rituals have remained almost unchanged. An "emperor", usually a child, is crowned in the parish church. With a sceptre and silver plate as insignia of the Holy Spirit, the "emperor" presides over the festivities that take place each Sunday for seven weeks after Easter. The seventh Sunday, Whit Sunday, the day of Pentecost when Christ's disciples were filled with the Holy Spirit, is the occasion of a great feast in the village.

The distribution of bread *for the Festival of the Holy Spirit originates in the donation of food to the poor introduced by saintly Queen Isabel (see p45). On the last day of celebrations, the seventh Sunday after Easter, a Holy Spirit soup is made from beef and vegetables and is handed out along with bread to everyone outside the local* império.

THE IMPÉRIOS OF THE HOLY SPIRIT

Império with Gothic windows in Terra Chã, Terceira (1954)

Flamboyantly decorated império in São Sebastião, Terceira (1918)

Simple império in Praia da Vitória, Terceira (1861)

The focus of the ceremonies is a small chapel or *império* (empire) which is used for the distribution of the Holy Spirit soup on the seventh Sunday. Here, the emperor's crown, sceptre and plate are displayed on the altar on the last day of the festivities. On Terceira, where the cult of the Holy Spirit is particularly strong, many of the 58 *impérios* are painted in bright colours every spring. Up to 500 islanders gather for a village feast accompanied by dancing, brass bands and lavish floral displays. In many places a *tourada à corda* will be held, where a bull, tied to the end of a long rope, is let loose in the street.

An emperor's crown on ceremonial display in an *império* on São Miguel

Traditional ox-drawn cart on the island of Graciosa

Graciosa ④

🏠 5,500. ✈ 2 km (1 mile) W of Santa Cruz da Graciosa. 🚢 Praia de São Mateus. 🛈 Praça Fontes Pereira de Melo, Santa Cruz (295-712 509). 🎉 Festas do Espírito Santo; Aug: Santo Cristo.

THE "GRACIOUS" ISLAND is one of the most peaceful in the Azores. Only 12 km (7 miles) long, most of its low-lying land is given over to farms and vineyards where ox-drawn carts and ploughs are still in use. The capital, **Santa Cruz da Graciosa**, on the northern coast, has a simple quayside backed by rows of stark, two-storey, whitewashed houses with wrought-iron balconies and oval windows. A small **Museu da Graciosa** recalls life on this sleepy island with a homely miscellany of toys, sea chests, kitchenware, wine presses, furniture and mementoes sent back by emigrants to North America. A building next door houses a whaling boat (see pp368–9).

The picturesque Monte da Ajuda that rises behind the town is capped by a 16th-century fortified chapel, **Nossa Senhora da Ajuda**, decorated with 18th-century tiles. Nearby, a small *vigia* (whalers' look-out) faces the sea.

In the southeast lies the island's principal sight, **Furna do Enxofre**, where visitors can descend flights of steps into the bowels of a volcanic crater. At the bottom is a huge cave with a deep, sulphurous lake and peep-holes where bubbling brews of evil grey liquid can be spied beneath the rocks. The best time to visit is late morning when the sun shines through the small cave mouth and lights the interior.

Above the cave, at **Furna Maria Encantada**, a natural tunnel through the rock leads to the edge of the crater. From here there are stunning views over the island. Treatments using the island's geothermal waters are available at the coastal resort of **Carapacho**, at the foot of the volcano.

🏛 Museu da Graciosa
Rua das Flores 2, Santa Cruz. 📞 295-712 429. 🕐 daily (Oct–Mar: Mon–Fri). 🕐 public hols. 🎫

🏞 Furna do Enxofre
2 km (1 mile) E of Luz, follow signs to Caldeira. 🕐 Fri–Wed. 🎫

The rich Baroque interior of Santa Bárbara in Manadas, São Jorge

São Jorge ⑤

🏠 11,000. ✈ 7 km (4 miles) E of Velas. 🚢 Velas & Calheta. 🛈 Rua Conselheiro Dr José Pereira 1, Velas (295-412 440). 🎉 23 Apr: Festa de São Jorge; Festas do Espírito Santo; Jul: Semana Cultural de Velas (Velas).

SÃO JORGE IS A LONG, thin mountainous island that stretches for 56 km (35 miles) but is only 8 km (5 miles) wide. On its north coast, sheer cliffs

drop 480 m (1,575 ft) to the sea. Over the centuries these cliffs have collapsed in places, creating tongues of land known as *fajãs*. It was on these coastal promontories that the island's Flemish colonists first settled in the mid-15th century.

Today many islanders on São Jorge are engaged in the production of a delicious, cured cheese, *Queijo de São Jorge*, exported to mainland Europe. The pace of life is leisurely and most visitors come here to enjoy the walking along the paths that climb up and down between the *fajãs*. The most popular route is in the northeast of the island from Serra do Topo 10 km (6 miles) down to Fajã dos Cubres.

Most of the settlements lie along the gentler south coast, including the capital, **Velas**, and **Calheta**, where the small **Museu de São Jorge** displays objects of local history such as the ornate breads baked for the Holy Spirit festival, a honey press, agricultural utensils and religious sculptures. West of Calheta, in the pretty village of **Manadas**, the 18th-century church of **Santa Bárbara** has an atmospheric carved and painted interior. In **Urzelina**, 2 km (1 mile) further west, the tower of a church buried by lava in 1808 protrudes defiantly from the ground. In the west of the island there is a pleasant forested picnic area at **Sete Fontes**, and on a clear day the nearby summit of **Pico da Velha** offers superb views of the central Azorean islands.

🏛 Museu de São Jorge
Rua José Azevedo da Cunha, Calheta. 📞 295-416 323. 🕐 Mon–Fri. 🕐 public hols.

Dramatic cliffs along the north coast of São Jorge

Pico ⑥

🏠 15,500. ✈ 8 km (5 miles) E of Madalena. ⚓ Madalena. 🚌 Avenida Machado Serpa, Madalena. 🛈 Rua Conselheiro Terra Pinheiro, Madalena (292- 62 35 24). 🎪 Festas do Espírito Santo (see p366); 22 Jul: Santa Maria Madalena; Aug: Festa dos Baleeiros.

THE FULL MAJESTY of Pico, the highest mountain in Portugal, becomes apparent when it is seen from the neighbouring central islands.

Rustic house and well on Pico made from black lava rocks

Only then does one realize how gracefully this volcanic peak soars out of the Atlantic, shooting up 2,350 m (7,700 ft) to form the summit of the greatest mountain range in the world, the Mid-Atlantic Ridge (see pp338–9).

The island's capital, **Madalena**, is a relaxed port that lies opposite Faial's capital, Horta. A regular ferry service crosses the 7 km (4 miles) between the two islands, making a day trip feasible. The entrance to the harbour is guarded by two rocks, Em Pé (standing) and Deitado (lying down) where colonies of birds have made their home.

Many people come to Pico to climb its eponymous peak, which in winter is often snow-capped and at other times can be wrapped in cloud. It is a strenuous climb, best done in

The summit of Pico's volcano

the company of a guide, and permission is required in advance. For further details contact the tourist office.

The other main draw to Pico in summer is whale watching. From **Lajes do Pico** groups are taken out in small boats for three-hour trips organized by the **Espaço Talassa**. They are guided by radio messages

In Pursuit of the Whale

EVERY SUMMER the waters around the Azores are visited by a great variety of whales and dolphins. Until 1984 whaling was a traditional part of Azorean life – in the 19th century American whaling vessels frequently called here to pick up crew for their expeditions, and from the 1870s the Azoreans took up large-scale hunting in their own waters. Flags were waved from clifftop *vigias* (lookouts) giving coded directions so that other villagers would not get to the prize first.

Since whaling was banned in the 1980s, the Azoreans have applied their knowledge gained from hunting to whale watching and conservation.

Scrimshaws are carvings made on the teeth and bones of whales and often depict whaling scenes. This fine example from the Museu do Scrimshau on Faial (see p370) shows the long, narrow boats called canoas that could hold up to 14 men.

Whale watching today takes place in small boats that allow fast and safe access to the whales. As well as trips out to sea, the whales can be observed from the vigias. These land-based towers afford spectacular views of the whales in their natural habitat. Expeditions run from Pico and Faial (see p370).

from men who scan the sea for a fluke (tail) from the former *vigias* (lookouts). The history of Azorean whaling is recalled at the **Museu dos Baleeiros**, also in Lajes, where boats, tackle and whalebone artefacts are displayed. The whales were processed at an immense factory on the north side of the island at São Roque do Pico. Closed down in 1981, the **Museu da Indústria da Baleeira** has been preserved as a piece of industrial heritage, retaining the boilers where the blubber was turned into oil.

A coastal road encircles Pico, offering a slow but rewarding drive that reveals the charm of this undeveloped island. Minor eruptions in previous centuries have covered parts of its landscape with black mole-hills of lava that the islanders christened *mistérios* (mysteries). The black lava has been used to build houses and grids of stone walls that enclose fields or shelter vines.

In some places, notably around **Cachorro** on the north coast, the eroded lava has formed curious arches in the sea.

Pico's famous *Verdelho* wine, which is similar to the one made in Madeira *(see p349)*, was once regularly exported to mainland Europe. In recent years there has been a revival of viticulture on the island and the production of new reds and whites – such as the much acclaimed *Terras da Lava* – now means visitors have a

refined alternative to the ubiquitous *vinho de cheiro* (wine of smell) traditionally drunk by the Azoreans.

Espaço Talassa
Rua do Saco, Lajes. 292-67 26 10.
daily.
Museu dos Baleeiros
Rua dos Baleeiros, Lajes. 292-67 22 76. Tue–Sun. public hols.
Museu da Indústria da Baleeira
São Roque do Pico. 292-64 20 96.
daily, Sat & Sun am. public hols.

West coast of Pico with Faial in the distance

MARINE LIFE IN THE AZORES

Some 20 species of cetaceans can be found in the waters of the Azores. These warm-blooded animals follow the warm currents of the Gulf Stream to feed in the region's abundant, unpolluted waters. Schools of playful and gregarious dolphins are often seen scything through the waves at incredible speeds, but the most impressive sights are sperm whales. These large, sociable animals dive to great depths for giant squid and live in family groups called pods. Like all whales and dolphins they must come to the surface to breathe and this is when whale-watching expeditions make their sightings.

Atlantic spotted dolphins, fast and graceful swimmers

Sperm whales
are huge, tear-shaped creatures,
the largest of the toothed whales. They can be seen breaching
(diving out of the water), spy hopping (raising their head
to have a look around) and socializing by rubbing bodies.

Pilot whales *belong to*
the dolphin family and are recog-
nizable from their strong blow of
up to 1 m (3 ft).

Risso's dolphins *have a*
squat head and light grey
colouring. Older ones are often
crisscrossed with white scars.

Bottlenose dolphins
are the best known. These playful
animals love to ride the waves at
the bow of a moving vessel.

Loggerhead
turtles, *born on Florida's*
beaches, are frequent visitors
to the warm Azorean waters.

Transatlantic yachts moored in the marina at Horta, Faial, with the pointed summit of Pico in the distance

Faial ⑦

🏙 16,000. ✈ 10 km (6 miles) SW of Horta. ⛴ Horta. 🚌 Rua Vasco da Gama, Horta. 🛈 Rua Vasco da Gama, Horta (292-292 237). 🎭 Festas do Espírito Santo (see p366); 1st–2nd Sun in Aug: Semana do Mar (Horta). 🌐 www.drtacores.pt

FAIAL WAS SETTLED by Flemish farmers in the 15th century and prospered with the development of Horta harbour as a stopover for ships and – more recently – flying boats crossing the Atlantic. Today it is a fertile island with an international atmosphere and a mild climate, famous as a yachting destination and for the endless rows of colourful hydrangeas that bloom in June and July.

Horta

Stretching around a wide bay, Faial's capital has been a convenient anchorage for caravels, clippers and sea planes over the centuries. Captain Cook commented on Horta's fine houses and gardens when he called here in 1775. Today, visiting crews crossing between the Caribbean and Mediterranean paint a calling card on the quayside and celebrate their safe passage in **Peter's Café Sport**. In the upstairs rooms of the café, an engrossing **Museu do Scrimshaw** exhibits engraved whales' bones and teeth dating back to 1884 (see p368).

In the **Museu da Horta** displays of antique furniture, portraits, nautical memorabilia and nostalgic photographs of the island's port are upstaged by miniature sculptures of liners and scenes of daily life, painstakingly carved from the white pith of fig trees. These virtuoso examples of a traditional island craft are by the Faial-born Euclides Silveira da Rosa (1910–79).

Ship's calling card on the quayside in Horta, Faial

Excursions for dolphin- and whale-watching (see pp368–9) in the waters around the island are organized by the **Espaço Talassa** company.

🏛 **Museu do Scrimshaw**
Peter's Café Sport, Rua T. Valadim 9.
📞 292-292 327. ⏲ daily. 📷
🏛 **Museu da Horta** Palácio do Colégio, Largo Duque A. de Bolama.
📞 292-293 384. ⏲ Sat & Sun pm.
⬤ 1 Jan, Easter, 1 May, 25 Dec. 📷
⚓ **Espaço Talassa**
📞 292-292 067. ⏲ Apr–Oct. 📷

Barren ash-covered volcanic landscape at Capelinhos, the westernmost point of Faial

Around the Island

Two viewpoints overlook Horta – to its south rises the volcanic peak of **Monte da Guia**, while the northern **Miradouro da Espalamaca** is guarded by a huge statue of Nossa Senhora da Conceição.

If the cloud cover permits, it is well worth driving 15 km (9 miles) to see Faial's central **Caldeira do Cabeço Gordo** – a vast green crater 2 km (1 mile) wide and 400 m (1,300 ft) deep. The path winding around its rim takes about two hours to walk and has magnificent views.

Faial's other spectacular natural sight is the **Vulcão dos Capelinhos** in the far west of the island. A volcano erupted here in 1957–8, smothering a lighthouse which can now be seen buried in ash. Around it lies a scorched and barren landscape that has, not surprisingly, been used as the location for a German post-nuclear holocaust film. The story of the eruption is told in the nearby **Museu dos Capelinhos** where photographs and maps trace the area's geological activity, showing how the black land is gradually coming back to life. Also shown are the lava formations created in the eruption.

🏛 **Museu dos Capelinhos**
Canto do Capelo. 📞 292-945 165.
⏲ Tue–Sun. ⬤ 1 Jan, 24, 25 & 31 Dec.

Flores ❽

🚶 2,000. ✈ 1 km (half a mile) N of Santa Cruz. ⚓ Lajes. 🚌 Centro de Saúde, Santa Cruz. 🛈 Rua Dr Almas da Silveira, Santa Cruz (292-592 369). 🎭 Festas do Espírito Santo (see p366); 24–26 Jun: Festas de São João; 19–22 Jul: Festa do Emigrante (Lajes).

OFTEN CUT OFF by stormy weather, the island of "Flowers" is a romantic outpost that was not permanently settled until the 16th century. A notorious hideout for pirates waiting to raid the treasure-laden Spanish galleons on their return to Europe, Flores was the scene of an epic battle in 1591 between the ship of the English commander Sir Richard Grenville and a fleet of Spanish ships. The battle was immortalized in a poem by Alfred Tennyson, *The Revenge* (the name of Grenville's ship).

This westernmost island of the Azores is 17 km (10 miles) long and extremely mountainous. Its name derives from the abundance of flowers growing in its ravines, and the prospect of wilderness draws adventurous walkers here during the summer. The capital, **Santa Cruz**, is enlivened by the enthusiastically run **Museu das Flores**, housed in the former Franciscan convent. Its displays include shipwreck finds, Azorean pottery, furniture and agricultural tools, as well as fishing rods and a guitar made from whalebone. The convent church of **São Boaventura**, erected in 1641, has a beautiful carved cedarwood chancel.

Hydrangeas growing in the mountains of Flores

The southern half of the island is the most scenic. The deep, verdant valleys are punctuated with dramatic peaks and volcanic crater lakes and caves. Yams and sweet potatoes grow in the fertile soil. The tranquil **Lagoa Funda** (Deep Lake), 25 km (15 miles) southwest of Santa Cruz, is a large crater lake at the base of a mountain. Visible from the main road just west of the lake, are the strange vertical rock formations of the **Rocha dos Bordões** formed by solidified basalt.

The winding road continues northwards over the mountains and, as the road descends towards the west coast, there are stunning views of the green valley and village of **Fajãzinha**. The resort of **Fajã Grande**, ringed by cliffs, is a popular base for walkers and impressive waterfalls plunge into the sea from the high cliffs. A short walk north from the town is the **Cascata da Ribeira Grande**, a towering jet of water that divides into smaller waterfalls before collecting in a still pool.

🏛 **Museu das Flores**
Largo da Misericórdia, Santa Cruz.
📞 292-592 159. ☐ Mon–Fri.
⬤ public hols.

Corvo ❾

🚶 370. ✈ ⚓ Vila Nova. 🚌 Rua da Matriz, Vila Nova. 🛈 Câmara Municipal, Rua J. da Bola, Vila Nova (292-596 115). 🎭 Festas do Espírito Santo (see p366); 3rd Sun in Jul: Sagrada Família.

CORVO LIES 24 km (15 miles) northeast of Flores. The smallest island in the Azores, it has just one settlement, **Vila Nova**, and is blissfully undeveloped, with only two taxis and one policeman. The entire island is the blown top of the marine volcano, Monte Gordo. An ethereal green crater, the **Lagoa do Caldeirão**, squats at its northern end. Its rim can be reached by road, after which there is a steep descent down to the crater floor 300 m (984 ft) below. In its centre, the crater is dotted with serene lakes and islands; a patchwork of stone-walled fields covers part of the slopes.

The island of Corvo seen from the rocky shore of Flores

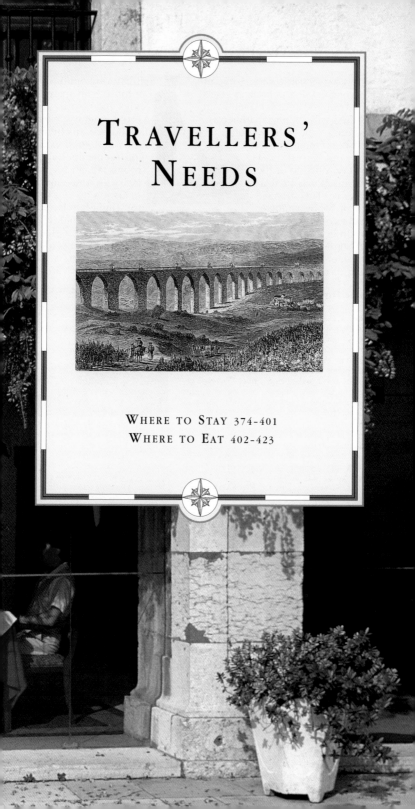

TRAVELLERS' NEEDS

WHERE TO STAY 374-401
WHERE TO EAT 402-423

WHERE TO STAY

PORTUGAL OFFERS a wide range of accommodation, from luxury hotels and restored palaces to family-run hostels and self-catering apartments. The majority of the country's hotels are in Lisbon, Oporto and on the Algarve and Estoril coasts. Elsewhere, outside of the main towns, hotels are relatively scarce. This shortage is made up for by a number of schemes offering accommodation in traditional or historic buildings often set in lovely countryside. These all require advance booking, as rooms are in short supply.

Porter at Lisbon's luxurious Lapa Palace *(see p382)*

Self-catering options include purpose-built apartments in cities and resorts, and converted country villas and farmhouses, all offering flexibility and good value. It is worth remembering that all rooms are cheaper outside high season. Accommodation in Lisbon divides between top-flight hotels and basic lodging with little choice in between. The hotels listed on pages 380–401 have been selected from every price category and represent the best value in each area.

TYPES OF HOTEL

HOTELS VARY considerably in quality, price and facilities. Not surprisingly, the highest concentration can be found in Lisbon and the Algarve, where there are hotels to suit most budgets. In towns and cities elsewhere in the country, there is usually a satisfactory range of accommodation.

There are several other types of lodging in addition to the conventional hotel, and the range of categories on offer can at first appear confusing.

An *albergaria* (inn) is usually found in towns or cities and offers lodging in pleasant, friendly surroundings, usually at a lower price than a hotel of a similar quality. The regional equivalent is an *estalagem*, which is often an old restored building of great character, set in its own grounds.

The modern *aparthotels* consist of self-contained apartments including a kitchen, combined with some hotel facilities, such as restaurants, bars and a swimming pool. This type of lodging offers great flexibility and good value, and is particularly well suited to families. *Apart-hotels* are mostly found in the tourist resort areas of the Algarve and the Estoril coasts.

POUSADAS

POUSADAS ARE country inns run by the state, of which there are around 40 throughout Portugal *(see pp378–9)*, with two on Madeira. Staying in a *pousada* is an excellent way to savour Portugal's history,

Bedroom at the York House Hotel in Lisbon, a converted 16th-century convent *(see p382)*

scenery and culture, and all *pousadas* offer very comfortable accommodation. They fall broadly into two categories. "Historical" *pousadas* are converted national monuments or other buildings such as palaces, which can sometimes have a very illustrious background. "Regional" *pousadas* are set in areas of local interest or fine scenery, such as in parks or reserves, and vary from the traditional to the very modern.

HOTEL CHAINS

AT THE TOP END of the hotel market, two small hotel chains offer the most luxurious surroundings and facilities. The grand **Hotéis Alexandre de Almeida** is the oldest chain in Portugal, founded in 1917. This group boasts the Buçaco Palace Hotel, a magnificent retreat built for the Portuguese monarchy. The **Hotéis Tivoli** have seven luxurious hotels in converted palaces in Lisbon, Sintra, Coimbra and Oporto.

Hotel Almansor in the resort of Carvoeiro, the Algarve *(see p397)*

◁ **Breakfasting beneath the wisteria at the Pousada de Palmela**

More modest accommodation is offered by **Choice Hotels**, who run two modern hotel chains: Comfort Hotels and Quality Suites. The latter offers more in terms of facilities and service, but Comfort Hotels have better facilities for disabled travellers. **Best Western** offer individually styled properties combined with quality service. **IBIS** hotels offer pleasant, simply furnished rooms with air conditioning and a standardized level of comfort throughout their hotels.

PENSÕES

P ENSÕES or guesthouses generally fall into the lowest price range and can often be excellent value, as well as offering a more relaxed environment than many hotels. At its simplest, accommodation in a *pensão* consists of a clean, basic room with a shared bathroom. At the more luxury end of the market, 4-star *pensões* can rival top hotels for comfort and service. *Pensões* may offer full-board accommodation that includes meals. A *residencial* is similar to a *Pensão*, and may offer breakfast with the room.

GRADINGS

M OST CATEGORIES of tourist accommodation are graded with a star rating, which ranges from one to five (five being the most luxurious). In theory, the stars awarded indicate the size, degree of comfort and facilities offered. The establishment has to adhere to a set of criteria to achieve and maintain its star rating. The system can be very misleading, however, with quality varying a great deal within each star rating and from one type of lodging to another. For instance, a three-star *pensão* will often be more comfortable and stylish than a one- or two-star hotel.

View from the Seteais Palace, Sintra, now a luxury hotel *(see p386)*

PRICES

I N PORTUGAL, establishments are free to decide their own prices, but all tariffs must be clearly displayed. It is sometimes possible to bargain for a better rate, especially outside the high season. As a rule, the cost of a single room is around 60 to 75 per cent of the cost of a double room. The most expensive areas to stay are the Algarve and Estoril coasts, and Madeira and the Azores, but on the mainland, prices drop outside the peak months of the summer. *Pousadas* charge two rates for low (Nov–Mar except New Year and carnival) and high (Apr–Oct) season. Between July and September is the most expensive time to stay.

NATIONAL TOURIST AGENCIES

A DVANCE BOOKING is essential for popular locations in high season, when much resort accommodation in the Algarve and around the Estoril coast is booked by tour operators.

Pousadas can be booked easily through the **Portuguese National Tourist Office** *(see pp426–7)* or **I.C.E.P.**, the Portuguese national tourism agency. Advance booking is essential for rural residences, as they often have only a few rooms. You can reserve rooms through the owners' associations listed in the directory on page 377 or through a travel agent. A deposit may be required, and generally guests must stay for at least 3 days.

Portugal has few roadside inns, so motorists should stay in towns or book rural lodging in advance. The **Direcção-Geral do Turismo** (State Tourist Office) publishes two annual guides that are available through National Tourist Offices: *Guia do Alojamento Turístico* (The Official Guide to Tourist Accommodation) and *Turismo no Espaço Rural* (The Official Guide to Tourism in the Countryside).

Reid's Hotel in Funchal, Madeira *(see p400)*

Casa do Campo, a manor house in Celorico de Basto *(see p393)*

RURAL ACCOMMODATION

THREE SCHEMES operated by *Turismo no Espaço Rural* (TER) enable visitors to stay with a family in rural Portugal. Properties in these schemes have to be registered with the State Tourist Office and will display the TER logo.

In the scheme run by the *Associação de Turismo de Habitação*, visitors may be treated as guests of the owners, often in private stately homes and manor houses. The highest concentration of properties is in the Minho, and there are also a handful in Madeira and the Azores. They vary from surroundings of antique opulence, with four-poster beds, to more modest farmhouses, and prices also vary accordingly. *Turismo Rural* (TR) offers visitors a chance to stay in rustic houses built in the local regional style, and *Agroturismo* (AT) offers rooms on family-run farms,

where guests are welcome to observe farm work. Many of these country properties are well off the beaten track, and it is important to obtain clear directions before setting out.

Each of the properties in these schemes is represented by one of three owners' associations, **ANTER**, **PRIVETUR** and **TURIHAB**, all of whom can send you information.

RESORT ACCOMMODATION

PORTUGAL'S RESORT accommodation is mainly situated along the Algarve and Estoril coasts. The most convenient way to book accommodation is to make prior arrangements through a travel agent or tour operator. Hotel prices can drop considerably outside high season, and it is often possible to get a very good deal at less popular times of the year, when there are also fewer crowds to contend with.

The tourist village or *Aldeamento Turístico* is a unique feature of resort areas such as the Algarve. These self-contained complexes offer well-furnished and fitted private apartments and usually provide a range of sports facilities, beaches, pools, restaurants, bars and sometimes a supermarket.

These complexes are rated as follows: Luxury (L), First Class (1ª) or Second Class (2ª).

Apartamentos Turísticos (Tourist Apartments) do not have the hotel-style facilities of the tourist villages but are ideal for those who require flexibility and independence. They are generally purpose-built modern buildings in resort areas that offer self-catering accommodation. These Tourist Apartments also carry one of three quality gradings.

The luxurious Marinotel at the resort of Vilamoura in the Algarve *(see p399)*

BUDGET ACCOMMODATION

YOUTH HOSTELS in Portugal *(Pousadas de Juventude)* are mainly dotted along the coast, and include two in the Azores. There are 22 in total and they are open all through the year, but advance booking is advisable in the summer. They require a valid IYHF card which can be obtained from any Youth Hostel Association. Facilities vary greatly, and may include the use of a kitchen, bar and swimming pool. Some also offer facilities for disabled travellers. Information is available from **Movijovem**, the head office of the Portuguese Youth Hostel Association.

Almost as cheap as youth hostels, and offering greater privacy, rooms *(quartos)* in private houses will invariably cost less than a *pensão*. This type of accommodation is often rented out in resorts, and lists of *quartos* are available from the local tourist office.

Dining room at Casa de Esteiró, rural lodging in Caminha *(see p393)*

CAMPING AND CARAVANNING

THERE ARE OVER 100 official campsites in Portugal in total. Most are along the coast, usually in attractive locations. The largest is at Albufeira in the Algarve, but most are small and quiet. There is a national chain of campsites run by the company **Orbitur**.

Generally you pay a rate for the tent and per person, and an extra charge for showers and parking. The Portuguese Tourist Office will provide lists of campsites and information. You will need an international camping carnet, available from motoring organizations or the **Camping and Caravanning Club** in Great Britain. This provides third party insurance cover and entitles holders to some out-of-season discounts.

Provided you show due care and consideration for the environment, it is possible to camp outside official sites in

São Miguel campsite, near Odemira in the Alentejo region

the countryside, except for the Algarve, where it is strictly forbidden to stray from the sites.

CHILDREN

CHILDREN ARE as welcome as adult visitors to Portugal and families are well catered for. Most hotels give children under eight years old a 50 per cent discount on the price of accommodation and meals.

DISABLED TRAVELLERS

HOTELS WITH facilities for the disabled are listed by the Portuguese National Tourist Office, who also produce a leaflet with useful information. Some campsites and youth hostels provide special facilities and these are listed by relevant organizations, and in a guide published by the **Secretariado Nacional de Reabilitação**.

DIRECTORY

HOTEL CHAINS

Best Western
UK 800-39 31 30.
Portugal 800-839 361.

Choice Hotels
UK 800-44 44 44.
Portugal 800-20 11 66.

Hotéis Alexandre de Almeida Rua Dr Álvaro de Castro 73, 1600-058 Lisbon.
21-799 19 35 .
FAX 21-793 04 45.

Hotéis Tivoli
Avenida da Liberdade 185, 1250 Lisbon. 21-319 89 00. FAX 21-319 89 50.

IBIS
112–114 Bath Road, Hayes, Middlesex UB3 5AL.
0181-283 45 50.
FAX 0181-564 78 94.

Enatur-Pousadas de Portugal
21-844 20 01
FAX 21-844 20 85
W www.pousadas.pt

NATIONAL TOURIST AGENCIES

Direcção-Geral do Turismo
Avenida António Augusto de Aguiar 86, 1069-021 Lisbon.
21-358 64 00.
FAX 21-358 66 66.

I.C.E.P
Avenida 5 de Outubro 101, 1070-051 Lisbon.
21-790 95 00.
FAX 21-795 09 61.
W www.portugalinsite.pt

Direcção Regional de Turismo dos Açores
Rua Ernesto Rebelo 14, 9900-112 Horta, Faial.
292-29 36 01.
FAX 292-29 20 06.
W www.dotacoves.pt

Direcção Regional de Turismo da Madeira
Avenida Arriaga 18, 9004-519 Funchal.
291-22 90 57.
FAX 291-23 21 51.
W www.madeiratourism.org

RURAL ACCOMMODATION

ANTER
Associação Nacional de Turismo no Espaço Rural, Travessa do Megué 4, 1º, 7000-631 Évora.
& FAX 266-74 45 55.

PRIVETUR
Associação Portuguesa de Turismo de Habitação, Largo das Pereiras, 4990 Ponte de Lima.
258-74 39 23.
FAX 258-74 14 93.

TURIHAB
Associação de Turismo de Habitação, Praça de República, 4990 Ponte de Lima.
258-74 16 72.
FAX 258-74 14 44.

YOUTH HOSTELS

Movijovem
Pousadas de Juventude, Avenida Duque d'Avila 137, 1050 Lisbon.
21-352 40 72.
FAX 21-352 86 21.

CAMPING AND CARAVANNING

UK: Camping and Caravanning Club
Greenfields House, Westwood Way, Coventry CV4 8JH.
02476-69 49 95.
FAX 02476-69 48 86.

Portugal: Camping and Caravanning Albufeira
Estrada de Ferreiras, 8200 Albufeira, Algarve.
289-58 95 05.
FAX 289-58 76 33.

Orbitur Interc mbio de Turismo
Rua Diogo do Couto 1, 8º, 1100 Lisbon.
21-815 48 71.
FAX 21-814 80 45.

DISABLED TRAVELLERS

Secretariado Nacional de Reabilitação
Avenida Conde de Valbom 63,1050 Lisbon.
21-793 65 17.
FAX 21-795 82 74.

The Pousadas of Portugal

Pousada symbol

THE CONCEPT of the *pousada* dates from the 1940s, when the Portuguese government decided to establish a national network of state-run country inns, offering "hospitality in keeping with the style and tradition of the region". *Pousadas* are often set in remote, scenic locations, and most have fewer than 30 rooms, so visitors can expect friendly, personalized service and a high degree of comfort. This map does not show all of Portugal's *pousadas*, just the 35 that are described in the listings on pages 380 – 401.

Pousada da Ria near the port of Aveiro has 19 bedrooms, most of which have balconies overlooking the sheltered lagoon of Ria de Aveiro (see p388).

d
Vila Ne
de Cerve

Viana
Caste

Pousada de São Pedro lies 13 km (8 miles) southeast of the picturesque town of Tomar and was originally built in the 1940s to house engineers working on the nearby Castelo de Bode dam. Overlooking the River Zêzere below the dam, the pousada reopened in 1993 after closing for extensive renovation (see p386).

Conde
a-N

P
Batalha

Pousada do Castelo, in the walled town of Óbidos, is situated in a beautifully restored palace inside the 15th-century castle keep. The pousada combines a medieval atmosphere with all modern comforts and a highly recommended restaurant (see p387).

P

ESTREMAI
AND RIBA

Queluz
P   TI
LISBON   LISI
CO
P S

Pousada de Palmela boasts an elegant interior, commanding hilltop views over the town of Palmela and the Atlantic Ocean, and an illustrious history. It is a thoughtful conversion of a monastery which was the headquarters of the Portuguese Knights of Santiago in the 13th century (see p385).

Sant
do Ca

Santa

Pousada do Infante occupies a spectacular clifftop position in the most southwesterly town of Europe, Sagres. The terrace restaurant of this purpose-built pousada has magnificent views over the Atlantic Ocean (see p399).

ALG

P

Pousada de Santa Marinha da Costa, *housed in a medieval monastery near the city of Guimarães, is one of Portugal's most impressive and historic pousadas* (see p393).

0 kilometres 50

0 miles 25

IO

ra do
no

Bragança

DOURO AND
TRÁS-OS-MONTES

Miranda
do Douro

ante

Pousada de Barão de Forrester, *named after JJ Forrester, an influential figure in 19th-century port production (see p252), enjoys a peaceful setting among vineyards in the small Douro town of Alijó (see p390).*

Almeida

ulo

Guarda

Oliveira do Hospital

Monsanto

THE BEIRAS

Pousada da Rainha Santa Isabel *dominates the town of Estremoz and the surrounding countryside. In the 13th century, the site of the pousada was home to King Dinis and his wife Queen Isabel (see p395).*

Marvão

ato

Sousel

Elvas

Pousada dos Lóios *in Évora has been converted from a 15th-century monastery. Adjacent to the remains of a Roman temple of Diana, it features an elegant dining room set in the original monastic cloisters and a Neo-Classical façade that dates from the mid-18th century (see p395).*

Alvito

Serpa

NTEJO

io Brás
e Alportel

Pousada de São Francisco *is located in the heart of the old Roman town of Beja at the centre of the sun-baked plains of the southern Alentejo. The building incorporates parts of a former Franciscan convent, dating back to the 13th century. It was opened as a pousada in 1994 (see p395).*

Choosing a Hotel

THE HOTELS in this guide have been selected across a wide price range for their good value or exceptional location. The chart gives a brief description of each hotel, highlighting factors which may influence your choice. Entries are listed by price category within the towns with colour-coded thumb tabs to indicate the regions covered on each page.

	CREDIT CARDS	RESTAURANT	GARDEN	SWIMMING POOL	NUMBER OF ROOMS

LISBON

	CREDIT CARDS	RESTAURANT	GARDEN	SWIMMING POOL	NUMBER OF ROOMS
BAIRRO ALTO: *Camões* Travessa do Poço da Cidade 38, 1° E, 1200. **Map** 7 A3. **(** *21-346 75 10*. **FAX** *21-346 40 48*. Conveniently located in the heart of the Bairro Alto, this hotel offers comfortable rooms and a friendly atmosphere. 🛏	€€				1€
BAIRRO ALTO: *Borges* Rua Garrett 108, 1200-205. **Map** 7 A4. **(** *21-346 19 51*. **FAX** *21-342 66 17*. The Borges, one of the few places to stay in the smart Chiado area, successfully combines elegant furnishings with pleasant surroundings. 🛏	€€	AE DC MC V			10
BAIXA: *Beira Minho* Praça da Figueira 6, 2° E, 1150. **Map** 7 B3. **(** *21-346 18 46*. **FAX** *21-886 78 11*. The spectacular views up towards the Bairro Alto from this simple *pensão* make up for the lack of facilities. 🛏	€				24
BAIXA: *Norte* Rua dos Douradores 159, 1100-205. **Map** 7 B3. **(** *21-887 89 41*. **FAX** *21-886 84 62*. Centrally located near Praça da Figueira, this *pensão* has few facilities and no breakfast but the rooms are neat and comfortable. Good value. 🛏 📺	€	MC V			36
BAIXA: *Alegria* Praça da Alegria 12, 1250-004. **Map** 4 F1. **(** *21-322 06 70*. **FAX** *21-347 80 70*. This small, good-value *pensão* offers clean and homely rooms and is set in a park-like square with a central fountain. 🛏	€€	AE DC MC V			3€
BAIXA: *Coimbra e Madrid* Praça da Figueira 3, 3°, 1100-240. **Map** 7 B3. **(** *21-342 17 60*. **FAX** *21-342 32 64*. A plain and simple *pensão* with rather sparse decoration. Some of the rooms, however, have magnificent views of the Castelo de São Jorge. 🛏	€€				32
BAIXA: *Duas Nações* Rua da Vitória 41, 1100-618. **Map** 7 B4. **(** *21-346 07 10*. **FAX** *21-347 02 06*. The "Two Nations" is a friendly place to stay, right in the heart of the Baixa, but the rooms overlooking Rua Augusta can be noisy. 🛏	€€	AE DC MC V			6€
BAIXA: *Florescente* Rua das Portas de S. Antão 99, 1150-266. **Map** 7 A2. **(** *21-342 66 09*. **FAX** *21-342 77 33*. For a *pensão* the rooms of the Florescente are extremely well equipped. The street is known for its many fine restaurants. No breakfast. 🛏 📺 🍽	€€	AE MC V			6€
BAIXA: *Nova Goa* Rua do Arco do Marquês de Alegrete 13, 1100. **Map** 7 C3. **(** *21-888 11 37*. **FAX** *21-886 78 11*. Just around the corner from Praça da Figueira, this *pensão* is like many in the vicinity: clean, comfortable and fairly basic. 🛏 📺	€€				42
BAIXA: *Restauradores* Praça dos Restauradores 13, 4°, 1250-187. **Map** 7 A2. **(** *21-347 56 60*. A very small and fairly basic *pensão* on the fourth floor of a building with a great location in the busy centre of the city. No breakfast. 🛏	€€				3€
BAIXA: *Suíço Atlântico* Rua da Glória 3–19, 1250-114. **Map** 7 A2. **(** *21-346 17 13*. **FAX** *21-346 90 13*. Tucked away in a small side street, this hotel has large old-fashioned rooms and public areas with stone arches and wooden beams. 🛏	€€	AE DC MC V			9€
BAIXA: *Internacional* Rua da Betesga 3, 1100-090. **Map** 7 B3. **(** *21-346 64 01*. **FAX** *21-347 86 35*. This hotel features modern and spacious rooms. Residents can relax in the hotel's large, comfortable TV lounge and small bar. 🛏 📺 🍽	€€€	AE DC MC V			5.

Price categories in euros for a standard double room per night, including breakfast: € under 35 €€ 35–60 €€€ 60–100 €€€€ 100–150 €€€€€ over 150	**RESTAURANT** The hotel has one or more restaurants open for lunch and supper, sometimes reserved for residents. **GARDEN** A garden, courtyard or large terrace for the use of hotel guests. **SWIMMING POOL** The hotel has its own indoor or outdoor pool. **CREDIT CARDS** Major credit cards accepted: *AE* American Express, *DC* Diners Club, *MC* MasterCard and *V* Visa.	CREDIT CARDS	RESTAURANT	GARDEN	SWIMMING POOL	NUMBER OF ROOMS

AIXA: *Portugal* €€€ ua João das Regras 4, 1100-294. **Map** 7 C3. **(** 21-887 75 81. **FAX** 21-886 73 43. hough plain on the outside, this hotel situated off Rua Martim Moniz is urprisingly elegant with stylish old-fashioned decor. 🛏 TV ▤	AE DC MC V				60
AIXA: *Roma* €€€ avessa da Glória 22a, 1°, 1250-118. **Map** 7 A2. **(** 21-346 05 57. **FAX** 21-346 05 57. his simple *pensão* has a fine location just off Avenida da Liberdade, con-enient for shops and sightseeing. There is a 24-hour bar service. 🛏 TV ▤	AE MC V				24
AIXA: *Metrópole* @ sales@almeidahotels.com €€€€ aça Dom Pedro IV 30, 1100-200. **Map** 7 B3. **(** 21-321 90 30. **FAX** 21-346 91 66. his turn-of-the-century building has been renovated in a style reminiscent * the 1920s. The result is a charming and elegant hotel. The famous uçaço wines *(see p210)* can also be bought here. 🛏 TV ▤	AE DC MC V				36
AIXA: *Orion Eden* @ lisbon@citadines.com €€€€ aça dos Restauradores 24, 1250-187. **Map** 7 A2. **(** 21-321 66 00. **FAX** 21-321 66 66. The modern Orion Eden offers apartments and studios, ree of which have been adapted for the disabled. 🛏 TV ▤ 🔌	AE DC MC V			●	134
AIXA: *Tivoli Lisboa* @ htlisboa@mail.telepac.pt €€€€€ v. da Liberdade 185, 1269-050. **Map** 4 F1. **(** 21-319 89 00. **FAX** 21-319 89 50. his large and elegant hotel has modern rooms and a huge two-level entral lobby. The suites are particularly spacious. 🛏 TV ▤ P	AE DC MC V	●	■	●	329
AIXA: *Avenida Palace* €€€€€ ua 1° de Dezembro 123, 1200-359. **Map** 7 B3. **(** 21-346 01 51. **FAX** 21-342 28 84. he Avenida Palace hotel, with its Neo-Classical façade and enviable central cation, offers both elegance and convenience. The luxurious interior ecoration retains many charming original details. 🛏 TV ▤ P	AE DC MC V				82
AIXA: *Tivoli Jardim* €€€€€ ua J. César Machado , 1250-135. **Map** 4 F1. **(** 21-353 99 71. **FAX** 21-355 65 66. he rooms of this smart hotel are well appointed with spacious athrooms and a mini-bar. An unusual round pool graces the garden ehind the hotel and there is use of extensive sports facilities. 🛏 TV ▤ P	AE DC MC V	●	■	●	119
AIXA: *Sofitel Lisboa* @ h1319@accor-hotels.com €€€€€ v. da Liberdade 127, 1269-038. **Map** 4 F1. **(** 21-322 83 00. **FAX** 21-322 83 10. he comfortable, modern Sofitel features an attractive piano bar called e "Molière", situated just off the lobby. 🛏 TV ▤ P 🔌	AE DC MC V	●			170
AMPO PEQUENO: *Lar do Areeiro* €€ aça Francisco Sá Carneiro 4, r/c, 1000-159. **Map** 6 E1. **(** 21-849 31 50. **X** 21-840 63 21. Conveniently located close to many shops, this *pensão* fers good-value accommodation that is clean and comfortable. 🛏	AE DC MC V				44
ASTELO: *Ninho das Águias* €€ osta do Castelo 74, 1100-179. **Map** 7 C3. **(** 21-855 40 70. he simple "Eagle's Nest" *pensão* sits below the castle walls. A stuffed agle greets visitors on the terrace that has amazing views. No breakfast.			■		16
ASTELO: *Solar do Castelo* W www.heritage.pt €€€€€ ua das Cozinhas 2, 1100-181. **Map** 7 C3. **(** 21-321 82 00. **FAX** 21-347 16 30. his luxurious hotel occupies a recently rennovated 18th-century ansion located within the castle walls. 🛏 TV ▤	AE DC MC V		■		14
NTRECAMPOS: *Quality Hotel Lisboa* €€€€ ampo Grande 7, 1700-087. **(** 21-791 76 00. **FAX** 21-797 47 61. pleasant hotel that caters for the business traveller. Features include a ealth club, gymnasium and jacuzzi. 🛏 TV ▤ P 🔌	AE DC MC V				84

		CREDIT CARDS	RESTAURANT	GARDEN	SWIMMING POOL	NUMBER OF ROOMS

Price categories in euros for a standard double room per night, including breakfast:
€ under 35
€€ 35–60
€€€ 60–100
€€€€ 100–150
€€€€€ over 150

RESTAURANT
The hotel has one or more restaurants open for lunch and supper, sometimes reserved for residents.
GARDEN
A garden, courtyard or large terrace for the use of hotel guests.
SWIMMING POOL
The hotel has its own indoor or outdoor pool.
CREDIT CARDS
Major credit cards accepted: *AE* American Express, *DC* Diners Club, *MC* MasterCard and *V* Visa.

ESTEFÂNIA: *Caravela* €€
Rua Ferreira Lapa 38, 1150-159. **Map** 6 D4. (21-353 90 11. FAX 21-357 17 51.
The rooms in this *pensão* have a slightly old-fashioned ambience. Each room has a direct outside line and there is a bar and TV room. 🛏 📺
AE DC MC V — Number of rooms: 45

GRAÇA: *Mundial* @ mundial.hot@mail.telepac.pt €€€€
Rua Dom Duarte 4, 1100-198. **Map** 7 B3. (21-884 20 00. FAX 21-884 21 08.
This hotel, located centrally off Praça da Figueira, has plain but comfortable rooms. The restaurant offers marvellous views. 🛏 📺 ▤ P &
AE DC MC V — Restaurant ● — Number of rooms: 25

GRAÇA: *Senhora do Monte* €€€€
Calçada do Monte 39, 1170-250. **Map** 7 D1. (21-886 60 02. FAX 21-887 77 83.
This *albergaria* is somewhat off the beaten track, but it is well worth the effort to find it. The rooms are fairly plain but the views, especially from the rooftop bar and garden, are simply the best in town. 🛏 📺 ▤
AE DC MC V — Number of rooms: 28

LAPA: *As Janelas Verdes* w www.heritage.pt €€€€€
R. das Janelas Verdes 47, 1200-690. **Map** 4 D3. (21-396 81 43. FAX 21-396 81 44.
A delightful *pensão* housed in an 18th-century ivy-covered mansion, once owned by the Portuguese novelist Eça de Queirós *(see p55)*. It has Neo-Classical decor and a peaceful, charming patio. 🛏 📺 ▤ P
AE DC MC V — Garden ■ — Number of rooms: 29

LAPA: *York House* €€€€€
Rua das Janelas Verdes 32, 1200-691. **Map** 4 D4. (21-396 24 35. FAX 21-397 27 93.
This enchanting *pensão* is housed in the 17th-century Convento dos Marianos. Set around a shady, plant-filled patio, the elegant rooms have wooden or terracotta floors and elegant antique furniture. 🛏 📺
AE DC MC V — Restaurant ● — Garden ■ — Number of rooms: 34

LAPA: *Lapa Palace* @ reservas@hotelapa.com €€€€€
R. do Pau da Bandeira 4, 1249-021. **Map** 3 C3. (21-394 94 94. FAX 21-395 06 65.
A gracious and charming hotel located in the city's diplomatic area. Each room in the Palace Wing is uniquely decorated in its own Portuguese style – from 18th-century Neo-Classical to Art Deco. 🛏 📺 ▤ P &
AE DC MC V — Restaurant ● — Garden ■ — Swimming Pool ● — Number of rooms: 94

RATO: *13 da Sorte* €€
Rua do Salitre 13, 1250-198. **Map** 4 F1. (21-353 18 51. FAX 21-353 18 51.
This well located *pensão* is situated close to Avenida da Liberdade and the Jardim Botanico. Breakfast is not included. 🛏 📺
MC V — Number of rooms: 22

RATO: *Amazónia* €€€
T. da Fábrica dos Pentes 12–20, 1250-106. **Map** 5 B5. (21-387 70 06. FAX 21-387 90 90.
Conveniently close to the city centre, this stylish hotel has elegant public rooms, large bedrooms and a piano bar. 🛏 📺 ▤ P &
AE DC MC V — Swimming Pool ● — Number of rooms: 19

RATO: *Lisboa Plaza* w www.heritage.pt €€€€
Travessa do Salitre 7, 1269-066. **Map** 4 F1. (21-321 82 18. FAX 21-347 16 30.
Built in 1953, and situated off Praça da Alegria, the traditional decor of this hotel is by the Portuguese interior designer, Graça Viterbo. 🛏 📺 ▤
AE DC MC V — Restaurant ● — Number of rooms: 11

RATO: *Altis* @ altishotel@hotmail.pt €€€€€
Rua Castilho 11, 1269-072. **Map** 4 F1. (21-310 60 00. FAX 21-310 62 62.
This huge hotel has every expected facility, including a rooftop grill and well-equipped health club with an indoor pool. 🛏 📺 ▤ P &
AE DC MC V — Restaurant ● — Swimming Pool ● — Number of rooms: 300

RATO: *Ritz Four Seasons* @ ritzfourseasons@.mail.telepac.pt €€€€€
Rua R. da Fonseca 88, 1099-039. **Map** 5 B5. (21-381 14 00. FAX 21-383 17 83.
The legendary Ritz is an elegant, comfortable hotel. Many of the rooms have balconies that overlook the Parque Eduardo VII. 🛏 📺 ▤ P &
AE DC MC V — Restaurant ● — Garden ■ — Number of rooms: 28

ROTUNDA: *Castilho* €€
Rua Castilho 40, 1250-068. **Map** 4 F1. (21-386 08 22. FAX 21-386 29 10.
An excellent-value *pensão* with good facilities and clean and comfortable rooms, some of which have three or four beds. 🛏 📺 &
DC MC V — Number of rooms: 25

ROTUNDA: *Jorge V* €€€
AE DC MC V — 51
Rua Mouzinho da Silveira 3, 1250-165. **Map** 5 C5. 【 21-356 25 25. ℻ 21-315 03 19.
This pleasant, comfortable hotel offers good value for the area. Roughly half the rooms have balconies, so request one when checking in. 🛏 TV ▤

ROTUNDA: *Nacional* €€€
AE DC MC V — 61
Rua Castilho 34, 1250-070. **Map** 5 B5. 【 21-355 44 33. ℻ 21-356 11 22.
This interesting glass-fronted hotel has comfortable rooms and extensive facilities. There are also two suites available. 🛏 TV ▤ 🅿 ♿

ROTUNDA: *Britânia* @ britania.hotel@heritage.pt €€€€
AE DC MC V — 30
Rua R. Sampaio 17, 1150-278. **Map** 5 C5. 【 21-315 50 16. ℻ 21-315 50 21.
Housed in a building designed by the architect Cassiano Branco in 1944, this delightful hotel has a beautiful marble lobby. 🛏 TV ▤ 🅿

ROTUNDA: *Capitol* @ sanaclassic.capitol@sanahotels.com €€€€
AE DC MC V ● — 57
Rua Eça de Queirós 24, 1050-096. **Map** 5 C4. 【 21-353 68 11. ℻ 21-352 61 65.
A comfortable hotel just off Avenida de Duque de Loulé. All the rooms are equipped with satellite television and mini bars. 🛏 TV ▤ 🅿 ♿

ROTUNDA: *Diplomático* €€€€
AE DC MC V ● — 90
Rua Castilho 74, 1250-071. **Map** 5 B5. 【 21-383 90 20. ℻ 21-386 21 55.
The Diplomático has spacious rooms with modern facilities and offers complimentary tea, coffee and chocolate in the rooms. 🛏 TV ▤ 🅿

ROTUNDA: *Rex* @ sanaclassic.rex@sanahotels.com €€€€
AE DC MC V — 68
Rua Castilho 169, 1070-050. **Map** 5 B4. 【 21-388 21 61. ℻ 21-388 75 81.
The Rex is located close to the Parque Eduardo VII. The rooftop restaurant has good views and offers a buffet breakfast. 🛏 TV ▤

ROTUNDA: *Veneza* €€€€
AE DC MC V — 36
Avenida da Liberdade 189, 1250-141. **Map** 5 C5. 【 21-352 26 18. ℻ 21-352 66 78.
The ornate staircase decorated with modern murals by Pedro Luiz-Gomes is the highlight of this spacious and comfortable hotel. 🛏 TV ▤ 🅿

ROTUNDA: *Le Méridien Lisboa* 🅦 www.lemeridien-lisbon.com €€€€€
AE DC MC V ● — 330
Rua Castilho 149, 1099-034. **Map** 5 B4. 【 21-381 87 00. ℻ 21-389 05 05.
Overlooking the Parque Eduardo VII from one of the city's seven hills, this hotel has comfortable rooms and spectacular views. 🛏 TV ▤ 🅿 ♿

SALDANHA: *Marisela* €
AE MC V — 19
Rua Filipe Folque 19, r/c, 1050-111. **Map** 5 C3. 【 21-353 32 05. ℻ 21-316 04 23.
Located in a quiet street very close to the gardens of Parque Eduardo VII, this good-value *pensão* has rather basic, but adequate, rooms. 🛏 TV

SALDANHA: *Horizonte* €€
AE DC MC V — 53
Av. António A. de Aguiar 42, 1050-017. **Map** 5 B4. 【 21-353 95 26. ℻ 21-353 84 74.
This large *pensão* offers good value for money for this area. The rooms at the front look out over Avenida da Liberdade and can be noisy. 🛏 TV ▤

SALDANHA: *VIP* €€
AE DC MC V — 54
Rua Fernão Lopes 25, 1000-132. **Map** 5 C3. 【 21-356 86 00. ℻ 21-315 87 73.
A simple hotel built over shops in a busy part of the city, the VIP is neat and tidy, although the decor is somewhat old-fashioned. 🛏 TV ▤

SALDANHA: *Hotel Marquês de Sá* €€€
AE DC MC V — 97
Av. Miguel Bombarda 130, 1050-167. **Map** 6 B2. 【 21-791 10 14. ℻ 21-793 69 83.
A pleasant hotel located in one of the most elegant areas of Lisbon, and a short walk from the Museu Calouste Gulbenkian *(see p76–9).* 🛏 TV ▤ 🅿

SALDANHA: *Príncipe* @ confortprincipe@mail.telepac.pt €€€
AE DC MC V ● — 67
Avenida Duque de Ávila 201, 1050-082. **Map** 5 B3. 【 21-353 61 51. ℻ 21-353 43 14.
Most of the rooms in this modern hotel have their own balcony. There is a small bar and lounge just off the lobby. 🛏 TV ▤ 🅿 ♿

SALDANHA: *Real Parque* @ info@hoteisreal.com €€€€€
AE DC MC V ● — 153
Avenida L. Bivar 67, 1069-146. **Map** 5 C3. 【 21-319 90 00. ℻ 21-357 07 50.
This impressive modern hotel, located on a quiet side street, has six rooms specially designed for the disabled. 🛏 TV ▤ 🅿 ♿

SALDANHA: *Sheraton Lisboa* €€€€€
AE DC MC V ● ● 375
Rua L. Coelho 1, 1069-025. **Map** 5 C3. 【 21-312 00 00. ℻ 21-354 71 64.
On one of the city's vantage points, Lisbon's Sheraton offers spacious rooms, a communications centre and a health club. 🛏 TV ▤ 🅿 ♿

Price categories in euros for a standard double room per night, including breakfast:

€ under 35
€€ 35–60
€€€ 60–100
€€€€ 100–150
€€€€€ over 150

RESTAURANT
The hotel has one or more restaurants open for lunch and supper, sometimes reserved for residents.

GARDEN
A garden, courtyard or large terrace for the use of hotel guests.

SWIMMING POOL
The hotel has its own indoor or outdoor pool.

CREDIT CARDS
Major credit cards accepted: *AE* American Express, *DC* Diners Club, *MC* MasterCard and *V* Visa.

	CREDIT CARDS	RESTAURANT	GARDEN	SWIMMING POOL	NUMBER OF ROOMS
THE LISBON COAST					
ALCÁCER DO SAL: *Pousada Dom Alfonso II* W www.pousadas.pt €€€€€ Alcácer do Sal, 7850. **(** 265-61 30 70. **FAX** 265-61 30 74. This atmospheric and historic *pousada* occupies a converted castle on a hilltop, overlooking the town and surrounding countryside. 🔒 TV 🗏 P 🕭	AE DC MC V	●	▨	●	35
CARCAVELOS: *Praia Mar* €€€€ Rua Gurué 16, 2775-581. **(** 21-458 51 00. **FAX** 21-457 31 30. This delightful hotel overlooks the Estoril coast's largest sandy beach. Modern and elegant throughout, the rooms are spacious and comfortable. The famed wines from Buçaco *(see p210)* are also available. 🔒 TV 🗏 P 🕭	AE DC MC V	●	▨	●	158
CASCAIS: *Solar Dom Carlos* @ solardecarlos@telepac.pt €€€ Rua Latina Coelho 8, 226. **(** 21-482 81 15. **FAX** 21-486 51 55. Set in a 16th-century mansion, this delightful hotel has a garden, historic chapel and comfortable, elegant rooms. 🔒 TV	AE DC MC V		▨		18
CASCAIS: *Baía* €€€€ Avenida 25 de Abril, 2754-509. **(** 21-482 76 00. **FAX** 21-486 72 26. A short walk from the town centre, the Cidadela is surrounded by gardens. Most of the rooms have spectacular views over the bay. 🔒 TV 🗏 P	AE DC MC V	●	▨	●	113
CASCAIS: *Casa da Pérgola* €€€€ Avenida Valbom 13, 2750-508. **(** 21-484 00 40. **FAX** 21-483 47 91. This Mediterranean-style mansion has rooms with stucco ceilings and marble floors. It closes from November until a week before Easter. 🔒			▨		11
CASCAIS: *Cidadela* €€€€ Avenida 25 de Abril, 2750. **(** 21-482 76 00. **FAX** 21-486 72 26. A short walk from the town centre, the Cidadela is surrounded by gardens. Most of the rooms have spectacular views over the bay. 🔒 TV 🗏 P	AE DC MC V	●	▨	●	113
CASCAIS: *Albatroz* €€€€€ Rua F. Arouca 100, 2750. **(** 21-483 28 21. **FAX** 21-484 48 27. Built in the 19th century as a retreat for the Portuguese royal family, the Albatroz sits perched on the rocks directly overlooking the ocean. Inside, the luxurious decoration is matched by excellent service. 🔒 TV 🗏 P 🕭	AE DC MC V	●	▨	●	46
CASCAIS: *Estoril Sol* €€€€€ Parque de Palmela, 2754-504. **(** 21-483 90 00. **FAX** 21-483 22 80. As well as marvellous views over the bay of Cascais, the Estoril Sol has a sea-water pool and a health club with Turkish baths. 🔒 TV 🗏 P 🕭	AE DC MC V	●		●	310
COSTA DA CAPARICA: *Praia do Sol* €€ Rua dos Pescadores 12a, 2825. **(** 21-290 00 12. **FAX** 21-290 25 41. A small hotel, the Praia do Sol offers well-appointed rooms conveniently located close to the beach in this popular resort town. 🔒 TV 🗏	AE DC MC V				53
COSTA DA CAPARICA: *Costa da Caparica* €€€€ Av. Gen. Delgado 47, 2829-506. **(** 21-291 89 00. **FAX** 21-291 06 87. This hotel, with an unusual semi-circular entrance, overlooks the beach. It has seven rooms adapted for the disabled. 🔒 TV 🗏 P 🕭	AE DC MC V	●	▨	●	353
ERICEIRA: *Vilazul* €€€ Calçada da Baleia 10, 2655-238. **(** 261-86 00 00. **FAX** 261-86 29 27. Only 500 m (550 yds) from the sea, this bright and airy hotel has panoramic views from the terrace and some of the bedrooms. 🔒 TV 🗏 P	AE DC MC V	●			21
ESTORIL: *São Cristóvão* €€ Av. Marginal 7079, 2765-480. **(** 21-468 09 13. **FAX** 21-468 09 13. This charming *pensão* is housed in an interesting old villa. Located on the ocean side of the Avenida Marginal, it offers spectacular views. 🔒 P			▨		14

ESTORIL: *Hotel Alvorada* €€€ — 52
Rua de Lisboa 3, 2765-240. ☏ 21-464 98 60. FAX 21-468 72 50.
Only a few minutes' walk from the beach, this newly decorated hotel offers friendly service and bright, well-appointed rooms. 🛏 TV 🍽 P ♿
AE DC MC V

ESTORIL: *Lennox Country Club* €€€ — 34
Rua Eng. A. de Sousa 5, 2765-191. ☏ 21-468 04 24. FAX 21-468 08 59.
Situated in its own lush gardens with panoramic views, this *estalagem* is perfect for golfers. 🛏 TV P
AE DC MC V

ESTORIL: *Hotel de Inglaterra* €€€€ — 52
Rua do Porto 1, 2765-271. ☏ 21-468 44 61. FAX 21-468 21 08.
Some rooms in this impressive early 20th-century mansion have lovely views over the Bay of Cascais or the Sintra Hills. 🛏 TV 🍽
AE DC MC V

ESTORIL: *Palácio* @ palacioestoril@mail.telepac.pt €€€€€ — 162
Rua do Parque, 2769-504. ☏ 21-464 80 00. FAX 21-468 48 67.
An elegant hotel with a prime location between the sea and the casino. It has an 18-hole golf course and tennis courts. 🛏 TV 🍽 P ♿
AE DC MC V

GUINCHO: *Estalagem Muchaxo* €€€€ — 60
Praia do Guincho, 2750-642. ☏ 21-487 02 21. FAX 21-487 04 44.
This rustic *estalagem*, with exposed beams and open brickwork, overlooks the ocean. The sea-water pool is built into the cliffs. 🛏 TV 🍽 P
AE DC MC V

GUINCHO: *Hotel do Guincho* €€€€€ — 29
Praia do Guincho, 2750-642. ☏ 21-487 04 91. FAX 21-487 04 31.
Perched on a clifftop overlooking the ocean, this atmospheric hotel with arched ceilings and medieval decor was once a fortress. 🛏 TV 🍽 P ♿
AE DC MC V

GUINCHO: *Senhora da Guia* €€€€€ — 42
Estrada do Guincho, 2750-642. ☏ 21-486 92 39. FAX 21-486 92 27.
Set in its own grounds with a sea-water pool, this charming *estalagem* is housed in a comfortable and relaxing manor house. 🛏 TV 🍽 P
AE DC MC V

MAFRA: *Castelão* €€ — 35
Avenida 25 de Abril, 2640-456. ☏ 261-81 60 50. FAX 261-81 60 59.
Convenient as a base when visiting the fabulous monastery in Mafra, this fairly small hotel is comfortable and clean. 🛏 TV P
AE DC MC V

PAÇO D'ARCOS: *Sol Palmeiras* €€€ — 35
Avenida Marginal, 2780. ☏ 21-446 83 00. FAX 21-446 83 99.
Housed in a 19th-century manor house, many of the rooms in the Sol Palmeiras are suites with views over the Tagus. 🛏 TV 🍽 P
AE DC MC V

PALMELA: *Pousada de Palmela* €€€€€ — 28
Castelo de Palmela, 2950. ☏ 21-235 12 26. FAX 21-233 04 40.
The fortified walls of this 12th-century castle now enclose a tranquil *pousada* with whitewashed rooms and many plants. 🛏 TV 🍽 P
AE DC MC V

QUELUZ: *Pousada da Dona Maria I* €€€€€ — 26
L. do Palácio Nacional, 2745-191. ☏ 21-435 61 58. FAX 21-435 61 89.
Once used by staff of the marvellous 18th-century Palácio de Queluz, today the "Clock Tower" is an impressive *pousada*. 🛏 TV 🍽 P ♿
AE DC MC V

SESIMBRA: *Hotel do Mar* €€€€ — 169
R. Gen. Humberto Delgado 10, 2970-628. ☏ 21-228 83 00. FAX 21-223 38 88.
This hotel, built on different levels on the cliffside, is surrounded by lush gardens. The presidential suite has a private pool. 🛏 TV 🍽 P ♿
AE DC MC V

SETÚBAL: *IBIS Setúbal* €€ — 102
Rua Alto da Guerra, 2914-518. ☏ 265-77 22 00. FAX 265-77 24 47.
Featuring the usual combination of IBIS comforts and economy, this hotel is surrounded by its own peaceful gardens. 🛏 TV 🍽 P ♿
AE DC MC V

SETÚBAL: *Pousada de São Filipe* €€€€€ — 16
Castelo de São Filipe, 2900-300. ☏ 265-52 38 44. FAX 265-53 25 38.
This historic castle, built by Philip II of Spain *(see p50)* in 1590, is an friendly pousada with fine views over the estuary. 🛏 TV 🍽 P
AE DC MC V

SINTRA: *Central* €€€ — 10
Praça da República 35, 2710. ☏ 21-923 09 63.
Heavy furniture and peeling paint give this hotel an old-fashioned atmosphere. It has an excellent position opposite the Palácio Nacional. 🛏
AE MC V

For key to symbols see back flap

Price categories in euros for a
standard double room per night,
including breakfast:
€ under 35
€€ 35–60
€€€ 60–100
€€€€ 100–150
€€€€€ over 150

RESTAURANT
The hotel has one or more restaurants open for
lunch and supper, sometimes reserved for residents.

GARDEN
A garden, courtyard or large terrace for the use of
hotel guests.

SWIMMING POOL
The hotel has its own indoor or outdoor pool.

CREDIT CARDS
Major credit cards accepted: *AE* American Express,
DC Diners Club, *MC* MasterCard and *V* Visa.

	CREDIT CARDS	RESTAURANT	GARDEN	SWIMMING POOL	NUMBER OF ROOMS
SINTRA: *Residencial Sintra* @ pensao.residencial.sintra@clix.pt €€€ T. dos Avelares 12, 2710-506. **[** 21-923 07 38. **FAX** 21-923 07 38. Heavy furniture and peeling paint give this hotel an old-fashioned atmosphere. It has an excellent position opposite the Palácio Nacional. ▪ **P**	MC V		▪	●	10
SINTRA: *Tivoli Sintra* @ reservas.tsintra.@mail.telepac.pt €€€€ Praça da República, 2710-616. **[** 21-923 35 05. **FAX** 21-923 15 72. The modern Tivoli Sintra, tucked away in a corner of Sintra's main square, has wonderful views across the valley, a bar and a boutique. ▪ **TV** ▪ **P** ▪	AE DC MC V	●			76
SINTRA: *Caesar Park* @ penhalongresort@mail.telepac.pt €€€€€ Estr. da Lagoa Azul, Linhó 2714-511. **[** 21-924 90 11. **FAX** 21-924 90 07. This huge, luxurious complex in the Sintra hills has a 9 and an 18-hole golf course, designed by Robert Trent Jones Jr, and a health club. ▪ **TV** ▪ **P** ▪	AE DC MC V	●	▪	●	177
SINTRA: *Palácio de Seteais* €€€€€ R. B. du Bocage 8, 2710-616. **[** 21-923 32 00. **FAX** 21-923 42 77. Just outside town, this elegant hotel occupies a delightful 18th-century palace with tastefully decorated interiors and a topiary garden. ▪ **TV** **P**	AE DC MC V	●	▪		30

ESTREMADURA AND RIBATEJO

ABRANTES: *Hotel de Turismo* €€€ Largo de Santo António, 2200-349. Road map C4. **[** 241-36 12 61. **FAX** 241-36 52 18. This hotel, decorated in bright, classic colours, is found in a very pleasant location surrounded by attractive gardens. ▪ **TV** ▪ **P**	AE DC MC V	●	▪		40
BALEAL: *Casa das Marés* €€ Praia do Baleal, Peniche, 2520. Road map B4. **[** 262-76 92 55. The family-run "House of Tides" is set on a promontory with dramatic sea views. Breakfast is served on the terrace above a cove. ▪ **TV** ▪ **P**					12
BARRAGEM DO CASTELO DE BODE: *Estalagem Lago Azul* €€€ Lago Azul, Ferreira do Zêzere, 2240. Road map C4. **[** 249-36 14 45. **FAX** 249-36 16 64. The rooms of this *estalagem* are functional but there are tennis courts and sailing boats and the lakeside setting is spectacular. ▪ **TV** ▪ **P**	AE DC MC V	●	▪	●	20
BARRAGEM DO CASTELO DE BODE: *Pousada de São Pedro* €€€€ Castelo de Bode, Tomar, 2300. Road map C4. **[** 249-38 11 59. **FAX** 249-38 11 76. Overlooking the River Zêzere, this pleasant *pousada* offers simple but tastefully furnished rooms and excellent regional cooking. ▪ **TV** ▪ **P**	AE DC MC V	●			25
BATALHA: *Pousada do Mestre Afonso Domingues* €€€€ L. do Mestre A. Domingues 6, 2440. Road map C4. **[** 244-76 52 60. **FAX** 244-76 52 47. This *pousada* stands next to the town's abbey, Batalha, and is named after its architect. The rooms are traditionally furnished. ▪ **TV** **P**	AE DC MC V	●			21
CALDAS DA RAINHA: *Caldas Internacional* €€€ Rua Dr.Figueiroa Rego 45, 2500. Road map B4. **[** 262-83 05 00. **FAX** 262-84 44 82. Patterned floor tiles in the reception area welcome the visitor to the efficient and modern Caldas Internacional Hotel. ▪ **TV** ▪ **P** ▪	AE DC MC V	●	▪		83
CONSTÂNCIA: *Quinta Santa Bárbara* €€€ 2250. Road map C4. **[** 249-73 92 14. **FAX** 249-73 93 73. A splendid 17th-century manor house, the Quinta Santa Bárbara has been converted into a distinguished hotel, with cosy, rustic rooms. The Gothic stone vaults of the former refectory now house the restaurant. ▪ ▪ **P**		●	▪	●	7
FÁTIMA: *Verbo Divino* €€ Praça Paulo VI, Aptdo 2, 2496-908. Road map C4. **[** 249-53 30 43. **FAX** 249-53 22 63. Built to guarantee a revenue for the Divine Word Missionaries, this is a large, simply decorated hotel for pilgrims to Fátima. ▪ **TV** ▪ **P**	AE MC V	●	▪		208

FÁTIMA: *Dom Gonçalo* @ hotel.d.goncalo@ip.pt €€€ | AE DC MC V | 42
Rua Jacinta Marto 100, 2495-450. **Road map** C4. ☎ 249-539 330. **FAX** 249-539 335.
A delightful *estalagem* that is set in charming, well-kept gardens and woods, and yet is still very close to the sanctuary. 🖥 📺 🍽 🅿

FÁTIMA: *Pousada Conde de Ourém* €€€€ | AE DC MC V | 30
Largo João Mansur Castelo, 2490 Ourém. **Road map** C4. ☎ 249-540 920.
FAX 249-542 955. Set in a restored cluster of medieval houses within the walled town of Ourém, this *pousada* is near Fatima. 🖥 📺 🍽 🅿

GOLEGÃ: *Casa da Azinhaga* @ jiai.v.saldanha@clix.pt €€€ | | 7
Azinhaga, 2150-021. **Road map** C4. ☎ 249-957 183. **FAX** 249-957 182.
This classic manor house, 7 km (4 miles) south of horse-loving Golegã, offers comfortable rooms in a pleasant ambience. 🖥 🅿

LEIRIA: *Leiriense* €€ | MC V | 24
Rua A. de Albuquerque 6, 2400-080. **Road map** C4. ☎ 244-82 30 54. **FAX** 244-82 30 73.
Found tucked away in the narrow side streets of the old area of Leiria, this *residencial* is clean, welcoming and quite charming. 🖥 📺 🍽

LEIRIA: *Dom João III* €€€ | AE DC MC V | 64
Avenida Dom João III, 240-164. **Road map** C4. ☎ 244-817 888. **FAX** 244-817 880.
The modern, well-equipped rooms of this hotel have views to the splendid *loggia* of the castle and over the River Liz. 🖥 📺 🍽 🅿

OURINHÃ: *Estalagem da Areia Branca* €€€ | AE DC MC V | 31
Praia da Areia Branca, 2530-214. **Road map** B4. ☎ 261-41 24 91. **FAX** 261-41 31 43.
This very comfortable *estalagem* sits perched on the cliffs overlooking the quiet beach of Areia Branca. 🖥 📺 🅿 ♿

NAZARÉ: *Mar Bravo* €€€ | AE DC MC V | 16
Praça S. Oliveira 70, 2450. **Road map** C4. ☎ 262-55 11 80. **FAX** 262-53 39 79.
In the heart of Nazaré this *albergaria* has panoramic views over this picturesque town and the beach. All rooms have balconies. 🖥 📺 🅿 ♿

ÓBIDOS: *Rainha Santa Isabel* €€€ | AE DC MC V | 20
Rua Direita, 2510. **Road map** B4. ☎ 262-95 93 23. **FAX** 262-95 91 15.
Enclosed within the walls of this pretty town, the attractive wood-panelled rooms of this *albergaria* contain lovely *azulejos*. 🖥 📺 🍽

ÓBIDOS: *Estalagem do Convento* $$$ | AE MC V | 31
Rua D. José D'Ornelas, 2510. **Road map** B4. ☎ 262-95 92 17. **FAX** 262-95 91 59.
Once a convent, the rooms of this tastefully converted *estalagem* are traditionally and elegantly furnished. Some have marvellous views. 🖥 📺

ÓBIDOS: *Pousada do Castelo* €€€€€ | AE DC MC V | 9
Paço Real, 2510-999. **Road map** B4. ☎ 262-95 91 05. **FAX** 262-95 91 48.
The novelist Graham Greene stayed in this stunning *pousada*, converted from a 15th-century royal castle. Book early as it is very popular. 🖥 📺 🍽

PENICHE: *Residencial Mili* € | AE DC MC V | 13
Rua José Estevão 23, 2520. **Road map** B4. ☎ & **FAX** 262-787 107.
In the charming town centre, this comfortable hotel is just a few steps from the fortress, fishing port and the town's main churches. 🖥 📺 🅿

SANTARÉM: *Vitória* €€ | AE DC MC V | 25
R. 2º Visconde de Santarém 21, 2000-197. **Road map** C4. ☎ 243-30 91 30.
FAX 243-328 202. A modest *pensão* handy for Santarém's main sights, the Vitória offers small rooms that are cosy and welcoming. 🖥 📺 🍽

SANTARÉM: *Quinta do Vale de Lobos* €€€ | V | 6
Azóia de Baixo, 2000. **Road map** C4. ☎ 243-42 92 64. **FAX** 243-429 313.
This restored 19th-century manor house, set among cedar trees, has traditionally furnished rooms and an inner courtyard. 🖥 🅿

SÃO MARTINHO DO PORTO: *Americana* €€ | MC V | 22
Rua Dom J. Saldanha 2, 2460-645. **Road map** B4. ☎ 262-98 91 70. **FAX** 262-98 93 49.
Conveniently located close to the sandy, sheltered beach popular with families, this friendly *pensão* offers pleasant rooms. 🖥 📺

SÃO PEDRO DE MUEL: *Mar e Sol* €€€ | AE DC MC V | 63
Avenida da Liberdade, 2430-501. **Road map** C4. ☎ 244-59 00 00. **FAX** 244-59 00 19.
Right beside the ocean and spectacular beach, this neat and unpretentious hotel offers rooms with seaviews in this popular resort. 🖥 📺 🍽 🅿 ♿

For key to symbols see back flap

<table>
<tr><td colspan="2">

Price categories in euros for a standard double room per night, including breakfast:

€ under 35
€€ 35–60
€€€ 60–100
€€€€ 100–150
€€€€€ over 150

</td><td colspan="2">

RESTAURANT
The hotel has one or more restaurants open for lunch and supper, sometimes reserved for residents.

GARDEN
A garden, courtyard or large terrace for the use of hotel guests.

SWIMMING POOL
The hotel has its own indoor or outdoor pool.

CREDIT CARDS
Major credit cards accepted: *AE* American Express, *DC* Diners Club, *MC* MasterCard and *V* Visa.

</td></tr>
</table>

	CREDIT CARDS	RESTAURANT	GARDEN	SWIMMING POOL	NUMBER OF ROOMS
TOMAR: *Santa Iria* €€€ Parque do Mouchão, 2300-586. **Road map** C4. 249-31 33 26. FAX 249-32 12 38. Wonderfully situated on an island park on the River Nabão, this discreetly elegant *estalagem* is near many of the city's sights. 🛏 TV P	AE MC V	●	■		14
TOMAR: *Hotel dos Templários* €€€€ L. Cândido dos Reis 1, 2304-909. **Road map** C4. 249-31 01 00. FAX 249-32 21 91. Overlooking the River Nabão and conveniently located in the city centre, this hotel offers tennis courts, a gym and a health club. 🛏 TV 🍴 P 🚪	AE DC MC V	●	■	●	176
VILA FRANCA DE XIRA: *Lezíria Parque* €€€ N1, 2600-203, Povos. **Road map** C5. 263-276 670. FAX 263-276 990. Close to the Lisbon to Oporto motorway (the A1), this attractive hotel has pleasant views over the River Tagus. 🛏 TV 🍴 P 🚪	AE DC MC V	●	■		71
THE BEIRAS					
ALMEIDA: *Morgado* €€ Bairro de São Pedro, 6350-210. **Road map** E2. 271-57 44 12. Found just outside the walls of the fortress at Almeida, this modern *pensão* is clean and comfortable, and very good value. 🛏 TV 🍴 P 🚪					12
ALMEIDA: *Pousada da Senhora das Neves* €€€€ Rua da Muralha, 6350. **Road map** E2. 271-57 42 90. FAX 271-57 43 20. Inside the star-shaped fortifications that enclose the town, this *pousada* has pleasantly furnished rooms, some with four-poster beds. 🛏 TV 🍴	AE DC MC V	●			21
AVEIRO: *Arcada* €€ Rua Viana do Castelo 4, 3800-275. **Road map** C3. 234-423 001. FAX 234-421 886. Located in a Neo-Classical arcaded building overlooking the central canal, the Arcada has character as well as all modern comforts. 🛏 TV	AE DC MC V				49
AVEIRO: *Mercure* €€€ Rua L. G. de Carvalho 23, 3800-211. **Road map** C3. 234-404 400. FAX 234-404 401. This hotel has been modernised in recent months and offers every modern amenity while retaining its charming small garden. 🛏 TV 🍴 P 🚪	AE DC MC V		■		45
AVEIRO: *Pousada da Ria* €€€€ Bico do Muranzel, Torreira, 3870-301. **Road map** C3. 234-860 180. FAX 234-83 83 33. This modern *pousada* has a peaceful location on the banks of the Ria de Aveiro. Most of the rooms have balconies overlooking the lagoon where the local painted boats *(moliceiros)* are moored. 🛏 TV 🍴 P	AE DC MC V	●	■	●	19
BUÇACO: *Palace Hotel do Buçaco* €€€€€€ Buçaco, 3050-261 Luso. **Road map** C3. 231-937 970. FAX 231-93 05 09. This extraordinary Neo-Manueline hotel, set in a luxuriant forest, was built as a hunting lodge for the last Portuguese kings. The grand interior offers attractive rooms, some with decorative *azulejos*. 🛏 TV 🍴 P	AE DC MC V	●	■		64
CARAMULO: *Pousada de São Jerónimo* €€€€ 3475-031. **Road map** C3. 232-86 12 91. FAX 232-86 16 40. This modern *pousada*, covered in ivy, offers well-appointed rooms and a delightful setting high up in the Serra do Caramulo. 🛏 TV 🍴 P	AE DC MC V	●	■	●	12
CASTELO BRANCO: *Rainha Dona Amélia* €€€ Rua de Santiago 15, 6000-179. **Road map** D4. 272-32 63 15. FAX 272-32 63 90. This pleasant modern hotel has comfortable rooms and an excellent location in the city centre close to the historical sights. 🛏 TV 🍴 P 🚪	AE DC MC V	●			64
CASTRO DAIRE: *Montemuro* €€ Termas do Carvalhal, 3600-398. **Road map** D2. 232-38 11 84. FAX 232-38 11 12. Located in the mountains between Viseu and the Douro, this modern hotel offers facilities for rafting and canoeing. 🛏 TV 🍴 P 🚪	AE DC MC V	●	■		80

CELORICO DA BEIRA: *Mira Serra* €€ AE DC MC V 42
Bairro de S. Eufémia, 6360. **Road map** D3. 271-74 26 04. FAX 271-74 13 82.
As the name Mira Serra suggests, this attractive and pleasant hotel has
stunning views of the Serra da Estrela mountain range. 📶 TV 🍽 P &

COIMBRA: *Internacional* € 27
Avenida Emídio Navarro 4, 3030. **Road map** C3. 239-82 55 03.
Conveniently located close to the railway station, and overlooking the
River Mondego, this *pensão* is welcoming but very basic. 📶 10 rooms. TV

COIMBRA: *Astória* €€€ AE DC MC V 62
Av. Emídio Navarro 21, 3000-150. **Road map** C3. 239-85 30 20. FAX 239-82 20 57.
A charming Art Deco hotel with a somewhat faded splendour, the Astória
has stylish rooms with fine views across the Mondego. 📶 TV 🍽 P

COIMBRA: *Bragança* €€€ AE DC MC V 83
Largo das Ameias 10, 3000-024. **Road map** C3. 239-82 21 71. FAX 239-83 61 35.
A slightly old-fashioned but very comfortable hotel located in the heart of
Coimbra. The suites have marble bathrooms. 📶 TV 🍽 P

COIMBRA: *Quinta das Lágrimas* €€€€ AE DC MC V 39
Santa Clara, Aptdo. 5053, 3041-901. **Road map** C3. 239-80 23 80. FAX 239-44 16 95.
A handsome 18th-century country house, famous for the "Fountain of Love"
where Pedro and Inês (*see p179*) used to meet in secret. 📶 TV 🍽 P &

COIMBRA: *Tivoli Coimbra* €€€€ AE DC MC V 100
Rua João Machado 4, 3000-226. **Road map** C3. 239-82 69 34. FAX 239-82 68 27.
This modern hotel in the heart of the city boasts an excellent health club
with a Turkish bath, massage and gymnasium. 📶 TV 🍽 P

CONDEIXA-A-NOVA: *Pousada de Santa Cristina* €€€ AE DC MC V 45
Rua Francisco Lemos, 3150. **Road map** C3. 239-94 12 86. FAX 239-94 30 97.
This modern *pousada*, situated in its own gardens, is a good base for
visits to Coimbra and the Roman ruins of Conimbriga. 📶 TV 🍽 P

COVILHÃ: *Hotel Serra da Estrela* €€€ MC V 40
Penhas da Saúde, 6200. **Road map** D3. 275-310 300. FAX 275-310 309.
Set in the Serra da Estrela, this modern hotel offers lodging in triangular
bungalows and facilities for horse riding and winter sports. 📶 TV P

CURIA: *Curia Palace Hotel* €€€ AE DC MC V 114
Tamengos, 3780-541. **Road map** C3. 231-50 13 00. FAX 231-51 55 31.
This elegant Art Nouveau palace is set in manicured gardens and features
a tennis court and mini-golf. Open April to October. 📶 TV P

FIGUEIRA DA FOZ: *Casa da Azenha Velha* €€€ 6
Caceira de Cima, 3080. **Road map** C3. 233-42 50 41. FAX 233-42 97 04.
This welcoming hotel has large, airy bedrooms and a lounge with an
open fire. The hotel also has a tennis court. 📶 TV 🍽 P &

FIGUEIRA DA FOZ: *Hotel Costa de Prata* €€€ AE 66
Largo Coronel Galhardo 1, 3080. **Road map** C3. 233-42 66 20. FAX 233-42 66 10.
Overlooking the sea, this hotel is brightly decorated throughout and has a
bar and breakfast room with panoramic views. 📶 TV 🍽

GUARDA: *Solar de Alarcão* €€€ 3
Rua Dom Miguel de Alarcão 25-27, 6300-684. **Road map** D3. & FAX 271-21 43 92.
This *turismo de habitação* occupies an intriguing granite house built in
1686. There is a chapel and the rooms are full of antiques. 📶 TV P

LUSO: *Astória* € AE MC V 8
Rua Emídio Navarro, 3050. **Road map** C3. 231-93 91 82.
This small *pensão* is a delight. The rooms are simply furnished but
comfortable, and the bar has a friendly atmosphere. 📶 TV

LUSO: *Grande Hotel* €€€ AE DC MC V 143
Rua Dr. Cid de Oliveira 86, 3050. **Road map** C3. 231-93 79 37. FAX 231-93 79 30.
Dominating the skyline of this attractive spa town, this elegant hotel has
sports facilities as well as access to the spa. 📶 TV 🍽 P &

MANGUALDE: *Casa d'Azurara* €€€ AE DC MC V 15
Rua Nova 78, 3530. **Road map** D3. 232-61 20 10. FAX 232-62 25 75.
Built in the 18th century, today the Casa d'Azurara is a friendly *estalagem*,
set in its own gardens, with many original features. 📶 TV 🍽 P

Price categories in euros for a standard double room per night, including breakfast:
€ under 35
€€ 35–60
€€€ 60–100
€€€€ 100–150
€€€€€ over 150

RESTAURANT
The hotel has one or more restaurants open for lunch and supper, sometimes reserved for residents.
GARDEN
A garden, courtyard or large terrace for the use of hotel guests.
SWIMMING POOL
The hotel has its own indoor or outdoor pool.
CREDIT CARDS
Major credit cards accepted: *AE* American Express, *DC* Diners Club, *MC* MasterCard and *V* Visa.

	CREDIT CARDS	RESTAURANT	GARDEN	SWIMMING POOL	NUMBER OF ROOMS
MANTEIGAS: *Pousada de São Lourenço* €€€€	AE DC MC V	●	■		21
MONSANTO: *Pousada de Monsanto* €€€	AE DC MC V	●			10
OLIVEIRA DO HOSPITAL: *Pousada de Santa Bárbara* €€€€	AE DC MC V	●	■	●	16
SABUGUEIRO: *Casas do Cruzeiro* €€					30
SÃO JOÃO DE AREIRAS: *Solar da Quinta* €€€	AE DC MC V		■		5
VISEU: *Melia Comfort Grão Vasco* €€€	AE DC MC V	●	■	●	111
ALIJÓ: *Pousada de Barão de Forrester* €€€€	AE DC MC V	●	■	●	21
AMARANTE: *Pousada de São Gonçalo* €€€	AE DC MC V	●	■		15
BRAGANÇA: *Classis* €€	AE DC MC V	●	■		20
BRAGANÇA: *Estalagem do Caçador* €€€	AE DC MC V	●		●	24
BRAGANÇA: *Pousada de São Bartolomeu* €€€€	AE DC MC V	●	■		28
CHAVES: *Aquae Flaviae* €€€	AE DC MC V	●	■	●	165

MANTEIGAS: *Pousada de São Lourenço* €€€€
Penhas Douradas, 6260-200. **Road map** D3. (275-98 24 50. FAX 275-98 24 53.
This traditional granite *pousada*, high in the Serra da Estrela, is ideal for hikers and others seeking a secluded retreat. ⛻ TV 🖩 P

MONSANTO: *Pousada de Monsanto* €€€
Rua da Capela 1, 6060-091. **Road map** D3. (277-31 44 71. FAX 277-31 44 81.
A friendly and attractive *pousada* in an ancient and famous village where the hillside houses are squeezed between giant boulders. ⛻ TV 🖩

OLIVEIRA DO HOSPITAL: *Pousada de Santa Bárbara* €€€€
Povoa das Quartas, 3404-909. **Road map** D3. (238-609 652. FAX 238-609 645.
A log fire and traditional decor add rustic charm to this modern *pousada* with views of the snow-capped Serra da Estrela. ⛻ TV 🖩 P

SABUGUEIRO: *Casas do Cruzeiro* €€
Apartado 85, 6270-990, Seia. **Road map** D3. (238-312 825. FAX 238-315 282.
Tucked in a village in a Serra da Estrela valley, the granite cottages of the Casa do Cruzeiro offer simple apartments with kitchenettes. ⛻ TV P

SÃO JOÃO DE AREIRAS: *Solar da Quinta* €€€
Póvoa dos Mosqueiros, 3440-458. **Road map** D3. (232 89 17 08. FAX 232 89 23 82.
This charming 400 year-old house has a large garden with a lake and each room is furnished with antiques. ⛻ P

VISEU: *Melia Comfort Grão Vasco* €€€
Rua Gaspar Barreiros, 3510-032. **Road map** D3. (232-42 35 11. FAX 232-462 444.
Located right in the centre of town, the comfortable Grão Vasco hotel has traditional decor and is surrounded by an attractive garden. ⛻ TV 🖩 P

DOURO AND TRÁS-OS-MONTES

ALIJÓ: *Pousada de Barão de Forrester* €€€€
Rua José Rufino, 5070-031. **Road map** D2. (259-95 92 15. FAX 259-95 93 04.
This *pousada* is in the heart of the port wine country and was named after the Englishman, James Forrester (1809–62), an advocate of "pure wine" *(see p252)*. Its sports facilities include tennis courts. ⛻ TV 🖩 P

AMARANTE: *Pousada de São Gonçalo* €€€
Aptdo. 286, 4604-909. **Road map** D2. (255-46 11 13. FAX 255-46 13 53.
Set in tranquil pine forests, the unusual semi-circular shape of this friendly *pousada* affords spectacular views of the Marão hills. ⛻ TV 🖩 P ♿

BRAGANÇA: *Classis* €€
Av. João da Cruz 102, 5300-178. **Road map** E1. (273-33 16 31. FAX 273-32 34 58.
A pleasant, modern and comfortable *residencial* just a short walk from the city centre, the Classis is particularly good value. ⛻ TV 🖩 ♿

BRAGANÇA: *Estalagem do Caçador* €€€
Largo Manuel Pinto de Azevedo, Macedo de Cavaleiros, 5340-219. **Road map** E1.
(278-42 63 56. FAX 278-42 63 81.
Located in a valley at the foot of the the Serra de Bornes, southwest of Bragança, this friendly and welcoming country inn has a pleasant interior. ⛻ TV P

BRAGANÇA: *Pousada de São Bartolomeu* €€€€
Estrada do Turismo, 5300-271. **Road map** E1. (273-33 14 93. FAX 273-32 34 53.
This popular *pousada* offers a panoramic view of the city of Bragança. Wooden furniture and stone walls add rustic charm. ⛻ TV 🖩 P

CHAVES: *Aquae Flaviae* €€€
Praça do Brasil, 5400. **Road map** D1. (276-30 90 00. FAX 276-30 90 10.
An impressive hotel that dominates the skyline of Chaves, the modern Aquae Flaviae has health and beauty facilities. ⛻ TV 🖩 P

CINFÃES: *Casa do Rebolfe*   €€€   5
Porto Antigo, 4690. **Road map** D2. & FAX 255-56 23 34.
Located east of Cinfães, near Porto Antigo, this 18th-century house beside the
Douro has been converted into a welcoming hotel.

ESPINHO: *Praiagolfe*   €€€€   AE DC MC V   132
Rua 6, 4500-357. **Road map** C2. 22-731 10 00. FAX 22-731 10 01.
Situated on the wide sandy beach, with views of the ocean, this hotel is
located next to a casino. There is a health club upstairs.

LAMEGO: *Hotel do Parque*   €€   AE DC MC V   42
Parque N. S. dos Remédios, 5100-025. **Road map** D2. 254-60 91 40. FAX 254-61 52 03.
Set in a grand whitewashed house next to the Santuário dos Remédios,
this hotel offers rustic rooms overlooking a chestnut forest.

LAMEGO: *Casa de Santo António*   €€€   AE   4
Britiande, 5100-360. **Road map** D2. 254-69 93 46. FAX 254-69 93 46.
Converted from a 17th-century manor house, with *azulejo* panels in
the chapel, Santo António offers quiet rural accommodation.

LAMEGO: *Villa Hostilina*   €€€   7
Almocave, 5100-192. **Road map** D2. 254-61 23 94. FAX 254-65 51 94.
Housed in a 19th-century farmhouse, Villa Hostilina offers tranquility
and charm and the use of a health club and tennis court.

MESÃO FRIO: *Casa d'Além*   €€   AE DC MC V   4
Oliveira, 5040-204. **Road map** D2. 254-32 19 91. FAX 254-32 19 91.
Originally a port wine-growing country estate built in the 1920s, this
family-run *quinta* has attractive interiors with original decor.

MIRANDA DO DOURO: *Pousada de Santa Catarina* $$$ AE DC MC V   12
5210-183. **Road map** E1. 273-43 10 05. FAX 273-43 10 65.
The spacious rooms of this *pousada* all have balconies and overlook the
peaceful Miranda do Douro dam.

OPORTO: *Residencial Santa Cruz*   €   AE MC V   17
Rua Santa Catarina 876, 4000-446. **Road map** C2. 22-205 71 99.
This good-value *residencial* is basic but it has both style and character.
The rooms have splendid views over the city centre.

OPORTO: *Hotel da Bolsa*   €€€   AE DC MC V   36
Rua F. Borges 101, 4050-253. **Road map** C2. 22-202 67 68. FAX 22-205 88 88.
The "Stock Exchange" hotel has an attractive façade and well-appointed
rooms, and is convenient for both shopping and tourist areas.

OPORTO: *Nave*   €€   AE MC V   81
Av. Fernão de Magalhães 247, 4300-190. **Road map** C2. 22-589 90 30. FAX 22-589 90 39.
This modern hotel is conveniently situated ten minutes walk from the
centre of town. The bedrooms have recently been renovated.

OPORTO: *Malaposta*   €€   AE DC MC V   37
Rua da Conceição 80, 4050-214. **Road map** C2. 22-200 62 78. FAX 22-200 62 95.
Tucked away on a quiet side street, and centrally located, the attractive
and modern Malaposta is a friendly, good-value hotel.

OPORTO: *Pensão dos Aliados*   €€   AE MC V   42
Rua Elísio de Melo 27, 4000-196. **Road map** C2. 22-200 48 53. FAX 22-200 27 10.
This excellent *pensão* with well-equipped rooms is located in the centre
of town in an impressive building recognized as a city landmark.

OPORTO: *São José*   €€   AE DC MC V   43
Rua da Alegria 172, 4000-034. **Road map** C2. 22-208 02 61. FAX 22-332 04 46.
One of several hotels in this busy street, close to the city centre, the São
José has a very pleasant style and ambience.

OPORTO: *Boa-Vista*   €€€   AE DC MC V   69
Esplanada do Castelo 58, 4150-196. **Road map** C2. 22-618 00 83. FAX 22-617 38 18.
As the name suggests, the charming Boa-Vista hotel has superb views
over the ocean. An enchanting tram takes guests into town.

OPORTO: *Holiday Inn Garden Court*   €€€   AE DC MC V   113
Praça da Batalha 127-130, 47-102. **Road map** C2. 223-39 23 00. FAX 222 00 60 09.
This modern comfortable hotel has adapted rooms for the disabled, and is
conveniently located for sightseeing.

For key to symbols see back flap

Price categories in euros for a standard double room per night, including breakfast:
€ under 35
€€ 35–60
€€€ 60–100
€€€€ 100–150
€€€€€ over 150

RESTAURANT
The hotel has one or more restaurants open for lunch and supper, sometimes reserved for residents.
GARDEN
A garden, courtyard or large terrace for the use of hotel guests.
SWIMMING POOL
The hotel has its own indoor or outdoor pool.
CREDIT CARDS
Major credit cards accepted: *AE* American Express, *DC* Diners Club, *MC* MasterCard and *V* Visa.

	CREDIT CARDS	RESTAURANT	GARDEN	SWIMMING POOL	NUMBER OF ROOMS
OPORTO: *Internacional* €€€ Rua do Almada 131, 4050-037. **Road map** C2. 22-200 50 32. FAX 22-200 90 63. A curious but pleasing combination of Baroque and modern styles in the reception rooms make this an interesting place to stay. TV	AE DC MC V	●			35
OPORTO: *Quinta da Granja* €€€ Rua Manuel Francisco Araújo 444, 4425-120. **Road map** C2. 229 71 01 47. Just five minutes from the city centre, this quiet hotel is housed in a grand granite 18th-century manor house. TV P	AE V		■	●	5
OPORTO: *Dom Henrique* €€€€ Rua G. de Azevedo 179, 4049-009. **Road map** C2. 22-340 16 16. FAX 22-340 16 00. Located right in the heart of the city, this hotel has 17 floors – two designated non-smoking – and a bar with a panoramic view. TV	AE DC MC V	●			112
OPORTO: *Ipanema Park* €€€€ R. de Serralves 124, 4150-702. **Road map** C2. 22-610 41 74. FAX 22-610 28 09. An elegant hotel in which each room has a view over either the city, river or Atlantic Ocean. Enjoy every conceivable convenience and a health club that includes an indoor pool and hydro massage. TV P	AE DC MC V	●	■	●	281
OPORTO: *Infante de Sagres* €€€€€ P. Dona F. de Lencastre 62, 4050-259. **Road map** C2. 22-339 85 00. FAX 22-339 85 99. This is a beautifully appointed city-centre hotel with public rooms full of antiques, a refined atmosphere and bedrooms which offer everything a discerning traveller expects from such a highly rated hotel. TV	AE DC MC V	●	■		74
OPORTO: *Porto Palácio* €€€€€ Av. da Boavista 4100-130. **Road map** C2. 22-608 66 00. FAX 22-600 63 97. This elegant hotel, situated in an affluent suburb of Oporto, offers all modern facilities including a comprehensive health club. TV P	AE DC MC V	●		●	250
OPORTO: *Tivoli Porto* €€€€€ Rua A. L. Vieira 66, 4100-020. **Road map** C2. 22-609 49 41. FAX 22-606 74 52. The modern Tivoli Porto, situated in the elegant suburb of Boavista, has comfortable rooms, most of which have a balcony. TV P	AE DC MC V			●	58
PESO DA RÉGUA: *Império* € Av. Vasques Osório 8, 5050-280. **Road map** D2. 254-32 01 20. FAX 254-32 14 57. In the heart of the port region, this modern *pensão* is located near Peso da Régua's harbour and has lovely views over the River Douro. TV P	MC V				33
PINHÃO: *Quinta de la Rosa* €€€ 5085, Pinhão. **Road map** D2. 254 73 22 54. FAX 254 72 23 46. This delightful farmhouse offers rooms as well as cottages to rent. The farm produces port, wine and olive oil and there are daily tours of the facilities. There is also a shop selling the produce. TV P	AE DC MC V		■	●	6
PINHÃO: *Vintage House Hotel* @ vintagehouse@mail.telepac.pt €€€€ Lugar da Ponte, 5085-034. **Road map** D2. 254-73 02 30. FAX 254-73 02 38. This elegant hotel, located on the river Douro, is built on the site of an old port lodge and is surrounded by majestic vinyards. Rooms each have a private balcony and the restaurant is excellent. TV P	AE DC MC V	●	■	●	43
SANTO TIRSO: *Quinta da Picaria* €€€ Guimarei, 4780. **Road map** C2. 252-89 12 97. Attractive and traditionally decorated rooms can be rented on this farm. It is an ideal base for those who prefer to stay out of town. P			■		4
TORRE DE MONCORVO: *Brasília* €€ 5160-287. **Road map** E2. 279-25 42 56. FAX 279-25 86 10. This neat and tidy *pensão*, offering all modern conveniences, is conveniently located on the main road through town. TV P	MC V		■	●	29

VIDAGO: *Vidago Palace Hotel* €€€€ | AE DC MC V | 83
5425-307. **Road map** D1. ☎ 276-99 09 00. ℻ 276-90 73 59.
This truly magnificent turn-of-the-century spa hotel, surrounded by forest, has a grandiose façade and a beautiful inside staircase flanked by marble columns. The bedrooms are also charming. 🍴 TV 🍽 P

VILA REAL: *Casa Agrícola da Levada* @ levada@netc.pt €€€ | AE V | 10
Timpeira, 5000-419. **Road map** D2. ☎ 259-32 21 90. ℻ 259-34 69 55.
Constructed in 1922 by the Portuguese architect Raúl Lino, this charming Art Deco house has elegant rooms and a lovely rose garden. 🍴 TV P ♿

VILA REAL: *Miracorgo* €€€ | AE DC MC V | 166
Av. 1º de Maio 78, 5000-651. **Road map** D2. ☎ 259-32 50 01. ℻ 259-32 50 06.
The modern Miracorgo is tastefully decorated and has superb views from the terrace of the deep ravine and river below. 🍴 TV 🍽 P ♿

MINHO

BARCELOS: *Quinta de Santa Comba* €€ | | 9
Lugar de Crujães, 4755-536 Várzea. **Road map** C1. ☎ & ℻ 253-83 21 01.
A spectacular 18th-century residence with wooden beams and granite stonework, this manor house has an elegant rustic charm. 🍴 P

BOM JESUS DO MONTE: *Hotel do Elevador* €€€ | AE DC MC V | 22
Tenões, Braga, 4710-455. **Road map** C1. ☎ 253-60 34 00. ℻ 253-60 34 09.
A luxurious hotel that derives its name from the 19th-century water-operated elevator that still takes visitors up to the sanctuary. 🍴 TV 🍽 P

BRAGA: *Comfort Inn* €€ | AE DC MC V | 72
Rua Damiana Maria da Silva 20, Ferreiros, 4700. **Road map** C1. ☎ 253-60 54 70.
℻ 253-67 38 72. Located a short distance from the city centre, and convenient for a quick stopover, this hotel offers the usual amenities. 🍴 TV 🍽 P ♿

BRAGA: *Dona Sofia* €€ | AE DC MC V | 34
L. São João do Souto 131, 4700-326. **Road map** C1. ☎ 253-26 31 60. ℻ 253-61 12 45.
Adjacent to a small square with a lovely fountain, this modern hotel is in the centre of Braga, close to the city's cathedral. 🍴 TV 🍽 P ♿

BRAGA: *Largo da Estação* €€€ | AE MC V | 51
Largo da Estação 13, 4700-223. **Road map** C1. ☎ 253-21 83 81. ℻ 253-27 68 10.
Located just outside the town centre, close to the railway station, this hotel offers some rooms with jacuzzi bathtubs. 🍴 TV 🍽 P ♿

BRAGA: *Turismo de Braga* €€€ | AE DC MC V | 132
Praceta João XXI, 4710-245. **Road map** C1. ☎ 253-61 22 00. ℻ 253-61 22 11.
This large hotel dominates a small square in the centre of town. Modern facilities and panoramic views are on offer here. 🍴 TV 🍽 P

CAMINHA: *Casa de Esteiró* €€ | AE DC MC V | 3
Vilarelho, 4910. **Road map** C1. ☎ 258-72 13 33. ℻ 258-92 13 56.
A restored 18th-century house set in its own magnificent garden, the Casa de Esteiró offers comfortable apartments and a cosy log fire. TV P

CELORICO DE BASTO: *Casa do Campo* €€€ | AE MC V | 8
Molares, 4890-414. **Road map** D1. ☎ 255-36 12 31. ℻ 255-36 12 31
A granite gateway welcomes visitors to this early 18th-century country house. The garden is said to contain the oldest camellia tree in Portugal. 🍴 P

GUIMARÃES: *Hotel de Guimarães* €€€ | AE DC MC V | 116
Rua E. Almeida, 4810-911. **Road map** C2. ☎ 253-42 48 00. ℻ 253-42 48 99.
A modern well-equipped hotel in the city centre that boasts a health club, gymnasium, sauna and massage facilities. 🍴 TV 🍽 P

GUIMARÃES: *Pousada de Nossa Senhora da Oliveira* €€€€ | AE DC MC V | 15
Rua de Santa Maria, Aptdo. 101, 4801-910. **Road map** C2. ☎ 253-51 41 57.
℻ 253-51 42 04. This *pousada* was once a distinguished aristocratic mansion in the old district of town. Inside, leather armchairs and antique paintings help preserve the original character of the house. 🍴 TV 🍽 P

GUIMARÃES: *Pousada de Santa Marinha* €€€€€ | AE DC MC V | 51
Lugar da Costa, 4810-011. **Road map** C2. ☎ 253-51 44 53. ℻ 253-51 44 59.
This marvellous building, once the 12th-century Santa Marinha da Costa monastery, has been carefully adapted to house this beautiful *pousada*. Original *azulejo* decoration adorns the sumptuous rooms. 🍴 TV 🍽 P

For key to symbols see back flap

Price categories in euros for a standard double room per night, including breakfast:
€ under 35
€€ 35–60
€€€ 60–100
€€€€ 100–150
€€€€€ over 150

RESTAURANT
The hotel has one or more restaurants open for lunch and supper, sometimes reserved for residents.
GARDEN
A garden, courtyard or large terrace for the use of hotel guests.
SWIMMING POOL
The hotel has its own indoor or outdoor pool.
CREDIT CARDS
Major credit cards accepted: *AE* American Express, *DC* Diners Club, *MC* MasterCard and *V* Visa.

	CREDIT CARDS	RESTAURANT	GARDEN	SWIMMING POOL	NUMBER OF ROOMS
PONTE DE LIMA: *Casa de Sabadão* €€€ Arcozelo, 4990. Road map C1. (258-94 19 63. An enchanting 18th-century country house set among vineyards. Rooms include two charming, isolated apartments in a converted mill. 🔒 P			■	●	6
PÓVOA DE VARZIM: *Mercure Póvoa de Varzim* €€€ L. do Passeio Alegre, 4490-428. Road map C2. (252-29 04 00. FAX 252-29 04 01. An elegant hotel in the centre of Póvoa de Varzim, right next to the casino and overlooking the beach. Guests can make use of the nearby Estrela golf course. 🔒 TV P &	AE DC MC V	●			86
VALENÇA DO MINHO: *Vale Flores* €€ Esplanada, 4930. Road map C1. (251-82 41 06. FAX 251-82 41 29. Located in the new part of town, outside the town's fortifications, this *residencial* is clean, functional and inexpensive. 🔒 TV	AE DC MC V				32
VALENÇA DO MINHO: *Casa do Poço de Valença* €€€ T. da Gaviarra 4, 4930. Road map C1. (251-82 52 35. FAX 251-82 54 69. Inside the Vauban-style fort, this handsome house has a spectacular interior that combines modern decor with antique furniture. 🔒 TV	AE		■		7
VALENÇA DO MINHO: *Pousada de São Teotónio* €€€€ Baluarte do Socorro, 4930-735. Road map C1. (251-80 02 60. FAX 251-82 43 97. The traditionally furnished rooms of this small *pousada* have enchanting views of the valley, across the River Minho to Tuy, in Spain. 🔒 TV 🍽	AE DC MC V	●			18
VIANA DO CASTELO: *Calatrava* €€€ Rua M. Fiúza Júnior 157, 4900-458. Road map C1. (258-82 89 11. FAX 258-82 86 37. Located conveniently close to the old centre of Viana do Castelo, this *pensão* is neat and tidy and has old-fashioned decor. 🔒 TV	AE MC V				15
VIANA DO CASTELO: *Casa dos Costa Barros* €€€ Rua de São Pedro 22–28, 4900. Road map C1. (258-82 37 05. FAX 258-82 43 83. This delightful house, which was constructed in the 16th century and has been owned by the same family since 1765, has an elegant interior and handsome stone carvings over the outside windows. 🔒 TV	MC V				10
VIANA DO CASTELO: *Hotel do Parque* €€€ Praça da Galiza, 4900-476. Road map C1. (258-82 86 05. FAX 258-82 86 12. A welcoming hotel located just outside the old town within its own attractive gardens, laid out around the swimming pool. 🔒 TV 🍽 P	AE DC MC V		■	●	124
VIANA DO CASTELO: *Pousada Monte de Santa Luzia* €€€€ Monte de S. Luzia, 4901-909. Road map C1. (258-82 88 89. FAX 258-82 88 92. Surrounded by eucalyptus and pine trees, this luxurious *pousada* has a spectacular vantage point over the town of Viana. 🔒 TV 🍽 P &	AE DC MC V	●	■	●	48
VIEIRA DO MINHO: *Pousada de São Bento* €€€€ Caniçada, 4850-047. Road map D1. (253-64 71 90. FAX 253-64 78 67. Set on the edge of the nature reserve of the Peneda-Gerês National Park, and overlooking the River Cávado, this ivy-clad *pousada* was converted from a hunting lodge. The interior retains a rustic style. 🔒 TV 🍽 P	AE DC MC V	●		●	29
VILA DO CONDE: *Hotel Sant'Ana* €€€ Azurara, 4480-160. Road map C2. (252-64 17 17. FAX 252-64 26 93. Within easy reach of Oporto airport, this hotel has a magnificent location on the banks of the pretty River Ave, which can be seen from the many rooms with balconies. 🔒 TV 🍽 P &	AE DC MC V	●	■	●	73
VILA NOVA DE CERVEIRA: *Pousada Dom Dinis* €€€€ Terreiro, 4920-062. Road map C1. (251-70 81 20. FAX 251-70 81 29. Built within the walls of the medieval castle at Vila Nova, this tranquil and charming *pousada* has spacious and pleasant rooms. 🔒 TV 🍽 P	AE DC MC V	●	■		28

ALENTEJO

ALVITO: *Pousada do Castelo de Alvito* €€€€€ — AE DC MC V — 20
Apartado 9, 7920-999. **Road map** D6. **(** 284-48 53 43. **FAX** 284-48 53 83.
This elegant *pousada*, housed in a restored 15th-century castle, has
stunning Gothic vaulting in the dining room and Manueline details
on the windows. Peacocks roam the tranquil gardens. 🔒 TV 🛏 &

BEJA: *Hotel Melius* €€ — AE DC MC V — 60
Av. Fialho de Almeida, 7800-395. **Road map** D6. **(** 284-32 18 22. **FAX** 284-32 18 25.
At the southern edge of the medieval town of Beja, this modern hotel is
pleasant and comfortable and offers exceptional value. 🔒 TV 🍽 P &

BEJA: *Pousada de São Francisco* €€€€€ — AE DC MC V — 35
L. Dom N. Álvares Pereira, 7801-901. **Road map** D6. **(** 284-32 84 41. **FAX** 284-32 91 43.
Originally a Franciscan convent founded in 1268, this attractive white
building is now a beautiful and luxurious *pousada*. 🔒 TV 🍽 P

CASTELO DE VIDE: *Garcia d'Orta* €€€ — AE DC MC V — 53
Estrada de São Vicente, 7320-202. **Road map** D4. **(** 245-90 11 00. **FAX** 245-90 12 00.
A discreet and attractive hotel with all the modern amenities and a
handsome restaurant offering good Alentejan cooking. 🔒 TV 🍽 P &

CRATO: *Pousada de Flor da Rosa* €€€€€ — AE DC MC V — 24
Flor da Rosa, 7430-999. **Road map** D4. **(** 245-99 72 10. **FAX** 245-99 72 12.
An architecturally outstanding adaptation of the 14th-century Mosteiro
de Santa Maria Flor da Rosa houses this elegant *pousada*. 🔒 TV 🍽 P

ELVAS: *Elxadai Parque* €€ — AE DC MC V — 41
N4, Varche, 7350-422. **Road map** D5. **(** 268-62 13 97. **FAX** 268-62 19 21.
A well-equipped complex situated on top of a hill just west of Elvas, with
a water park, sports facilities and an equestrian centre. 🔒 TV 🍽 P &

ELVAS: *Quinta de Santo António* €€€ — AE DC MC V — 30
Aptdo. 206, 7350-903. **Road map** D5. **(** 268-62 84 06. **FAX** 268-62 50 50.
This splendid *estalagem* has elegant 18th-century gardens. The long
buildings offer attractive, rustic accommodation. 🔒 TV 🍽 P &

ELVAS: *Pousada de Santa Luzia* €€€€ — AE DC MC V — 25
Avenida de Badajoz, 7350-097. **Road map** D5. **(** 268-63 74 70. **FAX** 268-62 21 27.
The pleasantly decorated Santa Luzia was the first *pousada* to open, in
1942, and has a pool and tennis courts. 🔒 TV 🍽 P

ESTREMOZ: *Pousada da Rainha Santa Isabel* €€€€€ — AE DC MC V — 33
Largo Dom Dinis, 7100-509. **Road map** D5. **(** 268-33 20 75. **FAX** 268-33 20 79.
This grandiose *pousada* has been beautifully integrated into the 13th-
century castle in Estremoz. The 17th- and 18th-century style furniture of
the rooms includes four-poster beds and coats of arms. 🔒 TV 🍽

ÉVORA: *Évorahotel* €€€ — AE DC MC V — 114
N114, Quinta do Cruzeiro, Apartado 93, 7002-502. **Road map** D5.
(266-73 48 00. **FAX** 266-73 48 60.
On the outskirts of the old town, this is an impressive modern hotel.
The well-equipped rooms all have a balcony. 🔒 TV 🍽 P

ÉVORA: *IBIS Évora* €€ — AE DC MC V — 87
Quinta da Tapada, Muralha, 7000-968. **Road map** D5. **(** 266-74 46 20. **FAX** 266-74 46 32.
Located just outside the walls that encircle the old town, this modern hotel is
basic, but has all of the usual comforts of an IBIS hotel. 🔒 TV 🍽 P &

ÉVORA: *Solar Monfalim* €€€ — AE MC V — 26
Largo da Misericórdia 1, 7000-646. **Road map** D5. **(** 266-75 00 00. **FAX** 266-74 23 67.
In the heart of the old town, this Renaissance house offers visitors
well-appointed rooms and a delightful atmosphere. 🔒 TV 🍽 P

ÉVORA: *Pousada dos Lóios* €€€€€ — AE DC MC V — 32
L. do Conde de Vila Flor, 7000-804. **Road map** D5. **(** 266-70 40 51. **FAX** 266-70 72 48.
Originally a 15th-century monastery, the simple rooms in this elegant
pousada were converted from the monks' cells. 🔒 TV 🍽 P

MARVÃO: *Pousada de Santa Maria* €€€€ — AE DC MC V — 29
Rua 24 de Janeiro 7, 7330-122. **Road map** D4. **(** 245-99 32 01. **FAX** 245-99 34 40.
This charming *pousada* is set in a cosy, whitewashed town house
with traditional painted furniture and friendly staff. 🔒 TV 🍽

For key to symbols see back flap

					CREDIT CARDS	RESTAURANT	GARDEN	SWIMMING POOL	NUMBER OF ROOMS

Price categories in euros for a standard double room per night, including breakfast:
€ under 35
€€ 35–60
€€€ 60–100
€€€€ 100–150
€€€€€ over 150

RESTAURANT
The hotel has one or more restaurants open for lunch and supper, sometimes reserved for residents.
GARDEN
A garden, courtyard or large terrace for the use of hotel guests.
SWIMMING POOL
The hotel has its own indoor or outdoor pool.
CREDIT CARDS
Major credit cards accepted: *AE* American Express, *DC* Diners Club, *MC* MasterCard and *V* Visa.

Hotel	Credit Cards	Restaurant	Garden	Swimming Pool	Number of Rooms
MÉRTOLA: *Casa das Janelas Verdes* €€ Rua Dr M. Gomes 38–40, 7750. **Road map** D6. 286-61 21 45. A pleasant hotel in a whitewashed Alentejan house in the centre of town. Water-sport facilities are available on the Guadiana River.			■		5
REDONDO: *Convento de São Paulo* €€€€€ Aldeia da Serra, 7170-120. **Road map** D5. 266-98 91 60. **FAX** 266-99 91 04. Set in the remote Serra de Ossa, this former 12th-century monastery is decorated with thousands of *Azulejo* panels and frescoes in all the rooms. Baroque and Renaissance fountains cool various patios. TV P	AE DC MC V	●	■	●	28
SANTA CLARA-A-VELHA: *Pousada de Santa Clara* €€€ Barragem de Santa Clara, 7665-879. **Road map** C7. 283-88 22 50. **FAX** 283-88 24 02. Overlooking the vast Santa Clara-a-Velha lake, this peaceful *pousada* is ideal for water sports, hiking and shooting. TV P	AE DC MC V	●	■	●	19
SANTIAGO DO CACÉM: *Pousada de São Tiago* €€€ Estrada de Lisboa, 7540-237. **Road map** C6. 269-82 24 69. **FAX** 269-82 24 59. This ivy-clad *pousada*, set in its own pleasant gardens, resembles a country villa and is an ideal base from which to explore the area. TV P	AE DC MC V	●	■	●	9
SANTIAGO DO CACÉM: *Pousada Quinta da Ortiga* €€€ IP8, Apartado 67, 7540. **Road map** C6. 269-82 28 71. **FAX** 269-82 20 73. This delightful farmhouse, just north of town and very close to the sea, is surrounded by 4 ha (10 acres) of land with stables. TV P	AE DC MC V	●	■		13
SERPA: *Pousada de São Gens* €€€€ Alto de São Gens, 7830. **Road map** D6. 284-54 47 24. **FAX** 284-54 43 37. A modern *pousada* located high on a hill overlooking the town of Serpa, the São Gens has spectacular views of the wide Alentejo plains. TV P	AE DC MC V	●		●	18
SOUSEL: *Pousada de São Miguel* €€€€ Serra de São Miguel, 7470. **Road map** D5. 268-55 00 50. **FAX** 268-55 11 55. This modern *pousada* is ideal for those in search of peace or outdoor pursuits. There are facilities for hunting and fishing. TV P	AE DC MC V	●		●	32
VILA NOVA DE MILFONTES: *Moinho da Asneira* €€€ Quinta do Rio Mira, 7645-014. **Road map** C6. 283-99 61 82. **FAX** 283-99 71 38. Rooms in the main house and hillside cottages of this country estate overlook the estuary of the River Mira and are close to the beach. TV P	AE DC MC V		■	●	20
VILA VIÇOSA: *Casa de Peixinhos* €€€ 7160. **Road map** D5. 268-88 13 48. **FAX** 268-98 21 48. This castellated 17th-century building with grand rooms is decorated in shades of ochre and red with Baroque statues in the pebbled patio. TV P			■		8

ALGARVE

Hotel	Credit Cards	Restaurant	Garden	Swimming Pool	Number of Rooms
ALBUFEIRA: *Alfagar* €€€€€ Alfagar, Semina Balaia, 8200. **Road map** C7. 289-54 02 20. **FAX** 289-54 19 79. On a cliff top overlooking the ocean, this attractive complex offers apartments with direct access to the Santa Eulália beach. P	AE DC MC V	●	■	●	210
ALBUFEIRA: *Falésia* €€€€€ Pinhal do Concelho, Praia da Falésia, 8200-911. **Road map** C7. 289-50 12 37. **FAX** 289-50 12 70. Located by Falésia beach, this hotel has brightly furnished and airy rooms and an atrium decorated with hanging plants. TV P	AE DC MC V	●	■	●	169
ALBUFEIRA: *Montechoro* @ comercial@grupomontechoro.com €€€€€ Rua Alexandre O'Neil, 8200-343. **Road map** C7. 289-58 94 23. **FAX** 289-58 99 47. A modern and stylish hotel surrounded by its own gardens, this hotel has extensive sports facilities and a health club. TV P	AE DC MC V	●	■	●	362

ALBUFEIRA: *Sheraton Algarve Pine Cliffs* €€€€€
Apartado 644, 8200. **Road map** C7. 289-50 21 00. FAX 289-50 19 50.
A pleasing hotel with *azulejo* decoration on the bedsteads, the elegant
Sheraton offers sports facilities and a lift down to the beach.
Cards: AE, DC, MC, V — Rooms: 215

ALJEZUR: *O Palazim* €€
N120, Aldeia Velha, 8670. **Road map** C7. 282-99 82 49.
This boarding house is in an attractive building with a terrace offering
wonderful views. The lounge is decorated with *azulejo* panels.
Rooms: 12

ALMANCIL: *Quinta dos Rochas* @ quinta-das-rochas@ip.pt €€€
Fonte Coberta, Caixa Postal 600-A, 8135-019. **Road map** D7.
289-35 03 50. FAX 289-39 91 98.
This small *quinta* (country estate) is conveniently situated close to the
beach and offers visitors the comforts of home, a friendly welcome and
peaceful, rural surroundings.
Rooms: 6

ALMANCIL: *Quinta do Lago* @ info@quintadolagohotel.com €€€€€
8135-024. **Road map** D7. 289-35 03 50. FAX 289-39 63 93.
This smart hotel has delightful rooms with views over the ocean, a health
club, golf concessions, and many other facilities.
Cards: AE, DC, MC, V — Rooms: 141

ALTE: *Alte* €€€
Montinho, 8100-012. **Road map** C7. 289-47 85 23. FAX 289-47 86 46.
In a peaceful inland location away from the teeming crowds on the coast,
the charming Alte Hotel boasts excellent views, pleasant gardens and a
shuttle bus that takes residents to the beach.
Cards: AE, DC, MC, V — Rooms: 30

ALVOR: *Pestana Carlton Alvor* @ pestanahotels@mail.telepac.pt €€€€€
Praia dos Três Irmãos, 8500. **Road map** C7. 282-40 90 00. FAX 282-40 09 99.
A large, superbly situated luxury hotel complex with gardens that lead
directly down to the beach, a heated sea-water swimming pool and easy
access to nearby golf courses.
Cards: AE, DC, MC, V — Rooms: 197

ARMAÇÃO DE PÊRA: *Vila Vita Parc* @ v.v.p@mail.telepac.pt €€€€€
Apartado 196, 8365-911. **Road map** C7. 282-31 02 00. FAX 282-32 03 33.
Set along a beautiful stretch of coastline in its own gardens with tropical
flowers, this luxurious hotel has direct access to the beach.
Cards: AE, DC, MC, V — Rooms: 182

CARVOEIRO: *Colina Sol* €€€€
Vale de Centianes, Praia do Carvoeiro, 8400. **Road map** C7.
282-35 08 20. FAX 282-35 86 51.
This large Neo-Moorish hotel complex with well-equipped apartments is
set in its own attractive gardens, overlooking the sea.
Cards: AE, DC, MC, V — Rooms: 124

CARVOEIRO: *Almansor* €€€€€
Praia Vale Covo, 8401-911. **Road map** C7. 282-35 80 26. FAX 282-35 87 70.
This hotel has a dramatic location perched above a small cove. The
secluded beach can be reached by a stairway at low tide.
Cards: AE, DC, MC, V — Rooms: 293

ESTÓI: *Monte do Casal* €€€€€
Cerro do Lobo, 8000-661. **Road map** D7. 289-99 15 03. FAX 289-99 13 41.
The elegant Monte do Casal has separate apartments set in a delightful
Mediterranean garden with eucalyptus and bougainvillea.
Cards: AE, DC, MC, V — Rooms: 13

FARO: *Alnacir* @ hotelalnacir@clix.pt €€€
Estr. Senhora da Saúde 24, 8401-500. **Road map** D7. 289-80 36 78. FAX 289-80 35 48.
A tidy, modern hotel, Alnacir is located on a quiet street close to the
centre of this busy town. Some rooms have a terrace.
Cards: AE, DC, MC, V — Rooms: 53

FARO: *Residencial Samé* €€€
Rua de Bocage 66, 8000. **Road map** D7. 289-82 43 75. FAX 289-80 41 66.
This quiet hotel, located east of the cathedral, offers clean modern rooms
with bathrooms and television.
Cards: AE, DC, MC, V — Rooms: 36

FARO: *Hotel Eva* €€€€
Av. da República 1, 8000-678. **Road map** D7. 289-80 33 54. FAX 289-80 23 04.
A modern and comfortable hotel with a hairdresser and a barber. Ask for
a room that looks out over the marina and the ocean beyond.
Cards: AE, DC, MC, V — Rooms: 148

FARO: *La Réserve* €€€€€
Santa Bárbara de Nexe, 8000. **Road map** D7. 289-99 94 74. FAX 289-99 94 02.
A luxurious hotel offering suites, all with private terrraces and sea views.
There are tennis courts and access to nearby golf courses.
Cards: AE, DC, MC, V — Rooms: 20

For key to symbols see back flap

<table>
<tr><td colspan="2">

Price categories in euros for a standard double room per night, including breakfast:

€ under 35
€€ 35–60
€€€ 60–100
€€€€ 100–150
€€€€€ over 150
</td><td>

RESTAURANT
The hotel has one or more restaurants open for lunch and supper, sometimes reserved for residents.

GARDEN
A garden, courtyard or large terrace for the use of hotel guests.

SWIMMING POOL
The hotel has its own indoor or outdoor pool.

CREDIT CARDS
Major credit cards accepted: *AE* American Express, *DC* Diners Club, *MC* MasterCard and *V* Visa.
</td></tr>
</table>

Hotel	Price	CREDIT CARDS	RESTAURANT	GARDEN	SWIMMING POOL	NUMBER OF ROOMS
LAGOA: *Parque Algarvio* Sítio do Carmo, N125, 8400-405. **Road map** C7. ℂ 282-35 22 65. FAX 282-35 22 78. Although located alongside the main Algarvian highway, this is a charming and good-value hotel with rooms around the pool. 🛏 TV P	€€	AE DC MC V	●	■	●	42
LAGOS: *Rubi-Mar* @ rubimaroi@hotmail.com Rua da Barroca 70, 8600-688. **Road map** C7. ℂ 282-76 31 65. FAX 282-76 77 49. The English-run Rubi-Mar is a friendly hotel overlooking the sea. Generous continental breakfast is served in the rooms. 🛏 TV	€€					8
LAGOS: *Marina Rio* @ marinario@ip.pt Av. dos Descobrimentos, Apartado 388, 8600-645. **Road map** C7. ℂ 282-76 98 59. FAX 282-76 99 60. Located in the eastern part of Lagos, this *albergaria* is modern and pleasant and has attractive views over the marina. 🛏 TV 🍽 P ♿	€€€	AE DC MC V			●	36
LAGOS: *Belavista da Luz* Praia da Luz, 8600. **Road map** C7. ℂ 282-78 86 55. FAX 282-78 86 56. The hotel overlooks the sandy Praia da Luz. Facilities include a health club and games room. Closed four weeks during Nov–Dec and three weeks in Jan–Feb. 🛏 TV 🍽 P ♿	€€€€	AE DC MC V	●	■	●	45
LAGOS: *Hotel Tivoli de Lagos* Rua A. C. dos Santos, 8600-678. **Road map** C7. ℂ 282-76 99 67. FAX 282-76 99 20. This pleasant complex has five restaurants, a health club and, during the summer, barbeques are prepared on the beach. 🛏 TV 🍽 P ♿	€€€€€	AE DC MC V	●	■	●	326
LOULÉ: *Loulé Jardim* Praça Manuel da Arriaga, 8100-665. **Road map** D7. ℂ 289-41 30 94. FAX 289-46 31 77. This small hotel on a quiet garden square is an appealing conversion of a classic town house, including a discreet rooftop pool. 🛏 TV 🍽 P	€€€	AE DC MC V			●	52
MONCHIQUE: *Abrigo da Montanha* Estrada da Fóia, 8550-257. **Road map** C7. ℂ 282-91 21 31. FAX 282-91 36 60. This *estalagem*, made from wood and bare stone, makes a peaceful retreat and a good base for walks in the Serra de Monchique. 🛏 🍽 P	€€€	AE DC MC V	●	■		16
MONTE GORDO: *Vasco da Gama* Avenida Infante Dom Henrique, 8900. **Road map** D7. ℂ 281-51 09 00. FAX 281-51 09 01. Set on the beach, this hotel has spacious rooms, each with its own balcony. There is also a children's pool and playground. 🛏 TV 🍽 P	€€€€	AE DC MC V	●	■	●	175
PORTIMÃO: *Bela Vista* Avenida Tomas Cabreira, 8500. **Road map** C7. ℂ 282-45 04 80. FAX 282-41 53 69. An attractive hotel situated above the popular Praia da Rocha, the Bela Vista is tastefully decorated with relaxing sofas and *azulejo* panels. There is also a terrace overlooking the sea. 🛏 TV P	€€€€	AE DC MC V		■		14
PORTIMÃO: *Le Méridien Penina* Caixa Postal 146, 8501-952. **Road map** C7. ℂ 282-42 02 00. FAX 282-42 03 00. This hotel is a golfers' paradise. Set in a lush garden, it has practice facilities, tuition and three championship courses. 🛏 TV 🍽 P	€€€€€	AE DC MC V	●	■	●	196
SAGRES: *Navigator* Rua Infante D. Henrique, 8650-381. **Road map** C7. ℂ 282-62 43 54. FAX 282-62 43 60. This hotel on the Sagres promontory has spectacular views. The rooms are individual apartments with all modern conveniences. 🛏 TV 🍽 P	€€€	AE DC MC V	●	■	●	56
SAGRES: *Pousada do Infante* Sagres, 8650-385. **Road map** C7. ℂ 282-62 42 22. FAX 282-62 42 25. Named after Henry the Navigator (*see p49*), this *pousada* has a superb location overlooking the ocean on the Sagres promontory. 🛏 TV 🍽 P	€€€€	AE DC MC V	●	■	●	39

São Brás de Alportel: *Pousada de São Brás* €€€€
Poço dos Ferreiros, 8150-054. **Road map** D7. 289-84 51 72. FAX 289-84 17 26.
This peaceful *pousada* is housed in a country manor north of Faro, with
spectacular views of the hills and the sea. 📶 TV ▤ P ♿
AE DC MC V — 33

Silves: *Quinta do Rio* €€
Sítio São Estêvão, Aptdo. 217. **Road map** C7. & FAX 282-44 55 28.
Only a few kms from the centre of Silves *(see pp332–3)*, this farmhouse is
still home to the Italian family that grow fruit trees here. Visitors have access
to the big garden and delicious dinners are available on request. 📶 P
AE DC MC V — 6

Tavira: *Quinta do Caracol* €€€
São Pedro, 8800-405. **Road map** D7. 281-32 24 75. FAX 281-32 31 75.
This 17th-century whitewashed country house is surrounded by the spacious
gardens of the *quinta* (estate) that include a tennis court. This is a
quiet and practical base from which to explore the coast and hilly
interior of the eastern Algarve. 📶 P
AE DC MC V — 7

Tavira: *Convento de Santo António* €€€€
Rua de Santo António 56, 8800. **Road map** D7.
281-32 15 73. FAX 281-32 31 75
This charming whitewashed guesthouse offers elegant rooms around the
shady patio, or pretty rooms converted from the monks' cells. 📶 ▤ P
AE — 7

Vila do Bispo: *Os Gambozinos* €€€
Praia do Martinhal, 8650. **Road map** C7. 282-62 01 60. FAX 282-62 01 69.
This attractive hotel, located on the isolated Sagres peninsula, stretches
along the sandy Martinhal beach, popular with windsurfers. 📶 P
— 17

Vilamoura: *Atlantis* @ hav.reservas@virtual-net-pt €€€€€
Rua do Oceano Atlántico, 8125. **Road map** C7. 289-38 16 00. FAX 289-38 99 62.
A stylish and modern hotel with views over the sea and extensive
facilities including tennis courts and a horse-riding club. 📶 TV ▤ P ♿
AE DC MC V — 305

Vilamoura: *Tivoli Marinotel* €€€€€
Aptdo. 65, 8125-911. **Road map** C7. 289-38 99 88. FAX 289-38 98 69.
This large and luxurious hotel boasts an exclusive "Presidential Suite".
The hotel overlooks an impressive marina and the ocean. There is a
wide choice of sporting activities available here, including tennis, golf
and horse riding. 📶 TV ▤ P ♿
AE DC MC V — 382

Vila Real de Santo António: *Guadiana* €€€
Avenida da República 94, 8900. **Road map** D7. 281-51 14 82. FAX 281-51 14 78.
A prettily refurbished 19th-century town house, this hotel is right in the
centre of town and has good views over the River Guadiana. 📶 TV ▤ P
AE DC MC V — 36

MADEIRA

Caniço: *Roca Mar* €€€
Caminho Cais da Oliveira, 9125-028. 291-93 43 34. FAX 291-93 40 44.
All rooms at the clifftop Roca Mar have large balconies from which to
enjoy the sea views. The hotel offers lively evening entertainments, as
well as access to sports facilities and a free minibus to Funchal. 📶 TV P
AE DC MC V — 100

Caniço: *Quinta Splendida* €€€€
Sítio da Vargem, 9125. 291-93 04 00. FAX 291-93 04 01.
The rooms of the Quinta Splendida, a villa complex set in the gardens
of a 16th-century mansion, are tastefully furnished. 📶 TV P
AE DC MC V — 141

Funchal: *Monte Carlo* €€
Calçada da Saúde 10, 9001-801. 291-22 61 31. FAX 291-22 61 34.
Housed in a gracious building with fine views from the rooms at the front,
this dignified hotel is a steep walk uphill from the centre. 📶 P
AE DC MC V — 53

Funchal: *Residencial Santa Clara* €€
Calçada do Pico 16b, 9000. 291-74 21 94. FAX 291-74 32 80.
Only a five-minute walk from the centre of town, this small, quiet hotel
has grand interiors and splendid views of the city and mountains. 📶
— 14

Funchal: *Windsor* @ hotelwindsor@netmadeira.car €€
Rua das Hortas 4c, 9050-024. 291-23 30 81. FAX 291-23 30 80.
A friendly, modern hotel located in the maze of narrow streets at the
heart of Funchal. Some rooms in this hotel face inwards to a quiet shady
central courtyard and there is a tiny rooftop pool. 📶 TV P
— 67

For key to symbols see back flap

	Price categories in euros for a standard double room per night, including breakfast:	RESTAURANT The hotel has one or more restaurants open for lunch and supper, sometimes reserved for residents.	CREDIT CARDS	RESTAURANT	GARDEN	SWIMMING POOL	NUMBER OF ROOMS

Price categories in euros for a standard double room per night, including breakfast:
€ under 35
€€ 35–60
€€€ 60–100
€€€€ 100–150
€€€€€ over 150

RESTAURANT
The hotel has one or more restaurants open for lunch and supper, sometimes reserved for residents.
GARDEN
A garden, courtyard or large terrace for the use of hotel guests.
SWIMMING POOL
The hotel has its own indoor or outdoor pool.
CREDIT CARDS
Major credit cards accepted: AE American Express, DC Diners Club, MC MasterCard and V Visa.

	CREDIT CARDS	RESTAURANT	GARDEN	SWIMMING POOL	NUMBER OF ROOMS
FUNCHAL: *Quinta da Penha de França* @ info@hotelquintapenhafranca.com €€€ Rua Imperatriz Dona Amélia 85, 9000-014. ☎ 291-20 46 50. FAX 291-22 92 61. This fine traditional mansion has grand rooms and sits in a walled garden. There is a modern 33 room extension nearby. 🛏 TV 🍽 P	AE DC MC V	●	■	●	76
FUNCHAL: *Quinta Perestrelo* €€€€ Rua do Dr Pita 3, 9000-089. ☎ 291-70 67 00. FAX 291-70 67 06. This mid-19th-century mansion offers luxurious accommodation and is filled with antiques and set in manicured gardens. 🛏 TV 🍽	AE DC MC V	●	■	●	37
FUNCHAL: *Quinta Bela Vista* €€€€€ Caminho Avista Navios 4, 9000-129. ☎ 291-70 64 00. FAX 291-70 64 01. Located 15 minutes by car from central Funchal, this 19th-century mansion has antique furnishings and large tropical gardens. 🛏 TV 🍽 P ♿	AE DC MC V	●	■	●	89
FUNCHAL: *Pestana Casino Park Hotel* @ cph.reservas@pestana.org €€€€€ Quinta da Vigia, 9004-513. ☎ 291-20 91 00. FAX 291-23 20 76. Madeira's liveliest hotel, with a casino, a cinema, cabaret and disco, was designed by Oscar Niemeyer (architect of the Brazilian capital, Brasília). The comfortable rooms have fine views. 🛏 TV 🍽 P	AE DC MC V	●	■	●	375
FUNCHAL: *Reid's Palace Hotel* @ reservations@reidspalace.com €€€€€ Estrada Monumental 139, 9000-098. ☎ 291-71 71 71. FAX 291-71 71 77. Founded in 1891, this elegant hotel is the haunt of wealthy and famous patrons. Furnished like a stately home, with chandeliers in the dining room, it enjoys prime clifftop views and palm-fringed pools. 🛏 TV 🍽 P	AE DC MC V	●	■	●	164
FUNCHAL: *Savoy* @ savoy.reservations@netmadeira.com €€€€€ Avenida do Infante, 9004-542. ☎ 291-22 20 31. FAX 291-22 31 03. Unobtrusive service is the hallmark of this luxury hotel with spacious rooms and leisure facilities such as boules and shuffleboard. 🛏 TV 🍽 P	AE DC MC V	●	■	●	337
PICO DO ARIEIRO: *Pousada do Pico do Arieiro* €€€ Santana, 9230. ☎ 291-23 01 10. FAX 291-22 86 11. Located on top of Madeira's second highest mountain, this *pousada* has stunning dawn views for those willing to rise early. 🛏 TV P	AE DC MC V	●	■	●	25
PORTO MONIZ: *Residencial Orca* € Vila Porto Moniz, 9270. ☎ 291-85 00 00. FAX 291-85 00 19. Atlantic waves batter the shore in front of this isolated hotel. Natural rock pools below the hotel are sometimes suitable for bathing. 🛏 TV P	AE DC MC V	●	■	●	12
PORTO SANTO: *Porto Santo* @ hotelpsanto@mail.telepac.pt €€€€ Campo de Baixo, 9400-015. ☎ 291-98 01 40. FAX 291-98 01 49. The premier hotel on Porto Santo makes up for the island's low-key attractions by providing a full range of sports facilities. 🛏 TV 🍽 P	AE DC MC V	●	■	●	97
RIBEIRA BRAVA: *Brava Mar* €€€ Rua Comandante Camacho de Freitas, 9350-209. ☎ 291-95 22 20. FAX 291-95 11 22. An ideal base for exploring the western part of the island, the Brava Mar is a modern hotel with mostly balconied rooms and friendly staff. 🛏 TV	AE DC MC V	●		●	70
SERRA DE ÁGUA: *Pousada dos Vinháticos* €€€ Ribeira Brava, 9350-306. ☎ 291-95 23 44. FAX 291-95 25 40. Book well in advance for this charming *pousada* geared to walkers and set in woodland just below the Encumeada Pass. 🛏 TV P	AE DC MC V	●	■		21
THE AZORES					
CORVO: *Casa de Hóspedes* € Estrada para o Caldeirão, Vila do Corvo, 9980. ☎ 292-59 61 30. Apart from private homes, this is the only accommodation available on the tiny island of Corvo. The rooms are clean but very basic.				■	5

FAIAL: *Quinta das Buganvílias* €€€ — AE MC V — 8
Castelo Branco, Horta, 9900. **(** 292-94 32 55. **FAX** 292-94 37 43.
This family-run *quinta*, near the airport has a rose garden, fruit orchard and commercial greenhouses filled with flowers. 🛏 TV ▤

FAIAL: *Estalagem Santa Cruz* €€€€ — AE DC MC V — 25
Rua Vasco da Gama, Horta, 9900. **(** 292-29 30 21. **FAX** 292-29 39 06.
Overlooking the sea, this 16th-century fort that once protected Horta has been turned into a cosy hotel adorned with antiques. 🛏 TV ▤

FLORES: *Ocidental* @ hotelocidental@hotmail.com €€€ — AE V — 36
Sítio do Boqueirão, Santa Cruz, 9970. **(** 292-59 01 00. **FAX** 292-59 01 01.
The main hotel on Flores is a functional block on the outskirts of Santa Cruz. Rooms are plain but most have balconies facing the sea. 🛏 TV P

GRACIOSA: *Santa Cruz* €€ — 19
L. Barão de Gaudalupe 9, S. Cruz da Graciosa, 9880-344. **(** 295-71 23 45. **FAX** 295-71 28 28.
A friendly hotel on a quiet square near the town centre. Accommodation on Graciosa is very limited so book well in advance. 🛏 TV

PICO: *L'Escale de l'Atlantic* W www.ciberacores.com/escale €€ — 5
Calhau Piedade, Piedade, 9930. **(** 292-66 62 60. **FAX** 292-66 62 60.
On the eastern tip of the island with views of São Jorge, this is a highly individual designer hotel with stylish rooms. ● *Oct–Apr.* 🛏 P ♿

PICO: *Pico* €€€ — AE MC V — 68
Rua dos Biscoitos, Madalena, 9950-334. **(** 292-62 84 00. **FAX** 292-62 84 07.
A modern, well-equipped hotel offering some rooms with balconies and views of the spectacular blackened peak of the island. 🛏 TV P

SANTA MARIA: *Praia de Lobos* €€€ — AE DC MC V — 34
Rua M, Vila do Porto, 9580. **(** 296-88 22 77. **FAX** 296-88 24 82.
A smart, efficiently run hotel in the centre of Vila do Porto, the Praia do Lobos offers modern facilities and a friendly welcome. 🛏 TV ▤

SÃO JORGE: *Hotel São Jorge* €€€ — AE DC MC V — 58
Rua Machado Pires, Velas, 9800-526. **(** 295-43 01 00. **FAX** 295-41 27 36.
On the outskirts of Velas, this is the only modern hotel on the island. The attractive rooms have balconies facing the sea. 🛏 TV ▤ P

SÃO MIGUEL: *Casa Nossa Senhora do Carmo* €€€ — 6
Rua do Pópulo Decima 220, Livramento, 9500. **(** 296-64 20 48 **FAX** 296-64 20 38.
A lovingly restored and secluded *quinta*, just to the east of Ponta Delgada. The rooms are full of antiques and family treasures. ● *Dec.* 🛏 P

SÃO MIGUEL: *Solar de Lalém* €€€ — 10
Estrada de São Pedro, Maia, 9625-332. **(** 296-44 20 04. **FAX** 296-44 21 64.
An elegant 19th-century manor house on the north coast that has been decorated in a simple style by its easy-going German owners. 🛏 P

SÃO MIGUEL: *Bahia Palace* €€€€ — AE DC MC V — 121
Água d'Alto, Vila Franco do Campo, 9680. **(** 296-53 91 30. **FAX** 296-53 91 38.
A large, isolated complex on the south coast with sports and conference facilities, the Bahia is often used by business travellers. 🛏 TV ▤ P

SÃO MIGUEL: *São Pedro* €€€€ — AE DC MC V — 26
L. Almirante Dunn, Ponta Delgada, 9500. **(** 296-30 17 40. **FAX** 296-30 17 44.
Built in 1812 for the American merchant Thomas Hickling, the São Pedro is now a gracious harbourside hotel furnished with antiques. 🛏 TV P

TERCEIRA: *Beira Mar* €€€ — AE MC V — 23
L. Miguel Corte-Real, Angra do Heroísmo, 9700-182. **(** 295-21 51 88. **FAX** 295-62 82 48.
Overlooking the harbour, this hotel has small, basic rooms but is excellently located for exploring the old heart of the city. 🛏 TV

TERCEIRA: *Quinta do Martelo* @ quintamartello@mail.telepac.pt €€€ — AE MC V — 10
Canada do Martelo 24, A. do Heroísmo, 9700. **(** 295-64 28 42. **FAX** 295-64 28 41.
An idyllic rural hotel with rooms decorated with island crafts and a restaurant serving Azorean dishes. Price includes car hire. 🛏 TV ▤ P

TERCEIRA: *Quinta da Nasce-Água* €€€€ — AE DC MC V — 14
Vinha Brava, Angra do Heroísmo, 9700-236. **(** 295-62 85 01. **FAX** 295-62 85 02.
Overlooking Angra do Heroísmo, this is a luxurious modern *quinta* in private grounds with large gardens, tennis and mini-golf. 🛏 TV ▤ P

For key to symbols see back flap

WHERE TO EAT

PORTUGAL IS the country to feast on all kinds of fish and seafood, from clams, lobster and sardines to tuna, swordfish and *bacalhau* (salted cod), the national favourite. All along the coast are restaurants dedicated to cooking freshly caught fish. The Portuguese are great meat eaters too and justifiably proud of such dishes as roast kid and sucking pig. Inland, meat is more

Sign for roast suckling pig at Mealhada *(see p412)*

plentiful and generally of better quality, with specialities varying according to region. Most restaurants are reasonably priced, and offer generous portions. Lisbon has plenty of cheap cafés and restaurants, as well as international ones, as does the Algarve. This introduction gives tips on types of eating places, menus, drinks and ordering to help you enjoy eating out in Portugal.

Drinks waiter at the Palácio de Seteais, near Sintra *(see p409)*

TYPES OF RESTAURANTS

EATING VENUES come in all shapes and sizes and at all price levels. Among the most reasonable is the local *tasca* or tavern, often just a room with half-a-dozen tables presided over by a husband-and-wife team. These are often frequented by locals and professionals at lunch

time, which is a good lead to follow. The *casa de pasto* offers a budget three-course meal in a large dining room, while a *restaurante* is more formal and offers a wider choice of dishes. At a *marisqueira* (found all along the coast), the emphasis is on fresh fish and seafood. The *churrasqueira*, a very popular concept imported from Brazil, specializes in spit-roasted foods, while a *cervejaria* (beerhouse) is the ideal place to go for a beer and a snack.

As a rule, hotel restaurants in Portugal are of surprisingly good quality. *Pousadas (see pp378–9)*, found throughout the country, offer a network of traditional restaurants, with the focus on local specialities.

Sign for Maria Rita's *(see p415)*

EATING HOURS

LUNCH IS USUALLY served between 1 and 3 pm when many restaurants, especially in cities, get very crowded. Dinner is served from 7–10pm in most places, but can be later in restaurants and *cervejarias* in major cities and resort areas such as Lisbon, Oporto and the Algarve. Another choice for a very late dinner would be to combine a meal with a show at a *fado* house *(see pp66–7)*, open from about 9:30pm to 3 or 4am.

RESERVATIONS

IT IS A GOOD IDEA to book ahead for expensive restaurants, and for those in popular locations in high season. Disabled people should certainly check in advance on facilities and access. Special facilities are generally lacking but most places will try to be helpful.

THE MENU

SOME RESTAURANTS, especially in tourist areas, offer an *ementa turística*, a cheap, daily-changing three-course menu served with coffee and a drink (glass of wine, beer, water or soft drink). This provides a full meal at a good price with no hidden costs. Lunch, *almoço*, is often a two-course fixed menu, consisting of a fish or meat main course with potatoes or rice and either a starter or a

The impressive interior of the Cozinha Velha *(see p407)* at Queluz

Sharing the local veal speciality at Gabriela's, in Sendim (see p413)

pudding. To sample a local speciality, ask for the *prato do dia* – dish of the day.

Dinner *(jantar)* may be two or more courses, perhaps followed by ice cream, fruit, a simple dessert or cheese. Casserole-style dishes, such as fish or meat stews or *porco à alentejana* (pork with clams), are brought to the table in a pot for people to share, as are large fish such as sea bass, which are sold by weight. One serving can easily be shared by two people and it is perfectly acceptable to ask for a *meia dose* or half-portion. Peculiar to Portugal is the plate of assorted appetizers – olives, cheese and sardine pâté – brought with bread at the start of a meal. Be aware that these are not included in the menu price, and may add substantially to the bill.

VEGETARIANS

VEGETARIANS WILL not eat as well as fish lovers, although local cheeses and breads can be excellent. In Lisbon or along the Algarve, vegetarians will benefit from ethnic restaurants. Chefs will usually be happy to provide something meatless, though this will probably mean simply an omelette or a salad.

WINE AND DRINKS

IT WOULD BE a shame to visit Portugal without sampling its two most famous fortified wines: port *(see pp252–3)* and Madeira *(see p349)*. Wherever you are, it is safe to order a bottle or jug of house wine to wash down your meal.

Otherwise, ask for the wine list, and choose one of Portugal's many native wines *(see pp28–9)*. Sagres and Super Bock are good beers and the bottled water is recommended. This comes either *com gás* (sparkling) or *sem gás* (still).

Relaxing at a seafront bar at Póvoa de Varzim in the Minho

CAFÉS AND CAKE SHOPS

CAFÉS ARE FUNDAMENTAL to Portuguese daily life and vary from modern white rooms to splendidly decorated, tiled and mirrored places where you can sit and talk or read the paper for hours. Many have tables outside. They make perfect meeting points and usually offer a range of snacks and sandwiches. At any time of the day a café is the obvious choice for a coffee break with a roll, croissant or cake. Do not miss the *pastelarias* (cake shops); the sweet-toothed Portuguese adore cakes, and the selections are excellent *(see pp147, 231 & 289)*.

PAYING THE BILL

IN MOST RESTAURANTS you have to pay a cover charge and it is normal to give a 10 per cent tip where service is not included. It is wise to check in advance whether or not a restaurant accepts credit cards.

CHILDREN

IN PORTUGAL, children are viewed as a blessing rather than a nuisance, so it is an ideal country for families to eat out together. Children's portions or half-portions at reduced prices are advertised or will be provided on request.

SMOKING

SMOKING IS WIDESPREAD and permitted in all public places in Portugal, unless there is a sign saying *proibido fumar*. No-smoking areas in restaurants are very rare.

COFFEE DRINKING IN PORTUGAL

Coffee is widely drunk in Portugal and served in many forms. The most popular is a small cup of strong black coffee like an espresso. In Lisbon and the South this is called *uma bica*; elsewhere ask for *um café*. A strong one is called *uma italiana*; for a weaker version, try *um carioca de café*. *Uma meia de leite* is half coffee, half milk. Strong coffee with a dash of milk is known as *um garoto escuro* (*um garoto claro* is quite milky). If you like your coffee with plenty of milk, ask for *um galão* (a gallon). This is served in a tall glass, and again you can order *um galão claro* (very milky) or *escuro* (strong).

Uma bica   **Um galão**

Choosing a Restaurant

THE RESTAURANTS in this guide have been selected for their good value, exceptional food or interesting location. This chart highlights some of the factors which may influence your choice. This chart lists the restaurants by region; the thumb tabs on the side of the page are colour-coded to correspond with the regional areas in the guide.

	CREDIT CARDS	LATE OPENING	OUTDOOR TABLES	GOOD WINE LIST

LISBON

ALCÂNTARA: *Espalha Brasas* €€€
Doca de Santo Amaro, Armazém 12. **Map 3** A5. ☎ 21-396 20 59.
Located in Lisbon's lively Docas area, this restaurant specializes in fish and serves cocktails. Enjoy eating outside in the summer. ● *lunch (Aug); Sun.*
Credit Cards: AE DC MC V — Late Opening ■ — Outdoor Tables ●

ALFAMA: *Hua-Ta-Li* €€
Rua dos Bacalhoeiros 109–115. **Map 7** C4. ☎ 21-887 91 70.
This is a large Chinese restaurant close to the docks that serves all the regular rice and noodle favourites. Fast and efficient service. ▤

ALFAMA: *Lautasco* €€
Beco do Azinhal 7a (off Rua de São Pedro). **Map 8** E4. ☎ 21-886 01 73.
Rustically decorated with wooden panelling and wagon-wheel chandeliers, Lautasco specializes in typical Portuguese cuisine. ● *Sun; 20 Dec–15 Jan.*
Credit Cards: AE DC MC V — Late Opening ■ — Outdoor Tables ●

ALFAMA: *Mestré André* €€€
Calçadinha de Santo Estevão 6. **Map 8** E3. ☎ 21-887 14 87.
Lively Portuguese restaurant offering delicious pork and fish dishes as well as excellent *churrasco* (spit-roasted meat) *(see p120).* ● *Sun.* ⬥
Credit Cards: AE — Late Opening ■ — Outdoor Tables ●

ALFAMA: *Restô do Chapitô* €€€
Costa do Castelo 7. **Map 7** C3. ☎ 21-886 73 34.
An extensive menu offers such international dishes as chateaubriand at this cheerful restaurant with a bar and fine views over the harbour. ● *Mon.*
Late Opening ■ — Outdoor Tables ● — Good Wine List ■

ALFAMA: *Sol Nascente* €€€
Rua de São Tomé 86. **Map 8** D3. ☎ 21-887 72 13.
On the main road up to the castle from Alfama, this restaurant has fine views over the Tagus. Try the seafood rice or the pork with clams. ● *Mon.* ▤
Credit Cards: AE DC MC V — Late Opening ■ — Outdoor Tables ●

ALFAMA: *Casa do Leão* €€€€
Castelo de São Jorge. **Map 8** D3. ☎ 21-887 59 62.
Beneath arched brick ceilings, inside part of Castelo de São Jorge *(see pp78–9),* this restaurant offers superb service and excellent traditional Portuguese cuisine. Sit outside to enjoy the magnificent views. ▤ ♬ *Wed–Fri.*
Credit Cards: AE DC MC V — Outdoor Tables ● — Good Wine List ■

ALFAMA: *Faz Figura* €€€€
Rua do Paraíso 15b. **Map 8** F2. ☎ 21-886 89 81.
A smart restaurant, where panoramic views of the river and city can be enjoyed from the covered terrace. Specialities include *cataplana* dishes *(see p121)* and *picanha* (steak grilled over an open fire). ● *Sat lunch; Sun.* ▤
Credit Cards: AE DC MC V — Outdoor Tables ● — Good Wine List ■

ALMADA: *Atira-te ao Rio* €€€
Cais do Ginjal 69–70. ☎ 21-275 13 80.
View Lisbon from the other bank of the Tagus and enjoy the restaurant's Brazilian specialities, including *feijoada à Brasileira* (bean stew). ● *Mon.*
Late Opening ■ — Outdoor Tables ●

BAIRRO ALTO: *Bota Alta* €€€
Travessa da Queimada 37. **Map 7** A3. ☎ 21-342 79 59.
The "High Boot" is an attractive restaurant with original paintings on the walls. The menu consists of traditional Portuguese dishes. ● *Sat lunch; Sun.*
Credit Cards: AE DC MC V

BAIRRO ALTO: *Casanostra* €€€
Travessa do Poço da Cidade 60. **Map 7** A3. ☎ 21-342 59 31.
Within the green, white and black interior of this Italian restaurant you can choose from a six-page menu full of delicacies. ● *Mon, Sat lunch.* ▤
Credit Cards: AE DC MC V

BAIRRO ALTO: *El Último Tango* €€€
Rua Diário de Notícias 62. **Map 7** A4. ☎ 21-342 03 41.
In this Argentinian restaurant the most popular choice is meat grilled over an open fire. It also has cocktails. ● *Sun lunch; 2 weeks in Jun; 2 weeks in Oct.* ▤
Credit Cards: MC V — Late Opening ■ — Outdoor Tables ●

Price categories are for a three-course meal for one with half a bottle of wine, including cover charge, service and VAT.
€ under 10 euros
€€ 10–15 euros
€€€ 15–20 euros
€€€€ 20–30 euros
€€€€€ over 30 euros

LATE OPENING
The kitchen stays open after 10pm, and you can usually have a meal up until at least 11pm.

OUTDOOR TABLES
Tables for eating outdoors, in a garden or on a balcony, often with a pleasant view.

GOOD WINE LIST
The restaurant will have a good selection of quality wines.

CREDIT CARDS
This indicates which of the major credit cards are accepted: *AE* American Express, *DC* Diners Club, *MC* MasterCard and *V* Visa.

	Credit Cards	Late Opening	Outdoor Tables	Good Wine List
BAIRRO ALTO: *Massima Culpa* €€€ Rua da Atalaia 35–7. **Map 4 F2.** (21-342 01 21. This restaurant has a simple, uncomplicated decor with a very Italian atmosphere, and offers numerous antipasti and pasta dishes. ● *lunch; Mon.* ▤	AE DC MC V	■		
BAIRRO ALTO: *Canto do Camões* €€€€ Travessa da Espera 38. **Map 7 A4.** (21-346 54 64. This small, tiled *fado (see pp66–7)* restaurant serves traditional Portuguese food and a range of international dishes. ● *Sun (Nov–Mar).* ▤ ♫	AE DC MC V	■		
BAIRRO ALTO: *Pap'Açorda* €€€€ Rua da Atalaia 57. **Map 4 F2.** (21-346 48 11. Both Lisboetas and tourists come here for the *açorda de mariscos* (bread stew and seafood), served in a light dining room. The menu is traditional Portuguese with some novel touches. ● *Mon lunch; Sun; 2 weeks in Jul; 2 weeks in Oct.* ▤	AE DC MC V			■
BAIRRO ALTO: *Tavares* €€€€€ Rua da Misericórdia 37. **Map 7 A4.** (21-342 11 12. Lisbon's oldest restaurant, Tavares, dates from 1784. Its reputation is maintained with dishes such as breast of partridge on toast with *foie gras* and fillets of sea bass *au gratin* with prawn sauce. ● *Sat; Sun lunch.* ▤ &	AE DC MC V			■
BAIXA: *Casa do Alentejo* €€ Rua das Portas de Santo Antão 58. **Map 7 A2.** (21-346 92 31. Set in a fine 19th-century house, this restaurant specializes entirely in Alentejan food such as *açorda alentejana* (coriander and bread soup). ● *1–19 Aug.*				
BAIXA: *Ribadouro* €€ Rua do Salitre 2–12. **Map 4 F1.** (21-354 94 11. Popular with the locals who flood in for a drink after work, this restaurant is part café and part bar, and offers a tremendous shellfish menu. ▤	AE DC MC V	■		
BAIXA: *Lagosta Real* €€€ Rua das Portas de Santo Antão 37. **Map 7 A2.** (21-342 39 95. Fish, and particularly shellfish, is the order of the day here. Shellfish casserole, lobster stew and a grilled seafood platter are house specialities. ▤	AE DC MC V	■	●	■
BAIXA: *Paris* €€€ Rua dos Sapateiros 126. **Map 7 B4.** (21-346 97 97. Open for nearly half a century, Paris offers a delicious mixture of Portuguese and Galician cuisine. Try the swordfish steak or the Alentejan pork. ▤ &	AE DC MC V			
BAIXA: *Solar dos Presuntos* €€€ Rua das Portas de Santo Antão 150. **Map 7 A2.** (21-342 42 53. An enticing window display of fish and shellfish draws diners inside. Caricatures of famous footballers adorn the walls. ● *Sun; 2 weeks in Aug; 1 week at Christmas.* ▤	AE DC MC V			
BAIXA: *Gambrinus* €€€€€ Rua das Portas de Santo Antão 23–5. **Map 7 A2.** (21-342 14 66. Renowned throughout Portugal, this is an exceptional and expensive restaurant. The service is impeccable, the cuisine delectable and the extensive wine list includes an array of vintage ports. ● *1 May.* ▤	AE V	■		■
BELÉM: *Já Sei* €€€ Avda Brasilia 202. **Map 1 A5.** (21-301 59 69. This has a beautiful location, right on the river, so it is pleasant in the summer; the seafood-based menu is good all-year-round. ● *Sun dinner; Mon.* ▤ ♫	AE DE MC V	■		■
BELÉM: *São Jerónimo* €€€€ Rua dos Jerónimos 12. **Map 1 C4.** (21-364 87 97. São Jerónimo is an elegant, spacious restaurant with 1930s decor. The excellent mixed menu of Portuguese and French cuisine includes skate in peach sauce and duck with nuts in wine sauce. ● *Sat lunch; Sun.* ▤	AE DC MC V			■

For key to symbols see back flap

....

	CREDIT CARDS	LATE OPENING	OUTDOOR TABLES	GOOD WINE LIST
Price categories are for a three-course meal for one with half a bottle of wine, including cover charge, service and VAT: € under 10 euros €€ 10–15 euros €€€ 15–20 euros €€€€ 20–30 euros €€€€€ over 30 euros **LATE OPENING** The kitchen stays open after 10pm, and you can usually have a meal up until at least 11pm. **OUTDOOR TABLES** Tables for eating outdoors, in a garden or on a balcony, often with a pleasant view. **GOOD WINE LIST** The restaurant will have a good selection of quality wines. **CREDIT CARDS** This indicates which of the major credit cards are accepted: *AE* American Express, *DC* Diners Club, *MC* MasterCard and *V* Visa.				
BELÉM: *Vela Latina* €€€€ Doca do Bom Sucesso. **Map 1** B5. 21-301 71 18. On the waterfront, this restaurant has a bar and terrace overlooking the Torre de Belém. The speciality is *cataplana rica do mar* (seafood). ● *Sun.* ▤ ♿	AE DC MC V	■	●	■
BELÉM: *O Nobre* €€€€€ Rua das Mercês 71a–b. **Map 2** D3. 21-362 21 06. Worth searching out on a day trip to Belém, O Nobre serves crab soup, game stew, partridge, fish with olives and roast pork with grapes. ● *Sun; Sat lunch.*	AE MC V	■		
CAMPO PEQUENO: *Chimarrão* €€€ Campo Pequeno 79. **Map 5** C1. 21-793 97 60. This Brazilian restaurant specializes in dishes grilled on an open fire. Try *rodízio* (unlimited amount of grilled meat) with salad, rice and black beans. ▤ ♫	AE DC MC V	■		■
CAMPO PEQUENO: *António Clara – Clube dos Empresários* €€€ Avenida da República 38. **Map 5** C1. 21-799 42 80. This wonderful old mansion offers a French-influenced menu in dining areas that were once individual rooms in the house. ● *Sun.* ▤	AE DC MC V			
CHIADO: *Adega do Ribatejo* €€€ Rua Diário de Notícias 23. **Map 7** A4. 21-346 83 43. This charming tavern, whose menu is strong on steak and fried fish, offers frequent and unmissable fado extravaganzas. ● *Sun.* ▤ ♫	MC V	■		
CHIADO: *Tágide* €€€€€ Largo da Academia Nacional de Belas Artes 18–20. **Map 7** B5. 21-342 07 20. An elegant restaurant with 18th-century tiles, a 17th-century fountain and a superb view over the Tagus. Luxurious dishes include marinated salmon, baby octopus in red wine sauce and partridge in port sauce. ● *Sat lunch; Sun.* ▤	AE DC MC V			■
ENTRECAMPOS: *A Gôndola* €€€ Avenida de Berna 64. **Map 5** B2. 21-797 04 26. A Gôndola is a charming restaurant offering a wide choice of dishes including Italian as well as Portuguese specialities. In the summer enjoy your meal in the pleasant surrounding gardens. ● *Sun.* ▤	AE MC V		●	■
ESTEFÂNIA: *Espiral* € Praça da Ilha do Faial 14a–b. **Map 6** D3. 21-357 35 85. This vegetarian restaurant, set in a pleasant square, has a plain interior but a large menu, with fresh juice drinks and organic wine. ● *1 Jan; 1 May.* ▤	AE MC V			
ESTEFÂNIA: *Clara Restaurante* €€€€€ Campo dos Mártires da Pátria 49. **Map 6** D5. 21-885 30 53. This is a spacious and luxurious restaurant in a green-tiled mansion, complete with garden terrace, fountain and fireplace. The excellent menu is predominantly traditional Portuguese. ● *Sat lunch; Sun; 1–15 Aug.* ▤ ♫	AE DC MC V		●	■
ESTRELA: *Conventual* €€€€ Praça das Flores 45. **Map 4** E2. 21-390 91 96. Decorated with religious antiques, this restaurant has an interesting menu that includes fried baby eels and ox tongue in egg sauce. ● *Sat lunch; Sun; Mon.* ▤	AE DC MC V			■
GRAÇA: *Via Graça* €€€ Rua Damasceno Monteiro 9b. **Map 8** D1. 21-887 08 30. Via Graça offers some fine views of the castle and the Baixa, and well-presented Portuguese cuisine. ● *Sat lunch; Sun.* ▤	AE DC MC V	■		■
LAPA: *Café d'Arte* € Rua das Janelas Verdes, Museu de Arte Antiga. **Map 4** D4. 21-396 09 30. This establishment provides an excellent opportunity to combine lunch with a museum trip in a fantastic riverside setting. ● *Mon; Tue & evenings (closes with museum).* ▤ ♿	AE MC V		●	

Lapa: *Picanha* €€€
Rua das Janelas Verdes 96. **Map 4 D4.** (21-397 54 01.
Picanha sells one dish: *picanha*, which is rump steak grilled on an open fire, served with potatoes, rice, salad and beans. ● *Sat; Sun lunch.* 🔲

Lapa: *Nariz de Vinho Tinto* €€€€
Rua do Conde 75. **Map 4 D3.** (21-395 30 35.
This restaurant offers top-class cooking and is famous for its casseroles and choice of regional dishes, including wild game in season. ● *Mon.* 🔲 &
AE V

Lapa: *Sua Excelência o Conde* €€€€€
Rua do Conde 34. **Map 4 D3.** (21-390 36 14.
The owner here can recite the menu in five languages. Classical Portuguese dishes served in a relaxed atmosphere. ● *Sat & Sun lunch; Wed; Sep.* 🔲 &
AE DC MC V

Lapa: *A Confraria* €€€€€
Rua das Janelas Verdes 32. **Map 4 D4.** (21-396 24 35.
This delightful hotel restaurant has a varied menu. Sit inside and admire the tiled walls, or outside below a towering palm in the flower-laden courtyard.
AE DC MC V

Lapa: *Ristorante Hotel Cipriani* €€€€€
Lapa Palace, Rua do Pau da Bandeira 4. **Map 3 C3.** (21-394 94 34.
This restaurant offers modern Italian and Mediterranean food in an elegant setting. There is a non-smoking section. 🔲 &
AE DC MC V

Rato: *Os Tibetanos* €€
Rua do Salitre 117. **Map 4 F1.** (21-314 20 38.
This vegetarian restaurant, in a Tibetan Buddhist centre, has much character and offers a tasty and inexpensive Tibetan menu. No smoking. ● *Sat; Sun.* 🔲
AE MC V

Rato: *Casa da Comida* €€€€€
Travessa das Amoreiras 1. **Map 5 B5.** (21-388 53 76.
A refined Lisbon restaurant with a charming patio, and an exquisite menu offering caviar, frogs' legs, goat, duck and pheasant. ● *Sat lunch; Sun.* 🔲
AE DC MC V

Rotunda: *Restaurante 33A* €€€€
Rua Alexandre Herculano 33a. **Map 5 C5.** (21-354 60 79.
Offering traditional Portuguese cuisine, this restaurant also has a small lounge with a country ambience and decor to match. ● *Sat lunch; Sun.* 🔲 🎵 &
AE DC MC V

Rotunda: *Pabe* €€€€€
Rua do Duque de Palmela 27a. **Map 5 C5.** (21-353 74 84.
Pabe looks like a Tudor house and serves Portuguese food. A medieval atmosphere is accentuated by wooden-beamed ceilings and copper tables. 🔲 &
AE DC MC V

Rotunda: *O Terraço* €€€€
Hotel Tivoli Lisboa, Avenida da Liberdade 185. **Map 4 F1.** (21-319 89 00.
This top-floor restaurant serves an innovative lunchtime special each day of the week. There are great views from the terrace. 🔲 🎵 &
AE DC MC V

Saldanha: *António* €€
Rua Tomás Ribeiro 63. **Map 5 C3.** (21-353 87 80.
This restaurant is a good stop for lunch. The cooking is straightforward, and includes steak and fries and roast chicken. ● *eve; Sun.* 🔲
V

Saldanha: *Cervejaria Portugália* €€
Avenida Almirante Reis 117. **Map 6 E5.** (21-314 00 02.
This atmospheric beer hall is the original of a small chain, the restaurant is popular with families and serves excellent shellfish and steaks. &
AE DC MC V

Saldanha: *O Polícia* €€€
Rua Marquês Sá da Bandeira 112a. **Map 5 B3.** (21-796 35 05.
A pleasant restaurant with an attractive bar, so named because the owner's grandfather was a policeman. The menu changes daily. ● *Sat eve; Sun.* 🔲
AE MC V

Saldanha: *Café Creme* €€€
Avenida Conde de Valbom 52a. **Map 5 B2.** (21-796 43 60.
An attractive, open and airy restaurant, Café Creme offers a wide choice of pastas, salads, cod, beef and grilled dishes. ● *Sat lunch; Sun.* 🔲
AE DC MC V

Xabregas: *D'Avis* €€
Rua do Grilo 98. (21-868 13 54.
Specialities at this restaurant, located east of the city centre, include cod with coriander and *migas* (bread dish with spare ribs). ● *Sun.* 🔲 &
AE DC MC V

For key to symbols see back flap

Price categories are for a three-course meal for one with half a bottle of wine, including cover charge, service and VAT:

€ under 10 euros
€€ 10–15 euros
€€€ 15–20 euros
€€€€ 20–30 euros
€€€€€ over 30 euros

LATE OPENING
The kitchen stays open after 10pm, and you can usually have a meal up until at least 11pm.

OUTDOOR TABLES
Tables for eating outdoors, in a garden or on a balcony, often with a pleasant view.

GOOD WINE LIST
The restaurant will have a good selection of quality wines.

CREDIT CARDS
This indicates which of the major credit cards are accepted: *AE* American Express, *DC* Diners Club, *MC* MasterCard and *V* Visa.

	CREDIT CARDS	LATE OPENING	OUTDOOR TABLES	GOOD WINE LIST
THE LISBON COAST				
CASCAIS: *Dom Manolo* €€ Avenida Marginal 11. 📞 21-483 11 26. A good-value mixed menu; the house speciality is *frango no churrasco* (spit-roast chicken). *Pastéis de bacalhau* (cod croquettes) are also good. ● Jan. ▤			●	
CASCAIS: *Os Navigantes* €€ Travassa dos Navegantes 13. 📞 21-486 86 31. This Portuguese restaurant is very popular with locals and is famous for its fresh fish and spit-roasted meats. ● Sun. ♿ (not toilets).	AE V	▪		▪
CASCAIS: *Estrela da India* €€ Rua Freitas Reis 15b. 📞 21-484 65 40. Some distance from the waterfront, this unpretentious Indian restaurant has a good choice of vegetarian dishes and a takeaway service. ● Mon. ▤	AE MC V			
CASCAIS: *Esplanada Santa Marta* €€€ Travassa do Enviado de Inglaterra 80. 📞 21-352 11 94. Known for its wide range of fish and shellfish dishes, as well as for a good choice of traditional Portuguese fare. During the summer the food is also served outside on a small terrace overlooking the sea. ▤ ♿	AE MC V	▪	●	▪
CASCAIS: *Casa Velha* €€€€ Avenida Valbom 1. 📞 21-483 25 86. With a recomended regional menu and charming rustic decor, Casa Velha also boasts a table always reserved for the president. ● Wed. ▤ ♿	AE MC V	▪		▪
CASCAIS: *Buchanan's Café, Bar and Restaurant* €€€€ Travessa da Alfarrobeira 2, 40. 📞 21-484 75 90. FAX 21-484 75 91 Located on the top floor of a building with stunning views over the new marina. High-quality modern European cuisine is served, with a choice of vegetarian dishes and fine wines. The café/bar has a fireplace. ● Mon (Oct–Mar). ▤	AE MC V	▪	●	▪
CASCAIS: *Eduardo's* €€€€ Largo das Grutas 3. 📞 21-483 19 01. Tucked away in a quiet corner, Eduardo's serves a mix of Belgian cuisine and Portuguese dishes, many of which are flambéed at the table. ● Wed.	AE MC V		●	▪
CASCAIS: *O Pescador* €€€€€ Rua das Flores 10b. 📞 21-483 20 54. A well-known seaside restaurant, decorated with old boats, nets and pictures of famous people who have eaten here. Specializes in seafood. ● Sun. ▤	AE DC MC V	▪	●	▪
ERICEIRA: *O Barco* €€€ Rua Capitão João Lopes 14. 📞 261-86 27 59. O Barco has sea views. The fish specialities include *feijoada de marisco* (seafood and bean stew) and seafood curry. ● Thu; 2 weeks in Jul & Dec. ▤	AE DC MC V			
ESTORIL: *Pinto's* €€ Arcadas do Parque 18b. 📞 21-468 72 47. Close to the Palácio Hotel, Pinto's is a mix of bar, cafeteria and restaurant. It serves pizzas and pastas, as well as a large selection of shellfish. ▤	AE DC MC V	▪	●	
ESTORIL: *Four Seasons* €€€€€ Hotel Palácio Estoril, Rua do Parque. 📞 21-468 04 00. Exposed beams and leather seats furnish this luxurious restaurant. Try the flambéed prawns with Pernod, cream and hollandaise sauce. ▤ ♪ ♿	AE DC MC V			▪
GUINCHO: *Estalagem Muchaxo* €€€€ Praia do Guincho. 📞 21-487 02 21. Overlooking Cabo da Roca, Muchaxo offers a good seafood menu. A popular dish is lobster in a tomato, cream and port sauce. ▤ ♪ Sat & Sun lunch. ♿	AE DC MC V	▪	●	▪

GUINCHO: *Porto de Santa Maria* €€€€€

Estrada do Guincho. [21-487 94 50.

This is one of the best seafood restaurants in the area. Choose your meal from the fish tanks and marble table where the best fish is displayed. ● *Mon.* 🍽 &

AE	
MC	
DC	
V	

MONTE ESTORIL: *O Sinaleiro* €€

Avenida de Sabóia 595. [21-468 54 39.

O Sinaleiro serves excellent food and is popular with locals. Try *escalopes à Zíngara* (in Madeira wine sauce with cream). ● *Wed; 2 weeks in Apr & Oct.* & 🍽

AE	
MC	
DC	
V	

MONTE ESTORIL: *O Festival* €€€€

Avenida de Sabóia 515d. [21-468 85 63.

This delightful restaurant serves an essentially French menu. Try the duck à l'orange or the sole filled with salmon mousseline. ● *Mon; Tue lunch; Jan.* 🍽

AE	
MC	
DC	
V	

PAÇO D'ARCOS: *La Cocagne* €€€€€

Avenida Marginal (Curva dos Pinheiros). [21-441 42 31.

One of the best French restaurants in Portugal, La Cocagne has refined decor, impeccable service, exquisite dishes and magnificent views of the ocean. 🍽

AE	
DC	
MC	
V	

PALMELA: *Pousada de Palmela* €€€€€

Pousada de Palmela, Castelo de Palmela. [21-235 12 26.

The converted refectory of the 15th-century monastery offers such delicacies as oyster soup or salt cod filled with bacon and coated in corn bread. 🎵 *Fri & Sat.*

AE	
DC	
MC	
V	

PORTINHO DA ARRÁBIDA: *Beira-Mar* €€€

Portinho da Arrábida. [21-218 05 44.

Enjoy specials such as *arroz de tamboril* (monkfish rice) and *arroz de marisco* (seafood rice) in this stunning seaside setting. ● *Wed (Oct–Mar); 15 Dec–15 Jan.*

AE	
DC	
MC	
V	

QUELUZ: *Cozinha Velha* €€€€€

Largo Palácio Nacional de Queluz. [21-435 61 58.

Set in the old kitchens of the Queluz Royal Palace, this spacious restaurant is famous for its typical Portuguese fare, such as pork with clams. 🍽 🎵

AE	
DC	
MC	
V	

SESIMBRA: *Ribamar* €€€€

Avenida dos Náufragos 29. [21-223 48 53.

Right next to the sea and offering fantastic views, Ribamar serves some unusual specialities; try fish with seaweed, or cream of sea-urchin soup. 🍽 &

AE	
MC	
V	

SETÚBAL: *Copa d'Ouro* €€

Rua João Soveral 17. [265-52 37 55.

A superb fish menu here features *caldeirada à Setubalense* (seafood stew) and *cataplana de tamboril* (monk fish steamed in its own juice). ● *Tue; Sep.* 🍽

AE	
MC	
V	

SETÚBAL: *Pousada de São Filipe* €€€€

Pousada de São Filipe, Castelo de São Filipe. [265-52 38 44.

This restaurant is part of a *pousada* that overlooks Setúbal and the Sado estuary. Its regional dishes include pumpkin cream soup and fried red mullet. 🍽

AE	
DC	
MC	
V	

SINTRA: *Tulhas* €€

Rua Gil Vicente 4–6. [21-923 23 78.

This rustic restaurant, decorated with blue and yellow Sintra *azulejos*, serves superb traditional dishes such as veal steaks in Madeira sauce. ● *Wed.* 🍽

AE	
DC	
MC	
V	

SINTRA: *Lawrences* €€€€

Rua Consigliéri Pedroso 39–40, Sintra. [21-910 55 00.

Set in the Lawrences Hotel, this restaurant has a wide-ranging international and Portuguese menu that changes daily. 🍽 &

AE	
V	

SINTRA: *Panorâmico* €€€€

Hotel Tivoli Sintra, Praça da República. [21-923 35 05.

Overlooking the lush, verdant Sintra valley, this restaurant offers a different speciality as a main dish each evening, as well as a regular menu. 🍽 &

AE	
DC	
MC	
V	

SINTRA: *Restaurante Palácio de Seteais* €€€€€

Avenida Barbosa du Bocage 8, Seteais. [21-923 32 00.

Set in an 18th-century palace, which is now a hotel, this restaurant has a daily-changing menu of international and traditional Portuguese cuisine. 🎵 &

AE	
DC	
MC	
V	

VILA FRESCA DE AZEITÃO: *O Manel* €€

Largo Dr Teixeira 6a. [21-219 03 36.

A family-run restaurant with a good-value menu. Specialities here are cod in cream sauce and *feijoada de gambas* (seafood and bean stew). ● *Sun; Oct.* 🍽

AE	
MC	
V	

Price categories are for a three-course meal for one with half a bottle of wine, including cover charge, service and VAT:

€ under 10 euros
€€ 10–15 euros
€€€ 15–20 euros
€€€€ 20–30 euros
€€€€€ over 30 euros

LATE OPENING
The kitchen stays open after 10pm, and you can usually have a meal up until at least 11pm.

OUTDOOR TABLES
Tables for eating outdoors, in a garden or on a balcony, often with a pleasant view.

GOOD WINE LIST
The restaurant will have a good selection of quality wines.

CREDIT CARDS
This indicates which of the major credit cards are accepted: *AE* American Express, *DC* Diners Club, *MC* MasterCard, *V* Visa.

	CREDIT CARDS	LATE OPENING	OUTDOOR TABLES	GOOD WINE LIST

ESTREMADURA AND RIBATEJO

ABRANTES: *O Pelicano* €€ Rua Nossa Senhora da Conceição 1. **Road map** C4. ☎ 241-36 23 17. Situated on the busy main square, O Pelicano serves good-value Portuguese food such as *bacalhau à Lagareiro* (breaded cod steak). 🍴	AE DC MC V			
ALCOBAÇA: *Trindade* €€ Praça Dom Afonso Henriques 22. **Road map** C4. ☎ 262-58 23 97. Located in a beautiful square next to the north wing of the monastery. Specials include *frango na púcara* (chicken stew). ● *2 weeks in May & Oct.* 🍴	AE MC V		●	
ALMEIRIM: *Toucinho* €€ Rua Timor 2. **Road map** C4. ☎ 243-59 22 37. A family-run restaurant with a reputation for fine country cooking. Try the home-made bread and the real *sopa de pedra (see p146)*. ● *Thu; Aug.* 🍴				
BARRAGEM DO CASTELO DE BODE: *São Pedro* €€€€ Pousada de São Pedro. **Road map** C4. ☎ 249-38 11 59. In a *pousada* dating from the 1950s, this restaurant has a regional menu that includes grilled trout and *chanfana* goat meat stewed in red wine. 🍴	AE DC MC V			▪
BATALHA: *Mestre Afonso Domingues* €€€ Largo Mestre Afonso Domingues. **Road map** C4. ☎ 244-76 52 60. This restaurant, found in the *pousada* named after the architect of the nearby monastery, serves such regional dishes as fried pork with turnip tops. 🍴	AE DC MC V		●	▪
CALDAS DA RAINHA: *A Lareira* €€€ Rua da Lareira, Alto do Nobre. **Road map** B4. ☎ 262-82 34 32. Located in a pine wood, A Lareira offers typical traditional Portuguese food such as *ensopado de enguias* (eel stew), *perdiz à Lareira* (partridge with chestnuts, fruits and vegetables) and home-made desserts. ● *Tue.* 🍴 ♿	DC MC V	▪		▪
CALDAS DA RAINHA: *Supatra* €€€ Rua General Amílcar Mota, 2500. **Road map** B4. ☎ 262-84 29 20. Once Portugal's only Thai restaurant, *Supatra* still attracts visitors from far and wide. Portuguese dishes are also served. ● *Mon; 2 weeks in May & Dec.* ♿	AE MC V	▪		▪
FÁTIMA: *Dom Gonçalo* €€€€ Rua Jacinta Marto 100. **Road map** C4. ☎ 249-53 93 30. Set in a charming hotel surrounded by its own grounds, not far from the sanctuary. Try the fillet of fish with prawn rice or the braised duck. 🍴 ♿	AE DC MC V			
FÁTIMA: *Tia Alice* €€€€ Rua do Adro. **Road map** C4. ☎ 249-53 17 37. One of the best restaurants in the area. The service is excellent and house specialities are Trás-os-Montes-style rice and duck rice. ● *Mon; Sun eve; Jul.* 🍴	AE MC V			▪
LEIRIA: *Tromba Rija* €€€€€ Rua Professores Portelas 22, Marrazes. **Road map** C4. ☎ 244-85 50 72. Well-known throughout Portugal, this restaurant serves excellent starters, including *ovos verdes* (a speciality egg dish), and a variety of *empadas* (pies). Main courses include partridge. ● *Mon lunch; Sun; 2 weeks in Aug.* 🎵 *Sat.*	AE MC V			▪
NAZARÉ: *Beira-Mar* €€ Avenida da República 40. **Road map** C4. ☎ 262-56 13 58. Beira-Mar has a delightful seafront setting. House specialities include *parrilhada de mariscos* (grilled seafood with garlic, butter and lemon). ● *Dec–Feb.*	AE DC MC V		●	
ÓBIDOS: *O Alcaide* €€ Rua Direita. **Road map** B4. ☎ 262-95 92 20. Try *coelho à Alcaide* (rabbit stew) or *bacalhau à Alcaide* (cod with potatoes and olive oil) at this rustic restaurant with panoramic views of the town. ● *Mon; Nov.*	AE DC MC V		●	

ÓBIDOS: *Castelo* €€€
Paço Real. **Road map** B4. **(** 262-95 91 05.
Located in the *pousada*, which is part of the fairy-tale medieval castle,
Castelo serves such regional delights as asparagus with smoked ham,
cabrito (braised kid) and *trouxas de ovos* (egg and sugar rolls). ▤

AE DC MC V			▪

ÓBIDOS: *Estalagem do Convento* €€€€
Rua D. José D'Ornelas, 2510. **Road map** B4. **(** 262-95 92 17.
Located within the hotel of the same name *(see p387)*, the restaurant serves
both international and Portuguese dishes. Only open for dinner. ● *Sun.* ▤

AE MC V			▪

PENICHE: *Estelas* €€€
Rua Arquitecto Paulino Montês 21. **Road map** B4. **(** 262–78 24 35.
Estelas has a large seafood menu and a selection of meat dishes. Try octopus
salad, seafood rice or a monkfish kebab. ● *Wed; 2 weeks in Oct.* ▤ &

AE MC V			▪

PENICHE: *Marisqueira Cortiçais* €€€
Porto d'Areia Sul. **Road map** B4. **(** 262-78 72 62.
Popular with locals, this rustic restaurant overlooks the beach and specializes
in seafood and shellfish dishes. ● *Wed (Sep–Jul); 2 weeks in Sep.* &

AE DC MC V		●	▪

SANTARÉM: *Central* €€
Rua Guilherme de Azevedo 32. **Road map** C4. **(** 243-32 23 03.
This Art Deco restaurant has been open since 1933 and is popular with
locals. Try the delicious *bife à Central* (steak in a mustard sauce). ● *Sun.* ▤

AE MC V			

SANTARÉM: *Mal Cozinhado* €€
Campo Emílio Infante da Câmara. **Road map** C4. **(** 243-32 35 84.
Do not be put off by the name, Mal Cozinhado (badly cooked). Dishes include
bacalhau com magusto (baked cod with green broth). ● *Sun (Jul–Aug).* ▤

AE DC MC V	▪		

SÃO MARTINHO DO PORTO: *A Casa* €€€
Avenida Marginal, Casa Azul. **Road map** B4. **(** 262-98 96 33.
Located at a pretty seaside resort with stunning views of the bay, this
charming restaurant specializes in seafood and shellfish dishes. ▤

AE DC MC V		●	▪

TOMAR: *A Bela Vista* €€
Fonte do Choupo 3–6. **Road map** C4. **(** 249-31 28 70.
A Bela Vista offers beautiful views of the river and castle, and excellent regional
specialities such as roast kid and *caldeirada* (fish stew). ● *Mon eve; Tue; Nov.*

		●	▪

TOMAR: *Calça Perra* €€€
Rua Pedro Dias 59. **Road map** C4. **(** 249-32 16 16.
This is a charming restaurant in the gardens of a 16th-century house in the
historic part of town. Specialities are grilled steak and duck with rice. ● *Wed.* ▤

		●	▪

TORRES VEDRAS: *O Pátio do Faustino* €
Largo do Choupal. **Road map** B5. **(** 261-32 43 46.
This rustic restaurant specializes in grilled fish. Decorated with antiques
and Roman-style amphorae, it has a pleasant atmosphere. ● *Sun eve.* ▤

VILA FRANCA DE XIRA: *O Redondel* €€€
Arcada da Praça de Touros. **Road map** C5. **(** 263-27 29 73.
This restaurant is housed in the elegant arcades of the town's bullring.
Traditional Ribatejo dishes such as *açorda de sável* (bread and shad fish stew)
are served. There is an excellent wine list. ● *Mon.* ▤ &

AE DC MC V			▪

THE BEIRAS

ALMEIDA: *Senhora das Neves* €€€€
Pousada da Senhora das Neves. **Road map** E2. **(** 271-57 42 83.
This restaurant, in the *pousada* inside Almeida's star-shaped fort,
serves dishes such as grilled cod in olive oil and braised kid. ▤

AE DC MC V			▪

AVEIRO: *Cozinha do Rei* €€
Rua Doutor Manuel Neves 66. **Road map** C3. **(** 234-42 68 02.
The Cozinha do Rei, one of the best restaurants in Aveiro, is often hired out
for functions, so check availability in advance. Dishes include seafood salad,
roast sea bass, and *ovos moles de Aveiro* (egg and sugar sweets). ▤

AE DC MC V			▪

AVEIRO: *Marisqueira O Mercantel* €€
Rua António Santos Lé 16. **Road map** C3. **(** 234-42 80 57.
Offering romantic views over the canal, this restaurant serves speciality sea-
food and shellfish dishes. A good meat selection is also available. ● *Mon.*

AE DC MC V			

<table>
<tr><td>

Price categories are for a three-course meal for one with half a bottle of wine, including cover charge, service and VAT:

€   under 10 euros
€€   10–15 euros
€€€   15–20 euros
€€€€   20–30 euros
€€€€€   over 30 euros

</td></tr>
</table>

LATE OPENING
The kitchen stays open after 10pm, and you can usually have a meal up until at least 11pm.

OUTDOOR TABLES
Tables for eating outdoors, in a garden or on a balcony, often with a pleasant view.

GOOD WINE LIST
The restaurant will have a good selection of quality wines.

CREDIT CARDS
This indicates which of the major credit cards are accepted: AE American Express, DC Diners Club, MC MasterCard and V Visa.

	CREDIT CARDS	LATE OPENING	OUTDOOR TABLES	GOOD WINE LIST
BELMONTE: *Belsol* €€ Quinta do Rio, off N18. **Road map** D3. 275-91 22 06. Situated near the Zêzere river, the pleasant restaurant of the Belsol hotel serves trout fresh from local streams. Any fish dish is well worth sampling. ▤	AE DC MC V			
BUÇACO: *Palace Hotel do Buçaco* €€€€€ Palace Hotel do Buçaco. **Road map** C3. 231-93 79 70. The dining room here is a Manueline fantasy, and the intricately carved balcony is unique *(see p210)*. Dishes include cod *au gratin* with cream and roast sucking pig from Bairrada. Buçaco's acclaimed wines are bottled in the basement. ▤	AE DC MC V		●	▪
CARAMULO: *São Jerónimo* €€€ Pousada de São Jerónimo, N230. **Road map** C3. 232-86 12 91. Found in a small *pousada* south of Caramulo, one of Portugal's leading health spas, São Jerónimo offers hearty fare such as kid stew and grilled octopus. ▤	AE DC MC V			▪
CASTELO BRANCO: *Praça Velha* €€€€€ Praça Luís de Camões 17. **Road map** D4. 272-32 86 40. Situated in the old part of town, in an old granary transformed by architects and interior designers, Praça Velha offers ambitious cuisine that combines traditional methods and modern creativity in fish and meat dishes. ● *Mon.*	AE DC MC V			
COIMBRA: *Adega Paço do Conde* € Rua Paço do Conde 1. **Road map** C3. 239-82 56 05. This cheap restaurant is full of character. Almost everything – meat, chicken, fish and squid – is barbecued on skewers on a large open grill. ● *Sun.* ▤	DC MC V		●	
COIMBRA: *Democrática* € Travessa Rua Nova 5. **Road map** C3. 239-82 37 84. Hard to find, but worth the effort. The back room has long benches and is a favourite hangout for university students. The house speciality is *arroz de polvo* (octopus rice). Food is served as long as there are customers. ● *Sun.* ▤	AE DC MC V	▪		
COIMBRA: *O Trovador* €€€ Largo da Sé Velha 15–17. **Road map** C3. 239-82 54 75. This rustic restaurant, set in the historic part of the town, offers excellent regional dishes such as *chanfana* (kid stew in wine sauce). ● *Sun.* ▤	MC V			▪
COIMBRA: *L'Amphitryon* €€€€ Avenida Emídio Navarro 21. **Road map** C3. 239-82 20 55. Set in the fine circular dining room of the Astória hotel amid 1920s decor, L'Amphitryon serves traditional French and Portuguese specialities. ▤	AE DC MC V			▪
CONDEIXA-A-NOVA: *Santa Cristina* €€€ Rua Francisco de Lemos. **Road map** C3. 239-94 40 25. A modern restaurant, aptly set in a modern *pousada* close to the famous ruins of Conimbriga. Regional specialities include braised kid with turnip tops, octopus rice and roast chicken with pepper sauce. ▤	AE DC MC V			▪
GUARDA: *O Ferrinho* €€ Rua Francisco de Passos 21–23. **Road map** D3. 271-21 19 90. A friendly restaurant that offers such regional specialities as spit-roasted goat. They also serve a variety of cod dishes. ▤	AE MC V	▪		▪
LUSO: *O Cesteiro* €€ Rua Monsenhor Raúl Mira 76. **Road map** C3. 231-93 93 60. In an attractive setting with pleasant decor, this rustic restaurant serves regional specialities such as *chanfana* (kid stew in wine), sucking pig and cod. ▤	AE DC MC V			
MANTEIGAS: *São Lourenço* €€€€ N232, Penhas Douradas. **Road map** D3. 275-98 24 50. Set in a *pousada* high in the Serra da Estrela, north of Manteigas, it specializes in local dishes such as red bean and cabbage soup and trout in onion marinade. ▤	AE DC MC V			▪

MEALHADA: *Pedro dos Leitões*　€€€
N1, Sernadelo. **Road map** C3. 231-20 99 50.
A handy stop for travellers. The speciality here is delicious *leitão* (roast sucking pig) roasted in a wood-burning oven and served with chips. ● *Mon.*
AE MC V

MONSANTO: *Pousada de Monsanto*　€€€
Rua da Igreja. **Road map** E3. 277-31 44 71.
In a well-preserved village, this traditional restaurant serves regional dishes such as broad bean and coriander soup, squid stew and rabbit with rice.
AE DC MC V

MONTEMOR-O-VELHO: *Ramalhão*　€€€€
Rua Tenente Valadim 24. **Road map** C3. 239-68 94 35.
Dine in a 16th-century manor house surrounded by antiques, and try such local specialities as *ensopado de enguias* (eel stew). ● *Sun eve, Mon; Oct.*
MC V

OLIVEIRA DO HOSPITAL: *Pousada de Santa Bárbara*　€€€
Póvoa das Quartas. **Road map** D3. 238-60 95 52.
This restaurant is located in a rustic mountainside *pousada* that looks out over the Serra da Estrela. Regional dishes include roast trout.
AE DC MC V

TRANCOSO: *O Museu*　€
Largo de Santa Maria. **Road map** D2. 271-81 18 10.
This elegant, stone-walled restaurant is in the old part of town within the castle walls. The roast kid is very popular.

VISEU: *Casablanca*　€€
Avenida Emídio Navarro 70–72. **Road map** D3. 232-42 22 39.
Situated near the historic city centre, Casablanca is decorated with pretty tiles, and serves a variety of fresh fish and seafood as its specialities. ● *Mon.*
AE DC MC V

VISEU: *Churrascaria Santa Eulália*　€€
N2, Repeses. **Road map** D3. 232-43 62 83.
South of Viseu, Santa Eulália is a spacious restaurant with a seafood-based menu. Try the fish kebab or the *feijoada de marisco* (beans and seafood). ● *Thu.*
AE DC MC V

VISEU: *O Cortiço*　€€
Rua Augusto Hilário 47. **Road map** D3. 232-42 38 53.
This is a stone-walled restaurant in the centre of town. The extensive and sometimes comic menu offers traditional Portuguese dishes, the speciality being *bacalhau podre apodrecido na adega* (rotten cod from the cellar!).
AE DC MC V

DOURO AND TRÁS-OS-MONTES

ALIJÓ: *Barão de Forrester*　€€€
Rua José Ruffino. **Road map** D2. 259-95 94 67.
Located in a *pousada* deep in port wine country, this restaurant has a regional menu that includes grilled octopus and pears with Muscatel wine.
AE DC MC V

AMARANTE: *Lusitana*　€€€
Rua 31 de Janeiro. **Road map** D2. 255-42 67 20.
Among the regional dishes served here is tripe cooked in wine and *Cabrito* (spit-roasted kid). Also enjoy splendid views over the River Tâmega.

AMARANTE: *O Almirante*　€€€
Rua António Carneiro. **Road map** D2. 255-43 25 66.
O Almirante combines excellent food with a friendly atmosphere. Among the house specialities are hake *au gratin* and veal with mushrooms.
AE DC MC V

AMARANTE: *São Gonçalo*　€€€
Pousada de São Gonçalo, Ansiães. **Road map** D2. 255-46 11 13.
Northeast of Amarante, São Gonçalo boasts a spectacular view down a long, deep valley, especially at sunset. On the menu are dishes such as trout stuffed with ham and pork with chestnuts, as well as some enticing desserts.
AE DC MC V

BRAGANÇA: *Solar Bragançano*　€€€
Praça da Sé 34. **Road map** E1. 273-32 38 75.
Solar Bragançano is housed in an old mansion overlooking the main square. Try the game dishes, such as *perdiz com uvas* (partridge with grapes) or *faisão com castanhas* (pheasant with chestnuts). ● *Mon in winter.*
AE DC MC V

CHAVES: *Carvalho*　€€
Alameda Tabolado, Bloco 4. **Road map** D1. 276-32 17 27.
Enjoy fine views from this pretty two-roomed restaurant with a charming garden. Try the roast kid or *arroz de fumeiro* (rice with smoked meats). ● *Thu.*
AE DC MC V

For key to symbols see back flap

Price categories are for a three-course meal for one with half a bottle of wine, including cover charge, service and VAT:

€ under 10 euros
€€ 10–15 euros
€€€ 15–20 euros
€€€€ 20–30 euros
€€€€€ over 30 euros

LATE OPENING
The kitchen stays open after 10pm, and you can usually have a meal up until at least 11pm.

OUTDOOR TABLES
Tables for eating outdoors, in a garden or on a balcony, often with a pleasant view.

GOOD WINE LIST
The restaurant will have a good selection of quality wines.

CREDIT CARDS
This indicates which of the major credit cards are accepted: *AE* American Express, *DC* Diners Club, *MC* MasterCard and *V* Visa.

	CREDIT CARDS	LATE OPENING	OUTDOOR TABLES	GOOD WINE LIST
CHAVES: *Leonel* €€ Campo da Roda. **Road map** D1. 276-32 31 88. Popular with the locals for its superb food. Try *bacalhau au gratin* (baked cod) or *açorda de marisco* (bread and shellfish stew). ● *Mon; 2 weeks in Jul & Nov.* ▤	AE DC MC V			
CINFÃES: *Varanda de Cinfães* €€ Rua General Humberto Delgado 20–22. **Road map** D2. 255-56 12 36. This cosy informal restaurant serves traditional Portuguese cuisine, and is popular with locals. The house specialities are roast lamb and baked cod. ▤				
ESPINHO: *Terraço Atlântico* €€€ Praia Golfe Hotel, Rua 6. **Road map** C2. 227-33 10 00. Few restaurants have such a wonderful panoramic ocean view as this one. Fish dishes are prominent on the menu, although the meats are not forgotten, and there are both red and white wines from every region of Portugal. ▤	AE DC MC V			▪
GIMONDE: *Dom Roberto* €€ N218. **Road map** D2. 273-30 25 10. This rustic, stone-walled restaurant is located on the riverside in the small town of Gimonde, 7 km (4 miles) east of Bragança. People come from far and wide to try the excellent game dishes and the roast kid. ▤ 🚻	AE DC MC V	▪	●	▪
LAMEGO: *O Tonel* € Estrada de Arneirós. **Road map** D2. 254-61 21 61. A friendly restaurant popular with locals, O Tonel offers good-value Portuguese cuisine, including baked cod and *espetadas* (meat kebabs). ● *Tue pm.*		▪		
LAMEGO: *Restaurante Turisserra* €€€ Complexo Turístico Turissera, Serra das Meadas. **Road map** D2. 254-60 91 00. This charming three-roomed restaurant, set in the tourist village 6 km (4 miles) north of Lamego, serves excellent traditional Portuguese fare. Enjoy the beautiful views of the Douro and surrounding hills. ▤	AE DC MC V			
LEÇA DA PALMEIRA: *Boa Nova* €€€€ Lugar da Boa Nova. **Road map** C2. 22-995 17 85. This modern restaurant overlooking the sea was built by one of Portugal's most famous architects, Siza Vieira. Try the baked sole or sea bass. ● *Sun.* ▤	AE DC MC V	▪		▪
LEÇA DA PALMEIRA: *O Chanquinhas* €€€€ Rua de Santana 243. **Road map** C2. 22-995 18 84. The restaurant is set in a large mansion with elegant dining rooms warmed by a cosy fireplace. The fish and desserts are excellent. ● *Sun; 3 weeks in Aug.* ▤	AE DC MC V	▪		▪
MIRANDA DO DOURO: *Balbina* € Rua Rainha Dona Catarina 12. **Road map** E1. 273-43 23 94. Well-known politicians sit with locals and Spanish holiday-makers to enjoy dishes such as *bife à balbina*, a steak of local *Mirandesa* beef. ● *Mon.*				▪
MIRANDA DO DOURO: *Buteko* € Largo Dom João III. **Road map** E1. 273-43 11 50. Set in the centre of town, Buteko's specialities include *posta Mirandesa* (veal) and *bacalhau à Buteko* (cod in the house style). ● *Sun (winter); 2 weeks in Jan.* ▤	DC MC V			
MURÇA: *Miradouro* €€ Pensão Miradouro, Curvas de Murça. **Road map** D2. 259-51 24 61. The small handwritten menu in this plain restaurant changes daily. Dishes include cod Miradouro, kid and roast sucking pig. ● *Tue; 15–30 Sep.* ▤ 🚻	MC V	▪	●	
OPORTO: *Adega Vila Meã* €€ Rua dos Caldeireiros 62. **Road map** C2. 22-208 29 67. This is a busy, family-run restaurant. Popular with locals Adega Vila Meã serves daily specials, as well as traditional favourites such as baked octopus and roast kid. ● *Sun; 3 weeks in Aug.* ▤				

OPORTO: *Chez Lapin* €€ | AE DC MC V
Rua dos Canastreiros 42. **Road map** C2. 22-200 64 18.
Beams, stone walls and numerous antiques give Chez Lapin a rustic feel. The
menu features fish and shellfish, plus a different Portuguese special each day. 🍽

OPORTO: *Filha da Mãe Preta* €€ | AE DC MC V
Arcos do Douro 2–3, Cais da Ribeira. **Road map** C2. 22-208 60 66.
Set into the arches by the river, this restaurant offers superb views and an
excellent choice of Portuguese food, including sardines. ● *Sun. Sep.* 🍽

OPORTO: *Tripeiro* €€ | AE DC MC V
Rua de Passos Manuel 195. **Road map** C2. 22-200 58 86.
Tripeiro – meaning "tripe eater" – is the name for a native of Oporto as well as
this famous tripe-serving restaurant. Seafood is also available. ● *Sun.* 🍽

OPORTO: *Bule* €€€ | AE DC MC V
Rua de Timor 128. **Road map** C2. 22-617 93 76.
Bule has charming views over a garden sloping down to the sea. The specialities
here are roast duck and other duck dishes. ● *First two weeks in Aug.* 🍽 ♿

OPORTO: *Casa Aleixo* €€€ | AE MC V
Rua da Estação 216. **Road map** C2. 22-537 04 62.
Run by the same family since 1948, this friendly restaurant offers excellent value.
Traditional dishes in include octopus and veal. ● *Sun; 3 weeks in Aug.* 🍽

OPORTO: *Mercearia* €€€ | AE DC MC V
Cais da Ribeira 32. **Road map** C2. 22-200 43 89.
Mercearia is set on two floors in an old building with arches, Portuguese food
and good service, a pleasant atmosphere and a daily special. ● *Tue in winter.* 🍽

OPORTO: *Dom Tonho* €€€€ | AE DC MC V
Cais da Ribeira 13–15. **Road map** C2. 22-200 43 07.
This is one of many restaurants on the historic quayside, in the shadow of the
Dom Luís bridge. The menu has a selection of regional Portuguese dishes. 🍽

OPORTO: *Dom Manoel* €€€€€ | AE DC MC V
Avenida Montevideu 384. **Road map** C2. 22-617 23 04.
Set in a mansion with views over the Atlantic, Dom Manoel offers *parrilhada
mista* (fish and shellfish mixed grill) and other seafood. ● *Sun; 2 weeks in Aug.* 🍽

OPORTO: *O Escondidinho* €€€€€ | AE DC MC V
Rua de Passos Manuel 144. **Road map** C2. 22-200 10 79.
This restaurant, located in the centre of Oporto, offers gourmet standard,
French-influenced cooking using only the finest ingredients. ● *Sun.* 🍽 ♿

OPORTO: *Portucale* €€€€€ | AE DC MC V
Albergaria Miradouro, Rua da Alegria 598. **Road map** C2. 22-537 07 17.
This is one of the most famous restaurants in the country. It has a wide array
of meat, fish and game dishes, and spectacular views over the area. 🍽

PESO DA RÉGUA: *Varanda da Régua* €€ | AE MC V
Lugar da Boavista, Loureiro. **Road map** D2. 254-33 69 49.
Enjoy panoramic views from this friendly, family-run place just north of Régua.
The menu offers superb Portuguese cuisine such as roast kid and baked cod. 🍽

ROMEU: *Maria Rita* €€ | MC V
Rua da Capela. **Road map** E1. 278-93 91 34.
This homely restaurant in a town house has rustic furniture and stone fireplaces.
Try the spicy sausage soup or the stewed duck with rice. ● *Mon; Wed eve.* 🍽

SENDIM: *Gabriela* €€€
Largo da Igreja 27. **Road map** E2. 273-73 91 80.
Gabriela's specialities inclde *posta à Gabriela* (veal steak) and smoked meats.
The restaurant is attractively furnished with wooden panels and an open fire. 🍽

TORRE DE MONCORVO: *O Artur* €€€ | AE DC MC V
O Lugar do Rebentão, Carviçais. **Road map** E2. 279-93 91 84.
Dishes at this charming, friendly restaurant situated outside Torre include
posta Mirandesa (thick grilled veal steak), baked cod and wild boar. 🍽

VILA NOVA DE GAIA: *Boucinha* €€€ | AE DC MC V
Avenida Vasco da Gama, Oliveira do Douro. **Road map** C2. 22-782 77 64.
Set in the stylish surroundings of an old *quinta*, this is an excellent restaurant.
Try the *cherne grelhado* (grilled stone bass) with a local wine. ● *Mon.* 🍽

For key to symbols see back flap

Price categories are for a three-course meal for one with half a bottle of wine, including cover charge, service and VAT:	LATE OPENING The kitchen stays open after 10pm, and you can usually have a meal up until at least 11pm.
€ under 10 euros	**OUTDOOR TABLES** Tables for eating outdoors, in a garden or on a balcony, often with a pleasant view.
€€ 10–15 euros	
€€€ 15–20 euros	**GOOD WINE LIST** The restaurant will have a good selection of quality wines.
€€€€ 20–30 euros	**CREDIT CARDS** This indicates which of the major credit cards are accepted: AE American Express, DC Diners Club, MC MasterCard and V Visa.
€€€€€ over 30 euros	

		CREDIT CARDS	LATE OPENING	OUTDOOR TABLES	GOOD WINE LIST
VILA REAL: *Espadeiro* Avenida Almeida Lucena. **Road map** D2. 259-32 23 02. Espadeiro offers superbly prepared regional dishes and local wines. House specials are *cabrito* (roast kid), cod Espadeiro and roast leg of pork. ● Mon. ▤	€€	AE DC MC V		●	
VILA REAL: *Cozinha do Vale* Casa de Campeã, Torgueda. **Road map** D2. 259-97 96 04. Set in the scenic Campeã valley, 8 km (5 miles) north of Vila Real, this modern restaurant offers local dishes and a good selection of wines. ▤ ♿	€€€	AE DC MC V		●	▪

MINHO

		CREDIT CARDS	LATE OPENING	OUTDOOR TABLES	GOOD WINE LIST
ARCOS DE VALDEVEZ: *Costa do Vez* N121, Quinta de Silvares. **Road map** C1. 258-51 61 22. In a pretty setting just north of Arcos, Adega serves traditional cuisine such as roast veal and *cozido à portuguesa* (meat stew). ● Mon; 15–30 Oct. ▤	€€€	AE MC V			
BARCELOS: *Bagoeira* Avenida Sidónio Pais 495. **Road map** C1. 253-81 12 36. A very popular restaurant serving Minhoto specialities, *rojões* (fried pork with potatoes) and kid stew, prepared with finesse in truly generous portions. ▤	€€	AE MC V			▪
BARCELOS: *Dom António* Rua Dom António Barroso 87. **Road map** C1. 253-81 22 85. Dom António's is a stone-walled place with rustic decor in the centre of town. House specials include grilled wild boar. ▤	€€	AE DC MC V	▪		
BRAGA: *Abade de Priscos* Praça Mouzinho Albuquerque (Campo Novo) 7. **Road map** C1. 253-27 66 50. Overlooking the leafy square beside the Catholic University, this restaurant offers excellent value and has a large menu ranging from curried prawns through to rabbit and braised veal. ● Mon lunch; Sun; 3 weeks in Jul. ▤	€€				▪
BRAGA: *Ignácio* Campo das Hortas 4. **Road map** C1. 253-61 32 35. Just outside the city walls, Ignácio is full of character. Enjoy a range of regional dishes amidst artefacts and antiques. ● Tue; 2 weeks in Apr; 2 weeks in Sep. ▤	€€€	AE DC MC V			
BRAGA: *Panorâmico do Elevador* Hotel do Elevador, Bom Jesus do Monte. **Road map** C1. 253-60 34 00. This is one of the most famous restaurants in the area. Enjoy the panoramic views of Braga and Bom Jesus, and its traditional local dishes. ▤ ♿	€€€	AE DC MC V			
BRAGA: *São Frutuoso* Rua Costa Gomes 168, Real. **Road map** C1. 253-62 33 72. A friendly restaurant just south of Braga which serves superb country food. Try the cod with corn bread or the stuffed veal. ● Mon & Sun dinner; 2 weeks in Aug. ▤	€€€	MC V		●	
CAMINHA: *Napoleon* Lugar de Coura, Seixas. **Road map** C1. 258-72 71 15. Just south of Caminha, Napoleon has a high standard of cooking and offers local, national and French dishes. ● Mon; Sun eve; 2 weeks in May; 2 weeks in Dec. ▤	€€€	AE DC MC V		●	▪
GUIMARÃES: *El Rei* Praça Santiago 20. **Road map** C1. 253-41 90 96. El Rei is a cosy place with a good-value menu and a pleasant atmosphere. Try the *bacalhau mistério* (cod surprise) – a house-invented speciality. ● Sun. ▤	€€	DC MC V	▪		
GUIMARÃES: *Solar do Arco* Rua de Santa Maria 48–50. **Road map** C1. 253-51 30 72. This elegant restaurant is located in a charming mansion in the heart of the city. Specialising in fresh seafood, Solar do Arco is famous for its *arroz de tamboril* (monkfish with rice). ● Sun dinner. ▤	€€	AE DC MC V	▪		▪

GUIMARÃES: *São Gião* €€€
Lugar de Vinhas, Moreira de Cónegos. **Road map** C1. █ *253-56 18 53.*
Found in a small village just south of Guimarães, São Gião offers tasty
dishes such as duck with olive sauce. ● *Mon; Sat lunch; Aug.* 🍽

PONTE DA BARCA: *Bar do Rio* €€ AE MC V
Fonte Velha, Praia Fluvial. **Road map** C1. █ *258-45 25 82.*
This is a charming wood-panelled restaurant with stunning views of the
River Lima. Try the specials of roast veal or cod *au gratin.* ● *Tue.* 🍽

PONTE DE LIMA: *Encanada* €€ AE DC MC V
Largo Doutor Rodrigues Alves. **Road map** C1. █ *258-94 11 89.*
This busy restaurant, overlooking the river, offers traditional Portuguese fare such
as *rojões à moda do Minho* (pork Minho style) and *vinhos verdes.* ● *Thu; May.*

PONTE DE LIMA: *A Carvalheira* €€€ MC V
Antepaço, Arcozelo. **Road map** C1. █ *258-74 23 16.*
Just south of Ponte de Lima, this friendly place is popular with locals. The
house special is *bacalhau com broa* (cod with maize bread). ● *Mon.* 🍽

PÓVOA DE VARZIM: *O Marinheiro* €€€€ AE DC MC V
Rua Gomes de Amorim, Estrada Fontes Novas. **Road map** C2. █ *252-68 21 51.*
An attractive restaurant in the shape of a boat and decorated with fishing
nets and buoys, O Marinheiro offers a fine seafood-based menu. 🍽 ♿

VALENÇA DO MINHO: *Mané* €€€ AE DC MC V
Avenida Miguel Dantas 5. **Road map** C1. █ *251-82 34 02.*
Above a café-bar, this modern restaurant has a wide, and relatively inexpensive,
array of fish and meat dishes. ● *Sun eve; Mon (except Aug); Jan.* 🍽

VALENÇA DO MINHO: *Pousada de São Teotónio* €€€ AE DC MC V
Baluarte de Socorro. **Road map** C1. █ *251-80 02 60.*
In a *pousada* within the old fort, São Teotónio offers a fantastic view across
the Minho valley to Tuy in Spain, and hearty local dishes such as kid stew. 🍽

VIANA DO CASTELO: *Camelo* €€ AE MC V
Rua de S. Marta 119–122, N202. **Road map** C 1. █ *258-83 90 90.*
In a village 1 km (half a mile) from Viana do Castelo, this gem of a restaurant
holds monthly festive banquets and offers summer dining under shady vines.
Try the *bacalhau à camelo* (house cod speciality). ● *Mon; mid-Sep–mid-Oct.* 🍽

VIANA DO CASTELO: *Casa d'Armas* €€€ DC MC V
Largo 5 de Outubro 30. **Road map** C1. █ *258-82 49 99.*
Behind a gracious and imposing façade, the stone and wood-panelled interior
of Casa d'Armas is enhanced by medieval-style decor. Expect only the freshest
fish and shellfish, and prime quality meats. ● *Wed; 2 weeks in Nov.* 🍽

VIANA DO CASTELO: *Cozinha das Malheiras* €€€ AE DC MC V
Rua Gago Coutinho 19–21. **Road map** C1. █ *258-82 36 80.*
Enjoy good traditional cuisine in this small and intimate restaurant in a former
manor house. The seafood dishes are recommended. ● *Tue.* 🍽

VILA PRAIA DE ÂNCORA: *Tasquinha Ibrain* $$$ AE MC V
Rua dos Pescadores. **Road map** C1. █ *258-91 16 89.*
Overlooking the harbour, this cosy place has excellent service and specializes in
seafood. Alternatively try the tasty *costeletão* (T-bone steak). ● *Wed.* ♿

ALENTEJO

ALANDROAL: *A Maria* €€€ AE DC MC V
Rua João de Deus 12. **Road map** D5. █ *268-43 11 43.*
An enchanting restaurant serving Alentejan dishes that include *cozido de grão*
(pork and chickpea stew) and *sopa de cação* (dogfish soup). ● *Mon; Aug.* 🍽

ALVITO: *Castelo de Alvito* €€€€ AE DC MC V
Pousada do Castelo de Alvito, Apartado 9. **Road map** D6. █ *284-48 53 43.*
A 15th-century castle with beautiful gardens and roaming peacocks
provides the picturesque setting for this fine restaurant. Try the cod
stewed with herbs or roast lamb cooked with spinach. 🍽 ♿

BEJA: *Dom Dinis* €€ AE DC MC V
Rua Dom Dinis 11. **Road map** D6. █ *284-32 59 37.*
Dom Dinis is a country restaurant specializing in grilled food, the most
popular dishes being the meat kebabs and veal chops. ● *Wed.* 🍽

<table>
<tr><td colspan="2">

Price categories are for a three-course meal for one with half a bottle of wine, including cover charge, service and VAT:

€ under 10 euros
€€ 10–15 euros
€€€ 15–20 euros
€€€€ 20–30 euros
€€€€€ over 30 euros

</td><td colspan="2">

LATE OPENING
The kitchen stays open after 10pm, and you can usually have a meal up until at least 11pm.

OUTDOOR TABLES
Tables for eating outdoors, in a garden or on a balcony, often with a pleasant view.

GOOD WINE LIST
The restaurant will have a good selection of quality wines.

CREDIT CARDS
This indicates which of the major credit cards are accepted: *AE* American Express, *DC* Diners Club, *MC* MasterCard and *V* Visa.

</td></tr>
</table>

	CREDIT CARDS	LATE OPENING	OUTDOOR TABLES	GOOD WINE LIST
BEJA: *Os Infantes* €€ Rua dos Infantes 14. **Road map** D6. 284-32 27 89. Os Infantes has a beautiful setting, fine decor and a good-value menu. Specialities include traditional Alentejo cuisine, partridge and hare. ▤	AE DC MC V			
CAMPO MAIOR: *O Faisão* €€ Rua 1° de Maio 19. **Road map** E5. 268-68 61 39. This cosy restaurant, with a fire and pictures of local life on the walls, offers a good selection of traditional dishes such as *cozido de grão* (pork and chickpea stew). Alternatively, try the house beef in mushroom sauce. ▤	AE DC MC V	▨		▨
CRATO: *Flor da Rosa* €€€€ Pousada da Flor da Rosa. **Road map** D4. 245-99 72 10. The restaurant is located in this marvellous *pousada* adapted from the monastery which is thought to date from the mid-14th century. Traditional regional favourites are served such as pig's trotters with coriander sauce. ▤	AE DC MC V			▨
ELVAS: *Pousada de Santa Luzia* €€€ Avenida de Badajoz. **Road map** D5. 268-63 74 70. Not far from the Spanish border, the large restaurant of this *pousada (see p395)* is popular with Portuguese and Spaniards alike. They come here to enjoy the large portions of *bacalhau dourado* and other traditional treats. ▤	AE DC MC V		●	
ESTREMOZ: *Águias d'Ouro* €€€ Rossio do Marquês de Pombal 27. **Road map** D5. 268-33 70 30. This cosy restaurant, on the first floor of an attractive town house, serves delicious pig's trotters in coriander sauce and lamb stew. ▤	AE DC MC V	▨		▨
ÉVORA: *Cozinha de Santo Humberto* €€€ Rua da Moeda 39. **Road map** D5. 266-70 42 51. Just off the main square, this is a real delight. A whitewashed cellar is adorned with antiques, and Alentejo dishes and local game are served. ● *Thu; Nov.* ▤	AE DC MC V			
ÉVORA: *Um Quarto Para as Nove* €€€ Rua Pedro Simões 9a. **Road map** D5. 266-70 67 74. This charming restaurant is situated in the old part of town. Among the menu's highlights are monkfish rice, hare rice and *açorda alentejana* (bread and coriander dish). ● *Wed; 2 weeks in Jul; 2 weeks in Nov.* ▤	AE MC V	▨	●	
ÉVORA: *O Grémio* €€€€ Rua Alcárcova de Cima 10. **Road map** D5. 266-74 29 31. A wonderful restaurant built into the city's Roman wall. Try the tasty hare stewed with beans. ● *Wed.* ▤	AE DC MC V			▨
ÉVORA: *Fialho* €€€€ Travessa das Mascarenhas 16. **Road map** D5. 266-70 30 79. Tucked away in a side street, this tasteful restaurant offers an interesting range of meat, fish, shellfish and game dishes. ● *Mon; 1–24 Sep.* ▤	AE DC MC V	▨		▨
MARVÃO: *Sever* €€ Portagem. **Road map** D4. 245-99 31 92. A pretty restaurant with excellent river views. The menu offers immaculately prepared regional specialities such as wild boar with clams and lamb stew.	AE DC MC V	▨	●	
MÉRTOLA: *Alengarve* € Avenida Aureliano Mira Fernandes 20. **Road map** D6. 286-61 22 10. This modest restaurant offers good-value regional cuisine such as pork cooked with chick peas and rabbit stew. ● *Wed; 2 weeks in Oct.* ▤	AE MC V		●	
MONSARAZ: *Casa do Forno* €€ Travessa da Sanabrosa. **Road map** D5. 266-55 71 90. Located near the main square of an attractive hill top town, Casa de Forno serves mainly regional dishes such as lamb stew and pork with clams. ● *Tue.*	AE MC V		●	

PORTALEGRE: *Quinta do Sauda*   €€€
Serra de Portalegre, 7300. **Road map** D4. 245-20 23 24.
Popular with the locals, this busy restaurant serves Alentejan specialities such
as a rich fish soup and a variety of pork dishes. 🔲 ⚫
AE
DC
MC
V

REDONDO: *Ermita*   €€€€
Convento de São Paulo, Aldeia da Serra. **Road map** D5. 266-98 91 60.
Inside a beautiful hotel, the Ermita offers a wonderful array of dishes such
as avocado with port and duck with olive sauce. There is also an unusual
mixed grill of stone bass, monkfish, shrimp and squid on the menu. 🔲 ⚫
AE
DC
MC
V

SANTIAGO DO CACÉM: *O Retiro*   €
Rua Machado dos Santos 8. **Road map** C6. 269-82 26 59.
A charming country restaurant with friendly service. House specialities are
duck rice and *bacalhau com natas* (cod in a creamy sauce). ⚫ *Sun.* 🔲
AE
MC
V

SERPA: *Molhóbico*   €
Rua Quente 1. **Road map** D6. 284-54 92 64.
A friendly local restaurant where the food is often outstanding. Try the
veal steak or the *cozido de grão* (pork and chickpea stew). ⚫ *Wed.* 🔲

SINES: *O Migas*   €€€
Rua Pero de Alenquer 17. **Road map** C6. 269-63 67 67.
Here a carefully chosen menu includes sole with bread and roe stew.
⚫ *Sat lunch; Sun; 2 weeks in Oct.* ⚫ *Sat lunch; Sun; 2 weeks in Oct.* 🔲
AE
DC
MC
V

VILA NOVA DE MILFONTES: *Marisqueira Dumas Mil*   €€€€
Off Avenida Marginal. **Road map** C6. 283-99 71 04.
This highly regarded fish restaurant serves a delicious *arroz de marisco*
(seafood rice) and *caldeirada de peixe* (seafood stew). 🔲
AE
MC
V

VILA VIÇOSA: *Os Cucos*   €
Mata Municipal. **Road map** D5. 268-98 08 06.
The setting in the municipal gardens is the main attraction of Os Cucos, though
it offers a good variety of grilled fish dishes as well. ⚫ *2 weeks in Aug.* 🔲 ⚫
AE
MC
V

ALGARVE

ALBUFEIRA: *Os Compadres*   €€
Avenida Dr Sá Carneiro, Edifício Cristina Pateo Sá Carneiro. **Road map** C7. 289-54 18 48.
This restaurant has a good atmosphere and friendly, relaxed service. The owner
is always around to offer advice on what to choose. ⚫ *Sun (Oct–Apr); Jan.* 🔲 ⚫
AE
DC
MC
V

ALBUFEIRA: *Marisqueira Santa Eulália*   €€€
Praia de Santa Eulália. **Road map** C7. 289-54 26 36.
Overlooking the beach, this modern restaurant serves typical Portuguese sea-
food dishes, including grilled monkfish, salmon and clams. ⚫ *Dec–Jan.* ⚫
AE
DC
MC
V

ALBUFEIRA: *La Cigale*   €€€€
Praia dos Olhos de Agua, 8200. **Road map** C7. 289-50 16 37.
Located by the beach, with a terrace and great sea views, this is a delightful
seafood restaurant serving both Portuguese and French dishes. 🔲
AE
DC
MC
V

ALBUFEIRA: *Ruína*   €€€€€
Rua Cais Herculano. **Road map** C7. 289-51 20 94.
Set in a restored early 19th-century building, Ruína is one of the best
restaurants in town. Specialities of the house are fresh fish and seafood.
Rooms are set aside for coffee and for listening to *fado.* 🔲
AE
DC
MC
V

ALMANCIL: *Ibérico*   €€€
Estrada Almancil, Vale do Lobo. **Road map** D7. 289-39 40 66.
Located near the vast Vale do Lobo complex south of Almancil, this place is full
of character and features an eclectic menu, with such dishes as smoked sword-
fish with horseradish sauce and cannelloni Ibérico (Iberian style). ⚫ *lunch.* 🔲
AE
MC
V

ALMANCIL: *Aux Bons Enfants*   €€€€
Sítio das Areias, Estrada de Almancil. **Road map** D7. 289-39 68 40.
Aux Bons Enfants offers French cuisine and an excellent selection of French
and Portuguese wines from 1934 up to the present day. ⚫ *lunch; Sun.* 🔲

ALMANCIL: *O Tradicional*   €€€€€
Estrada da Fonte Santa, Escanxinas. **Road map** D7. 289-39 90 93.
This excellent restaurant, south of Almancil, serves specialities such as steak in
Roquefort cheese sauce or duck breast with orange. ⚫ *lunch; Sun; Nov–Dec.* 🔲 ⚫
AE
MC
V

<table>
<tr><td>

Price categories are for a three-course meal for one with half a bottle of wine, including cover charge, service and VAT:

€ under 10 euros
€€ 10–15 euros
€€€ 15–20 euros
€€€€ 20–30 euros
€€€€€ over 30 euros

</td><td>

LATE OPENING
The kitchen stays open after 10pm, and you can usually have a meal up until at least 11pm.

OUTDOOR TABLES
Tables for eating outdoors, in a garden or on a balcony, often with a pleasant view.

GOOD WINE LIST
The restaurant will have a good selection of quality wines.

CREDIT CARDS
This indicates which of the major credit cards are accepted: *AE* American Express, *DC* Diners Club, *MC* MasterCard and *V* Visa.

</td></tr>
</table>

	CREDIT CARDS	LATE OPENING	OUTDOOR TABLES	GOOD WINE LIST

ARMAÇÃO DE PÊRA: *Santola* €€
Largo da Fortaleza. **Road map** C7. (282-31 23 32.
With panoramic seaside views, Santola has a pleasant atmosphere and is a reliable choice for seafood and shellfish dishes.
AE MC V — Late Opening ■ — Outdoor Tables ●

ESTOI: *Monte do Casal* €€€€€
Cerro do Lobo. **Road map** D7. (289-99 15 03.
The menu at this converted farmhouse restaurant includes a selection of vegetarian dishes and house specialities such as salmon in a white wine and dill sauce, and seafood with Monte do Casal sauce. ● *mid-Nov–mid-Feb.* ▤
MC V — Outdoor Tables ● — Good Wine List ■

FARO: *Adega Nortenha* €
Praça Ferreira de Almeida 25. **Road map** D7. (289-82 27 09.
This busy, unpretentious place overlooks a pretty square. Daily specials include *feijoada* (bean stew) and *caldeirada* (fish stew). ▤
AE MC V

FARO: *Dois Irmãos* €€
Praça Ferreira de Almeida 13–14. **Road map** D7. (289-82 33 37.
One of the most popular restaurants in Faro, the Dois Irmãos offers good quality cooking and efficient service. Seafood specialities include fish or meat *cataplana (see p288)* and a variety of fresh fish dishes.
AE MC V — Late Opening ■ — Outdoor Tables ●

FARO: *A Taska* €€
Rua do Alportel 38. **Road map** D7. (289-82 47 39.
Popular with locals, A Taska is a modest but cosy restaurant decorated as an old tavern. Try the eel stew or the pork with clams. ▤
AE DC MC V — Late Opening ■ — Outdoor Tables ●

FARO: *Camané* €€€€€
Avenida Nascente, Praia de Faro. **Road map** D7. (289-81 75 39.
Camané is a bright and spacious seafood restaurant located right on the waterfront. The house special is fried cuttlefish. ● *Mon; 2 weeks in Oct.* ▤ ♿
MC V — Late Opening ■ — Outdoor Tables ● — Good Wine List ■

LAGOA: *O Lotus* €€
Rua Marquês de Pombal 11. **Road map** C7. (282-35 20 98.
O Lotus offers good Portuguese cuisine such as marinated sardines, octopus and egg salad and *arroz de peixe* (fish rice). Desserts include chocolate mousse or *morgado de figo* (fig and almond paste cakes). ● *Sat.* ▤
AE DC MC V

LAGOA: *O Castelo* €€€
Rua do Casino 63, Praia do Carvoeiro. **Road map** C7. (282-35 72 18.
Booking is advisable in this cliff-top seafood restaurant surrounded by a pretty garden. Try the monkfish and prawn rice. ● *Mon; 10 Jan–10 Feb.* ▤
AE DC MC V — Late Opening ■ — Outdoor Tables ● — Good Wine List ■

LAGOS: *António* €€€
Praia do Porto de Mós. **Road map** C7. (282-76 35 60.
António is located in a pretty spot with good views of the ocean. It serves a mainly seafood menu in a friendly and relaxed atmosphere. ● *1 Jan–7 Feb.*
AE DC MC V — Outdoor Tables ●

LAGOS: *Dom Sebastião* €€€
Rua 25 de Abril 20–22. **Road map** C7. (282-76 27 95.
This rustic restaurant has an extensive menu offering traditional Portuguese fare such as smoked swordfish and kid stew in red wine. ● *1–25 Dec.* ▤
AE DC MC V — Late Opening ■ — Outdoor Tables ●

LOULÉ: *Bica Velha* €€€
Rua Martim Moniz 17–19. **Road map** C7. (289-46 33 76.
The oldest house in Loulé, dating from 1816, is the setting for this rustic, family-run restaurant. Specialities include lamb kebab, pork chop with apple sauce, and orange mousse for dessert. ● *Sun (except Aug); 2 weeks in Nov or Dec.*
AE DC MC V — Late Opening ■

LOULÉ: *Casa dos Arcos* €€€
Rua Sá de Miranda 23–5. **Road map** D7. (289-41 67 13.
Set in Loulé's historic centre, this restaurant is popular with tourists and locals alike. It serves good-quality seafood specialities and meat dishes. ● *Sun.* ▤
AE MC V

OLHÃO: *O Tamboril* €€€
Avenida 5 de Outubro 174. **Road map** D7.. 289-71 46 25.
Tamboril or monkfish is the speciality here, where you will find it and other
seafood served grilled, with rice or in stews. ● *Sat pm (winter only).* 目 ⑤

AE DC MC V

PORTIMÃO: *Cervejaria Lúcio* €€
Largo Francisco Maurício 33. **Road map** C7. 282-42 42 75.
Overlooking the river, this cheerful, noisy beerhouse is a popular meeting
place for locals and serves mainly fish and seafood dishes. ● *Mon.*

PORTIMÃO: *A Lanterna* €€€
Rua Foz do Arade Parchal. **Road map** C7. 282-41 44 29.
A variety of Portuguese dishes include smoked swordfish, clams in the
house style and almond mousse dessert. ● *Sun; Nov–Dec.*

MC V

QUARTEIRA: *Restaurante Suisse* €€
Estrada Quarteira-Almancil, Fonte Santa. **Road map** D7. 289-38 01 48.
Do not be put off by this restaurant's location, just south of Quarteira; inside it
has a charm all of its own. Amongst wooden beams and antiques you can order
from the varied Swiss-German orientated menu until midnight. ● *Mon.* ⑤

AE DC MC V

QUINTA DO LAGO: *Câ d'Oro* €€€€€
Hotel Quinta do Lago. **Road map** D7. 289-35 03 50.
This refined and elegant Italian restaurant serves Venetian specialities such
as *calamari e gamberi con verdurine di campo* (deep fried prawns, squid
and seasonal vegetables). ● *Lunch; Wed.* 目 ♬

AE DC MC V

SAGRES: *O Telheiro* €€€
Praia da Mareta. **Road map** C7. 282-62 41 79.
Enjoy the excellent service, and dining room with panoramic views and a
terrace. The house speciality is lobster rice. ● *Tue; 2 weeks in Nov or Dec.* 目 ⑤

AE DC MC V

SAGRES: *Pousada do Infante* €€€€
Pousada do Infante. **Road map** C7. 282-62 42 22.
With stunning views over the cliffs and ocean, this restaurant features
dishes like fresh fish fillets with mayonnaise and pork with clams. 目

AE DC MC V

SILVES: *Marisqueira Rui* €€
Rua Comendador Vilarinho 23. **Road map** C7. 282-44 26 82.
Popular with the locals, this busy town-centre restaurant is open until 2am. Menu
highlights are the seafood rice and selection of fresh fish. ● *Tue; 2 weeks in Nov.* 目

AE DC MC V

TAVIRA: *Quatro Águas* €€
Quatro Águas. **Road map** D7. 281-32 53 29.
Located just outside Tavira, Quatra Águas has superb views over the lagoon.
Try the house special "golden octopus". ● *Mon; 3 weeks in Nov.* 目 ⑤

AE MC V

VILAMOURA: *Sirius Restaurant* €€€€€
Vilamoura Tivoli Marinotel. **Road map** D7. 289-38 99 88.
Located in an elegant hotel, Sirius looks out over the marina and serves some
superb international and French-orientated cuisine. Indulge in beluga caviar
and vodka, escargots bourguignon or lobster thermidor. ● *Lunch.* 目 ♬ ⑤

AE DC MC V

MADEIRA

FUNCHAL: *Fim de Século* €
Rua da Carreira 144. 291-22 44 76.
Tiffany lamps help lend this restaurant its fin-de-siècle theme, and the fixed-
price menus offer the cheapest eating in downtown Funchal. ● *Sun lunch.* 目

AE DC MC V

FUNCHAL: *O Jango* €€
Rua de Santa Maria 166. 291-22 12 80.
O Jango is a cosy restaurant in a converted fisherman's house in the old town.
The good-value, fresh food includes bouillabaisse and paella. 目

AE DC MC V

FUNCHAL: *Londres* €€
Rua da Carreira 64a. 291-23 53 29.
This downtown restaurant has a typically Portuguese daily special, such as
bacalhau (salt cod) with olives or *cozido*, a hearty meat casserole. ● *Sun.* 目

AE MC V

FUNCHAL: *Marisa* €€
Rua de Santa Maria 162. 291-22 61 89.
An intimate old town restaurant that feels like a private home, as father and
son cook delicious paella or seafood rice and mother takes the orders.

AE DC MC V

For key to symbols see back flap

Price categories are for a three-course meal for one with half a bottle of wine, including cover charge, service and VAT:

€ under 10 euros
€€ 10–15 euros
€€€ 15–20 euros
€€€€ 20–30 euros
€€€€€ over 30 euros

LATE OPENING
The kitchen stays open after 10pm, and you can usually have a meal up until at least 11pm.

OUTDOOR TABLES
Tables for eating outdoors, in a garden or on a balcony, often with a pleasant view.

GOOD WINE LIST
The restaurant will have a good selection of quality wines.

CREDIT CARDS
This indicates which of the major credit cards are accepted: *AE* American Express, *DC* Diners Club, *MC* MasterCard and *V* Visa.

	CREDIT CARDS	LATE OPENING	OUTDOOR TABLES	GOOD WINE LIST
FUNCHAL: *Carochinha* €€ Rua de São Francisco 2a. **(** 291-22 36 95. Carochinha calls itself an "English" restaurant, but its eclectic menu includes a wide choice of dishes from various different countries. There is no roast beef, but the bread and butter pudding is excellent. ● *Sun.* ▤ ㅂ	AE DC MC V			▤
FUNCHAL: *O Tapassol* €€ Rua Don Carlos I 62. **(** 291-22 50 23. Booking is advised at this excellent small restaurant in the old town. Dine on quail, mussels, limpets or rabbit, choosing the indoor dining room for style, or the tiny roof terrace for a fun evening. ▤	AE DC MC V	▤	●	
FUNCHAL: *Caravela* €€€ Avenida do Mar. **(** 291-22 84 64. This smart seafront restaurant serves good local fish, such as tuna, scabbard fish and turbot, plus more expensive air-freighted seafoods. ● *Sun; 25 Dec.* ▤	AE DC MC V	▤		▤
FUNCHAL: *Casa dos Reis* €€€ Rua Penha de França. **(** 291-22 51 82. This is an intimate, quiet and sophisticated restaurant that offers a French-influenced menu. ● *Lunch.* ▤ ♬ ㅂ	AE DC MC V			▤
FUNCHAL: *Dom Filet* €€€ Rua do Favila 7. **(** 291-76 44 26. "King Fillet" specializes in beef served Madeiran style (cubed, skewered on a bay twig and grilled) or char-grilled Argentinian style. ● *Sun.* ▤ ♬ ㅂ	AE DC MC V	▤		
FUNCHAL: *Marina Terrace* €€€ Marina do Funchal. **(** 291-23 05 47. One of a run of outdoor restaurants by the yacht marina, this place serves dishes from simple pizza to lobster or grilled fish. ㅂ	AE DC MC V	▤	●	
FUNCHAL: *O Celeiro* €€€ Rua das Aranhas 22. **(** 291-23 06 22. O Celeiro offers candle-lit dining and a fish-based menu featuring several dishes for two, such as shellfish and lobster *cataplana*, and bouillabaisse. ● *Sun.* ▤	AE DC MC V			▤
FUNCHAL: *Dona Amélia* €€€€ Rua Imperatriz Dona Amélia 83. **(** 291-22 57 84. Flambé dishes, grilled fish and *espetadinhas* (small beef kebabs) on baywood skewers are the speciality of this prettily tiled restaurant. ▤	AE DC MC V	▤		
FUNCHAL: *Quinta Palmeira Gourmet Restaurant* €€€€ Avenida do Infante 17–19. **(** 291-22 18 14. In this fine 19th-century town house traditional Portuguese dishes are presented with flair, and the home-made ice cream is delicious.	AE DC MC V	▤	●	▤
FUNCHAL: *Les Faunes* €€€€€ Reid's Palace Hotel, Estrada Monumental 139. **(** 291-71 71 71. Madeira's finest restaurant offers stylishly presented international cuisine. Be sure to try one of their delicious desserts such as strawberry pancakes or *zabaglione* made with Madeira wine. ● *lunch; Sun; Apr–Oct.* ▤ ♬ ㅂ	AE DC MC V	▤		▤
RIBEIRA BRAVA: *Restaurante Agua Mar* €€ Vila Ribeira Brava. **(** 291-95 11 48. This informal restaurant offers a wide-ranging menu that includes Portuguese as well as French-influenced dishes. Perhaps the most popular choice is the simply grilled or fried fresh fish and shellfish. ● *Mon.* ㅂ	AE DC MC V	▤	●	▤
SANTANA: *Quinta do Furão* €€€ Achada do Gramacho. **(** 291-57 01 00. Sit next to the fireplace among antiques in this cosy restaurant overlooking the sea. Specials include steak in pastry and seafood kebabs. ▤ ㅂ	AE DC MC V		●	

Porto Moniz: *Orca* € | AE DC MC V
Residencial Orca, Vila Porto Moniz. (291-85 00 00.
Orca is made entirely of wood, apart from the large windows that enable diners to gaze out over the sea. Try the special of scabbard fish with banana.

THE AZORES

Corvo: *Traineira* €€
Largo do Porto da Casa. (292-59 62 07.
Currently the only restaurant on Corvo, Traineira is usually busy. The menu concentrates on fresh, locally caught fish. 🗏

Faial: *O Capote* €€ | AE MC V
Rua Conselheiro Miguel da Silveira, Horta. (292-29 32 95.
A lively and often crowded restaurant at the north end of the seafront, it is popular with both locals and yachties celebrating their return to land. 🗏

Faial: *Estalagem da Santa Cruz* €€€ | AE DC MC V
Rua Vasco da Gama, 9900-017, Horta. (292-29 30 21.
Housed within a converted fort alongside the hotel of the same name *(see p401)*, some claim that this is the best restaurant on the island. The cooking is of a high quality and uses good local ingredients. 🗏 &

Flores: *Reis* €€ | MC V
Rua da Boa Vista, Santa Cruz. (292-59 26 97.
Up in the hills above Santa Cruz, this is a clean and simple restaurant attached to the *salsicharia* (sausage shop) run by a local butcher.

Graciosa: *A Coluna* €
Largo Barão de Guadalupe 10, Santa Cruz da Graciosa. (295-71 23 33.
The owner of this small, idiosyncratic restaurant spent many years in Brazil and serves *feijoada* (bean and meat stew) and other Brazilian favourites. ● *Sun.*

Pico: *Terra e Mar* €€
Miradouro do Arrife, Terras, Lajes do Pico. (292-67 27 94.
This small cliff-top restaurant has a windmill and terrace. Serving simple fish and meat dishes, it is a good place to pause while touring the island.

Santa Maria: *A Candeia* €€
Cruz Teixeira, Vila do Porto. (296-88 20 63.
A Candeia specializes in hearty Azorean dishes like *caldo de nabos* (turnip soup) and *alheira e morcela* (garlic sausage and black pudding). Book a day in advance to be asssured of a table at this popular restaurant. &

São Jorge: *Manezinho* €
Furna das Pombras, Urzelina. (295-41 44 84.
A simple seaside restaurant that is popular with locals. Dishes include *ameijoas* (clams) from Fajã da Caldeira de Santo Cristo. ● *Mon.* &

São Miguel: *Alcides* €€
Rua Hintze Ribeiro 67–77, Ponta Delgada. (296-28 26 77.
An unpretentious but accomplished restaurant serving robust steak and chips fare, close to the Igreja Matriz de São Sebastião. ● *Sun.* 🗏

São Miguel: *Tony's* €€ | AE DC MC V
Largo do Teatro 5, Furnas. (296-58 42 90.
Tony's specializes in *cozido (see p231)*. The meat stew is slowly cooked in the hot volcanic rocks found around Furnas. Book at least a day in advance. 🗏

São Miguel: *Monte Verde* €€€ | AE V
Rua da Areia 4, Ribeira Grande. (296-47 29 75.
Monte Verde is a small, friendly restaurant with a first-floor dining room decorated with modern *azulejos*. Competent fish dishes include *tigelada de chicharro*, a stew made with thin, sardine-like fish.

Terceira: *Casa do Peixe* €€ | MC V
Estrada Miguel Corte Real, Angra do Heroísmo. (295-21 76 78.
Overlooking the harbour, the city's former fish market has been turned into an atmospheric restaurant with a full menu and friendly service. ● *Tue.*

Terceira: *Quinta do Martelo* €€€ | AE MC V
Canada do Martelo 24 , Cantinho, São Mateus. (295-64 28 42.
This is the place to go to try rich Azorean dishes like Holy Spirit soup (meat and vegetables in white wine) and *alcatra* (meat stew). ● *Wed.* 🗏 🎵

SURVIVAL
GUIDE

PRACTICAL INFORMATION 426-439
TRAVEL INFORMATION 440-449

PRACTICAL INFORMATION

TOURISM IN PORTUGAL is not as developed as it is in neighbouring Spain, but visitors are well catered for. The major tourist region is the Algarve, where the choice of resorts rivals anywhere in Europe. Portugal has many regional tourist offices

Sign for Tourist Information Office

and a good choice of hotels in cities and resorts. The Portuguese are a hospitable people and are keen for you to experience and enjoy their country. Travelling with a family is encouraged and restaurants and hotels will offer discounts for children (see p377).

WHEN TO VISIT

IN THE SOUTH of the country, the winter months are mild, but temperatures in July and August can be very high. The weather conditions in the north may not be suitable for visiting during winter, especially in the mountainous regions where it can be very cold. Between April and October, the north is pleasantly warm, although rain is not unusual. See pages 34–5 for more detailed information on Portugal's climate.

Christmas, Easter, July and August are the most popular holiday times in Portugal, with visitors and locals alike. At these times, especially in the south, rooms can be hard to find, and prices are generally higher. At other times of the year, good bargains can be found and the popular tourist areas are far less crowded.

Overall, spring and autumn are the best times to visit, when hotel rates are cheaper, the climate is pleasant throughout the country and there are not too many people.

CUSTOMS

ON 30 JUNE 1999, the intra-EU Duty and Tax Free Allowances, better known as Duty-free and mainly affecting such items as alcohol, perfumes and tobacco, were abolished. Consulates can generally provide up-to-date information on particular customs regulations. For more details on customs and other tax-related matters, see pages 436–7.

Bottles of port

VISAS

NATIONALS OF the European Union (EU) may stay for up to six months before applying for a residence permit. Those EU nationals wishing to stay longer than six months should contact the local frontier police to request a residence permit. Nationals of Australia and New Zealand need a valid passport or identity card and can stay for up to 90 days without a visa. American and Canadian nationals must apply for a 60-day visa before arrival. Anyone intending to study or work in Portugal needs a letter to prove they will be attending college or are in employment.

TOURIST INFORMATION

THE PORTUGUESE MINISTRY of Tourism divides the country into a number of touristic regions, which are separate from its administrative districts. All major cities or large towns within each touristic region have a **Government Tourist Office** (Posto de Turismo), as do the larger towns on Madeira and the Azores. This guide gives details of the relevant tourist information office for each sight. Here, visitors can obtain information about the region, town plans, maps and details on regional events. In some cases they will also sell advance tickets for local shows and concerts. Information about local hotels will be available from the tourist office, although they will not usually book the accommodation.

High season on a beach in the resort of Albufeira, in the Algarve

◁ **Fruit and vegetable stalls at the Mercado dos Lavradores, Funchal**

Signpost in the village of Marvão

Office opening hours vary as each tourist region is organized independently, but generally they follow the same opening hours as local shops. In more rural areas, offices are often closed at weekends, and may not offer the same information and services that can be found in larger towns. There are tourist offices at all the major airports, as well as in all cities and large towns. Visitors can also obtain information prior to travelling, from Portuguese tourist offices abroad. These offices will normally provide visitors planning a trip with a wide range of useful maps, fact sheets and tourist brochures.

Map of mainland Portugal showing the country's six tourist regions

MUSEUMS

THE MAJORITY of Portugal's museums are run by the state, although there are also a number of private ones. In addition to the main national museums and galleries, there are countless regional ones scattered around the country. These cover a range of topics, from the history of a region to the works of local artists.

ADMISSION CHARGES

MOST MUSEUMS in Portugal charge a small entrance fee, which varies from 200$00 to 500$00. These charges are sometimes reduced or waived altogether (or just in the morning) on Sundays and public holidays. Young people under 14 or pensioners (with proof of age) may obtain a 40 per cent discount. Those under 26 with a *Cartão Jovem* (youth card) or ISIC card (International Student Identity Card) are entitled to half-price entrance.

Museum tickets

Tourists to Lisbon may also purchase a Lisboa card, available from the airport, tourist offices, and travel agents. It allows entry to 26 of the city's museums (although not private museums, such as the Gulbenkian), and free public transport for a fixed period of time. Lisboa cards are valid for one two or three days.

OPENING TIMES

MUSEUMS ARE usually open from 10am–5pm from Tuesday to Sunday, with many closing for lunch either from noon to 2pm or from 12:30pm to 2:30pm. Smaller and private museums may have different opening times. Museums and some sights close on Mondays and public holidays. Major churches are open during the day without a fixed timetable although some may close between noon and 4pm. Smaller churches and those in rural areas may only be open for religious services and in some cases you may need to find the keyholder for admittance.

DIRECTORY

EMBASSIES AND CONSULATES

United Kingdom
Rua de São Bernardo 33,
1249-082, Lisbon. **Map** 4 D2.
21-392 40 00.

British Consulates
Funchal 291-22 12 21.
Lisbon 21-392 41 60.
Oporto 22-618 47 89.
Portimão 282-41 78 00.

Australia
Consular services are handled by the Canadian Embassy.

Canada
Avenida da Liberdade 196-200,
3º, 1269-121, Lisbon. **Map** 5 C5.
21-316 46 00.

Republic of Ireland
Rua da Imprensa à Estrela 1, 4º,
1200, Lisbon. **Map** 4 E2.
21-392 94 40.

US
Avenida das Forças Armadas,
1600, Lisbon. 21-727 33 00.

TOURIST OFFICES

Coimbra
Largo da Portagem, 3000,
Coimbra.
239-85 59 30.

Faro
Avenida 5 de Outubro, 8000,
Faro.
289-80 04 00.
www.rtalgarve.pt

Lisbon
Lisboa Welcome Center,
Rua do Arsenal 15,
1100-038, Lisbon. **Map** 7 A2.
21-031 27 00; toll free 800-296 296.
www.atl-turismolisboa.pt

Oporto
Praça Dom João I 43, 4050 Oporto.
22-205 75 14.
www.portoturismo.pt

In the UK:
22–25a Sackville Street,
London W1X 1DE.
09063-640 610.

In the US:
212-220 5772.

In Canada:
1 416- 921 7376.

Newspaper stall in the Brasileira Café *(see p90)*

LANGUAGE

PORTUGUESE RESEMBLES the Spanish language in many ways, and if you know Spanish you should have little difficulty reading Portuguese. However, Portuguese pronunciation is likely to sound very unfamiliar and spoken Portuguese sounds nothing like spoken Spanish.

The Portuguese are justifiably proud of their own language, and do not take kindly to being addressed in Spanish. Their own language is widely spoken throughout the world as a result of historical ties with Brazil and a number of countries in Africa. A phrase book containing the most useful words and phrases in Portuguese, along with their phonetic pronunciations, can be found on pages 479–80.

MANNERS

THE PORTUGUESE appreciate efforts by visitors, however small, to communicate in their language. A simple attempt at *bom dia* (good day), *boa tarde* (good afternoon) or *boa noite* (good night) will be gratefully received and is sure to elicit a friendly response.

The Portuguese are generally very open and amicable, particularly in the north of the country and in rural areas, and they are unerringly polite. It is considered polite to address

people as *senhor* or *senhora* and this formality extends to many job titles. Arts graduates are addressed as *doutor*, and science graduates as *engenheiro*. You are expected to shake hands when introduced to anyone new, although an informal kiss on each cheek between females and among young friends and acquaintances is more commonplace.

Although dress is generally relaxed, decorum should be observed when you visit churches and religious buildings, especially those in strongly Catholic areas: arms should be covered up and shorts should not be worn.

NEWSPAPERS AND MAGAZINES

ENGLISH-LANGUAGE newspapers, including the British *Financial Times*, the weekly *Guardian International*, and the American *International Herald Tribune*, are widely available on the day of publication. Other European newspapers are on sale a day late, although in the main tourist areas they may be found on the same day. Portuguese daily newspapers include *Diário de Notícias* and *Público*. *Correio da Manhã* covers the south and *Jornal de Notícias* covers the north. English-language

Portuguese dailies and the English APN

newspapers include the *Anglo-Portuguese News* (APN), aimed at the expatriate population in Portugal, and the *Algarve Gazette* and *Algarve News*.

RADIO AND TELEVISION

THERE ARE TWO state-owned Portuguese channels, RTP1 and RTP2, and two privately owned, SIC and TVI. Satellite television is available in several languages and the newspaper, *Anglo-Portuguese News*, has lists of programmes in English. The Portuguese radio station RDF broadcasts tourist information in English, French and German during the summer months. Madeira has its own TV channel and a radio service catering for tourists on 96 FM.

FACILITIES FOR THE DISABLED

FACILITIES IN PORTUGAL for the disabled are limited at present, although the situation is gradually improving. Wheelchairs and adapted toilets are now available at most airports and the main stations, reserved car parking is becoming more evident and ramps and lifts are gradually being installed in public places. In addition, Lisbon and Oporto have a dial-a-ride bus service. To book, phone and indicate when and where you want to be picked up, and your destination. The operators speak only Portuguese, so you may need to ask your hotel for help. There is a special taxi service in Lisbon, but it has to be booked long in advance.

A dial-a-ride bus for the disabled *(transporte especial para deficientes)*

Women travellers admiring the view from the castle in Lisbon

CONVERSION CHART

Imperial to Metric
1 inch = 2.54 centimetres
1 foot = 30 centimetres
1 mile = 1.6 kilometres
1 ounce = 28 grams
1 pound = 454 grams
1 pint = 0.6 litres
1 gallon = 4.6 litres

Metric to Imperial
1 millimetre = 0.04 inches
1 centimetre = 0.4 inches
1 metre = 3 feet 3 inches
1 kilometre = 0.6 miles
1 gram = 0.04 ounces
1 kilogram = 2.2 pounds
1 litre = 1.8 pints

WOMEN TRAVELLING ALONE

TRAVELLING ALONE in Portugal is fairly safe for women although common principles, such as keeping to well-lit, public areas after dark, still apply. Some areas of Lisbon, such as the Bairro Alto and the Cais do Sodré, are best avoided after dark, while resorts on the Algarve and Lisbon coasts tend to be the worst for unwanted attentions. Hitching anywhere alone is not safe; use taxis or public transport instead.

STUDENT INFORMATION

YOUNG PEOPLE aged 12–25 may buy a *Cartão Jovem*, (youth card), which costs about 1,100$00 and is valid for a year. It offers travel insurance and discounts for shops, museums, travel and youth hostels *(see p376)*. This card is supplied by the **Instituto Português da Juventude** (Portuguese Youth Institute). The International Student Identity Card (ISIC) provides the same benefits as the *Cartão Jovem* and can be bought in your own country.

RELIGION

ROMAN CATHOLICISM is the dominant religion in Portugal. Church services are held most evenings and every Sunday morning as well as on religious holidays. Sightseeing may be difficult (and is not encouraged) while services are in progress. Churches of other denominations, including the Church of England, Baptist, and Evangelical can be found in larger towns and cities. **St Vincent's Anglican Church**, which travels from place to place, holds a number of religious services in the Algarve.

PORTUGUESE TIME

PORTUGAL AND MADEIRA follow Britain in adopting Greenwich Mean Time (GMT) in winter and moving the clocks forward one hour from March to September (as in British Summer Time). In the Azores, clocks are one hour behind GMT in winter and the same as GMT in summer. The 24-hour clock is more commonly used throughout Portugal.

ELECTRICAL ADAPTORS

VOLTAGE IN PORTUGAL is 220 volts and plugs have two round pins. Most hotel bathrooms offer built-in adaptors for electric razors.

Worshippers leaving a church after mass in Trás-os-Montes

DIRECTORY

PLACES OF WORSHIP

St George's Church
Rua de São Jorge à Estrela 6,
Lisbon.
(21-390 62 48.

St James's Church
Largo da Maternidade de
Júlio Dinis, Oporto.
(22-606 49 89.

Lisbon Synagogue
Rua A. Herculano 59,
Lisbon.
(21-388 15 92.

St Vincent's Anglican Church (Algarve)
Apartado 135,
Boliqueime.
(289-36 67 20.

STUDENT INFORMATION

Instituto Português da Juventude
Avenida da Liberdade 194,
1250 Lisbon.
(21-317 92 00.

BUSES FOR THE DISABLED

**Lisbon
Carris**
(21-758 56 76. *(Orders may be placed 9am–5pm Mon–Fri.)*

**Oporto
Portuguese Red Cross**
(22-600 63 53. *(Buses for the Oporto area must be booked several days in advance.)*

Personal Health and Security

Pharmacy sign

IN GENERAL, Portugal is relatively free of crime, but simple precautions should always be taken. When parked, do not leave any valuable possessions in the car, and watch out for pickpockets in crowded areas and on public transport. Should you have serious medical problems, ring the emergency service number given in this section. For minor complaints, consult a pharmacy.

Police station at Bragança in the Trás-os-Montes region

WHAT TO DO IN AN EMERGENCY

THE NUMBER to call in an emergency is 112. Dial the number and ask for service you require – police *(polícia)*, ambulance *(ambulância)* or fire brigade *(bombeiros)*. If you need medical treatment, the casualty department *(serviço de urgência)* of the closest main hospital will treat you. On motorways and main roads, use the orange SOS telephone to call for help should you have a car accident. The service is in Portuguese; press the button and then wait for the operator who will connect you.

Motorway SOS telephone

Health. A booklet accompanies it, called *Health Advice for Travellers*, which explains what healthcare you are entitled to and how to claim for it. The E111 covers emergencies only, so visitors are advised to take out medical insurance for all other types of medical treatment. The **British Hospital** in Lisbon has English-speaking doctors, as do the international health centres in Estoril and Cascais, as well as a number of health centres throughout the Algarve. Details of these can be found in the local English newspapers.

normally only be available on prescription in many other countries. The sign for a *farmácia* is a green cross on a white background. They are open from 9am to 1pm and 3pm to 7pm. Each pharmacy displays a card showing the address of the nearest all-night pharmacy and a list of those with late closing (10pm).

PORTUGUESE POLICE

IN ALL MAIN CITIES and towns, the police force is the *Polícia de Segurança Pública* (PSP). Law and order in rural areas is kept by the *Guarda Nacional Republicana* (GNR). The *Brigada de Trânsito* (traffic police) division of the GNR, recognizable by their red armbands, is responsible for patrolling roads.

HEALTH PRECAUTIONS

NO VACCINATIONS are needed for visitors, although it is a sensible precaution to have had a typhoid shot and a current polio booster. Tap water is safe to drink throughout the country. If you are visiting during the summer, it is advisable to bring insect repellent, as mosquitoes, while they do not present any serious health problems, can be a nuisance.

PHARMACIES

PHARMACIES *(farmácias)* in Portugal can diagnose simple health problems and suggest appropriate treatment. Pharmacists can dispense a range of drugs that would

PERSONAL SECURITY

VIOLENT CRIME is extremely rare in Portugal, and the vast majority of visitors will experience no problems, but sensible precautions should

MEDICAL TREATMENT

SOCIAL SECURITY coverage is available for all EU nationals, although you may have to pay first and reclaim later. To reclaim, you must obtain an E111 form before you travel. This form is available at post offices throughout the UK or from the Department of

Traffic policeman

Male PSP officer

Female PSP officer

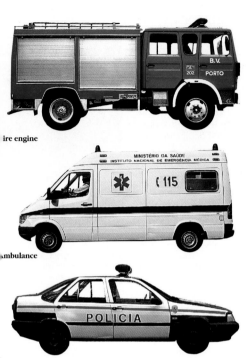

Fire engine

Ambulance

Police car

DIRECTORY

EMERGENCY NUMBERS

**General Emergency
(Fire, Police, Ambulance)**
(112.

**Assistentes Intérpretes
de Portugal**
Avenida da República 44 3°,
1269-098, Lisbon.
(21- 799 43 60.

British Hospital
Rua Saraiva de Carvalho 49,
1269-098 Lisbon.
(21-395 50 67.

Ordem dos Advogados
Largo de São Domingos 14, 1°,
1169-060 Lisbon.
(21-882 3550.

...be taken. It is advisable to arrange travel insurance for your possessions before you leave for Portugal. Thieves do operate, and care should be taken after dark in the Alfama, Bairro Alto and Cais do Sodré areas of Lisbon, in some of the resorts in the Algarve and in the Ribeira district of Oporto. Personal belongings should be protected and leaving anything inside a car, particularly a radio, is not recommended. When walking, hide wallets and carry bags and cameras away from the road so as not to tempt snatchers in cars or on motorbikes. If you are unfortunate enough to encounter thieves during your visit, do not attempt to resist and hand over your possessions immediately.

REPORTING A CRIME

IF YOU HAVE any property stolen, you should immediately contact the nearest police station. Theft of documents, such as a passport, should also be reported to your consulate. Many insurance companies insist that policy holders report any theft within 24 hours. The police will file a report which you will need in order to claim from your insurance company on your return home. Contact the PSP in towns or cities, or the GNR in rural areas. In all situations, keep calm and be polite to the authorities to avoid delays. The same applies should you be involved in a car accident. In rural areas you may be asked to accompany the other driver to the nearest police station to complete the necessary paperwork. Ask for an interpreter if no one there speaks English.

LEGAL ASSISTANCE

AN INSURANCE POLICY that covers the costs of legal advice, issued by companies such as Europ Assistance or Mondial Assistance, will help with the legal aspects of your insurance claim should you have an accident. If you have not arranged this cover, call your nearest consulate or the **Ordem dos Advogados** (lawyers' association) who can give you names of English-speaking lawyers and help you with obtaining representation. Lists of interpreters, if you require one, are given in the local Yellow Pages (Páginas Amarelas) under *Tradutores e Intérpretes*, or can be contacted through the **Assistentes Intérpretes de Portugal**, which is based in Lisbon.

PUBLIC CONVENIENCES

THE PORTUGUESE for toilets is *casa de banho*. If the usual figures of a man or woman are not shown, look for *homens*, *senhores* or *cavalheiros* (men) and *senhoras* or *damas* (ladies). Toilet facilities are provided at service stations every 40 km (25 miles) and at drive-in rest areas on motorways. In some cases you may have to pay to use ladies' toilets, but men's facilities are free.

Ladies' toilet sign

Men's toilet sign

Banking and Local Currency

BPI Bank Logo

YOU CAN TAKE any amount of foreign currency into Portugal but sums worth more than 12,450 euros should be declared at customs when entering the country. Traveller's cheques are the safest way to carry money in Portugal and may be exchanged at banks and bureaux de change, as well as some hotels and shops. You may find, however, that credit and debit cards are more convenient. They can both be used to withdraw currency, for a fee, from ATMs (automated teller machines) displaying the appropriate sign.

A 24-hour bank at Lisbon Airpor

BANKING HOURS

BANK OPENING HOURS are from 8:30am to 3pm, Monday to Friday, although many major branches in city centres and in tourist areas close at 6pm. Banks are closed at weekends and on public holidays.

CHANGING MONEY

MONEY CAN be changed at banks, at a bureau de change (câmbio) and in many hotels. The most convenient of these methods is to use banks as they are more common than bureaux de change and offer a better rate of exchange than hotels. However, service in banks can sometimes be slow and usually involves filling in a number of forms. In addition, some banks restrict currency exchange to their customers.

The quickest and most practical way of changing money is to use the electronic currency exchange machines found outside the branches of most major banks and at the main airports and railway stations. They have the added advantage of allowing you to change money outside normal banking hours. The screen in the centre of the machine displays the current exchan rates and gives instructions for use in several language:

CHEQUES AND CARDS

TRAVELLER'S CHEQUES are available from most bank or from branches of Thoma Cook and American Express offices. They are a safe way of carrying money, but in Portugal they are expensive to cash. Commission rates vary from bank to bank, so it is wise to shop around first

Although Eurocheques are less expensive than travelle cheques, they are no longer accepted by many banks an shops. Visitors now find it more convenient simply to use their debit card to withdraw cash from an ATM.

The credit cards that are most commonly accepted fo payment are Visa, American Express and MasterCard. These cards can also be use to withdraw currency at ban and bureaux de change. Be aware that charges vary from bank to bank.

CASH DISPENSERS

A PRACTICAL WAY of obtainin cash advances using yc credit card is to use the MB (Multibanco) ATM located o side banks, at railway station and in shopping centres. A transaction tax may be charge as well as a commission. Checking the rates is worth-while as tax and commission will vary. The cost of using a debit card for cash withdrawa may be less. Most ATMs acce Cirrus and Star debit cards.

Foreign currency is inserted here.

Exchange rates and instructions are shown on this screen.

Euro notes and coins emerge from these slots.

Language and currency is selected using these buttons.

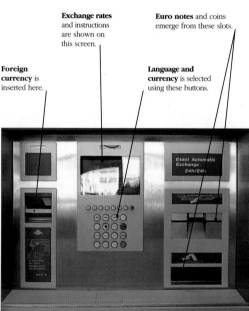

Currency Exchange Machine at Lisbon Airport
These machines provide a convenient way of changing foreign notes into euros at any time of day or night.

THE EURO

Twelve countries have replaced their traditional currencies with a single European currency called the euro. Austria, Belgium, Finland, France, Germany, Greece, Ireland, Italy, Luxembourg,

The Netherlands, Portugal and Spain chose to join the new currency; the UK, Denmark and Sweden stayed out, with an option to review their situation. The euro was introduced on 1 January 1999, but only for banking purposes. Notes and coins came into

circulation on 1 January 2002. A transition period has allowed euros and escudos to be used simultaneously, with national notes and coins being phased out by mid-2002. Euros can be used anywhere within the participating member states.

Bank Notes

Euro bank notes have seven denominations. The 5-euro note (grey in colour) is the smallest, followed by the 10-euro note (pink), 20-euro note (blue), 50-euro note (orange), 100-euro note (green), 200-euro note (yellow) and 500-euro note (purple). All notes show the 12 stars of the European Union.

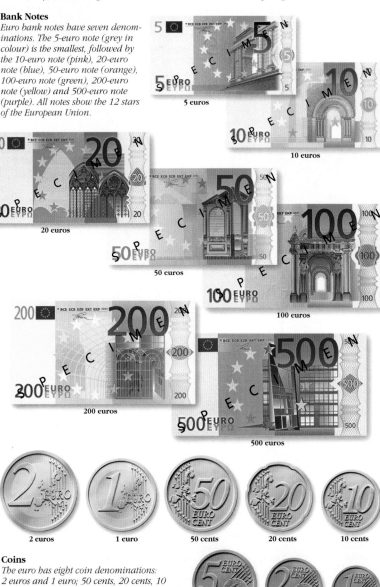

5 euros

10 euros

20 euros

50 euros

100 euros

200 euros

500 euros

2 euros

1 euro

50 cents

20 cents

10 cents

Coins

The euro has eight coin denominations: 2 euros and 1 euro; 50 cents, 20 cents, 10 cents, 5 cents, 2 cents and 1 cent. The 2- and 1-euro coins are both silver and gold in colour. The 50-, 20- and 10-cent coins are gold. The 5-, 2- and 1-cent coins are bronze.

5 cents

2 cents

1 cent

Using the Telephone

RECENT YEARS have seen a dramatic improvement in the Portuguese telecommunications system. Formerly, the antiquated equipment caused all manner of problems for visitors. Thankfully, it has been updated with the help of the latest technology, and visitors should now find that using the telephone in Portugal is relatively free of complications. Public telephones may be used for phoning internally or abroad, either with coins or cards. It is generally much more convenient, especially when making international or long-distance calls, to use card phones instead of coin phones.

English-style phone box

Post office *cabine* phone

USING A COIN PHONE

1 Lift receiver and wait for the dialling tone.

2 Insert coins into this slot one at a time.

3 The display shows amount of credit. If more money is required the message *"Inserir mais moedas por favor"* appears.

4 Key in telephone number and wait to be connected.

5 To make another call, press the follow-on call button.

6 Replace receiver after call. Unused coins will be refunded.

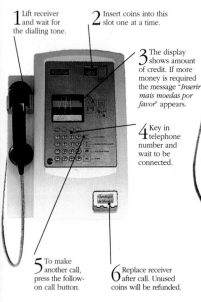

USING A TELECOM CARD PHONE

1 Lift receiver and wait for the dialling tone.

2 Insert phonecard arrow side up, or credit card magnetic strip down.

3 The screen will display number of units available, then tell you to key in telephone number

4 Key in number and wait to be connected.

5 If phonecard runs out in the middle of a call, it will re-emerge. Remove it and insert another one.

6 Replace receiver after call. When card re-emerges, remove it.

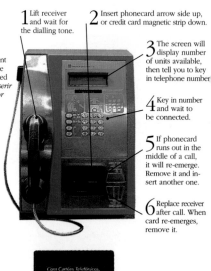

Com Cartões Telefónicos, dê outro Rumo às suas moedas!

TELECOM

Telecom card

TELEPHONING IN PORTUGAL

THERE ARE SEVERAL different types of pay phone in Portugal. Some use coins and others take cards. Coin-operated telephones may be found in the street, as well as in most bars, cafés, newsagents and other shops. During 2002 all phones will be adapted to accept the new euro coins, and are likely to accept denominations from 10 cents to 2 euros *(see p433)*. However, if you wish to call abroad it is far more convenient to use a card phone. These phones tend to be either red or blue and accept phone cards as well as credit cards. Telephone cards are available in different denominations from post offices, telecom company outlets, tobacconists and newsagents.

You can also call from post offices without having to have change. Simply queue at the cashier's window and you will eventually be directed to a booth *(cabine)*. Make your call first and then pay at the counter. The cost is based on how many units you have used and the rate is much better than in hotels. Some cafés, restaurants and bars now also use this method of paying for phone calls.

If you are going to call abroad, bear in mind that it is usually much cheaper to phone in the evening after 9pm or at weekends, when you will benefit from the off-peak rates.

PORTUGAL TELECOM

Telecom logo

Reverse Charge Calls

REVERSE CHARGE calls can be made from any telephone. Dial the *país directo* number or 172 for the country you wish to call. This number is listed in the opening pages of any telephone directory, after the list of city dialling codes for that country. This number will put you in contact with the local telephone operator. There are also separate numbers for calls to the USA using services such as AT&T, MCI and Sprint.

A new-style beige coin telephone covered by a shelter in Oporto

Dialling Codes

- To make a call within each town or region, and also to call from one town or region to another, simply dial the nine-digit number you require. You do not need to dial an area code first.
- To phone Portugal from abroad first dial 00 351, and then the number you require, for example, 00 351 21 for a number in Lisbon.
- To call abroad from Portugal, dial 00 and then the country code. The telephone code for US and Canada is 1; Ireland is 353; UK is 44; Australia is 61; and New Zealand is 64.
- Portugal's directory enquiries number is 118. For international directory enquiries dial 179.

Postal Services

Correios (postal service) logo

THE POSTAL SERVICE is known as the *Correios*. It is reasonably efficent: a letter sent to a country within the EU should take five to seven days, and a letter sent to the USA or further afield should take about seven to ten days. The *Correios* sign features a horse and rider in white on a red background.

Sending a Letter

FIRST-CLASS MAIL is known as *correio azul* and second-class mail is called *normal*. First-class letters are posted in blue postboxes and second-class post in red ones. At post offices there may be separate slots for national and international mail. There is also an express mail service called EMS, and for valuable letters, a recorded delivery service *(correio registado)* is available. Stamps *(selos)* can be bought from post offices or from any shop displaying the red and white *Correios* sign, and also from vending machines. These are found in airport terminals and in railway stations, as well as on the streets of large towns.

Portuguese stamps

Poste Restante

A MAIL-HOLDING service *(posta restante)* is also available at most major post offices. The envelope should carry the name of the recipient in block capitals, underlined, followed by *posta restante* together with the postcode and the name of the destination town. To collect the mail, take your passport and look for the counter that is marked *encomendas*. A small fee is charged for this service.

Post Offices

POST OFFICES are usually open from 9am until 6pm from Monday to Friday. Post offices in town or city centres have different opening times. These are 8am–10pm from Monday to Friday and 9am–6pm on Saturdays.

Portuguese Addresses

PORTUGUESE ADDRESSES often include both the storey of a building and the location within that floor. The ground floor is the *rés-do-chão* (r/c), first floor *primeiro andar* (1º), the second floor is expressed as 2º, and so on. Each floor is divided into left, *esquerdo* (E or Esqᵈᵒ), right, *direito* (D or Dᵗᵒ).

Information on   **First-class**
collection times   **postbox**

Portugal's Postboxes
First-class letters should be posted in blue (Correio Azul) *boxes and second-class letters in red boxes.*

Second-class postbox

Shops and Markets

Traditional arts and crafts have not been lost as a result of Portugal's modernization. Pottery, ceramics and tiles (*azulejos*) are produced everywhere with differing styles from town to town, while lace and embroidery are particularly good from Madeira. Cheeses, cured hams, sausages and wines can all be bought from local shops and markets; port, Madeira and spirits from wine shops or direct from the producer. Portugal is not an expensive country when compared with the rest of Europe, and prices are likely to be very reasonable for traditional craftwork and produce, especially away from the cities.

Serra cheese from the Serra da Estrela

produce, it also sells pottery, lace, rugs and clothes. At the regional markets throughout the country a range of local produce is on sale such as cheeses, breads and hams. In this guide, the market days are given in the information that precedes each town entry. Where a regular date is given, but that date happens to fall at a weekend, the market is held on the nearest weekday.

Choosing fresh, locally grown vegetables and fruit at a typical roadside stall in the Alentejo

Reclaiming Vat

Value added tax (IVA) can be reclaimed by non-EU residents who stay for less than 180 days. Ask for an *Isenção de IVA* form or invoice in triplicate, describing the goods, quantity, value and buyer's identity (best done where you see the "Tax Free for Tourists" signs). Present the forms at customs on departure.

Opening Hours

Shops open at 9am and close at 7pm and smaller shops or those in quieter areas normally close for lunch between 1pm and 3pm. Large shopping centres, which usually include a supermarket, restaurants and banks, have sprouted all over Portugal recently. Opening times for shopping centres are usually from 10am until 11pm daily (including Sunday).

Markets

A social and commercial occasion, the street market is integral to Portuguese life. It is usually held in the town's main square; ask for the *mercado* or *feira* if in doubt. Most markets sell a wide range of goods from food to household items and clothes, but you will also see sites devoted to antiques and local crafts. Roadside stalls are common, often selling produce from smallholdings. Most markets are held in the morning only, but in tourist areas they may go on until late afternoon.

Perhaps Portugal's largest and best-known market is the one in Barcelos (see p273) in the Minho, which is held every Thursday in the main square. As well as selling a vast range of household goods and local

Ceramics

In most cities you can buy as well as commission ceramic tiles and panels. Portugal has a long-standing tradition in ceramics, both for decorative purposes and for home use (see pp24–5). Styles range from elegant Vista Alegre porcelain to simple but classic terracotta crockery. Antique *azulejos* are highly sought after and very expensive, but you can buy reproductions of well-known historic designs at places such as Lisbon's Museu Nacional do Azulejo (see pp122–3).

Other Crafts

Portugal is well known for its delicate embroidery and fine lace, and the best-known source is the island of Madeira. On the mainland, the best lace and embroidery comes from towns in the Minho such as Viana do Castelo, also famous for its brightly printed shawls. Embroidered bedspreads are sold in Castelo Branco in the Beira Baixa, and colourful carpets, such as those from Arraiolos (see p301), are sold throughout the Alentejo.

Prices are very reasonable for knitwear, and woollen fishermen's sweaters from Nazaré (see p180), which are often hand-knitted, can be good value.

Ceramics at the market in Barcelos (see p273)

Filigree jewellery *(filigrana)* from the Minho is typically worn at festivals and is sold locally. Gold and silver threads are worked into fine, intricately designed brooches, earrings and pendants. In theory, all the gold sold in Portugal must be at least 19 carats.

Wickerwork is another speciality of Madeira that is produced in large quantities. Colonial-style garden chairs are much sought after. Woven baskets are produced throughout the country and make delightful souvenirs. Cork from the Alentejo *(see p313)* is used to make articles, such as mats and ice buckets.

Embroidered handkerchiefs and table mats in Caldas do Gerês, the Minho (see pp270–71)

Locally-made baskets for sale in the Beiras region (see p195)

REGIONAL PRODUCE

I N PORTUGAL every region has its specialities and it is best to buy fresh items in the region where they are made, although most of the better-known regional produce can be found throughout the country. Cured ham *(presunto)* from the north of the country is particularly good in Chaves *(see pp256–7)*, and smoked tongue sausages *(linguiça)* are a speciality of Oporto *(see pp236–41)*.

Regional cheeses include the delicious ewe's cheese Serra, which is produced from May to October in the Serra da Estrela *(see pp218–19)*, Ilha is a stronger, hard cheese from the Azores, and Queijinhos are small white cheeses produced in Tomar and the surrounding region *(see pp184–5)*.

WINES AND SPIRITS

A S WELL AS PRODUCING the well known fortified wines, port *(see pp228–9)* and Madeira *(see p349)*, Portugal has a wide range of good table wines *(see pp28–9)*. Among the best known are the rich red wines that come from the vineyards of the Dão region and the light *vinhos verdes* from the Minho.

It is usually possible to visit the port lodges and wine producers for tastings and guided tours *(see p247)* as well as to buy produce direct from them. Portugal's best-known spirit is *bagaceira* or *bagaço*, a fiery, clear drink distilled from grapeskins. Other spirits include *figo* (made from figs), *ginginha* (made from red cherries) and *medronheira*, a firewater distilled from arbutus *(see p289)*. If these are not to your taste, Portuguese brandies, such as *Macieira* and *Constantino*, are good and reasonably priced.

CLOTHING AND SHOES

P ORTUGAL HAS a thriving textile industry, but much of the country's production in clothes and shoes goes to supply well-known designer brands abroad. These clothes are not usually available in the shops. Some excellent-value seconds are on sale at local markets everywhere; a particularly well-known one is at Carcavelos between Lisbon and Estoril. Leather goods such as shoes, gloves, belts and bags can be good buys, but prices will reflect the quality of the product (and not all the leather goods on display will be Portuguese).

Shopping for gloves in the Chiado area of Lisbon (see pp92–3)

SIZE CHART

Australia uses both British and American systems.

Women's dresses, coats and skirts

Portuguese	34	36	38	40	42	44	46	
British	8	10	12	14	16	18	20	
American	6	8	10	12	14	16	18	

Women's shoes

Portuguese	36	37	38	39	40	41	
British	3	4	5	6	7	8	
American	5	6	7	8	9	10	

Men's suits

Portuguese	44	46	48	50	52	54	56	58 (size)
British	34	36	38	40	42	44	46	48 (inches)
American	34	36	38	40	42	44	46	48 (inches)

Men's shirts

Portuguese	36	38	39	41	42	43	44	45 (size)
British	14	15	15½	16	16½	17	17½	18 (inches)
American	14	15	15½	16	16½	17	17½	18 (inches)

Men's shoes

Portuguese	39	40	41½	42	43	44	45	46
British	6	7	7½	8	9	10	11	12
American	7	7½	8	8½	9½	10½	11	11½

Sporting Holidays and Outdoor Activities

ALTHOUGH IT IS A SMALL COUNTRY, Portugal offers an amazing variety of terrain, with sports and activities to match. Golf and tennis facilities have been well established for many years, and in the south the mild climate means that both sports can be enjoyed all year round. Other activities such as walking, cycling, riding and water sports are also widely enjoyed and easily arranged. Events are often organized on a local basis, so contact the regional tourist offices for the most up-to-date information on sporting facilities and events.

Walkers on the summit of Pico Ruivo in Madeira *(see p354)*

Windsurfing at sunset, Viana do Castelo *(see pp274–5)*

WATER SPORTS

SURFING, WINDSURFING and sailing are extremely popular along Portugal's 500 miles of coastline and around the Atlantic islands. The best beach for surfing is the world-famous Guincho, just outside Cascais

(see pp162–3), where international championships have been held. However, the ocean breakers there are only suitable for experienced surfers. More moderate conditons can be found in the Algarve resorts, where windsurfing boards and sailing dinghies can be rented and lessons easily arranged. In the Algarve, the marinas at Lagos and **Vilamoura** are important yachting centres.

For information on scuba-diving centres in mainland Portugal, and ones on Madeira and the Azores, contact the **Federação Portuguesa de Actividades Subaquáticas**.

Canoeing and kayaking are popular pursuits on many of the country's rivers, especially on the Mondego, the Zêzere and the Cávado. For further details, contact the **Federação Portuguesa de Canoagem**.

WALKING AND CYCLING

BOTH THE PARQUE NATURAL de Montesinho *(see p260)* and the Parque National da Peneda-Gerês *(see pp270–71)* are good areas for walkers, but some of Portugal's best walks are on Madeira and the islands of São Miguel and São Jorge in the Azores. In Madeira you can walk alongside the *levadas* (irrigation channels), some of which date back to the 15th century *(see p354)*. Following *levadas* allows access to parts of the island where no roads can penetrate.

Portugal is well suited to mountain biking, although the country's hilly terrain may deter the less fit. Bikes can be hired in the Parque Nacional da Peneda-Gerês, which has many scenic mountain routes.

GOLF COURSES IN THE ALGARVE

The majority of Portugal's best golf courses are concentrated in the Algarve, which has gained a reputation as one of Europe's prime golfing destinations. The mild climate ensures that a game can be enjoyed all year round, and many courses have been designed by leading professsionals such as Henry Cotton. Some of the top courses insist that players demonstrate a reasonable degree of proficiency, while others welcome golfers of any ability and provide excellent coaching. More serious golfers might consider booking a specialist package tour.

Immaculate fairway on Vilamoura II golf course

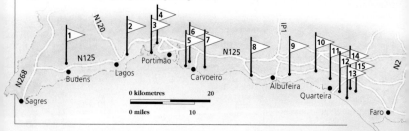

Golfers enjoying a game at Vale do Lobo in the Algarve

TENNIS AND GOLF

Tennis courts are found practically everywhere in Portugal and certainly alongside most tourist facilities. In the Algarve, most of the courts in tourist complexes are hard, although elsewhere many are clay. The larger Algarve resorts and a few other places offer tennis coaching holidays.

Portugal's resorts are famous for their golf courses, which include some of Europe's best. Many offer coaching for golfers of all abilities and specialist holidays are easy to arrange. Most courses are in the Lisbon area and the Algarve, but there are good facilities elsewhere.

1 Parque da Floresta (282-69 00 54).
2 Palmares (282-76 29 53).
3 Alto Golf (282-41 69 13).
4 Penina (282-42 02 00).
5 Quinta do Gramacho (282-34 09 00).
6 Vale da Pinta (282-34 09 00).
7 Vale de Milho (282-35 85 02).
8 Salgados (289-58 30 30).
9 Sheraton/Pine Cliffs (289-50 01 00).
10 Vilamoura I (289-31 03 41).
11 Vila Sol (289-30 05 05).
12 Vale do Lobo (289-39 39 39).
13 San Lorenzo (289-39 65 22).
14 Quinta do Lago (289-39 07 00).

Despite its rocky, mountainous terrain, Madeira has two fine courses: Santo da Serra in the east of the island and Palheiro Golf, high above Funchal.

Hoping for a catch at Praia da Adraga, near Colares (see p153)

FISHING

Along the coasts and rivers of Portugal are plenty of opportunities for the fisherman, from deep sea fishing off the shores of the Algarve, Madeira and the Azores, to angling in the mainland rivers for trout and salmon. You will need to obtain a licence, available from the **Instituto Florestal**.

HORSE RIDING

Portugal enjoys a famous riding tradition as a result of the country's fine Lusitano horses. In the Algarve, **Quinta dos Amigos** and **Vale de Ferro** are well-known riding schools. Other popular locations include the Alentejo, and the Peneda-Gerês National Park in the north of Portugal.

DIRECTORY

WATER SPORTS

Federação Portuguesa de Actividades Subaquáticas
Rua Frei Manuel Cardoso 39, 1700-206 Lisbon.
21-846 01 74.

Federação Portuguesa de Canoagem
Rua António Pinto Machado 60, 3º, 4100-068 Oporto.
22-600 78 50.

Marina de Vilamoura S.A.
8125-409 Quarteira.
289-31 05 60.

TENNIS AND GOLF

Federação Portuguesa de Golfe
Ave. das Túlipas, Ed. Miraflores 17º, 1495-161 Algés.
21-412 37 80.

Golf Holidays International
7th Floor, Regent House Hubert Road Brentwood, Essex CM14 4JE.
01277 228 980 .

Roger Taylor Tennis Holidays
85 High Street, London SW19 5EG.
020-8947 97 27.

FISHING

Federação Portuguesa de Pesca Desportiva
Rua Eça de Queirós 3, 1º, 1150-095 Lisbon.
21-314 01 77.

Instituto Florestal
Avenida João Crisóstomo 28, 1050 Lisbon.
21-314 48 00.

HORSE RIDING

Quinta dos Amigos
8135 Almancil.
289-39 52 69.

Vale de Ferro
Centro Hípico, Mexilhoeira Grande, 8500 Portimão.
282-96 84 44.

TRAVEL INFORMATION

Portugal, Madeira and the Azores have airports served by TAP, the national carrier. Major European airlines also fly to Lisbon and Oporto on the mainland. In addition, there are many charter flights operating in summer, especially to the Algarve, which are often sold as part of a package deal. Portugal's mainland rail network varies in speed and luxury, and there are many privatized bus services. Trains are cheap, and it is well worth cracking the complicated

Logo of
TAP Air Portugal

system of discounted tickets, although for most journeys, travelling by bus offers greater speed and flexibility. Driving on the mainland and the islands can be a hair-raising experience, both in cities and on twisting mountain roads, and Portugal has the highest road accident rate in Europe. On the islands, the smaller distances involved mean that it is sometimes more convenient for visitors to take taxis, but on the mainland, driving is the most flexible, albeit risky, means of transport.

Check-in at Lisbon Airport

ARRIVING BY AIR

Flights to mainland Portugal arrive at the international airports of Lisbon, Oporto and Faro. All are served by **TAP Air Portugal** and the first two also by the major European national airlines which run regular scheduled flights from cities such as Paris, Frankfurt, Milan, Rome and Madrid. Daily scheduled flights are operated by TAP and **British Airways**

from London, serving Lisbon, Oporto and Faro directly. Scheduled flights from Britain's regional airports and Dublin require passengers to pick up a connecting flight in London.

There are charter flights operating from all the major British airports to Faro, especially in summer, and a fair number also fly to Madeira, Lisbon and Oporto. **Aer Lingus** flies from Dublin to Gatwick or Heathrow, connecting to British Airways flights to Faro and Lisbon.

British Airways and TAP run scheduled flights to Funchal, in Madeira, from London. To fly to Madeira and the Azores from other European cities, you have to change in Lisbon for an internal flight *(see p441)*.

**Signs at the airport
for visitors' facilities**

LONG-HAUL FLIGHTS

Visitors from North America can pick up a direct **American Airlines** or **Continental** flight to Lisbon from Newark, New York as both sell tickets on TAP flights. Passengers going on to Faro, Oporto, Madeira or the Azores may pick up a connecting flight in Lisbon. **SATA** runs charter flights from Boston and Toronto direct to the Azores. Tickets should be booked in advance as the flights are popular. Other airlines, such as TWA, connect to major US hubs, where passengers can change planes for Lisbon. TAP and Brazilian airline Varig link South American cities such as Rio de Janeiro

Airport	Information	Distance to City Centre	Taxi Fare to City Centre	Public Transport to City Centre
Lisbon	21-841 35 00	7 km (4 miles)	1,500$00	20 minutes
Oporto	22-943 24 00	11 km (7 miles)	3,000$00	30 minutes
Faro	289-80 08 00	6 km (4 miles)	1,100$00	15 minutes
Funchal	291-52 49 41	18 km (11 miles)	3,600$00	30 minutes
Ponta Delgada	296-20 54 00	3 km (2 miles)	1,000$00	10 minutes
Horta	292-94 35 11	8 km (5 miles)	1,000$00	15 minutes

and Caracas with Lisbon and Oporto. There are no direct flights from New Zealand or Australia, and visitors from those countries will need a connecting flight from a European gateway such as London.

AIR FARES

AIRLINES OFFER many options on flights to Portugal, with prices varying according to class, season and the flexibility that the ticket provides. The cheapest scheduled flights from the UK are offered by GO! BA's periodic offers, such as their Everyday or Special Value fares, can be found by calling their bookings line. All such flights must usually be booked well in advance, as seats are limited, and it is wise to take out insurance against late cancellations, since refunds are not usually given.

Charter flights have fixed outward and return dates, and allow a maximum stay of one month only, but they are the cheapest way of getting to Portugal. Charter flights to Faro and other resort areas are the most frequent. Students and young people should consult agencies for youth travel, as these often have special deals on offer. Ticket prices are usually much higher in the summer and at Christmas and Easter.

TAP Air Portugal aircraft on the tarmac at Lisbon Airport

Shuttle service stop, Lisbon Airport

PACKAGE DEALS

SPECIALIST HOLIDAYS are now a popular option in Portugal. These include stays in manor houses and *pousadas*

(see pp378–9), short breaks to Lisbon and Oporto, tennis and golfing holidays in the Algarve and walking holidays in the Minho. These, together with package deals including hotel, villa or apartment accommodation, will often provide inclusive bus service to your destination from the airport. Fly-drive deals are also available, to the Algarve especially, that mean you spend less time at the airport dealing with paperwork. Car hire, when booked as part of a package deal, may be very reasonable. Travel agents sell these holidays but a list of companies specializing in them on the mainland and the islands is available from **ICEP**, the National Tourist Office.

INTERNAL FLIGHTS

TAP AND ITS RIVAL, **Portugália**, operate several daily flights between Lisbon and Oporto, and Lisbon and Faro. TAP also flies daily from Lisbon and Oporto to Funchal and from Lisbon to São Miguel, Terceira and Faial in the Azores. It runs daily flights between Funchal and Porto Santo, and between Funchal and Ponta Delgada on São Miguel, and SATA inter-links the Azores (see p447).

DIRECTORY

ARRIVING BY AIR

British Airways
London 【 0845-77 33 77.

Aer Lingus
Dublin 【 08459-73 77 47.

TAP Air Portugal
London 【 020-87 62 73 76.
Dublin 【 01-679 88 44.
Lisbon 【 21-843 11 00.

LONG-HAUL FLIGHTS

American Airlines
US 【 800-433 73 00.

Continental Airlines
US 【 800-525 17 00.

SATA
Boston 【 508-677 0555.
Toronto 【 416-515 71 88.

PACKAGE DEALS

ICEP
Portuguese Trade & Tourism Office,
22–25a Sackville Street,
London W1X 2LY.
【 09063-640 640.

INTERNAL FLIGHTS

Portugália
Lisbon 【 21-842 55 00.

SATA
Ponta Delgada 【 296-20 97 27.

TAP shuttle bus waiting to leave for central Lisbon

Travelling by Rail

T<small>HE</small> <small>PORTUGUESE</small> <small>STATE</small> <small>RAILWAY,</small> Caminhos de Ferro Portugueses (CP) provides an inexpensive, country-wide network. Quality of service can vary considerably, however, and much modernization to the system is still in the planning stage. The Alfa train between Lisbon and Oporto, via Coimbra, is fast and efficient, but for some other long journeys, such as Lisbon to Évora, it may be quicker and more comfortable to take the bus.

Carved arch over entrance to Lisbon's Rossio station *(see p82)*

ARRIVING BY TRAIN

T<small>HERE</small> <small>ARE</small> <small>TWO</small> main routes into Portugal by train. The first is to travel from Austerlitz station in Paris, changing at Irún on the French-Spanish border, then continuing on to the Portuguese border town of Vilar Formoso in the north. The train splits near Coimbra, heading north for Oporto and south for Lisbon, coming into Santa Apolónia station. The en-tire journey from London to Lisbon, using the Eurostar to reach Paris, takes 30 hours.

The alternative route is to travel on the overnight train from Madrid, passing through Marvão and Santarém, then on to Lisbon. Travel from Madrid into Lisbon takes 10 hours. This train, called the "hotel-train", has luxurious carriages, some of which have showers.

TRAVELLING BY TRAIN

M<small>OST</small> <small>AREAS</small> of Portugal are served by rail, although the more remote lines, such as Mirandela to Bragança, have sadly been made obsolete as new roads are built. A bus service covers any gaps in the system, although it is wise to confirm that the service you require exists before setting off.

There are several categories of train in Portugal. The most comfortable and quickest is the modern, high-speed Alfa, which travels between Lisbon, Coimbra and Oporto. The Rápido Inter-Cidades (IC), is only marginally slower, although less luxurious, and connects most im-portant towns and cities. Most smaller towns and villages throughout the country are served by the Regional and the Inter-Regional lines. As you would expect, these local lines are consider-ably slower than the Rápido and Alfa, and the trains are less comfortable, with fewer facilities. However, they stop at a great many more stations.

High-speed Alfa train at Santa Apolónia Station in Lisbon

CITY STATIONS

L<small>ISBON</small> <small>HAS</small> <small>FOUR</small> rail termini. **Santa Apolónia** station, on Avenida Dom Henrique to the east of the Alfama district, serves the north and all inter-national destinations. A new station, **Oriente**, close to the Expo site and on the same line as Santa Apolónia, was opened for Expo '98. For the south and east (the Algarve and Alentejo) you must cross the Tagus by ferry to catch the train from **Barreiro** station. The ferry departs from the terminal next to Praça do Comércio. West of here is the **Cais do Sodré** station, from where trains leave for Estoril and Cascais. The trip to Cascais takes around 30 minutes.

Logo for Caminhos de Ferro Portugueses

Rossio station, on Praça dos Restauradores, serves Sintra, about 45 minutes away, and destinations north along the coast as far as Figueira da Foz. However, the Lisbon to Sintra line is not safe at night.

Coimbra has two mainline stations: trains from Lisbon and Oporto stop at **Coimbra B**, a five-minute shuttle ride from the central **Coimbra A**.

Oporto has three mainline stations: trains from the south come into **Campanhã**, to the east of the city, trains from Guimarães, Vila do Conde and Póvoa de Varzim stop in the north of the city at **Trindade**, and trains from Bragança stop at **São Bento** in the centre. From here there is a shuttle service to **Campanhã** station.

Exterior of station at Santiago do Cacém with *azulejo* **decoration**

Departures board in Santa Apolónia Station, Lisbon

FARES

FARES WITHIN PORTUGAL are fairly cheap in comparison with other European countries, and there are numerous discounts available. Children

PORTUGAL'S PRINCIPAL RAILWAY LINES

under the age of four travel free, and those from four to eleven pay half-fare. There are also discounts for groups, students and pensioners.

First-class travel on Portugal's trains is 40 per cent more expensive than second class, and second-class travel, while fairly basic on some lines, is usually sufficiently comfortable.

Visitors who intend to do much travelling by train might consider buying a tourist ticket (*bilhete turístico*). This is valid for an unlimited number of journeys for 7, 14 or 21 consecutive days, and can be used on all the different types of train. Families can save money by using the *cartão de família*, which gives good discounts, but only on journeys over 150 km (90 miles). It works as follows: one member of the family pays full fare, other members over 13 years of age pay half the full fare, and those under 13 pay a quarter of the fare. An Interrail pass for young people under 26 gives unlimited travel on all European trains for a month, so will allow travel both to and within Portugal (if it is bought outside the country). The slightly more expensive Interrail 26-plus pass does not allow travel in Spain. For journeys within Portugal only, the Eurodomino pass offers unlimited travel for three, five or ten days, with a reduced rate for those younger than 26.

BUYING TICKETS

TICKETS FOR Alfa and Rápido (IC) trains can usually be booked up to 20 days ahead, although some services only offer 10-day advance bookings, so it is important to check first. Reservations can be made at stations or travel agents. If you want to buy a ticket the day you travel, arrive early as long queues at the ticket office are normal, especially during peak hours and holiday periods. It is important that you buy a ticket before boarding, otherwise you are liable to be fined on the spot by the conductor.

Comboios de amanhã e dias seguintes

Sign at ticket office showing where to buy advance tickets

Só para Comboios de hoje

Sign at ticket office showing where to buy tickets on day of travel

TIMETABLES

MAIN STATIONS in Portugal provide a complete rail timetable, the Guia Horário Oficial. This has details of all routes for IC, Inter-Regional and Regional trains, and a section in Portuguese only which details the tickets and discounts that are available.

DIRECTORY

RAILWAY STATIONS

Coimbra
Coimbra A (239-824 632.
Coimbra B (239-834 976.

Faro
(289-80 17 26.

Lisbon
Barreiro (21-207 48 07.
Cais do Sodré (800-203 067.
Rossio (21-393 37 47.
Oriente (800-201 820.
Santa Apolónia (21-881 62 42.

Oporto
Campanhã (22-519 13 28.
São Bento (22-200 27 22.

Driving in Portugal

Automóvel Clube de Portugal logo

PORTUGAL'S ROAD NETWORK includes an expanding motorway system, but some older main roads may be in need of repair, while minor roads can be very rough and tortuous. Traffic jams are a problem in and near cities. Never attempt driving in the rush hour, and be wary of reckless Portuguese drivers. Always carry your passport, licence, log book or rental contract, and car insurance. Failure to produce these *documentos* if the police stop you will incur a fine.

A steep road near Gouveia in the Serra da Estrela *(see pp218–9)*

Disembarking at Setúbal after crossing on the car ferry from Tróia

ARRIVING BY CAR

THE QUICKEST ROUTE is to cross the French-Spanish border at Irún and then take the N620 via Valladolid to Vilar Formoso in Portugal. To go to Lisbon or the Algarve, turn off at Burgos, head for Cáceres and then on to Badajoz.

Taking the car ferry to northern Spain from the UK reduces time on the road, but crossings are extremely long: 24 hours to Santander and 35 hours to Bilbao. **Brittany Ferries** travel to Santander leaving from Plymouth (March to November), and from Portsmouth (November to January). **P & O**'s Portsmouth-Bilbao line runs all year round, and all routes operate twice-weekly. There are no ferries travelling to Madeira or the Azores.

Driving time may also be reduced by using the Motorail link from Paris Gare d'Austerlitz to Lisbon, a twice-weekly service. Drivers load their cars one day, travel by passenger train the next, and pick up their cars on the third day. **French Railways** in the UK will supply information.

CAR HIRE

CAR HIRE AGENCIES may be found at Lisbon, Faro and Oporto airports and in main towns, and generally offer very reasonable rates. Local firms usually offer better rates than international ones, but you should check the condition of the car more carefully before you accept it, as well as the insurance coverage. You must have an international driving licence, be over the age of 23 and have held a licence for at least one year.

TRAVELLING AROUND BY CAR

MAJOR ROADS include EN *(Estrada Nacional)* roads, many of which have been up-graded to either IP *(Itinerário Principal)* or IC *(Itinerário Complementar)* roads. IP roads are much used by heavy goods lorries avoiding motorway tolls, and can be slow as a result.

Always fill up with petrol in town before setting off, as petrol stations can be scarce in remote areas. The best road maps are by Michelin or the Portuguese motoring organization, the ACP *(Automóvel Clube de Portugal)*.

PARKING

FINDING A PARKING space in cities can be difficult. If you do find a spot, leave the car facing the same direction as the traffic on that side of the road. Lisbon and Oporto have new underground car parks, while in Coimbra it may be best to park on the outskirts and take a bus to the centre.

PETROL

PETROL IS RELATIVELY expensive and the same price country-wide. Lead-free *(sem chumbo)* is slightly cheaper than 4-star (Super) and diesel is cheaper than both. Some pumps are self-service and colour-coded: green for unleaded, red for leaded and black for diesel.

Traffic queueing for the toll on the Ponte 25 de Abril, Lisbon

RULES OF THE ROAD

TRAFFIC DRIVES on the right hand side, continental rules of the road apply and the international sign system is used. Unless there are signs to the contrary, traffic from the right has priority at squares, crossroads and junctions. Cars on roundabouts travel anticlockwise, and have priority over waiting traffic. There is very little advance warning of pedestrian crossings.

Seat belts must be used and the alcohol limit is 5 ml per litre. Speed limits are 60 kph in towns and 90 kph on other roads (37 mph and 55 mph), and 120 kph (74 mph) on motorways. Breaking the speed limit incurs an on-the-spot fine.

A motorway toll – the left lane reserved for users of the Via Verde system

ESTORIL

SUL-PONTE

SETE RIOS

Signs in Lisbon for the coast, south via the Ponte 25 de Abril, and zoo

MOTORWAYS AND TOLLS

PORTUGAL'S EXPANDING motorway network (*see map on back endpaper*) links Lisbon with Braga and Guimarães in the north, and Oporto with Amarante. Another section goes from Lisbon to Torres Vedras, and a cross-country stretch runs east to the Spanish border at Elvas. Apart from some sections near Lisbon and Oporto, all motorways have

two lanes. Tolls are payable on motorways and on Lisbon's bridges, the Ponte 25 de Abril and the new Ponte Vasco da Gama. Do not use the Via Verde (green lane) at tolls; this is only for the use of drivers who subscribe to an electronic system allowing them to pay automatically.

BREAKDOWN SERVICES

THERE IS a reciprocal breakdown service between **ACP** and other organizations. To qualify, drivers should take out European cover with their own organization. Motorways have SOS phones, and if you use them, state that you are entitled to ACP cover. For drivers without cover, most towns have a garage with breakdown lorry.

CYCLING

THE SOUTH is the best area for cycling, but in summer the Alentejo can be too hot. If you plan on doing a lot of cycling, **Instituto Português Cartografia e Cadastro** sells good large-scale maps.

DIRECTORY

ARRIVING BY CAR

Brittany Ferries
0870-536 0360.

French Railways Motorail Department
0870-550 2309.

P & O
0870-242 4999.

CAR HIRE

A.A.
Castanheira/Budget, Lisbon
21-319 55 55.

Auto Jardim, Faro
289-818 491.

Budget, Oporto
22-607 69 70.

Europcar, Faro
289-823 778.

Hertz, Lisbon
21-381 24 30.

Hertz, Oporto
22-600 57 16.

Sixt, Lisbon
21-940 52 47.

BREAKDOWN SERVICES

ACP
21-942 91 03.

CYCLING

Instituto Português Cartografia e Cadastro
Rua Artilharia Um 107,
1070 Lisbon.
21-381 96 00.

ROAD NUMBERS

Roads in Portugal may have up to three different numbers. Thanks to a building and upgrading programme, former EN or *Estrada Nacional* roads can also be IP (*Itinerário Principal*) roads. A road with an E (*Estrada Europeia*) number indicates that it is also a direct international route.

The Bragança-Oporto road is now the IP4, part motorway (A4) and part dual carriageway.

IP 4

210

E 82

The road's original EN number (*Estrada Nacional*)

The **E82** is an international route, ending in Spain near Valladolid.

Travelling by Coach

The logo of EVA, one of the country-wide coach companies

Since the privatization of Portugal's bus network, the Rodoviária Nacional (RN), coach companies have multiplied and some routes are now even operated by foreign companies. Regional operators compete with each other to offer better services to more destinations, and as a result, many coach journeys, such as Lisbon to the Algarve, are quicker and often more comfortable than the equivalent train journeys. Coaches also cover the increasing number of defunct sections of railway, such as Mirandela-Bragança and Beja-Moura.

offers daytrips running from Lisbon to Évora and Coimbra, a cruise on the Tagus and a trip lasting three days to the Algarve. Pick-up points are at the main hotels or central locations. It is also possible to arrange longer trips to areas of historical or scenic interest.

In the Algarve, there are frequent coach trips to places of interest such as Loulé, Silves and Monchique, the southwest and the River Guadiana, and further afield to Évora and Lisbon. Tourist offices, hotels and travel agencies can help with these, and pick-up points are the main coastal hotels.

A Rodonorte coach, which covers the far north of the country

GETTING TO PORTUGAL BY COACH

Travelling to Portugal by coach is cheap but very time-consuming. **Eurolines** runs a weekly summer service from Victoria Coach Station in London to Oporto, avoiding Paris. Passengers change in Valladolid in central Spain, and the journey takes 31 hours in total. The London to Lisbon service, which runs all year, takes even longer. Passengers change in Paris and spend two nights on the coach.

TRAVELLING AROUND BY COACH

Coach operators in Portugal include **Renex**, who link Faro, Lisbon, Oporto and Braga, and **EVA** which covers the whole country. **Rodoviária Estremadura** connects Lisbon with Estremadura. In Vila Real, **Rodonorte** covers the extreme north, and **Rede Expressos**, based in Oporto, covers the inland areas of Portugal.

There is no central coach station in either Lisbon or Oporto as companies are private and operate separately, but the main coach terminus in Lisbon is on Avenida Casal Ribeiro. In Oporto, the main departure and arrival points are at Rua das Carmelitas and

Praça Dona Filipa de Lencastre. Information on routes and prices is available from tourist offices and travel agencies.

COACH TOURS

Bus and coach tours around Lisbon and Oporto are plentiful. **Citirama** runs sightseeing tours of Lisbon and its coast, and daytrips to sights such as Batalha, Sintra and Mafra. It also offers a night-time tour of the city, taking in the Jerónimos monastery and then dinner with a *fado* show. From Oporto, it runs tours of the Minho and Douro valleys, and a six-day trip to Lisbon. **Gray Line**, part of Citirama, also

A Cityrama coach on an excursion along the Lisbon coast

DIRECTORY

LONDON

Eurolines
52 Grosvenor Gardens,
London SW1W 0AU.
☎ 0207-730 82 35.

NORTHERN PORTUGAL

Rede Expressos
Rua Alexandre Herculano 366,
Oporto. ☎ 22-200 69 54.

Renex
Rua das Carmelitas 1, Oporto.
☎ 22-200 33 95.

Rodonorte
Rua D. Pedro de Castro, Vila Real.
☎ 259-34 07 10.

LISBON

Citirama
Avenida Praia da Vitória 12b.
☎ 21-319 10 70.

Gray Line
Avenida Praia da Vitória 12b.
☎ 21-352 25 94.

Renex
Rua dos Arameiros 15.
☎ 21-888 28 29.

Rodoviária Estremadura
Avenida Casal Ribeiro 18a/b.
☎ 21-357 05 50.

ALGARVE

EVA
Avenida da República 5, Faro.
☎ 289-899 700.

Travelling Around the Islands

O N THE ROCKY, MOUNTAINOUS ISLANDS of Madeira and the Azores, the pace of transport is necessarily slow, and some places are only accessible on foot. Driving needs care and patience, and you may find organized trips by coach or taxi are more relaxing and rewarding.

Inter-island aircraft on the runway on Pico

ISLAND HOPPING

T AP FLIES SEVERAL times a day between Funchal and Porto Santo in the Madeira group, and on the Azores, flights are operated by SATA *(see p441)*. Flights to Flores and Corvo are often disrupted by adverse weather conditions, so for extensive island hopping it is a good idea to insure against delays. SATA flights should be confirmed at least 72 hours before take-off.

Logo of the Azorean airline

The most useful ferry connections are between the five central islands of the Azores, especially the Faial-Pico run.

AROUND MADEIRA

B USES OPERATE throughout Madeira, but cater mainly for islanders' needs. However, companies such as **Intervisa**

and **Blandy** organize coach trips around the island. Taxis can be hired by the day or half-day, but car hire offers the most flexibility *(see p444)*. Book well ahead and allow plenty of time for journeys: roads are steep, tortuous and full of potholes. The new road along the south coast was finally finished in 1999, but many places are still accessible only on foot.

AROUND THE AZORES

C ARS CAN BE HIRED on all the Azores except Corvo, from firms such as **Ilha Verde Rent-A-Car**. Charges are high compared to the mainland and the roads are precipitous, so it may be more restful, at least on the smaller islands, to take a tour by taxi. Many drivers speak English, and they often make memorable companions. Before setting off on a day trip, you should agree a price, itinerary and return time. You should also offer to pay for the driver's lunch. Check the weather beforehand: if the mountains and calderas are concealed by

clouds, there is no point setting out. Buses are cheap but, as on Madeira, of little use to visitors. Tourist offices can supply information on coach trips by **Agência Açoreana de Viagens** and others, and also on boat trips along the coast. Bicycles can be hired, but the mountainous terrain makes cycling difficult. On the smaller islands you can usually hitch a lift with ease.

The best way to enjoy the Azores is on foot. Taxi drivers are willing to drop visitors off at the start of a route and pick them up further on. Detailed maps of the Azores are hard to find, so try to acquire one prior to arrival. Some routes are described in the specialist guidebooks sold locally.

DIRECTORY

MADEIRA

Blandy
Avenida do Mar 1,
Funchal.
(291-20 06 20.

Intervisa
Avenida Arriaga 30, Funchal.
(291-20 89 00.

AZORES

**Agência Açoreana
de Viagens**
Lado Sul da Matriz 68–9,
Ponta Delgada, São Miguel.
(296-28 54 37.

Ilha Verde Rent-A-Car
Praça 5 de Outubro 19,
Ponta Delgada.
(296-28 52 00.

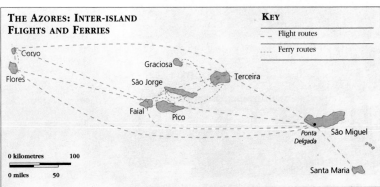

THE AZORES: INTER-ISLAND FLIGHTS AND FERRIES

KEY

- - - Flight routes

.... Ferry routes

Corvo

Flores

Graciosa

São Jorge

Terceira

Faial

Pico

Ponta Delgada

São Miguel

Santa Maria

0 kilometres 100

0 miles 50

Travelling within Cities

**Sign for Metro
in Lisbon**

M OST CITY CENTRES are small, so walking is by far the best way to explore them if you have both the time and inclination. Lisbon also offers a full range of transport options including a Metro system and funiculars, while the other cities are well served by buses, trolleybuses and taxis. Lisbon's Metro is being expanded, due for completion by the year 2001, and its trams are slowly being upgraded with smart futuristic models. Transport of any kind should be avoided during rush hour (8–10am and 5:30–7:30pm).

**Lisbon's Elevador da Glória
ascending to the Bairro Alto**

BUSES

B USES ARE A PRACTICAL way to travel round and see the main cities, though in Lisbon they are more expensive than the Metro. When boarding the bus, enter at the front door and exit by the central door.

For one-off trips you can buy your ticket from the driver, but it is cheaper to buy in multiples of 10, or a one- or three-day ticket, or a two-journey ticket for the same price as a single. Tickets must be validated in the machine *(obliterador)* near the driver when you board, or you will be liable to a heavy, on-the-spot fine. Every bus *(autocarro)* displays its destination *(destino)* at the front and each bus stop *(paragem)* has information about the route that the bus will take.

**Orange and white Lisbon bus
heading for Praça do Comércio**

TRAMS AND FUNICULARS

F UN WAYS of exploring Lisbon are by tram *(eléctrico)*, funicular or lift (both *elevador*), while Oporto has trolleybuses running down to the river and a tram route along the waterfront. In Lisbon, **Carris** runs a "hill tour" *(Linha das*

Colinas) by antique tramcar. Its *Linha do Tejo* tours the sights from Belém to the bullring.

Funiculars ascend from river level up to the Bairro Alto: the Elevador da Bica starts near Cais do Sodré station and the Elevador da Glória goes from Praça dos Restauradores. The Santa Justa lift *(see p86)* is also a useful means of transport, running between the lower Baixa area and the Bairro Alto.

BUS TOURS

I N OPORTO, **Gray Line** runs city tours at least twice a week, and more often in summer. They include a visit to a port lodge with tasting *(see p247)*. Tickets are sold at the Gray Line office, and the tourist office in Praça Dom João I, from where the buses depart. Citirama runs a once-weekly tour of Coimbra. They have no office there, but the tourist office can take bookings and enquiries, and the bus departs from just outside.

LISBON METRO

L ISBON'S METRO network is in the process of being extended. There are currently four lines operating, giving improved coverage of the city centre and suburbs, and by 2001 there should also be a link to Santa Apolónia station.

Tickets are inexpensive, and can be bought at a discount in books of ten, known as a *caderneta*. Tickets should be validated before going through the station barriers using the *obliterador* machine. The Metro operates between 6am and 1am, but rush hours should be avoided, as the Metro can get very crowded with commuters.

One of Lisbon's new set of longer, streamlined trams

Antique red tram operating the Linha do Tejo tour in Lisbon

TICKETS IN LISBON

Buses, trams, funiculars and the lift all accept the same tickets. Discounted ones can be bought from the Carris kiosks at Praça da Figueira, Santa Justa lift or Sete Rios station. Metro tickets bought from self-service machines at stations are cheaper, and multiple ticket purchases offer yet further discounts.

One-day metro ticket

One-day travel ticket

Two-journey ticket

The Lisboa card gives the holder access to 26 of Lisbon's museums, and travel on public transport for one, two or three days (see p427).

Lights showing which rate applies

"Taxi for hire" sign

Beige city taxi

TAXIS

TAXIS HAVE traditionally been black with a green roof, but these have been phased out in favour of a beige livery. They are relatively cheap and if you share the cost it sometimes works out cheaper than a bus or tram. You can flag a taxi down in the street or call a firm such as **Autocoope**. The meter is switched off for trips outside the city, so agree a price first. The cost of the journey is calculated according to the number of kilometres covered, and the starting rate is 250$00. A flat rate of 300$00 is charged for luggage, but only if it is placed in the boot. Do not pay extra otherwise. Rides between 10pm and 6am and those on Saturdays, Sundays and public holidays are at a higher rate. The two green lights on the roof indicate which rate is being charged: one light for the cheaper rate and two for the higher one. When the central light is on, the taxi is for hire.

Details about who to contact in case of a problem is on the rear left window of the cab.

DIRECTORY

BUS AND TRAM TOURS

Carris, Lisbon
Rua 1º de Maio 101,
1300 Lisbon.
21-363 20 44.

Coimbra Tourist Office
Praça da República,
3000 Coimbra.
239-83 32 02.

Gray Line, Oporto
c/o Avenida Praia da Vitória 12b,
1049-054 Lisbon.
21-352 25 94.

RADIO TAXIS

Autocoope (Lisbon)
21-793 27 56.

Radio Taxis (Oporto)
22-502 80 61.

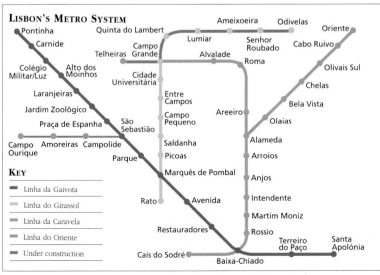

LISBON'S METRO SYSTEM

KEY

- Linha da Gaivota
- Linha do Girassol
- Linha da Caravela
- Linha do Oriente
- Under construction

(Stations: Pontinha, Carnide, Colégio Militar/Luz, Alto dos Moinhos, Laranjeiras, Jardim Zoológico, Praça de Espanha, Campo Ourique, Amoreiras, Campolide, Parque, São Sebastião, Quinta do Lambert, Telheiras, Campo Grande, Cidade Universitária, Entre Campos, Campo Pequeno, Saldanha, Picoas, Marquês de Pombal, Rato, Avenida, Restauradores, Cais do Sodré, Baixa-Chiado, Ameixoeira, Lumiar, Alvalade, Roma, Areeiro, Alameda, Arroios, Anjos, Intendente, Martim Moniz, Rossio, Odivelas, Senhor Roubado, Oriente, Cabo Ruivo, Olivais Sul, Chelas, Bela Vista, Olaias, Terreiro do Paço, Santa Apolónia)

General Index

Page numbers in **bold** type
refer to main entries

A

A.A. Castanheira/Budget
  (car hire) 445
Abbeys *see* Monasteries
  and Convents
Abd al Rahman 42
ABEP (Lisbon ticket agency) 65
Abrantes **188**
  hotels 386
  restaurants 410
Abrantes, Marquês de 104
Absolutists 37
ACP (Automóvel Clube
  de Portugal) 445
Addresses (Portuguese house
  numbering system) 435
Adega Machado
  (Lisbon *fado* house) 67
Adegas de São Francisco
  (Funchal) 347
Adoration of the Magi
  (Grão Vasco) **48**, 213
Adoration of St Vincent
  (Gonçalves) 97, **98–9**
Afonso, Dom (son of
  João I) 276
Afonso I, King *see* Afonso
  Henriques
Afonso II, King 38, 169
Afonso III, King 38, 44
  deposes Sancho II 44
  Estremoz 300
  Faro 44, 326
  Leiria 181
  Monsaraz 307
  Vila Nova de Gaia 247
Afonso IV, King 38
  murder of Inês de Castro 179
  Porto de Mós 180
  tomb of 74
  war with Pedro I 45
Afonso V, King 38
  captures Arzila 46
  marriage 175
  Monument to the Discoveries
  (Lisbon) 109
  Palácio de Dom Manuel
  (Évora) 305
  portrait of 99
Afonso VI, King 39
  deposed 51
  Palácio Nacional de Sintra 158
Afonso, Jorge 168
  *Apparition of Christ to
  the Virgin* 60
Afonso Henriques (Afonso I),
  King 38
  Alcobaça 142, 178

Afonso Henriques, King (cont.)
  Battle of Ourique 43
  Battle of São Mamede 43
  Cárquere 249
  Castelo de São Jorge
  (Lisbon) 78–9
  Castelo dos Mouros
  (Sintra) 157
  *Chronicles of Dom Afonso
  Henriques* 162
  Coimbra 202, 204
  declares independence 37
  defeats Moors 42, 43, 304
  Guimarães 280
  Lamego 250
  Leiria 181
  Minho 263
  Nossa Senhora da Oliveira
  (Guimarães) 280
  Óbidos 175
  Palácio Nacional de Sintra 158
  São Vicente de Fora 72
  Sé (Lisbon) 74
  statue of 78
  tomb of 202, 205
Afonso Sanches, Dom
  tomb of 272
Africa
  voyages of dicovery 48–9
  Portuguese colonies 54, 56–7
Age of Absolutism 52–3
Age of Discovery 17, **48–9**
  Manueline architecture 20
  Monument to the Discoveries
  (Lisbon) 108–9
Agência Açoriana de
  Viagens 447
Água, Museu da (Lisbon)
  see Museu da Água
Águas Livres Aqueduct (Lisbon)
  52–3, **124**
Air travel **440–41**
  travelling around
  the islands 447
Airports 440
Alandroal **300**
  restaurants 417
Alani 41
Albergarias (inns) 374
Albert, Cardinal-Archduke
  of Austria 50
Albert, Prince Consort 161
Albufeira 13, 317, **323**, 426
  hotels 396–7
  restaurants 419
Albufeira, Lagoa do 163
Albuquerque, Afonso de
  captures Goa 46, 47
  cenotaph 73
  Praça Afonso de Albuquerque
  (Lisbon) 102, 103

Albuquerque, Brás de 73
Albuquerque, Dom João de
  tomb of 200
Alcácer do Sal **169**
  hotels 384
Alcácer-Quibir, Battle
  of (1578) 47
Alcaníces Treaty (1297) 215
Alcântara (Lisbon)
  restaurants 404
Alcântara, Battle of (1580) 50
Alcobaça 142, 171, **178–9**
  history 43, 45
  restaurants 410
  tombs of Pedro I and Inês
  de Castro 44–5, 179
Alcochete 16, 149, **163**
Alcoforado, Mariana
  Lettres Portugaises 311
Alcohol
  customs allowances 426
Alcool Puro (Lisbon bar) 65
Alcoutim **331**
Aldeamento Turístico
  (tourist villages) 376
Alenquer **193**
Alenquer, Pêro de 193
Alentejo 14, 16, **290–313**
  climate 35
  hotels 395–6
  map 292–3
  restaurants 417–19
  Romans in the Alentejo 305
  vernacular architecture 18, 19
  wines 29
Alexander the Great 118
Alfama (Lisbon) **69–79**
  area map 69
  restaurants 404
  Street-by-Street map 70–71
Alfândega Velha (Funchal)
  Street-by-Street map 345
Alfonso VI, King of León
  and Castile 43
Algar do Carvão 365
Algarve 13, **314–31**
  beaches of the Algarve 286–7
  climate 35
  coach travel 446
  festivals 30, 32
  fishing 26
  flowers of the Western
  Algarve 319
  golf courses of
  the Algarve 438–9
  history 44
  hotels 396–9
  map 316–17
  restaurants 419–21
  vernacular architecture 18–19
Algarve Music Festival 30

Alijó
  hotels 390
  Port Country Tour 253
  restaurants 413
Aljezur **318**
  hotels 397
Aljubarrota, Battle of
  (1385) 142, 280
  Batalha **183**
  history 46
All Saints' Day 32, 33
Almada (Lisbon)
  restaurants 404
Almancil **324**
  hotels 397
  restaurants 419
Almançor, River 301
Al-Mansur 42, 44, 301
Almeida **215**
  Border Castles Tour 216
  hotels 388
  restaurants 411
Almeida family 188
Almeida, António de 52
Almeida, Leopoldo de
  statue of João I 85
Almeirim 190
  restaurants 410
Almendres 292
Almograve 312
Almohad dynasty 43, 44
Almondo, River 189
Almoravid dynasty 43
Almourol, Castelo de **189**
Al-Mu'tamid 322
Alpiarça **190**
Alte 315, **323**
  hotels 397
Alte, River 323
Alter do Chão **296**
Alter Real horses 296
Alto Alentejo
  climate 35
Alto das Caravelas 255
Alto da Memória 365
Alto do Trevim 209
Alto do Velão 255
Álvares, Baltasar 50
Alves, Diogo 124
Alvito 307
  hotels 395
  restaurants 417
Alvito, Barão de 307
Alvor **321**
  hotels 397
Amarante **248–9**
  festivals 31
  hotels 390
  restaurants 413
Amarante, Carlos 278
Ambulances 430, 431

Amélia, Queen 104, 108
Amoreiras Shopping Centre
  (Lisbon) 65, **114**
Al Andalus 42
Andrade, António de 50
Anes, Gonçalo 214
Anes, Pêro 346
Angola 55, 57
Angra do Heroísmo 361, **364–5**
Anjos 364
Anne, St 351
Anne of Hertford 350
Anos Sessenta (Lisbon) 65
ANTER 377
Antiga Confeitaria de Belém
  (Lisbon)
  Street-by-Street map 103
Antigo Paço Episcopal
  (Braga) 276–7
António, Lino 250
Antony of Padua, St
  (Santo António) **74**, 321
  Festas de Santo António 31
  Museu Antoniano (Lisbon) 75
  Santo António (Lagos) 321
  Santo António à Sé (Lisbon) 75
Apart-hotels 374
Apartamentos turísticos
  (tourist apartments) 376
Apparition of Christ to the Virgin
  (Afonso) 60
Aquariums
  Pavilhão dos Oceanos
    (Lisbon) 121
  Museu Oceanográfico
    (Portinho da Arrábida) 147
Aqueduto da Água de Prata
  (Évora) 305
Aqueduto das Águas Livres
  (Lisbon) 52–3, **124**
Aqueduto da Amoreira
  (Elvas) 297
Aquinas, St Thomas 326
Arabs 42
Arade, River 322
Araújo, José Ferreira 207
Archaeological Museum (Lisbon)
  see Museu Nacional de
  Arqueologia
Architecture
  azulejos (ceramic tiles)
    17, **22–3**
  Manueline 17, **20–21**, 106–7
  triangular houses
    of Santana 351
  vernacular architecture 18–19
Arcos de Valdevez 267
  restaurants 416
Arganil **209**
Arifana
  beach 286

Armação de Pêra
  hotels 397
  restaurants 420
Armed Forces Movement
  (Movimento das Forças
  Armadas) 57, 87
Armona 329
Arouca **198**
Arouce, River 208
Arqueologia, Museu Nacional de
  (Lisbon) see Museu Nacional
  de Arqueologia
Arrábida, Serra da
  see Serra da Arrábida
Arraiolos **301**
*The Arrival of the Relics of Santa
  Auta at the Church of Madre
  de Deus* 21
Arruda, Diogo de
  Convento de Cristo
  (Tomar) 20, **186–7**
Arruda, Francisco de
  Aqueduto da Água de Prata
    (Évora) 305
  Aqueduto da Amoreira
    (Elvas) 297
  Manueline architecture 20
  Nossa Senhora da Assunção
    (Elvas) 297
Arte Antiga, Museu Nacional de
  (Lisbon) see Museu Nacional
  de Arte Antiga
Arte Moderna, Centro de (Lisbon)
  see Centro de Arte Moderna
Arte Popular, Museu de (Lisbon)
  see Museu de Arte Popular
Arunce, King 209
Arzila 46
Associação Portuguesa
  de Tradutores 431
Assumption Day 33, 227
Augustus, Emperor 41, 208
Australian Embassy 427
Autocoope (Lisbon) 449
Automatic teller machines
  (ATMs) 432
Autumn in Portugal 32
Ave, River 248
Aveiras, Conde de 104
Aveiro 23, 195, **200–1**
  festivals 31, 33
  hotels 388
  restaurants 411
Aveiro, Ria de 23, 196, **201**
Avelar, Dom Francisco
  Gomes do 326
Avenida da Liberdade
  (Lisbon) **84**
Avis, House of 38, **46–7**, 183
  Alandroal 300
  Almeirim 190

Avis, João of *see* João I
Avis (car hire) 445, 447
Azambuja, Diogo de
tomb of 199
Azenhas do Mar 153
Azores 14, **358–71**
climate 34
festivals 30
formation of the Azores **338–9**
geology 338–9
Holy Spirit festivals **366**
hotels **400–1**
maps 10, **360–61**
Mid-Atlantic Ridge 338–9
restaurants 423
time zone 429
travel 447
volcanoes 338–9
whale watching **368–9**
whaling 368–9
windmills 19
Azulejos (ceramic tiles) 17, **22–3**
Museu Nacional do Azulejo
(Lisbon) 61, **122–3**
Azzolini, Giacomo 104

B

B. Leza (Lisbon club) 65
Baçal, Abbot of 259
Baía de São Lourenço 364
Bairro Alto and Estrela
(Lisbon) **88–99**
area map 89
hotels 380
restaurants 404–5, 406
Street-by-Street map 90–91
Baixa (Lisbon) 63, **80–7**
area map 81
hotels 380–81
restaurants 405
Street-by-Street map 82–3
Baixo Alentejo
climate 35
Balcões 351
Baleal 174
hotels 386
Bandarra (Gonçalo Anes) 214
Bank notes 433
Banking 432–3
Bar Pintaí (Lisbon) 65
"Barbarian" invasions 41
Barbizon School 93, 119
Barcelos **273**, 436
decorated ceramics 24
festivals 30, 226
hotels 393
restaurants 416
Barcelos, Count of
tomb of 251
Barcelos cock, legend of 273
Barragem de Bravura 321

Barragem de Valeira
Port Country Tour 253
Barragem do Castelo
de Bode **188**
hotels 386
restaurants 410
Barrancos 310
Bars and clubs
Lisbon 65
Bartholomew, St 45
Basílica da Estrela (Lisbon) **95**
Basto, Terras de 281
Bastos (prehistoric statues) 281
Batalha 142, **182–3**
history 47
hotels 386
Manueline architecture 21
restaurants 410
Battle of Ourique (Colaço) 23
Beaches
Beaches of the Algarve **286–7**
Cascais 162
Colares 153
Costa da Caparica 163
Estoril 162
Guincho 162
Ilha de Tavira 330
Nazaré 180
Península de Tróia 169
Porto Santo 357
Sagres 320
São Pedro de Muel 181
Serra da Arrábida 167
Sesimbra 166
Sines 312
Vila do Bispo 319
Vila Nova de Milfontes 312
Zambujeira do Mar 313
Beatriz, Dona
tomb of 74
Beatriz, Queen of Castile 44
Beatty, Hugh 321
Beckford, William 155, 165
Beco dos Cruzes (Lisbon)
Street-by-Street map 71
Beer 147, 403
Beira Alta 17
Beira Baixa
climate 35
Beira Litoral
climate 35
Beiras 14, **194–221**
climate 35
hotels 388–90
map 196–7
restaurants 411–13
vernacular architecture 18–19
Beja 284, **311**
hotels 395
restaurants 417–18
Belasco, Ângelo 92

Belém (Lisbon) **100–11**
area map 101
map 60
restaurants 405–6
Street-by-Street map 102–3
Belém, Torre de 20, 60, **110**
Beliche 320
beach 286
Belmonte **217**
Belvederes
Miradouro da Graça
(Lisbon) 75
Miradouro de Santa Luzia
(Lisbon) 72
Miradouro de São Pedro
de Alcântara (Lisbon) 94
Benedictines
São Bento (Santo Tirso) 248
Berbers 42
Beresford, Viscount 54
Berlenga Islands **174**
Bernardes, António de Oliveira
Christ Teaching in the Temple
(Misericórdia, Évora) 22
Convento da Esperança
(Ponta Delgada) 362
Life of the Virgin (Peniche) 174
Bernardes, Policarpo de Oliveira
Castelo de São Filipe
(Setúbal) 22, 168
Misericórdia church
(Alandroal) 300
Misericórdia church
(Chaves) 256
Museu Municipal
(Viana do Castelo) 275
Best Western Hotels 377
Bicycling 438, **445**
travelling around the
islands 447
Birds
Berlenga Islands 174
birds of the Tagus and
Sado estuaries 169
dovecotes of Montesinho 260
Reserva Natural do Estuário
do Tejo 163
water birds of the
Ria Formosa 329
Bisalhães 255
decorated ceramics 25
Biscoitos 365
Black Death 45
Blandy (coach tours) 447
Blandy family 347
Blandy's Gardens 347
Boa Ventura 342
Boats
ferries 444, 447
fishing 26–7
sailing 438

Boca do Inferno 162
Bocage, Manuel Barbosa
  du 85, 168
Boelhe 248
Boitac, Diogo
  Batalha 21
  Ermida de São Jerónimo
  (Lisbon) 111
  Igreja de Jesus (Setúbal) 168
  Igreja do Populo (Caldas
  da Rainha) 175
  Igreja Matriz (Golegã) 190
  Manueline architecture 20
  Mosteiro dos Jerónimos
  (Lisbon) 106
  Santa Cruz (Coimbra) 205
  Sé (Guarda) 217
A Bola (newspaper) 17
Bom Jesus do Monte 224, **278−9**
  hotels 393
Border Castles Tour
  (Beiras) **216**
Bosch, Hieronymus
  *The Temptations of
  St Antony* 96, **98**
Boticas 256
Boucher, François 119
Braga 263, **276−7**
  disabled taxis 429
  festivals 30, 226
  hotels 393
  map 277
  restaurants 416
Bragança 225, **258−9**
  citadel 258−9
  festivals 33
  hotels 390
  restaurants 413
Bragança dynasty 39, **299**
  tombs 72
Bragança, Dukes of 299
  Paço Ducal (Vila Viçosa)
  285, **298−9**
  Vila Viçosa 280, 298
Bragança, Dom Afonso,
  1st Duke of 258, 299
  Barcelos 273
  birth 217
  Paço dos Duques
  (Guimarães) 280
Bragança, Catherine of
  see Catherine of Bragança
Bragança, Fernando, 3rd
  Duke of 299
Bragança, Jaime 4th Duke of 299
Bragança, 8th Duke of
  see João IV, King
Braganza *see* Bragança
Brasileira, Café (Lisbon) 93
  Street-by-Street map 89
Bravães 267

Bravura dam 316
Brazil 46
  "discovery" of 37, 48
  gold discovered 51
  independence 54
  royal family flees to 53
Breakdown services 445
Brejoeira Palace 263
Brissos
  Megaliths Tour 306
British Airways 441
British Consulates 427
British Embassy 427
British Hospital (Lisbon) 431
Brittany Ferries 445
Buçaco 143, **210−11**
  hotels 388
  map 210−11
  restaurants 412
Buçaco, Battle of (1810) 54, 211
Buçaco Palace Hotel 21, **210**, 211
Budget (car hire) 445
Budget accommodation **376**, 377
Budget Travel 441
Bull-running
  Terceira 364
  Vila Franca de Xira 192
Bullfighting 17, **144−5**
  Campo Pequeno (Lisbon) 120
  Coruche 192
  Santarém 191
Bureaux de change 432
Burgundy, House of 38
Burgundy, Henry of
  see Henry of Burgundy
Buses
  bus tours **448**, 449
  in cities 448
  for the disabled 428−9
  travelling around the
  islands 447
Byron, Lord 155

C

Cabanas
  fishing 27
Cabeça da Neve 212
Cabeça do Velho 218
Cabeceiras de Basto **281**
Cabo Carvoeiro 174
Cabo da Roca 150
  Serra de Sintra Tour 154
Cabo de São Vicente **319**
Cabo Espichel **163**
Cabo Girão 357
Cabral family 217
Cabral, Fernão 217
Cabral, Gonçalo Velho 362
Cabral, Pedro Álvares
  Belmonte 217
  "discovery" of Brazil 48

Cabral, Pedro Álvares (cont.)
  Monument to the Discoveries
  (Lisbon) 109
  tomb of 191
Cabral, Sacadura 56
Cabril, River 255
Cacela Velha 317, **331**
Cachorro 369
Caesar, Julius 191, 311
Caetano, Marcelo **57**, 87
Café Brasileira (Lisbon) 88, 93
  Street-by-Street map 89
Cafés 403
Cake shops 403
Cakes
  bolo rei 33, 227
  Central Portugal 147
  Northern Portugal 231
  Southern Portugal 289
Caldas do Gerês 270
Caldas de Monchique 319
Caldas da Rainha **175**
  decorated ceramics 24
  hotels 386
  restaurants 410
Caldeira do Cabeço Gordo 370
Caldeira de Guilherme Moniz 365
Caldeira das Sete Cidades
  339, **362**
Caldeirão, Lagoa do 371
Caldeiras das Furnas 363
Calderas 339
Calheta **356**, 367
Camacha **348**
Câmara, João Gonçalves de 346
Câmara, Simão Gonçalves de 346
Câmara de Lobos 357
Câmara Municipal (Funchal)
  Street-by-Street map 345
Câmara Municipal
  (Sintra) 156
Cambridge, Earl of 307
Caminha **266**
  hotels 393
  restaurants 416
Camões, Luís Vaz de 46, **188**
  Casa Memória de Camões
  (Constância) 188
  cenotaph 73
  Os Lusíadas 16, 47, 152,
  188, 305
  Monument to the Discoveries
  (Lisbon) 109
Camões Day 33
Camping 377
Camping and Caravanning
  Albufeira 377
Camping and Caravanning
  Club (UK) 377
Campo Maior **296**
  restaurants 418

Campo Pequeno (Lisbon) **120**
hotels 381
restaurants 406
Canadian Embassy 427
Caniçal **350**
Caniço
hotels 399
Canova, Antonio 325
Canton 49
Cão, Diogo
birthplace 255
expeditions 48–9
Monument to the Discoveries
(Lisbon) 109
Cape St Vincent
see Cabo de São Vicente
Capela de São Pedro de
Balsemão (Lamego) 251
Car hire **444**, 445
Caramulinho 212
Caramulo **212**
hotels 388
restaurants 412
Carapacho 367
Caravanning 377
Carbonária (secret society) 54
Carcavelos
hotels 384
Cardoso, Amadeo
de Sousa 120
Carlo Alberto, King of
Sardinia 243
Carlos I, King of Portugal 39
assassination 55, 87
Buçaco Palace Hotel 210
royal yacht 108
tomb of 72
Vila Viçosa 298
Carlos I, King of Spain 47
Carlos of Évora,
Frey 98, 242
Carmelite Order 242
Buçaco 210
Igreja do Carmo (Lisbon) 92
Carmona, General 56
Carnation Revolution (1974)
14, 37, **57**
Carnaval 33
Carol, King of Romania 162
Carpets
Arraiolos 301
Cárquere 249
Carrasqueira 169
Carris (Lisbon) 449
Cars **444–5**
arriving by car 444
breakdown services 445
hiring **444**, 445
Madeira Wine Rally
(Funchal) 31
motorways and tolls 445

Cars (cont.)
Museu do Automóvel
(Caramulo) 212
parking 444
petrol 444
Portuguese Grand Prix
(Estoril) 32
rules of the road 445
travelling around the
islands 447
see also tours by car
Carvalhal, Count of 347
Carvalhelhos 256
Carvalho, Santos de 86
Carvoeiro
beach 287
hotels 397
Casa do Alentejo (Lisbon)
Street-by-Street map 83
Casa dos Bicos (Lisbon) **73**
Casa de Garcia de Resende
(Évora)
Street-by-Street map 303
Casa das Janelas Verdes (Lisbon)
see Museu Nacional de
Arte Antiga
Casa de João Velho (Viana
do Castelo)
Street-by-Street map 275
Casa dos Lunas (Viana
do Castelo)
Street-by-Street map 274
Casa de Mateus 225, **254–5**
Casa da Misericórdia
(Oporto) 240
Casa-Museu Fernando
de Castro (Oporto) 246
Casa-Museu Guerra
Junqueiro (Oporto) **240**
Street-by-Street map 238
Casa de pasto 402
Casa da Praça (Viana do Castelo)
Street-by-Street map 275
Cascais **162**
decorated ceramics 24
fishing 27
hotels 384
restaurants 408
Cascata da Ribeira Grande 371
Cash dispensers 432
Castelejo
beach 286
Castelo (Lisbon)
hotels 381
Castelo Branco **221**
hotels 388
restaurants 412
Castelo de Silves
festivals 31
Castelo de Vide **295**
hotels 395

Castelo-Melhor, Marquês de 84
Castelo Mendo 195
Border Castles Tour 216
Castelo Rodrigo
Border Castles Tour 216
Castile 44–5, 46
Castilho, Diogo de 205
Castilho, João de 20
Alcobaça 178
Convento de Cristo
(Tomar) 186
Igreja Matriz
(Vila do Conde) 272
Mosteiro dos Jerónimos
(Lisbon) 60, 106, 107
Castles
Abrantes 188
Alandroal 300
Alcoutim 331
Aljezur 318
Alter do Chão 296
Alvito 307
Arraiolos 301
Beja 311
Belmonte 217
Border Castles Tour **216**
Bragança 258–9
Castelo de Almourol **189**
Castelo de Arouce 209
Castelo da Foz (Oporto) 246
Castelo Lindoso 270
Castelo dos Mouros (Sintra) 157
Castelo do Queijo (Oporto) 246
Castelo de São Filipe
(Setúbal) 168
Castelo de São João
Baptista 365
Castelo de São Jorge
(Lisbon) 61, **78–9**
Castelo de São Miguel
(Guimarães) 280
Castelo de Vide 295
Castro Marim 331
Celorico da Beira 215
Chaves 256
Elvas 297
Estremoz 300
Évoramonte 301
Fortaleza de Santa Catarina
(Portimão) 322
Fortaleza de São Tiago
(Funchal) 347
Forte de São Brás
(Ponta Delgada) 362
Forte Ponta da Bandeira
(Lagos) 320
Leiria 181
Loulé 324
Marvão 294
Mértola 313
Mogadouro 261

Castles (cont.)
Monsanto 220–21
Monsaraz 307
Montalegre 256
Montemor-o-Novo 301
Montemor-o-Velho 199
Moura 310
Óbidos 45, 175
Palmela 166
Penamacor 220
Penedono 214
Penela 208
Pombal 181
Porto de Mós 180
Redondo 300
Sabugal 220
Santa Maria da Feira 198
Serpa 44, 310
Sesimbra 166
Silves 322
Sines 312
Sortelha 220
Tavira 330
Terena 14
Torres Novas 189
Torres Vedras 193
Viana do Alentejo 307
Vila Nova de Milfontes 312
Vila Viçosa 299
Castro, Fernando de
Casa-Museu Fernando
de Castro (Oporto) 246
Castro Daire
hotels 388
Castro Guimarães, Conde de 162
Castro Laboreiro 270
Castro Marim **331**
Catarina, Queen (wife of
João III) 107
tomb 107
Catarina de Bragança
see Catherine of Bragança
Cathedrals
Angra do Heroísmo 365
Aveiro 200
Braga 276
Coimbra 203, **204**
Évora 303, **304**
Faro 326–7
Funchal 345, **346**
Guarda 217
Idanha-a-Velha 221
Lamego 251
Leiria 181
Lisbon 61, **74**
Miranda do Douro 260
Oporto 236, 238, **240**
Portalegre 295
Setúbal 168
Silves 323
Viana do Castelo 275

Cathedrals (cont.)
Vila Real 255
Viseu 213
Catherine of Bragança
Convento de São Paulo
(Redondo) 300
marriage 51, 299
Porta da Rainha (Buçaco) 211
Catherine the Great, Empress 116
Catholic Church 16, 429
Cavaco Silva, Aníbal 39, 57
Cavaleiros (bullfighters) 144–5
Caves
Furna do Enxofre
(Graciosa) 367
Grutas do Escoural 306
Grutas das Lapas 189
Parque Natural das Serras
de Aire e Candeeiros 180
Celorico de Basto 281
hotels 393
Celorico da Beira **215**
hotels 389
Celtiberian tribes 40
Celts 40
Minho 263
Terras de Basto 281
Cemeteries
Cemitério dos Judeus
(Faro) 328
English Cemetery (Lisbon) 95
Central Portugal **140–221**
Beiras 194–221
Estremadura and
Ribatejo 170–93
horsemanship and
bullfighting 144–5
Lisbon Coast 148–69
map 142–3
regional food 146–7
Centro Cultural de Belém
(Lisbon) 65, **108**
Centro de Arte Moderna
(Lisbon) 120
Centro Equestre da Lezíria
Grande 192
Centum Cellas (Belmonte) 217
Ceramics
decorated ceramics **24–5**
Museu Histórico da
Vista Alegre
(Aveiro) 201
shops 436
Cervejarias (beer houses) 402
Cetóbriga 169
Ceuta 46, 48
Chagall, Marc 212
Chanterène, Nicolau
Mosteiro dos Jerónimos
(Lisbon) 106
Palácio da Pena (Sintra) 161

Chanterène, Nicolau (cont.)
Santa Cruz (Coimbra) 205
Sé (Évora) 304
tomb of 205
Chapitô (Lisbon) 64
Charles II, King of England
51, 299
Charola, Convento de Cristo
(Tomar) **186–7**
Chaves **256–7**
pillory 20
hotels 390
restaurants 413–14
Cheeses
Central Portugal 146
Monte 230
Rabaçal 146, 208
Serra **215**, 218
Southern Portugal 288
Chermayeff, Peter 121
Chiado (Lisbon) **92–3**
fire (1988) 92
restaurants 406
Street-by-Street map 90
Children
in hotels 377
in restaurants 403
Portuguese attitude to 15
China 46, 49
Choice Hotels Portugal 377
Christ Teaching in the Temple
(Bernardes) 22
Christian Reconquest **42–3**, 44
Christianity 41
Christmas 33, **227**
Christopher Columbus
(Ghirlandaio) 357
Churches 429
clothing in 428
see also Cathedrals, Igreja
*and individual saints' names,
towns and cities*
Churches in Lisbon
Basílica da Estrela **95**
Ermida de São Jerónimo **111**
Igreja do Carmo 91, **92**
Igreja da Graça 75
Igreja da Memória **111**
Madre de Deus 21, 123
Nossa Senhora da Conceição
Velha 20, **87**
Nossa Senhora dos
Remédios 71
Santa Cruz do Castelo 79
Santa Engrácia **73**
Santa Luzia 70
Santa Maria de Belém 101
Santo António à Sé **75**
São Domingos 83
São Miguel 71
São Roque 91, **92**

Churches in Lisbon (cont.)
São Vicente de Fora 50, **72**
Sé 61, **74**
Churchill, Winston 357
Churrasqueira restaurants 402
Cidade, Museu da (Lisbon)
see Museu da Cidade
Ciência, Museu da (Lisbon)
see Museu da Ciência
Cifka, Wenceslau 97
Cima da Conegliano 118
Cinema
Lisbon **64–5**
Cinemateca Portuguesa
(Lisbon) 65
Cinfães **249**
hotels 390
restaurants 414
Cistercians
Alcobaça 178
Convento de Arouca 198
Citânia de Briteiros 41, **281**
Citirama (coach tour
company) 446, 448
City travel 448–9
Clement V, Pope 185
Clement XI, Pope 103
Climate **34–5**, 426
Clothes
costume in the Minho 226
etiquette 428
shops 437
size chart 437
Clubs and bars
Lisbon 65
Côa, Parque Arqueológico
do Vale do 261
Côa, River 216, 220
Coach Museum (Lisbon)
see Museu Nacional dos Coches
Coach travel 446
Coches, Museu Nacional
dos (Lisbon)
see Museu Nacional dos Coches
Cock, Barcelos 273
Coelho, Eduardo 94
Coffee drinking 403
Coimbra **202–7**
bus tours of city 449
decorated ceramics 24
disabled taxis 429
festivals 30, 32
history 42, 43, 44
hotels 389
map 203
railway stations 442, 443
restaurants 412
Sé Nova 204
Sé Velha 204
tourist information office 427
Visitors' Checklist 203

Coimbra University 53, 143,
206–7
Coins 433
Colaço, Jorge
Battle of Ourique 23
Igreja dos Congregados
(Oporto) 241
Pavilhão Carlos Lopes
(Lisbon) 115
São Bento Station (Oporto) 239
Colares **153**
Serra de Sintra Tour 154
wine 28–9
Coliseu dos Recreios (Lisbon) 65
Columbus, Christopher 199
Casa de Colombo
(Porto Santo) 357
on Porto Santo **357**
Santa Maria (Azores) 364
Conceição Velha, church of Nossa
Senhora da (Lisbon) 20, **87**
Condeixa-a-Nova
hotels 389
restaurants 412
Conímbriga **208**
reconstruction of the
city 40–41
Conspiracy of the Nobles 46
Constância 188
hotels 386
Constitutionalists 37
Consulates 427
Contemporary Art, National
Museum of (Lisbon)
see Museu do Chiado
Convents *see also* Monasteries
and Convents
Convento de Arouca 198
Convento da Arrábida
(Serra da Arrábida) 151, **167**
Convento dos Capuchos
Serra de Sintra Tour 155
Convento de Cristo
(Tomar) 143, 184 **186–7**
Convento de Ganfei 266
Convento dos Lóios (Évora)
Street-by-Street map 303
Convento da Madre de Deus
(Lisbon) 122
Convento de Santa Clara
(Funchal) 346
Convento de São Paulo
(Redondo) 300
Conversion chart 429
Cook, Captain 370
Cook, Sir Francis 55
Corelli, Arcangelo 97
Corgo, River 255
Cork 313
Corpus Christi 33
Correia, Dom Paio Peres 330

Corte Real, Gaspar 48
Coruche 171, **192**
Corvo **371**
hotels 400
restaurants 423
Costa, Jorge da, Archbishop
of Lisbon 99
Costa, José da 318
Costa, Manuel de 164
Costa da Caparica **163**
hotels 384
Costa e Silva, José da 93
Costa Nova 195
vernacular architecture 18
Costanza, Infanta of Castile 179
Costume in the Minho 226
Costume Museum (Lisbon)
see Museu Nacional do Traje
Coudelaria de Alter 296
Coutinho, Gago 56
Covadonga, Battle of (722) 42
Covilhã 219
hotels 389
Crafts
markets 436
shops 436–7
Cranach, Lucas the Elder 98
Crato **295**
hotels 395
restaurants 418
Credit cards 432
in restaurants 403
Crime 430–31
Cristo Rei (Lisbon) **114**
Croft (port shippers) 228
Cromlech of Almendres
Megaliths Tour 306
Cromlech of Xerez 307
Cruz de Portugal
(Silves) 323
Culatra 329
Cunhal, Álvaro 174
Curia
hotels 389
Curral das Freiras **354**
Currency 432–3
Currency exchange 432
Curvo, Mendo 261
Customs allowances 426
Cycling 438, **445**
travelling around the
islands 447

D

Da Gama, Paulo 364
Da Gama, Vasco **108**, 193
Angra do Heroísmo 364
birthplace 312
cenotaph 73
expeditions 37, 47, **48–9**
Os Lusíadas (Camões) 188

Da Gama, Vasco (cont.)
  Monument to the Discoveries
    (Lisbon) 109
  São Gabriel (flagship) 327
  statues of 87, 312
  tomb of 106
  Vidigueira 310
Dalí, Salvador 212
Damascus, Caliphate of 42
Dance
  Lisbon **64–5**
  stick dancing 227
Dão
  wine 28–9
  vineyards 197
David, King of Israel 241
Delacroix, Eugène 190
Delgado, General 57, 311
Delors, Jacques 17
Delta Airlines 441
Deslys, Gaby 210
Deu-la-Deu Martins 267
O Desterrado (Soares dos
  Reis) 242
Deville, Antoine 215
Dia 25 de Abril 33
Dia dos Rapazes 227
Dia de Reis 227
Dia da Restauração 33
Dia do Trabalhador 33
Dialling codes 435
Diana (Houdon) **116**, 119
Dias, Bartolomeu 48, 193
Dinis, Júlio 199
Dinis, King 38
  Alcobaça 178
  Campo Maior 296
  Castelo de Vide 295
  Castelo Rodrigo 216
  castles 38, 216
  Coimbra University 206
  Elvas 297
  Estremoz 300–1
  Freixo de Espada à Cinta 261
  history **44–5**
  Leiria 181
  Marvão 294
  Mogadouro 261
  Monsaraz 307
  Óbidos 45, 174
  Order of Christ 185
  Palácio Nacional de Sintra 158
  Pinhal de Leiria 181
  Pinhel 216
  Portalegre 294
  Redondo 300
  Sabugal 220
  Serpa 44, 310
  Tavira 330
  Torre de Menagem
    (Beja) 311

Dinis, King (cont.)
  Trancoso 214
  Viana do Alentejo 307
Diogo de Castilho 205
Direcção-Geral de Turismo 377
Direcção Regional de Turismo
  dos Açores 377
Direcção Regional de Turismo
  da Madeira 377
Disabled travellers **428**
  in hotels 377
  in restaurants 402
  taxis and buses 428–9
Discounts, student 429
Discoveries, Age of the
  see Age of Discovery
Discoveries, Monument to the
  see Monument to the
  Discoveries
Dogs
  Portuguese water dog 329
  sheepdog of Castro
    Laboreiro 370
  sheepdog of the Serra 219
Dolmen of Comenda 40
Dolmen of Zambujeiro
  Megaliths Tour 306
Dolmen-chapel of São Brissos
  Megaliths Tour 306
Dolmen-chapel of Pavia 301
Dolphins 369
Domingues, Afonso 182
Dona Ana, Praia de
  beach 287
Douro, River 13
  Barragem de Valeira 253
  Miranda do Douro 260
  Port Country Tour **252–3**
  Port region 225, **228**
  River View of Oporto 242–3
  Upper Douro 233
Douro and Trás-os-Montes
  13, **232–61**
  climate 35
  festivals 227
  hotels 390–93
  map 234–5
  restaurants 413–16
  vernacular architecture 18
  wines 28–9
Dovecotes of Montesinho 260
Dressage 144
Drinks
  Central Portugal 147
  Northern Portugal 231
  in restaurants 403
  Story of Port 228–9
  see also Wine
Driving in Portugal 444–5
Driving licences 444
The Drunkards (Malhôa) 55

Duarte, Alfredo 67
Duarte, King 38
  Batalha 182, 183
  Leal Conselheiro 46
  portrait 46
Duas Igrejas 260
Dupra, Domenico 298
Durand, Antoine Sébastien 116
Dürer, Albrecht 190
  St Jerome **96**, 98

E

Eanes, Gil
  expeditions 48
  Lagos 320
  Sagres 320
Earthenware 25
Earthquake, Lisbon
  (1755) **62–3**
Easter 30, **226**
Ecce Homo 96
Edla, Countess 161
Edward, King of England 47
Edward VII, King of England 115
Eiffel, Gustave 86
  Dona Maria Pia railway bridge
    (Oporto) 55, 242
Eira do Serrado 354
Electrical adaptors 429
Eleonor of Aragon 99
Elevador do Carmo (Lisbon)
  see Elevador de Santa Justa
Elevador da Glória (Lisbon)
  Street-by-Street map 82
Elevador de Santa Justa
  (Lisbon) 61, **86**
  Street-by-Street map 91
  transport 448
Elvas 285, **296–7**
  festivals 32
  fortifications 297
  hotels 395
  map 297
  restaurants 418
  War of Independence 50–51
Embassies 427
Embroidery
  shops 436
Emergencies **430**, 431
Enatur S.A. (see ICEP) 377
Encontros de Fotografia
  (Coimbra) 32
England, João I's alliance
  with 46–7
English Cemetery (Lisbon) 95
Enoteca de Granjão 250
Enrique, Prince of Castile 198
Enrique II, King of Castile 331
Entertainment
  fado 17, **66–7**
  Lisbon 64–5

Entrecampos (Lisbon)
  hotels 381
  restaurants 406
Epiphany 33
Ericeira **153**
  hotels 384
  restaurants 408
Ermelo 255
Ermida de São Jerónimo
  (Lisbon) **111**
Eschwege, Baron von 57, 160
Escola de Rendas
  (Vila do Conde) 272
Escola Portuguesa de
  Arte Equestre (Lisbon) 144
Espadacinta 261
Espigueiros (granaries) 271
Espinho
  hotels 391
  restaurants 414
Essex, Earl of 326
Estádio da Luz (Lisbon) 65
Estádio José Alvalade
  (Lisbon) 65
Estado Novo (New State) 56
Estalagem (inns) 374
Estefânia (Lisbon)
  hotels 381–2
  restaurants 406
Esteves, Pedro 280
Estoi **325**
  hotels 397
  restaurants 420
Estoi, Viscount of 325
Estoril **162–3**
  festivals 32
  hotels 384–5
  restaurants 408
Estrada de Escarpa 167
Estreito de Câmara de Lobos
  festivals 32
Estrela district (Lisbon)
  see Bairro Alto and Estrela
Estrela, Basílica da (Lisbon) **95**
Estrela, Jardim da (Lisbon) **95**
Estrela, Serra da see Serra
  da Estrela
Estremadura and
  Ribatejo **170–93**
  bullfighting 144
  climate 32
  hotels 386–8
  map 172–3
  restaurants 410–11
  vernacular architecture 18–19
  wines 29
Estremoz 292, **300–1**
  decorated ceramics 25
  festivals 30
  hotels 395
  restaurants 418

Etiquette 428
Eurocheques 432
Eurodollar 445
Eurolines 446
Europe
  map 11
European Union
  Centro Cultural de Belém
    (Lisbon) 108
  Portugal joins 14–15, 17, 56–7
Eusébio 57
EVA (coach company) 446
Évora 41, 284, **302–5**
  hotels 395
  Megaliths Tour 306
  restaurants 418
  Street-by-Street map 302–3
Évoramonte **301**
Expo '98 **57**, 113, 120

F

Fabri, Francesco 82, 84
Fado 17, **66–7**
  O Fado (Malhôa) 67
Faial 334, 360, **370**
  hotels 400–1
  restaurants 423
Faïence 24
Fajã Grande 371
Fajãzinha 371
Falperra 277
Fantasporto (Oporto) 33
Farinha, Monte 281
Faro 285, **326–8**
  airport 440
  car hire 445
  history 44
  hotels 397
  map 327
  railway station 443
  restaurants 420
  tourist information office 427
  under Moorish rule 42–3
Farol 329
Fátima 16, **184**
  hotels 387
  pilgrimages 30, 32
  restaurants 410
  vision of the Virgin
    Mary 56, 184
Federação Portuguesa de
  Actividades Subaquáticas 439
Federação Portuguesa
  de Canoagem 439
Federação Portuguesa
  de Golfe 439
Federação Portuguesa de
  Pesca Desportiva 439
Feira de Artesanato
  do Porto (Oporto) 32
Feira da Ladra (Lisbon) **73**

Feira Nacional da Agricultura
  (Santarém) 31
Feira Nacional do Cavalo
  (Golegã) 32
Feira de Outubro (Vila Franca
  de Xira) 32
Feira de São Mateus (Elvas) 32
Feiras Novas (Ponte de Lima) 32
Feitoria Inglesa (Oporto) 240
Felipe I, King
  see Philip II, King of Spain
Felipe II, King
  see Philip III, King of Spain
Felipe III, King
  see Philip IV, King of Spain
Ferdinand the Great,
  King of Castile 202, 214
Ferdinand of Saxe-Coburg-Gotha
  (Dom Fernando II) 119, **161**
  Castelo dos Mouros (Sintra) 157
  Palácio da Pena (Sintra) 160
  Parque da Pena 57
Fernandes, Inês 217
Fernandes, Mateus 183
Fernandes, Vasco see Grão Vasco
Fernandine Walls (Oporto)
  Street-by-Street map 239
Fernando I, King 38
  death 44, 183
  Évora 305
  Fernandine Walls (Oporto) 239
  marriage 45
  Monsaraz 307
  peace of Alcoutim 331
Fernando II, Dom see Ferdinand
  of Saxe-Coburg-Gotha
Fernão, Infante 99
Ferragudo
  fishing 26
Ferreira, Adam Gonçalves 348
Ferreira, Eve Gonçalves 348
Ferries 444
  Azores 447
Fervença, River 225, 259
Festa da Coca (Monção) 31
Festa do Colete Encarnado
  (Vila Franca de Xira) 31, 192
Festa das Cruzes (Barcelos)
  30, 226
Festa da Nossa Senhora da
  Boa Viagem (Peniche) 31
Festa dos Rapazes (Bragança) 33
Festa da Ria (Aveiro) 31
Festa de São Gonçalinho
  (Aveiro) 33
Festa de São Gonçalo
  (Amarante) 31
Festa do Senhor Santo Cristo dos
  Milagres (Ponta Delgada) 30
Festa de Senhora da
  Consolação 32

Festa dos Tabuleiros
  (Tomar) 31, 184–5
Festas do Espírito Santo (Azores)
  see Holy Spirit festivals
Festas Gualterianas
  (Guimarães) 31
Festival da Cerveja
  (Fabrica do Silves) 31
Festival de Gastronomia
  (Santarém) 32
Festival Intercéltico do Porto
  (Oporto) 30
Festival do Marisco (Olhão) 31
Festival de Música de Sintra
  (Sintra) 31
Festivals 30–33
  festivals of the North 226–7
  Holy Spirit festivals in
  the Azores 366
FIAPE (Estremoz) 30
Fielding, Henry
  tomb of 95
Figueira da Foz 196, 199
  hotels 389
Figueira de Castelo Rodrigo
  Border Castles Tour 216
Figueirinha 167
Films see Cinema
Fire services 430–31
Fisgas de Ermelo 255
Fishing and fishing boats 26–7
  Museu Marítimo e Regional
  de Ílhavo (Aveiro) 201
  Olhão 328
  Sesimbra 166
Fishing holidays 439
Flemish School 193
Flor da Rosa monastery 295
  pousada 395
Flores 371
  hotels 401
  restaurants 423
Flower Festival (Funchal) 30
Flowers of Madeira 336–7
Flowers of the Western
  Algarve 319
Fogo, Lagoa do 363
Fóia 318
Folk music 64–5
Fonte Mourisca (Sintra) 156
Food and drink
  Central Portugal 146–7
  coffee 403
  fish 27
  Madeira wine 349
  Mercado 24 de Julho
  (Lisbon) 93
  Northern Portugal 230–31
  Serra cheese 215, 218
  shops 437
  Southern Portugal 288–9

Food and Drink (cont.)
  Story of Port 228–9
  wines of Portugal 28–9
  see also Restaurants
Forrester, Baron Joseph James
  243, 250, 252–3
Fortaleza de Santa Catarina
  (Portimão) 322
Fortaleza de São Tiago
  (Funchal) 347
Forte da Ínsua
  (Foz do Minho) 266
Forte Ponta da Bandeira
  (Lagos) 320
Forte de São João Baptista
  (Berlenga Grande) 174
Fósforos, Museu dos (Tomar)
  see Museu dos Fósforos
Foz, Marquês de 84
Foz de Odeleite 331
Frágil (Lisbon) 65
França 260
Francis of Assisi, St 74
Francis Xavier, St 92
Franciscan Order 74
Franco, General Francisco 56,
Franco, Francisco (sculptor) 344
  Cristo Rei (Lisbon) 114
Franco, Zé 152
Freixo de Espada à Cinta 261
French Railways Motorail
  Department 445
Frey Carlos 98, 242
Fronteira, Marquês de 125
Fronteira, Palácio
  see Palácio Fronteira
Fruit
  Southern Portugal 289
Funchal 335, 342, 344–7
  airport 440
  festivals 30, 31, 32
  hotels 399–400
  restaurants 421–2
  Street-by-Street map 344–5
Funda, Lagoa 371
Fundação Calouste
  Gulbenkian (Lisbon) 65
  see also Museu Calouste
  Gulbenkian
Fundação de Serralves
  (Oporto) 246
Funicular railways 448
  Bom Jesus do Monte 278
  Elevador da Glória (Lisbon) 82
Furado Grande 174
Furna do Enxofre
  (Graciosa) 367
Furna Maria Encantada 367
Furnas 363
Furnas, Lagoa das 363
Furnas do Enxofre (Terceira) 365

G
Gainsborough, Thomas 119
Galapos 167
Galleries
  see Museums and galleries
Galvão, Duarte 162
Garrett, João Almeida 93, 243
Geology of the Azores 338–9
Geraldo Sem-Pavor 304
  captures cities from
  Almohads 43
  Monsaraz 307
Gerês Mountains 270
Germain, Thomas 99
Germanic tribes
  invade Portugal 40–41
Geysers
  Furnas do Enxofre
  (Terceira) 365
Ghirlandaio, Domenico 118
Ghirlandaio, Ridolfo
  Christopher Columbus 357
Gil, Augusto 217
Gilão, River 330
Gilbert of Hastings 74
Gildemeester, Daniel 155
Gimonde
  restaurants 414
Giusti, Alessandro 152
Goa 48
  Afonso de Albuquerque
  captures 46, 47, 49
  India annexes 57
Góis, Damião de
  tomb of 193
Golegã 190
  festivals 32
  hotels 387
Golf 439
  golf courses in the
  Algarve 438–9
  Golf Holidays International 439
  Open Golf Championship 30
Gomes, António
  Tree of Jesse (Oporto) 241
Gomes, Diogo 48
Gonçalo, São (Amarante) 249
Gonçalo of Lagos, São 320
Gonçalves, André 198
Gonçalves, Nuno 109
  Adoration of St Vincent
  97, 98–9
Good Friday 33
Gothic style
  Manueline architecture 20
Graça district (Lisbon)
  hotels 382
  Igreja da Graça 75
  Miradouro da Graça 75
  restaurants 406

Graciosa **367**
  hotels 401
  restaurants 423
"Grande Lisboa" 60
Grão Vasco 213
  Adoration of the Magi 48, 213
  Annunciation 261
  Criação dos Animais 251
  Museu de Grão Vasco
    (Viseu) 213
  St Peter 213, 251
Gray Line (coach company)
  446, 449
Grenville, Sir Richard 371
Grutas do Escoural
  Megaliths Tour 306
Grutas das Lapas 189
Grutas de Mira de Aire 180
Guadiana, River 307, 331
Guarda **217**
  hotels 389
  restaurants 412
Guardi, Francesco
  *View of the Molo with the
    Ducal Palace* 119
Guimarães 263, **280–81**
  festivals 31
  hotels 393
  restaurants 416–17
Guincho 162
  hotels 385
  restaurants 408–9
Guitarra 66
Gulbenkian, Calouste 57, **119**
  Museu Calouste Gulbenkian
    (Lisbon) **116–19**
  Gulbenkian Foundation 119
  Planetário Calouste
    Gulbenkian (Lisbon) **105**
Guterres, António 39, 57

H

Hadrian, Emperor 296
Hapsburg dynasty 39
Health **430–31**
Hemingway, Ernest 348
Henrique, Cardinal-King
  39, 50, 304
Henrique, Infante Dom
  see Henry the Navigator
Henry of Burgundy 43
  Castelo de São Miguel 280
  Sé (Braga) 276
  tomb of 276
Henry the Navigator (Infante
  Dom Henrique) **49**
  birthplace 242
  Cabo de São Vicente 319
  cenotaph 73
  Convento de Cristo
    (Tomar) 186

Henry the Navigator (cont.)
  expeditions 46
  Lagos 320
  Madeira 350
  Monument to the Discoveries
    (Lisbon) 108–9
  Mosteiro dos Jerónimos
    (Lisbon) 108
  Order of Christ 185
  portrait of 99
  Sagres 320
  statue of 320
  tomb of 183
Herculano, Alexandre
  tomb of 107
Hertz 445
Hickling, Thomas 363
Hieronymites
  (Order of St Jerome) 106
Hilário, Augusto 213
Hill, Damon 32
Hiring cars **444–5**
Hispania 37, 40
História Natural,
  Museu de (Lisbon)
  see Museu de História Natural
History of Portugal **37–57**
Hitching 429
Holanda, Francisco de 185
Holbein, Hans the Elder 240
  *The Virgin and Child
    and Saints* 96
Holidays, public 33
Holy Spirit festivals
  in the Azores 30, **366**
Holy Week 30, **226**
Homem, River 270
Horses
  Alter Real 296
  Centro Equestre da Lezíria
    Grande 192
  Feira Nacional do Cavalo 32
  Golegã 190
  horse riding 439
  horsemanship and
    bullfighting **144–5**
Horta 360, **370**
  airport 440
  festivals 31
Hospitallers 295
Hot Clube (Lisbon) 65
Hotéis Alexandre de
  Almeida 377
Hotéis Tivoli 377
Hotels **374–401**
  Alentejo 395–6
  Algarve 396–9
  Azores 400–401
  Beiras 388–90
  booking 375
  budget accommodation **376**

Hotels (cont.)
  children in 377
  disabled travellers 377
  Douro and Trás-os-Montes
    390–93
  Estremadura and Ribatejo
    386–8
  gradings 375
  hotel chains **374–5**, 377
  Lisbon 380–83
  Lisbon Coast 384–6
  Madeira 399–400
  Minho 393–4
  pensões 375
  pousadas 374, **378–9**
  prices 375
  resort accommodation 376
  types of hotel 374
Houdon, Jean-Antoine
  Diana **116**, 119
House of Avis *see* Avis, House of
How to Use this Guide **6–7**
Huguet, David 182, 183
Huston, John 350

I

Iberians 40
IBIS (hotel chain) 377
ICEP (state tourist office) 441
  Pousadas de Portugal 377
Idanha-a-Velha **221**
Idrisi (Arab geographer) 322
Igreja do Carmo (Faro) 328
Igreja do Carmo (Lisbon) **92**
  Street-by-Street map 91
Igreja do Carmo (Oporto) 242
Igreja dos Clérigos
  (Oporto) 241
Igreja do Colégio (Funchal)
  Street-by-Street map 344
Igreja dos Congregados
  (Oporto) 241
Igreja da Graça (Lisbon) 75
Igreja da Memória (Lisbon) **111**
Igreja do Mosteiro
  (Leça do Bailio) 246
*For other churches see
  individual saints' names,
  towns and cities*
Ilha do Pessegueiro 312
Ilha de Tavira 330
  beach 287
Ilhéus das Cabras 359
Impérios of the Holy Spirit 366
Impressionists 119
India 49, 57
  Vasco da Gama 108
Inês de Castro 45
  children 47
  marriage 259
  murder of 45, **179**, 203

Inês de Castro (cont.)
  Santa Clara-a-Velha
    (Coimbra) 205
  tomb of 178–9
Inquisition 47, **51**
  Coimbra 202
  Évora 304
  Rossio (Lisbon) 85
Insect repellent 430
Instituto Florestal 439
Instituto Português
  Cartografia e Cadastro 445
Instituto Português da
  Juventude 429
Insurance
  legal assistance 431
  travel 431
International Algarve Car Rally 32
Intervisa 447
Iria, Santa 185, 191
Irish Embassy 427
Iron Age 40–41
  Citânia de Briteiros 281
  Murça 257
  Sanfins de Ferreira 248
Irrigation
  levadas of Madeira 354
Isabel, Queen (St Isabel,
  wife of King Dinis) 45, 204
  Estremoz 300
  Holy Spirit festivals 366
  Leiria 181
  marriage 174, 295
  Óbidos 174
  portrait of 99
  Santa Clara-a-Velha
    (Coimbra) 205
  tomb of 205
  Trancoso 214
Isabel, Queen
  (wife of Afonso V) 175
Islam 42, 48
Islands, Portugal's **332–71**
  Azores 358–71
  formation of the Azores 338–9
  landscape and flowers
    of Madeira 336–7
  Madeira 340–57
  map 334–5
  travelling around the
    islands 447

J

James, St 43
Jardim Agrícola Tropical
  (Lisbon) **105**
  Street-by-Street map 103
Jardim Botânico (Funchal) 346
Jardim Botânico (Lisbon) **84**
Jardim Botânico da Ajuda
  (Lisbon) **111**

Jardim da Estrela (Lisbon) **95**
Jardim do Palácio de Cristal
  (Oporto) 243
Jardim das Portas do Sol
  (Santarém) 191
Jardim Público (Évora) 305
Jardim do Ultramar (Lisbon)
  see Jardim Agrícola Tropical
Jardim Zoológico (Lisbon) **124**
Jazz in Lisbon 64–5
  Jazz em Agosto 31
Jean de Rouen
  Santa Cruz (Coimbra) 205
  Sé (Guarda) 217
  Torre de Anto (Coimbra) 203
Jerome, St
  Mosteiro dos Jerónimos
    (Lisbon) 106–7
Jerónimos monastery (Lisbon)
  see Mosteiro dos Jerónimos
Jervis, Admiral 319
Jesuits
  expulsion from Portugal 53
  Santarém 191
  São Roque (Lisbon) 92
  Sé Nova (Coimbra) 204
Jewellery shops 436–7
Jews
  Cemitério dos Judeus
    (Faro) 328
  expulsion from Portugal 46
  Museu Luso-Hebraico de
    Abraham Zacuto
    (Tomar) 185
  Tomar synagogue 185
Joana, Santa 200
Joanes, Domingues 212
João I, King 38, **46–7**
  Aljubarrota, Battle of
    46, **183**, 280
  alliance with England 46–7
  Batalha 182
  becomes king 44, 46
  birth 273
  Chaves 256
  defeats Castilians 46
  Guarda 217
  House of Avis 46–7
  Nossa Senhora da Oliveira
    (Guimarães) 280
  Palácio Nacional de Sintra 158
  Palmela 166
  regency 45
  statues of 83, 85
  tomb of 183
João II, King 38
  Conspiracy of the Nobles 46
  death 319
  Elvas 297
  and the House of Bragança
    299, 304

João II, King (cont.)
  maritime expansion 49
  portrait of 99
  Silves 323
  Viana do Alentejo 307
João III, King 38, 47, 185
  Convento da Madre de Deus
    (Lisbon) 122
  Convento de Cristo
    (Tomar) 186
  Crato 295
  Igreja da Graça (Coimbra) 202
  tomb of 107
  and Vasco da Gama 108
João IV, King 39, 217
  death 51
  Évora 305
  restoration **50–51**
  Santarém 191
  statues of 285, 299
  tomb of 72
  Vila Viçosa 298–9
João V, King 39, **52–3**, 99
  Aqueduto das Águas Livres
    (Lisbon) 53, 124
  Biblioteca Joanina
    (Coimbra University) 206
  Convento da Madre de Deus
    (Lisbon) 122
  extravagance 52
  Palácio de Belém (Lisbon)
    102, 104
  Palácio de Mafra 52–3, 152
  Palácio Pimenta (Lisbon) 121
  portrait 52
  Santa Clara-a-Nova
    (Coimbra) 205
  São Roque (Lisbon) 92
  Sé (Lisbon) 74
  Vila Viçosa 298
João VI, King 39, 165
  horsemanship 144, 145
  Olhão 328
  Palácio Nacional da Ajuda
    (Lisbon) 111
João de Castilho *see*
  Castilho, João de
João de Deus, São
  (St John of God) 301
John of Gaunt 46, 47
John Paul II, Pope 75, 184
José (son of Maria I) 95
José I, King 39
  Alter Real horses 296
  Coimbra University 207
  Igreja da Memória 111
  Palácio de Belém
    (Lisbon) 104
  Pombal's reforms 52
  silver tableware 99
  statue of 53, 86, 87

Josefa de Óbidos **51**, 98, 246
  birth 50
  O Coreiro Pascal 280
  *Mystic Marriage of
  St Catherine* 175
  Nossa Senhora da Assunção
  (Cascais) 162
Juan I, King of Castile 44–5, 183
Junot, General 53, 188
Junqueiro, Guerra
  Casa-Museu Guerra Junqueiro
  (Oporto) 238, **240**

K

Kapital (Lisbon club) 65
Karl I, Austro-Hungarian
  Emperor 162, 348
Kings and Queens 38–9
Knights Hospitallers 212
Knights of the Order of Christ
  see Order of Christ
Knights of Santiago
  Albufeira 323
  Cacela Velha 331
  Palmela 166
  Silves 322
Knights Templar 171, **184–5**
  Convento de Cristo 186–7
  Idanha-a-Velha 221
  Mogadouro 261
  Monsaraz 307
  Penamacor 220
  Pombal 181
  Santiago do Cacém 312
  Tomar 184–7
  see also Order of Christ
Kremlin (Lisbon club) 65

L

La Fontaine, Jean de 72
Lace 436
  Escola de Rendas
  (Vila do Conde) 272
Lagoa
  hotels 397–8
  restaurants 420
Lagos 284, **320–21**
  history 46
  hotels 398
  restaurants 420
Lajes 359
Lajes do Pico 368–9
Lalique, René 116
  Lalique Collection (Museu
  Calouste Gulbenkian) 119
Lamas de Mouro 270
Lamas de Olo 255
Lamego **250–51**
  festivals 32
  hotels 391
  restaurants 414

Landscape and flowers of
  Madeira **336–7**
Language 16–17, 428
Lapa (Lisbon)
  hotels 382
  restaurants 406–7
Largo da Porta de Moura
  (Évora) 305
Largo das Portas do Sol (Lisbon)
  Street-by-Street map 70
Largo do Chafariz de
  Dentro (Lisbon)
  Street-by-Street map 71
Largo do Chiado (Lisbon)
  Street-by-Street map 90
Laurence, St 324
Lavatories, public 431
Leandros, River 219
Leça da Palmeira
  restaurants 414
Legal assistance 431
Leiria **181**
  history 44
  hotels 387
  restaurants 410
Leo X, Pope 87
León and Castile,
  Kingdom of 42
Leonardo da Vinci 190
Leonor, Queen
  (third wife of Manuel I) 47
Leonor, Queen (wife of João II)
  Caldas da Rainha 175
  Convento da Madre de Deus
  (Lisbon) 122
  emblem 175
  Nossa Senhora da Assunção
  (Faro) 327
  statue of 87
Leonor Teles 45
Levada do Risco
  Rabaçal Walks 355
Levada da Rocha Vermelha
  Rabaçal Walks 355
Levadas of Madeira **354**
Lezíria 192
Lima, River 224, 227, 267
  Ponte de Lima 272
Lindoso 270
Lines of Torres Vedras **193**
Linhares 219
Linhas de Elvas,
  Battle of (1658) **50–51**
Lino, Raúl 23, 190
Liqueurs
  Central Portugal 147
  Southern Portugal 289
Lis, River 181
Lisboa *see* Lisbon
Lisboa à Noite
  (Lisbon *fado* house) 67

Lisbon 14, **58–139**
  airport 440
  Alfama 68–79
  Bairro Alto and Estrela 88–99
  Baixa 80–87
  Belém 100–11
  car hire 445
  churches *see* Churches in
  Lisbon
  coach travel 446
  disabled buses 428, 429
  disabled taxis 429
  earthquake 52–3
  entertainment 64–5
  festivals 31
  Further Afield 112–25
  museums
  see Museums and galleries
  history 44
  hotels 380–83
  maps 11, 60–61
  museums
  see Museums and galleries
  railway stations 442, 443
  Reconquest 43
  restaurants 404–7
  Street Finder 126–39
  tourist information office
  82, 84, 427
  travelling in 448–9
Lisbon Coast **148–69**
  climate 34
  hotels 384–6
  map 150–51
  restaurants 408–9
Listings magazines 64
Lobo, Silvestre Faria 165
Lodi, Fortunato 85
Lombo dos Reis 356
Lontra (Lisbon bar) 65
Lopes, Armindo Teixeira 246
  Museu Municipal Armindo
  Teixeira Lopes (Mirandela) 257
  statue of Eça de Queirós
  (Lisbon) 90
Lopes, Carlos 115
Lopes, Gregório 98, 184, 188
Lopes, João the Elder 274
Loreto (Madeira) 356
Loulé **324–5**
  festivals 30
  hotels 398
  restaurants 420
Lourinhã
  hotels 387
Lourosa 212
Lousã **208–9**
Love letters of a
  heartsick nun 311
Ludovice, João Frederico
  see Ludwig, Johann Friedrich

Ludwig, Johann Friedrich
  Palácio de Mafra 152
  Sé (Évora) 304
  Solar do Vinho do Porto
    (Lisbon) 94
Luís I, King 39, 55
  Cascais 162
  Palácio Nacional da Ajuda
    (Lisbon) 111
Luís Felipe, Prince
  assassination 55, 87
  tomb of 72
Luna family 274
Lusíadas, os see Camões
Lusiads, the see Camões
Lusitani tribe 40
Lusitania 40–41
Luso **209**
  hotels 389
  restaurants 412
Luso (Lisbon) 67
Lux (Lisbon club) 65

M

Macau 46, 49, 57
Machado de Castro, Joaquim 98
  Basílica da Estrela (Lisbon) 95
  Museu Nacional Machado
    de Castro (Coimbra) 205
  São Vicente de Fora 72
  Sé (Lisbon) 74
  statue of José I 53, 86, **87**
Machico 350
Machim, Robert 350
Madalena 368
Madeira 14, **340–57**
  climate 34
  crafts 436, 437
  festivals 32, 33
  hotels 399–400
  landscape and flowers
    of Madeira **336–7**
  levadas 354
  Madeira wine **349**
  map 10, 342–3
  Rabaçal walks **355**
  restaurants 421–3
  travel 447
Madeira Wine Rally (Funchal) 31
Madre de Deus, convent of
  (Lisbon) **122–3**
  rebuilding of portal 21
  see also Museu Nacional
    do Azulejo
Mãe d'Água das Amoreiras
  (Lisbon) 124
Mãe Soberana (Loulé) 30
Mafalda, Princess 198
Mafra 152
  hotels 385
  Palácio de Mafra 52–3, **152**

Mafra School of sculpture 52, 95
Magalhães, Fernão de
  (Ferdinand Magellan) 48
  birthplace 253
  Monument to the Discoveries
    (Lisbon) 109
Magalhães, Teresa 120
Magazines 428
  listings magazines 64
Magellan, Ferdinand
  see Magalhães, Fernão de
O Magriço 214
Maia, Manuel da 120
Mail services 435
Maiolica
  azulejo tiles 22, 122
Malhôa, José 121, 190
  The Drunkards 55
  O Fado 67
Malveira 152
Manadas 367
Manet, Edouard 119
Mangualde
  hotels 389
Manini, Luigi 211
Manners 428
Manteigas **219**
  hotels 390
  restaurants 412
Manuel I, King 38
  armillary sphere 48, 220
  banishes Jews 185
  Batalha 183
  Calheta 356
  Casa da Misericórdia
    (Oporto) 240
  Castelo de São Jorge
    (Lisbon) 78
  Convento de Cristo
    (Tomar) 187
  Crato 295
  expeditions 37, 46
  Funchal 346
  Machico 350
  Manueline architecture 20–21
  maritime expansion 48–9
  Monument to the Discoveries
    (Lisbon) 109
  Mosteiro dos Jerónimos
    (Lisbon) 60, 106
  Palácio de Dom Manuel
    (Évora) 305
  Palácio Nacional de Sintra
    158, 159
  portrait 37
  Praça do Comércio
    (Lisbon) 87
  Silves 323
  Sines 312
  statues of 87, 163
  tomb of 107

Manuel I, King (cont.)
  Torre de Belém (Lisbon) 110
  wedding 47
Manuel II, King 39
  Buçaco Palace Hotel 210
  Ericeira 153
  exile 54, 55, 299
  Palácio da Pena (Sintra) 160
  Palácio de Mafra 152
  tomb of 72
  Vila Viçosa 298
Manueline architecture 17,
  20–21, 60
  Mosteiro dos Jerónimos 106–7
Maps
  Age of Discovery 48–9
  Alentejo 292–3
  Algarve 316–17
  Azores 10, 360–61
  Azores: inter-island flights
    and ferries 447
  beaches of the Algarve 286–7
  Beiras 196–7
  Border Castles Tour 216
  Braga 277
  Bragança: the Citadel 258–9
  Buçaco 210–11
  Castelo de São Jorge
    (Lisbon) 78–9
  Central Portugal 142–3
  Coimbra 203
  decorated ceramics 24–5
  Douro and Trás-os-Montes
    234–5
  Elvas 297
  Estremadura and
    Ribatejo 172–3
  Europe 11
  Évora 302–3
  Faro 327
  fishing ports on the
    mainland 26–7
  Funchal 344–5
  golf courses in the
    Algarve 438–9
  Iberian Peninsula in 27 BC 40
  Iberian Peninsula in 1100 42
  Iberian Peninsula in 1200 44
  Iberian Peninsula in 1500 46
  Islands, Portugal's 334–5
  Lisbon 60–61
  Lisbon: Alfama 69, 70–71
  Lisbon: Bairro Alto and
    Estrela 89, 90–91
  Lisbon: Baixa 81, 82–3
  Lisbon: Belém 60, 101, 102–3
  Lisbon: Further Afield 113
  Lisbon: Greater Lisbon 11
  Lisbon: Metro system 449
  Lisbon: Street Finder 126–39
  Lisbon Coast 150–51

Maps (cont.)
  Madeira 10, 342–3
  Megaliths Tour 306
  Minho 264–5
  Northern Portugal 224–5
  Oporto 236–7
  Oporto: Cathedral District
  238–9
  Parque Nacional da
  Peneda-Gerês 270–71
  Port Country Tour 252–3
  Port region 228
  Porto Santo 343
  Pousadas of Portugal 378–9
  Rabaçal Walks 355
  Ria de Aveiro 201
  São Miguel 362–3
  Serra da Arrábida 167
  Serra da Estrela 218–19
  Serra de Sintra Tour 154–5
  Sintra 157
  Southern Portugal 284–5
  tourist regions 427
  Viana do Castelo 274–5
  Vila Nova de Gaia 247
  wine regions of Portugal 28
Marble
  marble in the Alentejo **300**
Mardel, Carlos 124, 205
Maria, Dona (wife of Manuel I)
  tomb of 107
Maria I, Queen 39, 72, 99, **165**
  Basílica da Estrela (Lisbon) 95
  exile in Brazil 52
  Palácio de Queluz 53, 164–5
  royal brig 108
  tomb of 95
Maria II, Queen 39, 161
  Angra do Heroísmo 365
  Teatro Nacional Dona Maria II
  (Rossio) 85
Maria Pia di Savoia 111, 158
Marialva 214
Marialva, Marquês de
  horsemanship 144–5
Mariana's window (Beja) 311
Marina de Vilamoura 439
Marine life in the Azores 369
Marinha, Museu da (Lisbon)
  see Museu da Marinha
Marioneta, Museu da (Lisbon)
  see Museu da Marioneta
Marisqueira restaurants 402
Maritime Museum (Lisbon)
  see Museu da Marinha
Markets **436**
  Barcelos 273
  Feira da Ladra (Lisbon) **73**
  Malveira 152
  Mercado dos Lavradores
  (Funchal) 347

Marta, Francisco 184
Marta, Jacinta 184
Martin, St 243
Martinhal 320
  beach 286
Martins, Deu-la-Deu 267
Martins, Manuel 324
Martins, Dona Teresa
  tomb of 272
Marvan 294
Marvão 285, **294**, 427
  hotels 395
  restaurants 418
Mary, Virgin
  Fátima 56, 184
  Santuário de Nossa Senhora
  da Lapa 214
Masséna, General 193, 215
Master of Sardoal 188, 205, 304
  Two Bishop-Saints **303**, 304
Match Museum *see* Museu
  dos Fósforos (Tomar)
Mateus, Casa de **254–5**
Mateus, 3rd Morgado de 254
Mateus rosé wine 28, 254
Matisse, Henri 311
Mealhada 209
  restaurants 412
Measurements
  conversion chart 429
Meca 193
Medical treatment 430
Megaliths
  Megaliths Tour 306
  Monsaraz 307
Meia Praia 321
  beach 287
Melgaço 267
Melides, Lagoa de 312
Memling, Hans 98
Mendes, Fernão 108, 258
Mendonça, Bishop João de 221
Meneses, Duarte de
  tomb of 191
Menhir of Almendres
  Megaliths Tour 306
Menhir of Bulhôa 307
Menhir of Outeiro 307
Menino Jesus (Arganil) 209
Menus 402–3
Mercado dos Lavradores
  (Funchal) 347
Mértola **313**
  hotels 396
  restaurants 418
Mesão Frio **250**
  hotels 391
Methuen Treaty (1703) 52
Metro (Lisbon) 448–9
MFA (Movimento das Forças
  Armadas) 57

Mid-Atlantic Ridge **338–9**, 368
Miguel, Infante 52
Miguel, King
  abdication 301
  Albufeira 323
  War of the Two Brothers 54
Militar, Museu (Lisbon)
  see Museu Militar
Milreu (Estoi) 325
Minas de São Domingos 313
Minho 13, **262–81**
  climate 34
  costume in the Minho 226
  hotels 393–4
  map 264–5
  restaurants 416–17
  vernacular architecture 18
Minho, River 266, 267
Mira, River 312
Miradouro da Espalamaca
  (Faial) 370
Miradouro da Graça (Lisbon) 75
Miradouro da Madrugada
  (São Miguel) 363
Miradouro de Santa Luzia
  (Lisbon) 72
  Street-by-Street map 70
Miradouro de São Pedro de
  Alcântara (Lisbon) 94
Miradouro do Sossego
  (São Miguel) 363
Miradouro da Vigia (Sintra) 156
Miranda do Douro **260**
  hotels 391
  restaurants 414
Mirandela **257**
Miróbriga 312
Misericórdia (Viana do Castelo)
  Street-by-Street map 274
Moby Dick, making of film 350
Mogadouro **261**
Moluccas 49
Monasteries and Convents
  Batalha 182–3
  Flor da Rosa 295
  Mosteiro dos Jerónimos
  (Lisbon) 102, **106–7**
  Mosteiro de Refojos
  (Cabeceiras de Basto) 281
  Mosteiro de Santa Clara
  (Vila do Conde) 272
  Mosteiro de Santa Maria
  de Alcobaça **178–9**
  Mosteiro de Tibães 277
  Pitões das Júnias 271
  Santa Clara-a-Nova
  (Coimbra) 205
  Santa Clara-a-Velha
  (Coimbra) 205
  Santa Marinha da Costa 281
  São João de Tarouca 251

Monção 265, **267**
  festivals 31
Monchique **318–19**
  hotels 398
Mondego, River 204
Mondim de Basto 281
Monet, Claude 119
Money **432–3**
Moniz, Egas
  heals Afonso Henriques 249
  tomb of 248
Moniz, Filipa 357
Moniz, Martim 79
Monsanto 15, **220–21**
  hotels 390
  restaurants 413
Monsaraz **307**
  restaurants 418
Monserrate **155**
  Serra de Sintra Tour 155
Montalegre **256**, 271
Monte **348**
  toboggan 344, **348**
Monte Brasil 365
Monte da Guia 370
Monte de Santa Luzia 275
Monte Estoril
  hotels 385
  restaurants 409
Monte Gordo
  beach 287
  hotels 398
Monteiro, José Luis
  Avenida Palace Hotel
    (Lisbon) 84
  Rossio station (Lisbon) 55, 82
Montemor-o-Novo **301**
Montemor-o-Velho **199**
  restaurants 413
Montes Claros, Battle of (1665) 51
Montesinho,
  Parque Natural de **260**
  dovecotes 260
Monuments
  Cristo Rei (Lisbon) 114
  Monument to the Discoveries
    (Lisbon) 108–9
  Praça Marquês de Pombal
    (Lisbon) 115
Moors 42–3
Morais, Cristóvão de 98
Morais, Graça 120
Mosquitoes 430
Mosteiro dos Jerónimos (Lisbon)
  60, **106–7**
  Museu da Marinha 108
  Museu Nacional de
    Arqueologia (Lisbon) 105
  Street-by-Street map 102
Mosteiro de Santa Maria de
  Alcobaça **178–9**

Mosteiro da Serra do Pilar
  (Oporto) 246
Mosteiro de Tibães 277
Mota, Rosa 57
Motorways 445
Moura 293, **310**
Moura, João 144
Moura Teles,
  Dom Rodrigo de 278
Mourão 307
Movies see Cinema
Movijovem 377
Mozambique 55
Mozarabs 43
Mumadona, Countess 200
Murça **257**
  hotels 391
  porca 40, 247
  restaurants 414
Al Musara, Battle of (756) 42
Museums and galleries
  (general) **427**
  admission charges 427
  opening hours 427
Museums and galleries
  (individual)
  Antigo Paço Episcopal
    (Braga) 276–7
  Câmara Municipal
    (Arraiolos) 301
  Câmara Municipal
    (Funchal) 345
  Casa da Cultura
    (Ribeira Grande) 362
  Casa Museu dos Patudos
    (Alpiarça) 190
  Casa-Museu Fernando
    de Castro (Oporto) 246
  Casa-Museu Guerra Junqueiro
    (Oporto) 238, **240**
  Casa do Paço
    (Figueira da Foz) 199
  Centro de Arte Moderna
    (Lisbon) **120**
  Escola de Rendas
    (Vila do Conde) 272
  Exposição Fotográfica
    (Horta) 370
  Fundação Abel de Lacerda
    (Caramulo) 212
  Fundação de Serralves
    (Oporto) 246
  Mértola 313
  Mosteiro de Tibães 277
  Museu Abade de Baçal
    (Bragança) 259
  Museu Abade Pedrosa
    (Santo Tirso) 248
  Museu da Água (Lisbon) **120**
  Museu de Alberto Sampaio
    (Guimarães) 280

Museums and galleries (cont.)
  Museu Amadeo de
    Sousa-Cardoso (Amarante) 249
  Museu de Angra do Heroísmo
    (Angra do Heroísmo) 365
  Museu de Arqueologia
    (Montemor-o-Novo) 301
  Museu de Arqueologia
    e Etnografia (Setúbal) 168
  Museu Arqueológico
    (Alcácer do Sal) 169
  Museu Arqueológico
    (Barcelos) 273
  Museu Arqueológico
    (Santarém) 191
  Museu Arqueológico
    (Silves) 323
  Museu Arqueológico
    (Sines) 312
  Museu Arqueológico and
    Biblioteca (Elvas) 297
  Museu de Arte Moderna
    (Sintra) 156
  Museu de Arte Popular
    (Lisbon) **109**
  Museu de Arte Sacra
    (Braga) 276
  Museu de Arte Sacra
    (Castelo Branco) 221
  Museu de Arte Sacra
    (Coimbra University) 206
  Museu de Arte Sacra
    (Funchal) 345, 346
  Museu de Arte Sacra
    (Lisbon) 91, 92
  Museu de Arte Sacra
    (Monsaraz) 307
  Museu de Artes Decorativas
    (Lisbon) 70, **72**
  Museu do Automóvel
    (Caramulo) 212
  Museu de Aveiro (Aveiro) 200
  Museu dos Baleeiros
    (Lajes) 369
  Museu da Baleia (Caniçal) 350
  Museu do Brinquedo
    (Sintra) 156
  Museu Calouste Gulbenkian
    (Lisbon) 61, **116–19**
  Museu do Caramulo 212
  Museu Carlos Machado
    (Ponta Delgada) 362
  Museu do Carro Eléctrico
    (Oporto) 246
  Museu de Cerámica
    (Caldas da Rainha) 175
  Museu do Chiado (Lisbon) **93**
  Museu da Cidade (Lisbon) **121**
  Museu da Ciência (Lisbon) 84
  Museu do Condo de Castro
    Guimarães (Cascais) 162

Museums and galleries (cont.)
Museu das Curiosidades
(Romeu) 257
Museu Dom Lopo de Almeida
(Abrantes) 188
Museu da Ericeira (Ericeira) 153
Museu de Etnografia e História
(Oporto) 240
Museu Etnográfico (Faro) 328
Museu Etnográfico
(Santa Cruz da Graciosa) 367
Museu Etnográfico
(Vila Franca de Xira) 192
Museu de Évora 303, 304
Museu das Flores
(Santa Cruz) 371
Museu dos Fósforos
(Tomar) 185
Museu de Fotografia Carlos
Relvas (Golegã) 190
Museu Francisco Tavares
Proença Júnior (Castelo
Branco) 221
Museu de Grão Vasco
(Viseu) 213
Museu de Guarda
(Guarda) 217
Museu de História Natural
(Lisbon) 84
Museu Histórico da
Vista Alegre 201
Museu da Horta (Horta) 370
Museu José Régio
(Portalegre) 295
Museu de Lamego
(Lamego) 251
Museu Luso-Hebraico de
Abraham Zacuto (Tomar) 185
Museu do Mar (Cascais) 162
Museu da Marinha
(Lisbon) **108**
Museu Nacional da Marioneta
(Lisbon) **93**
Museu Marítimo (Faro) 327
Museu Marítimo e Regional
de Ílhavo (Aveiro) 201
Museu Marquês de Pombal
(Pombal) 181
Museu Martins Sarmento
(Guimarães) 281
Museu Militar (Bragança) 258
Museu Militar (Buçaco) 211
Museu Militar (Lisbon) **73**
Museu Militar (Chaves) 256
Museu Municipal
(Estremoz) 301
Museu Municipal (Faro) 327
Museu Municipal
(Funchal) 344
Museu Municipal (Marvão) 294
Museu Municipal (Óbidos) 175

Museums and galleries (cont.)
Museu Municipal
(Portalegre) 295
Museu Municipal
(Porto de Mós) 180
Museu Municipal
(Santiago do Cacém) 312
Museu Municipal
(Torres Vedras) 193
Museu Municipal
(Viana do Castelo) 275
Museu Municipal Armindo
Teixeira Lopes (Mirandela) 257
Museu Municipal de Carlos
Reis (Torres Novas) 189
Museu Municipal Dr Santos
Rocha (Figueira da Foz) 199
Museu Nacional de
Arqueologia (Lisbon) 102, **105**
Museu Nacional de Arte Antiga
(Lisbon) 60, **96–9**
Museu Nacional do Azulejo
(Lisbon) 61, **122–3**
Museu Nacional dos Coches
(Lisbon) 103, **104–5**
Museu Nacional Machado
de Castro (Coimbra) 196, 205
Museu Nacional do Teatro
(Lisbon) 125
Museu Nacional do Traje
(Lisbon) 125
Museu Oceanográfico
(Serra da Arrábida) 167
Museu de Olaria (Barcelos) 273
Museu de Ovar (Ovar) 199
Museu de Peniche
(Peniche) 174
Museu de Pintura e Escultura
Martins Correia (Golegã) 190
Museu da Região Flaviense
(Chaves) 256
Museu Regional (Lagos) 321
Museu Regional (Sintra) 156
Museu Regional Rainha
Dona Leonor (Beja) 311
Museu Romântico (Oporto) 243
Museu de São Jorge
(Calheta) 367
Museu do Scrimshaw
(Horta) 370
Museu Soares dos Reis
(Oporto) 242–3
Museu da Sociedade de
Geografia (Lisbon) 83, **85**
Museu dos Terceiros
(Ponte de Lima) 272
Museu da Terra de Miranda
(Miranda do Douro) 260
Museu Tropical (Lisbon) 105
Museu do Vinho
(Biscoitos) 365

Museums and galleries (cont.)
Museu Visigótico (Beja) 311
Quinta das Cruzes
(Funchal) 346
Music
fado 17, **66–7**
Lisbon 64–5
Muslims 42, 48

N

Nabão, River 173
Napoleon I, Emperor 328
invasion of Portugal 37
Peninsular War 54
Nasoni, Niccolò
Bom Jesus (Matosinhos) 246
Casa de Mateus 254
Igreja dos Clérigos
(Oporto) 241
Igreja dos Clérigos
(Vila Real) 255
Sé (Oporto) 240
National Folklore Festival
(Algarve) 32
National Tile Museum (Lisbon)
see Museu Nacional do Azulejo
NATO (North Atlantic Treaty
Organization) 56
Natural History Museum (Lisbon)
see Museu de História Natural
Nazaré **180**
festivals 32
hotels 387
restaurants 410
Negreiros, José de Almada
56, 120
Nelson, Admiral 319
Nepomuceno, João Maria 21
New Kingdom 44–5
New State *(Estado Novo)* 56
Newspapers 17, 428
Nightclubs
Lisbon 65
Nisa
cheese 288
decorated ceramics 25
Nobre, Miguel 325
Northern Portugal **222–81**
Douro and Trás-os-Montes
232–61
festivals of the North 226–7
food and drink 230–31
map 224–5
Minho 262–81
story of Port 228–9
Nossa Senhora dos Aflitos
(Elvas) 297
Nossa Senhora da Agonia
(Viana do Castelo) 227, 275
Nossa Senhora da Assunção
(Elvas) 297

Nossa Senhora da Conceição
Velha (Lisbon) 20, **87**
Nossa Senhora da Graça (Évora)
Street-by-Street map 303
Nossa Senhora da Lapa 267
Nossa Senhora da Peneda
263, 270
Nossa Senhora da Piedade
(Loulé) 325
Nossa Senhora dos Remédios
(Lamego) 251
Nossa Senhora dos Remédios
(Lisbon)
Street-by-Street map 71
Noudar 310

O

Óbidos 16, 173, **174–5**
hotels 387
restaurants 410–11
vernacular architecture 18
Óbidos, Lagoa de 175
Óbidos Castle 45, 175
Oceanario de Lisboa
(Lisbon) 121
Odemira 291
Olaias (Lisbon)
restaurants 407
Olhão **328–9**
festivals 31
restaurants 421
Oliveira do Hospital **212**
hotels 390
restaurants 413
Open Golf Championship 30
(Open de Portugal de Golfe)
Opening hours
banks 432
museums 427
restaurants 402
shops 436
tourist information
offices 426–7
Opera **64**, 65
Oporto 14, 224, 234, **236–47**
airport 440
Barredo district 233
car hire 445
festivals 30–33, 226–7
Further Afield 246–7
history 42
hotels 391–2
map 236–7
railway stations 442, 443
restaurants 414–15
river view of Oporto 242–3
Street-by-Street map 238–9
tourist information office 427
travelling in 448, 449
Vila Nova de Gaia 247
Visitors' Checklist 237

Orbitur Intercambio de
Turismo 377
Ordem dos Advogados 431
Order of Brothers
Hospitallers 301
Order of Christ 45, **185**
Convento de Cristo
(Tomar) 186–7
Cross of the Order of Christ
20–21, 49
Tomar 143, 184–7
see also Knights Templar
Order of St Augustine 330
Order of St Jerome
(Hieronymites) 106
Order of Santiago
see Knights of Santiago
Ourém 184
Ourique, Battle of (1139) 43
Outdoor activities 438–9
Outeiro Machado Boulder 257
Ovar **198–9**
festivals 33

P

P & O 445
Pacheco, Lopo Fernandes
tomb of 74
Package deals
air travel 441
Paço d'Arcos
hotels 385
restaurants 409
Paço de Sousa 248
Paço dos Duques
(Guimarães) 280
Padrão (stone cross erected by
Portuguese explorers)
48–9, 108–9
Padrão dos Descobrimentos
(Lisbon) see Monument to
the Discoveries
Pais, Gualdim
Castelo de Almourol 189
Penamacor 220
Tomar 184
tomb of 185
Pais, Sidónio 56
Palaces
Buçaco Palace 21, 210
Paço Ducal (Vila Viçosa)
285, **298–9**
Paço dos Duques
(Guimarães) 280
Palácio de Belém (Lisbon)
103, **104**
Palácio dos Biscainhos
(Braga) 51, 277
Palácio de Brejoeira 28, 267
Palácio de Estoi 325
Palácio Foz (Lisbon) 82

Palaces (cont.)
Palácio Fronteira (Lisbon) **125**
Palácio de Mafra 53, **152**
Palácio dos Marqueses de
Ponte de Lima (Ponte
de Lima) 272
Palácio Nacional da Ajuda
(Lisbon) **111**
Palácio Nacional de Sintra
(Sintra) 142, 156, **158–9**
Palácio da Pena
(Sintra) **160–61**
Palácio Pimenta (Lisbon) 121
Palácio de Queluz 23, 53,
142, **164–5**
Palácio de São Bento
(Lisbon) **95**
Palacete Sá Sotto Mayor
(Viana do Castelo)
Street-by-Street map 274
Palácio da Bolsa (Oporto) 240
Palácio de São Lourenço
(Funchal) Street-by-
Street map 344
Palmela **166**
hotels 385
restaurants 409
Parking 444
Parks and gardens
Buçaco **210–11**
Casa de Mateus 225, **254–5**
Castelo de São Jorge
(Lisbon) 79
Jardim Agrícola Tropical
(Lisbon) 103, **105**
Jardim Botânico (Coimbra) 205
Jardim Botânico (Funchal) 346
Jardim Botânico (Lisbon) **84**
Jardim Botânico da Ajuda
(Lisbon) **111**
Jardim Episcopal
(Castelo Branco) 221
Jardim da Estrela (Lisbon) **95**
Jardim do Monte (Monte) 348
Jardim Municipal
(Angra do Heroísmo) 365
Jardim do Palácio de Cristal
(Oporto) 243
Jardim das Portas do Sol
(Santarém) 191
Jardim Público (Évora) 305
Jardim Zoológico (Lisbon) **124**
Madeira's gardens 336–7
Monserrate 155
Monte Palace Gardens
(Monte) 348
Palácio de Estoi (Estoi) 325
Palácio Fronteira (Lisbon) **125**
Palácio de Queluz 165
Parque Eduardo VII
(Lisbon) 113, **115**

Parks and gardens (cont.)
  Parque da Liberdade
    (Sintra) 156
  Parque do Monteiro-Mor
    (Lisbon) **125**
  Parque do Mouchão
    (Tomar) 185
  Parque das Nações
    (Lisbon) 121
  Parque da Pena 155, **157**
  Parque Terra Nostra
    (São Miguel) 363
  Praça do Príncipe Real
    (Lisbon) **94**
  Quinta do Palheiro Ferreiro 347
Parliament
  Palácio de São Bento
    (Lisbon) **95**
Parque Arqueológico do
  Vale do Côa 261
Parque da Pena **157**
  Serra de Sintra Tour 155
Parque Nacional da Peneda-
  Gerês 263, 264, **270–71**
  espigueiros (granaries) 224, 271
Parque Natural do Alvão
  234, **255**
Parque Natural de
  Montesinho 235, **260**
Parque Natural da Ria
  Formosa **329**
Parque Natural das Serras
  de Aire e Candeeiros 180
Parreirinha de Alfama
  (Lisbon *fado* house) 67
Passports 426
  theft 431
Pastelarias (cake shops) 403
Paúl da Serra **354**
Pauliteiros **227**, 260
Paula, Madre 121
Pavia 301
Pavilhão Chinês (Lisbon bar) 65
Pé Sujo (Lisbon club) 65
Pedra Bolideira 257
Pedras talhas
  (hewn stones) 306
Pedro I, Emperor of Brazil 54
  see also Pedro IV, King
Pedro I, King 38, 44
  Alter do Chão 296
  and Inês de Castro 45, 179, 259
  tomb of **44–5**, 178–9
Pedro II, King 39, 125
  deposes Afonso VI 51
  Serra da Arrábida 167
Pedro III, King 39, 164
Pedro IV, King 39, 72
  abdication 54
  Palácio de Queluz 164
  statue of 85

Pedro IV, King (cont.)
  War of the Two Brothers 54
Pedro V, King 39, 252
Pelourinhos (pillories) 195
Penafiel **248**
Penamacor 220
Peneda Mountains 270
Peneda-Gerês, Parque Nacional
  da *see* Parque Nacional da
  Peneda-Gerês
Penedono 214
Penela **208**
Penhas de Saúde 218
Peniche **174**
  festivals 31
  fishing 26
  hotels 387
  restaurants 411
Peninha
  Serra de Sintra Tour 154
Península de Tróia **169**
Peninsular War (1808–14) 54, 237
  Almeida 215
  Carrancas Palace (Oporto) 242
  Celorico da Beira 215
  Lagos regiment 321
  Lines of Torres Vedras 193
  Museu Militar (Buçaco) 211
Pensões (guesthouses) 375
Pentecost 30
Pereira, Afonso 184
Pereira, Fernão 198
Pereira, Nuno Álvares 184, 256
  Batalha 182–3
  Igreja do Carmo (Lisbon) 92
Perestrelo, Bartolomeu 357
Perfumes
  customs allowances 426
Pérignon, Dom 313
Personal health and security
  430–31
Peso da Régua 227, **250**
  hotels 392
  Port Country Tour 252
  restaurants 415
Pessoa, Fernando 56, 120
  statue of 93
Petrol 444
Pharmacies 430
Philip II (Felipe I of Portugal),
  King of Spain 39, 104
  Castelo de São Filipe
    (Setúbal) 168
  Spanish Armada 50
Philip III (Felipe II of Portugal),
  King of Spain 39
Philip IV (Felipe III of Portugal),
  King of Spain 39, 215
Philippa of Lancaster 47
  tomb of 183
Picasso, Pablo 212

Pico 334, **368–9**
  hotels 401
  restaurants 423
Pico Alto 339, 364
Pico da Velha 367
Pico do Arieiro 341, **351**
  hotels 400
Pico Ruivo 335, **354**, 438
Picota 318
PIDE (secret police) 56
Piero della Francesca
  St Augustine 96, 98
Pilarte, André 330
Pilgrimages
  Bom Jesus (Braga) 30
  Fátima 30, 32, 184
Pillement, Jean 242
Pinhal de Leiria 181
Pinhão 235
  hotels 392
  Port Country Tour 253
Pinheiro, Bishop António 259
Pinheiro, Columbano
  Bordalo 213
Pinheiro, Rafael Bordalo 175
  Zé Povinho 54
Pinhel
  Border Castles Tour 216
Pinto, Fernão Mendes 50, 199
Pires, Afonso 327
Pires, Diogo 199
Pires, Diogo the Younger 204
Pires, João 273
Pires, Marcos 206
Pisões 311
Pitões das Júnias Monastery 271
Pius XI, Pope 74
Planetário Calouste Gulbenkian
  (Lisbon) 105
Plants
  flowers of the Western
    Algarve 319
  landscape and flowers
    of Madeira 336–7
  see also Wildlife
Poço do Inferno 219
Police **430**, 431
Polinarda 189
Pombal **181**
Pombal, Marquês de
  Avenida da Liberdade
    (Lisbon) 84
  Baixa (Lisbon) 81
  bans Jesuits 53, 204, 304
  Coimbra University 53, 206, 207
  Faro 328
  Jardim Botânico (Coimbra) 205
  Jardim Botânico da Ajuda
    (Lisbon) 111
  Lisbon earthquake **62–3**

Pombal, Marquês de (cont.)
Lousã 208
mulberry trees 114
Museu Nacional de Arte
Antiga (Lisbon) 96
Peso da Régua 250
Pombal 181
Praça da Figueira (Lisbon) 85
Praça do Comércio (Lisbon) 87
Praça Marquês de Pombal
(Lisbon) 115
reforms 37, 52
statue of 87
and the Távora family 111
tomb of 111
Pombal (dovecote) 260
Ponsard, Raoul Mesnier du 86
Ponsul, River 221
Ponta da Piedade 321
Ponta de São Lourenço 343, 350
Ponta Delgada 361, **362**
airport 440
festivals 30
Ponta Ruiva 320
Ponte 25 de Abril
(Lisbon) 57, **114**
Ponte da Barca **267**
restaurants 417
Ponte de Dom Luís I
(Oporto) 55, **242–3**
Ponte de Lima 13, **272**
festivals 32
hotels 394
restaurants 417
Ponte de Vila Formosa 296
Poor Clares 205, 327
Porcelain
Museu Histórico da Vista
Alegre (Aveiro) 201
Porches Pottery 24
Port **228–9**
Baron Forrester 252
lodges 247
Peso da Régua 250
Port Country 225
Port Country Tour 252–3
Solar do Vinho do Porto
(Lisbon) 94
Vila Nova de Gaia 247
Portalegre **294–5**
restaurants 419
Portas Largas (Lisbon) 65
Portela 351
Portimão **322**
fishing 26
hotels 398
restaurants 421
Portinho da Arrábida 167
restaurants 409
Porto *see* Oporto
Porto Covo 312

Porto de Mós **180**
Porto do Abrigo (Sesimbra) 166
Porto Moniz **356**
hotels 400
restaurants 423
Porto Santo 341, **357**
Christopher Columbus
on Porto Santo 357
hotels 400
map 343
Portrait of an Old Man
(Rembrandt) **117**, 118–19
Portugal dos Pequenitos
(Coimbra) 205
Portugália (airline) 441
Post offices 435
Postal services 435
Poste restante 435
Posto de Turismo 426
Pottery *see* Ceramics
Pousadas 374, **378–9**, 402
Pousão, Henrique 242
Póvoa de Varzim 272
hotels 394
restaurants 417
Praça Afonso de Albuquerque
(Lisbon) 102
Street-by-Street map 103
Praça de Almeida Garrett
(Oporto)
Street-by-Street map 239
Praça do Comércio
(Lisbon) 81, **87**
Praça da Figueira (Lisbon) **85**
Street-by-Street map 83
Praça do Giraldo (Évora) 304
Street-by-Street map 302
Praça do Império (Lisbon)
Street-by-Street map 102
Praça Marquês de Pombal
(Lisbon) **115**
Praça do Município (Funchal)
Street-by-Street map 345
Praça do Príncipe Real
(Lisbon) **94**
Praça da República
(Viana do Castelo)
Street-by-Street map 274
Praça dos Restauradores
(Lisbon) **84**
Street-by-Street map 82
Praia da Adraga 153, 439
Praia de Arrifana 318
Praia dos Barcos 323
Praia do Cabedelo 275
Praia do Camilo 321
Praia do Castelejo 319
Praia de Dona Ana 321
Praia Grande 153
Praia das Maçãs 153
Praia de Mira 199

Praia de Monte Clérigo 318
Praia de Odeceixe 318
Praia da Oura 323
Praia da Rocha 315, 322
beach 287
Praia de São Rafael 323
Praia da Vitória 365
Prainha 350
Prehistoric Portugal **40–41**
Alentejo 291
Megaliths tour 306
Parque Arqueológico do
Vale do Côa 261
PRIVETUR 377
Public conveniences 431
Public holidays 33
Puppets
Museu da Marioneta
(Lisbon) 75

Q

Quarteira
hotels 398
restaurants 421
Queda do Vigário 323
Queima das Fitas
(Coimbra) 30, **207**
Queirós, Eça de 17, **55**
Coimbra University 206
statue of 90
Queluz, Palácio de 23, 53, **164–5**
hotels 385
restaurants 409
Quinta da Alorna 190
Quinta dos Amigos 439
Quinta da Aveleda 248
Quinta da Bacalhoa
(Serra da Arrábida) 22, 167
Quinta das Cruzes
(Funchal) 346
Quinta do Lago
restaurants 421
Quinta de Marim 329
Quinta da Pacheca 250
Quinta do Palheiro Ferreiro **347**

R

Rabaçal (Beiras) 208
cheese 146
Rabaçal (Madeira)
Rabaçal Walks **355**
Radio 428
Radio taxis 449
Railways **442–3**
Rainfall 34–5
Raphael 98
Rates 272
Rato (Lisbon)
hotels 382
restaurants 407
Realists 119

Rebelo, Domingos 362
Reconquest, Christian **42–3**, 44
Rede Expressos 446
Redondo **300**
  decorated ceramics 25
  hotels 396
  restaurants 419
Regeneration 54
Régio, José
  Museu José Régio
  (Portalegre) 295
Rego, Paula 120
Régua see Peso da Régua
Reguengos de Monsaraz 307
  decorated ceramics 25
Reis, Carlos 189
Religion 429
  festivals of the North 226–7
  Holy Spirit festivals 366
  see also Cathedrals and
  Churches in Lisbon
Relvas, Carlos
  Museu de Fotografia Carlos
  Relvas (Golegã) 190
Relvas, José 190
Rembrandt
  Portrait of an Old Man
  117, 118–19
Renex 446
Renoir, Pierre Auguste 119
Republic 54–5, 56
Republic Day 33
Resende, Garcia de
  Casa de Garcia de Resende
  (Évora) 303
Reserva Natural do Estuário
  do Sado 168–9
Reserva Natural do Estuário
  do Tejo 163
Reserva Natural do
  Paúl de Boquilobo 189
Reserva Natural do Sapal 331
Reserva Natural da Serra
  da Malcata 220
Resort accommodation 376
Restaurants **402–23**
  Alentejo 417–19
  Algarve 419–21
  Azores 423
  Beiras 411–13
  cafés and cake shops 403
  children in 403
  coffee drinking 403
  Douro and Trás-os-Montes
  413–16
  Estremadura and Ribatejo
  410–11
  Lisbon 404–7
  Lisbon Coast 408–9
  Madeira 421–3
  menus 402–3

Restaurants (cont.)
  Minho 416–17
  paying the bill 403
  reservations 402
  smoking 403
  types of restaurant **402**
  vegetarians 403
  wine and drinks 403
  see also Food and drink
Restoration (1640) **50–51**
Reverse charge telephone
  calls 435
Revolution (1820) 54
Revolution (1910) 54–55
Revolution, Carnation
  (1974) 14, 37, **56–7**
Ria de Aveiro 201
Ria Formosa, Parque
  Natural da **329**
  water birds of the Ria
  Formosa 329
Ribatejo see Estremadura
  and Ribatejo
Ribeira Brava **357**
  hotels 400
  restaurants 422
Ribeira da Janela
  Rabaçal Walks 355
Ribeira Grande 362
Ribeiro, António 92
Ribeiro Frio **351**
Ricardo do Espírito Santo Silva
  Foundation (Lisbon) see
  Museu de Artes Decorativas
Rio de Onor 260
Rio Mau 272
Risco Waterfall
  Rabaçal Walks 355
River view of Oporto 242–3
Road, travelling by **444–5**
Robillion, Jean-Baptiste
  142, 164–5
Roch, St (São Roque) 92
Rocha dos Bordões 371
Rock music 64–5
Rock paintings 294, 306
Rococo period 23
  Palácio de Queluz 164–5
Rodin, Auguste 93
Rodonorte 446
Rodoviária Estremadura 446
Rodrigues, Amália **67**, 125
Rodrigues, Simão 181
Roger Taylor Tennis
  Holidays 439
Roman Catholic Church 16, 429
Roman Empire 37, **40–41**
  Alentejo 305
  Alter do Chão 296
  Centum Cellas (Belmonte) 217
  Cerro da Vila (Vilamoura) 324

Roman Empire (cont.)
  Chaves 257
  Coimbra 202
  Conimbriga 40–41, **208**
  Milreu (Estoi) 325
  Minho 263
  Miróbriga 312
  Pisões 311
  São Cucufate 310
  Vila Cardílio 189
Roman temple (Évora)
  Street-by-Street map 302
Romarias (religious festivals)
  16, **227**
  Nossa Senhora da Agonia
  (Viana do Castelo) 31, 227, 275
  Nossa Senhora da Nazaré
  (Nazaré) 32
  Nossa Senhora dos Remédios
  (Lamego) 32, 251
Romeu 257
  restaurants 415
Romney, George 119
Rosa, Euclides Silveira da 370
Rossio (Lisbon) **85**
  Street-by-Street map 83
Rossio station (Lisbon) 55
  Street-by-Street map 82
Rotunda (Lisbon)
  hotels 382–3
  restaurants 407
  see also Praça Marquês
  de Pombal
Roupinho, Dom Fuas 180
Rua do Aljube (Funchal)
  Street-by-Street map 345
Rua Augusta (Lisbon) 86
Rua do Carmo (Lisbon)
  Street-by-Street map 91
Rua das Flores (Oporto)
  Street-by-Street map 238
Rua Garrett (Lisbon)
  Street-by-Street map 90
Rua do Norte (Lisbon)
  Street-by-Street map 90
Rua das Portas de Santo
  Antão (Lisbon)
  Street-by-Street map 83
Rua de São Pedro (Lisbon)
  Street-by-Street map 71
Rua Vieira Portuense (Lisbon)
  Street-by-Street map 103
Rubens, Peter Paul 119
Rulers of Portugal **38–9**
Rules of the road 445
Rural accommodation **376**, 377

S
Sabor 235
Sabrosa
  hotels 392

Sabrosa (cont.)
Port Country Tour 253
Sabugal **220**
Sabugueiro
hotels 390
Sado, River 169
birds of the Tagus and
Sado estuaries 169
Safety **430–31**
women travellers 429
Sagres 316, **320**
hotels 398–9
restaurants 421
Sailing 438
St Catherine (van der Weyden)
116, 118
St George's Church (Lisbon) 429
St James's Church (Oporto) 429
St Jerome (Dürer) **96**, 98
St Peter (Grão Vasco) 213
Saint-Léger, Comte de 311
St Vincent's Anglican Church
(Algarve) 429
Salazar, António 14, 37, 39
Beja 311
Belém (Lisbon) 102
car 212
Castelo de São Jorge
(Lisbon) 78
Cristo Rei (Lisbon) 114
New State 56
Paço dos Duques
(Guimarães) 280
Ponte 25 de Abril
(Lisbon) 114
retires 57
Saldanha (Lisbon)
hotels 383
restaurants 407
Salt
Alcochete 163
Aveiro 200–1
Salúquia 310
Salvi, Nicola 92
Sancha, Dona 258
Sanches, Rui 120
Sancho I, King 38, 44
Bragança 258
Coimbra 204
gold cross 45, 99
Guarda 217
Marialva 214
Montemor-o-Novo 301
Palmela 166
tomb of 205
Valença do Minho 266
Sancho II, King 38
Crato 295
deposed 44
Elvas 297
Estremoz 300

Sancho II, King (cont.)
Sesimbra 166
Sanfins de Ferreira 248
Santa Clara (Oporto)
Street-by-Street map 239
Santa Clara-a-Nova,
convent of (Coimbra) 205
Santa Clara-a-Velha,
convent of (Coimbra) 205
Santa Clara-a-Velha (Alentejo)
hotels 396
Santa Cruz (Flores) 371
Santa Cruz (quarter of
Lisbon) 78–9
Santa Cruz da Graciosa
(capital of island of
Graciosa in the Azores) 367
Santa Cruz do Castelo, church of
(Lisbon) 79
Santa Engrácia, church of
(Lisbon) **73**
Santa Luzia, church of (Lisbon)
Street-by-Street map 70
Santa Maria, island of
(Azores) 359, **364**
hotels 401
restaurants 423
Santa Maria, church of
(Lagos) 320
Santa Maria de Belém, church of
(Lisbon) 101
see also Mosteiro dos Jerónimos
Santa Maria da Feira **198**
Santa Marinha da Costa 281
pousada 379
Santana 341, **351**
restaurants 422
triangular houses 351
Santarém **191**
festivals 31, 32
hotels 387
restaurants 411
Santiago do Cacém **312**
hotels 396
restaurants 419
Santo André, Lagoa de 312
Santo António
see Antony of Padua, St
Santo António (Lisbon festival) 31
Santo António, church of
(Lagos) 321
Santo António à Sé, church of
(Lisbon) **75**
Santo Espírito (village on Santa
Maria, Azores) 364
Santo Espírito, Festas do
see Holy Spirit festivals
Santo Tirso **248**
hotels 392
Santos, Argentina 66–7
Santos, Lucia 184

Santuário de Nossa Senhora
da Lapa 214
Santuário de Nossa Senhora
da Piedade 209
São Bartolomeu do Mar 227
São Bento Station (Oporto)
Street-by-Street map 239
São Brás de Alportel
hotels 399
São Cucufate
(Roman site) 310
São Domingos, church of
(Lisbon)
Street-by-Street map 83
São Francisco, church
of (Évora) 304
São Francisco, church
of (Guimarães) 281
São Francisco, church
of (Oporto) 241
Tree of Jesse 241
São Frutuoso de Montélios
(Braga) 41, 277
São Gião, church of (near São
Martinho do Porto) 180
São João (festival in Oporto)
31, **226–7**
São João de Longos Vales 267
São João da Pesqueira
Port Country Tour 253
São João de Tarouca 251
São Jorge, Castelo de
see Castelo de São Jorge
São Jorge, island of
(Azores) **367**
hotels 401
restaurants 423
São Mamede, Battle of (1128) 43
São Martinho de Cedofeita,
church of (Oporto) 243
São Martinho do Porto 172, 180
hotels 387
restaurants 411
São Miguel, island of (Azores)
335, **362–3**
festivals 30
hotels 401
map 362–3
restaurants 423
São Miguel, church of (Lisbon)
Street-by-Street map 71
São Miguel (near Ponte
da Barca) 267
São Pedro see Peter, St
São Pedro, church of
(Faro) 328
São Pedro (festival in Lisbon) 31
São Pedro de Muel 181
hotels 387
São Pedro do Corval
decorated ceramics 25

São Rafael
 beach 287
São Roque, church of (Lisbon) **92**
 Street-by-Street map 91
São Vicente *see* Vincent, St
São Vicente (town in
 Madeira) **356**
São Vicente, Cabo de
 see Cabo de São Vicente
São Vicente de Fora, church
 and monastery of (Lisbon) **72**
Sardoal 188
Sarmento, Martins 281
SATA 441
Saudade 15–16, 17, **66**
Saxe-Coburg-Gotha, Duke of
 see Ferdinand of Saxe-
 Coburg-Gotha
Scarlatti, Domenico 97
Science Museum (Lisbon)
 see Museu da Ciência
Scoville, Mrs 167
Sé *see also under* Cathedrals
Sé (Lisbon) 61, **74**
Sebastião, King 39, **46–7**,
 98, 214
 expedition to Morocco 46–7
 tomb of 107
Secretariado Nacional de
 Reabilitação 377
Security **430–31**
Seia 218
Seixal 356
Seixas, José Figueiredo 242
Semana do Mar (Horta) 31
Sendim
 restaurants 415
Senhor Vinho
 (Lisbon *fado* house) 67
Senhora da Rocha
 beach 287
Sepúlveda, General 259
Sequeira, Domingos
 António de 98, 125
Sernancelhe **214**
Serpa 293, **310**
 history 44
 hotels 396
 restaurants 419
Serpa Pinto, Captain 55
Serra cheese **215**, 218
Serra de Açor 197, 212
Serra de Água
 hotels 400
Serra da Arrábida 166, **167**
 map 167
Serra do Barroso **256**
Serra do Cume 365
Serra da Estrela 143, **218–19**
 map 218–19
 Serra cheese 146, **215**

Serra da Estrela (cont.)
 sheepdog 219
Serra do Marão 250
Serra de Monchique 318
Serra de Montemuro 33, 249
Serra de Santa Bárbara 365
Serra de São Mamede **294**
Serra de Sintra Tour **154–5**
Serres, JT
 The Torre de Belém
 in 1811 110
Sesimbra 149, 151, **166**
 fishing 26
 hotels 385
 restaurants 409
Sete Frontes (São Jorge,
 Azores) 367
Seteais
 Serra de Sintra Tour 155
 hotels 375
Setúbal **168**
 hotels 385
 restaurants 409
Severa, Maria 66
A Severa (Lisbon *fado* house) 67
Seyrig, Teófilo 55
Sheepdog of the Serra 219
Shoe shops 437
Shopping **436–7**
 ceramics 24–5, 436
 clothing and shoes 437
 crafts 436–7
 opening hours 436
 regional produce 437
 VAT and taxes 436
 wines and spirits 437
Silva, Felipe da
 Tree of Jesse (Oporto) 241
Silva, Dom Pero da 318
Silva, Ricardo do Espírito
 Santo 70
Silva Meira, Domingos da 325
Silves 43, **322–3**
 restaurants 421
Silves, Diogo de 48
Silvestri, Silvestro 242
Sines **312**
 restaurants 419
Sintra 142, 150, **156–61**
 festivals 31
 hotels 386
 map 57
Sintra (cont.)
 Palácio Nacional de
 Sintra **158–9**
 Palácio da Pena **160–61**
 restaurants 409
 Serra de Sintra tour 155
Sintra, Treaty of (1808) 53
Sisinando 204, 208
Sítio 180

Sixtus II, Pope 324
Size chart 437
Smoking in restaurants 403
Soajo 270
Soares, Luís 24
Soares, Mário 39, 57
Soares da Silva, André
 Câmara Municipal
 (Braga) 276
 Nossa Senhora da Agonia
 (Viana do Castelo) 275
 Nossa Senhora da Lapa
 (Ponte da Barca) 267
 Palácio do Raio (Braga) 276
 Santa Maria Madalena
 (Falperra) 277
Soares dos Reis, António 242
 O Desterrado 242
Sobreiro 152
Socialist Party 57
Sociedade de Geografia, Museu
 da (Lisbon) *see* Museu da
 Sociedade de Geografia
Society for the Protection of
 Sea Mammals 350
Solar do Vinho do Porto
 (Lisbon) **94**
Solar do Vinho do Porto
 (Oporto) 243
Solomon, King of Israel 241
Sortelha 220
 restaurants 413
Soult, Marshal 242, 248
Sousa, Aurélia de 259
Sousa, River 248
Sousa-Cardoso, Amadeo de
 Museu Amadeo de Sousa-
 Cardoso (Amarante) 249
Sousel
 hotels 396
Southern Portugal **282–331**
 Alentejo 290–313
 Algarve 314–31
 beaches of the Algarve
 286–7
 map 284–5
 regional food 288–9
Spain, Portugal's relations
 with Spain
 history 44–51
Spanish Armada 50
Spanish rule **50–51**
Spas *see* Thermal spas
Speed limits 445
Spice trade 49
Spirits
 shops 437
Sports
 Lisbon 65
 sporting holidays and outdoor
 activities 438–9

Spring in Portugal 30
Sri Lanka 49
Staircase of the Five Senses
  (Bom Jesus do Monte) 224
Stick dancing 227
Stone Age *see* Prehistoric
  Portugal
Stoop, Dirk
  Terreiro do Paço 121
Student information 429
Suevi tribe 40, 41, 263
  Conimbriga 208
  Oporto 243
Sugar cane 356
Summer in Portugal 31
Sunshine 34–5
Surfing 438
Synagogues
  Lisbon 429
  Tomar 185

T

Tagus, River 13–14, 192
  Belém (Lisbon) 101
  birds of the Tagus and
    Sado estuaries 169
  ferries across 442
  Ponte 25 de Abril 114
  Santarém 191
  Vila Franca de Xira 192
Támega, River 249, 255, 281
Tangier 46
TAP Air Portugal 441
Tascas (taverns) 402
Tavares (Lisbon restaurant)
  Street-by-Street map 90
Tavira 18, **330**
  hotels 399
  restaurants 421
Tavira, Ilha de 330
  beach 287
Távora family 111, 257
Távora, River 214
Taxation
  Value Added Tax (VAT) 436
Taxis
  in cities 449
  for the disabled 428, 429
  travelling around the
    islands 447
Teatro da Trindade (Lisbon)
  Street-by-Street map 91
Teatro Nacional de São Carlos
  (Lisbon) 65, 93
Teatro Nacional Dona Maria II
  (Lisbon) 65, 85
  Street-by-Street map 83
Teixeira, Tristão Vaz 350
Telecom card phones 434
Telephones **434–5**
Television 428

Telheiro 320
Temperatures 34–5
Templars *see* Knights Templar
The Temptations of St Antony
  (Bosch) 96, **98**
Tennis 439
Tennyson, Alfred, Lord 371
Terceira 334, 359, **364–5**
  hotels 401
  restaurants 423
Terena 14, 300
Teresa, Dona (mother of
  Afonso Henriques) 43, 209
  tomb of 276
Teresa, St 200
Terras de Basto 281
Terreiro do Paço (Lisbon)
  see Praca do Comércio
Terreiro do Paço (Stoop) 121
Terreiro da Sé (Oporto)
  Street-by-Street map 238
Terzi, Filippo 50, 72
Textiles
  shops 436
Theatres
  Lisbon **64**, 65
  Museu Nacional do Teatro
    (Lisbon) 125
  Teatro Nacional de São Carlos
    (Lisbon) 65, **93**
  Teatro Nacional Dona Maria II
    (Lisbon) 65, 83, 85
Theme parks
  Portugal dos Pequenitos
    (Coimbra) 205
Theodomir, King of the
  Suevi 243
Thermal spas **209**
  Caldas de Monchique 319
  Castelo de Vide 295
  Chaves 256, 257
  Luso 209
  Vidago 257
"Thieves' Market" (Lisbon) 73
Tiago, São *see* James, St
Tiles *see* Azulejos
Time zones 429
Tipping
  in restaurants 403
Tobacco
  customs allowances 426
Toboggan, Monte 348
Todi, Luísa 168
Toilets 431
Tomar 143, 173, **184–7**
  Convento de Cristo **186–7**
  festivals 31
  hotels 388
  restaurants 411
Tonel 320
Tordesillas, Treaty of (1494) 46

Torralva, Diogo de 186
Torre 218
Torre de Aspa 319
Torre de Belém (Lisbon)
  60, **110**
  The Torre de Belém in 1811
    (Serres) 110
Torre de Menagem (Beja) 311
Torre de Moncorvo **261**
  hotels 392
  restaurants 415
Torreira 201
Torres Novas **189**
Torres Vedras **193**
  Lines of Torres Vedras **193**
  restaurants 411
Tourist information offices
  426–7
Tourist villages 376
Tours by car
  Border Castles Tour **216**
  Megaliths Tour **306**
  Port Country Tour **252–3**
  Serra de Sintra Tour **154–5**
Toyota Showroom (Funchal)
  Street-by-Street map 344
Toys
  Museu do Brinquedo
    (Sintra) 156
Trains **442–3**
Trajan, Emperor 208, 257
Trams **448**, 449
  Museu do Carro Eléctrico
    (Oporto) 246
Trancoso 214
  restaurants 413
Trás-os-Montes *see* Douro
  and Trás-os-Montes
Travel **440–49**
  air 440–41, 447
  Alentejo 293
  Algarve 317
  Azores 361
  Beiras 197
  buses 447, 448
  cars 444–5
  in cities 448–9
  coach 446
  Douro and Trás-os-Montes 235
  Estremadura and Ribatejo 172
  ferries 444, 447
  funiculars 448
  insurance 431
  Lisbon Coast 151
  Madeira 342
  Minho 265
  railways 442–3
  taxis 447, 449
  trams 448, 449
  travelling around the
    islands 447

Traveller's cheques 432
Tree of Jesse (Oporto) 241
Três Pastorinhos (Lisbon) 65
Trindade, Cervejaria
  Street-by-Street map 91
Trindade, Teatro da
  Street-by-Street map 91
Triangular Houses of Santana 351
Tristão, Nuno 320
Tróia peninsula
  see Península de Tróia
Tua
  Port Country Tour 253
Tua, River 257
TURIHAB 377
Turner, JMW 119
Turriano, João 205
Two Bishop-Saints (Master
  of Sardoal) 303, 304

U

Ucanha 251
Umberto II, King of Italy 162
UNESCO World Heritage sites
  Angra do Heroísmo 364
  Évora 302
  Sintra 156
United Kingdom
  Embassy 427
  tourist information office 427
Universities
  Coimbra 53, 143, **206–7**
  Évora 304
Urzelina 367

V

Vaccinations 430
Vale de Ferro (golf course) 439
Vale do Lobo (golf course) 439
Valeira dam 253
Valença do Minho **266**
  hotels 394
  restaurants 417
Valerian, Emperor 324
Valezim 218
Value Added Tax (VAT) 436
Vandals 41
Vanvitelli, Luigi 92
Vasco, Grão *see* Grão Vasco
Vasconcelos, Martim Mendes
  tomb of 346
Vauban, Sébastien
  le Prestre de 216, 266, 297
Vaz, Gaspar 213
Vegetarian meals 403
Velas 367
Velho, João 274–5
Vernacular architecture **18–19**
Vespasian, Emperor 41
Vetaça, Dona
  tomb of 204

Vez, River 267
Viana, Eduardo 120
Viana do Alentejo **307**
Viana do Castelo 224,
  274–5, 438
  festivals 31, 227
  fishing 27
  hotels 394
  restaurants 417
  Street-by-Street map 274–5
Vicente, Gil 47, 188
  Belém Monstrance 20
  statue of 85
Vicente, Dom Lourenço 276
Vicente, Mateus 75, 164
Victoria, Queen of England 161
Vidago 257
  hotels 393
Vidigueira 17, **310**
Vieira, Afonso Lopes 181
Vieira, Álvaro Siza 92
Vieira, António 50
Vieira do Minho
  hotels 394
Vieira da Silva, Maria Helena 212
*View of the Molo with the Ducal
  Palace* (Guardi) 119
Vila do Bispo **319**
  hotels 399
Vila Cardílio 189
Vila do Conde 264, **272**
  hotels 394
Vila Franca de Xira 13, **192**
  festivals 31, 32
  hotels 388
  restaurants 411
Vila Fresca de Azeitão
  restaurants 409
Vila Nogueira de Azeitão 167
Vila Nova (Corvo) 371
Vila Nova de Cerveira 266
  hotels 394
Vila Nova de Gaia 228, **247**
  map 247
  restaurants 415
Vila Nova de Milfontes **312**
  hotels 396
  restaurants 419
Vila do Porto 364
Vila Praia de Âncora 275
  restaurants 417
Vila Real **255**
  hotels 393
  restaurants 416
Vila Real de Santo António
  hotels 399
Vila do Touro 220
Vila Viçosa 285, **298–9**
  hotels 396
  Paço Ducal 298–9
  restaurants 419

Vilalobos, Maria
  tomb of 74
Vilamoura 15, **324**
  golf course 438
  hotels 399
  restaurants 421
Vilarinho das Furnas 270
Villages, tourist 376
Vímara Peres 42
Vincent, St 44, 72
  Adoration of St Vincent 98–9
  Cabo de São Vicente 319
  relics 74
  Sé (Lisbon) 61, 74
  statue of 70
Vineyards
  Port Country 225
  story of Port 229
  wines of Portugal 28–9
Vinhais 260
Vinhos verdes 28, 29
Vinte e Cinco (25) Fontes
  Rabaçal Walks 355
*The Virgin and Child and
  Saints* (Holbein) 96
Viriatus 40
Visas 426
Viseu **213**
  hotels 390
  restaurants 413
Visigoths 40, 41, 42, 263
Vista Alegre 201
  decorated ceramics 24
Vista do Rei 362
Viúva Lamego tile factory
  (Lisbon) 23
Volcanoes
  Azores **338–9**
  Furna do Enxofre
  (Graciosa) 367
  Vulcão dos Capelinhos 370
Voltaire 63
Vulcão dos Capelinhos 370

W

Walking 438
  levadas **354**
  Rabaçal Walks **355**
  travelling around the
  islands 447
Wamba, King 221
War of Independence
  (War of Restoration)
  50–51, 297
  Estremoz 300
  Moura 310
  Praça dos Restauradores
  (Lisbon) 82
War of the Two Brothers
  (1832) 54, 323
  treaty of Évoramonte 300

Water
  drinking 147, 403, 430
  levadas of Madeira 354
  thermal spas 209
Water sports 438, 439
Waterfalls
  Cascata da Ribeira Grande 371
  Fisgas de Ermelo 255
  Queda do Vigário 323
  Risco Waterfall 355
Watteau, Antoine 119
Wavrin, Jean de 47
Weather **34–5**, 426
Wellesley, Sir Arthur
  see Wellington, Duke of
Wellington, Duke of
  Abrantes 188
  Almeida 215
  Battle of Buçaco 54, 211
  Carrancas Palace (Oporto) 242
  Elvas 297
  Figueira da Foz 199
  Lines of Torres Vedras 193
  Mosteiro da Serra do Pilar
  (Oporto) 246
  Peninsular War 53, 54
  portrait of 193
Weyden, Rogier van der 240
  St Catherine 116, 118
Whales
  Caniçal 350
  Museu do Scrimshau
  (Horta) 370
  whale watching in
  the Azores **368–9**
  whaling 368–9
Wheelchair access
  see Disabled travellers

Wickerwork 437
  Camacha 348
Wildlife
  Berlenga Islands 174
  Cabo de São Vicente 319
  flowers of the Western
  Algarve 319
  landscape and flowers
  of Madeira 336–7
  Mértola 313
  Parque Natural da
  Ria Formosa 329
  Parque Natural das Serras
  de Aire e Candeeiros 180
  Parque Natural de
  Montesinho 260
  Reserva Natural da Serra
  da Malcata 220
  Reserva Natural do Estuário
  do Sado 168–9
  Reserva Natural do Estuário
  do Tejo 163
  Reserva Natural do Sapal 331
  Serra da Arrábida 167
  Serra de Monchique 318
  Serra de São Mamede 294
  whale watching in the
  Azores 368–9
Windmills 19
Windsor, Treaty of (1386) 46
Windsurfing 438
Wine Festival (Funchal) 32
Wines **28–9**
  Adegas de São Francisco
  (Funchal) 347
  Colares 53
  Madeira wine 349
  in restaurants 403

Wines(cont.)
  shops 437
  see also Port
Winery JM da Fonseca
  (Serra da Arrábida) 107
Winter in Portugal 33
Women travellers 429
World War I 56
World War II 56

X

Xabregas (Lisbon)
  restaurants 407

Y

Yacht Marina (Funchal)
  Street-by-Street map 344
Youth hostels 376

Z

Zacuto, Abraham 185
Zambujeira do Mar **313**
Zamora, Treaty of (1143) 43
Zarco, João Gonçalves
  Funchal 346
  Madeira 341, 350
  monument to 344
Zé Povinho (Pinheiro) 54
Zêzere, River 188, 219
Zoos
  Jardim Zoológico (Lisbon) 124
Zurbarán, Francisco 190

Acknowledgments

DORLING KINDERSLEY would like to thank the following people whose contributions and assistance have made the preparation of this book possible.

CONSULTANT
MARTIN SYMINGTON was born and brought up in Portugal. A freelance travel writer, he is the author of *New Essential Portugal* (AA), and contributed to *Eyewitness Great Britain* and *Eyewitness Seville and Andalusia*. He writes extensively on Portugal and is a regular contributor to the *Daily Telegraph, Sunday Telegraph* and other British national newspapers.

CONTRIBUTORS
SUSIE BOULTON studied history of art at Cambridge. She is a freelance travel writer and author of *Eyewitness Venice and the Veneto*.

CHRISTOPHER CATLING is a freelance travel writer and author of *Madeira* (AA) and *Eyewitness Florence & Tuscany*. He also contributed to *Eyewitness Italy* and *Eyewitness Great Britain*.

MARION KAPLAN has written for a wide range of magazines and newspapers. She has lived in Portugal and wrote *The Portuguese* (Viking/Penguin 1992). She also contributed to the *Berlitz Travellers Guide to Portugal*.

SARAH MCALISTER is a freelance editor and writer for *Time Out* guides and has spent much time in Lisbon and the surrounding area.

ALICE PEEBLES is a freelance editor and writer and has worked on several *Eyewitness Travel Guides*.

CAROL RANKIN was born in Portugal. As an art historian, she has lectured extensively on most aspects of Portuguese art and architecture and has acted as consultant for various cultural projects.

JOE STAINES is a freelance writer and co-author of *Exploring Rural Portugal* (Helm).

ROBERT STRAUSS is a travel writer and publisher. He worked for the Luso-British Institute in Oporto and has written several titles for Lonely Planet and Bradt Publications including the Portugal sections for *Western Europe* and *Mediterranean Europe* (Lonely Planet 1993).

NIGEL TISDALL is a freelance journalist who has written many articles on the Azores. He also contributed to *France, Spain* and *California* in the Eyewitness Travel Guide series.

EDITE VIEIRA has written many books on Portuguese food including *The Taste of Portugal* (Grub Street). She is a member of the Guild of Food Writers and broadcasts regularly for the BBC World Service.

ADDITIONAL CONTRIBUTORS
Dr Giray Ablay, Gerry Stanbury, Paul Sterry, Paul Vernon.

ADDITIONAL ILLUSTRATIONS
Richard Bonson, Chris Forsey, Chris Orr, Mel Pickering, Nicola Rodway.

DESIGN AND EDITORIAL ASSISTANCE
Gillian Allan, Douglas Amrine, Gillian Andrews, Vivien Crump, Joy FitzSimmons, Paul Hines, Esther Labi, Michelle de Larrabeiti, Felicity Laughton, Helen Markham, Rebecca Mills, Robert Mitchell, Adam Moore, Helena Nogueira, David Noonan, Alice Peebles, Marianne Petrou, Andrea Powell, Andrew Ribeiro-Hargreave, Alison Stace, Amanda Tomeh, Tomas Tranaeus, Fiona Wild.

INDEX
Hilary Bird.

ADDITIONAL PHOTOGRAPHY
Steve Gorton/DK Studio, John Heseltine, Dave King, Martin Norris, Roger Phillips, Clive Streeter, Matthew Ward.

PHOTOGRAPHIC AND ARTWORK REFERENCE
Steven Evans, Nigel Tisdall.

SPECIAL ASSISTANCE
Emília Tavares, Arquivo Nacional de Fotografia, Lisboa; Luísa Cardia, Biblioteca Nacional e do Livro, Lisboa; Marina Gonçalves and Aida Pereira, Câmara Municipal de Lisboa; Caminhos de Ferro Portugueses; Carris, Lisboa; Enatur, Lisboa; Karen Ollier-Spry, John E. Fells and Sons Ltd; Maria Fátima Moreira, Fundação Bissaya-Barreto, Coimbra; Maria Helena Soares da Costa, Fundação Calouste Gulbenkian, Lisboa; João Campilho, Fundação da Casa de Bragança, Lisboa; Pilar Serras and José Aragão, ICEP, London; Instituto do Vinho de Porto, Porto; Simoneta Afonso, IPM, Lisboa; Mário Abreu, Dulce Ferraz, IPPAR, Lisboa; Pedro Moura Bessa and Eduardo Corte-Real, Livraria Civilização Editora, Porto; Metropolitano de Lisboa; Raquel Florentino and Cristina Leite, Museu da Cidade, Lisboa; João Castel Branco G. Pereira, Museu Nacional do Azulejo, Lisboa; TURIHAB, Ponte de Lima; Ilídio Barbosa, Universidade de Coimbra, Coimbra; Teresa Chicau at the tourist office in Évora, Conceição Estudante at the tourist office in Funchal and the staff at all the other tourist offices and town halls in Portugal.

PHOTOGRAPHY PERMISSIONS

DORLING KINDERSLEY would like to thank the following for their assistance and kind permission to photograph at their establishments: Instituto Português do Património Arquitectónico e Arqueológico (IPPAR), Lisboa; Fundação da Casa de Alorna, Lisboa; Instituto Português dos Museus (IPM), Lisboa; Museu da Marinha, Lisboa; Museu do Mar, Cascais; Igreja de Santa Maria dos Olivais, Tomar and all the other churches, museums, hotels, restaurants, shops, galleries and sights too numerous to thank individually.

PICTURE CREDITS

t = top; tl = top left; tlc = top left centre; tc = top centre; tr = top right; cla = centre left above; ca = centre above; cra = centre right above; cl = centre left; c = centre; cr = centre right; clb = centre left below; cb = centre below; crb = centre right below; bl = bottom left; b = bottom; bc = bottom centre; blc = bottom left centre; brc = bottom right centre; bra = bottom right above; bla = bottom left above; br = bottom right; d = detail.

The work illustrated on page 120 tl, *Reclining Figure, 1982*, is reproduced by kind permission of the Henry Moore Foundation; the work illustrated on page 121b, *Terreiro do Paço* by Dirk Stoop, is reproduced by kind permission of the Museu da Cidade, Lisboa.

The publisher would like to thank the following individuals, companies and picture libraries for permission to reproduce their photographs:

MAURÍCIO ABREU: 33t/cr, 145tr, 338bc/br, 358, 360t, 364b/c, 365b, 366ca, 367c, 368tr/ca/cb, 370t, 371t, 399b; AISA: 38tr, 39tc, 39br, 56br, 106b; PUBLICAÇÕES ALFA: 186b. ALGARVE TOURIST OFFICE: 286tr; ALLSPORT: Mike Powell 57crb; ARQUIVO NACIONAL DE FOTOGRAFIA-INSTITUTO PORTUGUÊS DE MUSEUS, Lisboa: Museu Nacional de Arte Antiga/Pedro Ferreira 98t, 99t; Francisco Matias 49tl; Carlos Monteiro 46cla; Luís Pavão 39tl, 52clb, 53c, 60t, 96bl/br, 97b, 99c; José Pessoa 20bl, 21tr, 45c, 49tr, 50tr, 51t/clb, 96tl/tr, 97t/cr, 98b, 99b; Museu Nacional do Azulejo: *Painel de azulejos Composição Geométrica*, 1970, Raul Lino-Fábrica Cerâmica Constância 23tr; Francisco Matias 22b; José Pessoa 22cra/23cb/bl; Colecções Arquivo Nacional de Fotografia/San Payo 39tr; Igreja de São Vicente de Fora/Carlos Monteiro 39bl; Museu Nacional dos Coches/José Pessoa 39bc, 103bl, 144br, 145b; Henrique Ruas 104b; Museu Nacional de Arqueologia/José Pessoa 40t, 41ca/cb, 105c; Museu Monográfico de Conimbriga 41tl; Museu de Mértola/Paulo

Cintra 42cl; Igreja Matriz Santiago do Cacém/José Rubio 43tl; Museu Nacional Machado de Castro/Carlos Monteiro 44tl; José Pessoa 45tl; Biblioteca da Ajuda/José Pessoa 44cla; Museu de São Roque/Abreu Nunes 47tl; Museu Grão Vasco/José Pessoa 48bl; Universidade de Coimbra, Gabinete de Física/José Pessoa 52tr; Museu de Cerâmica das Caldas da Rainha/José Pessoa 54 cla; Museu do Chiado 55tl; Col. Jorge de Brito/José Pessoa 62/3tc; Col. António Chainho/José Pessoa 66b; Arnaldo Soares 66tr, 67tl; Museu Nacional do Teatro/Arnaldo Soares 66cl; Luísa Oliveira 67tr; Museu de Évora/José Pessoa 303 cra; TONY ARRUZA: 282–3, 38c, 44bl, *Portrait of Fernando Pessoa* by Almada Negreiros © DACS 1997: 56tr; 57br, 62/3c, 145ca.

JORGE BARROS S.P.A.: 226cr; INSTITUTO DA BIBLIOTECA NACIONAL E DO LIVRO, Lisboa: 37b, 46bca/b, 47crb, 50cb, 51br, 53br, 165bl, 183b; 283 (inset); GABRIELE BOISELLE: 144bl; BOUTINOT PRINCE WINE SHIPPERS, Stockport: 228br; THE BRIDGEMAN ART LIBRARY, with kind permission from Michael Chase: *Landscape near Lagos, Algarve, Portugal* by Sir Cedric Morris (1889–1982), Bonhams, London: 8–9; By permission of THE BRITISH LIBRARY, London: *João I of Portugal being entertained by John of Gaunt* (d), from de Wavrin's *Chronicle d'Angleterre* (Roy 14E IV 244v) 46/7c; © Trustees of THE BRITISH MUSEUM, London: 43cla, 48br, 54bl.

CÂMARA MUNICIPAL DE LISBOA: 51crb, António Rafael 62cl; CÂMARA MUNICIPAL DE OEIRAS: 52clb; CENTRO EUROPEU JEAN MONNET: 57tr; CEPHAS: Mick Rock 28crb, 29c; CERAMICARTE: 24bl; CHAPITO: 64tr; COCKBURN SMITHES & CIA, S.A. (an Allied Domecq Company): 228crb.

D & F WINESHIPPERS, London: 29bc; DIÁRIO DE NOTÍCIAS: 55cl; MICHAEL DIGGIN: 334t/b, 359t/b, 360b, 361t, 365t, 369t; DOW'S PORT 229cr.

EMPICS: Steve Etherington 32c; ESPAÇO TALASSA: Gerard Soury 368b; ET ARCHIVE: Naval Museum, Genoa 357b; Wellington Museum 193b; EUROPEAN COMMISSION: 433; GREG EVANS INTERNATIONAL: Greg Balfour Evans 287br; MARY EVANS PICTURE LIBRARY: 51bl, 63tr, 161b, 210b; EXPO '98: 57cra.

FOTOTECA INTERNACIONAL, Lisboa: Luís Elvas 33cl, 144tl/tr/cr; César Soares 27t, 38bl; LUÍZ O FRANQUINHO/ANTÓNIO DA COSTA: 337bla; FUNDAÇÃO DA CASA DE BRAGANÇA: 298t/c/b, 299bl; FUNDAÇÃO CALOUSTE GULBENKIAN: 64b; FUNDAÇÃO DA CASA DE MATEUS: Nicholas Sapieha 254b; FUNDAÇÃO RICARDO DO ESPÍRITO SANTO SILVA, MUSEU-ESCOLA DE ARTES DECORATIVAS PORTUGUESAS 72c.

JORGE GALVÃO: 57clb; GIRAUDON: 48c.
ROBERT HARDING PICTURE LIBRARY: 13b; Robert
Frerck 87br; KIT HOUGHTON: 32b; 145cb.

THE IMAGE BANK: Maurício Abreu 30bl; Moura
Machado 19t, 361b, 371b; João Paulo 31cb,
227cl, 363t; IMAGES COLOUR LIBRARY: 226b.

MARION KAPLAN: 144cl, 227t/cr.

LUSA: António Cotrim 67c; André Kosters 93t;
Manuel Moura 56bc, 357t; Luís Vasconcelos 92b.

JOSÉ MANUEL: 29br, 63br; ANTÓNIO MARQUES: 296c,
297b; ARXIU MAS: 50tl; METROPOLITANO DE LISBOA,
Paulo Sintra: *Four Tiles from Lisbon Underground
Station* (Cidade Universitária), Maria Helena Vieira
da Silva © ADAGP, Paris and DACS, London
1997, 56tl; JOHN MILLER: 21b; MUSEU CERRALBO,
Madrid: 42tl; MUSEU CALOUSTE GULBENKIAN, Lisboa:
*Enamelled Silver Gilt Corsage Ornament, René
Lalique* © ADAGP, Paris and DACS, London 1997,
116ca; 116t/ca/cb/b, 117t/ca/cb/b, 118c/b/t,
119b/t/c; MUSEU DA CIDADE, Lisboa: António
Rafael 62tl/bl/br; 63c/bl; MUSEU DA MARINHA,
Lisboa: 38br, 56cl, 108b.

NATIONAL MARITIME MUSEUM, London: 50ca;
NATIONALMUSEET, Copenhagen: 48tr; NATURE
PHOTOGRAPHERS: Brinsley Burbidge 336br, 337br;
Andrew Cleave 336clb/bl, 337bl; Peter Craig-
Cooper 329crb; Geoff du Feu 329b; Jean Hall
336bcr; Tony Schilling 336bcl; Paul Sterry 319c,
337bra/blc; NATURPRESS: Juan Hidalgo-Candy
Lopesino 32tl, 33br; Jaime Villanueva 24t;
NHPA: Michael Leach 369crb; Jean-Louis
le Moigne 329cra.

ARCHIVO FOTOGRÁFICO ORONOZ: 38bc, 42/3c, 43b,
46lb, 179br. Fotografia cedida y autorizada por el
PATRIMONIO NACIONAL: 42cb; THE PIERPONT MORGAN
LIBRARY/ ART RESOURCE, New York: 37t;
POPPERFOTO: 55b; POUSADAS DE PORTUGAL: 378t/cla.

NORMAN RENOUF: 374b, 379b; RCL, PAREDE:
Rui Cunha 30t, 31cl, 32tr, 65t, 332–3, 336cra,
337cra, 339tr, 365c, 366t/b, 377; REX FEATURES:
Sipa Press, Michel Ginies 57bl; MANUEL RIBEIRO:
22t; RADIO TELEVISÃO PORTUGUESA (RTP): 54t,
55clb, 56cr.

HARRY SMITH HORTICULTURAL PHOTOGRAPHIC
COLLECTION: 337cla; SOLAR DO VINHO DO PORTO:
252b; TONY STONE IMAGES: Tony Arruza 30ca;
Shaun Egan 286b; Graham Finlayson 41crb;
Simeone Huber 284b; John Lawrence 31b; Ulli
Seer 317t; 426b; SYMINGTON PORT AND MADEIRA
SHIPPERS: Claudio Capone 29cl, 229t/cla/bc/br.

TAP AIR PORTUGAL: 441t; NIGEL TISDALL: 339tl , 362,
363b, 364t, 367t/b, 370c/b, 447t; TOPHAM PICTURE
SOURCE: 57ca; ARQUIVOS NACIONAIS/TORRE DO
TOMBO: 36, 44bla, 267b; TURIHAB: Roger Day
376tl; 376b.

NIK WHEELER: 314; PETER WILSON: 30br, 31tr, 56bl,
68, 84tl, 93b, 226tl/r/cl; WOODFALL WILD IMAGES:
Mike Lane 169b; WORLD PICTURES: 287tc/bl.

Cover: All special photography except THE
IMAGE BANK: João Paulo FC cl.

Front Endpaper: All special photography
except MAURÍCIO ABREU tl; NIK WHEELER br;
PETER WILSON blc.

All other images © DORLING KINDERSLEY.
For further information see www.DKimages.com

DORLING KINDERSLEY SPECIAL EDITIONS

Dorling Kindersley books can be purchased
in bulk quantities at discounted prices for
use in promotions or as premiums.
We are also able to offer special editions
and personalized jackets, corporate
imprints, and excerpts from all of our
books, tailored specifically to meet your
own needs.

To find out more, please contact:
(in the United Kingdom)
SPECIAL SALES, DORLING KINDERSLEY LIMITED,
80 STRAND, LONDON WC2R 0RL;

(in the United States)
SPECIAL MARKETS DEPT,
DORLING KINDERSLEY PUBLISHING, INC.,
95 MADISON AVENUE, NEW YORK, NY 10016.

Phrase Book

IN EMERGENCY

Help!	Socorro!	soo-**koh**-roo
Stop!	Páre!	pahr'
Call a doctor!	Chame um médico!	**shahm'** ooñ meh-dee-koo
Call an ambulance!	Chame uma ambulância!	**shahm'** oo-muh añ-boo-lañ-see-uh
Call the police!	Chame a polícia!	**shahm'** uh poo-lee-see-uh
Call the fire brigade!	Chame os bombeiros!	**shahm'** oosh bom-**bay**-roosh
Where is the nearest telephone?	Há um telefone aqui perto?	ah ooñ te-le-**fon'** uh-**kee pehr**-too
Where is the nearest hospital?	Onde é o hospital mais próximo?	ond' eh oo **ohsh**-pee-**tahl'** mysh **pro**-see-moo

COMMUNICATION ESSENTIALS

Yes	Sim	seeñ
No	Não	nowñ
Please	Por favor/ Faz favor	poor fuh-**vor** fash fuh-**vor**
Thank you	Obrigado/da	o-bree-**gah**-doo/duh
Excuse me	Desculpe	dish-**koolp'**
Hello	Olá	oh-**lah**
Goodbye	Adeus	a-**deh**-oosh
Good morning	Bom-dia	boñ **dee**-uh
Good afternoon	Boa-tarde	**boh**-uh tard'
Good night	Boa-noite	**boh**-uh noyt'
Yesterday	Ontem	oñ-**tayñ**
Today	Hoje	ohj'
Tomorrow	Amanhã	ah-mañ-**yañ**
Here	Aqui	uh-**kee**
There	Ali	uh-**lee**
What?	O quê?	oo keh
Which?	Qual?	kwahl'
When?	Quando?	**kwañ**-doo
Why?	Porquê?	poor-**keh**
Where?	Onde?	oñd'

USEFUL PHRASES

How are you?	Como está?	**koh**-moo shtah
Very well, thank you.	Bem, obrigado/da.	bayñ o-bree-**gah**-doo/duh
Pleased to meet you.	Encantado/a.	eñ-kañ-**tah**-doo/duh
See you soon.	Até logo.	uh-**teh** loh-goo
That's fine.	Está bem.	shtah bayñ
Where is/are . . . ?	Onde está/estão . . . ?	ond' shtah/shtowñ
How far is it to . . . ?	A que distância fica . . . ?	uh kee dish-**tañ**-see-uh **fee**-kuh
Which way to . . . ?	Como se vai para . . . ?	**koh**-moo seh vy puh-ruh
Do you speak English?	Fala inglês?	**fah**-luh eeñ-glehsh
I don't understand.	Não compreendo.	nowñ kom-pree-**eñ**-doo
Could you speak more slowly please?	Pode falar mais devagar por favor?	pohd' fuh-lar mysh d-va-**gar** poor fuh-**vor**
I'm sorry.	Desculpe.	dish-**koolp'**

USEFUL WORDS

big	grande	**grañd'**
small	pequeno	pe-**keh**-noo
hot	quente	keñt'
cold	frio	**free**-oo
good	bom	boñ
bad	mau	**mah**-oo
quite a lot/enough	bastante	bash-**tañt'**
well	bem	bayñ
open	aberto	a-**behr**-too
closed	fechado	fe-**shah**-doo
left	esquerda	**shkehr**-duh
right	direita	dee-**ray**-tuh
straight on	em frente	ayñ **freñt'**
near	perto	**pehr**-too
far	longe	**loñj'**
up	suba	**soo**-buh
down	desça	**deh**-shuh
early	cedo	**seh**-doo
late	tarde	tard'
entrance	entrada	eñ-**trah**-duh
exit	saída	sa-**ee**-duh
toilets	casa de banho	**kah**-zuh d' **bañ**-yoo
more	mais	mysh
less	menos	**meh**-noosh

MAKING A TELEPHONE CALL

I'd like to place an international call.	Queria fazer uma chamada internacional.	**kree**-uh fuh-**zehr** oo-muh sha-**mah**-duh in-ter-na-**see**-oo-**nahl'**
a local call.	uma chamada local.	oo-muh sha-**mah**-duh loo-**kahl'**
Can I leave a message?	Posso deixar uma mensagem?	**poh**-soo day-**shar** oo-muh meñ-**sah**--jayñ

SHOPPING

How much does this cost?	Quanto custa isto?	**kwañ**-too **koosh**-tuh **eesh**-too
I would like . . .	Queria . . .	**kree**-uh
I'm just looking.	Estou só a ver obrigado/a.	**shtoh** soh uh vehr o-bree-**gah**-doo/uh
Do you take credit cards?	Aceita cartões de crédito?	kar-**toinsh** de **kreh**-dee-too
What time do you open?	A que horas abre?	uh **kee oh**-rash **ah**-bre
What time do you close?	A que horas fecha?	uh **kee oh**-rash **fay**-shuh
This one	Este	ehst'
That one	Esse	ehss'
expensive	caro	**kah**-roo
cheap	barato	buh-**rah**-too
size (clothes/shoes)	tamanho	taman'-ho
white	branco	**brañ**-koo
black	preto	**preh**-too
red	roxo	**roh**-shoo
yellow	amarelo	uh-muh-**reh**-loo
green	verde	vehrd'
blue	azul	uh-**zool'**

TYPES OF SHOP

antique shop	loja de antiguidades	**loh**-juh de añ-tee-gwee-**dahd'sh**
bakery	padaria	pah-duh-**ree**-uh
bank	banco	**bañ**-koo
bookshop	livraria	lee-vruh-**ree**-uh
butcher	talho	**tah**-lyoo
cake shop	pastelaria	pash-te-luh-**ree**-uh
chemist	farmácia	far-**mah**-see-uh
fishmonger	peixaria	pay-shuh-**ree**-uh
hairdresser	cabeleireiro	kab'-lay-**ray**-roo
market	mercado	mehr-**kah**-doo
newsagent	kiosque	kee-**yohsk'**
post office	correios	koo-ray-oosh
shoe shop	sapataria	suh-puh-tuh-**ree**-uh
supermarket	supermercado	soo-**pehr**-mer-**kah**-doo
tobacconist	tabacaria	tuh-buh-kuh-**ree**-uh
travel agency	agência de viagens	uh-jen-**see**-uh de vee-**ah**-jayñsh

SIGHTSEEING

cathedral	sé	seh
church	igreja	ee-**gray**-juh
garden	jardim	jar-**deeñ**
library	biblioteca	bee-blee-oo-**teh**-kuh
museum	museu	moo-**zeh**-oo
tourist information office	posto de turismo	**posh**-too d' too-**reesh**-moo
closed for holidays	fechado para férias	fe-**sha**-doo puh-ruh **feh**-ree-ash
bus station	estação de autocarros	shta-**sowñ** d' oh-too-**kah**-roosh
railway station	estação de comboios	shta-**sowñ** d' koñ-**boy**-oosh

STAYING IN A HOTEL

Do you have a vacant room?	Tem um quarto livre?	tayñ ooñ **kwar**-too **leevr'**
room with a bath	um quarto com casa de banho	ooñ **kwar**-too koñ **kah**-zuh d' **bañ**-yoo
shower	duche	doosh
single room	quarto individual	**kwar**-too een-dee-vee-doo-**ahl'**
double room	quarto de casal	**kwar**-too d' kuh-**zahl'**
twin room	quarto com duas camas	**kwar**-too koñ **doo**-ash **kah**-mash
porter	porteiro	poor-**tay**-roo
key	chave	**shahv'**
I have a reservation.	Tenho um quarto reservado.	**tayñ**-yoo ooñ **kwar**-too re-ser-**vah**-doo

EATING OUT

Have you got a table for . . . ?	Tem uma mesa para . . . ?	tayñ oo-muh meh-zuh puh-ruh
I want to reserve a table.	Quero reservar uma mesa.	keh-roo re-zehr-var oo-muh meh-zuh
The bill please.	A conta por favor/ faz favor.	uh kohn-tuh poor fuh-vor/ fash fuh-vor
I am a vegetarian.	Sou vegetariano/a.	Soh ve-je-tuh-ree-ah-noo/uh
Waiter!	Por favor!/ Faz favor!	poor fuh-vor fash fuh-vor
the menu	a lista	uh leesh-tuh
fixed-price menu	a ementa turística	uh ee-mehñ-tuh too-reesh-tee-kuh
wine list	a lista de vinhos	uh leesh-tuh de veeñ-yoosh
glass	um copo	ooñ koh-poo
bottle	uma garrafa	oo-muh guh-rah-fuh
half bottle	meia-garrafa	may-uh guh-rah-fuh
knife	uma faca	oo-muh fah-kuh
fork	um garfo	ooñ gar-foo
spoon	uma colher	oo-muh kool-yair
plate	um prato	ooñ prah-too
napkin	um guardanapo	ooñ goo-ar-duh-nah-poo
breakfast	pequeno-almoço	pe-keh-noo-ahl-moh-soo
lunch	almoço	ahl-moh-soo
dinner	jantar	jan-tar
cover	couvert	koo-vehr
starter	entrada	eñ-trah-duh
main course	prato principal	prah-too prin-see-pahl'
dish of the day	prato do dia	prah-too doo dee-uh
set dish	combinado	koñ-bee-nah-doo
half portion	meia-dose	may-uh doh-se
dessert	sobremesa	soh-bre-meh-zuh
rare	mal passado	mahl' puh-sah-doo
medium	médio	meh-dee-oo
well done	bem passado	bayñ puh-sah-doo

MENU DECODER

abacate	uh-buh-kaht'	avocado
açorda	uh-sor-duh	bread-based stew (often seafood)
açúcar	uh-soo-kar	sugar
água mineral	ah-gwuh mee-ne-rahl'	mineral water
(com gás)	koñ gas	sparkling
(sem gás)	sayñ gas	still
alho	ay-oo	garlic
alperce	ahl'-pehrce	apricot
amêijoas	uh-may-joo-ash	clams
ananás	uh-nuh-nahsh	pineapple
arroz	uh-rohsh	rice
assado	uh-sah-doo	baked
atum	uh-tooñ	tuna
aves	ah-vesh	poultry
azeite	uh-zayt'	olive oil
azeitonas	uh-zay-toh-nash	olives
bacalhau	buh-kuh-lyow	dried, salted cod
banana	buh-nah-nuh	banana
batatas	buh-tah-tash	potatoes
batatas fritas	buh-tah-tash free-tash	french fries
batido	buh-tee-doo	milk-shake
bica	bee-kuh	espresso
bife	beef	steak
bolacha	boo-lah-shuh	biscuit
bolo	boh-loo	cake
borrego	boo-reh-goo	lamb
caça	kah-ssuh	game
café	kuh-feh	coffee
camarões	kuh-muh-roysh	large prawns
caracóis	kuh-ruh-koysh	snails
caranguejo	kuh-rañ-gay-joo	crab
carne	karn'	meat
cataplana	kuh-tuh-plah-nuh	sealed wok used to steam dishes
cebola	se-boh-luh	onion
cerveja	sehr-vay-juh	beer
chá	shah	tea
cherne	shern'	stone bass
chocolate	shoh-koh-laht'	chocolate
chocos	shoh-koosh	cuttlefish
chouriço	shoh-ree-soo	red, spicy sausage
churrasco	shoo-rash-coo	on the spit
cogumelos	koo-goo-meh-loosh	mushrooms
cozido	koo-zee-doo	boiled
enguias	eñ-gee-ash	eels
fiambre	fee-añbr'	ham
fígado	fee-guh-doo	liver
frango	frañ-goo	chicken
frito	free-too	fried
fruta	froo-tuh	fruit
gambas	gam-bash	prawns
gelado	je-lah-doo	ice cream
gelo	jeh-loo	ice
goraz	goo-rash	bream
grelhado	grel-yah-doo	grilled
iscas	eesh-kash	marinated liver
lagosta	luh-gohsh-tuh	lobster
laranja	luh-rañ-juh	orange
leite	layt'	milk
limão	lee-mowñ	lemon
limonada	lee-moo-nah-duh	lemonade
linguado	leeñ-gwah-doo	sole
lulas	loo-lash	squid
maçã	muh-sañ	apple
manteiga	mañ-tay-guh	butter
mariscos	muh-reesh-koosh	seafood
meia-de-leite	may-uh-d' layt'	white coffee
ostras	osh-trash	oysters
ovos	oh-voosh	eggs
pão	powñ	bread
pastel	pash-tehl'	cake
pato	pah-too	duck
peixe	paysh'	fish
peixe-espada	paysh'-shpah-duh	scabbard fish
pimenta	pee-meñ-tuh	pepper
polvo	pohl'-voo	octopus
porco	por-coo	pork
queijo	kay-joo	cheese
sal	sahl'	salt
salada	suh-lah-duh	salad
salsichas	sahl-see-shash	sausages
sandes	sañ-desh	sandwich
santola	sañ-toh-luh	spider crab
sopa	soh-puh	soup
sumo	soo-moo	juice
tamboril	tañ-boo-ril'	monkfish
tarte	tart'	pie/cake
tomate	too-maht'	tomato
torrada	too-rah-duh	toast
tosta	tohsh-tuh	toasted sandwich
vinagre	vee-nah-gre	vinegar
vinho branco	veeñ-yoo brañ-koo	white wine
vinho tinto	veeñ-yoo teeñ-too	red wine
vitela	vee-teh-luh	veal

NUMBERS

0	zero	zeh-roo
1	um	ooñ
2	dois	doysh
3	três	tresh
4	quatro	kwa-troo
5	cinco	seeñ-koo
6	seis	saysh
7	sete	set'
8	oito	oy-too
9	nove	nov'
10	dez	desh
11	onze	oñz'
12	doze	doz'
13	treze	trez'
14	catorze	ka-torz'
15	quinze	keeñz'
16	dezasseis	de-zuh-saysh
17	dezassete	de-zuh-set'
18	dezoito	de-zoy-too
19	dezanove	de-zuh-nov'
20	vinte	veent'
21	vinte e um	veen-tee-ooñ
30	trinta	treeñ-tuh
40	quarenta	kwa-reñ-tuh
50	cinquenta	seen-kweñ-tuh
60	sessenta	se-señ-tuh
70	setenta	se-teñ-tuh
80	oitenta	oy-teñ-tuh
90	noventa	noo-veñ-tuh
100	cem	sayñ
101	cento e um	señ-too-ee-ooñ
102	cento e dois	señ-too ee doysh
200	duzentos	doo-zeñ-toosh
300	trezentos	tre-zeñ-toosh
400	quatrocentos	kwa-troo-señ-toosh
500	quinhentos	kee-nyeñ-toosh
700	setecentos	set'-señ-toosh
900	novecentos	nov'-señ-toosh
1,000	mil	meel'

TIME

one minute	um minuto	ooñ mee-noo-too
one hour	uma hora	oo-muh oh-ruh
half an hour	meia-hora	may-uh-oh-ruh
Monday	segunda-feira	se-goon-duh-fay-ruh
Tuesday	terça-feira	ter-sa-fay-ruh
Wednesday	quarta-feira	kwar-ta-fay-ruh
Thursday	quinta-feira	keen-ta-fay-ruh
Friday	sexta-feira	say-shta-fay-ruh
Saturday	sábado	sah-ba-doo
Sunday	domingo	doo-meen-goo

COUNTRY GUIDES

AUSTRALIA • CANADA • CRUISE GUIDE TO EUROPE AND THE
MEDITERRANEAN • CUBA • EGYPT • FRANCE • GERMANY
GREAT BRITAIN • GREECE: ATHENS & THE MAINLAND
THE GREEK ISLANDS • IRELAND • ITALY • JAPAN
MEXICO • POLAND • PORTUGAL • SCOTLAND
SINGAPORE • SOUTH AFRICA • SPAIN
THAILAND • GREAT PLACES TO STAY
IN EUROPE • A TASTE OF SCOTLAND

REGIONAL GUIDES

BALI & LOMBOK • BARCELONA & CATALONIA • CALIFORNIA
EUROPE • FLORENCE & TUSCANY • FLORIDA • HAWAII
JERUSALEM & THE HOLY LAND • LOIRE VALLEY
MILAN & THE LAKES • MUNICH & THE BAVARIAN ALPS • NAPLES WITH
POMPEII & THE AMALFI COAST • NEW ENGLAND • NEW ZEALAND
PROVENCE & THE COTE D'AZUR • SARDINIA
SEVILLE & ANDALUSIA • SICILY • SOUTHWEST USA & LAS VEGAS
A TASTE OF TUSCANY • VENICE & THE VENETO

CITY GUIDES

AMSTERDAM • BERLIN • BOSTON • BRUSSELS • BUDAPEST
CHICAGO • CRACOW • DELHI, AGRA & JAIPUR • DUBLIN
ISTANBUL • LISBON • LONDON • MADRID
MOSCOW • NEW YORK • PARIS • PRAGUE • ROME
SAN FRANCISCO • STOCKHOLM • ST PETERSBURG
SYDNEY • VIENNA • WARSAW • WASHINGTON, DC

NEW FOR AUTUMN 2002

INDIA • MOROCCO • NEW ORLEANS • TURKEY

FOR INFORMATION ON OUR NEW <u>EYEWITNESS TOP TEN</u> POCKET SERIES
AND ON
<u>DK TRAVEL MAPS</u> & <u>PHRASEBOOKS</u>

VISIT US AT
www.dk.com

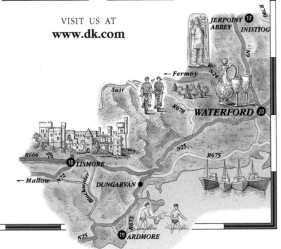

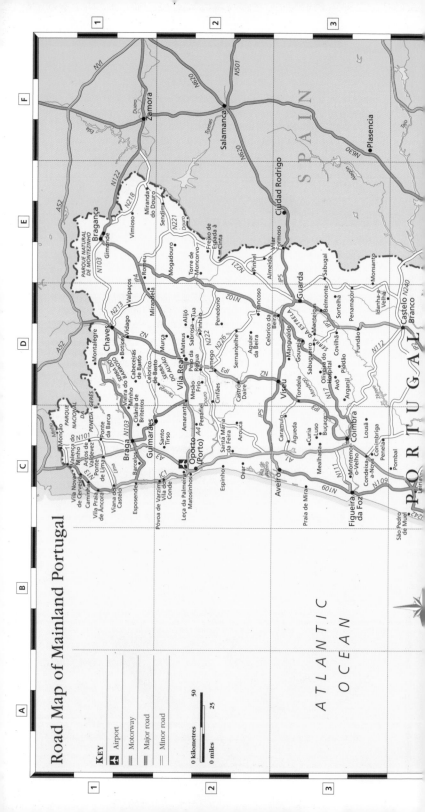